LA

RIVIERE

DE

SEINE

Fiſcher excudeba
Anno 1618.

Louise de Marillac

by the same author

MRS. SETON

SAINT CATHERINE LABOURÉ

Louise de Marillac

Joseph I. Dirvin, C.M.

FARRAR, STRAUS & GIROUX

NEW YORK

Nihil obstat:
    DANIEL V. FLYNN, J.C.D.
        Censor Librorum
Imprimatur:
    JOSEPH P. O'BRIEN, S.T.D.
        Vicar General, Archdiocese of New York
New York
May 6, 1970

The nihil obstat and imprimatur are official declarations that a book or pamphlet is free of doctrinal or moral error. No implication is contained therein that those who have granted the nihil obstat and imprimatur agree with the contents, opinions or statements expressed.

❧ *CONTENTS* ❧

◄§ *FOREWORD* ?►

It has been said that, within the two-thousand-year history of the Church, there were two saints who radically influenced its direction: Thomas Aquinas, who synthesized its philosophy and theology, and Vincent de Paul, who organized its charity. Like all such statements concerning complex organisms, this is an oversimplification: there were many schools and codices of teaching before St. Thomas and many organized arms of charity before St. Vincent. It seems true, however, that it has been God's way to bless these individual and isolated efforts against the day when an energetic and organizational genius should appear to unite them in dramatic, definitive style.

Such was certainly the case with the memorable synthesis of charity effected by Vincent de Paul in seventeenth-century France. Vincent grafted his tree, whose branches fill the world, upon many ancient roots and newer growths. An excellent example of the latter was the personal charity of Louise de Marillac, whose love for her neighbors and whose generosity to them were evident long before she met Vincent.

To some extent, it is regrettable that the great heart and original genius of this great woman have been obscured in the shadow of her friend, guide and co-worker. Of course, she would not think so; but history seems to have no patience with self-effacement when it hides extraordinary accomplishments.

However, Father Joseph Dirvin has set the record straight. He has accomplished this by citing the testimony of her contemporary, Gobillon, that she had cherished the thought of joining the Daughters of Charity even from the time of her marriage, by emphasizing the way she importuned Vincent for permission to establish the Company, and by asserting her personal contributions to their joint charitable and social works.

We are indebted to this quiet and humble woman for much of the highly efficient charity and social service practiced by both the modern Church and the modern world. Her instructions for the administration of hospitals, out-patient dispensaries, foundling homes, homes for the aged, and visiting-nurse programs are still of value in our day. Her warnings against the pitfalls of waste and mismanagement deserve our consideration. And, of course, her great motivating force of supernatural love of neighbor is as perennial as God Himself.

We are indebted to Louise, also, for the inner flame of her love, a spirit which has inspired young ladies to enter her beloved Company of Daughters. Today they number fifty thousand—by far the largest community in the Church. Other devoted women, almost three hundred thousand of them, join in the good works of the Ladies of Charity. It is clear from this biography that the flame of Louise's love was not confined by the walls of her community but reached out to enkindle the whole world— and, in the Providence of God, it still does. Thus we find that one of the first gifts Blessed Elizabeth Ann Seton gave her infant community of Sisters of Charity in Emmitsburg was a life of Louise, which she herself had translated. That gift has continued to inspire all Mother Seton's daughters with the charity and dedication and administrative ardor of Louise.

Thank God that the spirit of Louise and Vincent influences so much of the charity and social service in America and, in particular, in the Archdiocese of New York through the selfless efforts of the Daughters and Sisters and Ladies of Charity. May that spirit be quickened by the increased knowledge of Louise and her commitment portrayed by this biography. There is every reason to hope that it will, because our post-Conciliar age is committing itself more and more to universal charity and to the alleviation of the suffering of the poor, the wronged, and the neglected. We are all indebted to Father Dirvin for his patient application to the task of presenting the faith, confidence and love of Saint Louise de Marillac to our world.

TERENCE CARDINAL COOKE
Archbishop of New York

⊸§ *PREFACE* §⊸

It is incredible that there has not been, since the death of Louise de Marillac in 1660, a fully documented biography of this great lady who is responsible for much of the charity and social work and for legions of the dedicated workers of the past three centuries. Msgr. Baunard's biography of nearly a century ago comes closest to such a richly deserved tribute. It would seem that the world has taken Louise at face value when she protested to Vincent de Paul: "You know well, *mon père*, and our sisters also, that if anything has been done it has been by the orders your charity has given me"—for the world has never tired of broadcasting his achievements.

To compound the injustice, what has been written of Louise has too often contributed to the making of a somewhat false "image." Many factors have been involved: her faceless childhood, the arbitrary assumption that her adolescence was unhappy and frustrated, the abominable portraits, and especially the very real morbidity that characterized her young adulthood into the thirties. All in all, the young Louise seemed a poor candidate for the role of spiritual heroine. It was easy to assume that the dynamic Vincent de Paul had taken a weak woman and made her an automaton in carrying out, obediently, humbly, and without a thought of her own, his charitable plans. Such an assumption does little honor to Vincent, who grasped the potentialities of this woman from their first meeting, or to God who had prepared her for that meeting by an exquisite refinement in the furnace of suffering.

The greatness of Louise de Marillac can never be understood until this false image of a timid, dour, drab, and cheerless woman has been put aside. In undertaking this biography, my aim was to exorcise this disagreeable mythical creature and call up the real Louise. I went, therefore, to her letters and writings. No one, however he might try, can hide behind the pen. No one can help but reveal himself—personality, character, and qualities, good and bad—in letters, which are products of the most unguarded moments of life. And Louise does indeed reveal herself warmly in her more than 650 extant letters and numerous writings, which I was privileged to read in Paris and to compare meticulously line by line to the edition published in 1960, which, while uncritical, is faithful to the original.

Although Vincent de Paul has become far better known than Louise, mainly through Father Coste's fourteen-volume critical edition (crowned by the French Academy) of his some 3,500 extant letters, writings, and conferences, even he has been faulted by a selective process that often ignores his humanity. This neglect has been especially glaring in treating his relationship with Louise. It is to be hoped that the many quotes from their correspondence which are the central threads of this biography will establish, once for all, the delightful affection, intimacy, and dedication which made their cooperative ventures fruitful and permanent. The translations are my own, except for a certain few indicated letters and conferences.

The edited as well as the archival references have been cited for the convenience of the armchair scholar. All reference numbers have been avoided in the text so as not to interrupt the narrative, but sources are cited by reference to page and line at the end of the book.

My work has been made very pleasant by the wholehearted cooperation of good friends.

Father Raymond Chalumeau, C.M., archivist of the Congregation of the Mission, not only opened to me the archival and library wealth of the Parisian motherhouse but also shared with me his profound historical knowledge, accompanied me to the many existing places in the city where Louise and Vincent lived out their lives, and assisted me in collecting maps and illustrations. He crowned his invaluable help by reading the manuscript carefully and critically.

Sister Regnauld, archivist of the Daughters of Charity, was equally cooperative in affording me unlimited access to the Company's archives, suggesting pertinent sources, and, with the good offices of Sister Francis de Sales, American secretary, affording me every convenience for research.

I hold in grateful and affectionate memory Father Luigi Bisoglio,

C.M., late procurator general at the Holy See, who put at my disposal the valuable documentary testimony gathered for Louise's beatification and canonization which is preserved in the Congregation's archives in Rome.

From the start of my work seven years ago, Father William J. Casey, C.M., has given me the benefit of his interest, encouragement, and sound advice. Father James R. King, C.M., and Father Joseph Symes, C.M., worked long hours in checking the citation of sources and index. Indeed, so many of my confreres and sisters in religion have heartened me constantly by their never flagging interest in the progress of the work and by their prayers.

Dr. Edward A. Johnson, professor of English at St. John's University, has given selflessly of his time and expertise in reading the manuscript and offering suggestions.

In thanking all these good people for their unstinting help I have reserved until last His Eminence, Terence Cardinal Cooke, Archbishop of New York, who with his well-known kindness consented to write the foreword. That St. Louise may prosper his own far-flung charities in his great archdiocese is my earnest prayer in conveying to him my deep gratitude and filial obedience.

JOSEPH I. DIRVIN, C.M.

≈§ *Louise de Marillac* §≈

I

"My Cross ... from Birth"

France in 1591 was in desperate straits, having survived the thirty years of religious wars and the maternal maneuverings of Catherine de Medici, who had pitted Catholic against Huguenot, the *Liguers* against the *Politiques*, the crown against the nobility, Valois and Bourbon and Guise and Montmorency against one another—all for her weakling sons. War after war, battle after battle, but no peace—and, even more critical, no money. The crown was bankrupt, the nobles and merchants and lawyers impoverished because they were the unhappy creditors, and the peasants bled so white that many of them abandoned their little farms rather than pay the impossible taxes. Everyone hated everyone else. So blind and suspicious was *la belle France*, so disheartened and dispirited, that she did not recognize that one of her greatest kings, Henri de Navarre, had come to reign. The first of the Bourbon kings, he had succeeded to the throne two years before, in 1589, when Henri III had lost his life to an assassin while celebrating the final "peace" of the religious wars. But Henri de Navarre had not yet full possession of his kingdom. Paris was barred to him; it lay under the most horrible siege of its history. For Henri was a Huguenot, and the most fanatically Catholic of his subjects—led by the self-seeking Duc de Guise—refused to accept him. It would be another two years before Henri would settle the matter by turning Catholic.

It was in such a France that Louise de Marillac, who was to alleviate its miseries, was born on August 12, 1591. Earlier biographers tell us that Paris was her birthplace. Baunard, following Gobillon, her first biographer, asserts more precisely that she was born in the parish of St. Paul, "where . . . Guillaume, grandfather of Louise, 'had a great house' near the court and the Hôtel Saint-Paul, the king's palace of residence until the time of the League." But this hearsay evidence is somewhat thrown in doubt by the fact that Michel, Louise's famous uncle and son of Guillaume, was baptized in the Church of Saint-Nicolas-du-Chardonnet. Sister Geoffre, the famous nineteenth-century archivist of the Daughters of Charity, makes a better case for St. Paul's as the parish of the Marillacs —if not the birthplace of Louise—in her testimony before the beatification tribunal in 1895: "It appears very likely that it was the parish of Saint-Paul [where Louise was born]. It was, in fact, the burial place of the Marillacs: the body of M. Le Gras [Louise's husband] was carried there, even though he died in the parish of Saint-Sauveur. There M. de Marillac, father of the servant of God, was married for the third time [sic], and one cannot say that it was because it was the domicile of his new wife, for we learn from the marriage contract itself that she lived in the parish of Saint-Jean-en-Grève."

(An alternative birthplace may be conjectured—Ferrières-en-Brie in the Haute-Auvergne, where her father, Louis de Marillac, sieur de Ferrières et Farinvilliers, had his ancestral lands. It is accepted that he did not take up permanent residence in Paris until sometime between 1592 and 1594. The fact that a document providing for the child's future welfare was executed by her father's request at nearby Torcy-en-Brie favors the conjecture.)

Guy and Baunard both suggest that Louise's neurasthenic temperament came from a weakened mother who had lived through the siege of Paris, when the inhabitants were compelled to eat horses, mules, dogs, cats, rats, mice and, at the lowest point, even one another. But there is an explanation nearer to hand for Louise's nerves and insecurity. It is the unhappy circumstances of her birth. There seems little doubt that Louise was an illegitimate daughter of a proud and ancient house.

Louise's illegitimacy is evident from a number of incontrovertible facts. To begin with, she was born in the interval between Louis de Marillac's two marriages. Louis married his cousin Marie de la Rozière in 1584; she died childless in 1588 or 1589. He married for the second time in 1595, when Louise was already three years old; this second wife was a widow, Antoinette Le Camus, who had been married to Louis Thiboust, sieur de Bréau, and had had four children by him. Beginning with Gobillon in 1676, older biographers have pretended that the widow Thiboust was Louise's father's third wife, and have invented a "Marguerite Le Camus" as his second and the convenient mother of Louise. But Marguerite is a myth. Her name does not appear in the numerous and extensive genealogies of the Marillac family in the Archives Nationales, or in any other official document.

There is an alternative: there *was* a real Marguerite Le Camus, who was the mother of Louise—but not the lawful wife of Louis de Marillac. Certainly, an intriguing story lies behind the identical family name attributed by the biographers to Louis de Marillac's "second" and "third" wives. Were they related? Perhaps sisters, the unmarried mother and the wedded wife? Or was the name of the lawful wife invented for the unmarried mother deliberately to confuse the record and throw dust in the eyes of posterity? In any event, the first fact in establishing the circumstances of Louise de Marillac's birth is that her father never had a wife named "Marguerite Le Camus."

The second fact is that, ten days before his marriage to Antoinette Thiboust, the father, in settling an income on Louise, made her status quite plain. He called her *"ma fille, ma naturelle"*—"my natural daughter." Furthermore, Louise is not mentioned in the marriage contract of her father and the widow Thiboust, although the four Thiboust children are named—with the further information that they were being supported by public funds. (Marriage contracts of the age were mines of family information.)

Another fact is Louise's own marriage contract with Antoine Le Gras. Here again she is described as "the natural daughter of Louis de Marillac, in his lifetime *chevalier*, seigneur *en partie* de Farinvilliers." To her humiliation, there is no mention of her mother, although both father and mother of her husband are named. It is obvious that, before the law, neither Louise nor her mother existed. The absence of both their names in all the official Marillac genealogies is but supplementary proof.

Finally, when it was proposed to introduce the cause for beatification and canonization of Louise in 1895, the superior general of the Daughters of Charity, Father Antoine Fiat, hesitated until the Holy See assured him that the circumstances of her birth would in no way injure the cause. Every effort was made at the time to find a record of her baptism, which would have given us the name of Louise's mother and her marital status or the lack of it; but it could not be found. Father Fiat gave two reasons: all parish records, deposited at the Hôtel de Ville during the French Revolution, were subsequently destroyed by fire during the Commune of 1871; and similar records in the Bibliothèque Nationale have a lacuna for the years 1590–91. A tradition persists that a baptismal certificate or an authentic copy was once extant but was destroyed by some busybody with more sense of modesty and propriety than of history.

Absolutely nothing, therefore, is known of Louise's mother. This fact alone makes it probable that the mother was low-born, perhaps a servant. Had she been more gently born, it would have been hard to conceal her identity and, of more significance, Marillac could have married her. As it was, society decreed rigidly whom a nobleman might and might not marry. It was an age when family honor had to be jealously guarded, whatever the cost. Louise was to be a victim of this hypocritical code, caught between a grudging acceptance by the proud Marillacs and their resultant disapproval and coldness. Is it any wonder that she was nervous, withdrawn, and timid throughout the first half of her life?

Her father, then, is responsible for placing her in this half-world between honor and shame, for, despite her origin, he chose to recognize her as his daughter. This was, indeed, to his credit and to our gain. Had he not acknowledged her, she would have been a foundling, outside the orbit of respectable society, or perhaps a serving maid in some Marillac household: in either circumstance, her life's work would have been virtually impossible. But her father did acknowledge her and, illegitimate or not, she was a Marillac before the world; the only legal penalty attached to her birth was that she had no title of inheritance to her father's lands and moneys.

It is unfortunate that so little is known of this father. As head of a powerful house with the chancellor and a marshal of France for brothers, it would seem that the record of his life need not be so sparse. Brothers of celebrities are, indeed, often thrown into shadow, but seldom are they so obliterated that at least their vital statistics are not available to anyone who takes the trouble to look for them. Louis was a sieur of the realm and a councillor of the Parlement de Paris; yet little else is known about him.

The taint of his elder daughter's birth raises the suspicion that he might have been a libertine of whom his illustrious brothers were ashamed. Libertines were the order of the day in that licentious age— but be it said in defense of Louis's good name that there is no shred of evidence for this; not even his querulous and vituperative second wife made any such allegation. Louis was certainly not the only nobleman of his time to sire an illegitimate child (the King, Henri de Navarre, sired his quota). Furthermore, everything else we know of Louis is good: he acknowledged his sin publicly by giving Louise his name; he provided for her adequately and to all appearances cherished her with fond and fatherly affection. The most likely reason for his obscurity is that he was the sort of man content to remain out of the limelight. It is not possible to pinpoint the date of his birth, but the probable year would seem to be 1561 or 1562. He was the third of seven children born to Guillaume de Marillac, comptroller general and superintendent of finance to Henri III. At his father's death in 1573, Louis, not yet in his teens, succeeded to the title of sieur de Ferrières jointly with his elder brother, Charles. When Charles died in 1580, owing one hundred thousand livres, Louis, in order to clear the debt, found it necessary not only to relinquish his dead brother's portion of the family estates but also to transfer much of his own portion of Ferrières and the title to his brother Michel in return for the lesser title and inheritance of Farinvilliers. That he did not relinquish all, as Baunard asserts, is obvious from the fact that he deeded an annual rent and part of the lands of Ferrières to his daughter, Louise, in 1591. Whatever the details, Louis was never an independently wealthy man.

The Marillacs, known to recorded history since the thirteenth century, took their name from Marlhac, "near the town of Mauriac in the high country of the Auvergne." Their ancestral lands were part of the vast battlefield where Attila the Hun was routed in 431 by the allied arms of the Franks, the Merovingians, a remnant of the Romans, and a little band of Parisians sent to battle with the blessing of Sainte Geneviève. The first of the family of whom there is any certain knowledge was Bertrand, captured during the Hundred Years' War while fighting under the banner of Charles VI and held for ransom by Richard II of England. His son Sebastien raised the ransom money by selling the ancient *manoir de Marillac*; the bill of sale is dated May 7, 1382. The family recouped its losses during the fifteenth century by acquiring the lands and titles of Saint-Genès, Bicon and Mothe-d'Hermant. In the same century the Marillacs began their rise to power by tying their fortunes to the Bourbons, cousins of the kings of France and Princes of the Blood. Gilbert de Marillac became comptroller general to Madame Anne de France and Intendant to Charles de Bourbon. His son Gilbert succeeded him in his financial posts—the Marillacs seemed to have a talent for finance but this ability was not universal, especially when it came to their personal fortunes. A case in point is the third Gilbert, Baron de Poisat, grandson of the first and secretary to the famous Connétable de Bourbon. When that worthy betrayed François I by defecting to Emperor Charles V, Gilbert remained faithful to his king but had to work off his indebtedness to his patrons by embarking on an exhaustive history of the Bourbons that today is an indispensable source of information concerning that royal house.

This same Gilbert was the great-grandfather of Marguerite d'Arbouze, the renowned Abbess of Val-de-Grace, who died in the odor of sanctity in 1626. He had ten brothers and sisters, all talented in varying degrees, and it was this numerous clan that made the name of Marillac a household word in France. Three of them, Jean, Gabriel and François, were lawyers and councillors of the Parlement de Paris; Charles was Bishop of Vannes and then Archbishop of Vienne; Bertrand, a Franciscan, was Bishop of Rennes; Antoine and Catherine-Louise were religious; Guillaume, the grandfather of St. Louise, was, as has been said, superintendent of finances to Henri III; Julien was the only one who stayed at home in Auvergne and became *commissaire des guerres* there; Pierre, the black sheep who turned Huguenot, was disinherited by his father and died at Geneva. Archbishop Charles was the most brilliant member of the family. Like so many churchmen of the time, his main career was in statecraft; and he exercised his considerable political and diplomatic talents as chief of the privy council and ambassador to the courts of the Sultan Suliman at Constantinople, of Henry VIII at London, and of Emperor Charles V, notably at the Diet of Augsburg and at Rome. The family was to reach the acme of its power and influence in the person of Michel de Marillac, Keeper of the Seals; it was never again to attain to such a peak, yet it was not to lose its brilliance: Marillac blood flowed in the veins of the children of the Marquis de la Fayette and the Prince de Tarente.

Louise de Marillac thus belonged to a distinguished and powerful family, of whom Louis XIII said he "wished he could compose his Council entirely of Marillacs"; but she, saint and universal patroness of social workers, was its noblest ornament and the one it least regarded.

In August 1591 none of this, however, was of any help to Louis de Marillac. His newborn daughter had come into the world and she had no honorable mother; nor did he have a lawful wife to nurse and care for her. Yet he seems to have thought out well beforehand what he would do. Three days after the child's birth, on August 15, Louis appeared before Pierre Pivert, notary of Torcy-en-Brie, and settled upon "demoiselle Louise de Marillac, his daughter, a hundred livres of rent to be taken each year on St. Martin's Day in the winter from the goods of the donor, especially from part of the land and seignory of Ferrières; and beyond that he gave her nine workable acres and three *sizes* pieces of the territory of Ferrières in the plain."

At the time of this legal execution the child had been already baptized and named—apparently for her father—although all record of the deed, as we have shown, is lost. There is, of course, not the least doubt that she was baptized: Louise herself often dwelt lovingly on her baptism in her spiritual reflections and remarks. The document of donation also mentions as appended to it "a letter of the sieur de Farinvilliers addressed to his cousin, a religious at Poissy." Unfortunately, the letter is no longer extant. The "cousin" was undoubtedly Louis's aunt, Dame Catherine-Louise de Marillac, a Dominican nun of the royal Abbey of Saint-Louis-de-Poissy, where it is known Louise spent part of her childhood. The fact that such a letter was appended to a legal document executed three days after Louise's birth, and was given specific mention in the document itself, argues strongly for the hypothesis that Louise from infancy was placed legally in the care of her religious great-aunt.

The hypothesis makes sense. In the act of giving his illegitimate daughter the Marillac name, Louis had perforce to take her from her mother, if indeed the mother were still living. He had no way of taking care of her himself, and to leave her at home in the charge of a nurse or governess would surely invite talk and speculation. It is quite probable, too, that the fact of the child's birth was not generally known, and so the convent at Poissy would provide a home for the infant that was as discreet as it was honorable and safe. Beyond a doubt, such a solution to the father's embarrassment would be eminently satisfactory to the Marillac family, not least to his brother Michel, whose political star was beginning to rise.

Such disposition of wellborn little girls was common at the time, especially if, according to the vicious practice countenanced by the Church, the little girl was to succeed an aunt as abbess or prioress of the convent. A famous example is Mère Angélique Arnauld, who was brought as a child to Port-Royal; and Bremond cites the cases of Renée de Lorraine, daughter of the Duc de Guise and Catherine de Clèves, who was handed over to her aunt, abbess of Saint-Pierre, at the tender age of six weeks, and Anne de Plas, who was entrusted to her aunt, abbess of Faremou-tiers, two months after baptism. Not that so prestigious a future was in store for poor little Louise: the Gondi family, whom Vincent de Paul was to serve so well and they him, had as firm a hold on the monastery of

Poissy as they had on the See of Paris; Dame Jeanne de Gondi, sister of the Bishop of Paris and aunt of Vincent's patron, the General of the Galleys, was prioress of Poissy when Louise was placed there.

The hypothesis that Louise spent all her childhood from infancy within the convent at Poissy would answer a host of questions: why, for example, she never mentioned home or family life; why she seems not even to have known her stepmother, her stepbrother or her three stepsisters. Most of all, it would throw light on the fixation concerning the religious life that plagued her until she came to terms with herself at the age of thirty-nine. The hypothesis would obtain even if the letter to Dame Louise had been a sort of testament leaving the little Louise to her great-aunt's legal custody—not immediately, but in the event of her father's death or of a change in his way of life. Such a change took place on January 12, 1595, when Louis remarried. Louise seems to have had no part in this new life of her father. For this reason it is valid to suppose that she was at Poissy at least from the age of three. There can be little doubt that, throughout the most impressionable years of childhood, the monastery was her home.

It was a magnificent home, an opulent city whose stately buildings stretched along the Seine beside the forest of Saint-Germaine-en-Laye some six miles from Paris. Philippe le Bel established the monastery to honor the canonization of his grandfather, Louis IX, by Pope Boniface VIII in 1297, for St. Louis had been born and baptized at Poissy—he loved to sign himself Louis de Poissy—and the convent chapel marked the actual site of his birth. The Dominican nuns who took possession of it in 1304 were from the convent of Prouille, established by St. Dominic himself, and its first prioress was a granddaughter of St. Louis, Marie de Clermont, who had taken the Dominican vows at Montargis. More than one Princess of the Blood had been a nun of Poissy: Marguerite de France, daughter of King Jean; Marie de Bourbon, sister-in-law of Charles V; Marie, daughter of Charles VII; Isabelle d'Artois; Marie de Bretagne, to name but a few—and the great names of the kingdom were a commonplace in the community records. This could be said in a lesser degree of nearly every French convent, even to Louise's day and beyond; for a nun, if not of the nobility, was at least of good family, and brought with her a sizable dowry and the promise of lavish gifts to be bestowed on the monastery by her family and friends as long as she lived. Thus the monastery of Poissy was a rich treasury of every conceivable work of art—furniture, rugs, hangings, and sacred vessels of gold and silver studded with jewels. This symbolic intrusion of the world's wealth into the religious life of the late Middle Ages and the Renaissance often startles the modern Catholic used to the frugality, if not extreme poverty, of modern religious houses. Such worldly intrusion did not stop with material things but showed itself in a relaxation of rule and even in extravagant abuses. It was not uncommon for nuns to have regular calling days when they entertained in the convent parlors, or had meals of *haute cuisine* sent in from outside and served to them in their private suites, or even on occasion dressed in the height of fashion and danced at an especially gala *soirée*. Such nuns were not, of course, considered the mystics of their age, and no one was unduly scandalized at their antics; and even the genuinely pious nuns frequently lived in the genteel luxury of great ladies in retirement. The architecture of the convents almost demanded this style of living. Thus Christine de Pisan paid poetic tribute to the grandeur of Poissy in 1400:

> *So very beautiful, grand, vast, shining and serene is it,*
> *So well laid out, so finely architectured overall*
> *That the eye knows at once it was founded by kings,*
> > *And the great nobility,*
> *Who spared on it neither silver nor gold.*

What is most surprising is that genuine virtue, piety and even mysticism flourished amid such elegance and pomp. The nuns of Poissy had a solid reputation for regularity and holiness. They also had a reputation for learning. In an age when women, even those of the highest rank, were poorly educated—Marie de Medici and her young daughter-in-law, Anne of Austria, could scarcely read or write—the nuns of Poissy translated the Greek and Latin classics and turned the Scriptures and liturgical books into facile and often exquisite poetry. Ronsard himself praised the verses of Dame Anne des Marquets, who foretold a poignant, unforgettable moment to Hélène de Surgères, lady in waiting to Catherine de Medici:

> *When you are very old, in the evening, in candlelight,*
> *Seated by the side of the fire, spinning and weaving,*
> *Say, singing my verses in wonder to yourself,*
> *Ronsard celebrated me in a time when I was beautiful . . .*

Père Hilarion de la Coste recorded the literary achievement of Dame Louise de Marillac: the Office of the Blessed Virgin and the Seven Penitential Psalms turned into graceful French poetry; meditations for all the feasts of the year; and an "excellent" commentary on the Canticle of Canticles. It is evident that Louise suffered from no lack of religious training or of proper schooling at Poissy. God was all around her and her companions were dedicated to Him. She listened while they sang His praises in choir, and her lessons were full of Him: not only the basic catechism, but also the riches of the Bible, the antiphons and psalms of the liturgy, spiritual treatises, and lives of the saints. In learning to spell, she would try to assemble in proper order the letters that went to make up the names of places where He lived, and where He worked His miracles.

Spelling was not one of the strong points of the age: the approximate rendering of a word so that it was understood was quite acceptable, and variant spellings of the same word are common in a single document. According to this standard, her spelling was, indeed, better than average; her handwriting was clear and legible, her manner of expression simple and, when the occasion inspired it, either graceful and diplomatic or blunt and vigorous. Her formal education, added to her keen native intelligence, was more than adequate. Louise even acquired at Poissy a working knowledge of Latin: Vincent de Paul would pointedly, and with just a pinch of malice, refuse to translate Latin quotations for her.

She was well provided for in her convent home. She was fed and clothed and kept warm. She was instructed more than were other girls of her age and station. She received the deepest spiritual impressions, so deep as to last her all her life and to give her from these earliest years a thirst for perfection. But the most basic need was denied her: the need for normalcy, especially of family life with its warmth and affection, its parental discipline, and its taken-for-granted security. Any visitor to an orphanage who has seen love-starved outcasts running toward strangers with outstretched arms will know Louise's need and her lack. Perhaps her aunt tried to make it up to her, and probably the visits of the little girl's father were out-of-the-ordinary treats. The notion that he did not love her or do for her whatever his professional chores and undignified marital difficulties allowed is belied by the poignant testimony of his last will—that Louise "was his greatest consolation in the world, and that God had given her to him for his peace of soul in the afflictions of his life."

The complete impersonality of this little pensioner's childhood is symbolized by the blank it has left in history. She must have been at times unbearably lonely, without quite understanding why, for she had no normal standards by which to judge the urge for affection, for belonging, that rose unbidden within her. Years later, when older and wiser, she wrote: "God did me the favor of letting me know that His holy will was that I should go to Him by the cross. His goodness willed that I should be marked with it even from birth, not leaving me ever, at any age, without occasions of suffering."

II

Father's Death and
Her Marriage

Louise's father married for the second time on January 12, 1595, in the Church of St. Paul at Paris. His bride, the widow Antoinette Thiboust, had been born Antoinette Le Camus, the daughter of Jean, seigneur de Saint-Bonnet and scion of an old and respected Lyonnaise family. Her brother was governor of Etampes and the father of Jean Le Camus, Bishop of Belley, friend of François de Sales and famous in his own right as preacher and spiritual writer. It was not a happy marriage; much of the blame for its unhappiness must be laid (without exculpating Louis entirely) to Mme de Marillac. She was certainly devious and shrewd, and the facts of her life are not easily dragged out of the shadows which constantly obscure them. In any event, there seems to have been no peace in the Marillac household almost from the beginning of the marriage, a marriage whose violent history is recorded in a formal interrogation of Mme de Marillac, instigated by the complaint of her husband and conducted by court officials in 1601–2. Husband and wife hurled charges and countercharges at each other. He complained that she absented herself from his house for long periods of time in the company of "dissolute persons." She insisted that she was overworked and had fled to her mother's house with her husband's consent, returning when her mother died. There is a hint that her brother had threatened her by letter that, "if she did not behave as she should, he would be a man if her husband Marillac would not, and would put her behind four walls so that he would not suffer dishonor because of her." By her own testimony, her husband seems to have kept her a prisoner in his house from 1597 to 1600. When she complained that she was being deprived unjustly of Mass and the sacraments, he offered to bring in a priest to minister to her, but she protested piously that this would be contrary to the canons of the Council of Trent. The piety of her protest may justly be questioned, for she admitted a partiality to the Huguenot faith and later embraced it. On January 21, 1600, she left her husband's house for good and lived in various places with various people, good or bad, depending upon whose testimony is to be believed. The situation came to a boil in a certain house at Picpus where the "scandalous goings-on" are said to have brought down on her the *lieutenant criminel;* she insisted that the only scandalous goings-on were caused by her husband, who had broken down the door at three in the morning and had removed most of the furniture.

The sordid tale reached a climax on May 3, 1601, when Mme de Marillac was arrested and confined in the Hôpital St. Gervais, where she gave birth to a baby girl in December. The child was baptized in the Church of St. Gervais and named Innocente for the feast of her birth. Despite the mother's attempts to retrieve her dowry of six thousand livres by claiming that it was contingent on the consummation of her marriage which, she alleged, was rendered impossible by the impotency of her husband, the child was declared Louis de Marillac's legitimate heir and succeeded to his estates. Aside from this legal opinion, Mme de Marillac's charge is contradicted by her admission that she had "carnal relations" with her husband, and by the existence of Louise, whom Louis de Marillac had gone to great personal embarrassment and sacrifice to acknowledge.

It is a comfort to know that Louise, safe in her convent school, was shielded from such a *ménage à deux.* However, its scandalous history must have become common knowledge, and Louise's later awareness of it and consequent shame cannot be discounted as factors in her neuroticism.

Louis de Marillac died, a relatively young man, in his early forties, on July 25, 1604. Whether or not Louise was at his deathbed, she was in his dying thoughts; his last will and testament was signed two days before his death. He not only called Louise his "greatest consolation" and "peace of soul," as already noted, but he entrusted her with a last commission: ten écus of income from the land of Farinvilliers was to be given into her hands, that she might have three Masses offered and distribute alms for the repose of his soul. It was a poignant commission of love which the lonely, harried man could not leave to wife or stepchildren; and its poignancy is the more evident with the knowledge that it was the only way he could name this dearly loved daughter in his will.

Since he could not legally leave her a share in his estate, he had provided for her in what seems a frugal but adequate way. There were the hundred livres of annual income and the portion of the Ferrières land settled on her at her birth in 1591; and a further annual provision of 83 écus, settled on her before the father's second marriage. In addition, Louise's marriage contract mentions fifty livres of annual income awarded Louise by the chancellory of Paris on April 2, 1602, in interpreting a contract drawn up by her father on March 20, 1597; and a sum of 1,200 livres, which he gave her by legal contract of November 23, 1602 (this was in her possession at the time of her marriage, and may have represented a lump-sum dowry). Thus, Louis de Marillac provided for the support of his friendless little girl after his death, and for a suitable dowry to bring to her husband in a respectable marriage. He seems to have added to her security with each fresh matrimonial crisis in his life.

There can be little doubt that the death of her father left Louise alone and friendless at the age of twelve, except for her aunt, Dame Louise, and it is not certain whether Louise was still with her. The girl seems to have had no proper guardian. If Dame Louise had some such relationship when the girl was small, she obviously did not have it now when Louise was on the verge of leaving, or had already left, Poissy. Her uncle Michel is referred to in a legal document as *tuteur* of Louise's half sister Innocente, but not to Louise herself; in fact, their relationship, as reconstructed from five extant letters he wrote her, seems singularly cold and formal. She did have a caretaker for legal matters, a certain M. Blondeau, for two years, until she was declared to have reached her legal majority, on August 13, 1610; but it is obvious from the tenor of the language that he was court-appointed, and that the court's action was made necessary because her financial affairs had fallen into arrears through the lack of anyone to watch over them.

Between the years Louise spent at Poissy and her marriage in 1613, she lived for an indeterminate time in a Parisian *pension* conducted by a woman identified only as "a good, devout spinster." We have this information from Louise herself: she told it to her religious daughters, one of whom passed it on to Gobillon, her first biographer. There has been a great deal of confusion as to the nature both of this establishment and of its proprietress. This confusion has been generated by later biographers who have misunderstood the Sister's account and Gobillon's retelling of it and have distilled their misunderstanding into "facts" accepted without question but wholly unsupported by evidence. Thus, it has been taken for granted variously that it was a school for poor girls, or girls of a lower position in society, and one writer has even suggested that it was a kind of orphanage.

Schools for girls, in the generally accepted sense, were unknown at the time. Louise's own education was a notable exception and was certainly influenced by the uncommon learning of the religious ladies of Poissy. Neither the anonymous Sister nor Gobillon says that the establishment was a school. The Sister says merely that "Mlle Le Gras told us that, when she was young, she had been a boarder with a good, devout spinster, along with other young girls." Gobillon, writing either conjecturally or from still another source, says further that M. de Marillac "put her [Louise] at Paris in the hands of a clever and virtuous mistress that she might learn to do those things suitable to her position." Louise's biographers have unwittingly interpreted Gobillon's words in a financial context. The inference that a drop in fortune meant a drop in station was drawn, it would seem, from the fact that while at the *pension* Louise made articles (of clothing, apparently) that were sold commercially, and also did domestic work. But it is obvious that Louise did not do these things for herself, or because she was forced to do them, but for the mistress of the establishment and out of Christian charity: "The mistress being poor, she [Louise] suggested to her to take orders from merchants, and she worked for her, encouraging her companions to do the same. She even took upon herself the lowliest household chores, such as cutting wood and doing the menial tasks ordinarily confined to domestics." It seems quite plain that the narrator is recalling, for her own edification and that of others, that Louise gave evidence of her characteristic practicality, charity and humility even at an early age. It seems equally plain that the narrator is especially impressed that a noblewoman in her pursuit of virtue should stoop to tasks not consonant with her position in society.

Louise's progress in painting affords additional evidence that the *pension* was not a sort of "school of hard knocks," a domestic institute for girls destined to be ordinary housewives. Whether the mistress herself had a talent for painting, or whether Louise had instructors, we do not know. That Louise herself, without being in any real sense an artist, had more than a schoolgirl's talent for painting is certain because some of her work is extant. The subject matter of her paintings is wholly religious, thus giving proof of Louise's preoccupation with religion from her earliest years. Two watercolors—one, a young girl seated among trees and

flowers and in the act of tracing the Name of Jesus with the accompanying legend, "It is the Name of Him I love"; the other, the Good Shepherd surrounded by his sheep—are adolescent in conception and sentiment. They could have been painted by any pious, talented teenager.
M. D. Poinsenet has called attention to the unusual representation, in
the picture of the Good Shepherd, of the sheep drinking from the wound
in His side, and has indicated the probable source of Louise's inspiration: the Dominican monastery of Poissy. There Louise would have become acquainted with the spirituality of the great Dominican mystic, St.
Catherine of Siena, and with God's revelations to her concerning the
heart of His Son.

The identity of the "good, devout spinster" who was mistress of the
pension might help to solve the mystery of Louise's stay there. Was she
some faded gentlewoman, trying to support herself as respectably as possible with the only asset she had, her house? Gobillon calls her "clever"
as well as virtuous, and credits her with the ability to teach Louise "those
things suitable to her position." Or was she, as Calvet suggests, someone
more intimately connected with Louise? In an ingenious hypothesis, he
theorizes that this spinster of the *pension* might indeed have been
Louise's own mother. He argues his hypothesis well: Marillac, by providing the woman with the means of making a living, would have satisfied
his obligation to her; by placing Louise with her he would have both
restored to her their daughter and guaranteed the daughter's security.
The hypothesis nevertheless raises certain difficulties of its own. Since it
is a presumption that even Calvet subscribes to that Louise's mother
belonged to the lower classes, how could she teach Louise the niceties of
the girl's social station? A more serious difficulty will be found in
Louise's lifelong, absolute silence concerning her mother. It is hard to
imagine so tenderhearted, loving and impressionable a woman as Louise
so shutting her own mother out of her life as not to be impelled in some
way to allude to her. And to have known her mother would surely have
softened in her the prejudice of her class, held despite the circumstances
of her own birth, toward illegitimates: she remained adamant to the end
of her life in refusing them entrance into her congregation. The one
positive evidence the account of Louise's stay at the *pension* gives us is of
the practical turn of her growing sanctity. The years in the royal convent
had done their work.

Louise was growing to maturity in a flowering age, an age of religious
promise. Bremond's bursting volumes are refutation enough of the ac-

cepted picture of the early seventeenth century as an age of spiritual barrenness in France. The abysmal conditions of the provinces and the country places, so successfully attacked by Vincent de Paul, were real enough, but Paris was a different matter. A sterile soil could not have borne the planting of the Capucines and the Carmelites, or supported the footsteps of Bérulle, Condren, Olier, Bourdoise, Madame Acarie, the giant Vincent himself, and the host of lesser figures some of whom had an even greater prominence and influence than these in their lifetime. When the Spanish Carmelites came in 1604, even the austere Anne de Jésus, the mother of the band, wrote home to Spain: ". . . in Paris, a world of its own, there are abundant signs of religion, the frequenting of the sacraments recalls that of the Primitive Church; in fact, they are surprised not to see us communicate oftener." Religious vocations from noble families were abundant; among Louise's own contemporary cousins there were no less than two bishops, three priests and eight religious.

While the coming of the Carmelites to Paris was of great religious moment for France, another religious foundation was to have a more immediate and spiritually significant influence on the life of Louise de Marillac. This was the establishment in 1608 of the Capucines or Daughters of the Passion, who followed the Franciscan rule of St. Clare. Henri IV authorized the foundation to honor a vow made by the deceased Queen Louise de Lorraine. He left the details to the Duchesse de Mercoeur, who not only provided the religious with a new convent in the rue Saint-Honoré nearly opposite the monastery of their brother Capuchins but made of the formal ceremony of taking possession a religious spectacle which Paris would long remember. The ceremony began on the morning of August 2, 1606, when the twelve novice religious, barefoot, left the Hôtel de Mercoeur escorted by forty-eight Capuchin Fathers and twelve princesses, one for each Sister. A great crowd followed them to the Capuchin church, where Cardinal Pierre de Gondi and his nephew Henri, Coadjutor of Paris, awaited their arrival. After a word of welcome and exhortation, the Cardinal symbolically placed on each novice's head a crown of thorns. The whole assemblage, and the gaping crowd, then repaired to the Sisters' new chapel, where the new religious were clothed with the habit and listened to a sermon by the celebrated Capuchin mystic, Frère Ange de Joyeuse.

It was a sight to fire the imagination of youth—and Louise de Marillac was fifteen at the time. It is hard to imagine one of her age and temperament missing it, or not knowing every detail of it. Already oriented by her upbringing and her inclination to the religious life, Louise now set her young heart on joining the Capucines. Such a vocation had great appeal to her, for she had a bent toward self-effacement and austerity; her whole spiritual life was lived at the foot of the cross. Historically, this fact of her hankering for the hard life of the Capucines, when placed beside other long-known facts, illuminates hitherto dark and mysterious corners of her adolescent years. These facts, insignificant enough when taken separately, together point to an overwhelming probability. The isolated facts are these: Michel de Marillac, who was present when the Capucines took possession of their convent, had with his friend Bérulle assumed the habit of the Third Order of St. Francis; Michel's second son, Octavien, became a Capuchin in the monastery on the rue Saint-Honoré; the Hôtel d'Attichy, of which Louise's aunt Valence de Marillac, Marquise d'Attichy, was the mistress, was quite near the Capucine convent; Louise herself was a frequent visitor at the convent and was given the privilege not only of the parlor but of the convent garden, refectory and chapel, even to the point of being permitted to chant the office with the nuns; and, finally, her spiritual director was no less a personage than the noted Père Honoré de Champigny, provincial of the Parisian Capuchins, cousin of Madame Acarie and friend of Michel de Marillac. The links are undeniable. There was great rapport between the Marillacs and the Franciscan family, and Louise was very much a part of it.

Whatever had gone before which necessitated Louise's boarding out in the *pension*, there seems intriguing and insistent evidence that now, in her late teens, she was part of the Marillac circle, an accepted member of her family. It must never be forgotten that rank held undisputed sway in the society of the time, religious as well as secular. No unrecognized lay person could have free access to the inner life of a cloister, or ever hope to become an official part of that life—the lack of social status of the first Daughters of Charity, apart from their startling lack of cloister, was one of the reasons why they were hooted at by the very poor they had come to serve. Yet no ordinary lay person could have so distinguished a spiritual director as Père Honoré de Champigny, or boast of such friends and acquaintances as Ange de Joyeuse, Benoît de Canfield and Père Joseph du Tremblay, Richelieu's "Gray Eminence," as Louise certainly could. Add to all this the fact that Louise was later married from the Hôtel d'Attichy, and that, on their parents' deaths, the brilliant d'Attichy children were left to her charge, a responsibility that presupposes a far deeper obligation on her part than the convenient use of the d'Attichy home for an official marriage address, and the picture is complete. It seems inevitable to posit the Hôtel d'Attichy as Louise's home for several years before her marriage. It may be conjectured that the *pension* was a suitable alternative while her father was alive and had an official residence to which he could not bring her; but that, after his death, the family, whether reluctantly or not, came forward.

It need not challenge such a conjecture that between January 1608 and September 1610 several court actions were decided with Louise and her uncle Michel, in his role as *tuteur* of her half sister Innocente, as protagonists. It is not possible to determine the time when Louise left the *pension* and went to live at the Hôtel d'Attichy; nor is there any evidence concerning Michel de Marillac's relationship, close or distant, with his half sister Valence d'Attichy. In an order handed down at the Châtelet on January 2, 1608, Blondeau was designated as the *curateur* (legal guardian), "of the actions of the aforesaid demoiselle Louise de Marillac, to which is attached another sentence of the aforesaid Châtelet, of September 7, 1610, by which the sieur de Marillac, *tuteur* of Innocente de Marillac, daughter of the aforesaid deceased sieur de Farinvilliers, has been condemned to pay to the aforesaid demoiselle Louise de Marillac 250 livres of income on the one hand, 50 livres of income on the other, and 30 livres of income from yet another annuity, and to pay the arrears of these." Undoubtedly this settling of accounts had something to do with Louise's coming of legal age in 1610. (She reached the age of nineteen on August 28.) The fact that a councillor of the King, now bearing the title of "Master of Requests," had to be ordered to pay just dues to an orphan girl leaves a bad taste. The fact that he was also renowned for his sanctity and even mysticism does not help matters. Whatever the reason for his delay, it is recorded that Michel de Marillac paid his niece in full on September 17, 1610.

Caught up in the prospect of dedicating herself to God among the Daughters of the Passion, Louise made a private promise to join them. It was not a vow—Louise herself said so—but it was to take on the magnitude of a vow and was to terrorize her in unhappier years ahead. Such a promise, made in the enthusiasm and generosity of youth, should not be thought extraordinary; and Louise, at the time, felt quite confident of keeping it. She had not bargained on a denial but that is what she met with. Père de Champigny said no. Louise was not physically strong; all her life she would ail, and like many chronically ill people, she would live to a good age; but the austere life of the Capucines was not for her. God spoke, not only in the voice of her spiritual director but also in the official voice of him who had the last word in Capuchin affairs. And in the speaking there was a prophecy: "I believe," said he, "that God has other plans for you."

In her disappointment, Louise did not understand the import of these words. Instead she gave herself over to the plans of her family, which now turned upon a respectable marriage for her. Such a marriage would not be easy to arrange to everyone's complete satisfaction, because of Louise's tainted origin. However, what would be impossible for others was merely difficult for the Marillacs: not only was Uncle Michel a councillor of the King, but Uncle Octavien Dony d'Attichy was superintendent of finances, and Uncle Jean-Louis was the husband of Catherine de Medici, aunt of the Queen Mother.

That Octavien and Valence d'Attichy were the prime movers in the marriage arrangements is obvious from the context of a letter Louise wrote years later to their son-in-law, the Comte de Maure, concerning her own son. "By their direction," she wrote bluntly, "they caused me to engage myself in the manner of life which has put me in the state that I am [that is, a widowed mother]. Do not, I beg you, take what I tell you as complaining, O God guard me from that! for I would have been very happy if Divine Providence had wished their hope and design to succeed . . ."

It was not to be imagined that Louise's husband would belong to the *noblesse,* for no nobleman could be expected to marry beneath himself; but a man could be expected to marry above himself. And so it was that the husband selected for Louise was a rising young bourgeois. His name was Antoine Le Gras, and his future was promising enough, for he was already secretary to the Queen Mother and Regent, Marie de Medici. He was apparently no stranger to the Marillacs, since the two families came from the same part of the Auvergne. The Le Gras were long-time residents of Paris, and members of the family are listed as *marguilliers* (churchwardens or trustees) of the parish of Saint-Gervais from the sixteenth to the eighteenth centuries. They were of substantial fortune.

If it was a good marriage for M. Le Gras and enabled him to climb another rung of the ladder of society, what of Louise? Ironically, she who thus brought good fortune to her husband, she who had already suffered innocently for an origin not of her choosing, had still more to suffer. As a daughter of one of the most powerful families in the realm, she was forced now, in the proclamation of her marriage banns, to advertise her tainted birth to the world, and to bear henceforward the inferior title of *Mademoiselle* instead of the noble *Madame*, which was her familial right. The difference in station of husband and wife stands out in the signing of the marriage contract on February 4, 1613: "To speak for him and in his name," Antoine Le Gras had only his widowed mother; Louise was surrounded by the most brilliant of the Marillacs. They were listed in the contract as follows:

> There were present in their persons M. Antoine Le Gras, secretary of the Queen, mother of the King, son of the late noble man, M. Antoine Le Gras, while living Counselor and elected for the King in the election of Clermont in Auvergne, and of Demoiselle Marguerite née Atour his wife, his father and mother, dwelling at present on the rue des Francbourgeois in the parish of Saint-Gervais, to speak for him and in his name, on the one hand:
>
> And Demoiselle Louise de Marillac, natural daughter of the late Louis de Marillac, in his lifetime knight, seigneur *en partie* de Farinvilliers, in use and enjoyment of her rights, dwelling in the house of the Sieur and Dame d'Attichy, hereafter named to speak for her and in her name, on the other hand:
>
> The which parties of their good will recognized and acknowledged as lawful the future marriage which in the good pleasure of God is shortly to be made and solemnized in the face of Holy Church between these two, in the presence and with the advice of Messire Octavien Dony d'Attichy, counselor of the King in his Councils, Intendant of his finances and of the House of the Queen; dame Valence de Marillac, his wife; Messire Michel de Marillac, Counselor of the King in his Councils; Louis de Marillac, gentleman ordinary of the King's bedchamber; dame Catherine de Medici, his wife; demoiselle Cornelia Dony, widow of the late sieur Goriny; dame Geneviève Dony, wife of sieur le Comte de Chateauvillain; Messire Paul de Myremont, seigneur de Montigny; dame Victoire Scolary, his wife; and demoiselle Louise Hennequin, widow of seigneur de Vernoy, counselor in the Court of Requests of the Palace; all mutual friends of the aforesaid betrothed couple.

The wedding took place the next day, February 5, 1613, in the fashionable church of Saint-Gervais. M. François Board, doctor and regent of the faculty of theology, was Curé of Saint-Gervais at the time, and may well have assisted at the marriage of two such prominent parishioners.

So much for the legal and sacramental aspects of the marriage. But what were Louise's deepmost feelings? Almost certainly her marriage was not the culmination of a romance in the modern sense. In seventeenth-century France, marriages of ladies of rank were arranged. Not that Louise had no choice in the matter. Her father being dead, and she herself having attained her majority and "in use and enjoyment of her rights," she was her own mistress. It is probable that, the religious life beyond her reach, she accepted marriage as the normal course expected of her by God and by the circumstances of her social position. Undoubtedly she sought advice from both her spiritual director and her family, for she was always meticulous in this regard.

The marriage need not preoccupy our sympathy for a lonely and defenseless girl handed over, with grudging consent, to a man and a state of life she found distasteful. Louise was neither a misanthrope nor a puritan. Her nature was outgoing, her life given over to people. She was a creature of love, and she loved with all the ardor of a warm heart. Her letters to her religious daughters offer a continual testimony, filled as they are with affectionate greetings, anxious fussing, tender alarm and tears and, most often, a mother's fierce and shining pride. Her love for her son was at times so possessively human that it drew sarcastic rebuke from St. Vincent. Such a woman was not one to recoil from the thought of marriage. She probably liked Antoine Le Gras very much. Indeed, she may well have loved him from the very beginning; she certainly did at the end. No wife was more faithful, more loyal, more dedicated to her husband's comfort and interests. She wore herself out in nursing him through lingering years of illness. She brushed aside his faults, especially his peevishness, as of no account. She showed her love in deeds; and this is what love is all about.

It is because of Louise's first choice of the religious life, and its denial to her, that men have failed even to consider that her married life might have been eminently normal and happy, or have thought of it as an interlude, unfortunate but necessary, as a period of painful purification in preparation for her great enterprises. There is more than a hint of the truth in her later anxiety as to whether, because she had once promised herself to God, she should now leave her husband; it seems very much like the fear of one who might have to give up what she does not want to part with.

Antoine Le Gras was a good man. He was conscientious, hardworking, deeply religious and charitable to the poor. He would never make a brilliant noise in the world, for his personality was plain and his talents mediocre—qualities which would endear him all the more to a woman like Louise. It may be justly concluded, then, that it was a good marriage, and that Louise and Antoine were quite content.

III

Crisis

The first years of Louise's marriage were like summer lightning in their brilliance and evanescence. The marriage had brought her out, at twenty-two, into the most glittering of French society, the court itself. It was not her husband's doing, for he was only a secretary to the Queen Regent; it was rather that, as a married woman, she was able now, as she had not been as a spinster of tainted birth, to share in the royal favor then lavished on the Marillacs. This favor was due in part to Michel de Marillac's solid service to the Regency, but its chief motive was one that carried much more weight with the shallow, selfish Marie de Medici: Louise's uncle Jean-Louis had married, in 1607, the Queen's aunt, Catherine de Medici, and was thus uncle to Marie and grand-uncle to Louis XIII.

Innocent as she was of the ways of the world, Louise was not aware that she had been introduced into a fool's paradise. Marie de Medici's chief quality was stupidity. This quality, coupled with the vulgarity that was her trademark, kept France in dangerous ferment for almost twenty years, until Louis found the courage to put her down forever in 1630. Dedicated to her own comfort and interests, as was her cousin and predecessor Catherine de Medici, the Queen Regent was far less conscientious and well-intentioned. Like that disastrous lady, however, she favored her own countrymen. In the highest circles French was spoken with an Italian accent. Concini, the Maréchal d'Ancre, through his wife, the Queen's foster sister, Eleonora Galigai—her misshapen body readily suggested that the Queen kept her, in the current custom of royalty, as her pet dwarf—was in complete ascendancy. A shameless adventurer, he was soon cordially hated by noble and peasant alike, not because he was Italian but because he was greedy and arrogant.

Unfortunately, these two, the conceited and empty-headed Regent and her sycophant and irresponsible minister, were the two kites to which the Marillac fortunes were tied. It was only a matter of time until they should be dashed to the ground. But now, since the senseless and sacrilegious killing of Henri IV on May 14, 1610, by the demented Ravaillac, the living was high.

It was a heady society, this strange, artificial combination of nobles and lowborn upstarts Marie had gathered around her. As pleasure-mad and avaricious as the giddy Queen herself, they created a brilliant court, but the brilliance was like the flare of a candle before it goes out. Precisely because of their empty heads and frivolous, cruel hearts, they were dangerous to the French monarchy and to the French people, which was, in the noblest ideal of *la belle France*, to say the same thing. All the order which Henri IV had brought out of chaos was shattered, and the royal treasury so laboriously amassed by the great Sully was scattered to the winds in laughing largesse. The young King was completely ignored, his sacred person pushed aside to be trotted out on state occasions, when it was not unusual for his common mother to turn him over her knee and spank him like a street urchin for the amusement of the tittering court.

There were, of course, solid people, mostly the true nobility and the sober, practical *noblesse de robe*, the lawyers and councillors and intendants and members of the parlements; but these were forced to take a ceremonial part in the debacle because they were outnumbered and overruled. There were some worthy members of the new crowd, like the pious Catherine de Medici. And there were the perennial politicians like Michel de Marillac, a most seasoned courtier. His admirers have wasted thousands of turgid words and miles of tortuous rationalization in well-meaning efforts to reconcile the genuine piety and even saintliness of this remarkable man with his fancy political footwork. All in vain. There is no question of his administrative gifts or of his integrity and honesty in office; but, with all the facts in, it is a matter of record that he was a *Liguer*, then he was not; that he opposed Henri IV's accession, and that he helped arrange his triumphal entry into Paris; that he served Marie de Medici and, after Louis XIII had exiled her, became one of his most trusted lieutenants; that he despised the policy of Richelieu, helped to implement it, and was ready to supplant the Great Minister on the Day of Dupes. Indeed, attempts to "rehabilitate" Marillac are as unnecessary as they are futile: the French can separate private and public morality with Cartesian precision and a sincerity difficult for all non-Frenchmen to question and impossible for them to understand.

In and out of this musical-comedy court moved the great Cardinal himself, biding his time.

The newly married Le Gras bought or rented a *palais* or *hôtel*—what we would call a town house today—in the fashionable Marais-section parish of Saint-Merri on the right bank. For the first time in her life Louise did not have to watch her pennies. It is reported that, in a single year, the Le Gras spent eighteen thousand livres on the upkeep of their home—a far cry from the modest annual income of three hundred livres the young wife had lived on until now—and that they erected a turret, a status symbol of the day, on either this first house or a subsequent one in the parish of Saint-Sauveur. They had their circle of friends, of whom Louise's relatives were in the first rank. They were frequent visitors at the Hôtel d'Attichy, the Hôtel de Marillac, Uncle Michel's home on the rue Saint-Avoye, and the Petit Luxembourg, where Uncle Jean-Louis and his Medici wife had their suite.

There is no reason to assume that Louise despised the pleasant life of wealth and social acceptance her marriage had brought her. Guy shrewdly observes that she liked *"les belles choses."* And why not? She was wellborn. She had been raised in the elegance of Poissy. Her taste had been trained and refined by a classical education and the "things suitable to her condition" taught her by the mistress of the *pension*. All her writings reflect a delightful elegance, delicacy and discrimination. Certainly, Antoine Le Gras did not entertain lavishly or build his status turret against the wishes of his wife. Even in her widowhood, when she had begun to live a monastic sort of life in the world, Louise recognized the prior claim of the duties of her station: in the religious rule she wrote herself she proposed for her afternoons that she would work "for the Church, or for the poor, or for the good of the household, and the work will last until four o'clock. If I am obliged to make visits, or receive some, these hours will be thus employed."

Indeed, like St. Elizabeth of Hungary, Louise lived the life of the great Christian lady, dispensing the magnanimity the poor had come to expect from such a one. Gobillon records that from the first years of her marriage she visited "the sick poor of the parish where she dwelt. She took them soups and the remedies they needed, made their beds, instructed and comforted them by her exhortations, disposing them to receive the sacraments, and burying them after death. The parish of Saint-Sauveur, among others, where she lived as a widow, was the witness and object of all these acts of charity . . . Not content with relieving the poor in their homes, she visited them in the hospitals, bringing them treats over and above the necessities they received there, and rendering them with her own hands the lowliest and most demanding services."

There was an even more immediate witness to her good works. A woman servant of the Le Gras household attested that Louise "had a great piety and devotion for serving the poor. She brought them confections and sweetmeats, biscuits and other good things. She combed their hair, she cleansed their sores and vermin; she sewed them in their shrouds. She would leave her company to climb a hill [the Montagne Ste Genviève?], despite rain or hail, to help some poor man who shivered with the cold."

Characteristically, Louise, as she had in the *pension*, went beyond personal charity: she communicated her enthusiasm to others. "It was not enough for her personally to serve the suffering members of Jesus Christ," Gobillon testifies. "She wishes that other noble-born ladies share this honor with her; and she persuaded them by her urgings and example. It was thus that she tried out a great work she would one day launch for the solace of the miserable in the institution of a Company of Daughters, of which she has declared in writing she had conceived some design from the time of her marriage." Important and historic words. What was to come about some fifteen years later under the aegis of Vincent de Paul, the miracle of the Daughters of Charity, an idea so original that it flew in the face of public opinion and ecclesiastical tradition, was already stirring in the sedate head of this society matron from the Marais! The fact must be weighed thoughtfully in assigning credit for the foundation of the remarkable institute.

Second thoughts arise, too, about the organization of the Confraternities of Charity which were that institute's seedbed. There can be no question that, in God's good pleasure, they began under Vincent's hand, indeed, in his parish of Châtillon-les-Dombes, but the fact that the important first Parisian Confraternity was founded in Louise's parish of Saint-Sauveur and that its first membership was made up of her friends, whom she had brought together to serve the poor years before, suggests her strong influence in the work.

This holy influence made itself felt among the servants of her household, two of whom left her employ to enter religion: one with the Minims, and the other with the Benedictines of the new reform known as the Congregation of Saint-Maur.

The Les Gras' happiness was made complete in the first year of their marriage with the birth of a son on October 18, 1613. That the baby was premature in an age lacking the medical skill may account for his subsequent dull and often erratic behavior, behavior which was to cause his mother many heartaches. He was baptized the next day in the Church of Saint-Merri, and was named Michel-Antoine in compliment to the reigning Marillac and the infant's father. The godparents were René de Marillac, councillor of the King and Michel's son, and Louise's aunt Valence d'Attichy—mute evidence of the Marillac ascendancy and the Le Gras acceptance of it. Undoubtedly, Louise entered upon motherhood with the same enthusiasm she brought to everything. None of its sublimity or responsibility would have escaped her. Indeed, the remnants of her fierce grasp of both led Vincent de Paul, years later, to concede wryly: "You are more than an ordinary mother . . ."

The birth of this child in Louise's twenty-third year and the ninth month of her marriage brought a permanence and stability to the Le Gras' still strange and only partly explored married life. No matter how it had come about, through social arrangement or attraction or a combination of both, it now had a sense of finality that completely shut off the past and opened up a settled future. It brought Antoine a new seriousness of purpose and duty; it erased from Louise's mind every past hankering for the cloister; it drew them together in a knowing and loving bond that was exclusively theirs. In this shining moment of their common life there was no least suspicion of early death for the one or of agonizing doubt for the other.

Louise, in her last will and testament, describes Antoine Le Gras as "a man of good life, with a strong fear of God and exact in making himself irreproachable." In this laconic biography we have the sketch of a fastidious gentleman, anxious to a fault for his reputation and willing to earn it by meticulous observance of the divine and human laws and the social amenities. His family was noted for its charity and love of the poor, and had founded a hospital in Le Puy; Antoine himself was to evidence this family trait in his solicitude for the orphaned d'Attichy children. That, with it all, he was a son of Adam with faults like any man is attested to in a letter written by Louise after his death to his Carthusian cousin, Père Hilarion Rebours: "I will tell you that for a long time now, by God's mercy, he has had no longer any affection for matters which could lead to mortal sin and that he had a very great desire to live devoutly." There is the temptation to speculate concerning these "matters," but they are probably no more than the reaction of Louise's delicate conscience to the irritability to which Antoine's long illness made him prone —and which faded as death approached—and her overall regret that his more ordinary piety did not equal her own.

Her own piety had already climbed extraordinary heights. Her eagerness to express it in multiplied services to the poor and the sick came from deep wells of faith and religious practice. Hidden from her friends, these practices did not escape the sharp eyes of the servants. She made use of "hairshirt and discipline," the maid Delacour attested. "She pretended to eat at table but did not . . . As soon as her husband was asleep, she would get up to shut herself away in her oratory."

Louise herself is an even more trustworthy and meticulous witness. "I will work as hard as I can at mortifying my passions, especially those of vanity and too great impetuosity," she resolved in her *Rule of Life in the World*, "and to that end and to honor the sufferings of Jesus Christ I will take the discipline two or three times in the spirit of penance, and every Communion day I will wear in the morning the penitential cincture, and all day Friday. I will fast every Friday of the year; during Advent and Lent; all the eves of the feasts of Our Lord, the Virgin, the Apostles, and on every day commanded by the Church; and on the others which are not fast days I will eat only two meals, unless necessity or condescension obliges me otherwise."

Corporal penances like these can be extremely dangerous to an intemperate soul, and Louise had always to fight against a propensity to intemperateness in good. It is well to note, however, her tolerant and gracious bow to "necessity or condescension," and especially her choice of the word "obliges." Fortunately, her spiritual training at Poissy had been sound and she had always, from the beginning of her search for perfection, placed herself in the hands of solid spiritual guides.

It is impossible to identify all of them: it was Père de Champigny who directed her away from the cloistered life, and after 1614 or 1615 Jean-Pierre Camus, Bishop of Belley, was her chief director. He played a key role in her sanctity, not only because he guided her through the critical years which might be termed the dark night of her soul, but also because he led her to Vincent de Paul, who was to be, in the providence of God, the co-worker and captain of her life's achievement.

The Bishop of Belley—in his own right and by his intimacy with François de Sales famous in his time and in the history of French spirituality —was the "blessed Bishop of Geneva's" slavish imitator even to tone of voice and gesture until good-naturedly dissuaded from such folly by his idol. A man of flamboyant tastes, Camus was the embodiment of the baroque. His sermons were long tissues of purple passages, classical allusions, solid doctrine, literary curlicues, and anecdotes perilously close to bad taste. Enormously talented and energetic, he has left more than two hundred volumes to prove it, some sublime in their mysticism, some ludicrous in their thinly disguised romanticism. The judicious Bremond has written of him: "Jean-Pierre Camus is by no means the buffoon which a widely received tradition today represents him as being, and which would have considerably amazed the contemporaries of the famous Bishop of Belley . . . I do not ask that his innumerable spiritual treatises should be reprinted, but I do say that many of them seem to me excellent, and that no historian is justified in neglecting a writer who has had his thousands of readers and whose influence has been most valuable."

Far more intriguing than his claim to posterity's regard is the unlikely director-and-penitent relationship between this colorful prelate and the literal-minded Louise. How did it come about? Some biographers have traced a rather circuitous meeting through Michel de Marillac, who met François de Sales through Madame Acarie, and Camus through François de Sales. The truth may be much simpler. It is not at all proved, despite the few formal letters that passed between them and the social visits after her marriage, that Louise and her uncle Michel were close; it is a fact, however, that Camus was her stepmother's nephew. Whatever brought about the confluence of these two luminaries of the French religious revival of the seventeenth century, it was most original and memorable.

Camus came into Louise's life precisely at the time the freshness of her earthly happiness began to turn yellow at the edges. The first sign was the death in 1614 of her gallant kinsman, the Marquis d'Attichy; three years later, in 1617, his wife, Valence de Marillac, followed him. Her death was to have a profound effect on the lives of Louise and Antoine Le Gras because the seven orphan d'Attichy children, while left legally to the guardianship of their uncle Michel, became in fact the wards of the Le Gras. Michel's public life gave him no time for his nephews and nieces, and he asked the Le Gras to assume the responsibility for their upbringing. The d'Attichy children were to show themselves true Marillacs in their dedication to brilliance whether in the service of the Church or of the world, and the Italian blood inherited from their father added the piquancy that makes sensation out of achievement.

Henriette became, as Mère Angélique de Jésus, part of the ecstatic life of the Parisian Carmel instituted by her uncle Michel and his friends, Mme Acarie and Bérulle. Achille-Charles entered the Jesuits in the bright morning of their French resurgence, sparked by Père Coton's friendship and consequent influence with Henri IV. Louis, the familiar Père d'Attichy of French spiritual literature, was the chronicler of his Order of Minims and successively Bishop of Riez and of Autun. Antoine, the Marquis d'Attichy, who succeeded to his father's title, was a dashing man-at-arms whose recklessness got him killed in 1637. Anne, lady in waiting to Marie de Medici, stamped her beauty and passionate personality upon Paris and defied Richelieu, as her equally passionate husband, the Comte de Maure, defied Mazarin. Geneviève married Scipion d'Acquaviva, Duc d'Atri: their daughter Mlle d'Atri caused a furore in Paris over her alleged diabolical possession, a *cause célèbre* involving Vincent de Paul and Mère Angélique Arnauld, in a superstitous age which saw the auto-da-fé of the hapless Abbé Grandier and his "Devils of Loudun." Madeleine, the youngest d'Attichy, threw in her lot with Mme de Saint-Beuve's Ursulines and their audacious idea that women had as much right to an education as men.

This, then, was the lively brood left in the care of the gentle Louise and her clerkish husband. It was certainly in the Providence of God, for a hot head needs the guidance of a cool hand and the cool hand is often guided in turn by a heart of flame: there is delightful irony in the fact that the ladylike Louise showed herself more of a Marillac than any of them in the impact she made and continues to make on France and the world.

Before the young d'Attichy could be provided their brilliant futures, however, the state of the family fortune, which was vested largely in rich lands near Compiègne, had to be taken firmly in hand. Whether Mme d'Attichy had not been equal to the task of managing it after her husband's death is not clear, but it was in a precarious state. Antoine Le Gras gave it his full attention. As Louise tartly informed Père d'Attichy in 1644, when he insultingly asked if she had done nothing for her son, she "had failed in the duty of a good mother to my son" only in "not making known to him that my late husband had consumed everything, his time and his life, in looking after the affairs of [Père d'Attichy's] house, neglecting entirely his own property . . ."; and the harm done the Le Gras assets was complete. ". . . Since my widowhood I have been forced to seek help," she confessed to the Comte de Maure in

1649, "at least for the past ten or twelve years, as Monsieur and Madame de Marillac can well witness to you, and Madame their mother, to whom I owe great and special obligations, as well."

The time to give to the affairs of the d'Attichy was provided M. Le Gras by the unexpected fall from grace of his royal employer, Marie de Medici. On April 24, 1617, Concini was shot and stabbed to death in the courtyard of the Louvre by order of the young King and his favorite, the Duc de Luynes. The Queen Mother's reaction was typical. "This is the end," she cried with high drama. "For seven years I have been a ruler; now all I can hope for is a crown in heaven." When some lady in waiting asked, "How are we to tell the Maréchal's wife?" she screamed. "I have other things to think about; leave me in peace." On May 3 she went into exile to her castle at Blois amid the hoots and jeers of the ageless and omnipresent Parisian mob. The Marillac brothers survived the fall of the Regent; neither of them had yet reached a high enough eminence to fall to complete destruction. There is no evidence whatever to suggest that Antoine Le Gras went with Marie to Blois, but it would seem that he did not: his was only a minor post, easily filled; nor is there the least hint that Louise was left alone in Paris with the little boy Michel-Antoine, even for a short time; besides, this was the very time when Le Gras was attacking the problem of the d'Attichy finances.

How much of herself Louise had to give to the upbringing of the d'Attichy children is not clear. She makes no claim to having been their "stepmother." Her own son was her first responsibility, and the ominous signs of his delicate health and slowness to learn indicated that she would more than have her hands full. It is probable that the young d'Attichys were placed in the charge of a governess upon whom Louise kept a sharp yet motherly eye. Certainly the lifelong affection borne her by the Comtesse de Maure argues a more than perfunctory interest in the family on Louise's part; and it was Louise who arranged for the baby Madeleine to enter the Ursulines' school where her own half sister Innocente and her cousin Valence, Michel de Marillac's youngest child, had gone in 1607.

"I beg you to take her," Michel wrote, "after having learned from the mother prioress of Saint Ursula when it will be convenient for her to receive her. My wife or my daughter will make their carriage available when you have need of it." There is evidence that Louise played an active role in the management of the d'Attichy estate, probably in the years of her husband's illness, in the inquiries she made of her uncle Michel concerning the rights of slaughter, of sale, and of replanting the woods of the domain. It is the first evidence since her adolescent years in the *pension* of that remarkable taste and administrative talent that was to characterize the founding of the Daughters of Charity, a taste and talent God seems to give all religious foundresses in fulfillment of the qualities of the Strong Woman of the scriptures.

As often happens, the young d'Attichys were not always grateful to their guardian cousins. One of the boys, doubtless confident of his powers to be master of his own fate and feeling his adolescent oats, forgot his manners in impertinent letters to Antoine Le Gras. Calvet says that among other insolences he reminded Le Gras that his wife was once in need of the d'Attichy help. Smarting under the knowledge that this young ingrate was *her* relative, Louise with wifely indignation reported the matter to her uncle Michel and demanded a vote of confidence.

"Mademoiselle," answered the harried courtier, "I have seen my nephew's letters, at which I am very angry, and astonished that he has written in such terms. I beg both of you to excuse him; age and experience will moderate his spirit, for he is wellborn. M. Le Gras must not lose courage. The trouble that he takes will not fail of recognition. These accidents happen among persons to whom familiarity gives more liberty. I will not fail to speak to him about it when I see him." That "speaking to him" did not eradicate ingratitude from the d'Attichy forever is evident from the hauteur with which the then Père d'Attichy treated Louise when she sought his help for her son many years later.

In 1619 Louise had a great grace which was profoundly to affect her spiritual life and that of her future daughters. She met face to face the incomparable François de Sales. His *Introduction to a Devout Life* and *Treatise on the Love of God* had already become staples of her religious diet. Some biographers have treated this momentous meeting with suspicion, neither denying nor daring to affirm it. There seems no reason not to take Gobillon's word for it—he knew Louise personally and so many of her daughters, and his word on all other matters has been accepted without question. He says quite simply, in speaking of the mystical experience that came to Louise on the feast of Pentecost 1623: "She has declared in writing that she believed she obtained this grace by the merits of Saint François de Sales, for whom she had a great devotion, and who during his life had given her particular marks of affection and esteem, especially on the last trip he made to Paris, during which, having learned that she was ill, he honored her with several visits."

This last sojourn in Paris of the Bishop of Geneva from October 1618 to September 1619 was essentially a diplomatic mission. François de Sales had come in the suite of Cardinal Maurice de Savoie to facilitate negotiations for the marriage of Prince Victor Amédée of Piedmont with Princess Christine of France, sister of the King. The long visit became, as well, a spiritual experience for the French capital. The holy and genial Bishop is said to have preached three hundred times—Louise, hungry for the word of God, must certainly have heard such a preacher as often as she could—and all of the city's spiritual elite flocked to him. Even if no one had recorded a meeting between him and Louise, it would have almost certainly to be presumed, since she traveled in those circles where he would likely be found. Her director, Camus, was his closest friend; her friend and adviser, Mère Catherine de Beaumont, was superioress of his Visitation in Paris (which would lead to the presumption that Louise also met at this time Mère Jeanne de Chantal, who had come to Paris with François), and Michel de Marillac who had met the holy prelate at Mme Acarie's in 1602, would surely have seized as many opportunities as possible to renew so spiritually satisfying an acquaintance. It was very much in his character, moreover, for the saint to have paid the good Mlle Le Gras, friend of his friends, the courtesy of a visit when he learned through them of her piety and her illness.

His lasting impress on her spirituality, an impress passed on to her religious daughters and still evident in them, is the strongest argument of all for a personal acquaintanceship. It was not something caught from Vincent de Paul, as hindsight might suggest, for Louise did not meet Vincent, at least in the intimate role of spiritual confidant, until more than a year after her mystical experience of Pentecost 1623.

A curious relationship formed at this time by François de Sales was his connection with the fierce and austere Mère Angélique of Port-Royal. Not deep enough to be called a friendship, it nevertheless continued, in a series of letters, after his return to Savoie. The holy Bishop was intrigued by this strong woman with her grim love of God and her misguided capacity for good. It is interesting that he could not deter her by these written words from the same scruples and terrors that were soon to beset Louise, with whom he would have more success by his heavenly intervention after death.

The basic difference, of course, was in their personalities. Angélique Arnauld was essentially pitiless and cruel to herself and to others; Louise was essentially gentle and kind. It was not a question of strength in the one and weakness in the other: both were equally strong, but Angélique's strength was the strength of the battle steed that pride sits easily; Louise's was the strength of the humble beast of burden that draws willingly the load of others. Angélique was unafraid of pride; she used it for a goad. Louise was so afraid of it that she sank her spurs into it in anguish.

It was this earnest wish to efface herself, to lose herself in God—in which, it must be clearly recognized, God had an approving hand—that led her inevitably into a true dark night of the soul, and not what has, too often, been described as a stubborn self-entanglement with foolish scruples. These scruples and fears were to become the raw materials necessary to her purification; conquering them was her giant step toward sanctity. No one should be surprised that such little stones, negligible to the coarse, should afflict grievously a soul so refined and sensitive: they were as naturally abrasive to her genteel spirit as the luxurious temptations of St. Anthony to his desert austerity.

Those who have neatly and categorically labeled Louise neurotic and scrupulous during these formative years between 1619 and 1623, and who have unfortunately prevailed in creating this image of her before the world, have missed the point entirely. Neuroticism is complex and it may be that no one is wholly free from neuroses of one kind or another; but scrupulosity is another matter.

In flatly dismissing Louise as scrupulous, it would seem that her judges have failed to take into account, first, what is generally meant by scrupulosity, and second, the extraordinary purity of Louise's soul. Scrupulosity is an especially disagreeable spiritual disease, maddening to priest and penitent alike. It is caused and nourished by pride, in which the penitent-patient, behind his moral nit-picking, is secretly motivated by the desire that God have nothing "on" him. It can, and often does, coexist with mortal sin. To associate Louise with such a miserable form of spiritual immaturity is not only to fail to understand her, but to smear her good name.

Even, in these early years, Louise was sinless to a high degree. M. de Lestocq, Curé de Saint-Laurent and Louise's confessor for many years, gave strong testimony of this at her death: "O beautiful soul which takes with it the grace of its Baptism!" Gobillon, in recording his testimony, notes that "he had perfect knowledge by the general confession she had made to him." This same testimony was deposed and recorded in the process for Louise's beatification and canonization. Vincent de Paul, like any director in regard to his penitent, knew Louise's soul better than his own and witnessed to its purity, after her death:

> I asked myself: "What have you observed during the thirty-eight years you have known her? What did you see in her?" I remembered some little tiny fly of imperfection but, as for mortal sin, oh! never! The slightest stirring of the flesh was unbearable to her. She was a pure soul in all things, pure in her youth, in her married life, in her widowhood. She sifted her conscience in order to tell her sins and all her imaginations. She confessed her sins most clearly. I have never seen any who accused themselves of their sins with so much purity. She wept so that one had great difficulty in calming her.

Vincent might actually be describing the spiritual state of Louise during the years in question and, in a sense, he was. It is difficult, perhaps, for the ordinary mortal to comprehend the anguish caused within such a soul by the tiniest mote floating in the sunshine of its purity. Such souls see themselves differently from the general run of men and judge themselves more rigorously. The smallest imperfection is an enormity of evil in their eyes. Thus, Vincent de Paul could say of himself ironically that he "was a marvel, but a marvel of malice, more wicked than the devil, who merits to be in hell less than I . . ."; and when misfortunes befell the Company of Sisters, Louise was prompt and positive in blaming these misfortunes on her own "crimes." We say that such souls exaggerate; but not at all: they speak the truth, for they know the true ugliness and horror of the smallest smudge of imperfection seen against the blinding sinlessness of God.

Louise, while at times unduly agitated at the sight of her imperfections, was never scrupulous. Her fears had to be constantly quelled; she had to be assured and reassured; she had to fight her anxieties, bringing them, shamefaced, one by one to be dealt with by confessor or director— but, unlike the truly scrupulous, she was ever obedient, wanting to put them down no matter the cost in agonizing doubt, all the while waiting with what docility she could muster for deliverance in God's good time.

Quite simply, at the heart of Louise's trials was an overeagerness to be wholly good, with no admixture of the slightest evil, and that on the instant. She wanted instant perfection with what she herself labeled "a too great impetuosity." The wise Camus put his finger on it in warning,

"You have a certain spiritual avidity which needs to be controlled." It was this "spiritual avidity" that drove her to multiple penances and prayers and spiritual retreats and examens of conscience. "I am consoled to know that exercises of recollection and spiritual retreats are so useful to you and so much to your taste," the good Bishop wrote, smiling to himself, no doubt, "but it is necessary for you to take them like honey, rarely and in moderation."

Louise sought advice from her uncle Michel, probably (from the context of his replies) when she was writing to him about other matters or at times when she was cast down and her director was out of reach. Marillac's personal holiness and deep knowledge of spiritual things—his rapport with Mme Acarie, Cardinal de Bérulle, Antoine Du Val, the Capuchin mystics Benoît de Canfield and Ange de Joyeuse; in fact, all the Parisian spirituality of the day—made him eminently fitted to receive her confidences. He seems, however, to have given her cold comfort, either because of his formal nature, which could not bend to her highly personal anguish, or because he did not understand—a lack which can be forgiven him, since he was not her director and thus had no real knowledge of her soul. In any event, he fed her the general Bérullean doctrine of self-abnegation, without any specific application to her problems.

Thus, he wrote, on September 12, 1619: "Have patience and humiliate yourself before God . . . Dwell tranquil and humble in the sight of your faults . . ."; and on March 6, 1620: ". . . for the rest, Mademoiselle, it is good to learn from experience that God is not attached to our plans and propositions . . . The poor soul who knows itself such and accepts the knowledge in peace awaits from God whatever comes, without expecting it in one way rather than another. She is content to submit herself to God, and does not wish to prescribe to him the manner of leading her."

Louise knew all this and had ever practiced it as best she could. As Calvet has said well, at this point "she stood more in need of encouragement than of humbling." Closer to her need was her uncle's advice to imitate the patience of the humble soul: "She takes what comes . . . satisfied to do the best she can without grieving over what is beyond her, what is not in her power." Even here, Marillac was begging the question. Louise's anxiety was precisely concerned with what *was* in her power. Seeing the awful purity of God more clearly every day, she was terrified lest her imperfections—which, too, she saw ever more clearly—

her failure perhaps to correspond, as fully as God expected her to, to graces received, might be interpreted by her Beloved as conscious infidelities. The thought of infidelity, however unintended, is a horror, a blasphemy, not to be borne by those who truly love, whether man or woman, husband or wife, friend and friend, the enlightened soul and God.

Louise's trials were sharpened by the illness of her husband, which began in 1621 or 1622 and dragged on for almost four years. It is hard to define his ailment, for all illnesses of this time seem to be described in terms of fever; but from its slow progress, the patient's languishing state, his irritability, and the hemorrhaging at his death, it seems to have been a form of tuberculosis.

Louise waited on him hand and foot, night and day. His comfort and care was now her whole life. Terrible as it was, it was a great experience in loving for them both, and when he died she could say with her future daughter, Blessed Elizabeth Ann Seton, who thus described a last visit to her husband's grave-in-exile after a like long trial:

> I wept plentifully over it with the unrestrained affection which the last sufferings of his life, added to the remembrance of former years, had made almost more than human. When you read my daily memorandums since I left home, you will feel what my love has been and acknowledge that God alone could support it by His assistance through such proofs as have been required of it.

The proofs required of Louise's love were, in their place and time, as formidable as those required of the Blessed Elizabeth Ann—the endless nursing, the feeding, the vigils, the patient endurance of the sick man's helpless moods and petulance. Although the more reticent Louise did not record them, her friend and biographer did. "This charitable and faithful wife," wrote Gobillon, "showed him [Antoine] . . . a most tender affection, a most compassionate goodness, and a most compliant love, in trying to calm his spirit and sweeten his pains and sorrows." Louise's own indelible remembrance of her love, and these affecting years which crowned it, was in the yearly Mass she never failed to have said for Antoine on the anniversary of their marriage, in her bridling defense of him whenever his memory was impugned, and in the long and loving tribute to him written into her will more than thirty years later.

To test her to the breaking point, in the midst of this exhausting, long-drawn-out physical trial, the blackest part of her dark night now descended upon her with such smothering effect as to snuff out, if possible, her very soul. The most malevolent demons of doubt lurked in this horrible blackness.

Had she vowed to enter the Capucines back there half her lifetime ago? Or had she merely promised? Did Père de Champigny's rejection of her release her from her vow—or promise? Was she being punished for infidelity? Worse yet, had she, like Jonah, brought punishment on innocent people? On her son? It was evident that he was not as normal as were other boys his age. On her husband, who cherished her? The d'Attichy affairs had eaten deep into his fortune—this painful, debilitating illness . . .

It was easy for her in her physical and mental weariness to look on her life with dejection and almost despair. Time passed constantly, day and night without letup, before the eyes of a memory made myopic by trouble and pinched nerves, so that it seemed a continuous saga of hard luck with no touch of relief. The shameful birth; the lonely childhood; the struggling teens; the indifference, not to say hostility, of her relatives; the dashed hopes of convent peace; the social humiliations of her marriage; the backward child; the insolent and ungrateful wards; the sick husband. And, pounding incessantly through all, the haunting fear of infidelity to her divine Spouse.

Bishop Camus understood, and what is more, with his good nature and genial view of earth and heaven so akin to the view of his amiable friend de Sales, he was just the man to cheer her up, not by scoffing at her very real dejection but by trying to coax her to smile through her tears:

> Mademoiselle, my dear sister . . . I sympathize with you in the inertia of mind in which you find yourself because of the illness of your dear husband. Come, now, here is your cross! Why should I be sorry to see it on the shoulder of a daughter of the Cross? You lack neither skill, nor advice, nor books, nor intelligence, to carry it well.

This was certainly the vote of confidence she needed: she was fully capable of doing what she had to do; she needed, the good Bishop finished gently, only the determination to do it: "God wants you not to lack the courage." Then he got down to a specific problem. Pope Paul V had decreed a jubilee year, and to prepare herself to gain its indulgences, Louise's thoughts flew inevitably to a general confession. "There you go again! Ever the general confessions!" he jollied her. "Oh, how many times have I told you: short shrift to general confessions for your heart!

Oh, no, that is not what the Jubilee means for you, but for you to rejoice in God your Savior! for you to say: *Jubilemus Deo salutari nostro!*" This prelate knew that the eddies of darkness were not of her choosing. "I am always waiting," he wrote on another occasion, "for serenity to return to you after the clouds which prevent you from seeing the beautiful brightness of the joy which belongs to the service of God." And to deter her from delaying the lifting of those clouds by the slightest action of her own: "Do not make such great difficulties out of indifferent matters. Turn your gaze ever so little from yourself and fix it on Jesus Christ!"

Louise has left a humble and moving record of the climax of her great trial: "On St. Monica's Day [May 4, 1623] God gave me the grace to make a vow of widowhood if God should call my husband." A strange vow, indeed, which a modern biographer has scored as "repulsive" and "ridiculous." On the face of it, it is both; but the saint wrote down the history of it many years later when her soul was at peace and most wise in its judgment, and she stated in judicious retrospect without qualification that "God gave me the grace to make [it]." Her conviction cannot be brushed lightly aside. It would seem, therefore, that this vow might better be characterized a "mystery," as Augustine, St. Monica's great son, characterized Jacob's deception of his father, and other Church writers have characterized God's probing demand for the sacrifice of Isaac or His testing of St. Joseph in hiding from him the divine maternity of Mary.

There seems little doubt that this vow was made with the approbation of Bishop Camus. He was in Paris at the time—as we learn from his written permission, signed on May 8, 1623, "for Monsieur Le Gras and . . . Mademoiselle his wife" to read "the Holy Bible in French according to the translation of the Doctors of Louvain"—and Louise would hardly have failed to consult him, to whose counsel, by her own admission, she was firmly attached.

This mysterious vow actually precipitated the crisis. For three weeks there was a kind of peace, and then: "On Ascension Day following [May 25], I entered into a great desolation of spirit which lasted until Pentecost [June 4], because of a doubt as to whether I should leave my husband, as I wished to do in order to repair my first vow and have freedom to serve God and the neighbor."

The fear of the least infidelity to her divine Spouse, whom she had chosen long ago in her childhood and to whom she had bound herself tighter when she was sixteen by the promise to enter religion, brought on this new, agonized involution of doubt. Had she failed her divine Spouse? Had she unlawfully put an earthly spouse in His place? In her driven, confused condition, the next question—foolish when taken out of context—was painfully logical: did God want her, therefore, to separate from this man she had married, the father of her child? The very possibility must have brought her fresh anguish. Antoine was sick, he needed her; and no matter what had been in the beginning, their life together had brought her to love him.

It is indicative of Louise's anchorless desperation to do the most perfect thing God wanted her to that she now coupled to this doubt concerning her husband a further doubt as to whether, because of her attachment to Camus as a director, she should separate herself from him too! "I feared further that the attachment I had for my director might prevent me from taking another, thinking myself obliged to quit him . . ." The pitiless progression of these steps of doubt which, if capitulated to, would cast her wholly adrift, led inevitably to the most monstrous doubt of all: "I had great pain because of doubt concerning the immortality of the soul. These three uncertainties gripped my soul in agonies which [now] seem to me unimaginable." This horrible nadir of despair lasted through the novena of days during which the Apostles had barricaded themselves in the Upper Room in the same kind of unreasonable and unreasoning terror. Then the Holy Spirit, as He had come to the Apostles with His light and strength, now descended upon Louise in blinding deliverance:

> On the day of Pentecost, at Saint-Nicolas-des-Champs during holy Mass, all on the instant my spirit was cleared of these doubts. I was made to understand that I must dwell with my husband and that the time would come when I could make vows of poverty, chastity, and obedience and that this would be while living with others, some of whom would do the same. I understood further that this would occur at a place devoted to assisting the neighbor, but I could not imagine how it would come about, for such a thing would require going out and returning.
>
> I was also assured that I must be at peace insofar as my director was concerned and that God would give me another, who was then, so it seems to me, shown me in vision, and I felt a repugnance to accept him. I submitted, nevertheless, although it seemed to me that it would not be necessary to make this change yet.
>
> My third difficulty was banished by the assurance I felt in my soul that it was God who revealed all this to me and that, there being a God, I

must not doubt the rest. At that time, doubt concerning immortality was inclining me to a lack of belief in divinity.

I have always believed that I received this grace through the blessed Monsiegneur de Genève [François de Sales] for having, before his death, earnestly desired to communicate these troubles to him and having since felt a great devotion to him. I have received many graces through him, and at that time I had a special reason—which I cannot recall now—for believing that [I had received this one through him].

IV

Vincent de Paul

All was not over, and Antoine's illness had yet a long time to run its fatal course. Louise's anxious and sensitive nature, like St. Paul's "sting of the flesh," would last her lifetime and for the same purpose: to keep her humble. Both nature and soul were soon to be given into the keeping of another spiritual director of whom Camus had been only the precursor. This was the guide of her vision, her internal illumination, the promised one she had viewed with a pronounced distaste and holding back. His name was Vincent de Paul.

If Louise did not know him personally—the Hôtel de Gondi on the rue Pavée, where he lived, was not far from her own house in the same parish of Saint-Sauveur—she certainly knew him by reputation. House chaplain to the powerful de Gondi, grand chaplain of the Galleys, founder of the Mission and the Confraternities of Charity, his name was already one to be reckoned with in Paris.

He had been born in 1581 at Dax in Gascony. As a boy mounted on his rustic stilts, he had herded sheep and swine by that same Adour which was fed by the Gave, the river that swept by Massabielle in Lourdes where Bernadette Soubirous was to meet her "beautiful lady." When he showed an early leaning to the priesthood, his father, with the self-sacrificing faith of the peasant, sold a sorely needed yoke of oxen to send him to school in Dax. Having completed his studies at Toulouse with at least the licentiate in theology, he was ordained priest at only twenty by François de Bourdeilles, Bishop of Perigueux, at Château-l'Évêque on September 23, 1600.

Vincent was a good priest, but he was not averse to the material security which a modest benefice would bring him and his family. Soon after ordination he traveled to Rome to fight vainly for a contested benefice awarded him by his bishop. A few years afterward he was in Bordeaux on a mysterious errand which rumor says involved a bishopric proferred by the Duc d'Epernon, whose son was Vincent's pupil. He next learned of a small legacy left him by a good old woman, along with the right to collect some debts owed her. When one of the debtors decamped to Marseilles, Vincent went after him in hot pursuit, had him jailed, and got back what was now his. A sudden decision to return part of the way by sea was to begin for Vincent an adventure right out of the Arabian Nights.

Only a few miles off the coast, his ship was attacked "with such ferocity that two or three of our men were killed," he recorded, "and all the rest wounded. I myself was wounded by an arrow; for the rest of my life I shall feel it . . ." Taken to the Barbary Coast, Vincent and the captives were sold as slaves in the public market, "where the dealers came and inspected us much in the same way as a horse or an ox is inspected at a sale; they made us open our mouths to show our teeth, felt our sides, probed our wounds, made us walk, trot, run, carry a pack and then wrestle with each other to show our respective strengths . . ."

Vincent was luckier than many another slave: he was sold to a fisherman. But as he had "always been a very bad sailor," he was quickly got rid of to an old alchemist, who was "a very kind and humane man." The old man took to Vincent almost like a father to a son, even promising to give him all his knowledge and wealth if the priest would convert to Islam. When the old man died, he bequeathed Vincent to his nephew, who quickly sold him to a renegade Christian from Nice in Savoie. This man had three wives, and one of them, says Vincent, "a Turk by birth, was instrumental, through the boundless mercy of God, in drawing her husband out of his apostasy back into the Church and delivering me from my slavery." It was Vincent's singing of the Jewish psalm of exile, *Super Flumina Babylonis,* and the Salve Regina that won the woman's sympathy and started the train of salvific events that led to the escape of master, wives and slave in a skiff. They arrived at the French coast on June 28, 1607, and the renegade was reconciled to the Church at Avignon by the Vice Legate, Bishop Montorio. Vincent's meeting with Montorio was a fortunate one because alchemy was the Vice Legate's hobby, and he took Vincent to Rome with him, showing him every kindness in order to bilk him of the old Turk's secrets. "His Lordship is exceedingly anxious lest I should communicate these things to others and he hardly wishes me to talk to anyone," Vincent wrote. "He wishes to keep them for himself alone, desiring to have a reputation for this knowledge and on occasion to be able to show it off to His Holiness and to the Cardinals."

The years of Vincent's captivity (1605–7) were not lost years. Jean Calvet says of them that they left their mark on his life: "At Tunis he acquired the formulae of the various cures which he later passed on to the Sisters of Charity and were considered efficacious. At Tunis, too, he contracted that 'colonial fever'—his *fièvrotte*, as he used to call it—which was his constant trial. Because he had witnessed and felt in his own body a prisoner's complete wretchedness, he started the missions and established the consulates in Tunis and Algiers, set up what was to all intents a post office and a bank to put the prisoners in touch with their families, and with Captain Paul organized a military expedition against the Barbary Corsairs to bring to an end what was a scandal to the whole of Christendom. When at Marseilles he embarked on that short but disastrous voyage and went aboard the fatal felucca, one is tempted to inquire with Molière's character, 'What the devil is he doing there?' He went to get ready for his future work and to fulfill those mysterious designs of Providence which historians, with their hypotheses, explain so erroneously."

The next leg of the life journey mapped out by Providence for the young priest was a secret mission to Henri IV, presumably a verbal message to the King from Pope Paul V. Some historians have been bothered about the plausability of a young nobody of a cleric being employed in such high diplomacy, but it could be explained by the supposition that he may very well have been the only trustworthy French priest at hand. Out of this mission came an appointment to the court of the aging but still glamorous Queen Marguerite de Valois, ex-wife of Henri, as one of her almoners. On his rounds to distribute the lavish alms of this once-dissolute Queen with a weather eye on the hereafter, Vincent now saw at first hand the frightening misery of the Parisian poor. And he met Bérulle, the future Cardinal, who became almost at once Vincent's spiritual director, to be obeyed gladly by the disciple in all things.

Through the resignation of the parish of Clichy by an Abbé Bourgoing, one of Bérulle's first Oratorians, Vincent became pastor there. He had only one blissful year of what he would have liked for his whole priesthood when Bérulle peremptorily ordered him to leave his parish for the household of Philippe-Emmanuel de Gondi, Comte de Joigny, Marquis des Iles d'Or, Baron de Montmirail, Dampierre, et Villepreux, General of the Galleys and the King's lieutenant general for the fleet of the Levant. Here he was assigned to tutor de Gondi's three children, whom their aunt labeled "holy terrors." The youngest was the future, infamous Cardinal de Retz; but his future character must not be blamed on Vincent, for he was too young, unfortunately, to have had lessons from the saint. Vincent's love for the House of Gondi was such that years later he even sneaked this wretched Cardinal on a technicality into the respectable, holy assemblage of the clergy of the Tuesday Conferences.

Vincent's chief task in this eminent household soon became the care of the soul of Madame de Gondi, born Marguerite de Silly, daughter of the Comte de Rochepot, Seigneur d'Euville, Commercy et Folleville. This exceptional woman had a high and serious dedication to the things of the spirit, but she was truly scrupulous, tormenting her director with self-made difficulties that had to be resolved over and over again, refusing to let him out of her sight, and threatening him with the weight of guilt if she should die without the sacraments and be lost in his absence. She possessed many of the spiritual symptoms Louise had shown and was still to reveal even to Vincent, but the similarity is shallow; indeed, the very comparison highlights the basic strength and health of Louise's soul. Nevertheless, it was this good Madame de Gondi who was to point the way to Vincent's career of charity and in the process literally to establish the Congregation of Priests of the Mission.

Profoundly disturbed at the spiritual squalor of the country poor on her estates, she took Vincent with her on her tour of inspection, in January 1617, to Folleville. There he heard the confession of a dying man, esteemed the most pious in the village, who out of fear had been making bad confessions for half his lifetime—as he afterward confessed publicly. Appalled, Vincent preached in the village church on the twenty-fifth a sermon on general confession that met such a response that neighboring priests and Jesuit Fathers from Amiens had to be called in to cope with the avalanche of confessions. Out of these helpers Vincent formed on the spot the first mission band to bring the word and hope of salvation to a whole countryside that had never heard it. He soon saw clearly that the excellent effects of the mission would not last without a radical reform of the clergy, many of whom were so ignorant that they did not even know the words of absolution.

Thus were revealed to him the two cornerstones of his future Congregation: missions to the poor country people, and the education of the clergy. But the Congregation did not take substantial form until April 17, 1625, under the concerted action of the de Gondis led by the pious Madame Marguerite. The General of the Galleys and his wife provided the cash capital for the undertaking and the General's brother Jean-François, Archbishop of Paris, provided the motherhouse—a run-down college called the Bons Enfants, which the rector gave over in return for the promise of a life pension.

Despite the exhilaration of saving souls on occasion given him by the de Gondis, Vincent was stifling in the hothouse atmosphere of their great *hôtel* with its attendant pomp and circumstance. When Bérulle gave him the chance of escape to a parish in Châtillon-les-Dombes in 1617, he seized it with such unbelieving joy that he stole out of the house at night, lest the outcries of his good mistress constrain him. Her entreaties followed him in a barrage of letters; more to the point, her counterattack was trained on Bérulle too, where it soon found its mark. In a matter of months, scarcely the space of a mission, Vincent was back in his gilded cage.

But what he had accomplished in that time! First, he had made inroads on a pocket of determined Calvinists in the district, effecting important conversions, notably that of Jean Beynier, a rich bourgeois. Vincent's approach was brand-new and especially to be noted by our ecumenical age: he reached the hearts of Protestants, not with books and controversy, but with Christian love. It was the approach, anticipated by 350 years, of Pope John XXIII to the great Rabbi: "I am Joseph your brother." Secondly, Vincent had founded at Châtillon-les-Dombes the first of the Confraternities of Charity which were to sweep up nobleman and peasant alike in a revolutionary wave of Christian compassion that still washes through the chinks and crevices of the world. Vincent himself best describes its founding:

> Being near Lyon in a little town where Providence had called me to be parish priest, one Sunday, as I was vesting to say Mass, they came to tell me that in a house at some distance from any other, a quarter of a league away, everyone was ill, so that there was not one person well enough to look after the rest, and all in the greatest need. My heart was deeply touched. I did not forget to speak affectionately of them in my sermon, and God touched the hearts of all who heard, so that they were all moved with compassion for them in their trouble.
>
> After dinner that day, a group gathered in the house of a good spinster in the town, to see what help could be given, and everyone felt a wish to

go and see them, to comfort them in words, and help them in deed. After Vespers, I took a fine man, a citizen of the town, and we set out together to go there. All along the road we met women who had gone before us, and farther on we met others coming back. And since it was in the great heat of summer, these good women were sitting along the roadside to rest and cool themselves. At last, my daughters, there were so many that it looked like a procession. When I arrived I visited the sick, and went to get the Blessed Sacrament for those who needed it, not from the parish church but a dependency of a chapter of which I was head. After hearing their confessions and giving them Communion, I came to consider what could be done to help them in their need. I suggested to all these good people whose charity had brought them there, to club together, so that each should have a day to provide soup, not only for them, but for others who might need it later; that was the first beginning of this Charity.

The heart of its success lay in the simple, perfect balance of the human and the divine laid down in the first rule, written out in Vincent's own hand. That rule was the prototype of the many rules for many works to follow, and its spirit is evident in everything Vincent or Louise ever did:

She who is on duty for the day will bring in the dinner and carry it to the sick; as she enters, she will greet the patient cheerfully and charitably. She will set the bedtable over the bed, and put a cloth on the table, with a platter, a spoon and bread; she will wash the hands of the patient, and say grace; she will pour soup into a bowl and put meat on a plate, arranging everything on the said bedtable. She will then charitably invite the patient to eat, for the love of Jesus and His holy Mother; and she will do all things lovingly, as if for her own son, or rather for God, who will accept as done to Himself the good she does to the poor. She will address to him in this sense some few words concerning Our Lord, seeking to cheer him up, if he be very depressed; she will sometimes cut up his meat for him, and pour out his drink; and having settled him down to his meal, if he have someone else at hand, she will leave this patient, and go on her way, to find another to be likewise treated; remembering always to begin with those that are attended and to end with those that are alone, so that she may remain with these for a longer time.

It is impossible to say precisely when the director-penitent relationship of Vincent and Louise began, but it was after Pentecost 1623, and surely some time after, for Louise has given evidence of her satisfaction that she did not have to make a change of directors immediately. Vincent, in the first of his two conferences on Louise's virtues, July 3, 1660, recalled that he had known her for thirty-eight years—which may very well have been so—but if he meant in his capacity as her director, which the context of the words seems to imply, his apparent mistake must be ascribed either to the supposition that he was speaking in round numbers or to his old age and the blurring effect of time on memory.

The significant date for making a determination is October 29, 1623, when Camus wrote Louise some unexpected and depressing news. Antoine Le Gras had experienced a new crisis in his downward trend to death, and Louise had informed the Bishop of it and of how, for that reason, she especially looked forward to his presence in Paris for his annual Advent and Lenten courses of sermons.

"O God, my very dear sister," Camus replied in obvious distress, "what a blow to your heart! This dearly loved husband is thought to be dying, and this wretched father who writes you cannot come to Paris this winter. Do not sigh over yourself, my very dear daughter, but over me, who, separated from my country and my own, am relegated to an exile which has nothing attractive about it but the very attractive Will of God which renders everything attractive . . . So it is that I leave Paris and the two premier pulpits of Paris, where, to tell the truth, I do not deserve to appear, and that because it pleases the will of Him whose will is our life." Camus may have intended this vicarious salve—you think *you* have troubles—in way of teasing comfort, but some genuine self-pity seems to have escaped through the lines.

Other biographers have hesitated to point to Camus as the intermediary who brought Vincent and Louise together; but again, it would seem that Gobillon must be taken at his word: "He [Camus] believed that he could not confide her [Louise] to a wiser guide than the great Vincent de Paul, of whom Saint François de Sales, his friend, had given him the highest and most just notion. It is thus that by a secret disposition of the eternal Wisdom, this Prelate was happily the Author of the holy liaison which united these two great souls and their Companies, for the relief of the poor and the most arduous works of charity." It is probable, therefore, that through the good offices of the Bishop of Belley, Vincent de Paul assumed his lifelong care of Louise's soul in the late autumn of 1623 or soon after the start of 1624. To bring it about, the prelate must have had to employ his considerable charm and the memory of their mutual friend François de Sales, for Vincent seems to have been as reluctant as Louise, but for different reasons. He saw himself becoming more and more involved in a mission effort that would take him with increasing frequency away from Paris, and he was not anxious to complicate this effort with further commitments. He was already directing Madame de Chantal out of respect and obligation to her and the dead de Sales; and out of the same motives, he had accepted the guardianship of the Paris Visitation. Besides, his experience with the spiritual vagaries of Madame de Gondi had bred in him a deep caution lest he get himself so embroiled again. Could he have foreseen what was to result from this new encounter, he would have acquiesced at once and with fervor.

There is no correspondence between Vincent and Louise extant for the first year or two of their relationship, but this should not cause surprise, since he still lived close by at the Hôtel de Gondi and his direction would have been given face to face. Indeed, the entire body of their correspondence is regrettably small, considering its span of thirty-five years, because they saw each other frequently; we can be grateful for the little that we have to the fact that both of them, especially in the early years, traveled a great deal on the business of their respective communities, and that both of them were often ill.

Vincent's misgivings lest his absences from Paris affect the balance of so delicate a ministry as personal direction had not been rash. Louise was still terrified, in time of trouble, of recourse not being just around the corner. On one of Vincent's absences, perhaps the first in her experience, she dashed off a plea for help to the dependable Camus; but if she expected sympathy, she got none.

"Pardon me, my very dear sister," he answered with just a shade of annoyance, "pardon me if I tell you that you attach yourself a little too much to those who direct you, that you lean on them a little too much." He continued in fine irony: "Behold M. Vincent out of sight and Mlle Le Gras all in a heap and at loose ends! It is very necessary to see God in our directors and them in God. Sometimes, however, it is necesarry to see God all by Himself, who, without man and without [healing] pool, can cure us of our paralyses." Then, fearful that he has been too severe: "It is not, O dear soul, that it bothers me to guide or counsel you. Alas! no, on the contrary, for I hope that by this guidance you will guide me to heaven whither your example invites me more than my advice helps you along the road. It is just that I do not like to see those little weaknesses, those little clouds, in Mlle Le Gras's spirit, of which I take such great account, and which seems to me so clear and so strong."

God knew enough about Louise's inner strength, despite her own distrust of self, to will that she should be alone in the critical hour that had been building for four years. It was November 1625. Antoine's illness had suffered the crippling complication of a cerebral hemorrhage. Vincent had gone all the way to the South of France to carry to the General of the Galleys the sad news that his wife had died in June—Vincent had been with her at the end—and his duties as chaplain to the galley slaves had detained him there. Louise turned, as one woman turns to another in time of trouble, to her friend Mère Catherine de Beaumont.

"I suffer greatly with you in your sorrow, my very dear daughter," the Visitandine answered, "but I have no fear, for all that; I hope, rather, that the hand which dealt you the wound will heal you. O God, be then entirely at peace and courageous in supporting with patience what has been given you with such great love. Do you think that God would make you suffer for any other reason than to make you merit? You must leave the wherefore to Him and be wholly submissive to His good pleasure. Leave be, then, my dear child, and do not notice so much what you feel and suffer, but unite your will to the heavenly Father's to do and suffer all that pleases Him. Then, having done everything you could for your dear husband's health, leave the outcome to the good pleasure of God. I have no news at all of M. Vincent . . ."

The broken wife stayed at her post, torn with agony at each fresh agony of the poor sufferer. She bathed the sweating brow, kissed the fevered lips, coaxed between them the little nourishment they could take. And she prayed, silently in her heart, and aloud with him. Then, in the dragging hours of the night of December 20–21, the end came.

Louise relived the sad, loving memory of Antoine's last days in describing them for his Carthusian cousin, Père Hilarion Rebours:

> My very reverend Father, since you wish to know the graces the good God gave my late husband, after having said that it is impossible for me to make known all of them, I will tell you that, for a long time since, by the mercy of God, he no longer had any attraction for anything that could lead to mortal sin, and that he had a very great desire to live devoutly. Six weeks before his death he suffered a burning fever which put his life in great danger: but God, knowing how to show His power over nature, put him at peace; in acknowledgment of this grace, he made the resolution to serve God wholly all his life.
>
> He scarcely slept at all at night: but he had such patience that those looking after him were not the least inconvenienced. God wished Him to imitate the pains of His own death, for he suffered in his entire body, and lost all his blood. His soul was ever occupied in meditating on the Passion.

Seven times he hemorrhaged profusely from the mouth; and the seventh took his life on the instant.

I was alone with him to help him on this most important passage, and he showed, even to his last breath, that his soul was attached to God. He could not speak to me, except to say, "Pray God for me, I can no longer," words which will ever be engraved in my heart. I beg you to remember him when you say Compline; he had such a special devotion to it that he never failed to say it every day.

In the December cold of early morning Louise made her way through the dark streets to inform M. Jean Hollandre de Montdidier, Curé de Saint-Sauveur, of Antoine's death and to arrange for his funeral. It was right that this good pastor be the first to know, for he had visited the sick man all through his long illness and fortified him for death with the Last Sacraments. The grieving widow had need of comforting, too, and accepted it gratefully. Then she went to confession, heard the first Mass for the repose of Antoine's soul and received Communion for him, and for herself, that God would give her the strength she needed in her sorrow and, Gobillon adds, "to consecrate herself to [Jesus Christ] as her only Spouse." The time had come to pay her vow.

"Is it not most reasonable that I belong entirely to God, having belonged so long a time to the world?" she asked Père Rebours later. "I tell you then, my dear Cousin, that I vow it with all my heart, and in the way He pleases."

For some reason, Antoine's funeral was not held for ten days, according to Baunard, citing the *Journal de Christofle Petit, prêtre à l'église de S. Paul.* Such long delay between death and burial does not seem to have been the custom of the time; perhaps it was due in this case to the Christmas holidays and the time required to open and prepare the burial vault. The body was carried first to Saint-Sauveur for the requiem Mass, then to Saint-Paul, where it was laid to rest in the sepulchre of the Marillacs.

The faithful Camus sent a letter of condolence dated February 22, 1626. "At last, my very dear sister, the Savior of our souls, having placed your husband in His bosom, has placed Himself in yours," he wrote tenderly. "O heavenly Spouse, be ever that to my sister, who chose you as such when she was still divided . . . O God, my very dear soul, in this hour you must lean upon, you must hold fast to, the cross, since you no longer have your earthly support. Now you must call on God to remember His word. And what word, my very dear daughter? That He will be 'the father of the orphan and the judge of the widow': judge, my dear sister, to take her cause in hand, to judge her adversaries. Now we shall see whether you have loved God as you ought, since He has deprived you of him whom you greatly loved. Eternal peace and repose be to this dear soul for whom we pray; and consolation to yours from the Father of all consolation and the God of all mercies. Amen!"

This letter opened the floodgate of her woman's heart and brought a grief that left Camus, mere man as he was, completely bewildered: "I do not understand why your spirit is troubled and believes itself to be in darkness and abandoned. To what purpose? You are no longer divided. You determined long since to want only Him, and now that He has broken your bonds and you ought to offer Him a sacrifice of praise, you are astonished!" He ended with sublime spiritual advice which was beside the point, for Louise, for the moment, was but a grieving widow like any other. "Daughter of little faith, why do you doubt? I must say to you what Our Lord said to Mary at the resurrection of Lazarus: if you had more constancy you would see the glory of God upon you." What good is it to urge constancy on a woman worn out with long vigils and broken-hearted?

The bond that makes two people one flesh is not broken easily; nor did Louise ever forget, in all the years of a wholly new life in religion, that part of her lay buried in the church of Saint-Paul. She even came to see, by the illumination of God, a mystical relationship between her earthly marriage and her espousal to Christ, a sort of personal gloss on the parallel drawn by St. Paul between the bond of the Sacrament of Matrimony and the bond uniting Christ and His Church. Such an illumination came to her on a morning in the year 1630 as she was about to set out on a visitation on one of the Confraternities of Charity: "I left on St. Agatha's day, the 5th of February, to go to Saint-Cloud. At Holy Communion it seemed to me that Our Lord gave me the thought to receive Him as the Spouse of my soul, and more, that this would be for me a form of espousal; and I felt myself most strongly united to God in this consideration which struck me as extraordinary, and I had the thought to leave everything to follow my Spouse, henceforth to consider Him such, and to support the difficulties I would encounter as receiving them out of the community of His goods."

The boldness of this last figure reveals how deeply her soul was shaken; but in the very next sentence, with all the naturalness in the world, she turns from this divine sublimity to thoughts of her earthly marriage; and, as if in approval, receives a further grace from God. "Desiring to have Mass said on this day because it was the anniversary of my marriage, I deprived myself in order to perform an act of poverty, wishing to be entirely dependent on God in the action I was going to do. I gave no hint of this to my confessor, who said the Mass at which I communicated; but God permitted that, arriving at the altar, he had the thought to say the Mass for me in way of an alms, and to say the Nuptial Mass."

As Louise had told Père Rebours, her husband's last plea for prayers was indeed "engraved in her heart." Faithful to it all her life, she provided in her will that it be heeded even after her death by an anniversary Mass to be offered by a Vincentian Father each year on "St. Thomas' day before Noel," December 21, and by a solemn injunction to Michel-Antoine: "I beg my son to remember often to pray God for the repose of the soul of his father; and to hold in remembrance his good life—his strong fear of God and exactitude in making himself irreproachable; and above all else his patience in suffering the great evils that befell him in his last years, during which he practiced the greatest virtues."

Louise wrote this will twenty years after Antoine's death. She added a codicil eight years later, and even then the memory of "mon bon mari" was strong upon her.

V

"My Heart Could Not Conceal... from Yours"

Antoine Le Gras's death had ended with uncompromising finality a long chapter in Louise's life. At thirty-four she was a widow with a slow-witted son, who would soon be thirteen. Things had been changing gradually throughout Antoine's long illness. For four years the couple had rarely entertained or been entertained in the brilliant fashion of the early years. Louise had continued her charities, but she had not been able to give them the wholehearted attention she could give them now.

The Le Gras capital had dwindled: Antoine's illness and the d'Attichy estate had taken a hugh chunk of it, at least by the indirection of Antoine's neglect of his own affairs. Louise still had title to the small annual income left her by her father; signed over to her husband in her marriage contract, it now reverted to her. How much of it was available for her use is hard to say, for Louise's half sister, Innocente, now the wife of Jean d'Aspremont, seigneur de Vandy, seems to have been as remiss in paying what she owed Louise annually as her uncle Michel had been when he was her guardian. Louise, in her will, instructed her executors as to the possibility of a "claim upon the property of Madame de Vendy, who sold it to me in exchange for the rents which she owed me out of all her properties." Besides, a certain M. Gachier of Auvergne owed her "seven or eight hundred livres without the interest," from her lands there. "I recall," she added, "that immediately after the death of the late Monsieur Le Gras, Monsieur Gachier informed me that he wished to discharge this sum, and began to enter into payment, sending me a hundred livres or more"—and then with scrupulous honesty—"for which I do not remember whether I sent him a receipt." Despite M. Gachier's good intentions, his heirs still had the balance "in their hands" twenty years later. Louise had asked M. Bonnefoy, Gachier's grandson, for the money in vain, but "I have not wished to institute suit for it up to the present." She finished the history of this debt by "imploring my son again to get out of this affair in the most agreeable way he can." Even though she was a widow who badly needed the money, she would not cause anyone inconvenience or trouble.

Ironically enough, Louise's gradual withdrawal, through choice and circumstance, from a world she would never re-enter, took place at the very time the Marillac fortunes were entering on their final, flaring brilliance. Deep in the good graces of the Queen Mother, who had regained much of her influence over the vacillating King, Jean-Louis was rising in the army, and Michel was taken into the highest level of government, as a member of Richelieu's first council of government. The other ministers were Schomberg, Champigny—who shared the portfolio of finance jointly with Marillac—and Molé. The opposing views of Richelieu and Marillac were soon evident, and the long duel to the death was on.

Louise wisely set aside a fund for Michel-Antoine—"out of justice," she said—which, in 1645, had increased with the accrual of interest to "nearly four thousand livres." When this was done, there was still enough for mother and son to live respectably, at least for a few years. The pretentious house on the rue Courteauvilain was an encumbrance, however, and she let it go gladly; in any event, it did not fit with the new life of quasi-religion she had chosen. Her choice of a new place of residence was determined by the location of the motherhouse of the newly formed Congregation of the Mission, the Collège des Bons Enfants, which lay on the outskirts of Paris near the Porte Saint-Victor. Should she locate close by, she would be not only near M. Vincent but also in the midst of a rapidly growing colony of schools where she could send Michel. She chose an address on rue Saint-Victor in the parish of Saint-Nicolas-du-Chardonnet. She probably rented, since she moved successively to two other houses in the same street within five years.

Louise's change of residence did not by any means guarantee that Vincent would be at her beck and call, nor did she sincerely wish him to be—it was just that it took every ounce of her strength to fight down the panic when he was away. And he was away often. In the famous conference to his priests of May 17, 1658, during which he distributed the first printed copies of the rule, he tells in his homely fashion of the life of those early days: "[Madame de Gondi] at length wished to provide priests to continue the missions, and arranged for us to take over for this purpose the Collège des Bons Enfants, where we withdrew, M. Portail and I, and with us at first a good priest to whom we gave 50 écus a year. All three of us would go to preach and give missions from village to village. On leaving, we would give the key to one of the neighbors, or we would prevail upon them to sleep at night in the house . . ."

A myth has been perpetuated contrasting Louise's directors, the sunny Camus with the dour Vincent de Paul. Like all myths, it has its basis in the distortion of reality. The reality here is twofold: first, that when shown her future director in some form of supernatural enlightenment, Louise had a repugnance to accept him; and second, that Vincent by his own admission was a man "hard to approach and rather severe." The inference is that the first point derived from the second, that Louise hesitated to accept Vincent as her director because of the face he showed the world. Yet Louise never gave a reason for her repugnance. It is more probable that, as she and Camus both recognized, she was attached to the lively Bishop, felt comfortable with him, and dreaded the change, as everyone does, to something new. Vincent, again by his own testimony, was cured of the difficult disposition of his younger years during a retreat made in 1621, at least three years before he became Louise's director.

The reality is found in the solid evidence of their correspondence. Louise, on her side, was ever respectful and even reverential until the end of her life, but she never held back from saying what she had to or wanted to say, and at times with the Marillac vigor. Vincent, on his side, can never be accused of rudeness or even blameless crudity; he had the instinctive breeding of the peasant, which allowed him to take his place at court naturally, without any of the lessons his social betters often had to take. He was often firm in what he said, at times he was blunt, but he had taken well the measure of the woman he dealt with, her strength and resilience, her toughness of character and docility. It is interesting to contrast the deference of his approach to Madame de Chantal, for example, with the brusque intimacy, the honest affection and indeed, at times, the frank and manly tenderness of his rapport with Louise.

This brusque intimacy, the language of friends, is already evident in a letter of Vincent's written from Loisy-en-Brie on October 30, 1626: "I did not let you know of my departure because I left sooner than I expected, and because I should have caused you distress by letting you know I was leaving. Well, now! Our Lord will, if it so pleases Him, find what He is looking for, this little act of mortification, and will Himself act as your spiritual guide: yes, He will certainly do so, and in such a manner as to make you see that it is really Himself. So then, my dear daughter, be quite humble, submissive, and full of confidence, and always patiently await the manifestations of His holy and adorable Will . . . Please pray . . . especially for me, who do not answer all your letters, because I am not in a position to do what you request." Apparently, Louise wanted him to make a decision as to what she should do with her life, and he was waiting on the will of God before he made it.

In the meantime, he kept her and her friend Mlle du Fay—one of the first Ladies of Charity and related by marriage to Louise's aunt Marie de Marillac, Madame Hennequin—busy making clothing for the poor and vestments and ornaments for the Church.

On one occasion he thanked her with exquisite courtesy "for the very beautiful and welcome altar-cloth which your charity has sent us, and which seemed to cause my heart to overflow with pleasure, seeing your heart in it, the moment I entered the chapel, not having known it was there. This pleasure lasted all yesterday, and still persists, together with an inexplicable feeling of tenderness which has stirred up in me many thoughts which, if God pleases, I will tell you later. For the moment, I content myself with telling you that I pray to God to beautify your soul with His perfect and divine love, whilst you thus embellish His house with all these beautiful ornaments." It was natural that Louise's artistic gifts should be used for the Church, and in such a practical way. It is too bad that her handiwork is no more, for we should have enjoyed studying the designs she must have worked into her cloths and vestments, the kind of originality she showed in her paintings; Bernadette of Lourdes, who had also known the secerts of heaven, showed a like originality in working ecclesiastical ornaments and vestments.

Louise returned now, too, to her early love of painting, and her large oils, especially the famous "Lord of Charity," which the Daughters of Charity jealously guard in their motherhouse, date from these years. An exceptional feature of this painting, the depiction of the Heart of Christ shining through the clothing, has given rise to controversy as to whether, even before St. John Eudes and St. Margaret Mary, Louise had some glimmering of devotion to the Sacred Heart. If so, there is no evidence of it in her writings; as with the unusual representations of her early watercolors, so with this: some source might be found in the doctrine of St. Catherine of Siena learned at Poissy.

Vincent was also making use of Louise's good offices in widening the scope of his works of charity. Thus, on January 17, 1628, he gave her the following commission: "Be kind enough to perform an act of charity for the two poor girls whom we thought should leave here [Joigny], and whom we shall send to you eight days hence, begging you to direct them to some respectable woman who may find a position for them as domestic servants, if you do not know of any lady who needs them."

The intimacy their relationship had quickly reached was evident in a letter written probably in 1627: "What shall I say to you, now, of him whom your heart cherishes so dearly in Our Lord?" he asked unabashedly of himself in the third person. "He is improving somewhat, so it seems to me, but still suffers a little from his slight attacks of ague. However, he has been advised and urged to go to Forges [a health resort featuring mineral springs], and go there tomorrow . . . In truth, my dear daughter, it weighs more heavily on me than I can express, that so much must be done for one poor body . . . You will not speak of this matter to anyone, because nothing may come of it. My heart could not conceal it from yours, nor from our Mother at Sainte-Marie [Catherine de Beaumont], nor from Mademoiselle du Fay." Here, full-blown, is the unafraid affection of the saints—unafraid because it takes its rise from and subsists in God, as Vincent makes very plain in concluding this letter, "telling you that my heart will keep a tender recollection of yours in, and only for the sake of, Our Lord's Heart . . ." Its like can be found between Francis and Clare, François de Sales and Jeanne de Chantal, Elizabeth Seton and Antonio Filicchi.

The Confraternities of Charity were beginning to multiply, and Vincent must have thought of Louise in connection with them; but he was not sure whether this was what God wanted, and Vincent never moved until he was sure. There seems little doubt, however, from hindsight and from obscure hints, that Vincent was already thinking of bigger things for this remarkable woman than mere participation in the work of the Confraternities, and that inchoate ideas of the great achievement to come were already stirring in both their minds. God seems to have been showing His hand in a tenuous way, too, for even at this early date there is evidence that young girls were coming forward, offering to join themselves to Louise in her good works. Thus, in 1626 or early 1627, Vincent wrote: "You were mistaken, my dear daughter, in thinking I was of opinion that you should not accept the girl's proposal, because I had not thought of the matter at all; and I have not done so because I am quite certain that you wish, and do not wish, what God wills, and does not will . . . If His Divine Majesty does not let you see, and see in such a way that there can be no deception, that He desires anything further from you, do not think of, and do not allow your mind to be occupied by, any other such thing." And he dismisses the subject with typical dispatch: "Refer it to me, and I will think for both of us." It was the kind of positiveness she needed.

Again, Louise wrote, on June 5, 1627: "Allow me, Father, to importune you again on the subject of a girl, age twenty-eight, whom they wish to bring from Burgundy to give herself to me." Further on, she informs him of another one, age twenty-two, who "has been under the direction of the Reverend Fathers of the Oratory for four years, and is wholly a village girl." The volunteering of this last piece of information has special significance in light of St. Vincent's insistence, particularly in the early years of the Company, that its members should be drawn from among the simple, honest, hard-working, "good village girls." Louise finished: "I am not positive that she wishes to come; nevertheless, she has evidenced some desire to me. I beg you very humbly, Father, to advise me what I should do in the matter. The person who is going to Burgundy must leave Monday, and thinking you would return this week, I promised her a reply." When two girls three hundred miles away across France were in contact with a widow living in Paris about what seems to be some kind of charitable dedication, something certainly seems to have been afoot.

Provision for Michel-Antoine's schooling had now to be made. There were some thirty schools in the district where Louise was living, but the choice fell on the *petit seminaire*, or junior seminary, which Adrien Bourdoise had founded recently near the Church of Saint-Nicholas-du-Chardonnet. Louise informed Vincent of it on June 5, 1627: "At length, my most honored Father, after a little unrest, my son is at the college and, thank God, very happy and well; if such continues, I am very strongly in favor of it." These last words would seem to belie the common assertion that, from the beginning, it was Louise's idea that Michel should be a priest; she certainly clung to the conviction later, and was rebuked for it by Vincent. Now Vincent wrote back promptly his satisfaction at the move, and consoled the anxious mother, who was not only upset at this first separation from her son but worried about the expense of his board: "As for the *pension* . . . there is no help for it; he must enter by this door in order to get used to things. The board, according to my information, is 200 livres per person. I think there are some who pay more, but they will be satisfied with that."

Michel's contentment did not last long. In December 1627 and January 1628 his mother, who had been staying with Mlle du Fay to nurse her through an illness, wrote several letters to Vincent asking his "advice . . . in the matter of my son," but the letters were apparently lost. A subsequent one, dated January 13, reached him at Joigny, where he was giving a mission. She bewailed the fact that "whether God does not wish him [Michel] to persevere in the resolution to be an ecclesiastic, or whether the world opposes itself, his fervor is a great deal diminished." In Vincent's absence, she continued, she had hurried to their mutual friend Mère Catherine de Beaumont, who "advised me to place him simply as a pensionnaire with these good ecclesiastics."

Then she completely broke down, calling on God to "give me the grace of seeing your return, of which I have great need. Certainly, I have never felt your absence more sensibly, because of the need I have had since [your departure], in which I admit my weakness, assuring you, my Father, that if God does me the grace to recall the past, I would have no reason to boast. I ask strength from the assistance of your prayers, for the love of God, and thank you very humbly for the trouble you have taken to write me. I do not merit the honor of your remembrance, and God is very good to put up with me." And she ended with a great cry: "Oh! my most dear Father, offer my will to the divine mercy, for I wish by means of His holy grace to convert myself . . ." Here is abject self-abasement, but self-abasement of a Pauline nobility.

Louise, indeed, seemed to abandon reason when it came to her son. As Vincent once told her bluntly: "If you were a brave woman, you would rid yourself of your little maternal amusements and tendernesses. I have never seen a mother so much a mother as you. You are not a quasi-woman in any other thing." It was true. In everything else, despite her feminine sympathy and compassion, she thought and acted with a man's common sense and directness.

Now, however, in his reply of January 17, Vincent made an attempt to reason with her: "What shall I say to you about your son, unless that, just as too much assurance was not to be placed on his affection for the community [Bourdoise's seminary], so now one should not distress oneself too much because he experiences a dislike for it? Leave him alone, and surrender him entirely to what Our Lord may or may not will in his regard. The direction of such young and tender souls belongs to

Him alone: He is more interested in the boy than you are, because he belongs to Him more than he does to you . . . If anything else troubles you, write to me and I will reply."

Within a month, peace was restored all around. On February 23, Vincent dashed off a few lines to Louise before setting out on a short journey. He began by congratulating her for having disengaged her heart "from the too great attachment it had for the little one," and for having "adjusted to reason." One further detail was to be settled: whether Michel should resume the soutane or cassock. Vincent saw no problem, since to his knowledge Michel had not changed his mind about the priesthood: "God wishes whatever is for His glory and the salvation of souls." Mère de Beaumont's plan had evidently been abandoned, either because it was not feasible or, more likely, because Michel had overcome what looks suspiciously like a case of homesickness, a disease to which all young new seminarians are prone.

Louise had to contend with her own natural longing, and she faced up to it with courage and docility, albeit through tears. No one can miss the anguish in the resolution to "see my son no longer except as a child of God, nor to love him except as such, and for the love of God to suffer the privation of his sight."

She would suffer fresh agitations of soul precipitated by Michel's fits of restlessness, but from this time on, he was more or less safe and well cared for in various havens, leaving his mother free for God's service.

Her new life may be said to have begun with a solemn Act of Protestation, a blueprint for the future, made sometime after Antoine's death. The importance she attached to this Act may be gauged from the prescription in her *Rule of Life in the World:* "Every first Saturday of the month, I will renew my vows and good resolutions, reading my Protestation before or after Holy Communion—Saturday, in witness that I have taken the Blessed Virgin, because of my weakness and inconstancy, for my protectress"; and she adds a second reason, which is a symbol of her new spiritual orientation: "And also that by her intercession I may be able, for the rest of my days, to honor in her the esteem that God has for virginity over marriage."

It may reasonably be supposed that Louise would have prepared for so important an act by her favorite devotion, a retreat; and, indeed, the bones of the Act of Protestation are contained in the principal thoughts and resolutions found in the notes of what has been called for convenience her *Première Retraite:*

I must attach myself strongly to Jesus by the holiest imitation of His life . . .

I have resolved on every doubtful and irresolute occasion to consider what Jesus would have done [Vincent's influence is evident here: this was the lodestar of his own life] and to honor His subjection to His Blessed Mother. In the presence of the Blessed Sacrament I felt myself pressed interiorily to put myself in a state of holy indifference, so as to be better disposed to receive the call of God and to carry out His holy Will . . . I desire that His plans be entirely accomplished in me, and wish to offer my whole life to Him for that purpose . . .

All the actions of the Son of God are for our example and instruction, but principally His life of mingled action and contemplation.

Here was the cornerstone of the Company of the Daughters of Charity: the Sisters were to lead the life of the strictest religious in their houses, so that they would have a great fund of God to take out to the poor, all in imitation of the perfectly integrated life of prayer and action lived by Jesus Christ.

It was a Vincentian idea. The Saint of Charity begins every chapter of the Rule for his priests: "Just as the Son of God did . . . so, too, the missionaries shall . . ." and his simple injunction to his sons was that they be "Carthusians at home, and missionaries abroad." It may be justly suspected that a lack of balance between these two hinges of religious social service is the cause of the confusion, and at times personal shipwreck, in the modern apostolate. As the saint put it succinctly: "No one gives what he does not have."

Louise continued in her retreat jottings: "I should have a great confidence in God and assurance that His grace will be sufficient for me to carry out His holy Will, even when it seems difficult, provided that it be truly the Holy Spirit who invites me, the which I shall know through the advice He provides for me . . . a lively faith and full confidence that the plan of God for me will be accomplished so long as I allow myself to be led wherever He pleases."

In the fifth meditation of the retreat, she began to test the waters: "The example of [God's] most dear Son . . . induces me to resolve to help my neighbor as much as I can to understand [His law] . . . It is a great evidence of God's love for us to learn from His Son that we ought to be 'perfect as He is perfect.' He is sinless by nature, but I must hope from His mercy the firm will of sinning no more, and the grace to share in the virtues which are in Him by essence, not content to desire this good for myself, but for every soul created for His glory." Here was the ultimate goal of her future Company, the *raison d'être* of all good works, to bring salvation to souls, indeed—breathtaking grandeur of Louise's all-embracing love!—to "every soul created for His glory."

In the next meditation, her eyes are still alight with the vision: when the Master, after His Resurrection, summoned His Apostles by an interior call to repair to a mountain in Galilee where "He wished to show Himself to them," they were not content to go themselves, but "by their example and their words took along a great number of people; that which I must imitate as much as I can by procuring the salvation of my neighbor for the glory of God." This ultimate vision must never be lost sight of, this ultimate ministry of bringing souls to salvation must never be obscured by a too earnest scrambling to bring them even the basic necessities of life.

Louise finished this pivotal retreat, "waiting for as long as He pleases to learn what He asks of me."

Her Act of Protestation was then drawn up in the most official and solemn manner:

> I, the undersigned, in the presence of God eternal, having considered that, on the day of my sacred baptism, I was vowed and dedicated to my God to be His daughter . . .
>
> Considering, also, the immense mercy, love and kindness with which this most good God has ever sustained me in the desire to serve Him . . .
>
> Do detest with all my heart the iniquities of my past life, which render me guilty of divine *lèse-majesté*, and of the death of Jesus Christ, so that I merit more to be damned than Lucifer—
>
> Renew the sacred profession made to God for me at my baptism, and resolve irrevocably to implement and cherish it with more fidelity, giving myself entirely to Him for this purpose.
>
> I renew, also, the vow of widowhood I have made, and the resolution to practice the most holy virtues of humility, obedience, poverty, suffering and charity, to honor these same virtues in Jesus Christ which He has so often inspired in me by His love.
>
> Protesting, also, never more to offend God in any part of my being, and to abandon myself entirely to the design of His holy Providence for accomplishing in me His Will, to which I dedicate and sacrifice myself forever, choosing it for my sovereign consolation.
>
> If by my ordinary weakness it should happen that I contravene these holy resolutions—which may it never please God in His goodness to

permit—I implore from this moment the assistance of the Holy Spirit to give me the grace of immediate conversion, wishing nevermore to dwell an instant displeasing to God.

This is my irrevocable will, which I confirm in the presence of my God, of the Blessed Virgin, of my good Angel and of all the saints, and in the sight of the Church Militant, which hears me in the person of my spiritual Father, who, holding in my regard the place of God on earth, must aid me, if it pleases him, by his charitable guidance, in the execution of these resolutions, and make me accomplish the most holy Will of God.

May it please you, O my God, to confirm this consecration, to accept it as a fragrance, and as it has pleased you to inspire me to make it, give me the grace to perfect it . . .

Long live Your love and that of Jesus Crucified!

There are several noteworthy qualities in this protestation: its clarity —there is no mistaking the path of complete dedication Louise has laid out for herself, nor that she fully understood what the taking of that path entailed; its earnestness—she meant what she said; its prudence— she prepared for every contingency, and submitted the whole to "my spiritual Father," who will be her trusted guide. It is certainly not the work of a distraught or disoriented woman. Modern minds might find it artificial, yet these same minds draw up contracts and wills in the same way. It must be remembered, too, that such "acts" were a religious commonplace in the seventeenth century, which delighted in legal documents—even for marriages—and it may be near the truth to suppose that a sort of spiritual marriage contract was what Louise had in mind.

In the joyful *Vive!* of the closing we find for the first time that praise of Jesus Crucified which was the trademark of Louise's life and which she immortalized on the community seal in paraphrasing St. Paul: "The charity of Jesus Crucified urges us on."

A woman of action above all, Louise lost no time in spelling out her Act of Protestation by writing a *Rule of Life in the World,* which she prefaced, firmly but humbly, with the words: "In the name of God, may I attend to living thus, if it be permitted me." Throughout, the Rule is a manifestation of that longing for a regular life of consecration which God had promised her in the revelation of Pentecost 1623, a longing which gave her no peace but which she endured with heroic patience in waiting on the Will of God. This longing of the lover for final and binding union with the Beloved is in the opening words: "May there be ever in my heart the desire for holy poverty, so that, free of everything, I may follow Jesus Christ and serve my neighbor in all humility and sweetness, living in obedience and chastity all my life . . ."

Her first thought on awaking will be of God. From Easter to All Saints' Day she will rise at 5:30, and the rest of the year at six. As soon as she is up, she will make an hour's meditation, the points being drawn from the Gospels and Epistles and the life of the saint whose feast is celebrated that day. She will then recite Prime and Tierce of the Office of the Blessed Virgin—and at this point, the world intrudes: "If there is something to order in the household, I can do it while dressing."

"At 8:30 in summer and 9:00 in winter I will go to hear holy Mass; sometimes with the intention of the Church only, and sometimes aiding myself with points of meditation from *Philothea* [*The Introduction to a Devout Life*]." After Mass she will recite the rest of the Office of the Blessed Virgin. Back at home, she will work until eleven o'clock, when she will have dinner, preceded by some pious reading. "Precisely at noon, a few minutes of prayer to honor the moment of the Incarnation of the Word in the womb of the Virgin."

After dinner she will work "cheerfully" until four o'clock at the tasks Vincent has allotted her, for the Church, or the poor, or the household. These are also the hours for making or receiving visits, if need be. "At four o'clock, even if I am in town, if I am not too busy with charity or some necessary propriety, I will go to the nearest church to say Vespers of the Blessed Virgin and during them refresh my spirit to make afterward a half hour of prayer; then I will shut myself up in my house, occupying myself there as long as I can. If I have time between my prayer and six o'clock, I will work."

She will eat supper at 6:30, after having done some spiritual reading, which she will make use of to refresh her spirit or the conversation of "those I might be with." After supper, a half hour of recreation, and then a half hour of work. At eight she will go to bed, having first examined her conscience and said Matins of the Virgin for the next day. "Sometimes," she concluded simply, "I will examine myself as a Christian and a Catholic, and as a woman wishing to be devout."

Such was her order of day. Then there were general prescriptions: five decades of the Rosary daily; the practice of the Presence of God when the clock struck the quarter hour—a practice that would be incorporated in the community rule; self-mortification, especially by the prudent use of the discipline and, on specified days, a penitential cincture, and fast and abstinence; and two retreats twice a year, from Ascension to Pentecost—in commemoration of the great retreat of 1623—and during Advent.

This rule of life has been placed under many microscopes, some approving, some condemning; but examination by microscope isolates details and often exaggerates them. There is actually not more order here than is found in the lives of most men who rise and retire, go to the office or to the factory or, in the case of women, houseclean certain rooms and do their shopping on certain days at certain hours, have meals ready —all according to a personal schedule, none the less rigid for not being written out. The difference here is that more time is given to prayer, and all is done in the sight of God according to the saving formula of St. Paul: "Whether you eat or drink or whatever else you do, do all for the glory of God."

It must also be noted that this rule of life had Vincent's approbation: in an undated letter laying down instructions for a subsequent retreat Louise was to make, he cautioned her not to "take too many practical resolutions," but "rather strengthen yourself to the utmost in carrying out those you have already made with regard to your daily actions and duties." In fact, he probably amended it in its extant form: the provision of the Rule concerning the taking of the discipline "two or three times" fits very well with Vincent's admonition that she "not take the discipline," or, "if you do so, only three times a week."

The emphasis on devotion to Our Lady is not surprising: she figures prominently in Louise's writings and correspondence. A long jotting, in reality an informal theological treatise on the Immaculate Conception dating from the time of the Act of Protestation, shows admirably the precision and perception of Louise's mind. It begins with an unwonted acknowledgment of her spiritual awareness: "Would to God I could write all the thoughts His goodness gave me the grace to have on the subject of the Immaculate Conception of the Blessed Virgin, for the true knowledge I had of her merits, and the will to render her what I owe her, will never leave my heart." It continues with an orthodox Mariology, at times striking in the subtle originality of expression, that makes exaltation of, and devotion to, the Virgin inevitable.

Louise sees "the application of God's plan for the Incarnation of His Son out of the matter of this virginal body, in such wise that it would have no least blemish of original sin, since the divine Body of the Son of God would be formed in it." As woman, wife and mother, Louise fixes her awe not on the wonders wrought in the person Mary, but in her holy body. "The most pure body of the Blessed Virgin," she continues, "was the worthy lodging of the soul created in it, and the one and the other (her body and soul), ever pleasing to God, were ever enriched beyond her most pure conception with the merits of the death of her Son."

The Virgin's conception is also a triumph of God's omnipotence, "saving her without her being lost, not only by mercy but by justice, it being necessary for the Incarnation of the Son of God according to the plan made from all eternity for the redemption of the human race. We ought, then, to honor this holy conception which rendered her so precious in the sight of God, and to believe that it assures us of the Blessed Virgin's help in all our needs, since it seems impossible that the goodness of God should refuse her anything"; nor "would she ever ask anything of Him that was not for His glory and our good."

Enraptured by the "necessary consequence" of Mary's great privilege, the absence in her of "what excites to sin," Louise, who had known in almost unbearable measure that refinement of temptation which lures the soul to the greatest fall of despair, cries out in wonder: "Oh! what peace! what sweetness! what love! what lowliness in the soul of the Blessed Virgin, since it is this instinct which troubles us so much, which coaxes us continually to sin." She is also intrigued by the "purity of the holy Virgin's thoughts, never idle or given over to sinfulness."

Finally, deeply impressed that Mary did always the divine Will, "without omitting anything God asked of her," and was, in consequence, "full of virtue both in the matter and in the form of the whole being God had given her"—that which, at least in a shadow of imitation, Louise desired so passionately for herself—she resolved in a fervor of promise: "That is why, all my life, in time and eternity, I wish to love and honor her as much as I can."

It is at Christmastime, however, as she kneels before the crèche, that Louise's rapport with the Virgin Mother is ecstatically complete:

O holy time of grace, keep on generating joy and gaiety in our hearts! why do you not suffice to give us a lifelong love for a God so good! I want, O my God, to think often of this sacred time and to acknowledge Your great mercy in creating me after it had come to pass . . .

O Blessed Virgin, how admirable your virtue! There you are, Mother of God, yet reaping from it only lowliness and poverty . . . O my God . . . to say that she is the Mother of Your Son is to say all . . . It is not without reason that Holy Church calls her Mother of Mercy; she is Mother of Mercy because she is Mother of Grace . . .

I gaze on you today, most pure Virgin Mother of Grace, because you not only supplied the substance for the sacred Body of your Son, but gave Him to the world. You are Mother of Jesus, God and Man, who through His birth brought a new law to the world, the only law which brings eternal life. O Mother of the law of grace because you are Mother of Grace Itself!

Surely such rooted and flourishing devotion in Louise de Marillac, who was herself the "mother of many daughters," must be credited with that singular devotion of the Daughters of Charity to the Mother of God, gloriously rewarded by her and her Son in the apparitions vouchsafed two of them, St. Catherine Labouré and Sister Justine Bisqueyburu. It was not by chance that the Miraculous Medal and the Green Scapular, given through the one and the other to the world, both honor Our Lady's Immaculate Conception.

A *Deuxième Retraite* dating from the period of the *Première Retraite* is also extant. Its chief interest lies in the fact that it was certainly made under Vincent's explicit direction, after Louise first changed her address on rue Saint-Victor.

"As for your little retreat," Vincent instructed her, "make it quite peacefully, following the order in the *Introduction* of M. de Genève, but make your prayer only twice a day, an hour in the morning and a half hour in the afternoon, and read in the interval something from Gerson, or from the lives of the holy widows to whom you have a more special devotion; you may spend the rest of the time in reflecting on your past life and on your future . . . Perhaps I may make my own retreat at the same time. May God give us both the grace to make it well!"

Gerson was the perfect spiritual reading for Louise at this step of her development. A practical mystical master, he stipulated means to prepare for contemplation that well suited the "in-betweenness" of her state: to await the call of God, to know her temperament well, to be mindful of vocation and state in life, to strive for ever greater perfection, not to multiply occupations or be absorbed by them, to be calm and patient, to avoid extremes, for example, in the matter of abstinence.

Vincent wrote another letter on the eve of the retreat, adding details and making modifications. "It seems to me that you could not make your retreat at a more suitable time," he pointed out approvingly. "Religious of both sexes are, as a rule, making their retreat right now.

Begin, then, on Monday next, if you please. Three half quarters of an hour [Vincent meant to write "three half hours"] will be enough time to allow for your mental prayer every day, half an hour for each prayer; two in the morning, at eight and half past ten, and another at four o'clock . . . You will finish on Saturday evening, and will go to Mass every day. You may say that you are engaged, and put off those who may have necessary business to transact with you until immediately after dinner, and you may cut short such business affairs. You may go to Holy Communion next Thursday, and take as subject for your mental prayer only what M. de Genève places at the beginning of the *Introduction*. You will divide the points in such a way that they will suffice, and that you can make them all; you may make your prayer on some of them twice, according to the attraction Our Lord may give you. Read the New Testament, as well as the other readings I suggested to you. Write to me on every second day a summary account of all that takes place, and also of the state of your body and mind, and endeavor in all this not to be too anxious, but to do all things peacefully, as you may imagine the good M. de Genève used to do."

He concluded with that touch of tenderness now so characteristic: "I do not ask you to remember me in your prayers, because I have no doubt that, after little Le Gras, you put me in the first place; not indeed that I deserve it, but the knowledge which you have of my needs, and the charity which Our Lord has given you for me, makes me hope so." And, ever the director: "Adieu, then, Mademoiselle, take care of yourself during this retreat, so that you may allow us to advise you to make others."

Louise was very faithful to his injunctions; and it is interesting to compare her meditation notes with the order in François de Sales prescribed by St. Vincent. The tenor of her thoughts follows the line of the earlier retreat with emphasis on dedication, veneration of the neighbor, and waiting upon God's determination of her future. There is noticeable, however, a greater self-reliance, even a holy boldness. For example, she records "a great confidence that, despite my misery, He [God] will accomplish all in me," and states as her reason that "He has given me an interior assurance of it." Again, she renews her resolution of detachment because of "a strong sentiment that God asks it of me, in recalling that Our Lord said He had come to separate the father from the child and to make us renounce all attachment to creatures." There is no doubt where her thoughts lay as she wrote these words, or how hard they were to write.

She advances a most original reason for "hiding myself from the eyes of creatures to be known by God alone," that she may in turn "be ignored by the world and the devil." Her consequent resolution "to consecrate the rest of my days to honor the hidden life of Jesus on earth" drew Vincent's enthusiastic endorsement. "I will cherish in my heart the words that you wrote me of your generous resolution to honor the adorable hidden life of Our Lord, so like that for which He gave you the desire in your youth," he wrote feelingly. "Oh! my dear daughter, how this thought pulses with the inspiration of God, how far removed it is from flesh and blood! But, courage! it is the necessary attitude for a dear daughter of God!"

This central resolution of the retreat led inevitably to renewed prayer that the great longing of her life be satisfied: "Seeing that the common life had more need of [His] example, He gave it more time and the continual practice of evangelical perfection in that, being rich, He chose holy poverty and obedience to the Blessed Virgin and St. Joseph. I, though unworthy, beg Him for the grace to imitate this example of His" —and she capped her plea with a graceful and provocative exercise of the virtue of hope—"hoping from His goodness that, having given me the desire for so long a time, He will really grant it."

Several years were to pass before this grace was granted in its final form. In the meantime, however, God showed His will—in such a way as to satisfy St. Vincent that there "could be no deception"—for Louise to dedicate her life irrevocably to the service of the poor. There can be no other explanation than such a decisive turn of events for the momentous tone of Vincent's letter of the Seventh Sunday after Pentecost, July 30, 1628.

"Yes, indeed, my dear Mademoiselle, I do approve of it. And why not? Since Our Lord has given you this holy inclination," he wrote with an abruptness which was an anticlimax after Louise's three years of champing at the bit. "Go to Communion therefore tomorrow and prepare yourself for that useful review you suggest, and afterwards begin the holy exercises you have resolved on." The importance of what has happened is accentuated by his allowing matter-of-factly, indeed almost *de rigueur*, that she make a general confession and a retreat "out of season." His next words confirm it further: "I cannot express to you how ardently my heart desires to see yours to know what has come to pass in it, but I wish to mortify myself in this matter, out of love for God, with whose love alone I desire your heart to be occupied." And his closing reference to the good tree that brings forth good fruit is a crown of approbation: "Well, I imagine the words of today's Gospel have deeply touched you, so moving are they to a heart that loves with a perfect love. Oh! what a tree you seemed today in God's eyes, seeing that you have brought forth such fruit. May you be ever a beautiful tree of life, bringing forth fruits of love, and I, in this same love, your servant, V.D."

How joyfully these words must have rung in Louise's ears after the days and weeks and years of standing idly in the marketplace!

It was for Vincent now to decide how her life of dedication to the poor should begin, and he took the autumn and the winter and the spring to decide, or to plan the best execution of what he may well have decided already. The Confraternities of Charity were flourishing so well that new ones were springing up in a pattern that encircled Paris. The missions and their new congregation of priests were multiplying with the same joyous growth. Vincent's organizational acumen saw the danger: that this exuberant growth, if left untended, could dissipate its strength and bring death to the whole vineyard. It was getting beyond the care of his two hands; and so, thankful to God for the helper provided at just the right moment, he placed the visitation and administration of the Confraternities into the capable hands of this woman who had so gloriously proved herself.

VI

On the Roads of France

The years of Louise's waiting to begin her apostolate Gobillon has justly called a "novitiate." Not only was her soul purified, toughened and tempered in the hot fire of spiritual tribulation during these waiting years, but she was actively tried in the field of practical service; and the fact that it was in the unglamorous field of neighborhood charity and homework made it all the more useful as a test of her earnestness and staying power. As we have seen, the field was not new to her but the motivation was. She saw now, in the self-consuming efforts of Vincent de Paul, what she had always wanted to do herself. Thus Gobillon testifies: "As she saw up close the deeds of this apostolic man who worked without ceasing with his infant Company in every exercise of charity, she felt herself still more strongly impelled by his example . . . to cooperate to the last ounce of her powers in the great enterprises of this holy priest."

Now, however, the testing time of giving mere alms of money and clothing in support of the workers, the lowly apprenticeship of running errands of charity, was over. God had spoken, and Louise was taken into the heart of the work.

The state of her health may well have been one of the strongest reasons for Vincent's long hesitation. All her life her health baffled everyone, herself most of all. Always delicate, it seemed at times to tremble on the brink of swift decline, at times to go over and rush to the very door of death. Her precarious health was a chronic nuisance in the most serious sense of that word. Yet it withstood for sixty-nine years the battering of worry, anxiety, long hours of prayer, physical mortification, rough travel, the hard work and administrative tension of overlong days one after the other without letup.

The secret lay in Louise's wholehearted reliance upon God. She wrote of one of her confraternity visitations: "I was afraid to make the trip because of my infirmities, but felt strengthened at sight of the obedience which ordered me to go. At Holy Communion that day I was moved to make an act of faith, and this sentiment lasted long: it seemed to me that God would give me health so long as I believed that He could sustain me against all appearances, and that He would do so if I reminded myself often of the faith which made Peter walk on the water. And throughout the whole trip I seemed to act without any compliance of my own, much consoled at the thought that God wished me, despite my unworthiness, to make Him known to my neighbor."

Louise never pampered herself: when she went to bed it was because she could no longer stand or sit up; and even from bed the work of prayer and administration and dictation went on. She refused to let others pamper her, even St. Vincent. Once when he had counseled her to pray for better health, she wrote determinedly in her notes: ". . . I have done so, but in the same frame of mind as St. Fiacre, not wishing to be cured unless I could make good use of it."

At times special means had to be taken to conserve Louise's strength. One Lent, for example, Vincent directed her to obtain a dispensation from the law of abstinence, which at that time was binding for the whole penitential season: "For safety's sake, it would be better if you obtained a medical certificate that it is expedient both for you and your son to eat meat, and have it forwarded to the Chancellor of Monseigneur de Paris, whose name is M. Baudoin; he will arrange for the permission at once and without any difficulty." And he added with brisk logic, to forestall any protest: "As that is so, make no difficulty about eating meat. And now, insofar as I have power, I command you to do so . . ." He was so anxious about this dispensation that he added a postscript: "I beg you to see about this permission tomorrow morning, so that you may be able to eat meat from tomorrow onwards; because a fish diet is utterly unsuited to you." Louise had to submit to dispensations of this kind—from the law of the Church, from the rule, from her own resolutions—many times during her life. She never liked these exceptions. In her deep sense of her own unworthiness she often felt them uncalled for and even unjust; but she always obediently accepted them.

Vincent worried about her as much as she worried about him; for he, too, was a chronic sufferer but, except in the last years, generally not so seriously as she. It might be said without the least facetiousness that they showed their mutual affection by this mutual concern for each other's health.

We have seen already how, from the beginning of their friendship, he confided to her most familiarly the state of his health and the remedies he used; but, as might be expected, he was more preoccupied with her own well-being. He began an early letter: "Blessed be God, Mademoiselle, that you are better!" And a few lines down, with charming simplicity, for fear she would worry about his attending a long ceremony: "I do not fear the chapel as much now as in the summer [because of his tropical fever]." Another time, he tried to dissimulate his watchful concern: "I do not know how I came to imagine, during these past few days, that you were not well, seeing that I always think of you as being so. Now, thanks be to God, your letter has assured me . . ." On still another occasion he reproached her for hiding a recent indisposition from him, and commanded her "to take good care of your health for the love of Him . . ." This was the whole reason—the love of God—for their mutual anxiety: there was great work to do, and they must be well to do it. He admitted sheepishly to having been ill himself, but was "better, thank God. A little fever still hangs on, but it is ever diminishing, and my desire for your perfect holiness ever increasing," he finished with a nice turn of phrase he rarely had time for.

Louise gave exquisite expression to the reason for her setting out, never turning back, in service of the neighbor, "not only because of the reward Our Lord promises, as if it were done to Himself, but because the neighbor is His vicar, by a contrivance of love known to His goodness and which He has made plain to my heart."

She prepared for it as He had—by the desolation of the Garden of Gethsemane. "On St. Thomas's day," she recorded, "great depression of spirit because of my own vileness which seemed to me a sewer of pride and spring of self-love; destitution, self-ruin, abandonment by God, merited by my infidelities, pressing upon my heart so heavily that it made me suffer in my body; and sometimes, knowing myself esteemed by some, I believed myself for that reason unworthy that the most holy will of God be fulfilled in me." There may well have been an admixture of human grief in this spiritual dejection, for it was the anniversary of Antoine's death.

"The following Tuesday," she went on inexorably, "still in the same affliction, I saw myself the object of God's justice"—even as the Christ, the victim for sin—"and Holy Communion, along with all God's other graces in me, seemed the means for the triumph of His goodness through the execution of His justice"—He was heaping coals of fire on her head; nevertheless, His will, not hers, be done—"accepting this decree, I regained a little more tranquillity, having taken for my prayer, 'the peace of God surpasses all understanding.' "

On January 25, feast of the Conversion of St. Paul, the day on which the great charitable revolution had begun a dozen years before with a sermon preached by Vincent de Paul, Louise dwelt in her meditation on Jesus' destruction of "obstacles to His divine operations . . . both in this Apostle and in all the Gentiles," and "on the instant I felt my spirit ravaged with the greatest pain and most sensible sorrow."

Lent came, and the desolation continued, but she was equal to it. "I must remember not to seek tenderness or spiritual consolation in order to excite myself to the service of God," she wrote bravely, "but on the contrary I must offer myself to accept every rudeness and privation which seems prepared for my soul, with an entire abandonment to suffer every temptation it pleases God [to permit], and so to live and die if it be His holy will. "I have given myself to God, bowing to His Providence, if He should wish that for the rest of Lent I remain in interior desolation and even in affliction in order to honor the state of Jesus Christ which the Church presents to us."

What is so striking about this vivid and agonized retelling of a prolonged period of almost unbearable darkness is Louise's unwillingness to beg the question by a vague acceptance of whatever suffering God might send; she accepts rather this specific trial for a specific time, "the rest of Lent." This practical resolution—she is not going to presume upon her powers—reveals as nothing else could how much in earnest she was.

She had, it is true, toyed with vagueness, "to give myself to God in doing His holy will all my life, and to offer to Him the thought He gave me to make a vow to that purpose when it would be permitted me to do so." This was not permitted her; Vincent said no. When the time was assured, he would joyfully permit her to make the concrete vows of religion and also a fourth vow equally concrete—to spend her life in serving the poor.

In any event, the great day of beginning was at hand. In late April or early May 1629, Vincent informed her that "Father de Gondi [his former patron, who on the death of his wife had become a priest of the Oratory] has asked me to go at once to meet him at Montmirail. It will, perhaps, prevent me from the honor of seeing you, for I must leave tomorrow morning. Does your heart tell you to come there, Mademoiselle? If so, you must leave next Wednesday by the Châlons coach . . . which loads at the [Inn of the] Cardinal opposite Saint-Nicolas-des-

Champs; and we will have the good fortune to see you at Montmirail."
How she had waited for those words!

This welcome invitation was followed in a few days by the actual summons, solemn for all its matter-of-fact instruction: "Mademoiselle, I am
sending you the letters and memorandum which you will need on your
journey." Then, as if completely caught up in awareness of the memo-
rableness of the moment, Vincent conjured her: "Go forth, then, Mademoiselle"—he will never again address her as "my dear daughter," she is
now his partner—"go forth in the name of Our Lord." And he prayed
for her in beautiful paraphrase of the *Itinerarium Clericorum*:

> I pray the Divine Goodness to accompany you, to be your consolation
> on the way, your shelter against the heat of the sun, your protection from
> rain and cold, your soft couch in weariness, your strength in labor, and
> that, in the end, It may bring you back in perfect health, laden with good
> deeds . . .
>
> On the day of your departure, you may go to Communion to honor the
> charity of Our Lord, and the journeys which He made from, and in, that
> same charity; as well as the trials, contradictions, weariness, and labors
> which He endured . . .
>
> As to your question whether you should remain longer than we sug-
> gested: I think that two or three days in each place will suffice, for you
> can return there next summer, in case Our Lord makes it clear to you
> that you can render Him still further assistance. When I say two days, I
> mean your charity may induce you to spend some more time there, in
> case there is any necessity, and may also induce you to write to us . . .
>
> Adieu, Mademoiselle, remember us in your prayers, and above all, take
> care of your health, which I pray God may preserve, remaining in His
> love . . .

The first "Charity," as the confraternities were familiarly called, began
at Châtillon, not long after the first mission at Folleville. Now they were
intertwined as one work: wherever Vincent and his priests gave a mission, they established a Charity—the corporal work of mercy became the
enduring symbol of the spiritual work of mercy—and since the first missions were given on the Gondi estates, the first Charities were established there, too. The Gondi thus repaired magnificently the harm their
selfish countrymen, the Medici and the Concini, had done France.

The Charities were autonomous—except for the overall direction of
St. Vincent—and usually confined to the limits of a parish. They were
highly organized, but not according to a mold; the rules of each were

fashioned to its circumstances of place and need and personnel. Thus, for example, while the Charities existed only with the approbation and supervision of the proper ecclesiastical authorities, specifically the bishop and the pastor, if the pastor of a particular Charity was nonresident or showed small interest in the work, the Charity could choose a substitute priest for its director or chaplain. This priest-in-charge was not a spiritual figurehead—everyone worked in Vincent's enterprises!—he was held responsible for the exact observance of the rules; he sometimes shared the decision as to which poor and sick were to be helped; he was expected to visit the sick at least every two days; he supervised, and at times controlled, the treasury.

The body of the association was exclusively lay, and ran its own affairs. Long before the multiplication of lay institutes and the emerging layman of Vatican Council II, the Charity had some of the elements of both. The officers, usually a president and two assistants, were elected by the members for terms ranging from six months to three years. To be elected meant practically to assume a full-time, nonpaying job. The president actively directed the whole work, admitting by certificate the poor and sick to be cared for, and dismissing those who had recovered or found work, ordering the expenditures of the treasury, consulting with director, druggist, surgeon and apothecary. She had also to make a weekly visit to all her charges. Above all, she was a superintendent of nurses, and even a quasi-spiritual guide to her companions in the work: this is why she was called prioress or superioress; no one was ever allowed to forget the essential spirituality of the undertaking.

The assistant who acted as treasurer was as burdened as the president. She received and paid out all monies, entering them into two books, one for credits and one for expenditures, and had to render periodic accounts. She was the cellarer who kept all provisions and foodstuffs; in some cases she had even to keep chickens so that the sick poor could have fresh eggs. Since money is "the root of all evil," the post was as sensitive a one in the charities as it is in any organization, and it led to the eventual separation of men from women in the work. The women were always in the majority but, especially in the beginning, there were male volunteers, whom Vincent soon wisely organized into all-male confraternities of their own to look after the healthy poor, leaving the sick poor exclusively to the women. "Men and women together do not agree in the matter of administration," Vincent advised one of his priests. "The former wish to arrogate it to themselves and the latter won't stand for it. The conferences of Joigny and Montmirail were governed in the beginning by both sexes . . . but because of the common purse it was found necessary to remove the men."

The confraternities were supported largely by private contributions. Regular collections were taken up in the church or from door to door; poor boxes were placed both in the church and in the inns (was this the start of a worldwide custom still very much with us?), and the concierge invited patrons and overnight guests to contribute; in certain of the men's confraternities, members set aside one or two sheep from their flocks, branded them with the confraternity's insignia and turned over to the confraternity the proceeds from the sale of their wool and meat.

The members of the Charities were social workers and visiting nurses in the real sense and in the modern mold. Naturally they had not the same caliber of training; they were not professionals, but kindly men and women who donated their time, energy and personal resources of food and money for the love of God. The seeds of modern social service are nonetheless amazingly evident among them.

First of all, they were not accepted indiscriminately into the work. Since it was a work of true dedication to an ideal, in this case a spiritual ideal, they had to be of known piety and virtue, and their devotion was fostered within the confraternity by rule: they were to recite "a specified morning and evening prayer, to attend Mass daily if possible, to read daily a chapter of St. François de Sales's *Philothea*, to walk constantly in the presence of God, to practice humility, charity and simplicity towards all, and to receive the sacraments four times a year."

Membership was limited, usually, to not more than twenty members in a confraternity and frequently less, so that efficiency of administration would not suffer. While there was no specified period or method of training, members had adequate direction from the precise rule of the confraternity and the experience of older members. They were schooled in rudimentary forms of case investigation and case history. They were taught, for example, to distinguish between the deserving and the undeserving poor, to assess degrees of need, and seriousness and types of illness; they were especially cautioned about their approach to patients with infectious or contagious diseases. Simple records were kept of the sick nursed and the poor helped, of when they came under the care of the confraternity and when they were discharged.

Each member had her day on duty. If illness prevented her, the next on the list substituted for her; if some other reason, she had to get her own substitute. As she went off duty in the evening, she sought out her successor for the next day to give her the names of the sick, where they lived and the state of their illness.

Each new patient was visited immediately. The visitor went armed with fresh linen from the confraternity stores and, if necessary, made a second trip if eating and cooking utensils were lacking. In the meantime she had exhorted the sick person to go to confession, put a crucifix where he could see it, and summoned the priest. She then informed the next day's visitor, for it was the latter's duty to come now to clean the sick person's house in preparation for the Blessed Sacrament.

Menus were minutely detailed: as much bread as the sick person could eat, a bowl of soup, some veal or mutton on weekdays and chicken on Sundays and feasts, and a little wine. On abstinence days, eggs and fish were substituted for meat. The sick who could not eat solid foods were given broths and bread soups and boiled barley.

The obligations of the confraternity did not end with a patient's death. It was expected to pay for the funeral, to furnish a shroud if others did not, to have the grave dug, and to attend the funeral in a body, "taking . . . the place of mothers who accompany their children to the grave."

It can be imagined that, with so many details to be seen to by more or less simple people and with the comparative isolation of each Charity, there would be inevitable breakdowns in management. Periodic visits by capable administrators from outside were necessary to spot points of strain and weakness, to reform, to point out better methods. It is a measure of Vincent's esteem for Louise's talents that he set her to the task, "sight unseen."

Montmirail, her first visitation, mut have been a sobering experience. It was a long way to the west to Paris, over bad roads in a rough, lumbering stage that was a wholly different vehicle from the cushioned coaches Louise was used to in the sophisticated capital. It is no wonder that, by her own admission, she feared to undertake a second visitation that same year.

The lacelike delicacy of the French countryside in springtime hardly prepared her for its inhabitants. She knew the poor of Paris, who for all their obsequious beggary and dirty struggle to exist, were recognizable as human; they lived in the midst of civilization and it was bound to rub off at least a little. The country poor were chillingly different. Le Bruyère has caught them in his horrible portrait-in-words: "You see certain wild animals, male and female, scattered through the countryside, black, ghastly, scorched by the sun, rooted to the earth which they dig and turn over with invincible tenacity. They have a kind of articulated speech; and when they rear up on their feet they show a human face; and they are, in fact, men. At night they retreat into dens, where they subsist on black bread and water and roots. They spare other men the trouble of sowing, toiling and reaping in order to live, but receive as wages none of the bread they have sown." The grimness of life for these off-scourings of society has been captured also in the unsmiling faces by the brush of Le Nain. Thus had the constant wars and petty quarrels of the great nobles degraded the noble peasants of France, the backbone of their *belle patrie.*

Le Bruyère's use of the word "den" to describe their homes is not too harsh. These were hovels fashioned of dried mud, with no windows, floor or ceiling, filled with smoke which the defective chimney or simple hole in the roof could not carry off. The one touching ornament in them was the crucifix, or picture of Our Lady or the patron saint of the parish, or piece of blessed palm hung hopefully over the rude marriage bed.

The mechanics of Louise's first visitation to the country Charities must have been awkward: she had only the explicit written directions of M. Vincent and her own instinctive efficiency to go on. There is no extant record of the initial visitation, but there are detailed records of similar ones.

Louise was always accompanied by other women. She traveled by public conveyance—stage or barge—lodged at the cheapest inns and ate the cheapest food, not only from a sense of poverty, but to experience at first hand the lot of the poor. Her luggage contained very few personal effects but a great many linens and drugs for distribution. Nearly everything was at her own expense and she dispensed personal alms.

A visitation involved a great deal of talking, and as early as February 1630 Vincent was anxiously insisting that Louise inform him "precisely as to whether your lungs are not exhausted by so much speaking and your head by so much fuss and noise." Upon her arrival in the village, she would summon all the members of the confraternity to a general meeting. After she had gotten a good picture of the state of the confraternity's affairs from the reports of the officers, the complaints and observations of the members, and the answers to her own probing questions, she began the work of renewal by praising the good, reproving the bad, dealing with peculiar problems, but above all by encouraging everyone to a holier life, a deeper dedication, and to harder work. Vincent had cause for anxiety, for these sessions were indeed exhausting; it must be remembered that this was the era of the three-hour sermon—and what woman, not to say assemblage of them, was to be overborne in words by a mere man!

Louise must have literally overborne even the women of these country villages. Her quiet but fashionable dress, with its tapered waist and farthingale skirt and stiff collarette and mutton sleeves—she was as yet a woman of her class in the world of her times—her noble carriage and breeding, her elegant speech and evident learning, all marked her as a great lady. And a special quality of authority gave her first place even when she was accompanied by so brilliant a personage, for example, as Mme la présidente Goussault.

Plans for the renewal having been outlined, Louise proceeded to put them into effect by force of her own example. Now she was the superioress of the Charity, selecting the poor and the sick to be visited, assigning tasks, keeping records, examining the books. Now she was the treasurer, buying food, dispensing linen, making entries, preparing reports. Now she was the visitor of the day, sweeping the hovels of the sick, cooking their meals, feeding them, urging them to a more Christian life. She taught by doing. The confraternity members watched and learned.

One of her chief concerns was to provide education for the village girls. Some villages were sophisticated enough to have at least a nondescript schoolmistress: Louise would encourage her and show her how to improve her teaching. Most villages had no school of any kind; in these, Louise would select a likely candidate and begin laboriously to teach her so that she in turn could teach others.

It is interesting that at this very time Marguerite Naseau, the first Daughter of Charity, was engaged in the same kind of rudimentary education. "Marguerite Naseau, of Suresnes, was the first Sister who had the happiness of pointing out the road to our other Sisters, both in the education of young girls and in nursing the sick, although she had no other master or mistress but God," St. Vincent reminded his Daughters in 1642. "She was a poor, uneducated cowherd. Moved by a powerful inspiration from Heaven, the idea occurred to her that she would instruct children and so she bought an alphabet but, as she could not go to school for instruction, she went and asked the parish priest or curate to tell her what were the first four letters of the alphabet. On another occasion, she asked what were the next four, and so on for the rest. Afterwards, while she minded her cows, she studied her lesson. If she saw anyone passing by who seemed to know how to read, she would say: 'Sir, how is this word pronounced?' And so, little by little, she learned to read, and she then taught the other girls of her village. She afterwards made up her mind to go from village to village instructing the young, accompanied by two or three other girls whom she had taught."

Louise herself composed a catechism—long before the bishops of France provided one for their flocks—that reveals a penetrating knowledge both of theology and of the capacity of simple minds.

"Who created you and put you in the world?" it began by asking. "God, in order to love and serve Him, so that He can give us His paradise."

Of the Trinity it asked naïvely, "Who is the oldest and wisest? They are all equal . . ."

The definition of hell is exquisite: "It is a place where you never know God, where you never know love, where you suffer all kinds of torments." It was always first things first with Louise! The longevity of hell is described in simple language that would put a philosopher to shame: "It is longer than we know how to say, for it will never end."

In asserting the miraculous conception of Our Lord for these country children who grew up with the "facts of life" on their farms, the chaste widow was as forthright as they: "Who was His father insofar as He was man? He had none." "Who formed His body in the womb of the Blessed Virgin? The Holy Spirit." "Wasn't St. Joseph her husband? Yes, but he was given her to guide her and to live with her always as a virgin."

The schoolmistress in her showed in the answer to "How should we pray?" "We must pray peaceably, without turning our heads from one side to another, without thinking of anything but God."

And so it continued, instructing thoroughly, pastorally as well as theologically.

Louise had a basic reason for her "little schools": ignorance was a cause of damnation; but it was difficult to overcome ignorance unless you could read. Certainly the example of St. Louise, the foundress, and Marguerite Naseau, the first member of the Company, should give pause to the latter-day protestors against education's being a basic work of the Daughters of Charity.

It would appear that Louise first met Marguerite Naseau when she visited Suresnes on her second confraternity visitation in December 1629 and—as in hindsight was eminently fitting—that it was she who directed this touching and wonderful girl to M. Vincent. In a letter of February 19, 1630, Vincent asked Louise to let him know whether "that good girl of Suresnes who has visited you before and who works at teaching girls has gone to see you as she promised me when she was here last Sunday." Unknown to all three, God had already brought together the principals of a great work.

In this same letter Vincent was forced to quench once more Louise's anxiety for her son, an anxiety brought on, perhaps, by her first long absences from Paris. "As for Monsieur your son, I will keep an eye on him," he assured her, "but put yourself at rest, I beg you, since you can consider him under the special protection of Our Lord and His holy Mother by the fact of the many gifts and offerings of him you have made Them, and since he is a friend of the people of God and, therefore, nothing can happen to him. What shall we say about this too great tenderness?" he felt constrained to add. "It seems to me for certain, Mademoiselle, that you ought before God to work to rid yourself of it since it can only embarrass your soul and deprive you of the peace Our Lord desires in your heart and of that absence of affection for all that is not Him. Do it, then, I beg you, and so honor God who is charged with the sovereign and absolute good of Monsieur your son, and who does not wish you to interfere except in a dependent and peaceful way." The language of saints indeed: for who else would dare write so uncompromisingly to a woman working selflessly for God, and who but such a woman would accept it?

A few days later the rebuke was softened with an extraordinary compliment and promise. "How good it is to be a child of God, Mademoiselle," Vincent wrote in an exalted mood, "for He loves still more tenderly those who have this relationship to Him than you love your own, although as I can see you have more tenderness toward Him as quasi-mother of His children. Wonderful! We will speak about it on your return. In the meantime be full of confidence that she to whom Our Lord has given so much love for the children of others will merit that Our Lord have a wholly special love for her own . . ."

Louise was at Saint-Cloud and not very well; insisting upon her immediate return, Vincent commanded her to travel "not by water, but in a tightly closed carriage." Winter travel was especially hard on her, and she began to wear a face mask, which was very fashionable then, to protect her from the icy winds.

Back in Paris, Louise set about the work of establishing and giving

permanence to the confraternities there. One had already been established at Saint-Sauveur in 1629, and while Baunard gives Louise the
whole credit for the Parisian confraternities, there is no explicit evidence
that she was the founding spirit behind this first one. On the contrary,
she wrote at a later date to M. Vincent when regulations for the Charity
at Beauvais were under consideration: "I am sending back to you the rule
of Saint-Sauveur. I had not seen it. It seems to me that in the beginning
the whole confraternity was made to depend on M. le curé. I do not
know whether that would be apropos (for Beauvais)"—words which
would seem to indicate an unfamiliarity with the beginnings at Saint-
Sauveur. Certainly she had something to do with it subsequently, as she
did with all the confraternities of the capital, for she had a particular
acquaintance with the people and the conditions of her former parish.

This letter, which is quite long, is significant for Louise's firm opinions
concerning the administration of the confraternities: there is in it ample
proof that many of their highly successful methods and rules must be
ascribed to her genius.

It is certain that Louise was the foundress of the Confraternity of
Saint-Nicolas-du-Chardonnet, which began in 1630. Gobillon attests to
it, and Vincent congratulated her in these words: "As to your Charity, I
cannot tell you how consoled I am. I pray God to bless your toil and to
perpetuate this holy work." He ends the letter by asking playfully, "Does
not this console you, Mademoiselle? Can you say after this that you are
useless in the world?"

He was able to console her with better news about Michel-Antoine,
too, of whom, he said, one of the professors at the seminary "has told me
marvels." The exaggeration was surely harmless enough in the circumstances.

It was at Saint-Nicolas-du-Chardonnet that the poor under the
direction of Vincent and Louise were first served.

As early as June 1627 Louise had spoken of girls who wished "to come
from Burgundy to give themselves to me," presumably to help her in
the unorganized service of the poor which engaged her at that time, but
apparently because of Vincent's great caution nothing came of this. He
makes it quite clear that Marguerite was the first to serve in the Charities. Therefore she deserved to be called the first Daughter of Charity,
since her service led directly to the founding of the Company.

Louise's keen mind saw this eventuality even now in 1630 and her zeal
ran ahead to bring it about, but Vincent held her back. "I rejoice in the

provisions made for these good girls [others had joined Marguerite Na-
seau]," he assured her, "and I praise your desire to give them some organization, but do not give way to the thoughts you have. You belong to
Our Lord and to His holy Mother; hold yourself committed to them and
to the state in which they have placed you, while waiting for them to
indicate that they wish something else for you . . ."

Louise was obedient as always, she did not "give way" to her thoughts,
but the thoughts persisted—with good reason, for they were from God—
and they troubled her so that Vincent felt obliged some time later to
warn her to "rid your mind of everything that bothers you. God will take
care of things. You cannot be anxious without saddening (so to speak)
the Heart of God, because He sees that you do not honor holy trust
enough. Trust Him, I beg you, and you will have your heart's desire."

The beginning at Saint-Nicolas was hard, and Vincent was ready with
his encouragement. "Why, you are more than five women!" he reminded Louise in an obvious effort to cheer her up, and "you are good
managers, for you have spent only about half an écu." But he did not
ignore the difficulty: "You have few workers for a great deal of work," he
sighed. "Oh, well! Our Lord will work along with you."

With the coming of spring, Louise set off on another round of visitations, starting with Villepreux, where Vincent had established the confraternity in 1618. Here she made her first blunder. She started the visitation without calling on the curé, and his dignity was very much
offended. "It is extremely difficult, Mademoiselle, to do any good without arousing opposition," Vincent comforted her in her bewilderment
and distress; but went on with practical counsel: "As we are bound, insofar as in us lies, to soothe the injured feelings of others, I think you
would perform an act pleasing to God if you saw the parish priest and
excused yourself for having, without notifying him, spoken to the sisters
of the Charity and to the girls, and told him quite simply that you
thought you were free to act as you had at Saint-Cloud and other places,
that this would teach you your duty in future, and, in case he disapproved, you would let the matter rest. And my advice is that you should
do so. Our Lord will, perhaps, be more glorified by your submission than
by all the good you might effect there." It was a hard thing to ask of any
well-intentioned woman, but especially of a Marillac who was yet not
quite a saint in an age which was very touchy about its honor. But
Vincent knew his woman; Louise acquiesced gracefully and her charm
mollified the ruffled cleric.

The curé was not the only difficulty Louise encountered at Villepreux. She had to deal with truancy, too, but not of the usual kind. The simple villagers were actually frightened of this new thing called school, and Vincent counseled apparent withdrawal with a new, disguised approach. "Tell them," he advised blandly, "that it is not a school but an exercise of piety lasting several days."

He reassured her about "le petit Michel"—"I saw him two or three days ago on his way to his lesson, and he is well." His worry over her own health—she had thrown herself into the work at Villepreux to the point of making herself ill—was poorly disguised. "Blessed be God, Mademoiselle, that I learned of your recovery almost as soon as I learned of your illness," he began the letter cheerfully enough, but he was soon cautioning her to take some relaxation, and a few days later he openly confessed: "I am afraid you are doing too much . . . Take care, I beg you, Mademoiselle. Our Lord wishes you to serve Him with common sense; the opposite is called indiscreet zeal."

It was Louise's temperament, however, to give herself entirely to whatever she did, and she was so caught up with the poor that she hesitated to accept an invitation to visit her cousin Geneviève d'Attichy, Duchesse d'Atri, in September of that year. Vincent urged her to go, assuring her that "it is not to go needlessly when you visit a person of the quality of her who invites you"—a man of his time, Vincent always had a courteous but not servile respect for persons of rank—"and who perhaps has need of your advice to resolve something of great good. Go, then, Mademoiselle, go in Our Lord's Name and with His blessing!" he finished with Gascon vivacity.

But the useful was to be mixed with the agreeable: "If the occasion presents itself to do something in regard to the children there, do it cautiously," for he added rather acidly, "there is need of a great deal of it [caution] in that diocese. The authority of the lady of the place will, nevertheless, be yours in that of Our Lord . . . And you cannot be near the Charities of Beauvais without visiting them at your leisure."

It was vacation time, and Michel was to stay with M. Vincent in his mother's absence, but "after the ordinands have left ten or eleven days from now, because we have neither bed nor room for him."

On October 22, 1630, Louise was back at Montmirail, where she had begun her apostolate. Michel had returned to school and was very well, Vincent assured her—even M. Adrien Bourdoise, the rather grim rector, said so—but Vincent was especially happy over the improvement in

Louise's own health, although he continued to worry because she had to speak so much "in such penetrating air with your cold." A week later he was still fussing over the effect of the climate on her, but was satisfied that she had recovered sufficiently to stay on and finish the work.

This autumn of 1630 which saw Louise in full possession of a religious life of service saw also, curiously enough, the ultimate momentary success of the Marillac earthly fortunes and their final, complete destruction. Michel de Marillac's political career had progressed slowly and solidly through every vicissitude and setback for thirty years. It had taken a great leap forward with his inclusion in Richelieu's cabinet on August 27, 1624, and his appointment as Keeper of the Seals on June 1, 1626. That it should come now to a sudden, disastrous end is one of history's most fascinating turns of events. The key may lie in Marillac's age (he was now sixty-seven), and in his inability to dodge and feint with the brilliance of his political youth, or in a tired refusal to dissimulate any longer but to cling openly to what had always been his underlying ideal: the victory of the Catholic cause through loyalty to the Queen Mother and her allies.

It is amazing that so astute a politician as he should have so badly underestimated Richelieu and his hold over Louis XIII. The polite enmity of the Minister and Marillac came to a test in the Council of December 26, 1628, on the Italian campaign, which was designed to establish French influence in Italy against the Spanish and Austrian Hapsburgs. Richelieu with his farsighted wisdom knew the real enemies of France; it was futile to deal with the domestic Huguenot problem until the ultimate menace was driven off. Marie and Marillac and Bérulle held stubbornly to the narrower view. Richelieu won out and the fate of all was sealed—the Cardinal's glory and his enemies' disgrace.

Marillac should have seen the writing on the wall the following spring when the Minister, in a last effort at conciliation, offered Marillac's Capuchin son, Michel, the bishopric of Saint-Malo (which the pious young religious refused) and named his brother, Jean-Louis, a maréchal of France, but he continued on his intransigent way. So blind was he that, even after the death of his friend and ally, Bérulle—a lion in asceticism and a sheep in politics—on October 13, 1629, he allowed the Queen Mother to convince him that he could topple Richelieu and replace him.

The plot simmered for a year. The conspirator's chance came in September 1630 when the King fell suddenly ill at Lyons. Marie and her daughter-in-law Anne of Austria swooped upon the prostrate son and husband, who was perilously close to death. His death would have simplified things for Marie, for then her favorite son and fellow conspirator, Gaston d'Orléans, would be king; nor would Anne have grieved overmuch, for Louis had long thoroughly neglected her, following a miscarriage which he blamed on her carelessness. In the event of his death, it was more than casually planned to marry her to Gaston. Only the hated Richelieu stood to lose. But Louis lived, so the women merely switched to "Plan B," which was to poison the King's mind against his great Minister in the long hours of convalescence when they had his exhausted ear all to themselves.

By the time the King was able to travel to Paris, Richelieu was in perilous straits. On November 6 the Maréchal de Marillac, sharing the command of the French army in Italy with Schomberg and La Force, asked for leave to return to Paris. On November 9 the Cardinal's beloved niece, the Duchesse d'Aiguillon, went to the court to plead on her knees for her uncle before Marie and Louis. Marie insulted her, but Louis sent her away kindly enough.

The denouncement came swiftly and dramatically. When Louis went to visit his mother in the Luxembourg at eleven o'clock on the morning of November 10, she ordered all the doors bolted. Marie was exultantly sure of herself: alone with her son, who was completely unsure of himself now, she was confident that she could pull him away from his Minister and into her camp. But in the excitement of her apparent success she had forgotten one door, a little-used one in the corner. Now it opened quietly, and there stood the hated enemy, the great Cardinal himself. In this extremity he had taken the desperate ploy of appearing in the royal presence unbidden. As he sank to his knee before the King, Marie completely lost her head and began to scream like a fishwife in that shrill voice Louis had hated and feared all his life. It was too much for him now. Revolted by this vulgar display, he sternly ordered his mother to stop, raised the Minister to his feet and left the room.

As Richelieu went out of the palace he passed Michel de Marillac, who had excused himself from the Cardinal's summons that morning on a plea of illness, on his way to the Queen Mother. Marie had summoned him to assume the Cardinal's office.

All that day Richelieu was nervously poised for flight, while the friends of Marie and Marillac came trooping into the Luxembourg to congratulate the supposed victors. Then the King left suddenly for Versailles, sending word to both the Cardinal and Marillac to join him there. Significantly, Marillac's instructions were to await the royal pleasure in a village half a mile away. It is indicative of the human capacity for self-delusion that Marillac thought this a good omen. The waiting grew long, and at length Marillac realized that all was lost. He was at prayer in the village church when they arrested him. The Cardinal had won, secure in power until his death thirteen years later. A nobleman-adherent of the Queen Mother summed the day up in a sentence which has ever since characterized it in history: "It is the Day of Dupes."

The Maréchal Jean-Louis de Marillac at the head of the army in Falizo, Italy, was not forgotten. Richelieu was thorough: certainly no brother of his fallen rival should be left near guns and soldiers. So Schomberg was ordered to arrest him and send him back to Paris under guard.

The effect of all this on the proud Marillac pride, including Louise's own, can be well imagined. History has left no record of their intimate reactions to these first reversals, but their reaction to the final tragedy of the Maréchal supplies all defects.

Louise was away from Paris at the time, first at Montmirail and then at Beauvais. Beauvais had its own politics for her. Professional beggary had gone beyond all bounds there. Insolent hordes had made the streets, the church porches, even the churches themselves, unsafe. The forth-right Bishop, Augustin Potier—a brother of Mme la présidente de Lamoignon and a hopeful first minister after the death of Louis XIII until Mazarin drove him off—set up a campaign of controlled charity to eradicate this evil, and brought in St. Vincent to conduct it.

The saint did so with his usual dispatch and success, but not before he had been remanded to the Procureur Général of the King by the Lieutenant of the city. That worthy had indignantly protested that "about fifteen days ago there arrived in this city a certain priest named Vincent who, contemptuous of royal authority, had, without communicating with the royal officers nor any other body in the town who had an interest in the matter, brought together a great number of women whom he persuaded to band into an association to which he gave the special name of Charity . . ." The number of women thus assembled "to bring food and other necessities to the poor sick" was "about 300 or thereabouts," sputtered the self-important official, who remains anonymous to this day, ". . . and this must not be tolerated!" Apparently the Procureur Général thought the protest as funny as we do, for the Charity was flourishing in all eighteen parishes of the diocese when Louise arrived, although she was well forewarned to pick her steps so as not to tread on officious toes.

The Bishop himself could be something of a pitfall. Vincent cautioned her not to ask for his blessing, "since he has a strong aversion to ceremony and likes people to treat him in a frank and open way, but"—the saint added slyly—"with respect nonetheless."

The Parisian Charities were springing up like the grass between the cobblestones, and during this absence of Louise from the city another one, Saint-Benoît, was established. But Vincent was not wholly pleased with them. "I don't know what spirit causes each parish in Paris to desire to have something peculiar to itself and not to want to have anything to do with the others," he complained. "Each wishes to be a *salmigondis* [hodgepodge], taking something from Saint-Sauveur, something from our parish, Saint-Nicolas, and something else from Saint-Eustache." There was also a certain independence among the women of Saint-Benoît which worried him because of their inexperience, and he suggested that Louise exert her finesse to deal with it: "Consider whether it would be apropos for you to take the trouble to see this good *demoiselle* (a certain Mlle Tranchot) to stabilize her spirit so that she can strengthen the others. If you have visited her formerly, that would easily do for a pretext, for she would not bring it up to you, or to me . . ."

This letter mentions for the first time a girl of Villepreux, named Germaine, who was one of Louise's first schoolmistresses. They were kindred spirits in spirituality, for in a letter of the same period Vincent assured Louise—apparently about an extra Communion, for she was already receiving on Sundays, Tuesdays, and Saturdays—that "if Germaine is accustomed to communicate, I see no difficulty in your doing the same. Do it then, Mademoiselle."

At the same time he regulated her penitential practices: "If you cannot take the discipline and have a cincture of little silver roses Mademoiselle du Fay took back from me some time ago, use that in place of the discipline and of the hair shirt, which overheats the blood."

In this spring of 1631, young Michel was restless again. He was now thoroughly disaffected at the seminary of Saint-Nicolas-du-Chardonnet and there was nothing for it but to find a new place for him. Vincent was satisfied that there was reason enough for the change, but he wanted to defer it until Louise had returned from a scheduled visitation to Montreuil. "Tell him that you have decided to place him as a pensioner with the Jesuits [at their famous Parisian Collège de Clermont]," he wrote.

"It will be time enough upon your return to speak to these Fathers and to reserve him a place . . . so that he can be sent from the community [of Saint-Nicolas] to the Jesuits in his soutane without lodging with you."

"It will cost you more than it does now," he warned her and, knowing how cautious she was with money, partly because she had to be and partly because she considered what she had as belonging to the poor, he added laughingly, "*Mais quoi!* must we believe that one who loves holy poverty to a sovereign degree will not know how to impoverish herself?"

He kept promising during the weeks that she was at Montreuil that he would make the necessary arrangements at Clermont, but his missions and journeys and the retreats for ordinands kept getting in the way. Finally, at the beginning of Holy Week, he had good news for her: "I am assured of a place they have promised me for your son among the pensioners. The principal himself made the promise, and with very good will." And the week after Easter he was happy in the knowledge that Michel was satisfied, although Louise was still worried over the tuition.

This letter was an especially tender one. "I had promised myself the comfort of going to see you, but I have been forced to set out unexpectedly for the Vincennes woods," it began. "Your dear heart will forgive me, and on my return, God willing, we will talk over everything . . ." The news about Clermont followed, then some advice about a servant girl Louise thought of hiring. "There is no harm in having someone who is according to your heart," he assured her, "but I do not think she of whom you spoke to me is the one for you. You should get someone entirely new and devoted, someone who will honor and stand in awe of you, or who thinks the same as you do. Ask her of God . . ." And he finished: "Adieu, my dear daughter, be cheerful and gay. When I return we will speak further about this and about your trip to the fields. Don't let your heart murmur against mine because I go without talking with you, for I knew nothing of it until this morning."

Louise would have much to tell him: there had been problems at Montreuil over the collection for the poor because of troublemakers who scoffed at the work, the number of confraternity members had to be reduced, and a nascent confraternity had had to be absorbed into one already in existence. Vincent on his part would have news of several apostolic trips, and a scruple much like her own he had already asked her to pray over: a choice he had had to make between carrying out a promise and doing a charity for someone "who could do us neither good nor ill"; he had chosen to keep the promise, but was bothered lest he had followed his own inclination in the choice. And he would have to discuss with her the Charity of Saint-Sulpice, which needed her badly. "They have made a beginning," he had told her while she was still at Montreuil, "but things go so wretchedly, from what they tell me, that it is really a shame." And he had added hopefully, "Perhaps God is making the occasion for you to work there."

So it went, this evangelical life they had both embarked upon, this way of marking their souls and bringing them to perfection. There were even brighter, more glorious things in the future.

VII

The Execution of
Jean de Marillac

The day of Louise's great achievement, the founding of the Daughters of Charity, was drawing ever nearer. The idea had been long in her mind; indeed, it had become a burning desire; but Vincent had bade her time and again to stifle it. Even now, with the realization not much more than a year off, he bade her more firmly. "I beseech you, once for all, not to think about it until Our Lord shows that it is His will," he insisted, "and at present the sentiments which He inspires are quite to the contrary. Many good things are desired with a desire that seems to be according to God's will, and yet this is not always so. Still, he permits this in order that the soul may be prepared to be that which is desired. Saul sought a she-ass; he found a kingdom. St. Louis sought the conquest of the Holy Land, and found self-conquest and a heavenly crown. You seek to become the servant of these poor girls, and God wishes you to be His servant and, perhaps, the servant of many more than you would be in that way . . . Be at peace, then, Mademoiselle . . . I . . . bid you good night with as much tenderness of heart as I am in the love of Our Lord, your servant."

The command to stifle the thought was firm enough, but it did not shut the door. It was Vincent's way never to shut the door, but it was also his way never to open it wider until he was sure that the Lord willed it. As for Louise, she had once more to repress her longing and had once more to wait. She would try hard to obey—but the thought would not be stifled. And that was the Lord's way.

In the meantime, she had to deal with her own nature, to purify herself more and more so that when the Lord spoke she would be ready, worthy. Vincent had had to rebuke her for staying away from Communion one morning because of some "interior pain." "Don't you see clearly that it is a temptation?" he asked. "And must you in that case give the victory to the enemy of Holy Communion? Do you think to become more capable of drawing near to God by drawing away from Him rather than by approaching Him?"

And he had had to reassure her that her busy life for others was not preempting her first responsibility to her son, and that her frequent apprehensions for him were perfectly normal. "Oh! Our Lord surely did well not to choose you for His mother," he told her with delightful sarcasm, "for you cannot imagine that God's will is to be found in the maternal solicitude required of you by your son; or perhaps you think that will prevent you from doing God's will in something else; no, indeed, for God's will is not opposed to God's will."

In September, Louise was off on another round of visitations. Montmirail had become a sort of checkpoint, and she waited there for the letters of introductions she would need; then, starting with Mesnil, she went next to Bergier, then to Loisy, Soulières, Souderon and Villeseneux. There was a curious reference in Vincent's letter of instruction. "Put out of your mind the reason you have alleged for wanting to make this journey. You cannot know how it has saddened my heart," he wrote. "Oh! no, I am not made that way, thank God; for God knows what He has given me for you, and you will know it in heaven." What was worrying the sensitive soul of Louise? Was she afraid that she was becoming a bother to Vincent? Or was it something of greater import: was she afraid, perhaps, of their mutual affection? Certainly the fear, however nebulous, must at some time have crossed a conscience so delicate; and Louise's rugged honestly would have brought it into the open without hesitation. At any rate, whatever the scruple, Vincent had exorcised it.

Louise was detained at Montmirail for nearly two weeks, longer than she had anticipated. Vincent wrote to her there on September 13 in answer to a letter she had written him concerning one of the sisters of the Confraternity. "It doesn't matter that this woman has a bad reputation," he assured her. "Maybe it's false, or indeed that she has reformed. The Magdalen on the instant of her conversion became the Virgin's companion and Our Lord's disciple. Since I am a great sinner, I cannot reject those who have been such, so long as they show a good will." It was a wise and uncommon lesson in that pharisaical age.

The same letter bore disturbing news about two of Louise's dearest friends. Mlle du Fay was ill, and Vincent protested a little too much that "it is nothing." But Louise's Aunt Catherine was another matter. "The good Madame la maréchale de Marillac is very ill of stomach hemorrhages at Roule," he said bluntly, preparing Louise for the worst. "Honor the Blessed Virgin's patience; offer this sorrow to God. Would it not be a blessing for her to quit this earth of misery and go to enjoy the glory of heaven?"

The point was well taken, for, whatever the physical symptoms, Mme de Marillac was dying of grief over her husband's tragedy. All the Marillacs had been greatly upset since his arrest the previous year—this was why Vincent was ready with spiritual motivation—and with good reason. The Maréchal de Marillac had been in custody since his arrest— not in exile such as his brother Michel enjoyed at Châteaudun, where his daughter-in-law, widow of his son René, was permitted to keep house for him and minister to his needs—but in the hard custody of prison, awaiting trial.

All this time he had been, in fact, a hostage because the wily Richelieu knew that he might need one should the Queen Mother resume her plotting—which was a foregone conclusion. Michel de Marillac would make a poor hostage because the Cardinal could accuse him of no provable crime. It was different with Jean-Louis de Marillac, however, because like any and all military captains of the day he had made a tidy sum out of his posts. No matter that everybody did so and that the whole of France from the King down to the lowliest subject expected them to do so. Richelieu had a cause for indictment to be used when the occasion warranted. And the irony of it all lay in the fact that he found the cause for indictment in the stern *Code Michau* written by the Maréchal's own brother when he was Keeper of the Seals!

The suspense had been too much for the Maréchal's poor wife; she had broken under it and now lay dying. She was, in fact, dead when Vincent wrote; but he did not know it. A week later he broke the sad news carefully and tenderly: "Madame la maréchale de Marillac has gone to heaven to receive the reward of her deeds. Now, you had expected it. But, oh! Our Lord having wished it thus, we must adore His Providence and strive to conform ourselves in all things to His holy will. Surely I know well that your dear heart asks nothing better and that, if the interior part is affected, it will soon calm itself. The Son of God wept over Lazarus; why should you not weep over this good lady? There is no harm, provided that, like the Son of God, you conform yourself within to the will of His Father; and that I am sure you will do."

He broke off abruptly, asking for news as if to distract her: "But how are you? The penetrating air does not affect your health, does it? And Germaine"—he tried some gentle teasing here—"doesn't she complain that her children are at the mercy of M. Belin [he had taken over Germaine's school at Villepreux while she accompanied Louise on this visitation]? When are you going to Champagne? Is this good girl [Germaine] profiting from the trip? Do you hope to do some good there?" And after this barrage: "A word about all that, please?"

In a letter of this same period, St. Vincent impressed upon Louise a lesson he was ever to urge upon all his spiritual sons and daughters, the lesson of never obtruding themselves on a work under the pretext of zeal. "If Monseigneur de Châlons has not sent to seek you out and is in the neighborhood, it seems to me that you would do well to go to see him and tell him with simple good faith why Père de Gondi asked you to take the trouble to go to Champagne and what you are doing," he advised her, "and offer to retrench any part of your procedure, if he so pleases, and to quit it entirely if that is what he wants. Such is the spirit of God. I find no blessing except in acting thus. Monseigneur de Châlons is a holy man. You ought to regard him as the interpreter of the will of God . . ."

The good Bishop, as a matter of fact, decided that he had no need of Louise's services, and she quietly left the diocese.

She was away from Paris at a good time, for the plague was raging and some of her neighbors in the rue Saint-Victor had died of it. She must have been terrified to learn in mid-October that her son was sick in bed with "*un petit mal de tête*," but after purging and bleeding and other strenuous remedies of the day, he was, Vincent assured her, "cheerful and well-behaved . . . so as to edify us all. If he continues so, there will be reason to praise God and to hope that you are comforted." By the time Vincent wrote again two weeks later, Michel was recovered and back at Clermont.

Another misfortune befell Louise while she was away: she lost her rented room in M. Véron's house because he needed it for his son; but Vincent assured her that her friend Mlle Sevin, who was Véron's sister, was looking for a new lodging for her in the neighborhood and that Louise, if she returned before one was found, could stay with Mlle du Fay.

But these tribulations of daily living were as nothing compared to an incident which caused her acute embarrassment upon her return to Paris. Some anonymous gentleman was spreading it about that Louise had promised to marry him and was reneging on her promise. Naturally, she was greatly upset, but Vincent soothed her wounded feelings with words which have a hint of laughter behind them despite his opening protestation: "How troubled I am because you are upset! *Mais quoi!*" he continued, "such being the dispensation of Providence, what is the remedy for it? What real evil can you fear from it? So a man says that you have promised to marry him, and it isn't true. You are being slandered. You are suffering in your soul unjustly and without giving cause. Are you afraid people are talking about you? Let them! But be sure that all this is one of the greatest means of conforming to the Son of God you could have on earth and that you can gain by it conquests over yourself that you would never have otherwise. Oh! what vain complacencies are brought to nothing and what acts of humiliation are brought about by such an occasion! Indeed, nothing can result from it but what is excellent for this world and the next. Brace yourself interiorly then against the feelings of nature and the day will come when you will bless the hour that God tried you in such a way . . ."

It probably amused Vincent that Louise was forty years old and that she had been beseeching him for years to allow her some form of religious consecration; but the calumny was flattering for all that and vindicates Calvet's assertion that, "like all her family, she was handsome."

His commentary on her attractiveness is worth repeating: "The portrait that we have of her is based on a painting by Duchange, made from memory after her death. It is therefore separated by time from the model, but tradition declares it to be a faithful likeness. It depicts a face which is very regular, within the lines of a perfect oval. The veil, covering her head and part of her face, casts over her features a shadow which the artist has preserved but which tends to make her look plain, though we are informed that her expression was one of vivacious originality. The mouth is small, the lips thin, the chin prominent and firm. The eyes, lowered as is fitting in a nun, shine, as we may suppose, with a restrained fire. She so often spoke to her Daughters of Charity of the eyes, and of the manner of using them; of the obligation to mortify them out of doors, yet without closing them; of the fruitful meditation that may be made on the eyes of Jesus, which, as the Gospels tell us, were subject to His will—that we may well believe her own eyes to have been beautiful, clear, luminous, the mirror of an impassioned soul. Yes, we may say that she was beautiful." He might well have added that the face he so sensitively described was the face of a seventy-year-old woman from which the fresh glow of youth and character lines of middle age had long since faded.

Vincent's letter dealt also with a new problem concerning Michel: his mother was anxious to see him in holy orders as soon as possible. "We shall go to see him when you wish; but I do not think that you ought to make him take orders so soon," he dissuaded her, gently enough. "He is not old enough for sacred orders; and as for the four minors, there is no point of usefulness or utility for them yet, and he would have to suspend his studies to prepare for them, the which would cause him great harm." Vincent's stricture on age is amusing in light of the fact that the youth was only a year younger than Vincent himself had been when he was ordained priest at nineteen, according to the custom of the time but against the prescriptions of the Council of Trent. The fact was highly embarrassing to the Reformer of the Clergy!

The tragic fate of her uncle, the Maréchal de Marillac, was weighing heavily on Louise these days. That fate had been sealed by the stupidity of Marie de Medici. She had fled France, thoroughly beaten but not knowing it, and now threatened a treasonable revolt that would give Calais to the English. Hilaire Belloc has passed a considered judgment on this affair, which has by turns outraged and mystified historians: "Marillac was put to death in order to strike terror into those who proposed the seizure of Calais. Any determined government would have had to do what Richelieu did, or risk the realm . . . Putting Marillac to death at that moment meant that any one of the Queen Mother's agents caught in secret treason would die. So poor Marillac was like the owls and stoats which the gamekeeper nails to the barn door; a terror for the rest. In general it was an iniquity of State of the sort called necessary iniquity, and not personal to Richelieu and his regime."

On May 10, 1632—after a trial in the Cardinal's own house at Reuil by special commissionaries in place of the Parlement de Paris, whose competence it was to try maréchals of France—Jean-Louis de Marillac was beheaded in the Place de Grève for the crime of having profited from his military posts. The proud Marillacs had literally crawled to prevent it. One after another they had knelt to the Duchesse d'Aiguillon, a poor innocent who could not help them; to the implacable Cardinal; to the King, which is to say the same thing. Anne d'Attichy, Comtesse de Maure, can hardly be blamed for her savage reply to the Duchesse's inquiries after her, that she "could not bring herself to have anything to do with the niece of her uncle's murderer."

There is at least sketchy evidence that Louise had tried to do her part to save her uncle. Vincent assured her in a letter that "as for Monsieur de Marillac, I am in agreement to everything that you find good; but take care not to compromise yourself . . ." And again, "It would seem better for you to act in the manner you outlined to me, and to defer action rather than hazard all for nothing. Therefore, if between now and my return, you find someone trustworthy, act; if not, defer action. Our Lord is able for this affair, especially if you prefer to be at the foot of the cross where you are now and which is the best place in the world you could be. Prefer to be there, then, Mademoiselle, and fear nothing."

It is true, as Coste points out, that the Maréchal is not definitively identified as the Marillac in question; but since he was the most threatened at the time, it is at least valid to assume that Vincent referred to him. It is at least certain that the saint consoled Louise over the ignominious execution: "What you tell me of M. le maréchal de Marillac seems to me worthy of great compassion and does indeed grieve me. Let us honor within us the good pleasure of God and the good fortune of those who honor the suffering of the Son of God in their own. It doesn't matter how our relatives go to God as long as they go to Him. Indeed, the good use of this kind of death is the most sure way to eternal life." And he ended soothingly, "Do not weep, then; but bow to the adorable will of God." He was to tell her daughters, after her death many years later: ". . . She bore the loss of those who were dearest to her in all the world without manifesting any pain, although she felt it most deeply."

It had been a terrible scene at the home of Mme René de Marillac on the rue Chapon—a scene of which Louise was assuredly a part—when the headless body of the Maréchal had been carried there and placed in the chapel. Michel de Marillac did not live long after his murdered brother, dying in exile at Châteaudun on August 7 of that same year. Thus ended the earthly fame of the Marillacs; the heavenly fame was yet to come.

The wound was long in healing in Louise, but Vincent tended it with insistent cheerfulness. One day after he and his priests had moved to the priory of Saint-Lazare and he had returned on one of his frequent visits to the Collège des Bons Enfants, he sent her this note of mock reproach: "Here I am your neighbor since noon! For the last two hours I have sent to see whether you were at home, but you were off at your devotions. Therefore, if it pleases you to come right after dinner, we shall learn *viva voce* about what you have written us . . ." And he adds in mock-serious postscript: "I can only tell you that tomorrow I propose to blame you for letting yourself give way to vain and frivolous fears. Oh, when will you appreciate that you have been well scolded!"

A few days later he was apologizing with mock self-importance for not being able to see her, detained as he was by "a bishop-designate, a first president, two doctors, a professor of theology, and M. Pavillon [later Bishop of Alet] . . ." In the same note he expresses his pleasure that she has at last found "a fine lodging." Like any woman, Louise was eager for him to see it, and like any man—especially a man as busy as he—he had not got to it by the end of June: "*Mon Dieu*, Mademoiselle, how I offend you! I promised you yesterday that I would have the pleasure of going today to see your beautiful and holy paradise and that I would go to see Madame la présidente Goussault and Mademoiselle Pollalion, and here I have done neither one nor the other . . ." he wrote, sure of forgiveness.

The two noblewomen referred to, the one the widow of the President of the Chambre des Comptes de Paris and the other the widow of one of Louis XIII's gentlemen in waiting, were active in the work of the confraternities, and Vincent had plans for them to accompany Louise to "the Charity of Champigny, which badly needs you." She must leave at once for Villeneuve. "If neither of the ladies can go, I do not know whether you would be too uncomfortable in the boat to Joigny, which leaves on Saturday at eight o'clock. I think not, because it is covered."

The Charity at Villeneuve was in a sorry state. As early as the preceding October, Vincent had apprised Louise of the situation; and after Louise reached there he wrote, on July 7, 1632: "I do not doubt in the least that you will find great difficulty in reestablishing the confraternity, even more than you have told me; but blessed be God that there is so much hope that you will reestablish it!" He heartily approved her plan of attack, and had good news of helpers: "Mademoiselle Pollalion tells me that she hopes to be with you on Saturday, and I have written Madame Goussault that they have arranged for her to see the schoolmistress of Villeneuve on Saturday afternoon." He finished, obviously pleased: "O God! what a good little company! I pray Our Lord to bind your hearts into one, His own, and to strengthen you in your works."

With her usual abundance of energy, Louise did succeed in giving new heart to the languishing Charity; but Mme Goussault was totally unimpressed by the so-called schoolmistress. No one could be found at the moment to take her place, however, and Louise was forced to tell the mothers of her little scholars that she would send them a new schoolmistress as soon as she could find one. The dependable Germaine was considered, but who would take her place at Villepreux?

In thrashing things out, Vincent came up against a situation he would encounter again and again: the wounded dignity of the highborn ladies who assisted him. Goodhearted and pious though they were, they were at times constitutionally unable not to take offense at what they considered a lack of respect for their rank. Vincent was extraordinarily attuned to their nuances of feeling and was most considerate of them; but in his haste to get things done, and because he did not have to bother about such niceties in dealing with Louise, who was as highborn as many of them, he sometimes unconsciously offended noble sensibilities. Thus, he wrote to Louise: "It would be good for you to communicate with Madame Goussault and Mademoiselle Pollalion for their advice concerning Germaine. It is only two days ago that I paid any attention as to how we should act toward them, which, it seems to me, should be with cordiality and deference; and perhaps I offended them by having you make your last decision concerning the work without saying anything to them."

A new girl was found for the post of schoolmistress at Villeneuve. Vincent commented wryly that she "must be strong-minded; she will have much to put up with."

Louise at this time took on a new work, the relief of the galley slaves. Vincent had been their almoner or chaplain for ten years, and had done wonders in softening the harsh conditions of the Conciergerie and other Parisian prisons where they were held before assignment to their ships. Now in 1632 he obtained from the King and the aldermen of the city an old square tower near the Pont de la Tournelle between the Porte Saint-Bernard and the Seine, which he fitted out as a hospital for the galley slaves who were sick or infirm. He asked Louise and her good helpers to join him in alleviating their misery both in this impromptu hospital and in the actual prisons. It was not an easy thing to ask, because it meant exposing these sensitive women of breeding to the insults, curses, obscenities, and even physical violences of the worst criminal element of society. But again Louise and her friends were equal to the task.

"Charity toward these poor galley slaves has incomparable merit with God," Vincent reminded her thankfully. "You have done well to help them, and should continue to do so as much as you can until I have the good fortune to see you, which will be in two or three days. Consider a little whether your Charity of Saint-Nicolas would undertake the charge of them, at least for a time; you could aid them with the money you have left." And he ended proudly, "Oh, how difficult that is, which is what makes me throw out this challenge to your spirit of adventure."

The parish priests of Saint-Nicolas-du-Chardonnet showed great compassion toward the galley slaves confined in their parish and ministered to them with true pastoral zeal. After 1634, these parish priests were appointed as official chaplains to the prison.

In February 1633, Vincent and Louise suffered a great blow when Marguerite Naseau died of the plague. She had contracted the dread disease by lifting a poor sufferer into bed. "I have just learned scarcely an hour ago of the misfortune suffered by the girl who serves your guardians of the poor, of the doctor's opinion of her condition, and that you have visited her," Vincent wrote in haste to Louise. "I swear to you, Mademoiselle, that my heart was at once so strongly moved that, were it not nighttime, I would have left on the instant to go to see you . . ." He who was so cautious about Louise's health was so far from forbidding her for fear of contagion to go to the stricken girl that he congratulated her —and at the same time uttered a great prophecy: "No, Mademoiselle, do not fear [to go to Marguerite's bedside]," he wrote. "Our Lord wishes to avail Himself of you for something which regards His glory, and I think He will preserve you for that." And again, on February 24: "You can imagine, Mademoiselle, whether my heart is not suffering the pain of yours. As for danger to yourself, there is none, by the grace of God. It would be good to have the surgeon from the Santé visit Marguerite, in case the doctor makes some difficulty about going to see her. Monsieur Cotti [the doctor] frightens easily; and in any case it would be good to do it as soon as possible. Monsieur Bourdoise will see to it. Have him ask, please. He [the surgeon] will know what must be done; he has had experience . . ." Despite Louise's tireless nursing, despite anything anyone could do, Marguerite died in the Hôpital Saint-Louis. She died the very year the Daughters of Charity were to come into being. Although she was never, therefore, a formal member of the Company, she was by the emphatic testimony of the Founders the first member *par excellence*, the supreme model for the hundreds of thousands to follow her.

Vincent tried to divert Louise from her grief by sending her forth on another visitation to the Charities of Verneuil, Pont, Gournay, La Neufville-Roy, and Bulles.

In April, Mme Goussault traveled through the Valley of the Loire on a journey which seems to have combined visits to relatives with service to the poor and inspection of hospitals and other facilities for the sick and neglected. She wrote M. Vincent from Angers on the thirteenth a long letter amounting to a daily log or diary which is remarkable for its picture of the times and the people, and for the revelation of the good woman's own piety and dedication to the poor—a revelation made all the more charming by a certain naïve delight in her own goodness and amazement at her capacity for humility. The influence of Louise is seen throughout, especially in Mme Goussault's pious exercises practiced faithfully throughout the trip, for they will turn up later as part of the Daughters' devotional order of day:

Upon entering the carriage, I would say *In viam pacis*, and all would respond; then I would recall the points of mental prayer for them, after which we would say the Angelus.

Sometimes our first conversation would be about our meditation thoughts, and then, in a more recreational vein, about our distractions or our dreams; then Grandnom (her Intendant) would read for about half an hour from *The Pilgrim to Loreto*; then two of our girls would chant the litanies of the Holy Name of Jesus, and the rest of us would repeat what they had chanted. In passing a village, we would salute its guardian angel, and in the village where we stopped I would ask the special help of Our Lord.

At Etréchy . . . I met some children . . . and the thought crossed my mind that they were children of God. I experienced a great joy in having them say their Pater . . .

At Etampes . . . I got out of the carriage and went looking for the Hôtel-Dieu, which was at a great distance. I went on foot with only my servant and my footman. I spoke to a young religious who turned out to be the superior. I sat down to talk to her while my footman went to buy something for the sick; and when I spoke of the necessity of a director, she looked me up and down. I was dressed in a low collar, without *vertugadin* [a kind of farthingale skirt], like a servant. She asked me: "What sort of woman are you? Are you married? I have heard tell of a Mademoiselle [sic] Acarie, but I think that you are someone else." And she began to tell me how she had wished to be a hospital Sister, that they had chosen her as superior of six religious who are in need of reform, but that in two years' time she still had done nothing. I strongly encouraged her. She told me that she must go to Paris. I offered her my house. I have had a great desire to pray to God for her . . .

At Angerville there was no Hôtel-Dieu . . . but I met a number of poor persons who put their trust in me, and also some children and persons of quality who were struck with awe. I began by having them make the sign of the cross, which many did not know how to do, and it filled me with great pity. They seemed to be of good will.

At Artenay . . . I gave a long catechism lesson in the church, as I believe you advised me to do . . . I marveled at finding there nothing to my liking either for soul or body. Their Hôtel-Dieu is rich, so they told me, but the sick are not the better for it. There are few religious and these have servants who wait upon them too much . . .

At Blois I found a great deal of devotion, but the Hôtel-Dieu is not visited and is in wretched order. I spoke with one of my cousins who is very devout and he told me that Père Lallemant, superior of the Jesuits, had strongly exhorted them to visit it, but that perhaps God permitted that it be me who would come to inform them that in Paris ladies of quality went to the Hôtel-Dieu and so induce them to do likewise.

At Amboise . . . God gave me many graces. Their Hôtel-Dieu is poor. They take there all transient cripples and orphans, but no sick. There is a merchant there who has set up a foundation for a schoolmistress, whom I interrogated concerning the poor and asked her to come to see me the next day, which she did and was very much edified.

At Tours . . . I saw the most beautiful and the best-organized Hôtel-Dieu of any.

The good priest who said the Mass at Chouzé has real need, I think, to observe a mission; and I was minded to say something to M. d'Angers. The little children so poorly instructed! . . .

I have forgotten to tell you what we would do after dinner: sometimes we would recite our beads in two choirs, and every day the litanies of the Blessed Virgin . . .

Our recreation lasted well beyond our prayers. Sometimes we would play "Answer Yes or No"; and those who lost paid an Ave to those who won. We would sing Alleluia and other hymns, and so gayly that one of my tenant-farmers who was on horseback was delighted at us. I would give Catherine lessons in reading and pronunciation. Her replies and speech made us laugh until we cried. My father, it is so easy to serve God at this price.

At Angers, Mme Goussault was extremely pleased with her reception: great crowds thronged around her in the streets and the Ministers of Justice and all the principal people of the city came to call on her. She found the Hôtel-Dieu "in good enough order. A good bourgeois has made a vow to end his days in the service of the sick, who are in great need, and especially of their salvation. I have visited the prisoners twice . . . I gave them holy pictures and rosaries and would gladly have released them . . . What is annoying is that news spreads all over town and they make up news if there isn't any." On Sunday she taught the catechism to a group of young girls and then went out into the country to see whether the children were instructed and found to her satisfaction that their pastor had taught them well. On her return a certain Mlle Le Fèvre praised her extravagantly: "Everyone can see that you love the poor very much and that your heart is happiest when you are among them. You are twice as beautiful while you are speaking to them."

Mme Goussault, obviously elated, but with a certain honest and child-like pleasure, went on to tell St. Vincent: "My father, it is wonderful that God gives me the self-assurance to speak in front of never less than a hundred people with their pastor, and have them pay me compliments afterwards; even the good priest told me that he would think himself very lucky to be able to finish his days in my service without wages or recompense, but only to hear the words which fell from my lips."

This was a bit too much, and Vincent could be forgiven a smile as he read; but he knew the good woman and understood that she was just as sincere when she asked him, later on, to "root out my pride in whatever way it pleases you. I am ready to lose everything and to leave everything, preferring humility to all consolations and goods."

Louise's tour of the country Charities had not been protracted this time, and in April she was back in Paris, embroiled once more in the vagaries of her son. Michel could not decide what he wanted to do with his life. His latest whim was to quit his clerical studies. His mother, in great distress, informed Vincent. The saint answered guardedly, for a bout of his *petite fièvre* and a consequent bleeding had forced him to write through a secretary. He was apparently in great lassitude of mind from his illness, for he had forgotten to send the doctor to advise Louise whether she should allow "her girls" to enter a section of the city where the plague was raging, and he had forgotten also to draw up a schedule of meditations for one of these good helpers who was entering upon her retreat. He could not even recall what was in Louise's letter of the previous day, ". . . except in regard to the young man of whom you spoke to me [Michel] and about whom I will say that I do not think he ought to put aside the soutane in his present condition of uncertainty; it seems to me that he should stay as he is until he has definitely made up his mind, and that his good mother should not help him to make his decision." And he ended positively: "The ecclesiastical state is certainly best for him. If he holds to it, I think he will find peace."

Vincent had no sooner recovered from this latest attack than he suffered a fresh misfortune. His horse stumbled and fell, rolling on top of him. He was humbly grateful for "the singular protection of Our Lord" in this "most dangerous" accident, and characteristically blamed it on "the misuse of my life which has made [God] show me His punishing rod." He asked Louise to "help him obtain the grace of amendment for the future and to begin a new life." As for his injuries, he assured her, "nothing remains but a little sprain of the nerves of one foot, which now causes me but little pain."

Suddenly, a few days later in this same month of May 1633, comes the first hint that what Louise had long desired and prayed for and suffered exquisite agonies of frustration over—the gathering of her girls into an organized religious group—was close to realization. "As to the affair you are busy with," Vincent wrote, "my heart is still not sufficiently cleared of a difficulty which prevents me from seeing whether it is the will of His divine Majesty. I beg you, Mademoiselle, to recommend this affair to Him during these days in which He communicates more abundantly the graces of the Holy Spirit, indeed the Holy Spirit Himself." It was the season of Pentecost, Louise's happiest, most fruitful, time—and that was the best of auguries. "Let us persevere, then, in prayer, and as for yourself, be of good cheer."

Whatever the last-minute hesitation of this prudent man, it is evident that he saw the reality breaking through the clouds of doubt, and Louise's heart must have leaped as she read his words. It is remarkable that nothing in the previous correspondence prepares one for this momentous passage, except Vincent's occasional injunctions to wait for God's unmistakable revelation of His will. It is possible, of course, that the pertinent letters have been lost—Louise's letters of this time are almost completely missing and she might be expected to be more explicit on the matter—but it is too facile to postulate that of Vincent's numerous extant letters of this period only those referring to this important matter should have disappeared.

It is much more probable that, in his guarded way, Vincent reserved discussion of the topic for face-to-face meetings—even the reference just quoted needs authentic interpretation. No matter. The time had come and Louise was quietly, deeply happy.

VIII

The Great Achievement

The year 1633 was to be one of achievement for Vincent de Paul, too. On June 11 he wrote a simple note to Michel Alix, Curé de Saint-Ouen l'Aumône, which in effect established the famous Tuesday Conferences. "At last the little assembly of your other Messieurs les curés can be held here on Monday after dinner at two o'clock," he informed the priest, who had, perhaps, been waiting for this good news almost as anxiously as Louise had been waiting for hers. "I have very great hopes of this company," he added with a directness that made his words prophetic.

The Tuesday Conferences were weekly gatherings of priests and prelates, renowned and obscure—sometimes as many as 250 at a time—who met to plumb the profundity of their calling under the guidance of St. Vincent. These Conferences contributed greatly to the religious reform of seventeenth-century France through the formation of piety in their members and later, through Vincent's influence in the Council of Conscience, by the able bishops chosen from among them.

The second meeting was held on July 9 to draw up modes of procedure and to elect officers. It was then that Tuesday was decided upon for the regular meeting day. Vincent wrote of it, with his customary grace and deprecation of his own part in the affair, to an unidentified priest—perhaps M. Alix himself, who perforce had been absent. "God be blessed, Monsieur, for all the graces and benedictions He pours out upon your mission!" he began. ". . . Oh! how well the thought you did me the honor to communicate to me these past days has been received by Messieurs the ecclesiastics . . . ! We brought them together fifteen days ago and they resolved upon what you proposed with a singleness of purpose that seemed wholly from God. I began my discourse with the words you spoke to me, without naming you, except when it was necessary to make you of their number and reserve your place among them. They are going to meet again today. O Monsieur, there is much to hope of this company! You are its promoter and dedicated to its success for the glory of God. Pray for it, please, Monsieur, and for me in particular."

Louise was given this good news casually in an intimate note written from the Collège des Bons-Enfants the same morning. "I did not obey you in the matter of the little remedy last evening or [today], not indeed from want of respect for, or compliance with, your charitable advice," Vincent wrote, "but because of a certain hindrance. I wish to assure myself that you will excuse me, and, as well, for not having the goodness to see you before returning to Saint-Lazare because of a meeting of priests we have there today. Be assured, Mademoiselle, that I intend to use your remedies, and that I will return here from Saint-Lazare afterwards when we shall better give you spiritual direction than I could now. Meanwhile, please be careful to look after that slight cold you have and do not do so much the next time."

Louise's own great affair was progressing, as is evidenced by Vincent's freer way of referring to it—almost as a foregone acceptance—in a letter of early September. "Marie has very earnestly, fondly and humbly replied to me that she is ready to do whatever you wish and in the way you wish," he told Louise in especially happy mood, "and she is troubled only lest she lack the judgment, strength and humility for the task, but [says] that you will tell her what she must do and she will follow out your instructions to the letter. Oh, what a good girl she seems to me! Indeed, Mademoiselle, I think Our Lord has given her to you Himself so that she may serve Him through you." He continued in apparent reference to a reassuring illumination God had given Louise: "What shall I say about the remainder of your letter, except that I praise God for having consoled you on Saint-Lazare's Day at Bons-Enfants and that it seems to me that what He asks of you is to honor His holy Providence in your plan without hurrying or pressing forward. I will try to go to learn the thoughts God has given you about it. But as for Chartres, I cannot see my way to go, for we are tied down here with our more important business." This last was a reference to a long-standing devotion of Vincent and Louise to Notre-Dame-de-Chartres. It would certainly seem that they had planned a trip to her glorious cathedral to place the proposed foundation under her inspiration and protection.

Louise herself has written: "You have inspired us, O Lord, to choose your Blessed Mother as the only Mother of our little Company . . ." and goes on to state why: "Do you not know Your Eternal Father's design for this little Company? Do you not know that, in order for it to subsist, it has entire need of purity and charity? And from whom, after You, shall we learn these virtues if not from our Mother?" Turning to Mary, she made a fervent appeal: "Do not disdain us, O Mother of my God! We are your children by adoption . . ." and, confident that Mary would do nothing of the sort, she continued: "I am not wrong, holy Virgin, in thinking that you will agree to be our only Mother. We can pretend to the status of being your daughters because you are the Mother of Jesus who is our Brother and because we have vowed ourselves to be like Him."

The correspondence of the two saints is filled during these days with passing references to the foundation and its members. Thus, while on retreat at the end of the summer, Vincent wrote in alarm over Louise's health, scolding her for exposing herself too much to the heat: "I beg you, Mademoiselle, in Our Lord's name, do everything you can to take care of yourself, no longer as an individual, but [as] one in whom many have a stake . . . I think your good angel has already taken care of the matter you wrote about. For the last four or five days he has been in touch with mine concerning the *Charité* of your girls; for he has truly reminded me often to think about it, and I have given serious consideration to this good work; we will speak about it, with God's help, on Friday or Saturday if you do not inform me otherwise."

Some weeks later, advising her that it would be useless to go to Villeneuve because of the harvest and suggesting that she go to Vincennes instead, he broke off to exclaim: "But, then, these good women would be held back [from accomplishing their purpose of a common life] once more. I think it would be good for you to delay a little while longer . . . In the meantime, kindly send for [the girls] to come here for twelve or fifteen days, during which time you can instruct them through the schoolmaster. At the same time it will be good for them to learn that they must cultivate the spirit of indifference. Indeed, they must study to acquire solid virtue before they can do their work!"

There seems little doubt, at this writing, that "all things were prepared" for the great event which took place, simply and quietly, on November 29, 1633.

Looking at it from hindsight, the establishment of the Daughters of Charity was an evitable consequence of the establishment of the Parisian Confraternities of Charity. The city confraternities raised problems their country sisters never had. The country members were strong village women used to doing their own work. They had no need of servant-helpers to clean the rooms of their patients, to cook, to carry the heavy pans of meat and the pots of soup. Their sole need was for a schoolmistress, since their own education was negligible. It was different in Paris. There the members were wellborn ladies often of the highest rank. Their hearts were right, but their hands faltered. They knew little of the domestic arts; they had servants for such things. They soon grew tired of mounting to the third and fourth floors of rickety tenements, and had difficulty in coping with the squalor and disease they met there. Many of them were terrified of the rats and vermin and trembled at each new sickbed for fear of the plague. Even the stouter hearts among them were forced to give way before the protests of their husbands, understandably alarmed at the alien dangers their wives were exposed to daily. They began to take their servants along with them for the harder tasks and even to send them in their place. But this was no solution. The work was not of the servants' choice and they could not be expected, therefore, to put their hearts into it. There was very real danger of that true Christian love which was the soul of the work being lost.

It was at this point that the blessed Marguerite Naseau had come forward and offered herself with deep spiritual dedication. Others joined her; and it was in these strong-bodied country girls with hearts on fire with love for God and man that the solution was found—almost; for, as Gobillon puts it:

> It was soon recognized at Paris that these girls, despite their good will, could acquit themselves only imperfectly of their work; for, having no communion among themselves, nor any superior charged with their direction, they were neither trained for the service of the poor, nor sufficiently formed to exercises of piety; and besides, when it was necessary to change certain ones, or to offer them to new establishments, it was not easy to find those who were wholly amenable.
>
> To remedy these inconveniences, which could only increase as time went on, M. Vincent believed it necessary to unite these girls into a community under the direction of a superior . . . He could find no one more capable of this work than Mademoiselle Le Gras . . . He gave into her hands certain of these girls to lodge in her house and to live a common life. She resided then near Saint-Nicolas-du-Chardonnet, and she began this little Community in the year one thousand six hundred and thirty-three, the twenty-ninth of November, eve of Saint Andrew.

Louise describes this momentous beginning even more simply and intimately in speaking of it to her Daughters: "Was there ever anything more lowly in the eyes of the world than the beginning of your establishment? You can see in some of the conferences of our Most Honored Father that the beginning was the merest nothing. Some village girls had come to Paris, and were employed in carrying soup kettles and remedies; they were brought together in community and formed into the Company without changing anything of their way of life, neither in regard to their dress, or their simplicity, or their country roughness."

Gobillon must be revered as an early source, but the letters of Vincent and Louise are more primitive sources still; and on the strength of them it is entirely legitimate to question his crediting Vincent with the idea and the execution of the foundation.

Gobillon himself says, in treating of Louise's charity as a young married woman: "It was not enough for her personally to serve the suffering members of Jesus Christ, she wished that other noble-born ladies share this honor with her; and she persuaded them by her urgings and example. It was thus that she tried out a great work she would one day launch for the solace of the miserable in the institution of a Company of Daughters, of which she has disclosed in writing she had conceived some design from the time of her marriage."

The existence of this design, however vague, is proved from Louise's tentative approach to Vincent concerning the girls who "wished to give themselves" to her as early as 1626 and 1627—and Vincent's brusque dismissal of the question is significant. This design is the driving force of the *Rule of Life in the World* she made for her widowhood. It is implicit in the approval Vincent gave her wish to dedicate herself to the poor on July 30, 1628. But when the explicit question arises of organizing the country girls who came to serve the Parisian Charities, it is Louise who raises the question and Vincent who turns it aside: "I rejoice in the provisions made for these good girls, and I praise your desire to give them some organization, but do not give way to the thoughts you have. You belong to Our Lord and to His holy Mother; hold yourself committed to them and to the state in which they have placed you while waiting for them to indicate that they wish something else for you . . ." This juxtaposition of the two founders is even clearer in 1632, as Louise grew more insistent and Vincent more implacable: "I beseech you, once for all, not to think about it until Our Lord shows that it is His will," he writes bluntly, "and at present the sentiments which He inspires are quite to the contrary . . . You seek to become the servant of these poor girls, and God wishes you to be His servant and, perhaps, the servant of many more than you would be in that way . . ." There can be no question at this point of who saw more clearly the outcome. Even on the eve of the consummation, Vincent refers to it as "the affair you are busy with," and admits that "my heart is still not sufficiently cleared of a difficulty which prevents me from seeing whether it is the will of His divine Majesty."

Certainly Vincent had too much vision not to see that some sort of organization had to come about, and there can be no question that it was his supernatural prudence that made him delay until the will of God was clearly manifest; but there is ample evidence for crediting Louise with seeing the solution first and for pushing gently until it was adopted. In this sense, she is truly not just the first superior but the foundress of the Daughters of Charity.

To both Louise and Vincent the question was academic: God was the only founder of the Company. "Consider in its establishment the way God found to enable even the poorest women to exercise charity," Louise told her Daughters. "Who among you could have ever hoped to nourish the sick only, every day? Who could have dared continually to give them remedies and to dress their sores? Even more, who could have hoped to enter their houses freely to speak to them of their salvation, to make them see the evil state they were often in? As for me, I must admit to you that I could very well, with the grace of God, have desired it, but not hope for it; yet you see that this is what you do every day." And Vincent was even more explicit. "If Mademoiselle Le Gras or Father Portail [then director of the Company] or I have done anything, alas! it was only to put an obstacle in the way," he stated flatly in a conference of February 24, 1653. "God is the author of works of which the author cannot be found. I never even thought of it and consequently it is God Himself who has done it by Himself."

The first Confraternity of the Ladies of Charity established in Paris by God's inspiration was that of Saint-Sauveur. At that time a poor girl of Suresnes [Marguerite Naseau] had a devotion to instruct the poor. She had learned to read while tending her cows. She had procured an ABC, and when she saw anyone she asked them to point out the letters to her; then she spelled them out, little by little, and when people passed by she used to ask them to help her to put the words together; on their return, she used to ask whether that was what they told her to do. After she learned to read she went to live some five or six leagues from Paris. We went there to give a Mission. She came to confession to me and told me of her plan. When we set up the Charity here, she conceived so great an affection for it that she said to me: "I would like very much to serve the poor in that way."

About this time the Ladies of Charity of Saint-Sauveur, because they were women of rank, were looking for a girl who would carry soup to the sick. This poor girl, coming to see Mademoiselle Le Gras, was asked what she knew, where she had come from, whether she was willing to serve the poor. She gladly agreed to do so. She came then to Saint-Sauveur. She was taught how to administer medicines and render all necessary services and she succeeded right well. And that, Sisters, is how the Company began. No one ever thought of it. That is the way in which God's works begin; they are accomplished without anyone thinking of them. This poor girl had been guided in this way from her childhood. She was selected to establish a Confraternity of Charity in the parish of Saint-Nicolas-du-Chardonnet and, while there, slept with a girl who had the plague, which she caught. She was taken to the Hôpital Saint-Louis and died there. It was seen that this poor girl was so virtuous that others who presented themselves were accepted, and they did what she had done.

And that, my dear Sisters, is how God has brought about this work. Mademoiselle never thought of it, neither did I, nor Father Portail, nor this poor girl. Now it must be admitted—this is a rule laid down by St. Augustine—that when the author of a work cannot be discovered, then it is God Himself who accomplished it.

Allowance being made for the self-deprecation of the saints, and the consequent glossing over of facts which would challenge their humility, it is hard to quarrel with the providential logic of this simple recital. It was a recital Vincent made many times and in almost the same words to the Sisters; it runs through his conferences like a refrain.

The intentions of the founders in establishing the Company were characteristically clear-cut and spelled out over and over again on many occasions. "Although all Christians are obliged to serve God and do good to their neighbor," Louise reminded the Sisters, "they have employments of one kind or another which divert them; but as for you, God's goodness is so great that He has called you to a profession in which you have nothing else to do." And Vincent: "The spirit of the Company consists in giving itself to God to love Our Lord and serve Him corporally and spiritually in the person of the poor, in their own homes or elsewhere, to teach young girls and children and, in general, all those whom Divine Providence sends you."

While the founders in their humility considered the Company, in Louise's words, "the most worthless and contemptible in the Church to worldly eyes," they did not make the mistake of giving their humble Daughters an inferiority complex. Quite the contrary. Vincent assured them plainly: "I do not see any persons so well qualified to help the poor in every way as you." He rallied these first Sisters to the challenge of their vocation by instilling in them a holy pride in it: "To be true Daughters of Charity you must do what the Son of God did when He was on earth. And what did He chiefly do? After submitting His will, by obeying the Blessed Virgin and St. Joseph, He labored unceasingly for His neighbor, visiting and healing the sick and instructing the ignorant unto their salvation. You have the happiness to be the first who have been called to this holy work, you, poor village girls and daughters of working men. Since the time of the women who ministered to the Son of God and the Apostles, there has been no community established in God's Church with this end in view." How proud and startling a boast from the humblest of saints! It is hardly surprising that he added immediately as a natural consequence: "Humble yourselves thoroughly and resolve to render yourselves utterly perfect and holy, for you should not hope that those who will come after you, to follow your example, will be any better than yourselves, because, as a rule, like produces like. Do not, therefore, depreciate your state or life or rather do not dishonor it; do not, by your example, be the cause of imperfect girls being entrusted with such a noble duty."

On another occasion he warned them: "The more God asks of people, the greater the perfection they should have in order that they may carry out the orders of His divine Providence . . . You go, like the Apostles, from place to place, as Our Lord sends you, by the orders of your Superiors. You have undertaken to do what Our Lord did while He was on earth. Oh, Sisters, if you could only conceive what a degree of perfection your state demands!" And he proceeded to specify its demands unsparingly: "The Ursuline Nuns assist their neighbor by instructing and boarding their pupils, who, as a rule, are girls of some position; but you are bound to instruct the poor, whenever an opportunity of doing so arises, not only the poor children in your schools, but in general all poor persons whom you assist, and hence you should have the virtues of the Ladies of St. Ursula, since you do what they do. You should have the virtues of the nuns of the Hôtel-Dieu, those of the Carmelites, those of the Daughters of Holy Mary and, in general, all the virtues that are proper and necessary to all companies who profess to serve God, since He demands them all of you."

While they were to practice all the virtues of all religious, however, they were to resist to the death any thought or suggestion of being *de facto* religious in the canonical sense. ". . . If any mischief-maker or idolater were to appear among you and say: 'We ought to be religious; it would be much nicer,'" Vincent told them with his merciless gift for mimicry. "Oh! Sisters, the Company would be ready for Extreme Unction." And he continued earnestly: "Fear that, Sisters, and if you are still alive, prevent it; weep, groan, tell the Superior about it. For whoever says 'religious' says 'cloistered,' and Daughters of Charity should go everywhere."

Considering the uncompromising spirituality that both Vincent and Louise demanded of even the first Sisters, it is difficult to keep in mind that these Sisters were unlettered innocents from the country. They had need of every spiritual robustness, every prod to their sense of pride; for, especially in the beginning, they met with total unacceptance, indeed with hostility, from the Catholic populace and even from the poor they had come to serve.

"We scarcely dared to appear in the streets at the start," Louise recalled years later. And it was this very quality of being "Sisters" without a convent that caused all the trouble. They were a startling innovation in the Church. Vincent was quite right in asserting that when one said "nun" or "religious" in the seventeenth century, the Church and all its members immediately said "cloistered." This was why he established his Daughters not as a community of nuns but as a group of laywomen living a common life—in the beginning without vows of any kind and later and to the present day with private vows taken only for a year at a time. They must have mobility. They must be free to go to people without waiting behind convent walls for people to come to them. The Daughters of Charity were, in this sense, the first "nuns" in the modern world; for, nonreligious themselves, they breached the walls of cloister for others by conditioning the minds of people to welcome religious Sisters into the street and the marketplace; nonreligious themselves, they broke the path for the many teaching and nursing communities and congregations who go freely everywhere among men, bringing them God in word and deed.

Vincent described this new vocation in beautiful and memorable words. His magnificent (and, for future religious, prophetic) vision saw them as "having only for a convent the houses of the sick and that in which the superioress resides, for a cell a hired room, for a chapel their parish church, for a cloister the streets of the city, for enclosure obedience with an obligation to go nowhere but to the houses of the sick, or places that are necessary to serve them, for a grille the fear of God, for a veil holy modesty, making use of no other profession to assure their vocation than the continual confidence they have in Divine Providence and the offering they make to God of all that they are and of their service in the person of the poor . . ."

The citizens of Paris can be forgiven their lack of understanding toward these first Daughters of Charity: while they remained simple country girls assisting the ladies of the Confraternities in the role of servants, there was no problem; but once they presumed to come together to live a form of religious life, then they might be expected, as good religious, to stay at home! The populace did everything to enforce the tradition of centuries. They made fun, they shouted insults, they threw stones. Even the poor and the sick joined in, with that truculence, perhaps, that seeks to cover up the embarrassment of being treated kindly.

The mother and father of this brave little band were quick to sympathize and to console. "You must be convinced, my Sisters," Louise warned them with compassion, "that you will not lack petty annoyances, caused in part by the tempter our common enemy, and in part by yourselves and by the world and by the fact of your entry into the Company. The devil will not fail to lay snares for you; and to make them more formidable, he will pretend to you the most dreadful difficulties in everything you do . . . A little patience, my Sisters; all these are only clouds which for a time prevent you from seeing *how sweet God is to those who wish to love and serve Him* . . . Look upon these difficulties as proofs that they come to you from the hand of God, so as to reaffirm your resolution and your zeal. Embrace the cross generously . . ." It was the only possible motivation. Mere human comfort would have been cold and useless.

Vincent, for his part, gave the Sisters the supreme solace of the example of Jesus Christ: "My dear Sisters, if the Son of God endured sufferings, who would wish to be exempt from them? When he used to visit the poor, He passed in front of taverns where the people laughed and jeered at Him and He was deeply distressed at hearing the filthy songs and the insolent language used in such places. Ah! my Daughters, don't be surprised then if similar remarks are addressed to you and if, when you go through the streets, and even into houses, you meet with impudent people who insult you, seeing that the Son of God was not spared the same sort of treatment." His practical nature could not be satisfied with even this sublime comparison, but must go on to specify how the Sisters should conduct themselves in like circumstances: "Now, when you are spoken to in an improper way and find it hard to endure it, do not reply, but raise your heart to God and ask Him for the grace to bear it for love of Him, and go before Our Lord in the Blessed Sacrament and tell Him of your troubles."

He saw these unprovoked insults as means of humility "afforded you . . . by the very persons you will seek to benefit. O Sisters, you may expect that, because that is what usually happens. And if it did not happen to you, you would not be fully imitating the Son of God."

It is symbolic of the self-effacement of this first heroic little band that we do not know their names. (Even the house where Louise gathered them around her is gone. It was on the rue de Versailles between the rue Saint-Victor and the rue Traversière; the topography of the quarter is completely altered, but the probable site is the present 21, rue Monge.) Their number was probably four, if tradition is to be believed. We do know what they were like, however, for they were country girls. Vincent has left us a vivid and beautiful picture of these ideal souls whom "Divine Goodness has been pleased to choose . . . principally and in the first place, to be members of [the] Company":

> The spirit of true village girls is extremely simple—no cunning, no double-meaning words; they are not self-willed, or obstinate because, in their simplicity, they believe quite naturally what they are told . . .
>
> Country girls are remarkable for their great humility; they do not boast of what they possess, do not speak of their parentage or think they are clever, and act quite frankly. Although some possess more than others, they are not conceited but live on equal terms with all the rest . . . [They] desire only what God has given them, are not ambitious for more grandeur or riches than they possess and are satisfied with their food and clothing. Still less do they dream of speaking beautifully; they speak humbly. If they are praised, they do not know what is meant, and so pay no attention to praises. They speak with simplicity and truth . . .
>
> Country girls . . . are very temperate in the matter of food. Most of

them are satisfied with a little bread and soup, although they are unceasingly engaged in hard work . . .

Country girls . . . are also most chaste; they never remain alone with
men, never look them straight in the face, or listen to their cajolery. They
do not even know what cajolery means. If anyone told a good village girl
that she was sweet and pretty, her modesty could not tolerate it, and she
would not even understand what was meant . . .

[They] are most modest in their deportment; they keep their eyes cast
down and are modest in their dress, which is rough and cheap . . .

Have you ever seen any people more full of confidence in God than
good country folk? They sow their seed and then wait till God blesses
them with the harvest; and if God permits a poor harvest, they do not
cease from having confidence that He will provide them with goods for
the whole year. Should losses arrive, their love of poverty, out of submission to God, makes them say: "God gave it, He has taken it away:
blessed be the name of God." And provided they have enough to live on
(and that never fails them), they do not worry about the future . . .

There is no greater obedience than that of true village girls. They come
home from their work to have a meager repast, tired out and fatigued,
wet through and dirty, and they are barely at home when, if the weather
is suitable for work or if their father and mother tell them to go back to it,
they do so at once, without pausing on account of their weariness or
mud stains and without thinking of how they are treated.

This remarkable encomium, which was at the same time cleverly and
simply didactic, was given in a conference of January 25, 1643—to village
girls who had come to serve God in the city. The saint ended his reminder of their wholesome origin: "Blessed be God! Blessed be God,
Sisters! Remember this: namely, if I have ever said anything true and
important to you, it is what you have just heard. You should strive to
preserve the spirit of good and true country girls." It was an echo of
Christ's injunction: "Unless you become as little children, you shall not
enter the kingdom of heaven." Vincent insisted upon this basic simplicity in all who were admitted to the Company. "If girls of noble families
present themselves, wishing to enter your Company," he instructed his
Daughters, "O Sisters, they should do so in order to live, in body and soul,
like those who really and truly possess the virtues of village girls, as our
great Ste Geneviève possessed them, who is now so honored for her simplicity, humility, sobriety, modesty and obedience, and all the other virtues which we have remarked in good village girls. Oh! blessed be God!

But what am I saying, my Daughters! Were not these virtues practiced by One greater still, by the Son of God when on earth, and also by His holy Mother, whose life you should honor particularly in all your actions?"

Hard upon the founding of the Daughters of Charity came the establishment of another Vincentian institution which still flourishes—the Association of the Ladies of Charity. Like the Company of the Daughters, the Association too grew out of the Parisian Confraternities, and came into being primarily through a woman, Madame la présidente Goussault (she of the naïve humility), who—much more than the spiritually docile Louise—brought pressure to bear on Vincent to establish it. Once again, it was a case of Vincent's being assured of the will of God by the inevitability of events, and then taking over to give the institution its unique character and organization.

Geneviève Fayet had married in 1613 Antoine Goussault, seigneur de-Souvigny, councillor of the King and President of the Chambre des Comptes de Paris, and bore him five children. Widowed in 1631, she consecrated herself wholeheartedly to works of charity, especially, as we have seen, to the Confraternities. Her many visits to the sick of the Hôtel-Dieu—which at that time straddled the Seine immediately in front of and to the right of Notre Dame in a huge complex of buildings—convinced her that a great spiritual and material apostolate was needed there. The hospital was under the authority of the Canons of Notre-Dame, who deputed one of their number, called the Maître, as administrator, and was staffed by the Sisters of St. Augustine.

The spiritual chaos which horrified Mme Goussault—while partly the fault of the Maître, Nicholas Lesecq, who was an unprincipled scoundrel, and of the Sisters, who were left pretty much to their own spiritual devices even within their community—was in great measure the result of sheer size, meager funds, and certain foolish rules. The hospital was always filled to its capacity of 1,200 patients—piled two, three, and as many as six, in a bed—and, during the frequent epidemics that swept the city, tried to cope with twice that number. Fifty to a hundred new patients were admitted daily. The money available could provide adequately for only about a quarter of the patients.

Spiritual havoc was wrought by the admission rule which insisted that a patient must go to confession before being admitted. A patient was then officially considered to be prepared for death, and further spiritual ministrations were almost completely neglected. The Company of the Blessed Sacrament, a pious, powerful (and controversial) association of clerics and laymen—Vincent himself was a member—had tried to do something about this horrible situation by hiring in 1632 a layman and a priest to go to the hospital once a week, the one to catechize, the other to hear confessions; but, as the Apostle Philip said of the barley loaves and fishes, what were these among so many?

Madame Goussault went to Vincent to ask him to intervene, but he refused respectfully, politely and firmly. He knew better than to involve himself in a work already entrusted to others. The good lady was too used to wielding power and influence to accept Vincent's refusal without appeal. She went to the Archbishop of Paris, Jean-François de Gondi, who had authority over the Chapter of Notre-Dame and—she hoped—over Vincent, too. She calculated rightly, for the Archbishop approved her project and commanded Vincent to direct it. He then plunged into the work energetically and joyfully, for to him the voice of the Archbishop was the voice of God.

He called a meeting of the ladies in the early months of 1634 at the house of Madame Goussault. Besides the hostess there were present: Mme de Villesabin, widow of the secretary of commands to Marie de Medici; Mme de Bailleul; Mme Dumecq; Mme Sainctot, widow of the treasurer of France; and Mme Pollalion. Vincent informed Louise, who was not present at this first meeting, of the proceedings: "The project was agreed upon, and they resolved to hold another [meeting] next Monday; in the meantime they will offer the affair to God and communicate for that purpose, and each one will broach the project to married and single women of their acquaintance. How would Mademoiselle Guérin seem to you? Madame de Beaufort will join." Then he got to the point: "They will need you and your girls." It was the first offer of a ministry to the new Company—not that they had need of work: they were already deeply involved with the Confraternities when they banded together; and Louise must have now wondered how she was going to meet this new request. "They think that they will need four of them," Vincent continued. Here is possible evidence that, in the short space of two or three months, the Sisters had welcomed new recruits, although Vincent makes it clear that it will be "necessary to find a means of securing some. Think about the sister of that good girl you have. Speak to Michelle about it. I don't know whether the widow from Clayes would like it or

whether she would be right for it. But what to do with her children
. . . ?" He concluded realistically: "You see your work cut out for you.
Build up your strength as much as you can."

A short time later he relieved the pressure on her, at least for a time, in
telling her, "I think they will not take your girls for the Hôtel-Dieu. They
think that some of those who applied from the city will work out, and I
think with reason." He had even better news of another kind when he
wrote at the beginning of March: "Yesterday three fine girls from Argenteuil came to offer themselves to the Charity, recommended by an
ecclesiastic of whom I have heard and who will come to see me tomorrow on this matter. I did not send them on to you because it was too late
when they arrived; but they will go to see you on Wednesday, so they
tell me." He then proceeded to rule upon with indulgence, considering
the final rule of later years, certain requests made by members of the
infant community and referred to him by Louise: "I see no great inconvenience in Jacqueline's going to her brother's wedding; Marguerite of
Saint-Paul can do the same, and should direct to you a good, big girl she
spoke of; and Mademoiselle de la Bistrade and Madame Forest should go
to you to ask for the recall of Nicole because of her great shortcomings
and because Marie, who does all the work, can do so no longer unless you
give them someone in place of Nicole. They will, then, present both
requests to you, and Mademoiselle de la Bistrade promises to pay you for
Nicole's keep. I told her I would write to you about it. Think about it,
Mademoiselle, and consider whether this poor girl, so weak and unsuited
to the Charity, could earn her living by sewing or in some other way
when she will be a little stronger; and"—his perennial fear could never
go unspoken—"do everything possible, in the name of God, to improve
your health. I was very relieved that you did not go out yesterday. The
day you do go out, take something before going." He knew that unless
he commanded her, she would fast for Communion, no matter her
weakness. "Our Lord is a continual Communion to those who are united
to His will and non-will."

We find in this letter the intimate family custom—which lasted the
lifetime of the founders—of calling the Sisters by their given names or, if
there were two with the same name, of specifying them by the places
they hailed from or were stationed at at the time. It was only when the
Company grew numerous that, perforce, the usual form of "Sister" and
the addition of the family name came into general use. The letter also
contains for the first time the phrase "good, big girl," a phrase Vincent

was to use constantly in recommending candidates for the Company: his satisfaction at the evident physical strength of these country girls who were destined for such exhausting work was undeniable.

Louise had a great personal happiness, the realization of her dream of a lifetime, on March 25, feast of the Annunciation. Vincent permitted her to make an irrevocable vow which renewed her former vow of widowhood and "from that happy day forward [writes Gobillon] she offered to the Lord each month one of her Communions, to thank Him for having deigned to call her to a state where every moment of her life was consecrated to His glory and love." The Company has perpetuated the memory of that day so important to its life and growth by appointing it as the day when Daughters of Charity around the world renew their annual vows.

Negotiations had begun with the officials of the Hôtel-Dieu concerning the proposed ministrations of the Ladies of Charity. Vincent was a past master at this sort of thing, and carried it off with every nuance of courtesy and delicacy for the feeling of others. There was no rushing in, no tramping on toes. "Everything comes to him who waits," he wrote Louise. "That is usually true, and even more in the things of God than in other matters. It is not expedient that I be the one to speak to Monsieur le Maître . . . If Madame la présidente Goussault finds it apropos, she can say a word to him . . ." He was anxious for another meeting with the Ladies before they began their work, "both to give them some advice about it and to instruct them in how to teach the sick to make their examen [examination of conscience] in order to determine their sins."

Poor Nicole continued to be a problem. "It is greatly to be feared that she will never change, because of her age," he told Louise ruefully. "On the other hand, I am afraid to vote in favor of sending her away yet. Try a little privation from Communion; perhaps that will do some good; if not, *in nomine Domini.*" "In the name of the Lord"—they were his accustomed words of resignation or dismissal, for good or ill. "After you have done everything you could, if she does not amend, you shall send her away." It would seem that Louise with her woman's instinctive appraisal of other women could see no other solution; but Vincent had a man's tender heart for woman's foibles. His feeling was vindicated for the time: shortly afterward he wrote to inform Louise that "Nicole is doing better. That being the case, I think you would do well to assign Jacqueline to the Hôtel-Dieu, or better Jeanne; and whichever stays behind can serve your Charity [Saint-Nicholas-du-Chardonnet] with the girl from Grigny."

It is evident from the reference to the Hôtel-Dieu that the ladies had changed their minds about not using the Daughters of Charity to assist them in making the rounds of the patients. Vincent further referred to this change in the same letter in telling Louise that "it seems good to Madame Goussault that some thought be given to your taking up residence near Notre-Dame; think about it . . ." The idea was not carried out at the time, although the ladies did rent a room near the hospital for storing their supplies and for preparing food.

Vincent wrote in haste because he was leaving "against my heart for Villers with M. Lumaque [father of Mlle Pollalion and good friend of Vincent's], because I have not had the consolation of seeing you, due to our ordinands, among whom is M. le commandeur de Sillery. I assure you that, if you knew my pain, you would have pity on me."

The ordination of the Commandeur de Sillery was an especially happy occasion for Vincent, who as his spiritual director had converted him from a life of worldly brilliance to a wholehearted seeking after sanctity, and had induced him to give his vast fortune to the poor. Noël Brulart de Sillery, Knight of Malta and Commandeur de Troyes, had served as first equerry to the Queen, then as her chevalier of honor, and ambassador extraordinary to Italy and Spain, and to Popes Gregory XV and Urban VIII at Rome. In 1632 he turned his back on his career, sold his magnificent *hôtel*, pensioned off his servants, and put on the clerical soutane, residing during his preparation for the priesthood in a modest little house near the First Monastery of the Visitation. His financial generosity benefited these Sisters as well as the Priests of the Mission, the Jesuits, the Monastery of Sainte-Madeleine, and Carmel. He offered his first Holy Mass on Tuesday, April 13, 1634.

The little Company of Daughters was growing with an extraordinary rapidity for such a humble beginning—requests like "Tell me . . . if it suits you to have them send two good big girls chosen by Mademoiselle Pollalion for the Charity and who seem extremely good to me" appear with increasing frequency in Vincent's letters—and with this growth came the inevitable personality and character problems of which Nicole had been only the first. Fortunately, Louise had at hand the best advice in the world. "I have seen this good girl Madeleine," Vincent informed Louise in the late spring. "I think you have some work to do with her, since her passions are quite strong. But what of that! when such people have the strength to conquer themselves, they become marvels afterward . . .

"As to this good girl from Argenteuil who is melancholy"—that was a different matter. "I think you have reason to make a difficulty about receiving her; for it is a strange spirit, the spirit of melancholy." Besides, he felt that she had enough girls to look after for some time, and would have her hands full teaching them "to read and ply the needle . . ."

Louise left in late spring or early summer to visit the confraternities in the diocese of Beauvais. The trip exhausted her and on her arrival there she took to her bed. Vincent, much disturbed, importuned God "to give you the strength to serve Him in the mission on which He sends you." By the same post he sent her the rules of the Confraternities of Saint-Nicolas and Saint-Sauveur for possible adaptation to the needs of Beauvais.

Louise ran into problems in renewing the confraternities and establishing a new one. No one was surprised. Vincent had stirred up a hornet's nest when he first introduced the confraternities to the city, and now he reminded Louise, almost with unholy glee: "I told you emphatically, Mademoiselle, that you would meet with great difficulties in the affairs of Beauvais." She had been equal to them, however, for which he congratulated her: "Blessed be God that you have set things on the right road so happily! When the Charity at Mâcon was founded, everyone made fun of me and pointed me out with scorn in the streets; and when the thing was done, everyone dissolved into tears of joy: and the aldermen of the town showed me so much honor on my departure that, to circumvent it, I was constrained to leave secretly . . . And this is one of the better-organized Charities." He approved all she had done, and had sent a letter to that effect to the Bishop, Augustin Potier.

A few days later he informed her of another project to be undertaken: "I feel obligated by the alms of Madame la garde des sceaux [Séguier] to do what we can to establish the Charity in Saint-Laurent; but I must wait until you are here to work it out." Saint-Laurent was the parish in which Saint-Lazare was located and, later, the permanent motherhouse of the Daughters of Charity. The Charity in Saint-Paul was giving cause for anxiety: Marguerite, the Sister on duty there, was finding "the burden of this parish insupportable because of its vastness and the number of sick and because the ladies [of the Confraternity] do not go [on their rounds]."

The increasing number of works and the difficulties they bred weighed heavily on Louise. She was tired to death. In one of his letters to Beauvais, Vincent had begged her "to conserve the little health you have. I fear very much lest this great fatigue crush you." He had reason to fear, as Louise herself acknowledged: "I regret having lost the time [of vacation] Your Charity wished to give me," she wrote from Beauvais. "I have great need of some days to think a little in order to renew myself. I think, Monsieur, when the time comes to tackle the establishment of the Charity at Saint-Laurent . . . it will be necessary for me to stay there some days; I could well use the time, if you are agreeable"—and she broke off with a great cry of anguish that showed how truly weary she was in body and soul—"but, for the love of God, Monsieur, ask His mercy to make known my needs to you, otherwise I shall believe that He wishes to abandon me entirely . . ."

Rest had to be put off for a while, however, as she still had to go to Bulles, Clermont, and Liancourt, where she was to meet fresh difficulty. Vincent continued to enjoin her about her health. "Do not deny yourself anything in the way of nourishment during your hard work," he warned her. "I am always of the opinion that you do not eat enough." But he did not spare her, for all that. The work must be done; and there is always a great implicit faith throughout the correspondence of these two great souls that, despite Louise's wretched health, God would preserve her to do it. The very letter in which she admitted her state of near-exhaustion was itself a long report of the state of things at Beauvais and what she had done to reform them; its writing required enormous concentration and added much to her burden of weariness.

The problem at Liancourt was Madame la duchesse de Liancourt herself, who was insisting, outside the custom in any other Confraternity, that there be a central house for the distribution of all aid and remedies. "The proposal to establish the Charity seems good to me," Vincent wrote Louise there, "but I greatly fear that the house will ruin everything. The sisters of the Charity will easily excuse themselves from going to seek out the sick in their homes and will content themselves with taking the usual things to the Hôtel-Dieu, and the nurses will discharge their duties in the same way; so that, all of them contributing to the debacle, it will come about all the sooner."

Jeanne de Schomberg, Duchesse de Liancourt, was a good and charitable woman sincerely devoted to the poor. She received her "*chère amie*" Louise many times at her beautiful *château*—the friendship had, sadly enough, to be abandoned some years later when the Liancourts, under the influence of Pascal, Arnauld and Le Maître de Sacy, became champions of Jansenism—but, like any great noblewoman of the time, she was used to having her wishes obeyed without question. Vincent, therefore, tread gingerly in instructing Louise in how to deal with the establishment of this confraternity, whose organization left him very uneasy, especially as the Duchesse now decided, in addition to her first maverick idea, to establish it in several places at once. "I am afraid for the house, if Madame places the girls there now," he confided. "She will see after a while whether it is expedient for her to transport the sick there." The words are respectful, but the note of warning is evident. "It is hardly the time for establishing the Charity in several places"—but he added with resignation: "If Madame does not content herself with Liancourt for the present, I think she should establish it in two or three villages close by only." He saw a subtle way out: "Monseigneur de Beauvais wishes us to consider seriously the union of the Charity with the [Confraternity of] the Rosary throughout the whole diocese. Then Madame could establish and unite the Rosary and the Charity as a substitute for what she has decided upon." He summoned Louise home both for her own good and because of his dissatisfaction with the Duchesse's plans: "When you have finished at Liancourt and, if there is need, at Gournay . . . a little rest will be in order; and, while you are resting, we can work on the rule for Beauvais. I think, too, that it will be best at present not to settle the rule for Liancourt definitively, because of this house and the girls; but give them the ordinary rule, unsigned; experience will perhaps show what should be added or taken out. Our Lord having given the law of grace to men without writing it out, let us do the same thing here for a while."

By July, as Vincent informed Father du Coudray in Rome on the twenty-fifth, the Ladies of Charity had increased their membership to "a hundred or a hundred and twenty women of high quality." The original six had quickly been joined by Mme la chancelière Séguier, Mme la présidente Fouquet, Mme de Traversay, and Louise herself. Then, over the next few months, ladies bearing the greatest names in the kingdom came forward. An authentic list of the earliest members compiled before the end of the century includes Mesdames les duchesses d'Aiguillon (Richelieu's niece), de Ventadour, de Sully, and du Lude; Mesdames les marquises du Ubigeau, de Pienne, and de Palaiseau; Mme la baronne de Renty; Mesdames les présidentes de Lamoignon (and her daughter), de Herse, Nicolay, Amelot (and her daughter), Tubeuf, and de Maupeou;

Mme la chancelière Le Tellier; Mesdames de Miramion, Jolly, and Chevalier; and Mlle Viole. Led by the Queen, Anne of Austria, the Princesses of the Blood lent their names, their hands and their fortunes to the work: the beautiful Charlotte de Montmorency, Princesse de Condé, whom the gay Henri IV had tried to steal from her husband and who had fled with Condé into exile and later shared his prison; Louise de Bourbon, Duchesse de Longueville; and Marie d'Orléans, Duchesse de Nemours; as well as Louise de Gonzague, future Queen of Poland.

These great ladies, Vincent told du Coudray, "going four by four, visit eight or nine hundred poor every day, ministering to them with jellies, consommés, bouillons, preserves, and all kinds of sweets beyond the ordinary food the house furnishes them, in order to dispose these poor people to make a general confession of their past life and to see to it that those who die leave this world in a good state and those who recover make the resolution never more to offend God." The work had the undeniable blessing of God, he went on, and now, as a tangible pledge of God's approval, Mlle Aubry de Vitry requested that Father du Coudray obtain "for the women who make up the body of the Association and for those who support it with their alms . . . the indulgences that His Holiness has given to the Reverend Jesuit Fathers and the Fathers of the Oratory." This request, which Vincent made also for his own priests at the same time, showed how seriously he considered the Association of the Ladies of Charity to be a quasi-religious society. As a matter of fact, several of the first members founded religious societies of their own: Mme Pollalion, the Daughters of Providence; Mme de Villeneuve, the Daughters of the Cross; Mme Miramion, the Daughters of the Holy Infancy; and, of course, Louise, the Daughters of Charity.

The Association had no written constitution until near the end of Vincent's life, but there were written instructions from the beginning which made the visitation of the sick a religious ritual of ministry.

The Ladies were "to conduct themselves with great humility, meekness, and affability toward the poor sick, speaking to them in a familiar and cordial manner in order to gain them the more easily for God." They should "dress as simply as possible on the days on which they went to the Hôtel-Dieu, in order to appear poor with the poor, or at least far removed from vanity and luxury of dress, in order not to cause pain to these poor sick, who, seeing the excess and superfluities of the rich, ordinarily grieve the more on that account that they have for themselves not even the things that are necessary for them." Vincent always had an exquisite sensibility for the feelings of the poor.

As they entered the hospital, they were "to invoke . . . the assistance of Our Lord, who is the true Father of the Poor, through the intercession of the Blessed Virgin and of St. Louis, the founder [of the Hôtel-Dieu]."

Vincent very delicately avoided the possibility of the sick being wrongly instructed by ladies who thought they knew but did not, or of the sick being preached at or argued with, by preparing a little "catechism of the sick" which the ladies were to read to the patients. The following extract reveals how sensitively he precluded accusations, threats, in short anything that would offend, by the simple device of using the first person. "Is it long, my dear sister, since you went to confession? Do you think you would like to make a general confession, if you were told how it should be done?" the visitor would read out from the book. "I have been told myself that it was important for my salvation to make a good one before I die, both to repair the faults of my usual confessions, which I may have made badly, or to conceive a greater sorrow for my sins, by thinking on the more grievous ones I have committed in all my past life, and the great mercy with which God has borne with me, for He did not condemn me or send me to the fire of hell when I had deserved it, but waited for me to be penitent so that He might forgive me my sins and, in the end, grant me Paradise if I were converted to Him with all my heart, as I now really wish to be, with the help of His grace. Now you have the same reasons as I for making such a general confession and for giving yourself to God to live well for the future. And if you wish to know what you should do in order to recall your sins to mind, and then to make a good confession of them, I myself was taught to examine myself in the way I am now about to tell you."

At the end of the day the ladies were to go to the chapel before leaving the hospital, to adore there the Blessed Sacrament and to thank God for making use of them for His salvific purpose, and to pray that the sick instructed would make good confessions.

Although the Association of the Ladies of Charity needed no more than these practical guidelines in the beginning, the Company of the Daughters of Charity as a permanent institution within the religious structure of the Church had to have a book of at least basic rules. Besides, what was expected of these simple, unlettered girls had to be spelled out and drilled into them by dint of careful and patient explanation. That Louise worked out these first basic rules herself is evident from a note of Vincent's that he had received "your memorandum concerning the rule for your daughters, the which I have not yet had the leisure to read; I will do so as soon as possible." He went on to comfort her in her discouragement over the fact that all her daughters were not taking hold of their new way of life with the fervor she wished—proof of how necessary rules were. "As to what you tell me about them [the Sisters], I do not doubt that they are such as you describe; but you must hope that they will improve and that prayer will bring them to see their faults and encourage them to correct them. It will be good for you to tell them in what solid virtue consists, notably the interior and exterior mortifications of our judgment, our will, our memories, of sight, hearing, speech and the other senses . . ."

On July 31, 1634, in the last of a series of three conferences, Vincent explained the rules to eleven Sisters who had gathered around Louise at her home for the purpose—probably the entire community, since no Sister was stationed outside Paris as yet, and all would surely have been assembled for so important an occasion. He knelt to recite with them the *Veni Sancte Spiritus*, then began:

> My dear daughters, I said to you the other day, when I was speaking to you, that you have now been living together for some time with one object in view and that, nevertheless, you have not had so far any regulations for your mode of life . . .
>
> Providence has brought the twelve of you together here with the intention, as it would seem, that you should honor His human life on earth. Oh! what a favor to be a member of a community, for each member shares in the good that is done by all . . . It is for persons who have the same spirit and in this same spirit help one another to love God that His Son prayed, in the last prayer He uttered before His Passion when He said: "Father, keep them in Thy name whom Thou hast given me; that they may be one as We also are one." And so let us see, my dear daughters, how you should spend the twenty-four hours that go to make up the day, as the days make up the months and the months the years that will bring you to eternity.
>
> You should, as far as you can, observe the prescribed times, for it will be a great consolation to you, on rising, to think: "All my other Sisters, wherever they may be, are now rising for the service of God."
>
> You shall rise then at five o'clock, whenever your work with the Confraternity of Charity has permitted of your going to bed at ten, for you

must take care of yourselves so as to serve the poor and render your bodies what is justly their due. [Louise and Vincent were Christian lawmakers who knew that "the sabbath was made for man, not man for the sabbath."]

Your first thought should be of God: thank Him for having preserved you during the night; consider briefly whether you have offended Him; thank Him, or beg forgiveness; offer Him all your thoughts, the movement of your heart, your words and actions; resolve never to do anything to offend Him; and all that you will do during the day will derive its strength from this first offering made to God; for observe, my daughters, if you omit to offer everything to God, you will lose the reward of your actions . . .

The first thing you should do when you have risen and put on some clothes is to kneel down and adore God . . .

After you have dressed and made your bed, you will set about praying [he spoke of mental prayer or meditation]. O my daughters, this is the center of devotion, and you should eagerly desire to acquire thoroughly the habit of prayer. No, don't be afraid that poor village girls, ignorant as you think you are, should not aspire to this holy exercise. God is so good and has already been so good to you to call you to practice charity; why then should you think that He will deny you the grace you need to pray well? Don't let such an idea enter into your mind . . .

Go to Holy Mass every day, but do so with great devotion; conduct yourselves in church with great modesty and be an example of virtue to all who may see you . . . What do you think you should do during Mass? It is not only the priest who offers up the holy sacrifice but also those who are present, and I feel quite sure that when you have been well instructed, you will have great devotion to the Mass, for it is the center of devotion.

These words reveal with gentle pathos what primal clay Vincent and Louise had to work with to mold a great community. Their confidence was not misplaced. The Mass remains to the Daughter of Charity the center of her life, and she will go to any length to assist at as many Masses as she can. Even the Mass, however, was not to be preferred to the poor:

My daughters, remember that when you leave prayer and Holy Mass to serve the poor, you are losing nothing, because serving the poor is going to God and you should see God in them. [At another time he expressed it: "You leave God for God."] So then be very careful in attending to all their needs and be particularly watchful in respect to the assistance you may be able to render them for their salvation, so that they may not die without the Sacraments. You are not to attend to their bodies solely; you are also to help them to save their souls. Above all, urge them to make general confessions, bear patiently with their little fits of bad temper, encourage them to suffer patiently for the love of God; do not get angry with them and never speak to them harshly. They have enough to do to put up with their illnesses. Reflect that you are their visible angel guardian, their father and mother, and do not oppose them except in such things as are bad for them, for, in that case, it would be cruelty to yield to their importunities. Weep with them; God has made you their consolers . . .

The exercise of your vocation consists in the frequent remembrance of the presence of God and, to render this easy, make use of the reminder given by the clock when it strikes, and then make an act of adoration . . .

You shall make an examination of conscience before dinner for the space of one or two Misereres on the resolutions you took at prayer. Let these resolutions be, as far as possible, on the practice of some special virtue . . .

You should make good use of whatever free time you have after attending the sick; never be idle; study how to read, not for your own particular advantage, but so as to be ready to be sent to places where you can teach. How do you know what Divine Providence wishes to make of you? Always strive to be prepared to go wherever holy obedience may send you.

You shall keep silence from after the evening examination of conscience until after prayer the next day . . .

Go to bed modestly and sleep with a good thought in your mind. This will be a useful means of remembering God when you waken and, in the morning, your mind will be better prepared for prayer.

You shall go to Communion on Sundays and feast days and some other festivals, but always with your confessor's permission.

As obedience renders all our works perfect, there shall always be one among you who will hold the office of superior . . . Don't you think that's necessary? May God be pleased with your submission to her, in honour of His Son's submission to St. Joseph and the Blessed Virgin . . . By practicing obedience, you will learn holy humility, and by commanding out of obedience you will instruct others usefully . . . I should like to tell you, in order to stir you up to the practice of holy obedience, that when God placed me in the home of Madame the General's wife, I resolved to obey her as I would the Blessed Virgin, and God knows all the good it did me!

Honor the Ladies of Charity and always treat them with great respect; also, honor the sick and look on them as your masters."

Then, simply, and as a natural consequence of what he had been saying to these innocent girls about obedience, he began to appoint the first superiors of the little community. It would be a new experience for inexperienced people and the appointments were made, therefore, for a month only. "So now, Sister Marie [Joly], of Saint-Sauveur, you shall be the superior of your Sister [the troublesome Nicole] for the whole month, and Sister Michelle the superior of Sister Barbe [Angiboust], at Saint-Nicolas; Marguerite, of her sisters at Saint-Paul and you, Sister [Jeanne] at Saint-Benoît, your angel guardian shall be your guide. Mademoiselle La Gras will be superior at the Hôtel-Dieu." Finally, he enunciated the new principle of a motherhouse or central house for the whole Company, a principle unknown until then, since nuns lived out their lives within the walls of a particular convent: "Be very friendly with one another, and let those who belong to other parishes come here from time to time to be assisted in the observance of your rule."

After fervent exhortation to follow faithfully this simple rule of life given them by Louise, their mother, Vincent closed his conference by reminding them of the greatness of their vocation: "Well now, my daughters, consider what mercy God has granted you by choosing you to be the first members of this foundation. When Solomon determined to build God's temple, he used precious stones as a foundation to show the excellence of the work he had determined on. May God's goodness grant you the grace that you who are the foundation of this little Company may be eminent in virtue . . ."

Louise has subscribed in her own hand at the bottom of the conference notes that "all the Sisters then declared that they desired to follow the advice that had been given them and to practice the mode of life prescribed."

This solemn moment in the life of the infant community was concluded with a prayer offered by Vincent: "May the goodness of God be pleased so to imprint on your hearts and mine what I a wretched sinner have just said to you on His behalf, that you may be enabled to remember it well so as to practice it, and that you may be true Daughters of Charity. In the name of the Father and of the Son and of the Holy Ghost. Amen."

IX

"Mademoiselle's Girls"

The foundation was made and protected by the provisional rule; now began the endless process of growth and development. The twenty-six years left to Louise would be spent in fostering both by tireless attention to the daily tasks of spiritual direction and administration. Less and less time would she be able to give to tending the sick with her hands. It was her personal sacrifice for the advance of the kingdom.

From the beginning the Company was a close-knit little family, and even as its numbers grew, this intimate spirit was jealously preserved. It is interesting to note in this regard that one of the sufferings which binds a family closest, death, was visited on it in its very first days.

"So it has happened; here is the first victim God wished to take from among your Daughters of Charity," Vincent wrote tenderly to the bereaved Mother. "May He be blessed for it forever! I hope, Mademoiselle, that she is very happy, since she died in the exercise of a virtue which guaranteed her never being lost; she died in the exercise of divine love, for she died in the exercise of charity. I pray Our Lord that He will be the consolation of your house and of our most dear Sisters . . ."

His next words are a pathetic revelation of the poverty of the stricken little household: "It seems to me too inconvenient to defer the burial until tomorrow, considering that you have no extra room in which to put the [corpse], and it is to be feared that to provide one would cause too much inconvenience to our sick Sisters and yourself. You could ask [the curé de] Saint-Nicolas whether he could take care of things this evening . . ."

Louise's first thoughts had been of the dead girl's mother, who, poor as she was, had given her daughter to God. "I see no problem in giving the girl's clothes to her mother," Vincent assured her. "Nor does charity prevent you from providing for her, say twenty sols or a half écu a month." Sickness and death quickly became commonplace. This is not to be wondered at, since the Sisters' daily duties were arduous to the point of exhaustion, especially because hands were always wanting for the work and bodies were constantly exposed to disease of every kind.

Louise's heart was still sore from the loss of this first daughter when it had to bear an even greater grief—the death of her dear friend of many years, Mlle du Fay. A letter of Vincent's of this period gave Louise the dread news that "Mademoiselle du Fay is grievously ill." His terse comment speaks volumes for his compassion and understanding: "I do not ask you to offer her to Our Lord. I am quite certain that you will do so." It is not hard to imagine the depth of sorrow Louise was plunged into at the death of this principal sharer of her early years of charity.

It was summer and Michel, who had given his mother some peace for a time, was growing fretful again. He was now twenty-one and his thoughts were swinging once more away from the clerical life. "I will speak to Monsieur your son," Vincent promised Louise. "He should not lay aside the soutane lightly. If he does, he will have reason to be sorry. Even so"—Louise's peace of mind was more important to Vincent— "God, who does all things for the best, will turn it to His glory. You must be resigned to His divine Will in regard to everything. He is more the child of God than yours. Whatever happens will be for the best. Be ready then for any eventuality, and do not give in to him easily. If he leaves off the soutane, they will make fun of him, even at the college; and if he went some place else, he would lose everything, or at least run a great risk of doing so."

Vincent's advice to the young man seems to have prevailed for the time; but, shortly afterward, his mother suffered a new embarrassment when he decided to approach some relatives and family friends with certain "requests"—probably in regard to setting him up in life. Vincent was inclined to let him do so: ". . . I see nothing wrong in his making these proposals to your closest friends and near relatives. I think, however, that, to honor the humility of Our Lord, they should be small [requests] and for the purpose of freeing him from a great deal of worry. When he shall be on the benches of theology, that will be something else again." Michel went ahead with his plan, and on September 29, 1635, Louise wrote with warm gratitude to M. Nicholas Dehorgny at the Collège des Bons-Enfants: "You are too indulgent with me; I thank you very humbly for the honor you do my son; he is on his way to accept the benefit you have procured for him. God will see to it that he profits from it and is mindful of all your kindnesses."

Word of the new community had spread and, despite the first adverse reaction, more and more applicants were knocking on the door of the little rented house in the Faubourg Saint-Victor. The decision to keep or to turn them away had to be made quickly, and often with little knowledge of their backgrounds, since it was impossible to board them indefinitely and unfair to leave them adrift in Paris. "What shall I say about Mademoiselle Laurent?" Vincent asked in a letter of late June or early July 1635. "She appears to have good will; but her age makes me fearful; nevertheless, if you judge it apropos to let her go to the Hôtel-Dieu . . . for two or three days . . . and then to one or the other of your houses . . . but let her well understand that it is only on a trial basis . . ." Concerning a girl who had left another community, he advised Louise "to keep her if you find her to have the right intention. This entering and leaving religion indicates a certain instability; that is why you must be careful. But if you have some place to put her to test her vocation for a while, talk about it, please, with Madame Goussault." Louise was pleased with the girl and sent her to Vincent for his approval. He agreed that she "seemed to have judgment enough and a right will. The only difficulty is that she has been in religion; but she tells me that, even while entering it under persuasion, she had her heart set on the Charity. For that reason I think there is no danger in trying her out." The "good widow who accompanied her" was a different matter: "She strikes me as rude, very moody, and coarse. I think you should send her away very graciously, telling her you must think about it for a long time." An Italian girl who had applied, he suggested, should be "sent to the mother of that good girl of Mademoiselle Pollalion's at Villers"— presumably to better her French.

The illiteracy of the girls was a real problem. "*Mon Dieu!* how much I wish your girls to apply themselves to learning to read and to understanding the Catechism you teach them! Poor Germaine [the former schoolmistress of Villepreux] was wrong not to stay with you. She would have been a big help to you in this." Another problem was the occasional show of vanity. "I think that the time has come indeed to speak to this girl at the Hôtel-Dieu about her style and prettiness. But how will you go about it? To force her to change her mode of dress seems neither feasible nor expedient. She should lose her affection for being well dressed and neglect herself a bit." But, after confessing his perplexity, Vincent airily left Louise to "take care of it!"

Scarcely more than a year after its foundation, the community had to begin looking for new quarters. Their first motherhouse had been rented originally for Louise's small personal needs; it had managed to serve so long as the headquarters for the Company only because the members were scattered around Paris at their assigned Charities. The first reference to the intended move was in a note Vincent dashed off—"Four or five lines and no more"—on Palm Sunday, March 16, 1636. "I intend every day to go to consult with you," he complained to Louise, "but business keeps preventing me. It is over your lodging. Talk about it with Madame la présidente Goussault." The heavy press of affairs and chronic illness—his *petite fièvrotte* was flaring up with galling frequency —continued to prevent Vincent from taking an active part in the househunting. A short time later he was asking Louise whether "you have settled upon a house, and where have you taken it? Perhaps you are thinking that I have some reason which regards you personally for expressing the opinion that you should not take up residence in this neighborhood [of Saint-Lazare]. Oh! it is not that, I assure you. Here is the picture: we are surrounded by people who watch everything and judge everything. They would see us go into your house only three times and would have reason to gossip and draw unwarranted conclusions." He broke off to ask her: "When will you be free to go to the country to visit some Charities?" Louise's new duties were added responsibilities; her supervision of the Charities must go on.

A few weeks later, two specific houses were under consideration. "The house Madame Goussault spoke of is not the one I meant," Vincent told her. "The first is the finer, at a price of forty or fifty thousand livres, and the second seven or eight. The first would be scandalous for poor girls and the second too far removed from the church . . ." "Have you any money?" he asked. "A matter has come up for which we need fifteen hundred livres. If you have, we will repay you soon; if you do not, please don't trouble yourself about it."

In April the house they would settle upon first came under consideration. Vincent seems to have been the one who found it. "If you can come here next Tuesday morning with your girls, we will go to La Chapelle," he suggested to Louise. "It is a village near here, on the way to Saint-Denis . . ." This expedition did not immediately materialize, but he kept after her: "I have written Madame la présidente Goussault that I think you should go soon to see the house at La Chapelle and to decide whether you want to rent it. [The trip] would be a diversion for you, as well, for she believes, as I do, that the country air is good for you."

The two women were happy with the house, and the country air may have weighed heavily in their decision to take it, for there had been a great deal of sickness in the little house on rue Versailles. "Madame Gossault tells me that she executed the deed for the house yesterday," Vincent wrote at the beginning of May. "We must get together to decide whom you will take with you." He added a postscript to the effect that "the disposal of your present house must be deferred. I will keep in mind what you said about subletting it by private contract."

When Louise and her Daughters moved that same month of May 1636 to La Chapelle, it was a quiet little country village to the north of Paris; it has long since been engulfed by the sprawling city. Gobillon cites two advantages of the move: "the one the opportunity it presented for seeing and consulting with M. Vincent de Paul, who was not too far away; the other the opportunity to bring up the infant community in the spirit of servants of the poor and of forming them to the humble, simple and laborious life of the country, upon which they modeled their food, their clothes, and their work."

Baunard contends that Louise went to La Chapelle reluctantly, that her heart was torn at leaving "Saint-Nicolas, her Confraternity, her works," and the proximity to the "quarter where her son pursued his studies . . ." He bases his contention on a slightly misquoted passage from her *Pensées*: "No more self-will, but You reign only in me, O Lord! . . . I beg it with all my heart, supplicating your goodness not to regard the contrary dispositions in me, desiring the force of Your love to force, by its sweet violence, the consent of whatever senses of mine may be opposed to it. To go then to the new house with the design of honoring Divine Providence which leads me there, and to put myself in the disposition of doing there what this same Providence permits to be done. By this change of dwelling to honor that of Jesus and the Blessed Virgin from Bethlehem to Egypt and thence to other places, not wishing any more than They to have special dwelling places on earth." As Coste rightly points out, "there is nothing to prove that [these lines] were written in 1636; they are just as applicable to a previous change of abode, and to one even prior to the establishment of the Company." Besides, there is an intensely personal note in this extract; Louise, in 1636, would never have been so selfish as to omit all consideration of her Daughters.

In these short weeks of settling upon the house at La Chapelle and moving there, Louise was preoccupied once more with the vagaries of her son. His dissatisfaction of the moment with the clerical state and his approaches to his relatives and his mother's friends had apparently turned his thoughts to the possibilities of a military career or a secretarial post like his father's with royalty or nobility. Vincent and Louise prevailed upon him to determine his future by means of a retreat. "Monsieur your son has begun very well," Vincent assured the worried mother. "M. de Sergis on his return from the country took him in hand and put him to making his retreat. He tells me that he has ruled out the sword; there remain the ecclesiastical state and the palace; he will weigh the two of them and try to come to a decision." The youth, naturally enough, may have wavered toward the second, drawn by the glamour of court life—or at least his mother seems to have jumped to that conclusion, for, at the end of Michel's retreat, Vincent was forced to reprimand her severely. "I have never seen such a woman for taking certain things so very criminally!" he began in evident exasperation. "M. your son, you say, is proof of the justice of God upon you. You are indeed very wrong to entertain such thoughts, let alone put them into words. I have besought you on other occasions not to speak that way again. In the name of God, Mademoiselle, correct yourself in this and know once for all that these bitter thoughts are of the evil one and that those of Our Lord are gentle and sweet; and remember that the faults of children are never imputed to the fathers, especially when they have instructed them and given them good example, as you have done, thank God, and that Our Lord permits in His admirable Providence that holy fathers and mothers be torn to pieces inwardly . . . By the grace of God, that has not happened to you. On the contrary, you have reason to praise God for what M. Holden has told you, for it is the truth. M. your son is going to see M. de Sergis today, to make his confession to him and to tell him positively that he has decided to serve God in the ecclesiastical state, and certain other things which have greatly consoled me." And having thus reduced her to an anguished remorse, he added with maddening, and perhaps wilful, casualness: "But I don't remember now what they are."

Certain that this strong rebuke would be received with equal strength, he turned calmly to matters of business and ended by calling down "the peace of Our Lord" on her. Louise was human enough to smart under the rebuke, however, for Vincent had to reassure her a few days later that "you can certainly write to me about your son."

Louise and the Sisters had no sooner moved to La Chapelle than Vincent sent her on the visitation of confraternities he had been eager for her to undertake in the diocese of Beauvais, "where you will be a great deal more useful . . . than I." He was in a grumbling mood because he had been forced into making a canonical visitation of the Ursuline houses there. "O Mademoiselle, how that annoys me and how such time seems lost to a man who should be always with the poor country people! But!"—he added ruefully—"it is eight months ago at least that M. de Beauvais pressed me to do it; and because I have been so remiss, he no longer stays here when passing through, as he has been accustomed to do, nor does Monsieur Messier [Archdeacon of Beauvais] write to me . . . but let that go, and let us say: *mon Dieu!* Mademoiselle, how anxious I have been over your not going to take the air for so long a time and your continual work at the Hôtel-Dieu! . . . Couldn't you quite well go in the meantime to Grigny for seven or eight days and let Marie [Joly] manage the girls? She is serious and exact enough for that. Do it, I pray you, in my absence. I will speak of it to Madame Goussault, who is coming to Pontoise, and can bring you along. Mademoiselle Pollalion can also look in on your girls from time to time. If that is that, it would be good for you to visit, with Madame la présidente, the Charity of Villeneuve-Saint-Georges . . ."

With this letter Vincent sent back "the rules for the girls. They are so good that I have no wish to change anything." Louise was revising the rules as they went along so that they would be eminently practical and current. "Read them to them right away then," he bade her, "unless you judge it necessary for me to be there; in which case I promise faithfully that it will be one of the first things I do on my return, please God. It will be proper for the girls of this parish [Saint-Laurent] to be there at the time, so that all will be uniform."

Vincent foresaw a difficulty in Louise's going to Beauvais because of an invitation she had received to visit the Duchesse de Liancourt: "I give you no advice about Madame de Liancourt, except that, if she wishes to fetch you for seven or eight days only, you can do as you wish, but, the great being uncertain of what they are going to do, if she has not been in touch with you, you should in the meantime seize the opportunity for Grigny."

The Duchesse apparently contacted Louise at the last minute, for she went to Gournay while Mme Goussault made the visitation to Grigny. On Trinity Sunday, May 18, at an emergency assembly of the members,

Louise made a complete overhaul of the Charity of Gournay. She received Madame de Gournay as a new member, and reestablished her *château* as the Charity's headquarters; she checked on the observance of the rule; she presided at the election of new officers; and she resolved certain difficulties over the choice of sick to be ministered to. She did not report to Vincent on the visitation at once because she knew he was out of Paris; and on his return he wrote by special courier on the twenty-seventh, to "learn your news." He admitted that "you have reason to complain that I have not replied to what you wrote me about on your departure for Gournay. But what can you expect? These are my ordinary failings. I hope Our Lord will give me the grace to amend, if you do me the charity to forgive me."

Louise's health had been poor when she left, and Vincent was anxious to know how she was faring: "Do you need a doctor? If so, let me know; I will send you one. You have one at Senlis, a very able man who has treated the King and goes often to Liancourt because of the confidence Monseigneur and Madame de Liancourt have in him and rightly so. Spare nothing to engage him and to have him examine you thoroughly. Perhaps you have not taken enough money with you; if that is the case I will send you some."

He then gave her the news. Her son had been at Saint-Lazare for some days, and was well. Her Daughters at the Hôtel-Dieu were doing fine, except for "Henriette [Gesseaume], who is very lackadaisical. Marie [Joly] says it is because of your absence." Marie was looking after the Sisters at Saint-Nicolas and Barbe Angiboust after the Sisters at Saint-Sulpice, according to Louise's instructions. Isabelle Martin was feeling better. "The only help she has is that maid of Mademoiselle Viole's that they sent to stay with her, the one who scandalizes them because of her behavior with the boys who come to see her . . . She has a fractious and dangerous spirit. I went to see her yesterday to tell her that she could not bring boys into the house, but she did not take it well, and told me that she wanted to run away. We should be at peace, having done everything we could in the case."

He saved for the last a memorable happening which he was to recount with pride to the Daughters of Charity many times in the years to come. How Louise's heart must have swelled as she read of it! "Yesterday, being pressed by Madame de Combalet [the Duchesse d'Aiguillon] to send her a Sister, and because it was for her"—the Duchesse did as much, and in some ways more, for the Priests of the Mission and the

Daughters of Charity than Mme de Gondi and Mme Goussault—"I spoke to Marie-Denyse, because she seemed to me to be suitable; but she gave me an answer worthy of a girl who has a vocation from God for the Charity, to the effect that she had left father and mother to give herself to the service of the poor for the love of God, and prayed me to excuse her from changing that design to go to serve this great lady. After that I spoke to Big Barbe [Angiboust] without telling her for whom it was or for what task, and sent her to wait for me at the aforesaid lady de Combalet's, where I told her this good lady would employ her both in her service and for the poor of the parish. She began to cry, and when she had finally agreed, I handed her over to a servant girl of the aforesaid lady's. I was greatly astonished when immediately afterward she came back to me at M. l'abbé de Loyac's where I was visiting, and told me that she was awed to see so splendid a court, that she would not know how to act there, begged me to take her away from it, that Our Lord had given her to the poor, begged me to send her back to them. What especially amazed the Abbé was to see such contempt for the glory of the world. He urged me to tell this good girl to go back to the lady's house, and that, if she did not find it to her liking, she could return in four or five days to Saint-Nicolas. What do you think of that, Mademoiselle?" he asked exultantly. "Aren't you delighted to see the strength of God's spirit in these two girls and their contempt for the world and its grandeurs? You could not believe the encouragement it has given me for the Charity, nor the desire I have for you to return soon and in good health to work for it in good earnest." He finished fervently, still in his exalted state: "If you have need of my services, I would leave everything for that . . ."

Upon her return to Paris, Louise received into the Company probably the first of the ladies of quality who came to join the poor girls from the country, Madame Elizabeth Turgis. Louise was happy with her postulant, and Vincent concurred: "Blessed be God for all you tell me about Madame Turgis. I will go to hear her confession Saturday, after dinner, God willing. Give her, please, for her meditations between now and then the birth and life of Our Lord; she could continue then with the passion and some of His appearances, and you must not forget to prescribe the holy beatitudes two or three times . . ." His further prescriptions for Madame Turgis's postulancy provides a glimpse of the trial period given the candidates in these early years: "It will be good that at first you ask her to agree to observe what the girls do, to imitate them—and you will treat her as one of them—and finally to make a novitiate of some months: (1) to honor the infancy of Our Lord; (2) to give good example to these girls to do well, and to those of position who will come afterwards . . ."

That August, Richelieu's campaign to break the stranglehold on France of the Spanish and Austrian Hapsburgs and their German allies came home to Paris and its suburbs in a frightening way. Enemy troops led by the Bavarian General Johann von Werth and the young Cardinal-Infant Ferdinand of Spain, brother to the French Queen Anne of Austria, suddenly crossed the northern border and overran Picardy, driving the French back toward Paris. On August 5, they swept into the town of Corbie and by the fourteenth had control of the fortress there which protected the capital on the Amiens road. The French rout was intensified by crowds of fleeing peasants burdened down with whatever poor possessions they could carry, and by monks and nuns forced in terror from their monasteries and convents—intermingled with the exhausted troops, and all seeking the dubious safety of the capital.

Paris was suddenly a bedlam of soldiers and refugees, and Vincent and his priests at Saint-Lazare found themselves, he told Louise, "surrounded by arms which they are issuing to the soldiers from here." He described this military "invasion" of the house for M. Portail, who was in Pebrac:

> Paris is preparing for a siege by the Spaniards, who have invaded Picardy and are laying it waste with a powerful army of which the vanguard is only ten or twelve leagues away, and [the inhabitants] of the open country are fleeing to Paris; and Paris is so terror-stricken that many are fleeing to other towns. The King is trying nonetheless to raise an army to oppose the invaders, his own being outside of or at the borders of the realm; and the place where the companies are being trained and armed is right here where the stable, the woodhouse, the halls and the cloister are full of weapons, and the courtyards with soldiers. This day of the Assumption is not exempt from the tumult and clamor. The drums begin to roll as early as seven o'clock in the morning, and in the past eight days they have mustered seventy-two companies here.

Yet all the life of the other world went along its placid way: "Our whole company has continued to make its retreat, with the exception of three or four, in order to leave to work in distant places, so that, if the siege comes, the majority will not run the risk of being cooped up." Vincent himself was deploying his troops as expertly as any general: "I am writing to M. l'abbé [Jean-Jacques Olier] to allow me to send him four or five priests of the company and ask his charity for them. I will send another group to Messeigneurs d'Arles and de Cahors, and I hope to have them leave at once, before things get worse."

His plans were in vain, because on August 30 the government commandeered his priests as chaplains. He wrote on September 1 to M. de Sergis, who was already in the field at Luzarches: "Monsieur le chancelier [Pierre Séguier] sent me word by express messenger the day before yesterday to dispatch today or tomorrow twenty missionaries to Senlis . . . I told him we could not furnish so large a number, but maybe twelve or fifteen, and that I would send someone to receive his orders and transmit them to the others; I intend to send M. du Coudray tomorrow morning."

Vincent changed his mind and went himself to Senlis, where he personally offered the services of his priests to the King and had one of them pass on the monarch's orders to the others. He was highly pleased with the way his sons did their duty. "To have brought, by your efforts alone, such good fortune to three hundred soldiers who have so devoutly communicated, soldiers who are going to their deaths! . . ." he exclaimed in praising one of them. "By last Tuesday, nine hundred confessions had already been made in all the other army missions, without counting yours or what has happened since." On September 20, he informed M. Portail that "up until now four thousand soldiers have made their duty in the tribunal of penance," and he hoped that the ministrations of the missionaries would help in moving God to grant "success to the King's armies."

Louise and her little household at La Chapelle were doing their part in the national emergency by giving asylum to young girl refugees in fear both of their lives and of their virtue. It was a brave thing to do, for the Sisters were as defenseless as the girls; indeed, the presence of so many girls in the house made the Sisters all the more vulnerable if the Spanish came. It was one thing to be in Paris surrounded by French troops; it was quite another to be alone outside the walls of the city. Vincent wanted the Sisters inside the city—he told Louise: "It is impossible to leave you abandoned amid these alarms. It would be better for you to withdraw . . ." But there is no evidence that they did so; indeed, there is the contrary evidence of the refugees sheltered at La Chapelle.

Louise was as resourceful as Vincent, and had a mission preached to her guests, to calm them and to give them spiritual strength. The Charity at Liancourt also sent girls of the village to take refuge with

Louise. Vincent saw "no reason why you can't take them in . . . Madame de Liancourt can find other places to lodge them afterward."

Paris, at length, was spared through the bravery and constancy both of the King—who rode out to lead his troops in person, and, if need be, die in defense of the city—and of Richelieu—who, assailed at first by the mob, won their admiration by his swift measures for their safety—and through a lack of support on the Hapsburg side for the invaders. Corbie was recaptured by the King on November 14, and on the twenty-first he reentered Paris in triumph amid the cheers and shouted benedictions of his people.

Even during the weeks of ominous threat to the capital, life there and at La Chapelle went on much as usual. The Sisters made their daily rounds of the poor, their work increased certainly by the influx of refugees. Some of the Sisters sickened and died, despite their youth, under the harsh burden of it. Each new death was a fresh wound to Louise's heart, and her grief was immemorial proof of how dearly she loved them. "Console yourself by bowing to the adorable good pleasure of God," Vincent advised her on one such occasion. "I know it is easy to say; Our Lord's tears over Lazarus demonstrate how difficult it is to do. If you weep, that is nothing; afterwards you will be strong." At times he was alarmed for fear that her grief, on top of her delicate health, would make her seriously ill. "I beg you to pardon me for not going to see you in your sorrow," he wrote again. "It is the good pleasure of God, who loves you so much. O God! what a motive is God's pleasure! And what a motive yet again to consider that this good girl enjoys at present the reward of glory! Take refuge in that thought, Mademoiselle, and do not let it go . . . You would greatly comfort me if you would agree to rest yourself in bed during these two days."

Michel's approach to his relatives for assistance had caused his mother some unpleasantness with the d'Attichy cousins. Vincent had heard about it, although Louise had decided not to bother him with it. "I am sorry that I did not inform you," she excused herself later, "about the behavior of Père d'Attichy on the visit he made to Madame la duchesse [d'Atri, his sister] concerning my son, and which he had in mind for a long time without my knowing anything about it. Well, having met him at the Carmelites, where Madame la comtesse de Maure [another sister] had me go on business for her, he reproached me, asking what property my son would have, seeing that I would do nothing for him." It was a gratuitous insult and offended Louise deeply. It hurt her the more when the Comtesse de Maure, who had real affection for her, joined her brother in saying that "I knew Monsieur de Noyers [secretary of state] well enough to have spoken to him already [in behalf of Michel]."

It would seem that the d'Attichy had complained about her to Vincent, for her next words are obviously a defense, albeit a proud one, lit by a rare flash of the Marillac fire: "All that I have done was to write Père d'Attichy two days afterward and inform him that the only failure in my duty as a good mother to my son I could find was not to let him [Michel] know that my late husband had spent everything, his time and his life, in looking after the affairs of his [d'Attichy's] house, neglecting entirely his own; and that, to repair this fault, which I requested of him since he had decided to do so without my knowledge, that he take the trouble to tell the aforementioned lady that Monsieur de Noyers knew me through having seen me often at the home of Monsieur le garde des sceaux de Marillac, and that I believed Your Charity would give a recommendation for my son, if they would speak up in his behalf."

Angry as she was at the d'Attichy, she was even more anxious that Vincent not think ill of her. "Before God," she swore to him, "that is all I have contributed to this affair. I beg you very humbly to believe it. I would not have done anything at all if I had not run into these people unexpectedly; and my son knew nothing about it. I ask our good God to make known His will in this matter, and to make plain to you that I would rather die than hide anything from you . . ."

Vincent's reply, written across the bottom of Louise's letter, gave her complete assurance of his understanding and trust: he wondered that she had thought an explanation necessary, "as if it were unreasonable for a mother to look out for the welfare of her son. Would to God that I could do it myself! His goodness knows what a heart I bear you."

Now that Michel was leaning once more, in however vacillating a way, toward the priesthood, thought had to be given to where he would continue his studies. In early September, Vincent talked over possible theological schools with him. "I discouraged [any thought] of foreign universities," he reported to Louise, "and he agreed very willingly, because I think it fitted in with his own feeling, or perhaps you had told him that his feelings should take yours into account." At the end of October she wrote to inform Vincent, who was at Fréneville, that Michel had now made a definite commitment to continue his studies for the priesthood, and Vincent hastened, in a reply written on All Souls' Day, November 2, to tell her how much the news had consoled him, "more than I can express . . . Blessed be God forever who has given you this consolation, and me also, who am apprehensive for him [Michel] in every way, under any condition. So, then, he will soon begin his studies in theology. I pray God to give him a part of the zeal for the salvation of souls He has given to his mother and the grace He has invested her with for that purpose, entirely poor and lowly as she is."

Some days later Michel was eligible to stand for his degree in philosophy and Vincent assured Louise that, "if it is not too troublesome for M. your son to sustain the theses of all philosophy, there is no danger in letting him do so; it will make him study harder and train him in disputation." And he offered him hospitality at Bons-Enfant, "failing any other place he might find more agreeable . . ."

Louise was anxious to be rid of her former house in the parish of Saint-Nicolas-du-Chardonnet, but Vincent bade her have patience and "to keep the rent paid up from the common fund, for you may have need of it for your girls." In the meantime, it made a convenient meeting place for both the Ladies and the Daughters of Charity.

She was so ill at the time (September 1636) that he would not hear of her making her retreat, but sought to make it up to her by allowing her to make "your jubilee [it was a Jubilee Year], but do not fast; you are sick. M. le curé will dispense you. You can make your confession, and if you wish it to cover the time since the last general one and that I be of service to you for that purpose, I will consider putting off a little trip of seven or eight days until next week." The time was long gone when his frequent absences—and hers—sent her into panic.

One of the Sisters was stricken with the plague and was carried to the Hôpital Saint-Louis, where Marguerite Naseau had died, but by the grace of God she was spared to the Company. Another left, without saying a word to anyone. Vincent's only comment was: "Blessed be God! Oh! what a great crown she has lost!" He suggested to Louise that she be replaced with "Sister Geneviève, of the Hôtel-Dieu, and that you put in her place Madame Pelletier or Madame Turgis. Someone of substance is needed there because of the meetings in regard to the infants"—these were foundlings who were taken to the Hôtel-Dieu before going to La Couche, the official infant home of the city—"and to receive the Ladies. The first, Madame Pelletier, seems better to me for the post, both because she is suitable for either contingency and because that is Madame Turgis's neighborhood, which could be a temptation for her."

Almost immediately another candidate came forward to replace the

Sister who had not persevered. "This good little Marie, of Péronne, says that she would rather belong to the Charity than put herself in service to this good lady . . ." he told Louise happily. "If she perseveres and, as you hope, does well, keep her, if you wish."

Nicole continued to persevere, and was as much under everyone's feet as ever. "I greatly wish, Mademoiselle, that you could persuade this poor Nicole to go to live at Saint-Benoît or some place else," Vincent wrote in quiet desperation. "If she consents, you will have to write to Mademoiselle Viole for her agreement . . . Oh! What a good job done that will be, if you can manage it! To use your authority, it seems to me, would not be the way; it would have poor results. How to speak to her, I don't know." And thus throwing up his hands, he left Nicole again to Louise.

After her change from the Hôtel-Dieu, Geneviève developed a fear of falling ill, to the point that she would not even mingle with the other Sisters. Vincent thought to send her to the country, out of the plague-ridden air of Paris. "She told me that a little wine sometimes would be good for them," he reported to Louise, but added a word of caution: "I don't think, however, it would be good for you to let her grow accustomed to it."

The rule for the Charity at Liancourt, which they had purposely left in abeyance, had been weighing on his conscience; now it was at last ready and he sent it on to M. de la Salle there.

The Confraternities continued to expand in Paris. Louise wrote in December: "Madame de Beaufort tells me that the time is ripe to establish the Charity of Saint-Etienne, and that Monsieur le curé wishes it very much; and that to that end she and another lady would take up a collection during these feasts [the Christmas season]; which they have done. I ask you very humbly, Monsieur, to take the trouble to inform me whether I should begin it."

She continued with an outline of how she would go about it, which is a model of organization: "I have thought to instruct her, if you find it good, that the ladies who most desire this holy work seek out Monsieur le curé to tell him that, in order to begin well and persevere, they need to organize a number of persons for this holy exercise, both of quality and of mediocre station, so that the ones contribute more in the way of money, and the others willingly give more of themselves to visit the poor sick every day; and so that no one will be overburdened, the parish should be divided into two parts. In order to set about things usefully, it

will be first necessary for the said Sieur [sic] le curé to take the trouble
of having a very complete list [of names] drawn up by some ecclesiastic
who knows his parishioners, and afterwards to have a sermon on the
project given in his church, for which they can assemble all the ladies
named, announcing at the Mass, also, that all of whatever station who
wish to belong should go to the Assembly [of ladies], at which Assembly
the rule observed in the other parishes will be proposed."

She urged him to let her begin without delay, "because these good
ladies have been working up their enthusiasm for a long time, and I
believe we should strike while the iron is hot."

She finished reflectively: "Now that the end of the year is near, I very
much desire, if God gives me the life to begin another, that it be of a
kind fit for His service. I ask Your Charity to speak some words to me
about that, the poor being content with little, the which I would the
much more appreciate since I have been given to God by you . . ."

That same month of December 1636, the Daughters assigned to the
Hôtel-Dieu moved into an apartment alongside the hospital rented for
them by the Ladies of Charity so that they would not have to travel so
far every day. Vincent congratulated Louise jovially on December 30:
"God will bless you, Mademoiselle, for putting your girls on watch at the
Hôtel-Dieu and for everything that will come of that! But, in the name of
God, take care of yourself. You see the need we have of your puniness
and how your work goes on without you. I thank Our Lord, moreover,
for making your girls so good and generous. It is possible that His goodness makes up for what you call your failures toward them."

It had been foolish to think that Michel would settle down quietly to
the study of theology any more than he had settled down to anything
else. Only the month previous he had agreed to pursue his studies in
Paris. Now his eyes were roving abroad. "You must not listen to any plan
of [his] leaving Paris," Vincent warned Louise from Fréneville; and he
drove his warning home in a way to strike terror to her heart: "It is not
to be imagined how the majority of those who do, contract vices irre-
mediably, except when relatives offer their services in a special instance, as
for example some Jesuit or doctor relative in the particular locality. You
must try very sweetly and patiently to make him spend his time and
energy in putting his shoulder to the wheel." He finished with elaborate
diffidence, knowing well the effect of his words: "Nevertheless, I submit
what I have said to your better judgment . . ."

His advice had its effect, because on February 27, 1637, he was apologizing for having forgotten a stove for Michel's lodging in the capital. However, he reassured the youth's mother, he had instructed "Monsieur Soufliers to give him a warm little room . . . where he would be comfortable."

In the same letter he pointed out the need for Sister Barbe to have help at Saint-Leu, "at least so long as there are so many sick in that parish. You must consider whom you can give her, and think again about the Incurables." This hospital, founded by Cardinal de La Rochefoucauld for those incurably ill, was interested in procuring the services of the Company, but nothing ever came of it.

At this period we find the first mention of a work which quickly became identified with both Vincent and Louise, that of spiritual retreats for zealous laymen and laywomen, usually of the upper classes: "I am very agreeable to the retreat which Madame de Liancourt wishes to make at your house," Vincent assured Louise. "Mademoiselle Lamy would like to make one also. I want you to talk it over with Madame la présidente Goussault."

Gobillon comments on this new undertaking:

> This Servant of God [Vincent], persuaded of the need for these retreats, and zealous for the conversion and salvation of souls, wished to attract to them men who lived immersed in the world's business. It was with this in mind that he opened his houses to receive them; that he offered them his own person and those of his children to serve them; and that he prescribed wise exercises for their direction. His zeal never faltered in this, no matter how expensive it became. He even increased the work constantly; and we have read in his Life that, between 1635 and 1660, he received into the house of Saint-Lazare alone nearly twenty thousand retreatants.
>
> What this holy priest could do only for men, Mademoiselle Le Gras, who was pleased to walk in his footsteps, undertook for those of her own sex. She received into her house of La Chapelle all who presented themselves, whether to recover grace with God or to fortify themselves in virtue . . . Many ladies, and even of the highest quality, drawn by the odor of her virtues, left Paris . . . to spend some days in a village in order to converse with God; they quitted the sweetnesses and delicacies of life in order to think upon their salvation in a place of mortification and penance: and without regard of rank and quality . . . they entered into a house of servants of the poor to submit with them to the discipline of a superior, in order to learn to despise riches and glory by force of her instruction and example.

This apostolate to the rich and comfortable, the nobility and the bourgeois, carried on concomitantly with the basic apostolate to the poor, is very important in understanding the vocation of Vincent and Louise, which was essentially, like Christ's, a vocation to men and their most urgent needs—a vocation which very much concerned the fathers of Vatican Council II. Their first call was to the poor because they were, at the moment, the neediest; but, while never abandoning this first call, they did not hesitate to respond to other needs as they appeared.

Vincent carefully instructed Louise in how she was to direct her retreatants, "by giving them the order of day . . . by assigning subjects for their prayer, by listening to the accounts they give you in the presence of one another of their good thoughts, and by having reading at table during their meals, after which they can recreate themselves in a cheerful and modest way. The conversation can turn on things that have happened during their retreat, or of what they have read in holy narratives. If the weather is fair, they can walk a little after dinner. Outside of these two times, they should observe silence. It will be useful to have them write out the chief sentiments they have had in prayer, and they should prepare themselves for a general confession . . . Spiritual reading can be taken from *The Imitation of Christ* by Thomas à Kempis, pausing a little to consider each passage, and also something from [Luis de] Granada bearing upon the subject of their meditation. They could also read several chapters of the Gospels. It would be good, on the day of their general confession, if you would read them the prayer from Granada's *Memorial*, which is meant to stir up contrition. As for the rest, watch that they do not drive themselves too eagerly in these exercises. I pray Our Lord to give you His spirit for that."

The retreats quickly became popular, and rooms were often at a premium. On one such occasion when Louise was upset because she had no room for Mme Goussault when that special lady wished to come, Vincent jokingly expressed his fear "that Madame la présidente Goussault would fare badly sleeping in the street."

There is a curiosity in the ending of this letter. Vincent had first written, "I am, in all the stretch of my affection . . ." but had erased the words and substituted, "I am, in the love of Our Lord . . ." Coste is of the opinion that he made the change because he found the first phrase "too tender." He may indeed have thought better of it, but he did not take the trouble to erase it so thoroughly that Louise could not read it—and in any case it shows the bent of his heart. That he was not overly sensitive in the matter is obvious from the many frank avowals of his holy affection, and in particular a letter written at the same period—Sunday, May 24, 1637—approving the establishment of a Charity at La Chapelle, which assured Louise that he was "at home and abroad, now and for eternity, in the love of Our Lord, Mademoiselle, your very humble servant."

One of the most engaging qualities in Vincent and Louise during these first years of the Company was their compassion for the weaknesses of nature in the Sisters. They were well aware that these first recruits were basically raw country girls who could not be treated like sophisticated religious. Thus, in the fall of 1637, Vincent asked Louise whether she could send "one of your girls from the Hôtel-Dieu to replace Henriette" for a time; "I think you would do her not a small charity; for I doubt whether, without actually being ill, she could suffer the mortification of [not taking] this journey . . . I would be greatly consoled if she could have this consolation." He kept his wonderful patience with the troublesome Nicole, who once again had to be moved from yet another Charity where she had not worked out: "*Mon Dieu*, what shall we say of this poor, lapsed girl? Nothing, except to adore the most amiable providence of God."

A few weeks later there was a more serious disappointment. "A young blind girl from Argenteuil who governs the Charity there came to see me, along with a cousin of Barbe de Saint-Leu, and pressured me to consent that she [Barbe] join the religious who established themselves there a little while back [a convent of Bernardines]," he told Louise, "but I held firm against it. She is nonetheless receptive, however. It was her trip for her brother's marriage that did the trick." There can be no doubt that this defection—and that of another Sister at the same time—irritated him greatly. "So Barbe wishes to enter religion," he wrote sarcastically to Louise a few days later. "Hand her her papers [of separation] very sweetly, please. She will soon tire of it, or religion of her. As for this other girl of the Hôtel-Dieu, it is better to rid yourself of her sooner than later; the longer you wait, the more noise her going will make. Be assured of the truth of the matter and let the others understand that she can no longer remain, since she has not hesitated to plan secretly for some time to enter religion." He added rather wistfully: "If Barbe should persevere, she can thank her cousin and tell her, as she told you, that she has given herself to God in the person of the poor."

She was set upon leaving, however, but was afraid to do so until the matter of her vows was settled to her satisfaction. Some of the Sisters were already being permitted to consecrate themselves to the work by vow. "What you say about little Barbe's vow seems pointless," Vincent advised Louise, "because she is entering religion to help the sick and, as they tell her, the poor, and consequently under the terms of her vow. But if she is scrupulous about it, the bishop can dispense." He continued to insist that "she will often regret it and will give trouble to these good religious because of it. And if she should return, I don't know whether it would be good to take her back."

Despite their compassion, the founders felt the failures and weaknesses of their daughters keenly, and mutually consoled each other. "If the sweetness of your spirit has need of a dash of vinegar," Vincent reminded Louise wryly on All Saints' Day, "borrow a little from the spirit of Our Lord. O Mademoiselle, how well He knew how to taste the bittersweet when He had to!"

With the onset of the sharper weather, the indefatigable Mme Goussault fell ill. Both Vincent and Louise were apprehensive of her condition from the first, and visited her as often as they could. Vincent was concerned, too, about the effect of her illness on Louise. "I am worried for fear you will collapse again, after coming back from Madame Goussault's, as you did after your first visit," he wrote. "Be strong; you will have to be, at least in public."

The good woman rallied, and Vincent quickly passed on the good news to her friend and co-worker: "The night before last, Madame Goussault passed a great crisis of sweating and is improved since, so they tell me." And, in his relief, he drew a playful lesson: "Revive yourself the more; and the two of you can behold each other stronger. I have kept her informed of your indisposition. Oh my God, Mademoiselle, how sweet and firm her assent to God's will has been throughout her illness! To know her in health was nothing in comparison to knowing her in sickness."

Louise needed these glad tidings, for Michel, with no thought for his mother's troubles, was still making a nuisance of himself. Perhaps because she was his mother, she did not, or could not, recognize that his abilities were limited, and tended to be impatient with him for not getting on. Vincent admonished her in the most diplomatic way possible not to expect too much. "You must bear patiently with M. your son's state of mind and wait upon Our Lord's good pleasure to lead him into a way of life in harmony with what he proposes for himself [the priest-

hood]. Who will bear with a child if his mother does not, and to whom
does it belong to set each man to a task if not to God? Since he is not
studying and is not putting his hand to anything, I don't see much objection to your looking to M. de Riez [her cousin, Louis-Denis d'Attichy,
Bishop of Riez]. It is not a means to advance him, but to keep him
occupied and curtail his idleness, so this mother of all vices will not ruin
him. What kind of occupation is contemplated? It is that that makes me
hesitate. We ought to think about it a bit and recommend it to God,
and then we will talk it over. I told Madame Moran [housekeeper at
Bons-Enfants] to give him the room off the entrance."

As the year drew to a close, two "firsts" appeared on the horizon: a
new work for the Company, and its first mission outside Paris. Vincent
alluded to the proposed mission in a letter written to Louise in December: "You will see from the enclosure, Mademoiselle, that M. le curé de
Rueil prefers the girl from Nanterre to Barbe [Angiboust]. I adore Providence in that. We must employ her [Barbe] less and more usefully. M.
Lambert, who is at Richelieu [where the Cardinal was establishing a
house of the Priests of the Mission], is advising Madame de Combalet
[Duchesse d'Aiuguillon] to establish the Charity there, since two poor
women died there without help this past week. How would it seem to
you, Mademoiselle, to send Barbe and another girl there? Oh! how much
good could be done in that country! If you are a brave woman, you can
go there in the spring, by coach to Orléans, and by water as far as
Saumur, which is eight leagues [from Richelieu]. Everything is for the
best. We shall speak about it." Although the first considered, Richelieu
was not to be the first mission of the Company outside the capital.

The reference to the new work came, with that casualness that belied
the greatness of each of the Company's undertakings, in the mere part of
a sentence. After praising God that Louise's health had improved and
urging her "to eat eggs" lest she suffer a relapse, Vincent got down to the
business at hand: "Regarding the poor girl from Madrid [in the Bois de
Boulogne], I have been thinking of talking this affair over thoroughly
with M. le procureur général [Mathieu Molé], as well as a means for
helping these poor creatures at the Enfants Trouvés [La Couche, the
foundling home on the rue Saint-Landry]. Perhaps Madame Goussault
can advise you as to how we can manage the opportunity for that."

The opportunity was quickly found, for on January 1, 1638, Vincent
informed Louise that she would be asked "to make an effort for the
foundlings, if the means can be found to nourish them with cow's milk

and if you can take two or three of them for this purpose. I am consoled that Providence is calling upon you for this."

He sent her a New Year's greeting that was especially appropriate in the circumstances: "I wish you a new heart and an eternally new love for Him who loves us constantly and tenderly as if He were just beginning to love us; for all the good things of God are ever new and full of variety, although He Himself never changes. I am, Mademoiselle, in His love, with a like affection which His goodness wishes and which I owe for love of Him, your very humble servant."

X

The Shame of Paris

The work of the foundlings was the first modern organized attempt in the field of child welfare. It was also to become one of the major works of the Daughters of Charity.

Foundlings were illegitimate babies abandoned by their wretched mothers in church porches or other public spots, usually under cover of night, either because they could not support them or because they had no inclination to. The poor little things, if they survived exposure to all kinds of air and weather, were taken first to the Hôtel-Dieu, presumably for some kind of first aid, and then to La Couche, the government infant home established by Parlement at the Porte Saint-Landry near the bishop's palace. Like the patients of the Hôtel-Dieu, they were the charges of the canons of Notre-Dame, and laws and provisions were made for their care and support by the Parlement and the lords high justices of the city—for example, some of the more appealing were exhibited at the doors of Notre-Dame each Sunday to elicit the alms of churchgoers—but no one seems to have bothered much about the laws or about the infants themselves.

In 1638 La Couche was a national horror. A widow, who was the matron, and two hired servant girls were all the "mother" these sick and starving babies—some hundreds of them a year—had. There were few wet nurses to feed them—one woman would attempt to nourish four or five—because there was no money to hire them.

Vincent himself has detailed the atrocities practiced on these helpless innocents. "They give them laudanum pills to make them sleep . . ." Because of the lack of funds, the matron "is forced to give them [the infants] to the first ones who come along, and these bring about their deaths either through starvation or through evil practices [they were actually used as victims in the rituals of black magic and devil worship] . . ." Poor demented women "who have no children of their husbands or of the worthless men who keep them [as mistresses] steal them and pretend that they are their own . . . The cruelty practiced by Herod on the Holy Innocents" was practiced on these babies; they were sold "for eight sols a piece to scoundrels who break their arms and legs to excite the world to pity and the bestowal of alms, then leave them to die of hunger . . ."

"It is Paris's shame," he cried out with the righteous wrath of Christ toward the money-changers, "a thing we blame in the Turks, to sell men like beasts, for they sell these infants to anyone who wants them . . ."

The result of all this maltreatment was, Vincent stated flatly, that "they all die . . . In the past fifty years not one is known to have survived." And, he continued, "what is the culmination of all these horrors —many die without baptism."

To Louise must go the everlasting credit for attacking this incredible evil. "She began as usual by apprising M. Vincent de Paul of it . . ." Gobillon says. Vincent acted promptly, not waiting with his usual prudence for Providence to force his hand, as it were. He approached M. le procureur général Molé through Mme Goussault, and the canons of Notre-Dame through M. Molé. The canons, glad of any help—it must have weighed on their consciences whenever they allowed themselves to think of it—made a formal request to the Ladies of Charity to sponsor the reform.

With the Ladies' acceptance, Louise set to work at once to compose some guidelines for the project. "I am sending your notes back to you with my own," Vincent wrote her in early January 1638, "and beg you to add to or change mine, and to take the trouble to copy it at your leisure and send the whole thing back to me . . ."

The work could not have been started at a worse time, for both Vincent and Louise were extremely busy, and she was ill again, besides. "I am worried about your night fever," he fretted, "and implore you to spare yourself as much as you can for Our Lord and His work. It seems to me, however, that you are less ill this winter than others, especially when you stay in town, and this gives me some comfort."

The stream of candidates for the Company continued without letup; and Vincent wrote of one of them that, "if she has a strong vocation, her village of Nogent will need her in time." He was to be disappointed and to exclaim in outrage, "O *mon Dieu!* how this poor creature has deceived me!" In the same letter, scarcely breaking the stride of business, he reprimanded Louise for what his keen eye had detected for wounded woman's feelings in something she had written him about the officers of one of the Charities and herself. "What reason have you for saying that you were not mentioned in the matter?" he demanded. "You must guard against the vice of singularity, because it has its roots in vanity, and that in pride, which is the vice of all vices."

He noted in a postscript that he was going "to hear the confession of Mademoiselle d'Atri." This lady, the daughter of Louise's cousin the Duchesse d'Atri, had recently given Parisian society an exotic and delicious morsel of gossip to chew on. Ardently religious to the point of fanaticism, she had not the firmness of will to carry out her good intentions. This sorry trait brought on such a violent attack of scruples and repugnance for the things of God that she was judged to be possessed by the devil, and one of the diocesan officials had commissioned Vincent to exorcise her. The exorcism was never performed because the black mood left her. A year or so later she built herself a little hermitage at Port-Royal—she was by now an enthusiastic Jansenist and supported the heresy with her great fortune—where she stayed until the community was dispersed in 1669. She died in retirement in 1676, the year M. Gobillon brought out his biography of her sainted cousin Louise.

The work of the foundlings got off to a slow start due to its novelty and to the revolutionary attempt—which did not succeed—to avoid the expense and inconvenience of securing wet nurses by feeding the babies cow's or goat's milk. M. Sebastien Hardy, sieur de la Tabaize, and his wife, a Lady of Charity, were fired with enthusiasm for the project and, as is frequent in such cases, proceeded to make nuisances of themselves. "They are pressuring me in an unbelievable way from M. Hardy's quarter," Vincent told Louise. "He blames me for all the delay . . . What problem would there be in your buying a goat and making a wider experiment?" Louise refused to be pushed. "Please do not get upset over the nourishment for the little babies, whom we do not have with us yet," she replied calmly on January 17, "for ours will suffice very well for the time you indicate and longer."

After a false start in December, the first mission of the Company outside Paris was about to be launched at the request of a source that could not be denied, the court itself. "They are asking us for a Sister of Charity for Saint-Germain-en-Laye, where a mission is in progress and where the Charity was established last Sunday," Vincent informed Louise. On the advice of Richelieu, the King had selected Nicolas Pavillon, future Bishop of Alet and a member of the Tuesday Conferences, to preach this mission to the court and himself attended several of the sermons. The permanent Charity, which was the normal outcome of such a mission according to the custom established by Vincent de Paul, was placed under the leadership of Madame de Chaumont, lady in waiting to the Queen. Although the ladies of the court eagerly joined in the project by doffing their finery for soberer garb and waiting in person on the poor and sick, their husbands—as had happened already in Paris— protested their participation, alleging that they might carry contagion to the royal family. This dire possibility upset the King, but the Queen scoffed at it and staunchly backed her ladies in their charitable ministry. The gentlemen tried a different tack, accusing Pavillon of comparing the King to the Beast of the Apocalypse, and stirring up the King's musketeers by sowing the rumor among them that the preacher did not want them to have any salary perquisites. The uproar was only settled after Pavillon defended himself in a lengthy document and, that failing, appealed his defamation, with the King's permission, to the Sorbonne, which gave him justice. Nothing was to defeat the work of the Charities.

"What do you think about sending Barbe [Angiboust] . . . to train these good women?" Vincent asked Louise. "They have a special reason for wanting her because of the soldiers the King wishes to be ministered to . . . Oh! how I wish you could go!" he exclaimed, "but, indeed, God draws more glory from you as you are! To get back to Barbe. Could you give her a companion, or would you rather send her alone? The former would be better . . ."

Louise concurred in sending Barbe and a companion. Barbe was with Louise at La Chapelle at the moment because she had been sick; but Louise hastened to assure Vincent that "both of us are much stronger. I think it would be very good for her to have the honor of seeing you before she leaves. Shouldn't some attention be given to the bits of furniture she will need?" Louise was filled with happiness over the "marvels" the procurator of the Charity of La Chapelle and the Sisters "are doing today . . . for the feast of the Holy Name of Jesus. They—themselves—" she emphasized proudly, "want me to ask you to arrange for a sermon for them at Vespers . . . They would like Monsieur de la Salle, but you mustn't think they wouldn't welcome another. I join my prayer to theirs so that they will be encouraged to persevere."

In early February Vincent announced that "Monsieur de la Salle has informed me of the arrival [at Saint-Germain-en-Laye] of your girls [Barbe and her companion] and that he will introduce them today to the sisters of the Charity. Madame Chaumont told him that she will give them an écu for food as a start. I told him that wasn't necessary, that there would be other provision for them. Give me a word of advice in this matter, please."

He then turned to the question of the foundlings. "Mademoiselle Hardy is constantly pushing me to assemble the Ladies, who have given her their word to contribute. If I don't do it, I will have much to regret; if I do, it will be against my judgment. I doubt if it would succeed the way things are; for she expects the Ladies to go to the foundling home [La Couche] and to work everything from there and according to the established order. My thought is that it would be better to put aside consideration of this home, as it must render so many accounts and has so many difficulties to overcome, and to make a new establishment, leaving that one as it is, for some time at least. What do you think? If I thought she would agree to the experiment you propose of a nurse and a goat at your place—enough!"

This was only one of his troubles, and he poured them all into Louise's sympathetic ear. He had not had the time to complete the establishment of the Charity at La Chapelle because of "the business of the Temple"—the foundation of a seminary in the Maison du Temple which M. le commandeur de Sillery was trying to effect much too fast for Vincent's sense of prudence. A similar precipitate activity had brought to grief a laudable foundation sponsored by the Company of the Blessed Sacrament, he told her, but cautioned her that "all this is confided to your heart alone, and no other." Jean Paradis, the Curé de La Chapelle, was ill and his recovery uncertain—"O mon Dieu, what that means to us! Madame Goussault had a fever the day before yesterday that they were afraid would continue. Take care of your health, I beg you." A postscript revealed how upset he was over de Sillery's seminary: "They are forcing me to hurry the Temple affair, and I dread its quick collapse. I say it over and over again, and nonetheless they brush it aside. Humility obliges me to defer and reason makes me fear. In nomine Domini!"

Mlle Hardy's plan for La Couche was overruled and a beginning was made by removing twelve babies from there to temporary quarters in the Faubourg Saint-Victor—Louise's own house, which Vincent had wisely insisted upon her retaining. Mme Pelletier was put in charge—an unfortunate choice because she made trouble from the start. She went to Vincent on a Tuesday in February "about her furniture. She wants it set up in a private little room. She would not hear of putting it elsewhere. I told her that we would speak about it, but that it was necessary to hold all things in common and to shun singularities. Such language, however, seems rather strange to her."

She had, indeed, a plan of her own, which was to rule the roost without interference despite the fact that the Ladies of the Hôtel-Dieu had decreed that "the house depend upon the superioress of the Daughters of Charity"—Louise. She began to intrigue against Louise and the ladies by insinuating herself into the confidence of highly placed ecclesiastical and civil officials and managed to convince them for a time that she was ill-treated. Louise, however, had "confidence that the good God would draw glory from this vexing situation." And she was right. Nothing or no one would stand in the way of His will.

Vincent assured Louise that "we have adopted your directive for the foundlings at two assemblies of the officers of the Charity of the Hôtel-Dieu, and next Sunday we will communicate the directive, which I have drawn up in the manner of a rule, to Madame Pelletier to see whether she will submit to it. This will be done at Madame Goussault's in the presence of the officers."

It was a pathetic commentary on the fate in store for the babies left behind at La Couche that the twelve removed to Louise's house were chosen by lot. Scarcely had they been taken in when fresh complications arose. "Sister Turgis [who had replaced La Pelletier] is very upset because the sergeant of M. de Castillon's company came to inform her that he is going to send as many as a corps of soldiers to billet in the foundlings' house," Louise informed Vincent. "They will make a terrible racket. If you find it proper for her to refuse to admit them, Your Charity might enlist the influence of Madame la duchesse d'Aiguillon or Madame la chancelière [Séguier] to obtain the help of the Queen . . ." Vincent sent back a reply by the messenger who had brought Louise's letter. He was sending the letter on to Mme Séguier and addressing a protest in the name of the Ladies of Charity to the chancelier himself. There was more danger than noise to be feared: ". . . the gendarmes could not live in your house . . . without danger to the purity of the girls or without scandal." Since Vincent knew there was little chance of immediate action, he advised Louise to "go to M. your curé and ask him to try to get the *habitants* to billet the gendarmes some place else."

Mme Séguier could do nothing to remove the soldiers and Vincent turned to the Duchesse, who as the Cardinal's niece was, after the

Queen, probably the most powerful woman in the kingdom. The problem was eventually solved by hastening the removal of the babies to a permanent home taken for the purpose on the rue de Boulangers. As in the case of La Chapelle, Mme Goussault joined Louise in the house-hunting. They found what they wanted quickly, spurred on by the nuisance of the soldiers; in a very few days Vincent was telling Louise that "you have your work cut out for you as regards the transferal of the foundlings and the regimen to be adopted in their new establishment. I pray you, Mademoiselle, to work on it tomorrow and to send back to me on Saturday what you have done. I informed Madame Pelletier that they wish her to be dependent on you for the conduct of the work. She replied that I must make clear in what she is dependent on the officers and in what on you. It seems to me that in purely temporal matters she should be answerable to the good woman; but in spiritual matters, such as the direction of the girls, the nurses, the little runaways who are increasing in number"—even at this early stage, apparently, all the foundlings were not nursing infants—"she should defer to you, and to this end advise you from time to time of what is going on, say each week or at least every fifteen days."

It is not surprising that in addition to the difficulty of securing nurses—they had gone outside Paris into the country in their search—the first problem to be dealt with was the death and burial of all too many of these frail little creatures. "Blessed be God for taking this little soul in a state which makes it possible to believe that it is very happy," Vincent wrote in the first weeks. And again: "I think it would be good to bury this little infant in the cemetery and to send to ask M. le curé to come to see you so that you can tell him how the matter stands while you wait to be advised as to procedure. What comes to my mind at present is to give something annually to M. le curé and to the gravedigger to bury all. For today, ask him to send M. his vicar to handle matters and to give orders to the gravedigger to dig the little grave . . ." It was necessary to decide on a standard procedure immediately because a short time later Vincent was expressing his "astonishment at the death of so many of these little creatures . . ." Louise had her own opinion of the cause—which, unfortunately, has not been recorded—and Vincent conceded that "there might be something in what you say . . . We must take counsel seriously and at once as to what is to be done." He instructed Madame Traversay "to fill the empty places with no more than seven little babies, some from the Hôtel-Dieu and some from La Couche, until you have another nurse, a goat and a cow."

Far more important than these temporal details, however, was the spiritual motivation that must inspire the Sisters in raising these abandoned children. "These little children belong to God in a very special manner," Vincent told them, "because they have been abandoned by their fathers and mothers . . . They belong to God alone, who takes the part of father and mother and provides for all their wants. Consider, my daughters, what God has done for them and for you. From all eternity, He singled out this century in which to inspire a number of ladies with the idea of assuming the care and control of these little ones whom He regards as His own, and from all eternity He has chosen you, my daughters, to serve them . . . God takes [great pleasure] in the services you render these little children, as He also does in their little prattlings, nay, even in their little cries and wailings. Each of these cries touches the heart of God with pity. And you, my dear Sisters, when they begin to cry and you soothe them . . . do you not give pleasure to God? Look upon yourselves as their mothers. What an honor to consider yourselves the mothers of children of whom God is the father! . . . You will, my daughters, by doing so, resemble in a way the Blessed Virgin, because you will be at one and the same time both mothers and virgins." The Daughters of Charity have ever taken him at his word, and so much maternal affection do they lavish on these little love-starved outcasts that their hearts are often cruelly wrenched at the separation when they must leave them to serve obedience elsewhere.

There is no question but that Vincent meant it to be this way. "Apart from the merit and recompense which God bestows on you for serving these little children, a sufficiently strong motive for tending them with care and diligence is that there is at times a certain pleasure in doing so," he suggested with his knowledge of the susceptibility of the human heart, and he added, no doubt with a smile: "And I am persuaded that you often feel fond of them. O my daughters, you cannot have enough affection for them. You may be quite certain that you will not offend God by loving them too much, because they are His children, and the reason why you devote yourselves to their service in His love. Accustom yourselves to look upon these little children in that light [of being their affectionate mothers] and it will help to lessen the trouble you have to take in dealing with them, for"—he assured these willing girls—"I know quite well that there is trouble." He described the trouble with great perception:

> Someone will say to me: "What! Am I to look after dirty, squalling brats, the children of wicked mothers who have brought them into the world while actually offending God, and then abandoned them?" O my daughters, you will have a great recompense . . . You will repair in a way the offense which those sinful mothers committed by thus abandoning their children . . . They are dirty, no doubt, and, moreover, the very thought of their mothers may inspire you with a slight feeling of loathing. It is quite true, my daughters, that the work is very troublesome, but where is there not trouble? When you were in the world, had you no troubles? If you were still there, would you not have some? Oh! there are trials and troubles in every walk of life. But in the case of those who serve little children . . . the pain is followed by such a great reward that the trouble involved should be deeply loved . . .
>
> Suffer courageously then, my dear Sisters, the little pains to be met with in this employment, for I know there are pains, but, above all, take care that from the moment they begin to stammer, they pronounce the name of God . . . Get them to talk frequently of our good God among themselves; tell them about Him yourselves, in little words adapted to their capacity; whenever you bring them anything which they look on as good or beautiful, tell them, and get them to say, that it is our good God who has given it to them . . .
>
> Endeavor to imprint strongly on their minds a knowledge of their obligations toward God and a great desire to be saved. The good you do will not end with their time here, because, if they live, they will have work to do in the world; if they marry, they will give good example to their families and neighbors; if they withdraw from the world, how can they fail, with the good habits acquired from their infancy, to be most virtuous and to give edification to others?

At the same time that the founders of the Company were inaugurating the work of the foundlings, they were taking concrete steps to train the Sisters to teach school. Vincent had been worried from the beginning over the illiteracy of most of the first Sisters, particularly in view of the fact that teaching, especially of the catechism, was essential to their ministry.

Schools had taken a priority in Louise's plans in the early days of the village Charities. One of the first things she had done on moving to La Chapelle was to establish a school for girls in the house; and she personally taught catechism to the girls and women of the village on Sundays and feast days. Now the time had come to give the Sisters formal teacher training. "We must give some thought at least to teaching the girls how to conduct a school," Vincent wrote. "This woman says that she has conducted them in this city and elsewhere. We must see whether we should make a start with her." Louise was dissatisfied with such a hit-and-miss approach: she wanted something more professional and suggested sending the Sisters to learn from the Ursulines, who were already firmly established in the field. Vincent had his usual objections to the Sisters' mingling with religious, but Louise won her point and he subsided, but not without a parting grumble: "I do not expect very much from this communication of the Ursulines with your girls. Please see to it, nevertheless."

Daily problems arose inevitably and had to be dealt with. The father of a girl who had been sent home had been pestering Vincent to take her back. "Are you agreeable?" Vincent asked Louise. "If so, tell him to have her speak with me." A Sister, Marie of Saint-Sulpice, "has two thicknesses of bed curtains," he complained on another occasion. "It is because the house is so new and the windows badly fitted. When winter is over, there must be a rule about that. None of the rest of us have the like."

Another case was more serious. "Jeanne, the Daughter of Charity of this parish [Saint-Laurent], has committed a great many faults, for which reason Monsieur le curé [Lestocq], the officers and M. de Vincy have decided today that she must be changed," Vincent reported to Louise in March. "I ask you, Mademoiselle, to send us another with a sweeter and more accommodating disposition, and do it tomorrow morning so that she [Jeanne] will not have time to intrigue . . . for it is unbelievable how capable she is of it. But I think nonetheless that we must begin again with her at the Hôtel-Dieu or some place else, so that justice be accompanied by mercy." Despite his inclination to mercy, he could scarcely contain himself when he thought of Jeanne's misdeeds. "Would you believe that she slapped Jacqueline?" he asked. "And that she has had her own way in everything and that she has done several things without a word to anybody, such as treating a sick person without permission? And what is worse, she informed the Lenten preacher of certain failings of the ladies and wanted him to preach to them?" The offender was sent home to La Chapelle.

There was better comfort in another Sister Jeanne. "The ladies of Saint-Sulpice have a marvelous attachment to their Sister Jeanne," Vincent reported with satisfaction. "It would hurt them to remove her"; but he added with renewed caution because of the humiliation caused by her namesake: "We must apprise her of her faults."

"You are right to destine Marie-Denise for Saint-Etienne," he continued, but added disconsolately: "I distrust that Charity because of the attitude of the persons who work in it, especially the men."

He was still plagued by the fact that he had not got around to completing the establishment of the Charity at La Chapelle. "Ask God to give me the time to work at it," he implored Louise. "It is my pitiful fate. I have no time. God give me eternity!"

This anguished cry found an echo in Louise's heart. She, too, had no time; but in her overburdened day first things came first. Those who knew her well, notably Gobillon and Louis Abelly, have testified that she had "a love, or rather an extraordinary ardor, for prayer. Since she had an elevated mind and solid judgment formed both by the study of philosophy and by voluminous reading, and a tender heart penetrated by God, she entered into it with strength, sublimity and wholehearted affection . . ." Over and above the daily meditation prescribed by rule, she prayed extra hours on Wednesdays and all the days of Lent; and the inexhaustible subject of her prayer on these special days was the death of the Son of God. The marvelous purity of soul effected by this assiduity in prayer, reviewed and made more limpid by periodic retreats of three or four days (and a ten-day withdrawal from the world, insofar as duty allowed, between Ascension and Pentecost), continued throughout her life.

In March 1638 Vincent sent her an urgent plea to attend an assembly of the Ladies of Charity at the home of Mme Goussault. Sisters were going to be requested for the Parisian Charity of Saint-Etienne-du-Mont: he was anxious to learn from her at the meeting whether it was true that "you know some good, dedicated girls who are disposed to offer themselves for the spiritual assistance of women in the [hospital's ward of the] Legate"—the most pestiferous ward of all—in place of the fourteen ladies. That seems to me most desirable, because everyone is constantly fearful lest these ladies fall ill.

"What they tell me is true," he confided, "that things are going badly at the Hôtel-Dieu and it is to be hoped that your health will permit you to spend two or three days there. See to it." He trusted her completely.

Her son was ill, but Vincent hoped that a minor bleeding by the surgeon would restore him. Afterward, he admitted, Michel looked "pale and this trouble with his hand is rather painful," but he had high hopes for his application to duty: "He assures me that he realizes the excellence of the priesthood . . ." It is possible that the youth was pledged to the Diocese of Alet, because Vincent assured the mother that "he had promised M. Pavillon to work at the resolution he has taken."

A letter of this period reveals an ironic switch in Louise's relations with the Marillacs: they had arranged her marriage; now she was a party in arranging the marriage of her cousin Michel de Marillac, grandson of the late Garde des Sceaux, to Jeanne Potier, niece of the Bishop of Beauvais. "I am going to see Madame de Marillac [widow of René]," Vincent told her in reporting on the progress of a certain unidentified matter. "If she believes me, she will put an end to it. It would be good for her piety to fortify herself in this satisfaction she wishes. It would be a source of blessing for her son's affair. That is what I propose to tell her. But do not inform her of my opinion, please, until I have seen her and reported to you on the success of our interview of today. Monsieur de Beauvais spoke of consulting with the two of us together [himself and Louise] about [the marriage]. We will arrange it."

With the coming of spring, Vincent was anxious for Louise and Mme Goussault to see how the country Confraternities had fared through the enforced separation from headquarters caused by the severe winter—but they were both ailing. "They tell me you are better," he wrote Louise hopefully. "I praise God and pray Him to give you back the strength necessary to go to the country this spring." Mme Goussault, he told her reassuringly, was also better "and looking forward to the good weather and an increase of health so that she can travel to the country."

On March 22 he informed M. Lambert aux Couteaux that "Monseigneur le cardinal has bid me tell you to establish the Charity at Richlieu and that he will give something toward it annually until it can subsist on the ordinary collections . . ." And he promised "to send you the Daughter of Charity." This was Barbe Angiboust, whom he had already recalled from Saint-Germain-en-Laye for the purpose. She returned to Saint-Germain for some months when it became obvious that she was not needed yet at Richelieu.

Mme Goussault was already in the country and had sent back word that "they wish, without making the request at this time, for three [Sisters] for the hospital at Angers." This, the Company's first hospital, was to be an important foundation. Madame invited Louise to join her at Grigny, and Vincent assured Louise that God had inspired the invitation.

Before she left, Louise received a letter whose boldness horrified her. It came from the Sister from whom Vincent had expected so much when she entered the Company only the preceding January. "I believe we must act promptly with this poor girl," Louise told Vincent, "who has so won the hearts of the villagers that, rumor has it, they would not accept another if she were removed. She has hoodwinked everybody for a long time and especially two old bachelors named Messiers de la Noue, from whom she accepts comforts and with whom she makes good cheer over a bottle of wine and cakes. I beg you very humbly and for the love of God to consider the embarrassments of this bad affair, of which I believe myself to be the cause. I beg you to pray our good God to pardon me."

"You are shocked at seeing the treason of this poor creature," Vincent replied in surprise. "We will see many more [traitors], if we live; and, indeed, we will not suffer as greatly from ours as Our Lord did from His. Let us submit graciously to His good pleasure in what we are faced with. We must get her to return, either by my writing her myself, or by sending the lady foundress to her, or a priest from here; for she must in the end withdraw. You should see the letter she has written me! O *mon Dieu*, how this poor creature has deceived me! Please give me your thinking in the matter, as to whether Barbe [Angiboust] might be more suitable for winning her over, or better, whether, if your health permits, you could take little Jeanne [Lepeintre] there and install her in her place." As an afterthought he suggested that the offender might be lured away with a sop: "If she wishes to set herself up in Nogent [her home village], Madame de Brou, M. de Vincy's cousin, could take care of everything."

It was characteristic of Louise to blame herself when anything went wrong in the Company. "May it please Your Charity to remember the paper you promised me to help me in speaking to our Sisters two or three times each week to try to encourage them," she wrote on one occasion. "It seems to me that I merit the greatest punishments for all their failings: ask God for someone who could serve them better; indeed, I beg this of you with tears in my eyes. How many years have passed since God did me the grace of speaking to me through you, and I am what I am!" Vincent replied on the bottom of the letter to her humility with sardonic humor: after promising to speak to the Sisters the following week and several other people in the meantime, he rejoined, "And as for you, in the name of God, Mademoiselle, forgive me if I do not speak to you as soon as that; I will when I can."

At times Sisters had to be reluctantly withdrawn from certain posts because the ladies of the particular confraternity took a dislike to them. "I wrote M. de la Salle to have M. le curé de Saint-Germain send the girl back," Vincent informed Louise in one such instance. "Madame de Chaumont wrote to me about her at the insistence of Mademoiselle Chemerault . . . We should do what we can to [defend] her, but we must give way under pressure when the powers-that-be mix themselves up in things."

At the end of August, Louise set off again with Mme Goussault to visit the country Charities. Vincent wished them godspeed and playfully enjoined Louise "to be very cheerful with [Madame]. Force yourself to lighten somewhat that little seriousness which nature has given you and grace has sweetened . . ."

It was not hard for her to follow his advice at the moment, for her son had made her happy with new resolutions to apply himself. She had offered to visit her friend Mme de Liancourt to help her with her painting, and the Duchesse was looking forward to the pleasant days they would spend together.

With September the time had come for Barbe Angiboust to go to Richelieu "because of the number of sick . . . The illnesses are not contagious. For that reason, could you not give us [also] our Sister Louise from here [Saint-Laurent]?" Louise gladly lent her namesake to be one of the foundresses of this important new house. Travel was far from precise then, as the schedules for these two pioneers reveal. "They should take the coach to Tours," Vincent suggested, "and there inquire after a man who ordinarily acts as guide to those who wish to go to Richelieu: they should avail themselves of his services and hire a donkey or a little cart to get to Richelieu, which is about ten leagues distant." He was very anxious for them to be on their way as soon as possible. Enclosing fifty livres for the trip, he explained carefully that it cost "twelve livres for each coach passenger as far as Tours. I always instruct our people here to reserve a place on the first one leaving." He gave them a handsome reference to the Priest of the Mission who was pastor at Richelieu, M. Lambert aux Couteaux: "Here are two Daughters of Charity, who come to you to comfort the ladies of the Charity and to help the sick poor; they both know how to conduct schools for little girls; when the sick diminish in number, one of them can do that and the other can return here. Madame la duchesse d'Aiguillon has advised me that she has written to M. de Grandpré to provide them with lodging. I hope she will give instructions for their maintenance, too, or perhaps His Eminence will. In the meantime, please furnish them with what they need for their nourishment."

The Sisters left Paris, armed with this letter of introduction, on October 2, 1638. Their departure lifted Vincent to extraordinary heights and he broke forth in holy eloquence: "*Bon Dieu*, Mademoiselle, what good fortune for these good girls thus to go forth to advance where they go the charity Our Lord exercised on earth! Who will know, seeing them together in the coach, these two covered-heads, that they go to a work so admirable in the sight of God and the angels that the God-Man found it worthy of Himself and His holy Mother? Oh! how heaven will rejoice to see it and how magnificent their reward will be in that other world! How they will hold up their heads on judgment day! Indeed, crowns and empires seem trash to me compared to the crowns they will wear." The affectionate nickname of "covered-heads" was an allusion to the tight white peasant coifs they wore with their gray serge dresses—the costume of the country women in the villages surrounding the capital, which was most naturally and almost without conscious thought adopted as the dress for all the Sisters.

The father, anxious that his beloved daughters lose nothing of their promised glory, took over as he continued: "It only remains to instruct them to comport themselves like the Blessed Virgin on their journey and in their behavior; often to see her as present before or beside them; to act as they imagine the Blessed Virgin would; to meditate on her love and humility, and to be very humble in the sight of God and cordial with each other, models to all and a disedification to none; to perform their little exercises every morning, either before the coach leaves or on the road; to carry some little book to read from at times, at others reciting their chaplet; to join in conversations that are of God and in none that are worldly, much worse loose, and to stand firm against the familiarities that men might wish to take with them. They should sleep in a room apart, which they should ask for at the inns, or with honest women if there are such in the coach . . .

"On reaching Richelieu they should go first to salute the Holy Sacrament, then M. Lambert, receiving his orders and endeavoring to put them into practice with regard to the sick and the children who will attend the school, observing the little daily exercises they have been practicing. They should go to confession every eight days only, unless some principal feast comes along during the week. They should try to profit the souls while they tend the bodies of the poor. They should honor and obey the officers of the Charity and show much respect to others, animating them to love their holy work; and going on in that way, they will find that they are leading a very holy life and that from poor girls they have become great queens of heaven."

These fervent, beautiful instructions and apostrophes were to be repeated over and over with variations to other Daughters of Charity setting out for other missions in the years ahead, but their wisdom, beauty and enthusiasm would never fade. This mystical, often ecstatic, letter—and others like it—is testimony to a great truth: that this towering figure of Church and state, this paradoxically humble Vincent de Paul, intimate of kings and queens and prelates, bared the most secret spiritual chamber of his heart—which most men are too protectively shy to reveal to anyone—to only one person in all the world, to his co-worker and dearest friend, Louise de Marillac.

While the Sisters were leaving for Richelieu, Louise was in another crisis over her son. He had told M. de la Salle that he was studying for the priesthood only because his mother wished it, that he wished he were dead—and his mother, too—but that, nevertheless, he would take minor orders to please her. Vincent had first written Michel's ungracious remark about Louise, then erased it to spare her feelings; however, knowing she could decipher the words if she wished, he added lamely: "I believe that he would rather die than wish your death."

Despite this unpleasant and unnecessary note, the point was, as Vincent bluntly asked Louise, "Is this a vocation?" Whether the youth's feelings and words were "from nature or the devil, his will is not free to decide for itself in such an important matter, and you ought not to wish it." It seems apparent that Vincent at least suspected undue influence on the mother's part, because he set out in frightening detail his own experiences with forced vocations: "Some time ago a good child of the city took the subdiaconate in that state of mind and could not pass on to the other orders. Do you want to expose M. your son to the same danger? Let him be led by God; He is more his Father than you are his mother and loves him more than you do. Let Him have the conduct of the affair. He well knows how to call him at another time, if He wishes, or to give him work suitable to his salvation. I often recall to mind a priest who was with us who had taken the order of priesthood in this trouble of spirit. God knows where he is now . . . !" Confident in the luminosity of her prayer, he enjoined her in a postscript to make it on the subject of "the wife of Zebedee and her sons, to whom Our Lord said, when she pressed Him to establish them: 'You do not know what you ask.' "

The terrified mother was crushed spiritually and physically under the weight of her son's unfeelingness and her own misguided zeal. Vincent consoled her with great tenderness: "I render God a thousand thanks for the goodness with which you carry your cross, and pray Him to preserve you in perfect health. I have word from M. your curé that you communicate at home, and ignore the fact that you do not feel a great desire to receive. Our Lord does this expressly, as I hope, so that you have the merit of obedience joined to that of the love you bear Him and which I hope His goodness will give you."

Characteristically, her remorse seems to have taken the extravagant form of divesting herself of everything so that Michel would have the means to make his life as he liked, but Vincent would not allow it. He loved her son "more dearly than I can tell you," he avowed, "but I do not like your giving way to the too tender thoughts you bear him, because they are against reason and consequently against God, who wishes mothers to give part of their goods to their children, but not to deprive themselves of everything."

He sent a book of poetry to relieve the tedium of her illness, but charged her "to read or have read only two or three sonnets a day at different and widely separated times," so as not to tire herself.

With his usual maddening inconsistency, Michel now assured Vincent that he intended to persevere in his vocation and would probably enroll at the Sorbonne. Louise had been torturing herself with thoughts of his taking off to parts unknown and losing his soul in the process. In an effort to reassure her, Vincent conveniently forgot that he himself had raised such phantoms in her mind only a year or so before. "Please be at peace," he admonished her blandly, "and what is more, should what you fear come to pass, you must even then adore the Providence of God in his regard and believe that the journey or change of condition will contribute to his salvation and perhaps to his greater perfection. Alas! Mademoiselle, if everyone separated from his parents were in danger of perdition, where would I be?"

Vincent always exerted himself to the utmost for Michel from sincere fatherly affection and a desire to set Louise's mind at rest, and a short time later he was assuring her that M. Georges Froger, rector of the seminary at Saint-Nicolas, would accept the young man "without title, which is a favor against the formalities." It is not usual, even now, for a seminary to accept a candidate for the priesthood who does not have assurance of financial support when ordained, either from a diocese or from a religious community or an ecclesiastical benefice. Vincent cautioned Louise, however, in case "some difficulty should arise . . . to hold [assurance of an income for Michel from her own resources] in readiness." He felt constrained to add, with little conviction, that there was "no change that I know of in the intentions of my aforesaid lord your son."

That the aforesaid lord's intentions were not so crystal-clear, however, is evidenced by the report of a consultation Vincent held with Père Hilarion Rebours, Antoine Le Gras's Carthusian cousin. "M. your twice-cousin de Rebours came here yesterday," he informed Louise. "We were in complete agreement that the ecclesiastical state was the best thing for M. your son; secondly, that his bent seemed toward that more than toward the world; thirdly, that it was perhaps this young man who had mixed him up and brought on the revival of his little aversion to the community of Saint-Nicolas; that, despite all this, if things are represented to him properly, reason should reassert itself; that there is danger in catering to his whim of wearing a short gown, unless he is going to the country, for it is ever important for him to be modest." But Vincent was practical—and charitable: "If he persists in his present way despite everything, *in nomine Domini*, we must give him a helping hand." Vincent was not, however, a fool: "But to give in easily to a reversal of the disposition he has shown all his life toward the ecclesiastical state because of the influence of this debauched young man on his state of mind is not, I think, right." He finished with his exquisite sensitivity: "Be then at peace on that score, I beg you, Mademoiselle. Our Lord will dispose everything. Have no fear, nor let us act hastily."

Michel's evil genius seems to have been a certain Comte de Mony, whose name, even years later, caused Louise to prick up her ears. "Who is this Comte de Mony whom he [Michel] is going with?" she asked Sister Hellot in a letter written from Nantes on August 21, 1646. "Is he an acquaintance of the ladies with whom he is staying, or is it one of his former acquaintances . . . ? Please do not let on to him that I asked, but if it is one of his former acquaintances, I beg you to discourage this trip."

No one could blame Vincent for an occasional show of exasperation with the muddled affairs of Michel Le Gras. He was doing his best to settle him in life; and when, on top of all, Michel's mother occasionally raised objections to his plans, his aggravation was ill-concealed. Now, for example, she found fault with a lodging Vincent had in mind for the youth, and he answered her shortly: "I know you have many things against this [landlord] and I have taken them into account; but there is my opinion." It was in this same letter that he bade her leave off her "maternal amusements," and "strengthen your body and soul in view of so many occasions of doing good." But, as so often happened when he rebuked her sharply, his courtesy was the more gracious. "God knows," he added, "that I am yours and that you are mine . . ."

Since 1634 when the promising grape harvest was trampled underfoot to make a battleground for the endless wars, Lorraine had become a barren corner of hell. The peasantry, preyed upon day in and day out by roving bands of robbers, fled to the walled towns for safety. No one tilled the fields, and the resultant famine was so total that nearly eighty villages were deserted and those who stayed behind to prowl their ruins like animals subsisted on human flesh. Vincent deployed his priests and brothers into the disaster area with money and seeds for new planting in a heroic recovery effort.

Many of the Lorrainers took refuge in Paris, where Louise joined Vincent in his efforts to rehabilitate and relocate them. "Here are three poor Lorrainers who arrived last night," he wrote her on many like occasions. "One is a child. You must try to place her in the Refuge, and perhaps the old lady also." All were not worthy of the charity shown them. Louise reported such a one to Vincent in July 1639: "The Lorrainer who spoke to you Saturday at the Hôtel-Dieu has not found a situation; she has been staying at the Hôtel-Dieu a good two weeks for that purpose. What are we going to do with her? Please do not give her any money. I have asked Sister Geneviève to supply her needs. She could ask for nothing better than to live there, do nothing and have money. I see so much disorder everywhere that, it seems to me, I am completely crushed. Nonetheless, I live in hope and the will to confide myself with Saints Martha and Mary to Divine Providence."

She had, indeed, a blessed optimism where human weakness was concerned. She was still worrying along with that poor misfit, Sister Nicole.

"Since you think Nicole will soon correct herself, make another try of her . . ." Vincent wrote resignedly, but added cautiously, "I think, however, you should wait some days."

She had no patience, however, with what she considered betrayal. On May 16, 1639, she had occasion to write to the mother superior of the convent in Argenteuil to which Sister Barbe had defected, and she seized the opportunity to let the good mother know her feelings concerning this chosen "one of the Sisters Servants of the sick poor of the Parish Charities whom God called and placed in that state eight years ago. I have not wished to believe, Madame, that it was you who gave the order to turn her from her vocation, not being able to imagine that those who know the importance of it would wish to undertake to oppose themselves to the designs of God and to put a soul in danger of her salvation by giving up the assistance of the abandoned poor, who are in all kinds of need and who could not be better helped than by these good Sisters who, detaching themselves from every interest, give themselves to God for the spiritual and temporal service of these poor creatures whom His goodness so very much wishes to have as His members. God grant, Madame, that she whom you already have in your house may serve you well, and to her peace. I prefer to believe that she was not called to the state in which she found herself; otherwise she would be culpable indeed. But, Madame, permit no longer, I beg you, that they be accepted with your permission, for that could be a source of temptation to a number of others . . ." The words were polite, but Louise's defense of her Company as every bit as much a divine vocation as the convent, and the acerbity of her condemnation of those who would tamper with it, must have caused the mother superior some uncomfortable moments!

Nor could Louise abide arrogance. There was Jeanne who had "beaten her companion." Vincent and Louise expelled her from the community on the spot, putting her, out of kindness, however, with the Sisters at Saint-Sauveur "until she could find a position." Vincent insisted on her dismissal and the justice of it being a lesson to all: ". . . Let the others know that it is not the first time she has struck someone, and that she was pardoned the other times, but that it would be too great a scandal if it were said that Daughters of Charity fought like dogs and cats." Jeanne got the wind up and disappeared. The sordid incident depressed Louise greatly and, on top of it, some of the most promising of her young daughters sickened and died. Vincent was deeply touched at her depression and wrote to comfort her: "You appear to me to be under great stress of heart. You fear lest God be angry and no longer want the service you render Him because He takes your girls. That is very wrong, Mademoiselle. It is a sign that He cherishes it since He makes use of it in such fashion, for He treats you like His dear spouse the Church, at whose beginning He made the greater part of it die not only by natural death but even by sufferings and torrents. Who would have said, seeing it, that He was angry with these young and holy plants? Do not, then, believe such a thing any longer, but the contrary.

"Since you feel as you do," he continued with that delicacy so characteristic of him, "I will look for this Big Jeanne, or, if you know where she is, send her to me, please.

"It is not in character for you to be so apprehensive over my departure," he admonished her gently—she could never forebear fretting over his health—and assured her that his trip would be broken up into easy stages: "The longest I foresee is the trip to Pontoise tomorrow."

Within a few days he had found the Sister with the ready hand and reported to Louise that he "had let this Big Jeanne know last evening that she must depart . . . Act sweetly in this matter, but with firmness and dispatch."

On July 4 he wrote anxiously from Troyes, where he was making a visitation of his missionaries: "I cannot express how grieved I am over your suffering caused by the return of your headache. *Mon Dieu*, Mademoiselle, could it be the air at La Chapelle that brings on this illness? I beg you to ask the doctor for his opinion and, if it is that, to leave at once and take a house in our faubourg if you can find one to suit you, or in the city . . . Please, Mademoiselle, do this at once, and everything possible to make yourself well." Louise did not, in fact, move from La Chapelle until 1642.

Mme Goussault was ill again, also, and Vincent besought Louise to send him "two lines" about her condition. The good woman was well enough the following month to make a tour of the country Charities, but she was mortally ill, and the tour was her last. Not long after her return to Paris, Vincent was writing gravely to Louise: "I have just come from seeing Madame Goussault, who is not grievously, but dangerously, ill. She knows it, too, and has told me so. We must beseech God for her. Her heart is constant in its unquestioning acceptance of the will of God. I have let Madame la chancelière [Séguier] know. She said that she would send you her carriage tomorrow."

The end came on September 20 in the evening. Vincent was at her

side, had been with her all day. That morning she had said to him: "Oh!
sir, I was thinking all night about the dear Sisters. If you only knew how
highly I esteem them. Oh! what things has God not revealed to me
about them!" She saw them standing before God, who "demanded great
things of them." And she exclaimed with joy: "Ah! how they will multiply and do good! Ah! how happy they will be!"

So died the first superioress of the Ladies of Charity and a true mother
of the Daughters of Charity. She has a living memorial among them in
the title of "Sister Servant" borne by their superioresses, for it was the
only title she would accept for herself. Her greatness has the best testimony in the friendship of Vincent and Louise, who held her up as a
model to Ladies and Daughters of Charity alike as long as they lived.
Louise wrote to Sister Barbe Angiboust and Sister Louise at Richelieu on
October 26, 1639: "I have no doubt that you have felt the loss we have
all suffered in the death of Madame la présidente Goussault. Our obligations to her ought to serve to make us imitate her so that God may be
glorified."

XI

To the Sick Poor
and the Prisoners

Mme Goussault died happy in the thought that her last request had been granted: the Company would accept the charge of the Hôpital-Saint-Jean at Angers. Three Sisters had been appointed to the pioneer band—Claude Carré, Marguerite Lavalle and Barbe Rouelle, and were preparing to depart when the holy godmother of the Company died.

Like so many already established works taken over by the Company, the Hôpital-Saint-Jean was in a woeful state due to the absolute neglect of its administration. Its governing body, along with the sheriffs and citizens of Angers, had only recently besought the King to do something, since "the sick were destitute of all help." The poor themselves avoided the hospital unless carried there bodily.

The negotiations for the Sisters had been confided to the vicar general of Angers, M. Guy Lasnier, Abbé de Vaux. De Vaux's early ecclesiastical career had been worldly indeed; and it was only when curiosity had led him to Loudun to see with his own eyes the bizarre happenings there in the reputedly haunted convent of the allegedly possessed Ursulines, and, as the story goes, one of the tormented nuns publicly proclaimed some of his most secret faults, that he turned resolutely to God. He had met Vincent de Paul in 1635 when he made a retreat at Saint-Lazare, and they had become friends. They had, besides, mutual friends in Mme de Chantal and Jean-Jacques Olier. Back in Angers, M. de Vaux introduced the Tuesday Conferences to the priests of Anjou.

This relationship with Vincent was providential, because M. de Vaux was essential to Vincent's acquiescence in sending his Daughters so far away as Angers from their motherhouse and superiors. They were entrusted wholly to the keeping of de Vaux, for all practical purposes, as is evident from Louise's weekly letters to him over a period of twenty years

—and both Vincent and Louise were completely satisfied with the arrangement.

Shortly after Mme Goussault's death, a letter from Angers begged the Sisters to come at once, and Vincent instructed Louise "not to put off sending the girls, even though the Act [of Establishment] has not been executed." Louise thought the foundation important enough for her to establish personally, but Vincent was afraid of her making the long journey in her precarious state of health. His fears were vindicated when she had a relapse which made her feel for the first time that death might not be far off. "*O Jésus*, Mademoiselle," he cried in alarm, "it is not time yet. Lord God! the world has too much need of you! In God's name, do everything possible to be well and to treat yourself better."

He had some news that would surely rally her: "Monsieur your son told me last night that he was going to Monsieur de Saint-Nicolas to take the examination [for tonsure]. He seems to be absolutely determined." And he went on to explain tactfully that Michel had not been to see her because "his long cloak was ripped . . . and he is having it repaired. Perhaps he does not wish to see you until he can come as one bound to the Church . . ." It would seem either that Michel and his mother were still estranged or that he had grown completely thoughtless of her feelings.

It was, perhaps, during this illness that Vincent sent Louise a touching note. "If you wish me to have the boon of visiting you in your illness," he wrote, "tell me so. I have imposed a rule on myself not to go to see you without being summoned for something necessary or useful." Perhaps it was the eternal caution of the honest male, or the absolute self-abnegation of the saint, or both. In any case, his diffidence makes plain their intimacy.

Word came to the sick woman that Barbe Angiboust and Louise at Richelieu were experiencing the difficulties of two disparate personalities forced to live at the closest quarters. She roused herself to a long letter of reproach. "I have heard what I have always feared," she wrote sorrowfully, "that your little work, which has succeeded so well in solacing the sick and instructing girls, has done nothing for your perfection . . . Think, my dear Sisters, of what you do. You are the cause of Our Lord being often offended rather than glorified . . ." Then she began to detail maternally but firmly the specific offenses of each: "You, Sister Barbe, by your little cordiality to the sister God has given you, by your petty disdains, and the lack of support for her weaknesses . . ." These faults were especially reprehensible because Barbe had forgotten that, "when you were appointed as her superior, it obliged you to a mother's responsibilities . . ."

She turned then to Louise: "And you, dear Sister Louise, look at you, fallen again back into your bad habits! What do you think your state in life is? A life of freedom? Certainly not. It has to be one of continual submission and obedience." She was not to pay visits or make pilgrimages, as she had been doing, or "do anything or go anywhere without the permission of Sister Barbe, whom you have accepted as your superior . . ."

As usual, Mademoiselle blamed the faults of these daughters ultimately on "the bad example I have given you in the practice of the virtues I recommend to you; I beg you, good Sisters, not to recall it, and to ask pardon for me and the grace to correct myself . . ." The mother had had hard things to say, but she knew the worth of her daughters: "Know, dear Sisters, that I look forward to your reconciliation, after a renewal of affection, because you have, both of you, open hearts . . ." They had indeed. Vincent was able to write from Richelieu on November 24: "I have seen Sister Louise for a moment in the church; she is ecstatic at the hope of seeing you. I have not yet seen Sister Barbe. Things are going better, thank God."

As soon as Louise was up and about again she was impatient to set out for Angers, but an outbreak of the plague in Richelieu made Vincent ask her to put off the journey until he had returned to Paris. Louise replied that God had indicated that, despite the fact that the plague had spread to Angers itself, she was to go there at once. "Since Our Lord gives you the impulse to go to Angers, go *in nomine Domini*," he wrote back. "Whomever He protects is well protected." That settled, Vincent began to fuss over the details of the journey, so as to cause her as little discomfort as possible:

> If it please you to take the Châteaudun coach, you will pass through Chartres, where you can make your devotions. From Châteaudun it is perhaps eleven leagues to Orléans and maybe less to Notre-Dame de Cléry, where you cross the river, or even closer, if I remember rightly. That way you will avoid the public road except for three or four leagues near Orléans, where I recommend that you stop. To go there, you must hire a cart at Châteaudun . . . I have instructed our Brother Louistre to escort you wherever you wish to go; he will leave on Tuesday. See if you can arrange to go with him . . .

It would be good, on your return trip, to visit the Charity at Richelieu, which is eight leagues from Saumur, where you will find Notre-Dame des Ardilliers [he knew how delighted she would be with the shrines]. From Richelieu you will take a carriage for Tours, which is a good ten leagues from Richelieu by that route. As soon as you arrive at Orléans, you should go to the wharfs to find a boat . . .

At Angers Louise was to lodge with relatives of Mme Goussault, "whom she besought constantly in her last illness to assist you." Vincent enclosed a rule for the Sisters to follow at the Hôpital, of which she was "to make a fair copy and change as you find necessary." The first thing they were to do was to love God "sovereignly and to perform their duties for love of Him, and the second, to cherish one another as sisters united in the bonds of His love, and the sick poor as their lords, because Our Lord is in them and they in Our Lord." Here, indeed, was Vincentian doctrine lifted in one piece from the Gospels: the greatest and the first commandment, and the second like unto it. They have been drawn to a divine state, the rule continues, the grandeur of which elevates Vincent's spirit and makes him speak in the uncompromisingly Mosaic tone of the divinely appointed lawmaker:

> They will study to despise what the world esteems, and to esteem what the world despises, for the love of Jesus Christ who has given us the example; and to that end, each one will seek complete contempt and mortify herself in all things and will prefer the vile and abject employments to the honorable . . .
> They will renounce carnal affection for their relatives and their native place, and will transform it into a spiritual affection, according to the counsel of Our Lord who tells us that we cannot be His disciples unless we hate fathers and mothers, and that no prophet is without honor except in his own country . . .
> They will be faithful to the observance of their rule and to the way of life proper to their little Company . . .
> Poverty will be jealously guarded among them as a means of preserving them in their vocation . . . Each will always choose for herself the poorest; they shall have no money or anything, either in their own rooms or elsewhere . . . They will neither receive nor give any present. They will content themselves with living, dressing and sleeping according to what is given them. In brief, they will keep in mind that they were born poor, that they must live in the poor, for the love of the poorest of the poor, Jesus Christ Our Lord . . .
> They will use every imaginable precaution to preserve their chastity

. . . They will not speak alone with men, not even with priests or the religious of the house. They will keep always to plainness of dress and hairdo.

They will obey their superiors in this city of Paris as regards discipline and interior conduct, and Messieurs les administrateurs as regards exterior conduct, specifically their hospital rules for assisting the poor, and the superioress among them as regards the implementation of their rules and, in general, in everything she orders them to do: and their obedience shall be prompt, cheerful, entire, constant, persevering in all things, and with the submission of their own judgment and will . . .

Here was the solid, unyielding rock of sacrifice upon which these simple, unlettered, spiritually unsophisticated girls built lives of joyful, dedicated perfection, heroic in their striving and in their accomplishment, and their reward—there could be no reward adequate except eternal life, endless, unshadowed bliss. Their heroicity lay in the drab, harsh, daily, day-long tasks of soul and body.

"They will rise at precisely four o'clock in the morning," and after having made their spiritual exercises and discharged their household chores, "at six o'clock they will report to the sick ward, empty the pots, make the beds of the sick, mop the wards, administer medicines." To protect themselves from infection or faintness, "they should take a little bread and a finger of wine," before entering the hospital, "and on Communion days should sniff a little vinegar, or massage their hands with it." The rules continue:

At seven o'clock they should give the sickest a breakfast of soup or a fresh egg, and the others a little butter or sliced apple. Afterward they should hear holy Mass, if they have not heard it at five o'clock, and should take great care to serve soups at the precise times to the sick who have taken medicine.

Those who need to eat something can do so after that. Then they shall return to the sick, instructing the ignorant in the things necessary for salvation . . .

They shall take great care that the sick poor have what is necessary, their meals at the hours scheduled, liquids when they need them, and sometimes sweets to eat.

At ten o'clock, they will go to the infirmary to give the sick their dinner and to serve them . . . They should give them veal and mutton with a little beef in the dish at dinner, and some roast and boiled meat at supper . . . Those who cannot eat solid foods should be given soups

and fresh eggs alternately every three hours, in such a way that they will
have four soups and three eggs a day.

After the poor have been fed, the Sisters will have their own dinner;
then someone will return to "try to bring the sick some recreation," and
to nursing chores, while the others work at whatever tasks the superioress
has assigned them. "At four o'clock they will give the baths, change the
sheets of those who have soiled them, empty the pots, and freshen the
beds a little without making the sick get up."

Supper will be served at five. The sick who are ambulatory must be
put to bed by seven, and "some wine and little sweets shall be ordered
according to the needs of the sickest . . . At eight o'clock the Sisters
will withdraw, leaving one in the infirmary on watch to assist the sick
and help the dying die well . . . She will spend the night watching,
reading, and sleeping sometimes when the poor are quiet. The others
will retire to their employments preparing what must be done the next
morning, and will go to bed precisely at nine o'clock . . ."

After such an arduous day, the exhausted girls must have slept
soundly; and tomorrow would be another arduous day, and all the days
after, succeeding one another endlessly, stretching away into the years.

Vincent had had good cause to worry about the effect of the trip on
Louise's health; she arrived at Angers exhausted and immediately came
down with a cold. He himself had been traveling back to Paris in short
stages, stopping for business on the way. He arrived in the capital on
December 11, fully expecting to find Louise there. "*O mon Dieu!* how
anxious I am for you and your daughters!" he wrote her the very next
day, "Please, above all things else, take good care of yourself in the midst
of the great dangers which confront you at Angers." The plague had not
abated in the least.

Louise's first difficulty at the hospital was minor, but one which could
prove very annoying as time went on. A goodhearted young girl had been
helping to tend the sick and had taken it for granted that, with the
advent of the Sisters, she would continue living there. This was out of
the question, for it would interfere with the privacy of community life.
But what was to be done, without offending her? Louise's prudence
found a way, and she was able to assure M. l'abbé de Vaux early in
January 1640 that "our good girl is entirely disposed to do whatever
pleases you, and if I am not mistaken, she will give you good service." In

the short time that she had known the girl, Louise had taken a motherly interest in her and, therefore, cautioned the abbé: "She tells me that, ever since she has served in the hospital, she needs some wine when she works; but half a pint a day will be sufficient for her."

At the last minute Louise had decided to take Sister Jeanne Lepeintre with her for Angers, and Vincent was happy with her choice. He was unusually concerned about her safety because of the virulence of the plague, and recommended that she have a postulant from Richelieu accompany her home. "I am rather concerned about your going to Richelieu . . ." he confessed. "Our dear Sisters have stopped visiting the sick and the schools. The Monday I left, a little girl died who had attended their school the previous Saturday. If you go there, stay only a day, please." He knew why she was so set on stopping at Richelieu: it was to satisfy herself that all was well between Barbe and Louise. "Your letter has done wonders for them," he assured her. "They are well at present and happy, provided they see you."

At Angers Louise found that, despite the fact that she had sent three Sisters originally and had supplemented them with Jeanne Lepeintre, more were still needed for this 200-bed hospital. She had put Madame Turgis in charge of the motherhouse and Vincent now went there to talk the matter over with her "and to begin to give their obediences to the girls you are asking for." He disagreed, however, with some of her choices: "I do not think we should speak to Marie [Joly] of Saint-Germain, or to the one at Saint-Paul. I will try to send you the others as soon as I have a little talk with Madame Turgis. There is much to be said for and against. Alas, *mon Dieu!* what we must do for Nantes, where we must send some girls at the earliest date possible."

Sister Henriette had proved unsatisfactory and Vincent was not sure what to do with her. He put it frankly, "I cannot make something from nothing." To his way of thinking, she should not go to Saint-Germain-en-Laye, where they had talked of sending her: "I am going to dispatch someone else to Saint-Germain and keep her here [at La Chapelle] to make her realize her fault."

Louise was so impressed by the magnitude of the challenge at Angers that she thought of Madame Turgis herself for the mission. Vincent, however, "found a difficulty" in sending her. He thought it better to "send you Geneviève [Caillou], who was close to you here, or perhaps Marie [Matrilomeau], who was at the Enfants Trouvés." In the end

Louise had her way, and Madame Turgis left for Angers, along with Barbe Toussaint and Clémence Ferré.

Louise's condition worsened. Vincent saluted her "on this last of the month and of the year 1639" in a peculiarly exalted mood from which all anxiety was absent, almost as if he knew she was to be long spared for their work. "There you are ill by order of the Providence of God," he began simply. "His holy name be blessed! I hope of His goodness that it will glorify itself in this illness as it has in all the others; and that I ask of Him without ceasing both at home and abroad wherever I may be. Oh, how I wish Our Lord would let you see how every heart is affected, and the tenderness of the officers of the Charity of the Hôtel-Dieu when I told them of it the day before yesterday at a little assembly!" Exaltation did not, however, blunt his common sense: "As for your return trip, it must be by litter; we will send you one when you are ready for it." He sent a letter to de Vaux by the same post to thank him for his kindness to Louise, who, at his insistence, was staying in his house. "I do not recommend her to you, Monsieur," he wrote graciously. "Your letter has shown me that you think of nothing else, and she has written me as much." And he begged the Abbé to consider him henceforth "as someone God has given you."

Louise's illness was stubborn and kept her in bed all through December and January. Her absence was keenly felt at La Chapelle and Vincent himself seemed at uncommonly loose ends. To begin with, letters from Angers were unaccountably delayed or lost and, when they did arrive, gave little specific news on the progress of the patient. "*Mon Dieu*, Mademoiselle," he grumbled good-naturedly on January 17, "see how you oblige me to write entirely in my own hand! *Mais quoi!* You tell me nothing of the state of your illness!"

Some of his letters did not get through promptly either, but he insisted that he had "written every week, and the last only three days ago." He stoutly reassured her time and again that "your daughters are well and do well, too." But, at the same time, he lamented, "Oh, how your presence is needed here, not only for your girls, who are well enough, but also for the general business of the Charity." He fretted continually over the means of travel she should employ on her return trip, changing his mind about the litter in favor of a carriage with "two good strong horses," because it would be more comfortable. "I beg you, Mademoiselle, to spare nothing; and, whatever it costs, to take whatever will be the easiest for you." A week later he was apologizing for forgetting to tell her that he "would send a coach for you, except that there are three leagues of bad road between Chartres and Le Mans which cannot be traveled at this season, joined to the fact that we cannot divert the coaches from their ordinary routes without an outcry from the public." He was really free to do so, because Cardinal Richelieu had signed over to his Congregation the revenue from the Loudun coaches as part of the endowment of the Congregation's house at Richelieu.

Despite her illness, Louise was negotiating the agreement between the administrators of the hospital and the Company. Vincent instructed her to sign it as "Directress of the Daughters of Charity, servants of the sick poor of the hospitals and parishes, at the good pleasure of the Superior General of the Congregation of Priests of the Mission, Director of the aforesaid Daughters of Charity." Should the administrators ask for the letters of establishment of the Company, she was to reply that "there are none, other than that which has given competency to the above-mentioned Superior, Director of the Confraternities of Charity, as has been done everywhere, notably in that diocese [Angers] at Bourgneuf, on the lands of Madame Goussault—so I recollect, although I am not absolutely certain—and at Richelieu in the Diocese of Poitiers." The mention of Richelieu would be quite enough, and Vincent knew it.

The letters of agreement were signed on February 1. Vincent had urged Louise "to leave Angers in haste, the minute this was done." But her weakness from the long bout of sickness, the affairs of the hospital and the establishment of a confraternity, all conspired to delay her. Vincent was brimming with delight at the news of her recovery and of the proposed confraternity when he wrote on February 10: "Blessed be God that you are in better health and are planning your return. Oh, how you will be received and with what great desire you are expected! I praise God that the ladies of that city have agreed to establish the Charity of the Hôtel-Dieu, and pray Him to grant success to this holy enterprise in His honor." This hospital confraternity at Angers was the first to be modeled explicitly on the Confraternity of the Hôtel-Dieu of Paris.

Various affairs were awaiting her return. There was some thought of removing the Sisters' motherhouse from La Chapelle. "I have been much occupied at prayer this morning with a house at La Villette [another Parisian suburb] and find it has a number of advantages," Vincent informed Louise on February 4. "Monsieur le curé offers his rectory. We shall see about it." He did not know what to do about "the sister of Marie of Saint-Germain, who stutters. She seems to be a good enough girl, but I don't know whether she has the proper spirit. Her good sister is pressing us to take her." He had already received two other girls because they had been waiting a long time for Louise's return. The beginning of a new apostolate with the galley slaves was especially awaiting her. "You will come in the nick of time . . ." he told her elatedly. Claude Cornuel, one of the King's financial ministers, had died recently and left an annual income of six thousand livres for the work. The bequest would support the ministrations of the Daughters of Charity and of the priests of Saint-Nicolas to the prisoners.

By the time Louise left Angers for Tours, she had settled on the personnel for the hospital: Elisabeth Martin, superioress; Madame Turgis, Cécile-Agnès Angiboust [Barbe's sister], Clémence Ferré, Madeleine Monget, Geneviève Caillou, Marguerite François, Marie Matrilomeau, and Barbe Toussaint. M. l'abbé de Vaux, who had showered every kindness on her and the Sisters, multiplied it by sending her off in his own coach with his personal lackey in attendance. She sent the coach back from Tours with profuse thanks; she had decided there to hire a light carriage to take her to Paris by way of Orléans. She had no reason now to stop at Richelieu because Vincent had arranged for M. Lambert to send Sisters Barbe and Louise in the priests' cart to visit her at Angers.

Louise's serious illness had belatedly shaken Michel enough to make him stop thinking about himself for the moment. When his mother had begun to talk about coming home, he had come forward with the offer to go and fetch her. "If you will let me know the day you can be at Chartres—if you take that route—he can go there to meet you," Vincent wrote on January 28, "and there, if you are strong enough, you can transfer to the coach." Three days later he wrote her in haste to tell her that "M. your son offered yesterday to go to you at Angers, but I did not judge it necessary . . ." Michel did not go to Angers. We do not know whether he met his mother at Chartres. But, undoubtedly, after so much aridity of feeling on his part, his offer alone was enough to make her happy.

Louise had missed an important assembly of the Ladies of Charity held on January 10 but, Vincent consoled her, "you can be sure that you were not forgotten." Mme la princesse de Condé and Mme la duchesse d'Aiguillon had been present. "Never have I seen a company so grand, or so united in modesty," he wrote happily.

The years of work with the foundlings had scarcely made a dent in the overall situation and now Vincent, after much thought and prayer, had decided to dare the responsibility for all the abandoned infants of the city. He had called the meeting of January 10 to persuade the Ladies to support him. He prepared his plan of approach carefully. First he described graphically the dreadful condition of these poor little creatures and the inevitability of their fate. Then he raised objections that might be made against the project. *It was the business of the high justices and not of private persons, especially women.* He admitted as much, but submitted practically that it would take a lawsuit to make them undertake it. Who would institute the lawsuit? And in the meantime, "these poor little creatures die." *God has condemned many of these little creatures because of their birth, and it is for that reason, perhaps, that He orders no one to do anything about them.* He had nothing but contempt for such an objection. It was because man had been cursed by God through Adam's sin, he replied, that Our Lord became man and died, assuming responsibility for these little creatures cursed by His Father. The identification of the unfortunate children with the rest of mankind was adroit. The third objection, he agreed, was the hardest to answer. *The work was too costly to undertake: 550 livres were barely sufficient to support six or seven children, and from two to three hundred of them were abandoned each year.* Vincent's answer was simple: to do what could be done.

He was not above using the sensational to motivate these good women. There might be found among the foundlings, he suggested, some "who would become great personages and great saints. Remus and Romulus were foundlings, suckled by a wolf. Melchisedech the priest was, according to Saint Paul, without genealogy; that is to say, without father or mother, or in other words, a foundling. Moses was a foundling [rescued] by Pharaoh's sister."

The meeting was a complete success. He reported to Louise: "They have resolved to receive all foundlings."

The work for the relief of Lorraine went on, directed by Vincent and his priests in the field and aided by Louise and her Daughters in Paris. Vincent had sent Brother Mathieu Regnard on fifty-three trips into the devastated area, carrying on each trip from twenty thousand to fifty thousand livres. Despite the omnipresence of bandits, who on occasion stopped and searched him, Regnard never lost a sou of the poor's money. So famous were his hairbreadth escapes and the obvious protection of God over him that, for example, the Comtesse de Montgomery would not venture to travel from Metz to Verdun until assured that Brother Mathieu would escort her.

The Charities in Paris became way stations where female refugees fortunate enough to reach the safety of the city stayed until more permanent quarters could be found for them. Sending a poor woman and her little daughter to Louise on one occasion, Vincent suggested delicately that she "give the child and her mother to Our Lord," and promised in return that "He will render good account of you and your son."

Vincent did not confine his charity to the poor of Lorraine, but extended it also to the displaced nobility who had fled to Paris, often with little more than the clothes on their backs. The Baron de Renty was his chief co-worker in this apostolate, and they were joined by the Duc de Liancourt, the Comte de Brienne, and the Marquis de Fontenay—whose wives aided as assiduously the efforts of the Ladies and Daughters of Charity—and by the Duchesse d'Aiguillon, whose influence and personal fortune were inexhaustibly at the command of Vincent and Louise and who had taken the refugee religious of both sexes for her personal project.

Home in Paris, Louise looked anxiously back to Angers. "I have promised myself to learn your news every week either from yourself or from someone else," she wrote the Abbé de Vaux on March 23. She begged him to excuse her importunity, "for I am so prone to commit faults that it does not astonish me, hoping that, as I am good for nothing, God can and very often will draw His glory from people like me so as to make known that His power has no need of creatures for the fulfillment of His designs." She was sending him three more girls "on Tuesday without fail," and she assured him with simplicity that they were "the elite of those who remain after we have taken care of something very urgent nearby."

She was still not completely satisfied with the letters of agreement. "Would it not be apropos, Monsieur," she asked de Vaux anxiously on March 26, "to put back among the articles the one taken out which attests to the freedom of Messieurs les administrateurs to send the girls back and of us to withdraw them, so as to make clear that Monsieur Vincent has never had any design of taking the hospital over?" The fear had been raised by a recent action of Madame Turgis, who, Louise said, "was wrong not to buy what the Fathers wished. If you judge it proper, please command her to make her apologies. I am very fearful lest these gentlemen allow themselves to be persuaded to listen to gossips."

She worried about Madame Turgis's health. "I believe, Monsieur, that she needs some medication to prevent a serious illness," she confided to de Vaux on April 27, "but she must be ordered, for she has a great repugnance to dosing herself." She was grateful for the intimacy of the Abbé's reports: "You have consoled me with what your kindness has taken the trouble to inform me about Sister Marie [Matrilomeau]. I am well aware of her restless mind." The plague still raged in Angers and several of the Sisters, so vulnerable to contagion in the fetid sick wards, fell ill—Marguerite François worst of all. "Please, Monsieur," Louise wrote in anguish, "tell me whether our poor Sister Marguerite is dying or has died happy, for from the news I have of her condition, I cannot hope any other thing than death for her." Even as Louise asked, M. de Vaux was writing the sad news: "The poor deceased died with simplicity and made all the acts of virtue God inspired in her, but the good disposition of her heart was itself an act of many virtues."

Louise suggested to de Vaux that "the mind of our Sister Clémence may be strengthened when the organs of her body, weakened by her sickness and its remedies, are. It is my opinion that a multitude of things should not be asked of her, especially as regards her memory and imagination. Let her go without making meditation for a long time." It was excellent psychiatric advice long before its time. Louise had a really phenomenal knowledge of her daughters and the peculiarities of each and treated them accordingly, because they were indeed, every last one of them, her daughters.

While she was happy that they had a good father in de Vaux, she did not want them to overburden him with their troubles or lean on him too much. On the other hand, she told him, it would be "very wrong for them to wish to hide their difficulties if you, Monsieur, and the gentlemen command otherwise." And she insisted that he must not "always be telling me only the good things about them. Do not be afraid, I beg you, Monsieur, to let me know their failings, too."

Another assembly of the Ladies of Charity to implement their decision taken for the foundlings was held in the latter part of April. It began with a satisfying report on conditions at the Hôtel-Dieu: both the Ladies and the chaplains were performing their duties faithfully; the spiritual instruction of the sick and the personal devotions of the Ladies were being carried out in a most edifying manner; five heretics had also been converted, of whom three had died exemplary deaths.

As for the foundlings, there were natural difficulties caused by the transferral from governmental to private control. Suitable quarters was one problem: some of the children were at the little foundling asylum on the rue des Boulangers, some at La Chapelle, and some still suffered the miserable conditions of La Couche. The major problem was money. Vincent's basic solution was the same as before—trust in God and do what could be done. But he added a further practical suggestion, that the Ladies take up a collection among themselves. "If six of you ladies have for the past ten months kept alive 2,500 poor who would have died in Lorraine, by giving 2,500 livres each month," he pointed out, "what ought we not hope for?"

The motives he urged upon them for undertaking the difficult, nay heroic, task—and herein lies the secret of its eventual success—were entirely spiritual: they were serving God in these babies; they were glorifying Him; they were cooperating with Him in the salvation of souls; they were edifying the whole church and one another and at the same time withdrawing themselves from the spirit of the world; they were blotting out their past sins and preventing present ones; they were guaranteeing themselves a happy death—like Mme Goussault's; they were bringing God's blessing on their families.

The good women sighed, and with the best will in the world they rolled up their sleeves to tackle the enormous task afresh.

Mme de Vertamon, a cousin of Louise, alarmed her companions by reporting that the high justices wished to retain final authority over the foundlings. The report may have been true; if it was, the illustrious gentlemen must have beat a hasty retreat before the aroused and even more illustrious women because they came forward graciously to grant "anything they wished," including the supplying of nurses and financial support in the form of a tax on all merchants. Chancelier Séguier promised to make the offer official with his signature and seal.

Louise suffered a long and serious relapse in May and was in grave danger. As she lay between life and death, her thoughts were continually with the exiles in Angers and through a secretary she kept up her correspondence with de Vaux. Sister Madeleine [Monget] owed a debt "to a good priest, her cousin, who is in town and is pressing hard for payment because he needs it. Just send me her promise [to pay]," she directed the Abbé, "and we will give the order [of payment]." Three days later, on May 29, she was alarmed over the illness of "our poor Sister Elisabeth [Martin]. I am not sure that this is not weakness from a former illness. If it is, Monsieur, I think that, on the advice of a doctor as to her strength, it would be best to send her back to us." To Elisabeth herself she wrote: "How I suffer in your suffering! I would that you sweeten it by the thought that you find yourself in the state in which God wishes you to be . . . Consider, then, that God wants you to be cheerful and at peace . . . Call to mind, dear Sister, that you have been in this condition before and that God gave you back your health when He wishes you to serve Him." Despite her sympathy for the stricken superioress, Louise did not forbear to complain that "you have not written to me by your own hand once since I left. Do so, if you are able. But tell me your troubles very frankly. I will read and understand everything."

There was another crisis over Michel, but the nature of it is obscure. Louise begged Vincent's advice concerning "a reply which I am pressed to give my son," urging her "great need" to see him. He seems to have rebuffed her with the injunction to trust in God, but she returned to the attack with a rare show of Marillac stubbornness, pleading that in this instance he did not understand. "Forgive me my violent apprehension of that one thing I have always feared most in that person of whom I have spoken [her son]," she wrote in extraordinary agitation of mind. "My thoughts on this subject [which increase my grief] are the reason why the consolation God gives me through your kindness is not apparent to you. If you believe that I have had the direction of Divine Providence over my life, in the name of God, my most dear Father, do not abandon me in this need without doing me the charity to make known my delusion to me so that I will not die impenitent." There could be no doubt of the agony gnawing at her heart. "I forgot to ask you very humbly," she continued, "to say holy Mass tomorrow for my son, and to do whatever it pleases God to inspire you to help him out of this great trouble I believe him to be in. You would have great compassion if you could see the thing as I do." Having said what she had to say, she finished with her usual spirit of submission: "I do everything I can to enter into the thoughts you have done me the honor to suggest to me."

Some young girls of Angers, attracted by the selfless dedication of the Sisters, came forward to offer their services as nurses' aides in the hospital. M. l'abbé de Vaux was not sure of Louise's mind in the matter, but he might have known that there would be no jealousy or possessiveness on her part. "I assure you, Monsieur," she wrote, "that I have had great consolation and suffer no displeasure in these good girls who have thought to associate themselves with us in this good work if it is God's will. My desire to have associated with us only those who are truly called and with no temporal interest in view allows for a great deal of flexibility." Her spirit was indeed the spirit of Christ who rebuked those disciples who complained about "outsiders" working miracles in His name.

Marguerite de Gondi, Marquise de Maignelay and sister of the former General of the Galleys, sent Vincent an appeal for help for the poor on her lands at Nanteuil-le-Haudoin. "Some time ago," she began, "I wrote to Mademoiselle Pollalion to ask of Mademoiselle Le Gras whether she could do the charity of supplying a good schoolmistress for the girls of this place; but [stipulated] that she be able to teach a trade, since, if that were not the condition, the inhabitants here would make difficulties about leaving a schoolmaster's where it did not cost much and where girls were taught with boys—a thing sufficiently dangerous, as you know . . . Mademoiselle Le Gras informed Mademoiselle Pollalion that they could send two, one of whom would look after the sick . . . and that they would be subject to change as in other places. We will accept all the conditions that you and she judge proper." The request for the schoolmistress was forgotten a few days later with a crisis that had arisen in the local confraternity. "The servant we have is so charitable," the Marquise wrote in a sarcastic fury, "that, despite the fact that she has been paid up to the sixth of next month, she wishes to leave us at the end of this one, and I do not want to hold her one hour against her will." She begged him to send one of the Sisters at once. They would lodge her and pay a hundred livres for her services. She wrote again three days later to say that they had found a replacement and that he need not send the girl asked for. He and Louise apparently decided to send her anyway, if the Marquise would allow her the time to make a retreat before she left. Mme de Maignelay's reply has been lost, and it is not known whether the girl went.

Louise was up and around again, but far from well. It was her natural condition. Daily life went on much as usual. The new missions of Richelieu and Angers had already proved seedbeds of vocations to the Company, and postulants came also from Beauvais and from some unnamed place as far away as "twenty-two leagues from here." Vincent had heard rumors of complaints that the Sisters at Angers were appropriating some of the foodstuffs given for the poor. Whether the rumors were true or not, he insisted, "we must make a rule that they cannot, under any pretext whatsoever, eat what is set aside for the poor." Louise and he were thinking of replacing the two Sisters at Richelieu, with a further thought of appointing Barbe Angiboust superioress at Angers. In the meantime, he spoke his mind on a matter that had arisen at Richelieu. "It is important," he told Louise, "that your girls . . . should not enter- tain M. Durot or his brother. Everything must be done to let him know politely that it is not expedient for us to have visits except for necessary business."

On July 5, Vincent began that long series of regular conferences to the Sisters at the motherhouse which would end only with his death. He had given them many conferences during the past seven years, but at spo- radic intervals. As he put it, "urgent business has prevented me until now from helping you, but the remorse of conscience which I often feel has caused me to make a resolution to speak to you every fortnight . . ." He defined in this memorable conference, which has been preserved in Louise's own hand, what it meant to be a Daughter of Charity: "To be true Daughters of Charity, it is necessary to have given up everything— father, mother and the hope of establishing a household. The Son of God teaches us this in the Gospel. It is also necessary to give up self, for it we leave all things but retain our own wills, we do not surrender our- selves; nothing has been done. To be Daughters of Charity is to be Daughters of God, daughters who belong entirely to God, for whosoever is in charity is in God and God in him."

Two weeks later, on July 19, he told them:

You have been guided by tradition, my daughters, in all that you have done during these past years but, with the help of God, you shall at some future time be provided with your little rules . . . Reflect, my daughters, on the greatness of God's design in your regard, and the grace He be- stows on you, by even now enabling you to serve so many poor people in so many different places. To do this entails different sorts of regulations. The daughters in Angers have theirs; one sort is needed for those who serve the poor little children, another for those who serve the poor in the parishes, another for those who serve the poor convicts, and still another for those who remain at home, whom you should look upon and love as your own family. And all these rules should be based upon the general rule of which I now wish to speak.

The rule he referred to was the basic and flexible rule composed by Louise in 1634 and explained to the first Sisters by Vincent on July 31 of that same year. Throughout the remainder of July and well into August, he continued his commentary on the rule. This emphasis must have prompted a new attempt to write it in final form, because he was trying at this time to find "some moments for the rule." Later on, he informed

Louise that he had "read what you have given me and find it good. What made it appear otherwise was due to my not distinguishing in my mind among the employments of the girls." Here is further proof that the rule was largely of Louise's authorship. Her own commentaries on it are pungent and reflect not only her practical mind but also the innocent simplicity of the first Sisters.

One of the minor officials of the house was called, appropriately enough, "the awakener." She should have, Louise advised, "a special devotion to her good angel for help in awaking herself a little before four o'clock . . . She must bear in mind that she should not be like the clock she depends on, which does not go whither it calls others, but as she is the first to arouse others, she must also arouse herself, not only to be the first in chapel, but also to where she is going and what she is going to do there."

The portress will be so efficient as "not to let the bell ring twice, prompting herself to diligence by an act of love and by the thought that, if God should send her to purgatory and did her the mercy of releasing her to enter into Paradise, she would be very vexed to be kept waiting to enter." The next prescription involved positive heroism in a woman: she should "guard against curiosity when someone enters and sits down to wait, never seeking news. If they wish to tell her some, she shall adroitly turn the conversation, and if she cannot prevent hearing it, she shall not tell it to the other Sisters . . ."

The cook shall think of "the joy Saint Martha and Saint Joanna of Chusa had when they prepared a meal for Our Lord . . ." She shall take such pride in her cooking as to "make up for the better morsels eaten elsewhere." When she ladles out the food as well, she shall "give the Sisters what is necessary, and save the leftovers, charity requiring the one and the virtue of poverty the other. And when she notices that some Sisters are unwell or have no appetite, she shall give them the best and what she judges good for their indisposition." Louise noted wisely that she will "need great charity and prudence not to give more to some than to others . . . If she knows that a certain Sister, by temperament, thinks that she needs something different from what is given to her, she should ask the Sister superioress whether she should satisfy her . . ." When a Sister is really sick, that is a different matter: then she must "take special pains to make good soups, realizing that it is rather the care with which it is cooked than the quantity of food that renders it palable to the sick."

Louise, knowing the vagaries of human nature, especially of women living in community, warned the poor cook "not to be dejected or upset at the complaints some Sisters might make about the food, not even if these malcontents accuse her of treating herself better than others . . ." At such time she should remember "how much they murmured against Our Lord" and how He rejoiced at it, "not considering them blamable."

The Sister assigned to wait on table shall "take great care not to make noise in the refectory, and shall let in neither dog nor cat nor chicken . . ."

The Sister infirmarian is enjoined to practice a special meekness, for Louise knew well that, as often as not, "it could happen that the sick might complain about her; in which case she should show no resentment, excusing them because of their illness and the restlessness they suffer and even looking for some means of doing what they wish . . ." And if, through impatience, the sick Sisters should speak rudely to her, "she should act as if she had not heard it or she should sweetly beg pardon, honoring the reproaches the Jews made Our Lord when He healed their sick on the sabbaths." At the same time the infirmarian was to encourage her sick Sisters to be greatly submissive to the will of God, to have confidence in His love, and to make good use of their sufferings. And Louise suggested this beautiful exhortation: "Sister, do you not think, lying there in your bed, of the sufferings of our sick poor, often alone as they are on their straw, without fire, without sheets, without covering, without any comfort or consolation? Are you not happy in the favors God has given you?"

The Sisters who assisted the Ladies of Charity at the Hôtel-Dieu and the foundling asylum were obliged to "a greater perfection than the others, especially because of the example of humility and charity given them by persons of quality, and by reason of the purity and obedience preached to them by the poor little innocents through their presence alone."

While the Sisters who engaged in specific works already had more or less detailed rules, the general rule of the Company was not to be written in its final form for some years, despite Vincent's good intentions. In the meantime they were, he said, honoring "the way in which the Son of God acted when He established His Church, for He spent thirty years of His life without appearing in public, labored for only three years, and left nothing in writing to His Apostles."

There is no precise date for the start of the Company's apostolate to the galley slaves, but it certainly began early in 1640. One day in February, Vincent had sent Louise, still detained at Angers, a note only two lines in length: "We are awaiting you with the affection that Our Lord knows. You must come for the galley slaves." M. Cornuel's bequest had at last made it possible to enlist the Daughters in the work.

The Ladies of the Charity of Saint-Nicolas-du-Chardonnet had lent their assistance a few years back, and the Company of the Blessed Sacrament had done what it could but was driven off by the parish priests, who resented this trespass on their domain but were doing nothing themselves to help these most abandoned of their parishioners. Only when, through Vincent's influence, these poor wretches were moved to the prison of La Tournelle in the parish of Saint-Nicolas did they receive anything approaching adequate spiritual aid from the good, zealous priests there.

The work with the galley slaves was a fearsome work indeed. The misery of these outcasts is beyond the imagination of our comfortable age. They were chained in dark, airless dungeons without the mercy of a moment's sight of the blue sky or a restorative breath of clean air. They ate bread and drank water because they could not afford to buy the simplest food at the exorbitant prices extorted by the jailers. Worst of all, there was no hope of even eventual release, because the warden conveniently forgot to write down alongside their names the length of their sentences. It is no wonder that they despaired and blasphemed. It is no wonder that they turned brutish and savage and fierce like the most crazed of animals, or that their jailers became as degraded as they and attacked them wildly at will.

It is eloquent testimony to the character of the first Daughters of Charity that Vincent and Louise sent them to minister to such depraved beasts. "Although the work with the galley slaves is one of the most difficult and dangerous, both because of handling money and because of the nature of the persons you must mix with there," Louise warned the Sisters selected for this apostolate, "it is also one of the most meritorious and pleasing to God when it is done as it should be, because you exercise in a high degree the corporal and spiritual works of mercy for the most miserable in body and soul you could possibly imagine. That is why those called by God to this holy work ought on the one hand to try to render themselves worthy by the practice of the virtues required for it and by an exact observance of their rules, and on the other to excite themselves to and possess great confidence in Our Lord Jesus

Christ . . ." It was a service done "to His own Person, and consequently He will not fail to supply in return the graces necessary to sur-
mount all difficulties they might encounter in it, to say nothing of the
rich crown reserved for them in heaven."

She urged upon the Sisters, as their basic safeguard, "a great modesty
and reserve." They should pretend not to hear the mockery directed at
them. They should respond to insolence either by keeping in good coun-
tenance or by leaving the room. Such control required heroic patience,
she admitted, but it could be achieved through prayer for the offenders,
"as Saint Stephen prayed for those who stoned him." They must never
lose control to the point of complaining or answering back as rudely as
the prisoners themselves; on the contrary, they should show them nothing but sweetness and compassion, "seeing their pitiable state." This was
the core of Christianity, which could be reached only by those completely committed to it.

While the galley slaves must have first consideration—with Louise the
poor always came first—the safety of her daughters was certainly not
forgotten. They must, she urged with that wise maternal heart of hers,
say special prayers to the Holy Spirit several times a day "in order to
cleanse well their thoughts, words, and actions, particularly in time of
temptation to impurity if it should come." She knew well that it was
their greatest danger amid such brutish and obscene men. But they must
not be afraid. They were "like the rays of the sun which pass continually
through dung without being the least soiled." God would preserve them
as He did "the three children in the fiery furnace." It is fascinating how
she spoke always to these innocent children of the fields in the child's
language of pictures and invariably chose the most graphic.

Her lessons were well learned. Years later, Sister Jeanne Luce testified
of Barbe Angiboust, in one of those delightful dialogues with Vincent
that were a feature of his conferences: " 'Father, I lived with her in the
Hospital for Convicts. She showed great patience in bearing with the
annoyances that had to be encountered there on account of the bad
temper of those men. For, although they were sometimes so angry with
her as to throw soup and meat on the ground, shouting at her whatever
their impatience suggested, she bore it all without saying a word and
gathered up what they had thrown down, looking just as pleasant as if
they had not said or done anything to her.'

" 'Oh, what a feat! [Vincent exclaimed] to appear as pleasant to them
as she had previously been.'

" 'Father, not only that, but on five or six occasions she prevented the jailers from beating them.' "

Then the charism of the teacher seized the old man (it was in 1658) and he began to instruct a second generation of servants of the poor from the living textbook of the first: "Well, now, Sisters, if there are any here . . . who wished to oppose those poor men, rendering them evil for evil and insult for insult, they should feel very sorry, seeing that one of your Sisters who wore the same habit as yourselves, when the meat which she brought them was thrown at her, never said a word, and would not allow the jailers to beat the prisoners . . . Learn from our Sister how to bear patiently with the poor. When Our Lord was loaded with insults, He made no reply, but it is said of Him that He was like a lamb led to the slaughter, never opening His mouth or complaining. Learn then from Him never to reply to insults." And he finished with a piece of practical wisdom: "If you act otherwise, you will only embitter men and give them reason to offend God all the more."

While the law seems callously to have abandoned the galley slaves to their fate, it often busied itself with the foundlings. Sometimes the unfortunate women who abandoned their ill-gotten babies were caught in the act and punished with a lawsuit by the high justices. Louise wrote to Vincent on October 1 about such a case: "Friends of the mother of one of our infants are pressing to settle the suits instituted against her . . . A benefactor and the master of the woman [a serving girl] have entered the affair." Louise wanted to know whether, "as an example to others, the ways of justice should not be allowed to take their course, which would certainly have shock value, or whether to take the kinder way of allowing her to pay the expenses incurred and to take her child back . . ." The woman, she assured him, "would do the child no harm, but would raise him as she should, and would give the house an alms if I should name the sum." Louise leaned to the latter course. Vincent agreed, but cautioned her, in order to avoid further trouble, to consult the Ladies of Charity.

In the same letter she informed him that Madame Turgis had returned from Angers and brought another postulant with her. There had been trouble in the house at Saint-Germain-en-Laye and Louise informed the superioress firmly that "we cannot keep discontented people in the house, or anyone who will disedify the other Sisters." If the culprit wished to stay, she "should change her ways," and know that she was "in no condition to serve the poor, at least for several years."

The move from their present motherhouse was now determined upon. Vincent had advertised the fact in the summer. But Louise had no intention of leaving what she had until she found something better. She was, therefore, upset when Madame de Villeneuve, who was also house-hunting, was told of "a house at La Chapelle." Louise did not know, she informed Vincent, whether the house in question "might not be ours." If so, she asked, "wouldn't it be wise to list all its inconveniences for you, and what it can accommodate, before leaving it, so that we will have no regrets?"

Vincent bade her go to the landlord immediately to ask whether the house had been put on the market. In the meantime, he assured her, he had someone looking for a better house in La Chapelle.

Public knowledge that the Sisters were thinking of moving brought the usual horde of salesmen, and Vincent warned her against them: "I would have nothing to do with the lumber merchant. His kind are prone to ruin themselves and I have never known them, except for one at Troyes, not to fall in the end flat on their faces. As for the other fellow, I don't know what to say, except that this quantity of new houses makes me suspect that he is a contractor, and that type ordinarily allow their businesses to fall into confusion." He was in great hopes that M. le commandeur de Sillery, who had died on September 26, had left them enough in his will "for the house we must buy for the girls."

On All Saints' Day he apprised her of "a little house at La Villette. There is only an acre and a half, including house and garden . . . It is the last house in the village . . . on the church side and not as far from it as your present house is. They are talking about four or five thousand francs. It has a complex of one or two lodgings with barn and stable in the manner of the country, and air on one side and in the rear. It is the only place for sale at La Villette. See what you think of it."

On November 28 Louise paused in her busy life to look back with gratitude on the years of the Company. She reminded Vincent content-edly:

> It was on such a day as tomorrow that the first girls began to live in community, even though they did so poorly for five or seven years. This evening a thought came to me that causes me to rejoice, which is that by the grace of God they are better than they were at the beginning, that, after the few years which I hope remain to me on earth, those God will give will draw upon these even more blessings because of the good

example these have given them. It is what I wish with all my heart and ask of our good God, and will until my last hour.

It was a modest—and proud—appraisal. The same glow of achievement lay in Vincent's heart and he expressed it in reply with the utmost simplicity: "Never have I been as full of the realization of the hand of God upon your daughters as lately."

XII

Army Nurses
and Schoolteachers

It would never have crossed the minds of either Vincent or Louise that
it was the force of their own dedication and the communication of their
own hard rule of life that had made Jeanne d'Arcs of charity out of the
rawboned girls who had come trustfully to them with nothing to offer
but strong backs and good will. Nor would it have occurred to either of
them that the leap to high sanctity had been accomplished the more
easily because of their solicitude for every need and care of their daughters, even the weakest.

Thus Vincent wrote his chagrin to Louise that the Ladies of the Charity of Saint-Laurent "are complaining about Marie and her ways and
want someone else. How can we dismiss her . . . ?" He was especially
understanding and patient with newcomers. He recommended that one
of them be given "a lot of work to channel her energies. She is a very
good girl with a good reputation in her own country who has persever-
ingly served her mistress for seven or eight years . . . Some spirits do
not adjust at first to all the little regularities. Time takes care of everything."

One of the "little regularities" that took getting used to was the uniformity of dress, and Vincent was at a loss with a "good Angevin girl"
who could not grasp its importance. "I think we shall have to wait a bit,"
was all he could say.

Dress was not the most important problem with recruits from Anjou.
The Parisian climate did not agree with them: it was hard to exchange
the sunshine of the Loire Valley for the cold and dampness of the capital. In welcoming two more girls sent by Abbé de Vaux, Louise expressed the hope "that they will escape the weaknesses to which Angers
girls who have come to this climate are subject . . ." Two who had

come earlier "have been incurably ill since their arrival . . . and are now on their deathbeds."

The problem was especially vexing because Anjou was very fertile in vocations to the Company. Louise had, indeed, to remind the good Abbé of the importance of refusing candidates who were "not proper." He should be on his guard, she cautioned, "lest it be a desire to see Paris that prompts them to come, or a need to insure their livelihood." She insisted that they be "very strong." Six had presented themselves recently "of which some were rather weak and others young. They were very good girls but not ready to render the total service necessary for the poor."

Always jealous of her daughters' rights, especially their right to privacy, she communicated to de Vaux her dissatisfaction with the arrangement for a certain Mme Terrier to live at the hospital. "Is there no way of shutting the gate of the alley which separates her room from the Sisters' small kitchen?" she asked. As for a doctor's complaint that the Sisters were not accompanying him on his hospital rounds, she stoutly defended them against it: "That is Monsieur Nabulo's chore and he does not fail to perform it, as I understand, and he is properly careful to let the Sisters know the needs of the sick."

Vincent had a request for an entirely new work: Sisters were needed at Sedan to nurse wounded soldiers. "I have written that perhaps you could go there [to look over the situation]," he told Louise, but he admitted practically that it would be foolish for her to "expose yourself to so much danger at such a season as this." He was particularly anxious to answer this call for a reason beyond the care of the soldiers: the Sedan country was "a new Christianity. M. le duc and Madame la duchesse [de Bouillon] are recent Catholics. Heresy established its throne in that principality ninety years ago. Oh, how I wish you were in good health! But winter is here. We mustn't think about it."

Even though, perforce, he put aside all thought of sending Louise herself to Sedan, he persisted in his determination to send a Sister there as soon as possible. On January 31, 1641, he mentioned Marie Joly for the work and instructed Louise to cast about for someone to replace her at Saint-Germain-l'Auxerrois because "she should leave in five or six days." It was the beginning of that nursing apostolate in the wars of the world which would later earn the Sisters, notably in the Crimean and the American civil wars, the title "Angels of the Battlefield."

The urgent need at Sedan made Vincent act with uncharacteristic haste and the inevitable mistakes attendant on such a course rose to plague him. The curé and the Ladies of the Confraternity of Saint-Germain were not at all happy about losing Marie but did not dare oppose Vincent in the matter. When her replacement, probably the only Sister available, proved woefully inadequate, they soon found their tongues and descended upon Saint-Lazare with "great remonstrances." Vincent ungallantly shifted the blame and the responsibility to Louise. The hapless girl sent to Saint-Germain, he said, "doesn't know anything, not even where the house of the ladies is . . . It is up to you to find some means of withdrawing her and of putting someone in her place or, better, to give them yet another one who knows how to prepare the medicines and has had some experience. This proves how necessary it is that you move to this parish [Saint-Laurent] and how trained all your girls must be."

Louise in reply had her own complaints. Marie had returned to La Chapelle "with full good will" but worn out with all the work she had had at Saint-Germain. "I am very apprehensive of her going [to Sedan] all alone and no longer having the company of her Sisters," even though "she is a good sort" who would go "without a murmur," Louise wrote. "The resolution which I recollect your taking never to send out a Sister alone has so taken possession of my mind that it appears necessary to me that someone go with her." It was the perfect riposte, but Louise was not satisfied until she had buttressed it with reasons which stand as a beautiful monument to her concern for her daughters: "She could fall sick on the roads, or encounter wicked persons who, judging evil of her, could make it unpleasant for her. And, since everyone has feelings and it is no little thing that these good girls have left everything, she could suffer much opposition, and not being able to comfort herself, there is danger of discouragement; and I fear, too, that that would cause others to say that no one bothers much about these girls since they leave them entirely alone." As far as living expenses, the good people of Sedan need be responsible only for the one they asked for, who could share her food with the other, and they "could earn the rest," for example, by taking in laundry.

She had in mind for Marie's companion "big Sister Claire . . . She has a docile enough temperament and I think they would get on well together." The drawback was that she could not read, and perhaps it would be better to send someone who could, because such a one "could hold school for the poor little girls."

Vincent capitulated in favor of sending two Sisters to Sedan and, since Claire could not read, a third who was "less needed in this city [Paris]." The Ladies of Saint-Germain had asked for a certain Sister who had been stationed there formerly, but Louise would not give them their way. She sent Françoise Carcireux and Vincent acquiesced in her decision.

The motherhouse was becoming less and less adequate for the growing Company, and Louise more and more anxious to move. She and Vincent had decided, as mentioned previously, to locate the new motherhouse near Saint-Lazare in the parish of Saint-Laurent as most convenient for both of them in their busy lives, and were willing to rent while waiting for the opportunity to buy.

A flare-up of his perennial fever had prevented Vincent from pursuing the matter. It was probably his illness that caused his annoyance at what he considered her importunity: "I see you carried away by human sentiments in that, finding me ill, you think that all is lost for lack of a house. Oh, woman of little faith and submission to the direction and example of Jesus Christ! This Savior of the world relies on His Father for the regulations and affairs of the whole Church, and you think He will fail us as regards a handful of girls whom his Providence has manifestly raised up and brought together! Go, Mademoiselle, and humble yourself very low before God."

There can be no doubt that the problem of the house was a thorn in his side, because a short time later he was writing again: "We must continue to pray for the house, which does not trouble me so much as [to find] the means of establishing you here [Saint-Laurent] immediately by renting. O Jésus! Mademoiselle, your work does not depend on a house but rather on the continuation of God's blessing on it."

Despite the cramped quarters, lay retreats were still being conducted at La Chapelle and efforts were made even to tailor the spiritual exercises to the special needs of individuals. Thus Vincent snatched a few minutes from his crowded day to outline points of meditation for a young girl who was about to be married. He was anxious to know at the end of February whether Louise's health would permit her to direct the retreats of Mme Le Roux and Mme Lotin, and reminded her that the latter great lady was used to meat at her meals. Retreatants were not admitted sight unseen. Louise asked Vincent about a certain lady whose name she did not know that had been recommended by the curé of Saint-Germain-l'Auxerrois; Vincent cautioned her not to receive her until she had learned her name and credentials. On the other hand, he requested her to admit "an actress who wishes to leave off her way of life and retire to the country" and to mark the change by a retreat.

The Company suffered another defection at this time in the person of Sister Maurice, who sent for her mother to come to Saint-Sulpice and take her home. Vincent was with the Duchesse d'Aiguillon when the news was brought, and that great lady cried out that "it was the bad treatment the girls received in the parish and that she would want to leave, too." The parish of Saint-Sulpice had, indeed, the worst reputation in Paris.

Barbe Angiboust had been recalled from Richelieu and was sent now to replace a Sister who had been proven unfit for the work of the galley slaves, although Vincent expressed his fear that the work might be too much for Barbe's physical strength.

He was much edified by "a good demoiselle from Arras" who had come to join the Company, and found her "very interior," so much so that he wondered how she might take to a life of activity. He fully believed, however, that "the Lord will supply for her needs." He was not so sure about a Marguerite de Turenne, who had come from Saché: he found her "too vacillating," but instructed Louise to "speak with her, and if you are still satisfied with her you can admit her." Two others, one from Liancourt and one from Nanteuil, were put off.

Although Louise wore the simple gray serge dress of her daughters, Vincent was loth to allow her, because of her frail health, to put off her noble widow's coiffe of black, which entirely covered her head and neck, in favor of the tight white cap the other Sisters wore. Her "singularity" was a great humiliation to her and, during her Pentecost retreat of 1640, she decided to exchange her coiffe for the headdress of the others. She fell immediately and violently ill. Vincent consoled her in a note that said "I told you so" and "don't blame me" in the most charming manner possible. "Blessed be God, Mademoiselle," he wrote, "for all He has been able to do for you in your retreat, and for depriving me of the consolation of seeing you during it. I am well enough, thanks be to God, and able to offer you tomorrow to Our Lord in the new exterior and interior state to which the divine love has disposed you. He supplied for and did divinely what men could not do humanly. Did He perhaps permit on purpose that I should not see you, so that I should not put my scythe in the harvest? I pray that He animate you wholly with His spirit, and your two daughters also, all three of you ill together."

Louise was not the only one whose health was affected by the lack of protection afforded by the cap, or *toquois*. Vincent, despite his sympathy for the problems of frailer Sisters, held strictly to a uniformity of headdress. In 1641, for example, he told Louise to warn Jeanne Lepeintre against the danger of vanity in supplementing her cap with a handkerchief or bandanna. In 1646, however, he saw a solution to the problem of giving the more infirm better protection from the elements while preserving the peasant "look," by allowing them to wear the white cornette affected by certain peasant women. In 1685, M. Joly (third superior general) made the cornette obligatory for all, and its gleaming white wings became the Sisters' "trademark" and a familiar symbol of charity until a few years ago when the Sisters adopted a blue coiffe reminiscent of Louise's own.

Elisabeth Martin's health had grown much worse and Louise was heartsick, she told Abbé de Vaux, at being separated from her in her need, for "I believe her to be a good and true servant of God." She decided that it was necessary to replace her as superioress at Angers and told de Vaux to choose between Cécile-Agnès Angiboust and Madeleine Monget. He chose Sister Madeleine, and Louise, writing to Sister Elisabeth, hinted delicately that she could help the transition of administration and discourage any lack of loyalty toward her successor: "Be very careful, I beg you, and do not trouble yourself about what goes on in the hospital when you are not there. If the Sisters speak to you in a particular way, stir up in them affection for and confidence in Sister Madeleine."

Mme Pelletier had had two years to repent of her pride and now sought readmission to the Company. Vincent decided to take her back, but Louise was reluctant. "I am sending your reply to Madame Pelletier by Sister Turgis," she wrote obediently, "but I am so wicked that I have very much wished this word of her return so soon had not been given."

Louise's own poor opinion of herself led her at times into fits of despondence over the inevitable failings of her daughters. It was not a true despondence—her faith was too real for that, and her wretched health probably had as much to do with it as anything—but it allowed her to unburden her heart to Vincent for the human-divine comfort from a friend that the holiest soul occasionally needs. Thus she wrote now: "My little experience and capability prevent me from making Your Charity foresee the dangers I often see of the whole Company perishing little by little almost as soon as it is established, the which often gives me Agar's fears for the death of her son lest she [have to] watch him die—but more justly than she, since my sins are the cause of all these disorders. I very humbly beg your pardon for the overload of trouble I give you. If I thought only of the will of God I would try to view all these dangers in peace . . ."

The negligible quality of her feelings was underscored by the important work assumed by the Company in May. In a formal petition to M. des Roches, Chantre de Notre-Dame de Paris, dated May 9, 1641, "Louise de Marillac, widow of Monsieur Le Gras, Secretary to the Queen Mother of the King, calling attention to the large number of poor in the Faubourg Saint-Denis," expressed the desire "to busy herself with their instruction." She gave as her reason the fear that their ignorance would lead to "the malice which renders them incapable of cooperating with the grace of salvation." There were, she admitted, the *Petites Écoles*, but the poor had no money for tuition, and in any case the rich did not want them to mingle with their own children. At the end her feelings got the better of her and she forgot the legal language to tell M. des Roches fervently that, if he would grant her request, "these souls bought with the Blood of the Son of God will be under obligation to pray for you, Monsieur, in time and eternity."

She waited three weeks for his reply, but when it came it was, to her great joy, favorable. In virtue of his authority over all "the *Petites Écoles* of the city, the faubourgs, and the suburbs of Paris," and "after our own inquiry, communication with your curé [of Saint-Laurent], the evidence of all others worthy of credence, and with knowledge of your life, morals and Catholic religion, we grant you the necessary license and give you the faculty of opening and operating schools in the aforesaid Saint-Lazare section of the Faubourg Saint-Denis, charging you to instruct poor girls only and no others, and to raise them in good morals, grammatical letters and other pious and upright exercises, having previously accepted your word to run the aforesaid schools diligently and faithfully according to our statutes and ordinances."

Thus were inaugurated the same free schools for the poor of Paris that the poor of the villages had long enjoyed.

Through his friendship with Louise, M. l'abbé de Vaux had become interested in seeing her uncle Michel's translations of the Psalms and the Book of Job, and had asked her to procure them for him. She did not know whether the Psalms were still in print, she informed him, but since "my son tells me that Monsieur your nephew will be returning imme-

diately, I will entrust him with the copy I have if I cannot find another."
The translation of Job, she said, had never been published. The "devils
of Loudun" were still at their work there, and de Vaux's interest in them
had not lessened. He shared it, in fact, with all of France, and Louise
was not above satisfying her own curiosity. "I would be very pleased,"
she told him, "to learn from you on your return from Loudun some
truth about that place."

On August 7 Louise had a letter from Marie Joly at the soldiers' hospital in Sedan which gave her great happiness. "I have read from it to our
Sisters everything that could encourage them by her example," she informed Vincent. "They strike me, as they say, like soldiers at the sound
of the alarm, especially Sister Henriette, who, although she is in retreat,
would rather leave today than tomorrow." She asked him to write Marie
some words of encouragement, but he felt that it would be "dangerous"
to write—perhaps because of war censorship. He suggested that they
"wait a little until I have seen M. le comte's chaplain."

Louise asked a personal favor of Vincent—that she be able to speak to
him "by Saturday or Sunday at the latest, in order to prepare myself to
begin my fifty-first year, which I enter upon on Monday, the feast of St.
Clare, if God spares me." Vincent was leaving for Nanterre the next
morning, Thursday, and would not be back until Sunday evening; "after
that we will have the pleasure of seeing you."

At the end of the summer he made a trip to Richelieu and returned
with disturbing news. Elisabeth Martin (whom Vincent and Louise
often called Isabelle) had been sent there to recuperate, replacing Barbe
Angiboust as superioress. Vincent found her "perfectly well in body, but
she is unhappy living in a house where there is no observance. Her companion is a poor creature. I don't know whether there might be a means
of finding her a position. She has only four or five girls [in the school]
and does not visit the sick. What most mortifies Isabelle, our good Sister, is that she herself does not visit the sick because for some time they
have employed her in ministering to forty or fifty ordinands, concerning
which situation I have instructed M. Lambert that he is not to employ
her in such a manner any longer. This good girl seems to live for her
return here or to Angers."

A suitable new motherhouse for the Sisters had been found at last. It
was actually two houses joined together and stood on rue Faubourg-Saint-
Denis opposite the Church of Saint-Lazare. One consisted of "a cellar,
two low halls, four chambers, of which two were below and two above, a

garret, a stable, a courtyard enclosed with walls and in the courtyard a well." The other contained "a low hall, an attendant kitchen, a large chamber, two paneled chambers with an attic above covered with tiles, a porte-cochère serving as the entrance to both houses. There is a porch with a slate roof, and walls enclose the whole property."

The Ladies of Charity had considered a suggestion of Mme de Lamoignon to invest capital of 45,000 livres and to rent a house for the Sisters with the interest; but that seems to have been before this house was found at a sales price of 12,000 livres. It is not known whether the Ladies had a share in its financing.

The deed of sale was signed on September 6, 1641, by the owners, a bourgeois named Jean du Maretz and his wife, and by the Congregation of the Mission as the purchaser. The signatories for the Congregation were Vincent de Paul, Antoine Portail, Antoine Lucas, Jean Dehorgny, François Soufliers, Léonard Boucher, and René Alméras. The down payment was 6,600 livres, with the agreement to pay 300 livres a year interest on the remainder. The Congregation sold the house to the Company of the Daughters of Charity in 1653. It was to be the mother-house of the Company until the Sisters were dispersed and the house confiscated during the French Revolution. Napoleon allowed the Sisters to regroup in 1800 and gave them a house on the rue de Vieux-Colombier. In 1815 they moved to their present motherhouse at 140, rue du Bac, the former town house of the Comtes de la Vallière.

On October 15 Vincent gave the Sisters a conference "for no other purpose than to teach you about the Jubilee" that Pope Urban VIII had proclaimed because of the "universal need for it which is apparent throughout the whole Christian world." The purpose of the Jubilee, Vincent told the Sisters, was to supply them "with the means to recover God's grace which we have lost by sin, to recoup our strength and to compensate for the good we might but have not done." For them it meant a serious examination of conscience. "Are you better now than when you entered the community . . . ? Have you not lost much if for the last four, seven or eight years you have not advanced in the spiritual life, in the correction of your faults and the mortification of your senses?" One of the Sisters raised the difficulty of finding the time to make her meditation, and Louise, who took down the conference, noted that "because the service of the sick often prevents Sisters in parishes from making their prayer, M. Vincent with his usual charity suggested that the hours of rising and retiring should be changed."

With little fanfare, apparently, another foundation had been made at Fontenay-aux-Roses. The first mention of it is a casual reference in a letter of Vincent's to Louise in October: "A Fontenay man has told me marvels in praise of your poor girls."

A letter of this period is the earliest example of a form of correspondence Louise employed when Vincent was especially busy or ill. She would number a series of questions to which she wanted replies, and he would write his answers between the lines or in the margin. For example, she wrote: "I forgot to tell you that Madame Traversay has sent to ask me to remind you about the galley slaves' paper to be taken to Monsieur le procureur général"; and Vincent replied, "I will send the paper to Madame Traversay." One of the new recruits at Saint-Lazare, "a poor little man," Louise called him, "had in his great goodness and simplicity" been advising one of the Sisters, a fellow Norman, and had instructed her to call on him; but "I have not dared give her permission without your order. He also gave her some statues, but I think he himself was not permitted to have them. I have held them awaiting your order. This priest is new here and did that through simplicity," Vincent noted on the margin. "You did right to hold the statues."

The next matter was much more important: M. l'abbé de Vaux had been prompted by the episcopal approval of a new community in Angers to ask "whether it would not be fitting for Messieurs les administrateurs to ask Monseigneur d'Angers to approve the service and house of the Sisters at the hospital. The Sisters excuse themselves from speaking to him until a trial has been made, for fear that the Fathers might get the idea of wanting them to be religious." Louise herself was afraid that, "now that Sister Elisabeth is no longer there, the rest might be easily persuaded." In his reply Vincent pointed out that the Sisters did not need the same kind of approval as the new religious. "In the meantime it must be remembered that Monseigneur d'Angers has given his approval to these girls; otherwise they couldn't stay there." The administrators should do nothing until Sister Elisabeth's return.

In a postscript Louise made mention of "her good fortune in seeing Madame Chantal." It was that saint's last visit to her daughters in Paris; within a few weeks she was dead. The other saint, Louise, in her humble pleasure at the visit, had only amazement "at what our good God does for me who am so faithless to Him and so full of sins."

A note of this period also gives the first evidence of a custom of centuries, now fallen into opprobrium, of superiors opening the mail of their "subjects"—an appelation equally out of fashion. "Here are our Sister Marie's letters, which I have judged it appropriate to open," Vincent wrote. "After you have seen them, enclose them in an envelope, please, with two lines in your hand to these ladies to the effect that I have opened them because it is the custom that we see the letters our girls write and receive."

Life was getting more and more complicated both for Louise and for him. She was off on another round of visitations, now of a more personal nature than her visitations of the Charities, because she went as religious superior of an ever growing number of houses. "Are you angry with me for not having my news since your return?" Vincent asked her. "The continual entanglements I have here have prevented my going to see you. Today I intended to visit Monsieur Villecot, but with the hour for me to go to Saint-Marie [convent of the Visitation] on top of me before I knew it, I did not go. Meanwhile, I hope you will excuse me . . ."

Mme de Chantal died on December 13. Before she left Paris in the early part of November she had had a last long consultation with Vincent, her director and friend, and superior of her Parisian monasteries for the past twenty years. She had asked him to prepare her for death and had made a general confession. "Monsieur Vincent is a saint," she had written afterward to the motherhouse at Annecy. News of her last illness had reached Vincent close on the actual moment of her death and he solemnly swore to what followed, speaking of himself humbly in the third person:

> This individual [himself] told me that, having news of the extremity of the illness of our deceased, he fell on his knees to pray to God for her, and that the first thought that came to him was to make an act of contrition for the sins she had committed and ordinarily commits, and that immediately afterward there appeared to him a little globe of fire which rose from the earth and merged in the upper region of the air with another larger and more luminous globe, and the two of them reduced to one were raised higher, entering and blazing within another globe infinitely greater and more luminous than the others, and that he was let know interiorly that the first globe was the soul of our worthy Mother, the second that of our blessed Father [François de Sales], and the other the Divine Essence, that the soul of our worthy Mother had been reunited with that of our blessed Father and the two of them with God their Sovereign Principle.
>
> He said further that, celebrating holy Mass for our worthy Mother immediately upon word of her happy passing, and being at the second

Memento where the dead are prayed for, he thought it well to pray for her, since she might be in purgatory because of certain words she had spoken some time ago which seemed to contain venial sin, and on the instant he saw the vision again, the same globes and their union, and there dwelt in him the interior sentiment that this soul was blessed, that she had no need of prayers.

Vincent forgot, in attempting to disguise his identity in this disposition written just before his death, that he had identified himself as the seer of this vision shortly after it occurred, in a letter to Bernard Codoing. It is the only supernatural happening recorded in the lifetime of this active saint.

He used the occasion of a funeral service held for Mme de Chantal in Paris to console Louise for slights she had suffered from the officers of one of the Charities. "You will suffer many others . . . if you live, which I hope," he told her. "We were informed yesterday at the obsequies for the late Madame de Chantal that one of her own religious had spoken ill of her throughout twenty years."

During a conference-dialogue held on the feast of the Epiphany, in 1642, Vincent learned that certain Sisters were scandalized by the defections in the Company, especially when the defectors had been members almost from the beginning. "My daughters," he explained gently, "no one should be surprised at the fact that some Sisters have left. You know quite well how patiently they have been borne with: sometimes they were changed to another house, sometimes Sisters were changed because it was thought they would get on better with certain Sisters than with others; they were even assigned to the villages to see whether in any way they could be induced to persevere in their vocation. If, after all, they could not acquire self-control, would you wish to keep them at the risk of harming the whole community?"

Other Sisters were downcast because people jeered at their vocation and told them they were wasting their time and even that they were "shirkers" who "remained in the Company to lead an easy life." Vincent instructed them to reply to such scoffers simply: "We desire to serve God faithfully, and also the poor at the expense of ourselves."

M. l'abbé de Vaux had asked Louise's opinion of certain devotional exercises the Sisters at Angers wished to adopt. "You embarrass me, Monsieur," she replied, "to wish my poor advice to interfere with the direction your goodness should give our Sisters . . ." Nonetheless, she gave it obediently and humbly: "I believe Sister Madeleine could easily say two decades of the chaplet a day, which with the three on Saturday would make a Rosary a week. As for sleeping on straw, that seems to me more the shadow of mortification than the reality. As for our Sister who wishes to join the Confraternity of Saint Francis, that would oblige her to go out, and it seems to me that the Company they belong to places them in all other confraternities. Nevertheless, Monsieur, if you do not find it inconvenient for her to go out, there is nothing here prohibited by the rules . . . I am very opposed to what you say about the one who asks for penitential cinctures" for the Sisters, adding that she believed some of them already had them. "Your goodness will please avail them of these when you judge fitting. There are so many circumstances to consider in this matter that no definite rule can be made." But they were never to fail to observe "the fasts of the Church and abstinence on Wednesdays."

"It would be injurious, I think, for the Sisters to go into the sick wards in the morning without eating," she continued with the advice de Vaux had requested of her. "On fast days I think they can get by with the help of a little wine or by putting up with the inconvenience . . . As for those who ask to hear Mass outside the house, they cannot do so if a Mass is said in the hospital at nine or ten o'clock. This is the practice at the Hôtel-Dieu, for I am afraid of the habit of going out."

As has been seen, the hospital administrators could be petty in their complaints about the Sisters, and on such occasions Louise, like the true mother she was, rose quickly to their defense. For example, on January 28, 1642, she informed de Vaux that "our Sister Madeleine does not speak of the faults of which they accuse them, so I find it difficult to see how they could do better than they are doing, in light of the fact that they have too many people ordering them around. One of the things I told these Messieurs les Maîtres was that they would never be fully satisfied with the service our Sisters render the sick if they did not let them do it, for too often one commands and another forbids . . . I am sure that there is still some envy breeding these murmurs in the town."

A Sister named Anne who had been sent to Fontenay now refused a transfer to another mission and Louise sent Vincent word that there might be a lawsuit over it "because Monsieur du Ruisseau and the principal citizens seem to be the ones who wish to keep her there." Things did not come to such a pass. The girl was persuaded to return to the motherhouse and after a retreat regained "more than ever her will to live and die a Daughter of Charity." Louise wondered whether the girl had been talking to her namesake, Anne Hardemont, who had been imploring a change from the notorious Charity of Saint-Sulpice. Although Louise freely admitted that "the gentlemen involved in this Charity have great contempt for them [the Sisters]," she could do little about the situation at the moment except to encourage Anne to suffer it for the sake of the work.

Since Vincent was about to leave for Richeleu and Louise had a great many questions to ask him—twenty in all—she sent him a questionnaire this time, with space between the questions for the answers. Perversely enough, he wrote most of his replies in the margin! Should Sister Henriette (who had shown such enthusiasm for nursing wounded soldiers) be sent to Sedan along with Sister Gillette (Joly, sister to Marie)? *I think so.* Should Sister Barbe Angiboust, who was ill, remain with the galley slaves or should a third Sister be supplied to make things easier for her? *I think you should do so* (send a third) *in any case. You will need only two in a few days. The prisoners will be leaving soon* (for Marseilles). What should be done about withdrawing Sister Anne from Saint-Sulpice? *Take care of it.* What was to be done about Sisters who speak about leaving at the first inconvenience they suffer? *In the first conference I give we will try to remedy this defect, please God.* Should the Ladies buy or rent a house for the children in his absence? *As they wish.* Would it be well to bring all the Sisters together to talk over their work, its successes and its failures? *Try it, please.* And so on. His last reply was couched in the playfulness he sometimes allowed himself—probably because Louise's seriousness often begged for teasing: Would he not come to bless them all so much in need of his encouragement? *I will try to come at the last minute, telling you in the meantime that you are* [a] *woman of little faith and that I am your servant.*

The Sisters were in their new house. It is not certain when they made the move, but they were still at La Chapelle in the late autumn of 1641, waiting for the necessary alterations to be finished. Due either to the age of the house or to a flaw in its construction, the ceiling of the large room in which the Sisters and the Ladies of Charity were accustomed to hold their meetings fell, on the eve of Pentecost, June 7, 1642. Remarkably, no one was injured, although Louise had been in the room only a moment earlier, preparing for a meeting with Vincent and the Ladies. A Sister had come to warn her about an ominous creaking of the central beam; she had brushed aside the warning until an older Sister had come to beg her to leave. She was hardly out of the room when the ceiling—

which was also the floor of the room above—came crashing down. Referring to the accident four years later, Vincent was still marveling at the
Providence of God in removing Louise from danger in time and in delaying the arrival of the Ladies and himself.

Knowing Louise's readiness to assume the blame for any and all calamities in the Company, he hastened the day after the accident to reassure
her by comparing this near-tragedy to the "fall of the tower of Jericho,"
which, he said, was caused "not by the sins of the people, or by those of
their fathers and mothers, but to show forth the glory of God. And,
indeed, I tell you the same, Mademoiselle, that this accident was not
sent either because of your own sins or because of the sins of our dear
Sisters, but to warn us—those of us who will listen—to live so well that
we will not be surprised by death, and to give you by means of this
happening a new motive for loving God more than ever, because He
preserved you as the apple of his eye in the midst of an accident that
must have buried you in the rubble if God by His amiable Providence
had not turned the blow aside."

Surprisingly enough, Louise has recorded in her spiritual notes that
"although, miserable as I am, I should have recognized that this had
happened through my sins, the thought never struck me, neither at the
time nor afterward; but I ever said and held firmly in my heart that it
was a grace from God given for a reason we were ignorant of and that
God by means of it was asking something of both [the Priests of the
Mission and the Company of the Daughters]—trusting to His goodness
to make it plain to our Most Honored Father."

She is specific as to what she thought this "something" was: "It
seemed to me that this had happened as a great sign for the solid establishment of this little family. I have understood that this accident, which
must be called a favor, should be a notification to our Most Honored
Father to establish an intimate union of our community with his institute according to the Will of God, their interests being the same."

This is a very important reference in establishing the primacy of
Louise's role in the foundation of the Company. This primacy has already been demonstrated historically, but the "intimate union" which
Louise here calls for is much more important as the heart and soul, the
nourishing force, of the Company: throughout the centuries it has been
an essential means, recognized as such by the Sisters themselves, of preserving in the Company the spirit of Vincent de Paul. It has been the

extension in time of the vital rapport between him and Louise. And it was Louise who conceived it, insisted upon it, and worked to establish it, often against the mysterious indifference of Vincent himself. Another historic incident occurred that June—almost as an afterthought—during Vincent's conference on obedience. Enumerating those whom the Sisters were bound to obey, he came to the superioresses.

"That reminds me, my daughters," he broke off, "to tell you that some days ago I happened to be in a convent of nuns of the Annunciation Order, I think it was, and I noticed that their superioress was called Ancelle. The word *ancelle*, my dear Sisters, comes from the Latin word *ancilla* and means handmaiden or servant, and it was the title assumed by the Blessed Virgin when she told the angel she consented that the will of God should be fulfilled in her in the mystery of the Incarnation of His Son. This led me to think, my dear Sisters, that in future, instead of calling Sisters 'superiors' and 'superioresses,' we should employ the title 'Sister Servant.' What do you think?" our most dear Father asked some of the Sisters. His proposal was accepted. He also said: "That is the title given to the Holy Father and all his pronouncements begin thus: 'Urban, Servant of the servants of Jesus Christ, etc.' " And also the superioress of the Company of the Hôtel-Dieu, when it was first founded, took that title. Dear Madame Goussault wished them to do so.

Thus came about the community practice, so modern in its emphasis on service, of addressing the superioress as Sister Servant.

Louise's heart was not reserved only for her daughters but went out to every good soul in need. In several letters to Abbé de Vaux she besought his charity for a certain widow who had shown great generosity to the Church. "She makes me pity her," she told him, "and I am sure that if you took the trouble to speak to her you would recognize the need she has to withdraw from the world for some years at least." Again, Louise urged that this good woman be shown her "delusions of mind. I think that she would avail herself of the solid advice you would give her, having had experience of the usefulness of what she has received from others who do not understand her . . ." If de Vaux did not agree that she should withdraw as a pensioner into a monastery, perhaps "she would resolve to live in the world in true widowhood, and make it apparent in her exterior. That would be of great advantage to her . . ." Louise's own widowhood had awakened her sympathy for this young girl. She was able to report to de Vaux at a later date that the girl,

Madame Raffy by name, had gone to live safely with her father and mother "just as you advised her to do."

The Sisters at Angers were about to make their retreat, and Louise informed de Vaux that they were to make use of the readings that had become her standards and the Company's—François de Sales, Luis de Granada, and Gerson—and to meditate on the life and death of Our Lord, imitating the manner of life of Him and His holy Mother, "who are their patrons," in the resolutions taken.

On July 5, Louise wrote the news of the Company to Jeanne Lepeintre, who was the schoolmistress at Saint-Germain-en-Laye. Sister Anne, who had caused such a furore at Fontenay, had gone, humbly repentant, with Sister Jeanne Dalmagne to Nanteuil in answer to the renewed request of the Marquise de Maignelay. Louise was prudently going to recall her to the motherhouse for the feast of the Assumption so as to strengthen her resolve. There had been another accident and another remarkable escape from death. One of the newly arrived Sisters had "fallen into the river while washing linen at the Hôtel-Dieu and by a very special grace of God was pulled out." Doing one's laundry in the Seine was apparently as popular then as it is now.

Always solicitous to let her daughters know the state of their families' health and fortune, Louise next told Jeanne that her "father and step-mother are well but their business is doing badly. I think the mill is bankrupt again. I have asked Sister Turgis to go herself to find out for certain, and also whether they are in need. Do not upset yourself. Only recommend them to God. I will let you know what I find out, and we will look after things." She finished by begging Jeanne to take care of her health and advised her to "be bled for your inflammation. I know no other remedy except to take frequent baths. *Bonjour*, dear Sister, and you also, good Sister Baptiste; take care of one another as much for the health of the body as for the health of your souls."

The next day Louise informed Vincent of complaints from the Sisters that she would not let them unburden their consciences. "Examining myself," she wrote ingenuously, "I can remember only two such occasions, the one when M. Thibault came to ask for two or three of his acquaintance, one of whom was little Sister Claude, who at the time could not have her fill of talking about the pain she was suffering over a sin she had confessed, and I advised her not to speak to him about it; and another time, when I told our Sister Louise, who greatly delights in talking, and often, about austerities, not to speak of them but to hold to the practice of those which were permitted . . ." Vincent in his reply showed little interest in such complaints and implied his complete confidence in her judgment.

The Sisters at Saint-Sulpice were still a cause for worry and Louise proposed to remedy matters by sending there Sister Henriette, who had apparently not yet departed for Sedan, and recalling Sister Catherine to the motherhouse. Vincent agreed to the solution.

In the letters of Vincent and Louise from this period, and in earlier ones, it becomes increasingly clearer that Antoine Portail, Vincent's first recruit for the Mission and his close friend and associate all their lives, was becoming ever more deeply involved in the affairs of the Daughters of Charity. This is further evident from Vincent's conferences to the Sisters, which indicate that Portail, from the earliest years of the Company, either accompanied the saint to the conference hall or substituted for him. It is certain that he was officially appointed by Vincent to be the first Director of the Sisters other than himself, but it is impossible to assign a specific date to the appointment.

This good, shy little priest was born at Beaucaire on November 22, 1590. While a student at the Sorbonne, in 1610, he met Vincent de Paul and never thereafter was far from his side. Vincent prepared him for the priesthood, entrusted him with the first apostolate to the galley slaves, and took him along on the first missions to the poor country people. He died in 1660, preceding in death Louise and Vincent, who also died in the same year.

On September 1, feast of St. Vincent de Xaintes, patron of Vincent's native diocese, Louise sent him a feast-day greeting and received a gracious reply and a memorable lesson concerning the ever present tension between prayer and good works. "Thank you for the interest you take in devotion to my patron saint," he wrote, "and I pray God to give your faith what my misery is unworthy to obtain for you. Ask pardon of Him, please, for my lack of devotion caused by the lack of preparation. I have been entangled in business all this morning without being able to say even a little prayer and with many distractions. Judge how you must wait for my prayers on this holy day." It sounded bitter, but it was not. "Nonetheless, this does not discourage me, because I put my confidence in God and certainly not in my preparation or in my business; and with all my heart I wish the same for you since the throne of the goodness and mercy of God rests on the foundations of our miseries. Let us, then, trust in His goodness and we shall never be confounded, as His word assures us."

Vincent would have been embarrassed by the formality of the note that went to Louise, apparently by the hand of a secretary, some days later: "Mademoiselle Le Gras will take the trouble, please, to inform me of whom she is going to send to Saint-Germain if she withdraws Sister Perrette for Fontenay," it began. Jeanne Lepeintre had received some article without permission and Vincent had ordered her to beg pardon of her community. "She asks to make her retreat; it seems good to me to permit it." A few days later he wrote himself to say that "since you have your reasons for sending Perrette to Fontenay, do so, please, and send the one from Normandy to Sister Henriette and the other of whom you spoke to me to Saint-Sulpice, and the one from Le Mans in place of Perrette." He had his doubts about Louise's choice for Saint-Sulpice; however, he said, she should please herself in the matter.

Having taken care of this business, Louise set out for Liancourt to visit her friend the Duchesse and the confraternities in the neighborhood. The way she was forcing her frail body alarmed Vincent anew—he made her, in fact, delay her journey until she had "taken the waters" imported from a noted medicinal spa—and he now implored her: "In the name of God, Mademoiselle, do not push yourself. If Madame [de Liancourt] finds it good for you to visit the Charities of these villages, speak but little. It is all the talking that makes me fear for you on these visitations."

From Liancourt Louise wrote a charming letter to Sister Madeleine and the others at Angers, urging the qualities of her special patroness on each. As Sister Servant, Madeleine was to take the Good Shepherd Himself for patron. Sister Marie-Marthe was to imitate, naturally enough, the sisters of Lazarus: as Mary she should be "in a state of great purity, sweetness and modesty, ready to please everyone"; as Martha she was "obligated to a great exactitude of her Rule in all its details." And Sister Cécile, "oh, how peaceful and sweet she must be in order to sing sweetly the praises of God in imitation of her holy godmother!" Sister Brigitte should be steadfast in pain and perseverance for the accomplishment of God's designs in her. Sister Françoise must make up for the weakness of her body with strength of soul.

Requests for the services of the Daughters were growing constantly and Vincent suggested to Louise that she "would do well to bring some girls back with you, if any with vocations present themselves and you judge them suitable." The administrators of the hospital at Angers were asking for four more Sisters, but Louise did not have them to send. Vincent himself wanted a few for Louise's former parish of Saint-Gervais but she informed him that, while "we have a fair number of girls, I do not think they have had enough training . . ." However, if he would give her two weeks, she could arrange to send Sister Henriette to supplement the hired personnel there.

The ladies of the confraternity were not satisfied with this and Louise began to think of Henriette for a new mission at Issy, but was also minded to send her to Fontenay, which had a school and the Sister assigned there did not know how to read. The foundation at Issy was off to a bad start because the sponsors, who had asked for the Sisters, failed to support them when they arrived and they found themselves with as little means of subsistence as the poor themselves. Louise brought Sister Jeanne home from Issy in January 1643. On February 9, the curé of the village appeared on her doorstep to ask for Jeanne's return. "I gave him to understand that I would wait until I was clear in my own mind as to whether they intended to continue this confraternity and I told him very plainly the reason for my doubts," Louise reported to Vincent, hastening to assure him that she had done so with tact and respect. "He should speak to Mademoiselle de Montdésir and inform you of what she wants. He tried hard to place the blame on us for the little the Sisters have had since they have been at Issy." Sister Jeanne, or a replacement, went back eventually, but the foundation was never a success and was closed in 1649.

Mme de Lamoignon and her daughter Mme de Nesmond had just returned from a visit to the hospital in the royal town of Saint-Denis and carried a request for Daughters of Charity in case the religious community then in charge would not accept certain conditions being proposed by the administrators. The ladies felt sure that the hospital would be offered to the Company and asked whether protocol demanded that they "merely thank the Queen, recommending the work to Her Majesty, or do her the honor of making her its protectress." They were very premature to fuss over so minor a point, for the Sisters would not go to Saint-Denis until 1645.

When Louise wrote to the Abbé de Vaux on February 10, she was worried about "Sister Claude and Sister Barbe, Sister Madeleine having informed me that they often think of leaving. I do not know, Monsieur, whether they speak to you or Monsieur Ratier about it. I ask you very humbly, if you judge fitting, to obtain their permission to report the matter to Monsieur Vincent . . ." A month later her worry had not been relieved. "I do not write to these two Sisters . . . not knowing whether I should," she told the good abbé. "I am vexed at the weakness Sister Madeleine has shown." She reproached him for not having reported it, "which is the reason why I have not spoken to her. As for changing her, I have not yet ascertained from Monsieur Vincent the length of time they [Sisters Servants] should be in office. I expect Monsieur Lambert to make a tour of your neighborhood, at which time, Monsieur, please take the trouble to confer with him about all your problems."

With this letter Louise began to use the quote from St. Paul which became the motto of the Company and was incorporated in its official seal: "The charity of Jesus Christ Crucified urges us on."

Elisabeth Martin's health was not yet fully restored and she remained at Richelieu. Louise prescribed for her, besides frequent purging, "a large glass of barley water, well boiled but very clear throughout," sweetened with honey or sugar, to be taken daily morning and evening. On the question of beverages for Elisabeth's companion, she was less than enthusiastic: "It seems to me, Sister Anne, that you have mentioned to me something about taking wine. In the name of God, do not get used to it, for despite what I know of you I believe it can cause you much harm."

Toward May, Louise received word from M. de Mondion, Curé de Saché, that Jeanne Dalmagne was dying at Nanteuil. Louise was anxious to send someone from the motherhouse to her side, but Vincent thought it would be easier for Elisabeth Martin to go from Richelieu, if she were able. Elisabeth went, taking with her from Louise a touching letter of farewell to the dying Sister. "If it is the most holy will of God to take back your soul," Louise wrote, "His holy name be blessed for it. He knows the regret I have at not being able to assist you in this last act of love I believe you are making, that of giving your soul very willingly to the Eternal Father in the desire of honoring the moment of the death of His Son. Our good Sister Elisabeth goes to assure you of the affection of all our Sisters and of their desire that you remember them in heaven when God will have shown you that mercy, and Sister Anne-Marie especially, who sends her deep regret at not being able to render you the last services. Be mindful, then, my most dear Sister, of the needs of the poor

Company to which God has called you. Make yourself an advocate before His goodness that it please Him to accomplish His designs in it and, if His kindness permit, pray our good angels to help us. *Bonsoir*, my most dear Sister. With all my heart I beg Jesus Crucified to bless you with all the virtues He practiced on the Cross, and am in His most holy love, my most dear Sister, your very humble Sister and servant."

Jeanne did not die. When Elisabeth entered the sickroom she greeted her with the resolution to return with her to the motherhouse: "I am going with you." She did, indeed, recover sufficiently to be carried back to Paris in a litter and spent her last months surrounded with the consolations of home.

On June 8, Louise informed Vincent that Mme Pelletier had come to tell her that M. l'abbé de Buzay, youngest of the children of Vincent's old patron, Père de Gondi, was to be named coadjutor to his uncle, the Archbishop of Paris. This far from exemplary abbé (the future, notorious Cardinal de Retz) was, in fact, named to the post on June 13. Mme Pelletier, Louise confided, "had thought of my son, and without saying anything to me, had spoken to the Révérend Père Emmanuel [de Gondi], who told her to find out from me whether I indeed wished him to propose him [Michel] for my said Sieur Buzay's [sic] service—I do not know whether as an almoner or in some other capacity better suited to him. Since this was not in any way my doing, I thought, Monsieur, that I should not fail to take the liberty to ask you what I should do in this matter and, if you judge it feasible, to beg you very humbly to do us the charity of helping us. I think that if my son had something to distract him from the melancholy which is, in my opinion, the cause of all his difficulties, they would disappear. He has ever seemed in my eyes to fear God and to wish to acquit himself faithfully of whatever was committed to him."

There can be no doubt of the poor mother's wish, and the last, patently false statement as to her son's fidelity of purpose lay bare for a piteous moment her inmost suffering heart. Vincent's reply has been lost, but it is not hard to surmise that the evil-living de Retz would have been the last person to whom Vincent would have confided anyone as unsophisticated as Michel or, conversely, to imagine that brilliant and cynical prelate putting up with him for a minute.

Since the Ladies of Charity had determined upon taking over the entire work of the foundlings of Paris, a search had been in progress for a larger house than the one on rue des Boulangers. Louise now wrote on

June 12 to tell Vincent that "Mesdames Souscarrière, de Romilly, and Traversay have been to your house to report to you that Monsieur le chancelier [Séguier] had received them very well and had advised them that, to get possession of the Château de Bicêtre, it was necessary to speak to the Queen and submit a brief." This huge, rambling pile outside the walls of the city had been built upon the site of an old castle by Louis XIII as a veterans' home.

Vincent was the ladies' choice to be their spokesman to the Queen, Louise said, and they also desired his advice as to who should present the brief and to whom. They were also anxious for him to act promptly, lest someone else get to the Queen first. It is ironic, in light of Louise's later opposition to this white elephant of a refuge, that she should be the one to bring it to Vincent's attention in the ladies' behalf.

Elisabeth Martin, who had returned to Richelieu after her errand of mercy, was again seriously ill and Louise, who knew illness so well, wrote to comfort her: "Two things can help us greatly [in time of illness]: one is the love we should have of honoring the suffering of God's son, and the other is the frequent thought that this life is of short duration and sufferings well cherished will lead us happily to eternity." Nevertheless, such a Christian attitude neither prevented nor excused one from "asking with great confidence for the help you need."

There was another kind of help not so easy to ask for or accept—especially for one of Louise's birth—financial help. Yet she saw the Providence of God "which does not disdain sinners" in the visit of Mme de Marillac, granddaughter-in-law of her uncle Michel, because she "thought I was in need. She begged me to speak frankly since she could advance me the sum Madame her mother had offered to give me every year. I told her my difficulties in all simplicity but [assured her] that I would need nothing if only my son had some employment." Michel, who was now twenty-nine years old, seems at this point to have abandoned all thought of the priesthood and was idling about, supported by his mother and Vincent, who were thinking at the moment of speaking to the Bishop of Beauvais in his behalf.

Since the care of the wounded soldiers at Sedan was exhausting work and the Sisters assigned there were virtually cut off from the rest of the Company, Louise saw to it that they had occasional relief by bringing them home to rest. She had just recalled Marie Joly to the motherhouse and, sensitive to the fact that Marie's sister Gillette, who had been left behind, would be low in spirits at the separation, she now wrote to console her: "I have no less envy to see you here than you have to be here, but it is only right that Sister Marie have the first choice and afterwards you shall come."

Shortly after the start of the new year, 1644, Vincent was forced to take to his bed once more and Louise took the occasion to chide him familiarly: "So our good God wishes you to be ill. May He be blessed for it! But does He not also wish that you have the charity for your body that you have for the poor? If I may dare to say so, my Most Honored Father, I tell you that He wishes it absolutely." Despite his illness, which hung on for more than a month, and despite her chiding, the indefatigable man refused to let up, Louise confided to Abbé de Vaux on February 23 when she wrote to remind him to give M. Lambert, who had arrived there, "a complete picture of our Sisters' situation and also all the complaints against them." By March 21, de Vaux had written to tell her that he had high hopes of the visitation, and she was happy and relieved, but cautioned him, since he was leaving Angers for a few weeks, to make the Sisters understand that they must obey absolutely whomever he left over them in his absence; if necessary, she added, she would have Vincent himself "command this submission." The good order of this outpost community was ever on her mind.

She was still uneasy about Sister Madeleine's capability in the post of Sister Servant and would dearly love to have restored Elisabeth Martin to the post, but Elisabeth was still ailing. This was the reason, Louise told de Vaux on April 19, that "we do not know whether we should send her back, but we will send Sister Turgis in her stead for three months. I think that will do. And we will recall Sisters Barbe, Geneviève, Clémence, and Sister Madeleine to stay with us while Sister Turgis is there." The other replacements would leave "no later than the beginning of next week." She besought de Vaux to accustom the administrators to the Sisters being changed, "promising them that in this way they will give better satisfaction," and that hopefully "the poor will be better served according to their [the administrators'] desires. I assure you, Monsieur, that to arrive at this we are withdrawing Sister Turgis reluctantly from the foundling asylum, where she is very much needed because of the superior intelligence necessary for this work."

The search for a new lodging for the foundlings was still in progress and Louise had her eye on a house "next to Saint-Laurent," she informed Vincent in May. She was more concerned with her own interior life at the moment, however. "I cannot help telling you that I am greatly distressed today over a fear about predestination because of certain thoughts I had during prayer," she wrote. "It has oppressed my spirit so, that I have been moved to make an act of submission to the designs of God for myself and my son, that we be ever objects of His justice."

She was making her annual Pentecost retreat, and although she had forgotten to ask Vincent's permission to go to Communion daily, she had presumed to do so because of the blanket permission he had given her to communicate whenever her health permitted. Despite the fact that she now protested that she "did not dare to continue without your permission," she was quite evidently growing in the spiritual courage to make her own decisions. This courage is evident in the recounting of her fear about predestination: she merely mentions it to Vincent without the piteous cries for help of former years. She had already countered it with her "act of submission."

Sister Claude at Angers was still being tormented with temptations against her vocation and Louise wrote in May to comfort her. "I suffer with you in the pain I know you feel in your downheartedness and sadness," she assured the poor girl. "I hope that you are making good use of it in your interior. It is what I pray God with all my heart to give you the grace to do. I wish, most dear Sister, that you would tell me the thoughts that come to you. I might try, having had like thoughts, to be of service to you. Do try, please, to distract yourself from them as soon as they come."

The Sisters were still being criticized by envious spirits in the town, but Louise was satisfied, from a letter of Sister Turgis', that no great harm was being done.

On June 29 Louise besought the Abbé de Vaux to continue to remember Vincent in his Masses: "He has more need of it than ever. I am very much afraid of him dying under the load. He has his ordinary fevers constantly and his work besides." Vincent's duties had increased with the death of Louis XIII on May 14 of the previous year. Anne of Austria had summoned him to her husband's deathbed to assist him to die well. After the King's death, she had refused to allow Vincent to leave the court, appointing him her confessor and spiritual director. Soon afterward she had named him to the Council of Conscience, which she had set up to look after the ecclesiastical affairs of the Kingdom, notably the appointment of bishops. His fellow members on the Council were Cardinal Mazarin, who had succeeded as First Minister upon Richelieu's death in 1642, the Prince de Condé, Bishop Augustin Potier of Beauvais, and Bishop Philippe Cospeau of Lisieux. It can be imagined, the visitors and correspondence this newfound eminence and power, however unsought, brought the already overworked saint—people who wanted favors, people with axes to grind, to say nothing of those who came lawfully and validly. Louise might well worry about him.

The next day, June 30, Louise herself was adding to Vincent's burdens, but it could not be helped. She was unusually downcast for fear she had offended God by not communicating "for a long time" and felt that only by speaking with him could she drive out the fear. She had done all she could herself, she said, reminding him that he knew that to be in such a state "is not ordinary with me."

Historically, the interest of this note lies in the imprint it bore in the sealing wax of a heart enclosing the representation of Jesus Crucified—the first known use of the seal of the Company.

During Abbé de Vaux's absence from Angers, very real troubles had settled in among the Sisters. On July 26, Louise wrote them a grieving letter: "I can no longer hide from you the sorrow of my heart at the knowledge I have that there is much to be desired among you. Why, my poor Sisters, must our enemy prevail over you? Where is the spirit of fervor that animated you at the beginning of your establishment at Angers which gave you such great esteem for Messieurs your directors . . . ? Is it not contrary to all reason that you should seek anything opposed to their advice and guidance? I speak both of spiritual and temporal superiors. Where is the sweetness and charity that you ought to preserve at all costs for our dear masters the sick poor?" She went on to warn them against vanity, which could insinuate itself even "beneath these poor habits and vile headdresses . . . under the appearance of propriety and neatness." She refused to believe that they "would entertain any thought against your holy vocation" or would wish "to speak to those who could harm purity or the love you owe to God . . .

"Renew yourselves, then, dear Sisters, in your first fervor; and begin with the desire of pleasing God, reminding yourselves that He has led you by His Providence to the place where you find yourselves and brought you together to help one another to perfection." For this reason they should above all bear with one another:

> If our Sister is sad, if she is a bit cranky, or too prompt, too slow, what do you expect her to do?—it is her nature. And even though she often makes the effort to conquer herself, she cannot prevent her inclinations from rising often to the surface.

I will never leave off conversing with you in the sight of God, so great is my desire to render you pleasing to His goodness.

She had not heard by August 24 whether the Sisters had received this letter and wrote of her anxiety to Sister Turgis: "I am greatly astonished to learn that because of small contradictions some have entertained the thought of returning to Paris before obedience calls them . . . ! You do indeed suffer embarrassment when Messieurs les Pères mortify you in front of your masters the poor. Give them no reason for it. Do so well that they will find nothing to criticize. And if sometimes you feel that you have done nothing wrong or some of these gentlemen reprove you too rudely for your taste and you feel it discredits you with the sick, humble yourselves in suffering patiently, afterwards privately give your reasons and ask them to tell you your faults. If you act in such a way, I assure you, my Sisters, there would not be a single Sister of ours who would not be happy to be in your place."

She badly needed Sister Turgis back in Paris and confided to the Abbé de Vaux that she was of the opinion that there would be little resistance from the hospital administrators, "who had not been very happy" to have her in the first place. The administrators were anxious to have Elisabeth Martin back, but it seemed to Louise that "this poor girl would be better off, perhaps, in this climate [of Paris]. Barbe Angiboust, she told de Vaux, had "all the qualities necessary for the governance of that little troop [at Angers]."

Vincent was about to leave for an extended stay at Richelieu. On the eve of his departure Louise sent him a pathetic note informing him that her son's little servant had come to tell her that Michel had sent him back to Paris the day before and that the servant had no idea where his master might be. "You can imagine my grief, which I very humbly beg you to comfort," she wrote. Did anyone at Saint-Lazare know anything of Michel's whereabouts? She dreaded his permanent disappearance "without my knowing where he is." Her anguish was increased, she said, by having to trouble Vincent, "but it is impossible for me to look for comfort anywhere else." She ended with a cry from the depths of her heart: "How great is my sorrow! If God does not help me I do not know what I shall do! Help me to hold fast to Jesus Crucified . . ."

Despite her personal troubles, which, except to confide in Vincent, she usually kept to herself, she gave her fullest attention to the affairs of the Company. There is a suggestive reference in a letter she addressed to Vincent at Richelieu concerning "the execution of an article contained in the little memorandum I sent you before you left." This may well be a reference to the formal petition for approbation of the Rule, which was now ready for such action. The suspicion is enhanced by her request "to make the trip to Chartres in your absence in order to recommend to the Blessed Virgin all our needs and the proposals I have made you." No major step was taken in the Company without the blessing of the Virgin of Chartres.

Louise was at Chartres from October 14 to 17 and gave Vincent an account of the visit when she returned: "The Saturday Office was offered to God in the Chapel of the Blessed Virgin as something I owed him for several favors received through her goodness. Sunday's was for the needs of my son. Monday's, the day of the dedication of the Chartres church, was an offering to God of the designs of His Providence for the Company of the Daughters of Charity, giving the aforesaid Company wholeheartedly to Him and asking for its destruction the minute it should undertake anything against His holy will, asking for it, through the prayers of the Blessed Virgin, Mother and Guardian of the aforesaid Company, the purity of which it had need."

By December 2 Louise had news of her son but received little comfort from it. "I am completely crushed over my son, who arrived on Saturday in the company of the Comtesse de Maure. She has informed me that she gave him a note on Sunday and that he should have come to see me, and that she does not know where he is. What shall I do?" she wrote in sorrow to Vincent. It was one thing to know the faults of your flesh and blood; it was quite another for your relatives to know them.

On December 11 Vincent gave the Sisters a conference on "The Inordinate Love of Self." Louise, as usual, took notes to be fleshed out later. He spoke of "the empty satisfaction one may take in clothes, and the pleasure which flesh and blood would like to take in eating . . . Almost all of you, like the first Sisters, are of humble birth and, consequently, such foolish satisfactions are not natural in your case, nor have you been accustomed to them from your youth. How fortunate you are, and myself also, that God has shown us His favor in choosing us from the dregs of the world to serve Him!" He took note, also, of the highly born in the Company: "Even if you were of noble birth, as some of you are, you should never presume on it, and you are just as much obliged as the rest to rid yourselves of all that sensitiveness and sensibility which you acquired by nature and training."

It was a revolutionary doctrine for the age. It was equally revolutionary for noblewomen to join themselves in absolute parity with illiterate country girls. And Louise had shown the way.

XIII

Establishment and Rule

On January 15, 1645, Vincent introduced a custom which was to become deeply cherished in the Company and which still persists in various derivative forms. This was the discussion at the usual conference time of the virtues of a recently deceased Sister. Actually this colloquy was an astute form of spiritual pedagogy which at the same time gave the Company a hagiography of its own and wove into it the strong, biding thread of tradition.

The Sisters themselves were the chief eulogists, for they had lived and worked with the deceased. Vincent contented himself with interjecting comments and summing up at the end. Louise listened proudly to what God had wrought in her daughters—how often the living betrayed their own goodness in speaking well of the dead!—and she spoke only when Vincent asked her to, which he invariably did before his own summation.

The first Sister to be honored in this fashion was Jeanne Dalmagne, who had died the previous March 25. It was a good first choice, for she was a remarkably spiritual soul. She had come to the Company under a great inspiration of God, despite an invitation from the Carmelites that she become one of them and from the Princesse de Condé, who offered to gain her entry into any convent she chose. A Sister who had been with her at Nanteuil testified that "she cured incurable patients in a miraculous manner of their various sores and wounds. And yet she had no experience, for very frequently she did not know where to begin or what she should do; she used then to turn to God and afterwards say: 'Oh, what a good teacher God is!'"

One poor girl, eaten away by scrofula and shunned by all because of the stench of her disease, became a symbol of Jeanne's heroic service. "She used to go twice a day to clean and dress the sick girl's sores, although she was ill herself," her companion told the assembled community. "The bad smell sickened her very much and increased her own weakness. When I was told of her condition and chided her for acting as she had done, she told me that her weakness was due to her own want of courage, and that, as she could not render great services to God, the least she might do was to exercise herself in the little opportunities she had to serve the modest poor."

And so the dialogue went on, everyone entering into it with a holy enthusiasm and admiration, the shy and backward encouraged by Vincent's approbation: "Oh, isn't that beautiful, my daughters!" Oh my daughters, have you not felt very happy to hear this account?"

Louise had climbed now to a great, serene plateau of sanctity, to the spiritual Eden of illumination and union. Its advent was, perhaps, signaled in a note written, significantly, during her Pentecost retreat of 1645. Having asked Vincent's permission to attend his Mass the following morning [May 26], she continued in a state of exaltation: "This advent of this great feast has a very special frame of reference for me because of all the singular favors God has done His Church and, as far as I am concerned personally, because of what His goodness did for me twenty-two years ago which has rendered me so happy as to have that rapport with Him which Your Charity knows. I sense in my interior I know not what disposition which, so it seems to me, wishes to unite me more firmly to God but how I do not know. Please tell your poor daughter and servant, my Most Honored Father, what you think of it in the name of Jesus by whom we are what we are."

Because many of the Sisters were ill, Louise had to interrupt her retreat to minister to and comfort them. Nevertheless, the thread of her illumination was not broken. On June 3 she told Vincent with a holy eagerness that she "did not know how to wait any longer . . . to tell you of my state [of soul] during these days of my retreat . . . Oh good God! what reason I have to acknowledge and recognize that I do nothing worth anything! Yet my heart is not embittered for all that, even though it has reason to fear lest the mercy of God grow tired of extending itself to one who has ever displeased Him. Today is the anniversary of the collapse of our floor, tomorrow that of the day on which God once let me know His will and on which I yearned for *His holy love to give itself to my heart as a perpetual law*." She added a postscript dictated by maternal intuition, recommending Michel to Vincent's prayers because "it has occurred to me to ask whether he has a great cross in his room."

At this period the correspondence between the two friends begins to grow less frequent. Both of them are more caught up in their own affairs: Louise with her daughters, and Vincent with his sons and with the spiritual affairs of the Kingdom. Besides, their houses were only a few steps apart now. If her letters to him outnumber his to her, it is probably because he was less frequently at home and she was forced more and more to leave messages for him.

Writing to Sister Madeleine at Angers on June 27, Louise confessed her affliction at the faults Madeleine had humbly admitted to her. She was especially distressed because it was the responsibility of the Sister Servant to give the example to the others, but she begged Madeleine to be comforted and not to "consider this fault in anger [at yourself]; rather, admire God's goodness in letting you suffer this little fault in order to learn to humble yourself more perfectly than you have in the past." She then addressed herself to all the Sisters, urging each to be more than "a Daughter of Charity in name," and ended by prostrating herself in spirit before them: "My dear Sisters, you know that because of my age [she was now fifty-four] I have inveterate habits, which is why I have great need of the assistance of your prayers." It was a long letter and what it cost Louise to write it is betrayed in her sending her regards to Abbé de Vaux and M. Ratier because "I haven't health enough to write them."

Since most of the girls who entered the Company to serve the poor were poor themselves, a dowry such as was expected of those who entered religious orders was not required of them. Nevertheless, if a girl of better means wished to join the Company, there is evidence that Louise asked a dowry of her. Thus on July 11, 1645, she complained to Vincent of a mother who was reneging on a dowry for her daughter, despite the fact that Louise had acquainted her with "the little means I have of taking care of the motherhouse . . . I know well that most of the girls here bring nothing, [but] if what she says is true, could she not give a sizable dowry from her estate for a daughter of such a station, even if she had only half of what she claims to own in the country?"

On July 26 Louise wrote to Vincent in great distress of spirit. She was anxious first of all about Vincent himself. His latest illness had caused ulceration of the legs and Louise was not at all happy with the treatment he was receiving for it. "If you were one of our poor," she told him, "it seems to me that our 'Monsieur Deure's Strong Water' would have cured you by now and that the ointments, powerful as they are, only irritate the infection and keep it running." Then she was profoundly saddened and worried about Michel, who, it would seem, had been consorting with a girl who had been arrested and forcibly constrained in the convent of the Magdalens. "I do not know, my Most Honored Father, whether the good priest at the Daughters of the Magdalen has spoken to you," she asked. "He is pressing for a decision on the girl's release and seems convinced of her conversion, saying that she promises him to think no more of him with whom she is smitten [Michel], that she wants to go back to her own country. I have since recalled that that was the resolution they took together before their capture, and that the letter I showed Your Charity later shows that her suggestion to him is, after the marriage, either to enter into partnership with this girl's parents, who sell wine, or to go back to her country to live in peace but in idleness. Her intention then—by all appearances, if she can be believed—is to seek him out as soon as she is free."

Louise was therefore of the opinion that things were "now what they were at the beginning," and her heart was breaking. "The thought that I am very near the time of dying is always with me and although I wish sincerely, if God wishes it, that I leave all my little business at loose ends and in a sorry state, I cannot leave off suffering over it." The worst she feared seems not to have occurred, to judge from Michel's respectable marriage a few years later.

She was depressed also because "our little Company was never weaker . . . I don't know, Most Honored Father, whether it is because we have not had you among us for a long time, but we are infirm. I beg Your Charity very humbly to recall the proposal I made you of having a conference every week, to be given by one of your gentlemen . . . One Sister could come from each parish at a time, to prevent the poor from being incommoded."

The Ladies of Charity had been actively pursuing their plan to obtain the Château de Bicêtre for the foundlings. At the same time, Louise had been strengthening her opposition to the plan because she believed it would "interfere . . . with the execution of God's plans . . ." At Vincent's request she now, on August 19, drew up her objections in writing:

> The place was so big that even in two years' time not half of it would be in use . . .
> The cost of proper renovations would be exorbitant . . .
> It had been the haunt of evil men who would continue to lurk in its remotest parts even after the Sisters had moved in . . .
> There would be danger on the roads for the Sisters obliged to travel constantly to and from between there and Paris . . .

It was too far to carry children in arms and the bad terrain made it difficult even to transport them by horse or donkey, especially in bad weather . . .

The daily trips to the city would require more Sisters and they were not available . . .

The Sisters assigned there would find great difficulty in attending the conferences at the motherhouse; to move the motherhouse to Bicêtre would raise the same problem for the Sisters assigned to the parishes and the Hôtel-Dieu . . .

Her arguments were cogent, but she was a wise woman who knew her sex well. The ladies would have this huge, rambling pile. Therefore, in retreat, as it were, she contented herself with firing a last volley at their pocketbooks:

If, notwithstanding all these difficulties, we must go, it will be necessary, at least every winter, for two men to live there; daily Mass will have to be said in the chapel, and fonts erected for baptizing the babies. This will exhaust the fifty livres given for that purpose. It will be necessary further to have some kind of little cart with a horse for transporting the children; this would solve many problems. One of the men could drive it, and this being the case it will be necessary to pick the men carefully, because of their communication with the nurses and the Sisters.

At the same time that Louise was fighting her solitary rear-guard action against this preposterous and gigantic undertaking she and Vincent were readying a formal petition to Jean-François de Gondi, Archbishop of Paris, for ecclesiastical approbation of the Company. "Here is the draft for the girls' establishment," he wrote Louise at the end of summer. "It contains three things: 1º the hand Providence had in instituting them; 2º their manner of life up to the present; 3º the rules of their confraternity or association. I included the first two so that Monseigneur l'archêveque and the gentlemen of his council will be informed of everything . . . Read over the comment on the draft. On your advice I have suppressed many things I could have said. Let us leave it to Our Lord to let everyone know about it and let us for our part remain hidden."

Louise acted promptly and to the point in this matter of such importance to her: she saw nothing to be gained in praising her daughters overmuch in the document; Vincent had forgotten to list the hospitals at Sedan and at Saint-Denis, which had been taken over on August 2; she thought that it should be stated that the Sisters "in the villages serve as much by the instruction of children as by [nursing] the sick and healing the wounded"; and she asked whether it should not be explained that "the money kept in the common fund is used to buy the necessary material for clothing the girls at the motherhouse and even in the parishes so that their habit can be kept uniform." The petition listed all the current missions of the Company:

Saint-Germain-l'Auxerrois, Saint-Nicolas-du-Chardonnet, Saint-Leu, Saint-Sauveur, Saint-Médéric [Saint-Merri], Saint-Etienne, Saint-Sulpice, Saint-Gervais, Saint-Paul and others where the confraternity [of Charity] is established and operated with benediction . . . Besides the work of the aforesaid girls in the parishes, there are three of them employed by the Ladies of Charity of the Hôtel-Dieu . . . Further, there are ordinarily ten or twelve at least employed in raising the little foundlings of the city and two or three in assisting the poor galley slaves. And beyond those employed in such works in this city there are others at the Angers hospital, at Richelieu, at Saint-Germain-en-Laye, at Sedan, and for a short while now at the Hôtel-Dieu of Saint-Denis-en-France, and in other country places . . . In order to furnish girls for all these places and for other places requesting them, the aforesaid demoiselle [Louise] has others in training with her, ordinarily more than thirty, whom she employs, some to instruct poor little girls who come to school at her house, some to visit the sick of the parish [Saint-Laurent] to take them food or medicine or to nurse them, some to do the bleeding and dress the wounds of the poor from outside [the parish] who come to them for these services, some in sewing or in other similar work, some in learning to read or write, some in housework . . .

It was indeed an impressive inventory of service to have been achieved in less than a dozen years. The actual words of petition were beautiful and artless:

Our Lord so blesses the little service they perform in their simplicity that there is cause to bless Him for the success achieved in such fashion that one clearly sees accomplished in them what Scripture says about God being pleased to communicate Himself to the simple and humble and to make use of the least and lowliest to perform deeds great and exalted, and that it is Himself who has called and approved them and He who has inspired their little way of life. All of which makes it easier to believe, in addition, that the voice of the people which is the voice of God gives its approbation not only because of the usefulness to the public of their works but even more because of the good odor they diffuse by means of their good lives. And what gives more authenticity than these is the fact that all has been done in virtue of the consent and permission Your Grace gave the suppliant [Vincent], prelatial approbation being the most certain mark of a true vocation and a good work.

Because works which concern the service of God ordinarily die with those who begin them unless there be some kind of spiritual bond among the persons who perform them, and because the suppliant to whose direction these women have ever been confided up to the present by the power Your Most Illustrious Grace has in your graciousness given him fears that such might happen: therefore, Monseigneur, it seems desirable to me that it please Your Charity to erect into a confraternity this company of girls and widows and to give them for a rule the following articles by which they have lived up to the present and propose to live by in the future under the name of Daughters and Widows of Charity, servants of the poor . . .

There is some confusion as to whether this petition was actually submitted to the archbishop at this time: even Coste is self-contradictory on the point. In any event, Louise was not happy with the prescription in the appended rules which provided for "an ecclesiastic who will be deputized by Monseigneur de Paris for the direction of the aforesaid girls and widows." She was already firmly committed to the principle that the Company of Daughters and the Priests of the Mission should form a double family with the superior general of the priests at its head.

Early in 1646 she petitioned Vincent that "Daughters of Charity" be settled upon as the name of the institute, "a name which is omitted perhaps by inadvertence in the memorandum of the terms of *Establishment*." And she continued: "Will not this absolute expression of *dependence upon Monseigneur* harm us in the future, giving as it does the freedom *to withdraw* us from *the direction of the Superior General of the Mission?* Is it not necessary, Monsieur, that by this *establishment Your Charity be given to us as perpetual Director?*" She was concerned, too, about lumping the approval of the rules with the establishment of the Company. "In the name of God, Monsieur," she pleaded, "do not allow anything which hastens ever so little the day of withdrawing the Company from the leadership God has given it; for you can be sure that it will not, for all that, be more than it is, and the sick will not be better aided, and I believe therefore that the will of God will not be done any better among us . . ."

Louise's anguish over Michel had not been assuaged by October 28, for in a letter of that date she asked Abbé de Vaux to pray "for someone close to me because of whom I am in very great affliction out of entirely human reasons and even more out of the fear I have for his salvation; and because it is to all appearances an irremediable evil, it will take the omnipotence of God to make it right . . ."

Three more small missions, at Serqueux, Maule, and Crespières, were begun almost simultaneously with the taking over of the hospital at Saint-Denis. They were either of little importance or ran smoothly or both, for they are scarcely mentioned in the correspondence of the two saints.

The Sisters at Liancourt—Jeanne-Christine, Jeanne Pangoy, Jeanne Celon, and Mathurine—were making what Louise considered an unnecessary fuss about the manner of performing their duties there and she rebuked them with unwonted acerbity: "I must tell you that I resent very much the trouble you give me with the difficulties you propose in carrying out so holy a work. It is ten years, I think, since it was begun and by Sisters who had much less intelligence than you, and things were hard in a way entirely different from now because there was no one to show them the way . . ." And she dismissed the matter curtly: "By the grace of God I have encountered no contradictions since we have had Sisters at Liancourt. I hope that His goodness will continue this grace."

Louise was a sharp-eyed mother who made frequent note of the places where her daughters' spiritual life needed patching. In a memorandum jotted down early in 1646, she listed subjects that might be treated in conferences with profit: "What the state of Daughters of Charity is and with what dispositions girls should enter . . . What thought they must give . . . to the nourishment of and the bestowal of alms on the poor . . ." The next items reflected a discontent as old as religious life, that of being stationed at "headquarters" and deprived of "front-line" duty: "Whether the girls do not deceive themselves with the strong desire of serving the poor in the parishes and at the Hôtel-Dieu in such a way as to make them discontented with living at the motherhouse . . . Whether those at home have not the same merit as those who actually serve the poor. What care and affection the girls should have for the rule of the motherhouse and its practice . . ." The list concluded on a deeply personal note: the love and forebearance Sisters should have one for the other; their willingness to accept correction humbly and even to have their failings reported to the superioress; the divisive force of murmuring and grumbling.

Vincent dealt with these suggested topics in a series of conferences stretching over the next few months. He was most grateful for these and all suggestions because the increased tempo of his life and works left him little time to think and still less to prepare. He actually opened the conference of February 13, 1646, by asking the Sisters what the topic was! But his vast experience and deep prayer life were themselves inexhaustible wells of preparation from which he drew readily and with ease.

Before starting his formal treatment of the subject that Tuesday afternoon, he asked a Sister about her narrow escape from death the Saturday before. The secretary recorded his remarks:

"My daughter, what happened? I heard a house had fallen down. In what part of the city was it? Were you inside or outside? On what day did it happen?"

The Sister replied that, on the last day of fleshmeat [before Lent], when she was taking a pot of soup to one of her poor, as she was going up the stairs, a water carrier in front of her cried out: "We are lost!" She was between the first and second floors and as soon as the poor man had uttered these words the house began to fall, and our poor Sister, quite dismayed, drew aside into the corner of the stairs. The neighbors, overcome with fear, ran off at once for the Blessed Sacrament and for Extreme Unction so that they might be administered to those capable of receiving them. But more than thirty or forty persons were piteously crushed beneath the ruins, and only a little child about ten or eleven years of age was saved.

The spectators, seeing our poor Sister in what seemed to be inevitable danger of death, shouted out to her to throw herself into their arms. Ten or twelve prepared to rescue her. She handed them down the can of soup at the end of a fair-sized pole and then, relying on God's mercy, threw herself into the cloaks they held out for her. Without being able to explain how she had been transported, she found herself, by a special providence of God, safely out of danger and, trembling all over, set off to serve the rest of the poor.

M. Vincent, after listening attentively to the whole story, grieved over the fate of those who had perished beneath the ruins of the house, and after observing that our Sister's fear was quite legitimate, seeing herself threatened with danger so near at hand, he cried out, with his hands raised aloft to heaven:

"O my God, if the fall of this house is so dreadful, what, my daughters, will it be like on the Day of Judgment, when we shall see an innumerable number of souls miserably hurled into hell for all eternity? O my God! what will it be like? Ah! Blessed be God, my daughters!"

It was to lessen the number of the lost that the Sisters had come together. As one of them said toward the end of the conference, "The Sacraments should be given to the poor before anything else." The active work of charity, noble and necessary as it was, was only a means to this nobler, more necessary work.

One of the Sisters made the very practical point that, when they had disposed the poor to accept the grace of salvation, "very frequently the priests paid no attention to them." Vincent's answer was a lesson in tact: "O my daughter, take great care never to believe they neglect this duty but, when you have informed them, then your conscience is free in the sight of God . . . If [the poor] grow worse, you might then give the parish priest a second intimation, but above all you should not do so by way of complaint, but gently. You might say to him: 'Your Reverence, this poor man is getting worse. I am afraid he may not recover. I thought I was bound to let you know.' And tell him so peacefully and quietly." We can picture Vincent afterward as he crossed the road to Saint-Lazare shaking his head in frustration at the obstacles his lazier brethren put in the way of saving souls.

Antoine Portail seems now to have been in full exercise of his office as Vincent's lieutenant in directing the affairs of the Company. Louise wrote to him on March 20 at Mans, where he was giving a mission, reminding him to be alert to anything in the preaching of his confreres that might be helpful to the Sisters, and gave him the community news: "Sister Anne has given up at last and withdrawn from us, and Big Anne from Richelieu, as soon as she saw we were going to dismiss her. She stole away just yesterday, but we don't know where. You can decide, Monsieur, whether we have need of the help of your holy prayers . . ."

M. Portail was going to visit the Sisters at Angers before his return to Paris and Louise primed him on what he might expect and might do there. It was M. de Vaux's opinion, she told him, that "all our Sisters at Angers have the tacit intention of returning some day to Paris." She felt that the restlessness among the Sisters stemmed from the fact that outsiders were making them think that they needed more spiritual communication than was the custom of the Company and, she observed tartly, "this amusement makes them desire conversation with others than those who have been appointed their directors . . ." She herself had had for some time an assistant to help her with the affairs of the Company and she was freer than before to deal personally with the Sisters' problems, she told him; this availability had already made for an improvement in the life of the motherhouse and she hoped that it would be used to make a happier life at Angers.

On March 24 Louise sent Vincent a picture of Our Lady, painted perhaps by herself, as "an ornament for an altar dedicated to her beautiful name, in way of asking her for fresh assistance for my son, of whom I have had no news since the seventh of the month—which gives me great pain." Vincent misunderstood her intention and she clarified it some days later: "It is not my intention at all that the picture of the Blessed Virgin be either for our oratory or for the foundling asylum, but that it serve as an ornament for an altar dedicated to the Blessed Virgin to repair in some way for the faults of my son, and to be paid for by some rings that I still have. That is why, Monsieur, I beg you very humbly to agree that this satisfaction be made in your church, having been so grieved that my son had used one of your houses for committing his offense."

While making this reparation for her son, her thoughts turned to a legacy she wished to leave her daughters: a little chaplet for "the devotion which three years ago I asked permission of Your Charity to practice and have practiced privately." She had "in a small casket a number of these little chaplets with the topics for meditation written on a piece of paper, to leave to all our Sisters after my death, if Your Charity will permit. No one has ever heard of it. It honors the hidden life of Our Lord in his state of imprisonment in the womb of the Blessed Virgin and congratulates her on her good fortune during these nine months; and the three small beads salute her under her beautiful titles of Daughter of the Father, Mother of the Son and Spouse of the Holy Spirit. That is the gist of this little devotion that by the grace of God . . . I have not failed to practice since the time noted . . . and this little exercise, according to my intention, is to ask God by the Incarnation of His Son and the prayers of the Blessed Virgin for the purity necessary to the Company of Sisters of Charity and the constancy of this Company in carrying out His good pleasure."

Sisters had been asked to staff a hospital already established at Le Mans and M. Portail made the final arrangements for this new foundation while he was there. It was not to be of long duration, despite the fact that Louise considered it of "great importance . . . especially since it was arranged by your gentlemen [the Priests of the Mission] . . ."

She proposed Jeanne Lepeintre for Sister Servant, and her companion to be chosen from among Sisters Claude and Geneviève, who had been at Angers, and Sister Andrée. In the end she sent all four. They left Paris on May 4, 1646, fortified by a farewell conference from Vincent and a little rule written out for them by Louise. The rule enjoined "Sister Jeanne Lepeintre to carry to Le Mans a heart filled with charity both for the sick poor and for the Sisters . . ." The Sisters were to "remember the advice of Monsieur Vincent and especially that of having no communication with men, even ecclesiastics, without necessity and in no other place than the church or the hospital. They must remember to preserve among themselves a great sweetness and support of one another, with open hearts and great confidence in the Sister Servant in regard to all their needs."

It is interesting that Vincent's instructions for choosing a confessor for the Sisters at Le Mans laid down only that he be "a good confessor, very spiritual, old, and prudent, who will be careful to follow the line of direction proper to them . . ." while Louise believed it "necessary" that he be a Priest of the Mission.

A financial accounting dated May 2, 1646, throws light on the support of the motherhouse. "I have totaled all that the Sisters of the parishes have brought to the motherhouse in 1646," Louise reported to Vincent. "It amounts to 1,129 livres 12 sols; and over and above that, forty-three girls were furnished with habits and linen. I think nearly four hundred livres remained for the motherhouse after expenses were taken out, not counting the linen and habits made by the Sisters stationed in the house. I believe, Monsieur—if Your Charity would say something about it— that it would be good for our Sisters to understand that what they bring just about covers expenses . . . I am not sure whether the entire Company should be informed—because of the lack of discretion of some, especially those who tell too freely all that they know—that their thrift is very beneficial to the motherhouse." It was the old fear of how much and how many to tell in view of the constant supply of imprudent babblers.

The Sisters arrived at Le Mans only to find that the religious community already serving the hospital would not accept their authority. M. Portail had been too hasty in summoning them and they sat idle for two weeks while the controversy raged around them. If it were not resolved, Louise suggested on May 25, they could be sent to Angers, where the administrators had requested four more Sisters and where Sister Marie Despinal was on her deathbed. She wrote in the same post to console her embarrassed daughters: "It is enough that God knows that we are ready to work whenever it pleases Him to employ us."

M. Portail decided on June 1 to abandon the attempt to install the Sisters. He kept two for Angers and sent the others back to Paris. "I believe they are not less loaded down with merits by their not doing than if they had performed heroic actions," he told Louise in a rather transparent effort to make the best of things. "If they have done nothing more than preach by means of their modesty and equanimity of spirit in the midst of turmoil, the time and money expended on their journey has not been ill-spent."

Louise asked M. Portail before he left Le Mans "to speak to Madame du Clos, who is forever writing to our good Sister Jeanne de la Croix and giving her scruples over having left her mother." She besought him to find out once and for all "whether her mother does need her or her sister Renée, the one you sent last and who tells us that the mother herself begged you to receive her."

The first council meeting in the history of the Company was held on June 28, 1646. Aside from Vincent, Louise and M. Alméras, Vincent's assistant who was sitting in for M. Portail, the names of those present are not recorded. Beyond a doubt they were the officers of the Company and we may presume, from the minutes of this meeting and from the officers named in an instruction written by Louise a short time later, that they were Jeanne Lepeintre, Anne Hellot and two others. These others may have been senior Sisters of the house, two of whom were sometimes invited to such meetings.

Vincent began by outlining the procedure to be followed in this and subsequent meetings. They were to start by invoking the Holy Spirit in "the antiphon *Veni Sancte* with its verse and prayer" and to end with an antiphon of the Blessed Virgin, *Sancta Maria, succurre miseris,* or better, *Sub tuum praesidium.*"

He cautioned them, "before coming, to have nothing to say, not preoccupying your mind with one opinion or another; nor to discuss among yourselves your sentiments of affection or aversion, letting the spirit of God work in you; nor to deliberate among yourselves: 'I will say this or that,' but to express ingenuously whatever God will inspire you with. Do you know why, my daughters? Because, if your mind is made up as to one opinion or another before you come, it will not be free to judge clearly about what is proposed . . ."

The matters discussed in the meetings were to stay there because "the soul of God's business is secrecy." Louise was to preside in his absence and, after explaining each matter and the reason for discussing it, to ask the opinions of the others, first those on her right, then those on her left.

A recalcitrant Sister, "poor Jacqueline," has the dubious honor of being the first order of business proposed at a general council of the Company. Vincent presented the facts: "She is a warped soul who causes many little disturbances, for which reason she must no longer remain in the Company. She complains constantly and this can upset weak spirits who are not yet 'on' to her. She has no taste for the truth, making up ridiculous stories wherever she may be, and this can cause much harm. If anyone opposes her wishes, she makes herself unbearable. She is incapable of correction and, what is more—it seems to me and I regret to say it—she cannot achieve her salvation here, and would do better by herself. To sum up, my daughters, she has no common sense. On the other hand, you ought to consider that she is a girl who has rendered great service to the poor and is one of the oldest, indeed I think among the first who began to serve them in the Company. For that reason it might seem better to keep her."

"How does it seem to you, Sister?" he asked the first. The Sister thought that because of Jacqueline's years of service she should be kept but should be sequestered from the community. A second Sister agreed and suggested that it be done by sending her to serve in a village by herself. A third rejected the idea of sending her to a village and thought she might be left at the motherhouse to do whatever she wished and to be taken care of "for the love of God." A fourth was of the same opinion, adding that others would not imitate her bad example, seeing that she was kept only out of charity.

Then Vincent turned to Louise, who thought she must be dismissed. Her presence in the motherhouse would be a very bad example to others, she said; since it was impossible for her to be quiet, she would stir up discontent, especially among newcomers, who were always the most vulnerable. And Louise concurred in Vincent's fear for her salvation if she was allowed to remain; perhaps Mme de Lamoignon would employ her in one of her good works or a position might be found for her at Les Petites Maisons, the city's asylum for the insane: in either case the Company would support her, "because this good girl, in the midst of all her caprices, has ever held fast to her resolution to serve the poor . . . and left her own country for that purpose." After calling on M. Alméras, who agreed that Jacqueline should be dismissed but was noncommittal as to what disposition was to be made of her, Vincent made the decision that she should indeed either be dismissed or be persuaded to withdraw voluntarily. What she was to do afterward was not so clear. "Oh, well," he finished, "we don't have to resolve that today." And he turned to other matters.

On May 18 the administrators of a hospital at Nantes had written Vincent to implore "six of your Daughters of Charity . . . [whom] we will receive according to their rule and establishment at Angers." On the twenty-eighth, Louise expressed her fears that a division of authority between the *maître* of the hospital and the administrators might cause the Sisters the same embarrassment they were then suffering at Mans, but the difficulty was resolved and Louise herself conducted the first band of Sisters to Nantes, leaving Paris on July 26.

She first wrote out instructions for her assistants at the motherhouse. In her absence Jeanne Lepeintre was to be "Sister Servant of the entire Company," and she and Sister Anne were to look after the outpatients and the pharmacy and were to oversee the ministrations to the sick of the parish of Saint-Laurent. Sister Marguerite Le Soin would retain her post as portress and Sister Marguerite of Vienne would be the cook, "although she may from time to time go to the poor." Another Sister Marguerite was expected back from Angers: "after she has had some rest, put her on retreat with anyone else who might wish to make one." Sister Jeanne Fouré was to be assigned to the hospice of the foundlings as infirmarian with Sister Jeanne-Baptiste, and "you will give one of the two Sisters who are with Sister Antoinette to Sister Vincent if she so wishes and if she thinks the Ladies will not be annoyed at their being changed so often . . . It is my express wish that Sister Rose await my return to make her retreat because she is rather scrupulous and must be handled differently from the others." Certain Sisters, by Vincent's orders, were to be sent on visitations of the Parisian houses: "Sister Henriette to Saint-Sulpice; Sister Geneviève of the Hôtel-Dieu to Saint-Barthélémy, Saint-Séverin and Saint-Etienne; Sister Barbe, Saint-Gervais and Saint-Jacques-de-la-Boucherie; Sister Antoinette, Saint-Jacques-du-Haut-Pas; Sister Hellot, the galley slaves and Saint-Leu."

Vincent had second thoughts about these visitations: at a July conference he decided to make a trial of "two or three at first and see how it works out." His usual caution had asserted itself because, as he told the

Sisters, "the art of conducting a visitation is no slight matter, and there are very few persons capable of carrying one out in such a way as to make it acceptable. It is one of the most difficult things to do well . . . One must be so prudent, so gracious, so gentle, so silent—ah! as silent as the confessional."

Louise set out with the Sisters for Nantes on Thursday, July 26. Vincent had given them a conference on the Monday before, and on Wednesday Louise had gone to receive his final instructions and his blessing. The Sisters destined for the new mission were Elisabeth, Claude, Marguerite Noret, Catherine Bagart, Perrette of Sedan, and Antoinette of Montreuil. Sister Turgis went along to be Sister Servant at Richelieu, and François Noret as Louise's companion for the return trip.

The first leg of the journey was made by coach to Orléans. Louise's health was good for a change and she was in high spirits. "We all made fun of ourselves in the Orléans coach," she wrote, "and were very gay without by the grace of God failing in the observances, except that during the times of meditation and silence we would let ourselves be overcome by sleep, for which we would sometimes blame the heat." They did not fail to visit the sick along the way, "in the name of the entire Company as a continuation of the offering of our services and duties to God in the person of the poor," and to teach catechism whenever the opportunity offered.

Louise wrote to Vincent from Orléans, but the letter was delayed. On August 4 he complained in a short note that he had no news of the travelers. "Everybody wishes you were here," he told Louise, "and I don't know what to answer those who are asking for you. I am more anxious than anyone and can get news from no one but yourself. I am so afraid lest the great heat and the discomfort of the coach have overcome or at least greatly weakened you that I am awaiting your news with great impatience . . ."

The Loire was so low that the Sisters could not take a boat at Orléans as they had planned but had to go by road to Meung, which took them five days. On the way they stopped overnight at Cour-sur-Loire, Mont-Louis, and Ablevoie, where Sister Turgis left them to go on alone to Richelieu. At Tours they rejoiced in a delay of six or seven hours which gave them an opportunity they had hoped for, "of visiting the places of devotion and the relatives and friends of our Sisters from the area."

Louise wrote on July 30 "from the boat, near Tours," to M. Portail at Saint-Méen concerning the canonical establishment of the Company, which was being negotiated with Archbishop de Gondi: "Monsieur Lambert has sent us a copy of the petition to Monseigneur de Paris with the chief portions of our Rule appended; but this is not the complete [Rule], which Monsieur Vincent gave us after explaining it in a conference and which Your Charity promised to send me. In the name of God, Monsieur, please send it, for we have no copy."

Vincent himself wrote to Portail about both the Daughters' and the Priests' rules on August 12, and alerted him to be ready to return to Paris to help with the final drafts. The reason for the sudden decision to submit a new request for approbation—Louise would never have left Paris if such important business had been planned—was that an opportunity had arisen which Vincent did not want to miss. The Archbishop had left the city and would be away for some time, and Vincent's old friend de Retz, the coadjutor, enjoyed full vicariate powers, including "the power to approve our rules."

The Sisters' journey continued through Saumur to Les Pont-de-Cé, where they "had the honor . . . of being thrown out of the inn because of arriving very late and of not wishing chickens killed lest it put us in the situation of having to eat them on Friday. We needed rest badly and . . . met a very accommodating woman, the wife of a surgeon, who graciously rescued us." They arrived at Angers on Friday and put up at "the inn closest to the hospital." The Sisters there were "greatly consoled to see all our Company."

Abbé de Vaux had reported to Louise in June that certain Sisters, especially Sister Perrette, had resisted his orders—and in front of outsiders. She believed him, of course, and took action, but at the same time her instinctive maternal defense of her daughters came very much to the fore. "While I do not wish to believe that Sister Perrette is entirely innocent of the faults of which she is accused," she told de Vaux, "nevertheless I find it very hard to persuade myself that she wished to soil her reputation ever so little." And again two weeks later: "I doubt very much whether our poor Sister Perrette was as criminal as they try to make her appear. She is of a very free temperament . . . but has no evil will." Nonetheless, Louise decided on this August stopover at Angers that it would be better for all concerned to transfer Sister Perrette.

They stayed on at Angers until Monday. When they were on the point of leaving, a short business duel ensued between Louise and the administrators, from which she emerged the victor. "The gentlemen had been waiting for me to bring up the matter of the four Sisters they had asked for," she later told Vincent. "It was they who brought it up, giving us to understand—in order to get out of paying the cost of their [the Sisters'] journey, I think—that it was our Sisters who had made the request and that they themselves were indifferent. I showed as much indifference as they and told them in leaving that, if they wished it, we would do our best to send [the Sisters]."

Louise and the Sisters stopped, at M. de Vaux's request, to visit the Ladies of Charity in the little village of Ingrande. The Ladies had prepared a big dinner for them but, since they could not stay, Mlle Gouain packed it in hampers to take with them, for which Louise was profoundly grateful since funds were running low. This same Mlle Gouain had asked repeatedly to join the Company but had not been accepted. The previous May, Louise had informed M. Portail: "I believe, Monsieur, that the good Sister [of the confraternity], Mlle Marie Gouain, will seek you out to ask once more to come to us. Please do not give her any hope, Monsieur, but make it plain that she can say that she belongs to the Company and that the service she renders God in His poor earns her this association." Mlle Gouain may very well have been the first affiliate of the Company. Affiliates by reason of exceptional service to the Company are privileged to share in its prayers and good works.

The low water in the river slowed the last leg of the voyage considerably and it was the afternoon of Thursday, August 18, before the boat docked at Nantes. The whole town turned out to welcome them. As Louise put it: "All the families of Nantes had been waiting with impatience for the arrival of our Sisters, and for a day or two before, ecclesiastics and women had been gathering in the streets, thinking they must come at any minute . . ." The Sisters were escorted to the hospital by cheering crowds who fought for the honor of drawing their carriage. Louise's pleasure was evident as she described for Vincent this triumphal and deafening welcome. The memory of it still glowed in her when she wrote him three days later:

> I do not know what will happen to this foundation, of which I have not yet seen the thorns of popular murmur but only the unbelievable applause of everyone . . . Would to God, my Most Honored Father, I had the power and love to recognize the care of divine Providence over us! Oh, how loudly I would sing His praises! I must stop short and content myself with asking the heavenly court to render to God the glory it can. It is up to you, our Most Honored Father to whom our good God makes known his protection over us, to supply our lack.

When the administrators of the hospital wished to show Louise special deference, however, she would have none of it. "They had prepared a private room for us near our Sisters' room," she wrote, "the which I refused and asked to be allowed to have no more privacy than our Sisters had, and this [the administrators] in their goodness granted me."

An attempt was made—which later proved most unsuccessful—to avoid future conflicts in administering the hospital. "From the very day of our arrival," Louise recorded, "all the Messieurs le Pères gave us full power in the hospital, both as regards the care of the sick and in making sure that the servitors made their submission, instructing our Sisters to dismiss those who did not satisfy them by obeying their orders. The servants were discharged at once and our Sisters put in command of everything. There was a good ecclesiastic, chaplain of the house, without whose orders nothing was done, and the gentlemen decided to remove him as soon as the Sisters were well established and replace him with the confessor to the religious of Sainte-Marie." Louise was too wise and too tactful, however, to parade prerogative. "God gave us the grace never to exercise the power these gentlemen gave us, by doing anything without informing them and obtaining their consent," she said.

The Sisters were indeed great news in Nantes and women of every rank flocked to see them. Even the heads of the Protestant sects came; and the cloistered religious begged the Sisters to visit them so that they might talk to them and inspect their habits. An association of Ladies of Charity like the one at the Hôtel-Dieu in Paris sprang up immediately to supplement the ministrations of the Sisters by bringing the sick poor the delicacies and sweets the Sisters could neither afford nor spare the time to distribute.

On August 13 Louise wrote to M. Portail to warn him to let Sister Anne rather than Sister Marguerite introduce the wearing of the white cornette, which was now being permitted, for the latter had, she said, "a great inclination to make an impression" and while she was "devout and wise" she was also "rather vain" and had a way of "speaking at length about humility in such a way as to attract praise." Louise did not mean to belittle the girl, she insisted: these were natural traits and "I count on grace to draw good out of them."

She was anxious for news of the motherhouse and amazed that she had not received any letters from Jeanne Lepeintre. Her health continued so excellent, she confided happily to Jeanne, "that there is no longer any fear of my undertaking long journeys." She had had no word from her son and "but for Brother Ducournau [who had written from Saint-Lazare about Michel] I would have been greatly upset." At the moment, however, nothing could disturb her bubbling spirits, which showed themselves in a postscript: "I greet all our dear Sisters in general and individually and embrace them with all my heart. I have written to Sister Hellot, Sister Jeanne de la Croix and someone else—oh, yes, Sister Torneton; and I complained to Sister Anne for not having written to me. I am sure that Sister Louise would want to write to us and a little word from her hand would comfort me. Little Sister Anne could add a word, too. And Sister Marguerite of Vienne—oh, I renounce her if she doesn't write me a word, too! My wish for her today is a good-sized slice of melon for the community. Sister Françoise [wants to know] whether Sister Anne has received the gravel she sent for her pigeons."

As so often happens, their letters crossed, and Louise sent a second letter hard upon the first, to answer questions which Jeanne had raised. The little Sister at Sedan who was ill should be brought home. Sisters should not come to stay at the motherhouse without being invited. As for Sister Geneviève at Saint-Germain, who was experiencing some "little problems": "It is not so long ago that I spoke with her . . . She is a very good girl . . . If you see her, comfort her, for she is rather sensitive." She begged Jeanne, further, to "comfort all the weak and help those in distress, speak to each one."

Despite her wish to have one of Vincent's priests at Nantes for the Sisters' confessor, Louise agreed in a letter of August 21 that "divine Providence would wish us to follow Your Charity's order" by accepting "for ordinary confessor the [confessor] of the religious of the Visitation, who has agreed to come to the hospital as chaplain." The Visitandines did not know yet that he was leaving them, she told Vincent, and although she did not think they would blame her for his loss she was going to visit them, nonetheless, to explain that neither she nor the Sisters had anything to do with it.

Vincent had written again on August 14. He had still no letters from Louise, but a Visitandine at Orléans and M. de Vaux at Angers had assured him that the travelers had been well when they saw them. He had no instructions for her negotiations with the administrators of the hospital, because of his confidence that "Our Lord will give you sufficient light and wisdom." He could tell her now that her son had been gravely ill but was out of danger and on the way to recovery. He had offered Michel the hospitality of Saint-Lazare or the services of two Daughters of Charity to nurse him at M. Vacherot's clinic. Michel had chosen the latter. He finished by telling her with rueful humor that the Ladies of Charity "have declared war on me for letting you go [to Nantes], especially Madame de Nesmond. If you return healthy—as I hope from the goodness of God—peace will be quickly restored. So I beg you to conserve your strength as much as you can!"

Louise was most grateful for his goodness to Michel. "It is a great comfort to me," she wrote in obvious relief. "The day I had the honor of your dear letter I had been moved very strongly to give him to God, abandoning him entirely to Him, which helped me very much to bear the news Your Charity sent me." At the same time she was "annoyed that my son did not accept the honor of your offer to take him into your house. *Mon Dieu!* I think I shall never cease asking for his entire conversion. It seems to me that this illness of his is more dangerous than he thinks; but I fear even more that he turns a deaf ear and does not permit himself to be afraid lest that force him to a happy change."

While she felt Michel's condition as keenly as ever, the panic it would have caused in the past was absent. This calm self-possession, so hard fought for and now permanent, was also evident in her resolution not to delay her return to Paris, much as she would have liked to fuss over the establishment of the hospital until all was perfection, lest she be "satisfying myself without necessity and fall ill." But she would not stop at Le Mans, as a churchman there bent on recalling the Sisters wished her to, she told Vincent, "unless Your Charity commands me and tells me what to do." His Charity did neither.

She was amused at the reaction of the Ladies of Charity to her trip. They should be "very satisfied with me," she wrote with mock seriousness, "since I have not failed to write to them. I am amazed at so much fuss, since I do not merit it. Why does God who knows that permit it? To keep me humble."

Her newfound assurance was unmistakable. It was the reason why she did not hesitate to describe for Vincent "the honors they render me here," adding with a wholly new and delightful sarcasm: "In the name of God, make no mistake about it: they take me for a great lady! I think there is scarcely a lady of quality who has not come to call and some have even made special trips from the surrounding countryside. Oh, how I shall burn for that one day, and what a comedown I shall have!"

On the same day she wrote to Sister Hellot, who had given her all the details of Michel's illness. She was of the opinion, she told the good

Sister, that his attack had been caused by "too much weight and an extreme natural weakness." She was convinced of God's goodness, for she knew very well from what Sister Hellot had told her that Michel "had been in grave danger of choking to death on the instant." She was, she finished, "under great obligation to all our Sisters and I thank them with all my heart for their dear affection, which they could never have shown in a more feeling way."

Turning to spiritual problems Sister Hellot had confided to her, Louise assumed a half-playful sternness. She would start on the return trip in a week, she told the good Sister, so "get ready to hear a catalogue of your faults. Do you think I wish to accept a heart to have for my own that gives way to so many fears and imaginations as to read like a novel? I tell you that if it no longer follows what divine Providence tells it, if it listens only to so many apprehensions, I want no part of it. What would I do with it? In the meantime I desire wholeheartedly its return to God, its witness to Him that it wants only what He wants, that it would like in the future to perform acts of prowess and generosity. But since that cannot come about without giving a great push to nature, let us content ourselves for the present with acquiescence, let us with submission to God leave in doubt everything which is unclear." It was tender advice given affectionately.

On that very day Vincent was writing to inform Louise of a new foundation that had come about suddenly: "The Queen has commanded us to send her two Sisters for the Charity at Fontainebleau, which command we have obeyed, choosing Sister Barbe [Angiboust] with another [Anne Scoliège], who, I think, may have to be brought back because she is too young." Barbe was assigned to look after the poor and the sick, and Anne to the school.

Sister Hellot had informed Louise that her friend the Duchesse de Liancourt had suffered a great loss in the death of her son. Louise wrote back on August 25 to ask Sister Hellot "to inform me if you learn how the dear child of this holy family was killed. Our Sisters at Saint-Sulpice could find out something by going to visit Madame de Ligniéres." By the time she wrote to Vincent on the twenty-eighth, she had the news that this only son, the Comte de la Roche-Guyon, had fallen in the siege of Mardyth. As a mother with an only son herself, she told Vincent, she understood that "it would be a great sorrow for a long time to this good mother." As for that grief of another kind Michel brought her daily, she went on, she had clung to the hope that his recent illness might have taught him a lesson, "but from what they tell me he is gadding about and even sleeps away from home. He has written to me and I detect a new resentment at having been checked and, in my small opinion, he has put and continues to put a guard on his heart lest it come to a knowledge of the actual state of his soul. I contemplate all this evil, but tranquilly enough, and it seems to me that I no longer have anything to do with him except for my great desire for his salvation."

The illness of Sister Marie-Marthe at Angers meant that another Sister would have to be added to the four already requested, plus two more who, it had become clear, were needed at Nantes, making "seven whom we must request of Divine Providence. God be eternally glorified for the blessings He showers on our little Company! I hope always for its increase because Your Charity is so strongly bent on its perfection. I cannot express the consolation my heart has from that, God making plain to me that I am in no way necessary and very little useful." She closed in this same artless vein of sincere self-abnegation: "You know all my shortcomings, not the least my infidelities which prevent me from performing scarcely any exercise of devotion. Always with people and looking after my health! It is to my shame."

Vincent sent her the notes Sister Hellot had taken down at his latest conference and asked her to review them and send them back. "I have read over some of them. I confess to wincing a bit at two or three." But he did not say whether he blamed the secretary or himself for his pain.

It was October before all details of the establishment were ironed out and the official agreement signed between the Company and the administrators of the hospital. A few days later, Louise and Sister Françoise Noret set out for home. They took the river boat as far as Angers, a voyage of four days, but the wind and water were so violent that there was real danger of shipwreck and after several frights Louise decided to take a carriage from Angers to Paris.

The hospital administrators at Angers again brought up the matter of the four additional Sisters and Louise seized on their obvious need for them to extract the promise of a new washtub and piping for the laundry and of servants to do the wash, with which the Sisters had been overburdened in addition to everything else they had to do. The administrators tried to regain their position by insisting that journeys of Sisters returning to the motherhouse be paid by the Company, but Louise would not agree unless the Company had recalled them: if the administrators should make the request, they must assume the expense.

As soon as possible after her return, Louise sent the two extra Sisters she had promised for the hospital at Nantes, and with them a solicitous letter to Elizabeth Martin and all the Sisters. "Do you read your rule and your offices?" she asked. Do you recite evening and morning the prayers for the sick and the *Benedicite* and grace at meals? Have you napkins at the bedsides of your sick? Do you minister to them properly? But especially, my dear Sisters, do you have a great love for their salvation? It is that above all that Our good God looks for from you . . ."

Louise reminded Elisabeth Martin that one of the Sisters she had sent, Henriette Gesseaume, was old, "but the deference and respect you should have for her should not keep you from assisting her in the desire she has to be of good service during the little time Monsieur Vincent assigns her to work for her perfection. You should treat her then like any of our other Sisters. She will run the pharmacy and train Sister Claude for it. She will do everything the others do . . . Please, dear Sister, be very careful to give her work. She has promised me to do everything you tell her to . . . She needs great gentleness and to be corrected of her faults with much charity." At fifty-five, Louise understood the old and their need for extra kindness without coddling.

In another letter to Elisabeth Martin dated November 18, Louise reported the death of Sister Mathurine at Saint-Denis, and called attention to the suffrages for the dead common to all religious institutes: "Do not forget the holy custom of going to Communion for the repose of her soul."

Sister Turgis at Richelieu missed Louise, who hastened to comfort her tenderly: "Dear Sister, please do not think of the distance between us but consider rather that we are intimately united, with no possibility of ever being separated, because the closeness engendered by holy love knows no separation." She went on to encourage her to "give great care to the instruction of youth and to keep good order in your school." One of the postulants from Richelieu, Sister Michelle, "a truly good girl," had come to an untimely death and Louise asked Sister Turgis to "assure her parents that she made a good end, which should comfort them a great deal." Louise had herself been ill, but promised to write to Michelle's father when she was able. The girl had been ill for two weeks and had suffered "a little martyrdom, which she bore with admirable patience." Several days before her death she had asked "for signs that she would die a true Daughter of Charity, the which Monsieur Vincent granted her." Whether these "signs" were formal admittance into the

Company or the taking of vows, they had brought the dying girl "ineffable consolation."

On November 20, 1646, Jean-François-Paul de Gondi, Coadjutor of Paris, signed as his uncle's vicar the act which formally established the Company as a confraternity. Louise's objections to the first draft had been ignored in the approved document, except that the Coadjutor, while retaining absolute and perpetual control over the Company for the Archbishops of Paris, had named Vincent as its director for his lifetime. It was the first giant step, nevertheless, and while Louise would continue her campaign to have the ultimate act of ecclesiastical approbation reflect the safeguards which she firmly believed to be the will of God, she was supremely happy at this first official sign of His favor.

XIV

"This Poor Company Suffers Much"

God had given Louise exceptional health when she needed it for the rigorous journey to Nantes and back, but once home she relapsed into her usual borderline state of serious illness and was "even in danger, from what they say." The business of the Company went on, nonetheless, when she was able to put her hand to it.

A letter of January 31, 1647, mentions two new houses, one at Chars and one "near Melun." The Chars mission had been founded at the request of the Marquise d'O, wife of the Duc de Luynes; it also had the favor and support of Madame la présidente de Herse. The first Sister Servant was advancing in years and Louise urged her to the perfect practice of the Rule for the special reason that the "time for working will pass swiftly for you, because of your age, and will leave you cause for regret, and because, being with a younger Sister, you are obliged to be an example to her." She was anxious to know whether the Sisters had "any work from the town. Be very mindful that it is the practice among us to earn our keep . . . God does not dispense us from the need to earn our bread not only that we may be easy and free from anxiety but in order that we may work all the harder to imitate His Son."

Barbe Angiboust had been appointed the first Sister Servant of the new hospital at Fontainebleau. Among her four companions was Anne Scoliège, who was mistress of the school which had long become a fixed part of each new foundation. After the first few weeks, when the house had been put in running order, Louise asked Anne to report on "the way she handles the instruction of the little girls . . . Sometime ago Monsieur Vincent spoke to me about our Sisters employed in teaching and indicated his desire that they all use the same method." She was happy that Barbe had heard from her parents before she left, and sent her the additional good news that her sister Cécile at Angers was well.

In a letter of March 10 to Sister Turgis at Richelieu, she had family news of another kind. Her sister, "the widow," she told her, "has remarried during these Mardi Gras days [to] a young man about twenty-five years old, and gives as the reason, to help him with his school." The noncommittal report smacked of disapproval and of the assurance that Sister Turgis would not be overjoyed either.

On Easter Day, April 21, Louise was moved to make Vincent some considered suggestions for the betterment of the Company. "This poor Company suffers much under my miserable direction," she lamented. "May I not hope that God will deliver it soon from this captivity which is so great an obstacle to the perfecting of its work?" Her further proposals were that Vincent write a letter to all the Sisters at Nantes for the internal good of the house, and that he promulgate "our little rules so that they may be read from time to time in the Company." Her son's perennial restiveness was causing her such constant worry that she could not forbear bringing it up even in this letter which dealt exclusively with basic community needs. Would not Vincent speak in his behalf concerning some new venture to the Comtesse de Maure? *"Mon Dieu!* how my pride has made me suffer in this affair," she excused herself sadly, "and what great peace would ensue if I were rid of it!"

Vincent promulgated the rules in a conference on May 30. This six months' delay after the official Act of Establishment can hardly be ascribed to the press of Vincent's duties: he could, for that matter, have made the promulgation at a conference given on February 2. The delay seems rather to have been due, as Coste suggests, to protocol or to the founders' hopes of effecting certain modifications.

Vincent wrote the desired letter to the Sisters at Nantes on April 24 from his Congregation's farm at Orsigny. The letter was a masterpiece of gentle correction and persuasion. It began by praising them for the very real progress they had made: the good example they were giving "to those left behind at the motherhouse"; "the good girls you have drawn there from Nantes"; "the sick poor you have brought to a good way of life"; all the others "you have reconciled to God" and especially so many "who are now happy in heaven and who pray without ceasing for your dear souls." It was the truth, he assured them, that "reams of paper" would not suffice to list all the good they had done and were doing.

Despite all this, they were tormented by temptations! It was the natural condition, he told them bluntly. Even the Son of God was tempted, in order that He might prove "His love for His Father and for the sanctification of His Church." But, the Sisters would object, other people might be tempted from time to time, but they themselves were tempted "constantly, in every place and, as it were, by every person they came in contact with!" "It is God's good pleasure, dear Sisters," he replied, "that those blessed elite souls He cherishes so much be tempted and afflicted every day." Are we not commanded to take up our cross daily? "Notice the word *daily*, dear Sisters!"

Very well, they might counter, they could suffer the faults of externs, but it was their own Sisters, those who should be their consolation, who were their "pain, cross and affliction." And who else would be, he rejoined sardonically—"those who are far away . . . ? From whom and by whom had Our Lord to suffer if not His Apostles, disciples and the people He lived among who were the people of God?"

But when the contradiction came from "your Sister Servant, from her coldness, her discomfitures, her reticence, her never saying a gracious word—when she does speak . . . it is with sarcasm and to find fault"—that is what cannot be borne! (Elisabeth Martin was ill again and therefore these allegations were probably true, the fruits of her illness; but the real cause of the trouble was Catherine Bagart, who had sowed dissension among the Sisters and between them and the Sister Servant.)

Vincent responded vigorously that "we are very weak or ill when we need to be flattered by our superiors in everything that they say and command . . ." He finished, in his usual way, with positive corrective measures to be taken: the Sisters should meditate on what he had written; they should confide absolutely in their confessors; they should avoid seeking human consolation from one another; and they should write to inform him of the good sentiments God would inspire them with when they had prayed and had gone to confession and Communion. He gave the letter to Louise so that Jeanne Lepeintre might take it with her when she left for Nantes on May 8. "I must tell you in wholehearted simplicity, dear Sisters, the thoughts this dear letter inspired in me while reading it," Louise wrote approvingly to her daughters. "O my Sisters, the sweetness of style, the catalogue of graces God has given you and us, the instructions his [Vincent's] goodness has so gently given you . . . !"

On June 21 she wrote to M. Portail, who was in Rome on business. He had been taken ill there and she expressed the hope, in a rare witticism, that he "would not mistake *Paradis* for *Paris*, for I am of the opinion that the perfection God asks of the entire Company waits upon your charitable advice and direction." She envied his being "at the fount of Holy Church and nears its head, the Holy Father of all Christians," whose blessing she "as [his] child, however unworthy," greatly desired. Because of her "age and infirmities, which increase every day," she asked Portail to procure for her and for all the Sisters a papal blessing with a plenary indulgence applicable at the hour of death.

Peace was finally restored in Lorraine and both Louise and Vincent were trying to finish up their ministry to the refugees. Some few still lingered on in the capital, including three religious lodged with Louise. "Can't you induce them to return to their monastery?" Vincent asked her. The Duchesse d'Aiguillon had obtained a hundred écus from the superintendent of finances to send them back but, Vincent cautioned, they were not to have the money unless they went.

On June 24 Louise wrote Vincent, who had been called unexpectedly to Freneville, of her "surprise at your going before giving us the necessary orders for the departure of our Sisters to Montreuil." The Comte Charles de Lannoy, governor of Montreuil-sur-mer, had requested Sisters and Louise had selected Anne Hardemont and Marie Lullen. Louise's implied reproach to Vincent was hardly called for, because he had given detailed advice to the two Sisters in council meetings held on June 19–20.

Always practical and farsighted, Louise had focused on the precise point upon which they would need the most instruction: "how to conduct themselves toward M. le Comte because, having nothing special to do and a great interest in this establishment, he will be with them often." The key to maintaining the proper relationship, Vincent said, was to remember at all times that M. le Comte held the place of God at Montreuil and especially at the hospital. But this was not getting to the heart of the matter, Louise insisted: "M. le Comte is extremely frank and open to the point that he would speak freely to a child . . ." Since it was to be expected that he would speak just as freely to the Sisters, it was to be feared that they, not used to being taken into the confidence of the great, might fall into the trap of being too familiar with him. Ah, Vincent replied, in that case there were two safeguards: neither of the Sisters should reciprocate the Comte's openness by giving away community confidences or the secrets of family living; and they must perform perfectly as true Daughters of Charity, remembering that so outspoken a man would be as ready with blame as he was with praise. Louise wrote out a long instruction of her own for the departing Sisters, expanding upon Vincent's advice and especially upon the danger of self-complacence and upon the absolute union they should maintain in imitation of the Holy Trinity. She suggested to them, also, a specific application of her own devotion to the guardian angel: that they facilitate their work and their rapport with the people by "having devotion to the guardian angels of all the souls in the town." It is no wonder that these poor, unlettered first Daughters of Charity were able to accomplish so much, for they worked literally as the arms of God, steeped in Him as they were by the spiritual motivation given them by their father and mother so that they thought of themselves only as His servants and helpmeets. Anne Hardemont and Marie Lullen left for Montreuil two days later.

The Sisters transferred from Angers had arrived at the motherhouse, one of them sent back in disgrace, and Louise reported to Vincent that "the accused poses as the most innocent person in the world. I do not dare write to her father until I know what Your Charity wants us to do with her." And, she told him further, Sister Marguerite Tourneton had defected to the Augustinian Sisters who conducted the Hôtel-Dieu. She had stolen away the previous Sunday "without saying a word, and the Mother Prioress has written me that she went to the Hôtel-Dieu this morning to receive her . . . I have made no reply and will not until your return. God alone knows the state of my poor mind in the midst of all these disorders, for it seems as if the good God wishes to destroy us entirely. I merit it and am amazed that His justice defers the execution so long. Just so His mercy sweetens my soul—that is enough for me."

The whole community was upset over Sister Tourneton's defection. "All our poor Company is in great sorrow, amazed and frightened over the loss of our Sister," Louise wrote. "Everybody is whispering about it on the sly, for no one dares speak out . . ." Sister Tourneton soon repented of her faithlessness, humbly asked to return and was taken back. She died the following year.

Louise summed up the press of her duties in a letter written that same day to Barbe Angiboust at Fontainebleau. "You have good reason to complain about me," she began familiarly, "for it is indeed too long a time since I have written to you, without being able to pinpoint what has prevented me, except the affairs that often arise unannounced: the death of poor dear Sister Louise of Saint-Jacques de la Boucherie, the illnesses of several others and the departure of some, joined to the hope

I had from time to time of sending you a Sister without being able to find one, for while she might do passably here, when it comes to sending her some place else we would not know whom to choose because those who are suitable for one thing are not suitable for another." She had, nevertheless, found someone at last, Sister Jeanne-Christine, the bearer of the letter.

At least everything was going well with Sister Turgis and Sister Anne at Richelieu. "You would not believe the consolation Monsieur Vincent had, and I also, at reading your letter," Louise wrote them happily. She ascribed it all to "the good direction you receive" from the Priests of the Mission.

Despite Louise's objections to the Château of Bicêtre as a foundling home, the will of the Ladies of Charity had prevailed with Vincent and the Queen, and he wrote an order for the transfer of the first children there on July 7, 1647. "Mademoiselle Le Gras is requested by the Ladies of Charity to send tomorrow, Sunday, at one o'clock, four children, two boys and two girls, with two Daughters of Charity to Bicêtre . . ." the order ran. "Madame Truluy will go with a carriage to fetch the children . . . and the necessary linen." There was also to be a little inaugural ceremony, for Mme Truluy was to stop first either at Mme de Romilly's or Mme la chancelière Séguier's, where the other ladies would be assembled, and all would then escort the children and the Sisters to Bicêtre. It is amusing to note that the order mentioned that the ladies would like "Mademoiselle Le Gras . . . to be of the party," but added hastily that such would not be necessary.

Louise probably did not join the inauguration parade. Indeed, a few days later she wrote Vincent a curt and angry note. "Experience has at length shown that it was not without reason that I feared taking up residence at Bicêtre," she began abruptly. "These ladies want the impossible from our Sisters. They have set aside as their quarters tiny rooms where the air will grow stale almost immediately, having passed over the larger rooms. But our poor Sisters dare not open their mouths! They not only do not want Mass said [there] but expect our Sisters to go Gentilly to hear it. And who will take care of the children in the meantime? And who will do the chores? Here is Sister Geneviève [Poisson]. I beg you to take the time to speak with her. She will tell you all about the trouble they have and the pretensions of these ladies." And she ended with what can only be construed as a threat: "I am very much afraid that we will have to give up the care of these poor little babies." Vincent's reply, unfortunately, is lost; but not long afterward Louise herself went out to Bicêtre and stayed there until she had brought some kind of order out of the chaos.

Before she left, however, the long-simmering unrest at Nantes exploded. Jeanne Lepeintre had been sent as a visitor extraordinary to investigate the situation, making visitations at Fontainebleau, Richelieu, and Angers on the way. The plan was for M. Lambert to meet her at Nantes, where the two of them would join forces to bring about peace, but the slowness of travel and communication did not allow the plan to gel. On July 10 word came to Louise that Elisabeth Martin was at Angers!

"There must be some great necessity since you did not wait for permission," she wrote Elisabeth posthaste. "Beyond that, it would not enter my mind that Sister Elisabeth would be guilty of such an infidelity." She and Vincent demanded to know the reason for the trip at once and Elisabeth was "not to budge from Angers" until she had written them and received a reply. Louise next fired off a letter to Jeanne Lepeintre at Nantes with the order to bring Sister Turgis there from Richelieu if she was needed, and another to Sister Turgis to hold herself in readiness. "*Mon Dieu!* dear Sister," Louise cried out to Jeanne, "what need you have for graces to do what God has committed to you!" Her agitation increased with information she received that "a girl had died without assistance, and that it had happened because several of the Sisters were out in the town! If that is true I am astounded, for they should never go out. *Mon Dieu!* Sisters, we have reason to humble ourselves, seeing this occasion for gossip and contempt among the citizens of Nantes, who have called us to prevent small disorders in the house of God and we profane it, at least in the opinion of men, and that by attachment to our own self-love and self-satisfaction! I want you to do penance, and I assure you that whenever people speak to me of the good done by our Company I will blush with shame at the thought of the disorder of Nantes!" She went on to plead with Jeanne: "Tell our Sisters that the people of Nantes clamor against them more than they think and about things of the greatest moment. The devil dearly loves such pastimes, but he will not prevail as long as they regroup and unite together under the Cross like chicks under their mother when the hawk hovers above them."

By July 20 she had heard from Jeanne, who confirmed her worst fears. "Everything you tell me about what our Sisters have done is entirely contrary to the agreement we signed with the Messieurs les Pères, such as going out to market," she wrote in sorrowful reply. "They should go out only for fish and fowl, and that could be done in less than an hour. As for fruits, herbs, eggs, etc., they should be brought to the house by vendors, and butter is part of the provisions the Messieurs les Pères promised to supply to the house, along with wood, wine, vinegar, oil and other necessities." Jeanne had not told Louise the whole story, either because she was afraid to or because, falling ill shortly after her arrival, she had not had time to learn it.

Louise's agony was evident in a letter of July 30 which began: "It seems to me that M. Lambert is a long time getting to Nantes." She still clung to the hope that much of what was reported was rumor and dictated by envy. Catherine Bagart had written to her and Louise asked Jeanne to "assure her . . . that I am still the same toward her as she has known me to be and that the friendship God has given me for her has not diminished." Despite her previous avowal that she would ever hold her head in shame over the disturbances at Nantes, she was pathetically eager to tell the Sisters there that the mother of one of the Sisters from Montreuil "never had more comfort than to know that her daughter belonged to our Company." Some of the rebellious Sisters had resented Louise's strictures on leaving the house and alleged her own conduct in this matter, reducing her to the humiliation of having to defend herself: "It is true that I have given myself the liberty of taking some meals at the monasteries of the Daughters of the Blessed Virgin [Visitandines] when I have been on the road. But, dear Sister, great care must be taken not to make a custom out of this. My weaknesses and travel difficulties have caused me to commit faults into which, dear Sister —please!—you need not fall, nor all our dear Sisters!" She certainly never committed these "faults" without Vincent's permission and advice —or, even so, without shame.

The bombshell came with the report written by M. Lambert to Vincent on July 26. "I can assure you that our Sisters have been greatly upset," he began, "and, indeed, if they have committed certain small faults, the occasions the Providence of God has sent them have been great opportunities for proving their souls." After this pious introduction he got down to facts: "The Sister Servant was at variance with the confessor, and vice versa—and openly. Each had his faction both inside and outside the house. It is enough to tell you that for you to know all the rest, especially since everything said on one side or the other did not always agree with the truth but was very much dictated by emotion. We

have sent away three of our Sisters: two to Paris, Sisters Catherine Bagart and Antoinette Larcher; the other to Richelieu, Sister Isabelle
[Elisabeth Martin] . . . It has been necessary to make this transfer not
only of our two Sisters but of Sister Isabelle also, who, while an excellent
girl, has at the same time greatly contributed by imprudence to all the
little disorders which have occurred. Sister Henriette, who had a horrible
fight with the good gentleman chaplain, although he was quite innocent,
is still here . . ."

The Sisters would be provided with a new confessor, he continued, so
as to make matters easier all around. Despite what had happened, the
"Messieurs les Pères . . . are full of good will toward the Sisters and indeed, if God does us the grace to let them live in perfect rapport, there
will be a little establishment here which will sanctify the Daughters of
Charity greatly, because I think God will permit them to suffer a long
time yet from outsiders." He urged that the Sisters sent to Paris be received kindly, "for they are not guilty of the evils they have been suspected of and, had they been directed properly, I believe wrongdoing
would never have been imputed to them."

It was surely the weight of all the troubles at Nantes that made Louise
write Anne Hardemont at Montreuil that "you make me somewhat
nervous seeing the applause of all the people"—although she wrote
proudly to Nantes: "Our Sisters at Montreuil are wonderful, by the
grace of God!"—and was perhaps the reason for her pretended petulance
in writing to Sister Turgis: "Please tell Sister Anne that we will not be
good friends until she writes to me. I will not allow [you] to greet her
[for me]."

Once at Bicêtre, Louise was mollified, if not wholly convinced, as to
the possibilty of continuing the work of the foundlings there. "It is true,
my Most Honored Father," she wrote on August 22, "that a great deal of
good is to be hoped for this work, if it pleases Our good God to continue
His holy blessings." After looking over the situation she had decided that
she "should not return until I can leave behind a schoolmistress," who
was in training. In the meantime Louise herself had assumed the
teaching chores and expressed a wish for "alphabet charts" which "could
be put against the walls—this is the Ursuline method . . ." A few days
later she was still pressing a Sister at the motherhouse to "tell Monsieur
Vincent, please, that if he comes across alphabet tables to send them to
us."

November 20, 1647, anniversary of the approbation of the Company, moved Louise to write Vincent that "it seems to me that God put my soul in a great peace and simplicity at prayer, very imperfect prayer on my part, although I made it on the subject of the necessity that the Company of the Daughters of Charity be ever successively under the direction that Divine Providence has given it in both *spirituals and temporals*. Concerning which I think I understood that it would be better for His glory that the Company fail entirely than to come under any other direction, since that would seem to be against the will of God . . . I hope that, if Your Charity has understood from Our Lord what He seems to me to have said to you apropos of Saint Peter, that it was upon [the Congregation of the Mission] that He wished to build this Company, it will persevere in the service He asks of it for the instruction of little ones and the comfort of the sick." There is something inspired in her conviction that Vincent's Congregation was essential to the survival of the Daughters of Charity.

On October 30 Vincent convened an important council meeting whose significance he stressed in his opening remarks. "My daughters," he began, "we must deal with certain matters that Mademoiselle Le Gras regards as essential to the Company. If something is to be done about them, it is better to do it now rather than later. Things are not hardened yet. Mademoiselle Le Gras is living. What is done now will remain forever, and if things are allowed to drift, when they wish to remedy them at some future time—say, in thirty, forty, fifty years, if the Company should last that long—they will say: 'That's the way it was done at the beginning, that's the way it will continue to be done. Monsieur Vincent was there. Mademoiselle Le Gras. And they approved its being done in that way.' For this reason, if anything is to be done for the perfection of the Company it should be done as soon as possible."

The first question considered was whether the Sisters should teach boys as well as girls in their schools. It was decided in the negative, the chief reasons being Church and royal ordinances against it, although Vincent adduced rather perfunctorily certain moral dangers also. The reasons for this decision, which was clung to well into modern times and which is still followed in regard to orphan boys older than infants, are interesting in assessing the controversies on the subject which have arisen in the Company from time to time. The second question raised was whether the motherhouse and the village Charities should accept pensioners. Louise made a distinction: she judged it impractical, indeed "impossible," to accept pensioners in the motherhouse or in the parish

Charities, but "practically necessary" to accept them in the village Charities because the ladies who financed them wanted it. M. Lambert, who was now Vincent's assistant, demurred and Vincent agreed with him. "We must take none, oh, none at all!" he stated flatly. The most important decision was the last taken up. Vincent made his usual presentation of the question:

> We have now to consider whether there should be a Sister appointed to direct those newly come [to the Company] . . . It is of great significance for the good of the Company, and has always been a universal practice. This is the way it was done formerly in individual houses and especially at the Hôtel-Dieu: a new girl would be entrusted to an older [Sister] who would train and look after her. But it was noted that "nieces" tied themselves to their "aunts," as they called them, in such a way as to make for partialities that divided the house. Therefore it has been thought better to appoint a mistress in charge of novices and to put them all together and to call the place a *novitiate*. If there is anything that is necessary for the advancement of the Company, it is this. Whom have you decided upon, Mademoiselle?

There was no consultation in this matter: it was a *fait accompli!* Louise promptly ignored Vincent's air of ignorance and reminded him that they had already decided that the first mistress of novices was to be Julienne Loret, who was present. Turning to her, Vincent asked with a smile: "O Sister, what have they done to you? It is the first office after superioress and the most important. It has to do with forming girls capable of serving God in the Company, with rooting them in virtue, with teaching them submission, mortification, humility, the practice of their rules and all the virtues. Oh, marvelous! We will give you rules to follow —you should let them make certain exercises by themselves and, if possible, in a separate place." He admitted that it would not be possible at the moment for the novices to have their own exercises, or their own sleeping quarters, but he saw no great problem in that so long as the mistress assembled them each day for a special instruction.

On November 28 Louise wrote Sister Turgis and her companion at Chars of her happiness at "the good understanding and holy peace between you which is so necessary for Christian living . . ." She added with unwonted gaiety: "You are living gloriously, dear Sisters, to have sabots [wooden shoes]. She will be the better housewife for whom they last the longest. You must keep us informed about them!" She broke the news of the deaths of "little Sister Jeanne from Saint-Méen" and "poor

Sister Salome, who is a great loss to us." Sister Michelle was "still gravely ill, as well as many others at the motherhouse and in the city, so that we have more need for God to send us girls than ever."

She counseled Anne Hardemont at Montreuil to have "a great esteem for your neighbor: for the rich because they are above you, for the poor because they are your masters." She also had very exact instructions as to how Anne was to teach the catechism to her little pupils: "Never use the expression 'Do your catechism' [or] 'Come to catechism' . . . but say only 'Let us do some reading,' and then, holding the book, you can make familiar explanations—never anything high-sounding. You know well how easy it is to make a mistake . . ."

Jeanne Lepeintre had succeeded in restoring peace to the house at Nantes, but she was worried for fear Catherine Bagart, who had left the Company in a huff at her transfer, might turn up there. Even if she did, Louise wrote Jeanne, "there is no reason for you to be upset. I do not think she will have the effrontery to go to the hospital . . . I have done all I could for her, procuring her a good mistress . . ." She bade Jeanne tell Sister Marguerite Noret "that all her people are well. Her sister Françoise has received her letter. And Sister Jeanne's father is well, too, thank God."

In January 1648 Louise went again to stay at Bicêtre. Despite her dislike of the place, she put her whole heart into the effort to make it succeed. She asked Vincent on the seventeenth to send the brother baker from Saint-Lazare "to help build a good oven and to find us someone who will know how to use it. We should also start to sell the wine. There has been a great loss of barrels and bottles in this quarter because of the soldiers. If we wait too long, it is to be feared that it will not be so easy to sell." The ladies wanted to wait until they could procure cheaper wine to mix with what they had, but Louise did not like the idea because "we would need a boy to do it and he could abscond with all the profit," and if the Sisters tried to do it themselves "they would have to be very careful not to do the wrong thing, which would be very difficult to avoid." She never raised the question whether such a practice might be unjust or not!

She could not forbear to complain to Vincent again that "*the work* of our poor Sisters here is almost unbelievable, not only because it is very hard but also because of their natural repugnance for this kind of work." Prejudice died hard. Louise understood, however. "For this reason we must in strict justice assist them, encourage them and make them understand what they do, that it is their work before God, and also help them with prayers. I have more need than any, being the most infirm in body and courage . . ."

A week later she reported the somber news that "fifty-two babies have died since coming here. Fifteen or sixteen more do not gain." And she added with a trace of sarcasm: "I trust that when everything shall have been arranged according to the wishes of these good ladies they [the infants] will not go off so quickly." Funds were badly needed and Louise asked for begging sermons in the Parisian parishes, "for when people see this magnificent place for little babies and [know] that it is governed by persons of exalted station, most of them will think that it is richly endowed."

Vincent was ever her tower of strength and she deeply clung to his kindness, "which does me so much good. It seems to me that when I allow myself to be carried away by my fears, which put me in the same state as real afflictions would, I need to be managed quite roughly. You will see from my son's letter, which I am sending you, my weakness on that side, ever the cause of grief to me—which creates the great need I have of your charitable assistance."

Sister Turgis wrote from Chars to inquire whether she might use Cardinal Robert Bellarmin's Catechism to instruct the children. "I know no catechism more thorough than Monsieur le cardinal Bellarmin's," Louise replied, "but it would seem that Monsieur Lambert does not think it wise for us to make use of it to teach little children or even older girls, advising me that it is suitable only for curés. And to tell you the truth, dear Sister, it could be very dangerous for our Company to wish to attempt to speak learnedly, not only as regards our private interest, which is inclined to vanity, but for fear of teaching errors. Monsieur Vincent's wish is that we go along simply and you know how we should defer to him and to his orders. Nevertheless, I will speak to him about it."

Vincent's reply repudiated M. Lambert's opinion and voiced great confidence in his daughters. "There is no better catechism than Bellarmin's, Mademoiselle," he said, "and when all our Sisters are familiar with it and teach it they will teach only what they should teach since they are called to teaching and will know what curés should know." He then proceeded enthusiastically to direct Louise "to explain it to our Sisters so that all will be acquainted with it and will so absorb it as to be capable of teaching it . . . They could seize upon nothing more solid than that book. I am very happy that we have spoken about it . . ."

Writing to Jeanne Lepeintre on March 27, Louise expressed "great compassion for our dear Sister Louise. Tell her, I beg you, that her mother and sister are well. Try to find out whether her malady proceeds from a dissatisfaction with being so far away." She missed Jeanne and told her so fondly: ". . . If Sister Jeanne Lepeintre could stay at Nantes and come to Paris, too, I would wish it with all my heart."

When she wrote again on May 6 she was satisfied that "Sister Louise shows love for her vocation. I think if she had any problem she would say so. Not that she is incapable of having problems, but since she does not complain, it is clear that her troubles are not voluntary but are borne in an effort to mortify herself." This was a wise mother indeed who could read her daughters' hearts no matter the distance that separated them!

On May 13 she spoke to Vincent in behalf of two faithful daughters, Sister Andrée and Sister Catherine de Gesse, who were leaving for new missions at Crespières and Maule. They had "a long time ago asked Your Charity to be allowed to give themselves to God by vows," she reminded him. "Six or seven years in the Company, they have never evidenced any distaste but on the contrary have always given good example. If it please Your Charity, permit them to hear Mass and perform this holy action tomorrow morning before they leave."

In June, the first of the famous Wars of the Fronde broke out. It began as a battle between the Queen Regent and Parlement. Anne of Austria herself was not unloved of her people—she was kind, gracious and pious—but her Minister, Cardinal Mazarin, was hated. To begin with, he was a foreigner—which did not admittedly carry the stigma for, or arouse the suspicions of, the natives of a country that it would today, but he possessed a craftiness which natives invariably assign to aliens. Nor did he have the saving graces of wisdom and dignity which were the hallmarks of his great predecessor Richelieu, while surpassing him in rapacity. To make matters worse, he had an obvious hold over the Queen. Indeed, the question whether or not they were secretly marrried —Mazarin was not in holy orders—has never been solved. The question is of great interest to friends of Vincent de Paul because he was the Queen's director, and it has even been alleged that he witnessed the conjectural marriage. Interrogated by his secretary Brother Robineau about rumors to this effect which were all over Paris, Vincent replied with perhaps too much vehemence, "It is as false as the devil!" But what was false? That the marriage had taken place, or that Vincent had performed it? A provocative sentence appears in a letter he wrote Louise on September 5, 1648: "I believe what they say about the person you understand me to speak of is false." The context allows us at least to surmise that he was speaking of Anne of Austria.

Both Parlement and the nobles had been cool to Anne since she had retained Mazarin as her Minister after the death of her husband, Louis XIII, in 1643. The coolness needed only a pretext to break into open rebellion. The pretext came at last in 1648 over new taxes which Parlement refused to register. On Mazarin's advice, Anne banished Broussel as the instigator of this insolence, without pausing to remember that Broussel was popular with the people. Barricades were thrown up all over Paris and she was forced to recall him. Parlement and the nobles became conscious of their power—almost, for they never had the sense to unite—and waited for another pretext. It came with a second blunder of the Queen's: she secretly spirited the young King Louis XIV out of Paris. Now the person of the King was France to the people, and the Parisians erupted in fury when they learned that he had been taken away from them. Their fury increased with the rumor that Mazarin meant to starve the city and Parlement into submission.

A few days after the return of Broussel, Louise was writing to Jeanne Lepeintre about Vincent: "If you knew the great burdens he has because of his charities to the poor refugees, you would pity him, but his goodness does not complain and never lets up." Her only other allusion to the ferment in the city was to express her sadness "that we will be so long a time without having news of each other." The refugees she referred to were villagers from the countryside surrounding Paris who had been forced from their homes by the ravaging army of the Prince de Condé. Condé was ostensibly protecting the royal family, who were in residence at Reuil.

Despite the stage of semi-siege, Louise left Paris toward the end of summer to visit the confraternity at Liancourt and her friend the Duchesse. She was marooned there for a while and wrote to Sister Hellot at the motherhouse of her "pain at being separated from one's friends when one believes them to be in danger." And in a note to her son written on the same sheet—she apologized to Sister Hellot, "I write in a place and time that forces me to make use of your envelope"—she reiterated her "great anxiety and . . . great dissatisfaction at not being in Paris."

She used the time of her exile well, writing to her daughters scattered abroad. On September 5 she had words of consolation for Julienne Loret on the deaths of several of the young novices: "How deeply Our good God touches you in the persons of your little creatures!" she exclaimed tenderly. "How happy you are, dear Sister, that so many souls leave your arms to appear before God and praise Him eternally!" She had to break the news gently to Anne Hardemont at Montreuil that one of her postulants, Anne Varon, "does not give much hope of being suitable for the Company. Consider, in case she must be separated from it, whether it is not better to send her back than to keep her at Paris, where there are more lost girls than ever." War was a poor climate for virtue.

A few days later she was greatly alarmed at "the rumor going round the country that there has been clamor and death in the streets of Paris." And she besought Julienne Loret: "In the name of God, dear Sister, give me news as quickly as possible of Monsieur Vincent and of my son and our Sisters . . ." Despite her agitation she did not forget the rule of "business as usual," instructing Julienne to ask Sister Hellot to "send me the rule for Chantilly and [copies] of the accounts of expenditures for the hospital and for Madame de Liancourt." The Chantilly establishment had been made some months before, under the patronage of the Duchesse. Louise was also anxious to know the progress of her son's "affair"—apparently some job opportunity for which Louise's "good friend," Mme Musnier, was prepared to speak in his behalf.

On the same day Louise wrote also to Sister Hellot, begging news of "Monsieur Vincent, Monsieur Holden [an English priest who had been chaplain to her uncle Michel], Monsieur de Marillac [her cousin], and my son. I am in such great anguish that if I had a carriage I would return from here today. Hide nothing from me, I beg you!" But her chief thought was of the Company and the motherhouse. "Put away for safekeeping as much as you can of the little we have," she counseled Sister Hellot, "but the best thing you can do is to have recourse to God. I ask that for the time being one or two of our Sisters be always before the Blessed Sacrament to pray for assistance for so many good souls and to appease God's anger upon us. If Monsieur Vincent is of the opinion that my son should retire into Saint-Lazare, I ask him very humbly to do him this favor . . . Remember me to all our dear Sisters. They must not be afraid, but have a great submission to the justice of God and His holy will."

Vincent reassured her in a letter of September 5: "Blessed be God, Mademoiselle, for the solicitude God gives you for your dear daughters and for me in the midst of these popular emotions! Here we all are by the grace of God without Our Lord finding us worthy to suffer anything in the event." His next lines seemed to indicate that he had tried to use his influence with all parties—Parlement, the nobles; the court, and the people: "Be assured for the rest that there is nothing that I thought should be said that I have not said. The trouble is that God has not blessed my words—although I believe what they say about the person you understand me to speak of is false. I have honestly tried to speak to them like the good angels who give advice without getting themselves upset when no use is made of their insights." He promised her, also, that he "would try to say a word to M. le comte de Maure." The Comte was deeply embroiled in the Fronde and it is conceivable that Louise wished Vincent to caution him. Vincent finished by offhandedly granting her permission to visit an old friend—she never failed to ask—"If you wish to spend some time with Madame de Saint-Simon, why not?" The Marquise de Saint-Simon was the mother of the famous court gossip of Louis XIV's reign.

Louise had no sooner returned to Paris than news reached her from Fontainebleau that Barbe Angiboust had been ill since October 7, and, Louise told Vincent tearfully, "yesterday someone from Saint-Germain-l'Auxerrois told us that her [Barbe's] confessor had informed a woman of the parish that she was going to die and had been given Extreme Unction. Permit us, Monsieur, because of this news to send a Sister there today, because we have written, and one of our Sisters left here eight days ago to be her companion there, and we have heard nothing." Vincent replied promptly, "very much moved at the grave illness of our poor Sister Barbe. It would be a charity to send a girl, and an encouragement to the others. You should send her by coach if there is one available, Mademoiselle, or by water as far as Melun, where there is a carriage at the Port-Saint-Paul on Mondays or Tuesdays. From there she will have to go on foot through the woods to Fontainebleau, where there is no danger at present because the court is not there . . ." Anne Hardemont, who was visiting Paris at the time, went and to the joy of all found Barbe much improved.

Louise received another alarm that October with a report that M. Portail, who was traveling back to Paris from Marseilles, had died at Nantes. This report, too, was premature. "God be blessed, Monsieur; that His goodness has spared you amidst so many dangers . . ." Louise wrote him happily on October 8.

A sad blow fell in December, however, with the death at Chantilly of Sister Turgis, who had been one of Louise's strongest arms almost from the beginning of the Company. Louise's grief was all the deeper because her death had come as a shock. Sister Turgis had been ill all that autumn but had improved, and the Sisters had not informed Paris of her relapse. Louise sent the Sisters at Liancourt to Chantilly to see whether they could make use of any of the dead Sister's clothes, but strictly forbade them "to touch her little strongbox." That was to be sent back to the motherhouse at the earliest opportunity, along with her "chaplets, books of hours, papers and other private possessions."

In December also, Louise was faced with the very serious problem of a lack of funds for the foundlings. Many of the Ladies of Charity whose families were caught up in the Fronde on one side or the other were facing financial ruin and could no longer give with their usual generosity. On December 15 she told Mlle de Lamoignon: "I understand only too well the extreme need of the poor infants and their nurses"; but she excused herself from approaching Mme la chancelière Séguier and others for help because, she said, she did not wish "to bring further sadness to tender and charitable hearts. There is nothing more for me to say except that the Ladies of the Company seem to me more the mothers of these little ones than their real mothers and to be suffering now the same grief as the mothers of the little Innocents when the massacre befell them, not be able to offer a remedy." She suggested that Mlle de Lamoignon call a plenary assemblage of the ladies to arrange for collections in all the churches of the city. They might accomplish together, she said, what they could not do alone.

Paris had known a very uneasy peace throughout the autumn, and as the end of the year apporached, it grew uneasier still, fed by fresh rumors of the marriage of Mazarin and the Queen, by the Coadjutor de Retz, who dearly loved machination as another man might love hunting or chess, and by the universal hatred of the Cardinal Minister. Nervous about her own safety and that of the young King, Anne now spirited him away from Paris again, this time to Saint-Germain-en-Laye. A great part of the court followed them. The departure had the effect of lifting the lid from the pot, and bloodshed and looting spewed forth once more.

Louise was terrified for her daughters at Bicêtre. Nonetheless, she rallied them courageously to show great confidence in God. Their virtue was in very real danger from the licentious soldiers and the riffraff of war, but she expressed her own trust that God would give them "courage enough to die rather than allow God to be offended," and that their modesty would "proclaim that you belong to the King of Kings to whom all powers bow." She had very practical advice for them to follow. "Make all the Sisters stay together," she told the Sister Servant, "and take special precautions with the older girls, whom you must keep always in sight or locked in the schoolroom . . . I do not doubt that each of you has thought to make a good confession . . ." After she had finished the letter, she was afraid that she might have frightened them unnecessarily with this last observation and she added a postscript: "When I mentioned going to confession, it was not my wish, dear Sisters, to put the fear of death in you," she wrote. "Oh, no, no! But to help you stay always in the grace of God so that His eye will be ever upon you."

It is no wonder that with death all around her in the Faubourg Saint-Denis she should seem to be brooding on it these days. On January 1, 1649, she reminded Sisters Brigitte and Marie at Chantilly that "death comes so soon that it seems to me, dear Sisters, that the expectation that our turn will come soon should always be before our eyes." In the previous two weeks two Sisters had died at the motherhouse and others were gravely ill—"so, dear Sisters, we ought to pray always for all our Company so that our prayers will help each one to die well."

With the fresh outbreak of violence, Vincent now decided to take a bold hand. Aghast at the horrors this foolish war had let loose on Paris and especially on the poor, and conscious of the responsibility he had by reason of his influence with the Queen, he decided to make a desperate ploy for peace. In the cold dark before the dawn of January 14 he stole out of the city, accompanied only by his secretary, Brother Ducournau, bound for Saint-Germain. At Clichy the travelers were ambushed by soldiers but their lives were spared when a grizzled native recognized his pastor of nearly twenty-five years before. The Seine was swollen but their horses managed the crossing. Anne admitted Vincent to her presence at once and listened to him willingly despite the fact that he pleaded with her to dismiss Mazarin for the sake of peace and that normally she would never brook criticism of the Minister in her presence. Vincent next bearded the Cardinal himself, who received him politely and even promised to resign if his colleague Le Tellier should concur with Vincent's advice. Nothing came of it. As Vincent told Antoine Portail the following week, he had hoped "to render some little service to God, but my sins made me unworthy."

Word of Vincent's "flight" from the beleaguered capital got around quickly enough and was wholly misinterpreted. *The Queen's confessor knew what side his bread was buttered on! Had he not married her to the hated Italian?* As Vincent put it to Portail ruefully, he was now "completely useless for anything." But with his usual philosophical acceptance of things as they were, he decided to spend the time of his enforced exile—he would have been torn apart as a traitor if he had attempted to reenter the city—in visiting the houses of his priests in Brittany.

His realization of the magnitude of the mindless rage of the anti-royalist soldiers and the Parisian populace against him came with the news that his community's farm at Orsigny had been completely pillaged; only a small herd of sheep and two horses were saved. And at the very time he was writing to M. Lambert not to put on sale "the wheat stored in the granaries of Saint-Lazare" but to "put it out at interest under the good God to earn an alms for the poor," he did not know that some six hundred soldiers had taken over the buildings, sacked them, sold some of the wheat and set fire to the woodpile.

His visitation was not going well either. He got only as far as Fréneville and was marooned there for a month by the extraordinary cold and snow. He wrote from there to Louise on February 4, praising her courage in defending her house despite the wild melee across the street in his.

A week later he confided to the Ladies of Charity his fears lest the Fronde and the enmities it had raised among them cause them to abandon their good works. "It seems indeed that private miseries could dispense us from alleviating public ones . . ." he wrote, "but really, Mesdames, I do not know whether that would satisfy God, who could say to us what St. Paul said to the Corinthians who found themselves in similar circumstances: 'Have you resisted even to blood?' Have you, at least, sold some of your jewels? What do I say, Mesdames . . . ? It is because of the excellence of your incomparably kind hearts that I speak so."

On March 2 the Duchesse d'Aiguillon wrote him from Saint-Germain to inform him that representatives of the court and of the Parlement were about to meet in an effort to effect peace. The names of the opposing arbitrators are eloquent testimony to the divisions the war had brought about in society and hence among the Ladies of Charity. The parliamentarians include Molé, de Mesmes, de Nesmond, Le Cogneux,

Viole, Longueil, Menardeau, Le Cocq, Bitault, and Lefèbvre; the cour-
tiers Condé, Mazarin, Séguier, and de la Rivière. A Te Deum had been
sung that very day, the Duchesse reported, to celebrate the peace of
Westphalia, which had finally brought to a close the horrible Thirty
Years' War.

Elisabeth Martin, who had been ailing for so many years, died in
March at Richelieu and Vincent wrote from Le Mans to tell Louise how
"greatly moved" he was at her passing. Here was one more pioneer gone,
a Sister who, despite her occasional failings, had served Louise and the
Company well in the hardest posts. Things were going much better at
Angers, Vincent reported, due mainly to the capable leadership of
Cécile Angiboust. Proof of this, he pointed out in a letter written from
there on March 23 after he had concluded a visitation of the house, was
that the only fault he could find in the Sisters was their occasional breaking of the "grand silence" after night prayers.

He was anxious over Louise's news that "your poor girls and foundlings are still besieged by a large army at Bicêtre." These were Condé's
troops, which had not disbanded because, while peace had been concluded on March 11, it had not yet been ratified by Parlement. Ratifica-
tion was finally given on April 1.

Soldiers tried to break into Bicêtre several times, sending the Sisters
into paroxysms of terror, but their faithful adherence to Louise's instructions saved them from harm. Writing on Easter Monday, April 5, Vincent praised God "for the preservation of our Sisters at Bicêtre and Saint-
Denis," but he was very saddened at Louise's description of "the devastation of Bicêtre and the poverty of the children . . . Since the place is
uninhabitable, it is to be hoped that Parlement or the city would provide
another, but clearly they will not. Such should be requested, nevertheless, if the Ladies agree—and their opinion should be sought. Ask them,
please, through Mademoiselle de Lamoignon . . ." He was especially
anxious to enlist the support of the greatest among them, such as the
Princesse de Condé, the Duchesse d'Aiguillon, and Mme de Brienne.

On April 9, news reached him that the children had been removed
from Bicêtre and he was "anxious to know where they have been put.
Mon Dieu! what trouble that transfer must have given you!" he exclaimed sympathetically to Louise. The children were lodged for the
time being at the Sisters' motherhouse, which must have resembled the
Old Woman's Shoe of the nursery rhyme. But, Louise told Vincent,
they "were getting ready to return to Bicêtre one of these days . . ."

Vincent had suffered an accident on his way from Le Mans to Angers. His horse slipped while fording a small river and fell on top of him. Pinned beneath the animal, he would have drowned but for the prompt action of one of his priests. Hearing of it belatedly, Louise had written, anxious for news, to Abbé de Vaux on March 31. Vincent himself now reassured her that, aside from a good drenching from which he caught cold, he had not suffered any great injury—which was remarkable, considering his sixty-eight years.

When he arrived at Nantes on April 18 he discovered that the Sisters there had just been through a harrowing persecution. "They accused them of an infinity of things," he told Louise, "the principal one being that they appropriate for themselves what belongs to the poor." The calumniators were three priests, and a layman whose wife had taken offense at something a Sister had said to her. The aldermen of the city conducted an investigation and exonerated the Sisters. But that did not stop the accusers, who went to the Bishop with their lies. The Bishop, not a great friend of the Sisters, was disposed to reopen the case, but Vincent deterred him, defending the Sisters vigorously. "I find much to be desired in them," he told the prelate frankly, "but by the grace of God they are innocent of the things they have been accused of."

He was, indeed, very unhappy with their community life, and catalogued their faults for Louise: "1° They have forgotten the observance of regularity. 2° They are not exact in prayer, in spiritual reading, in examens of conscience, or silence. 3° They have little charity among themselves as regards either obedience or the support of one another and, to tell the truth, as regards applying themselves to helping the sick." Evil days had certainly fallen upon this community which had gotten off to such a promising start. It was not the fault of the Sister Servant, Jeanne Lepeintre, Vincent hastened to assure Louise, for she was "a very good girl, judicious and sweet, [although] some of the Sisters think she has not enough foresight . . ." It was rather the fault of Henriette Gesseaume, the older Sister sent as pharmacist some months before, and a Sister Marie. Henriette was "hard-working and full of charity," Vincent judged fairly, "but with scant respect and little or no submission to the Servant, and quarrelsome with the doctor and a number of people . . ." It was "absolutely necessary" to recall her, he said, and to dismiss Sister Marie from the Company. As for Marie, Louise had reminded Vincent that "we have tried her in several places and when sending her to Nantes I told her it was her last chance." Despite the calumnies circulated at

Nantes about the Sisters, Vincent was asked while he was there to make another foundation at nearby Vannes but replied that "it could not be thought of, at least so soon." Indeed, Louise was hard put to find a replacement for Henriette and asked Jeanne Lepeintre whether one of the other Sisters could not substitute for her for the time being.

Arriving at Richelieu on his return journey, Vincent found that the Duchesse d'Aiguillon had sent a coach and two horses to bring him to Paris and further discovered to his shame that it was an outright gift, which, because of his age and infirmities, he was forced to accept by order of the Queen.

The plight of the foundlings lay heavy on his heart. He had resolved, he told Louise, to call "a general assembly of the Ladies in order that they might decide whether to appeal to the Queen for a general collection or to present a request to Parlement for their needs in the name of the officers—that would give the matter more prestige than your name alone."

He begged Louise in a postscript "not to be upset over M. le sheriff." Michel had been so hapless in finding a job that Vincent had created the post of Sheriff of Saint-Lazare for him; his duties were to look after the legal interests of the benefice and its dependencies. Michel was now thirty-six years old and his mother saw no hope for his salvation except in getting him married; and, characteristically, once she had decided upon a course of action, nothing would do until it was accomplished. "Don't you see the extraordinary care Our Lord has taken of him without you?" Vincent twitted her affectionately. "Let His divine Majesty take care of things. He knows well how to show the mother, who has care of so many children, His satisfaction in her by looking after this one, and will not allow her to run ahead of or surpass Him in goodness."

Michel, like most beggars, was not to be satisfied with the provision Vincent had so kindly made for him but had an eye on a post in the Court des Monnaies. It was Vincent's opinion that "it would be better for M. le sheriff to go cautiously at first and not use up everything he has in procuring this post. Perhaps it will be sold very dearly." It was indeed. The price was so high that Michel had reluctantly to give up all thought of it.

M. Portail was back in Marseilles, delayed there by his community's business, and Louise wrote on May 16 to tell him how impatient the Sisters were for his return. If he could not come soon, would he write them a letter, she asked, "to be read while waiting for the conference to begin."

With Sister Marie gone from Nantes, Henriette Gesseaume was much more docile and plans to recall her to Paris were left hanging. Louise, in fact, greeted her very warmly in a letter of June 6 addressed to Jeanne Lepeintre, and begged Jeanne "not to let her wear herself out in her pharmacy."

She was obviously happy to be able to tell Jeanne and the Sisters that their Company had been increased by fifteen postulants since Easter.

The Sisters at Nantes were still undergoing harassment from their enemies, and Louise gave them the only comfort she could: that they must suffer in submission and silence, that their only thought must be for the hospital and the poor. As late as August, it was uncertain whether the continued persecution might drive the Sisters out, in which eventuality Louise strictly forbade them to leave without letting her know, because, she said, other more appreciative persons wanted their services in that part of the country.

Peace had come to Paris and with it the penchant of people to forget, or perhaps the ability to see things in their true light, so that Vincent was able to return quietly and without notice on June 13. The capital was still completely disorganized, however, as Louise told Anne Hardemont on July 23. "If you knew the difficulty of finding jobs for people in Paris at the moment—it is incredible!" she wrote. "It looks like the war will be with us for a long time yet. On the other hand, Sister, when the war began, it seemed that the parishes must send all our Sisters away and yet Divine Providence saw to it that alms were given for the sick and bashful poor, more than anyone had dared hope. The lady officers seemed to have more care in finding wheat for their poor than for themselves."

On August 18 she gave Jeanne Lepeintre the welcome news that "our good King arrives in Paris today, which gives joy to all hearts. Pray fervently to God for the Church and for all France . . ."

Sisters Charlotte Royer and Françoise Carcireux had been sent recently to Richelieu and were homesick for the mother house. In an unusually teasing vein, Louise asked them:

> Isn't it true that you have been crying ever since you left Paris, and that if you could speak to that wicked Sister Louise who sent you off, you would tell her what you thought of her? For lack of that, write me

everything: you can be sure that I will devour your letter. Sister Julienne has not failed to write to your [Sister Charlotte's] father as you asked her. He is well, and your mother, thank God, and both send their love. I hope to leave tomorrow for Liancourt. I will not fail to tell them all your news, and ask them if they want you to write and to send them a big basket of raisins. There, Mademoiselle is making fun of me—isn't that what you are saying? Oh! I think you have come to your senses and will weep no more. Be very happy, then, that Our good God does His will in you. I say the same to dear Sister Carcireux, informing her, too, that Monsieur her father is well, thank God . . . In the name of God, dear Sisters, be very brave in working out your perfection, forgetting your homeland and your hearth so as to live in peace in the land He has shown you by holy obedience.

With her usual tenacity Louise continued to busy herself in arranging a marriage for Michel. On August 30 she wrote Vincent from Liancourt to inform him that one possibility had failed to materialize because "all the family on one side and the other are spoken for." Mme de Romilly had been lending a hand, however, and had learned that "the family of Monsieur Portier who lives opposite Saint-Paul is all we could wish for. She will speak to you on their behalf. I ask very humbly, most dear Father, that you do not speak of property unless she brings it up, because those who have spoken about this matter have told him that the parents were satisfied as regards property. And one should be careful in all such matters not to say exactly what one has because it would be detrimental if the affair fell through. Hopes for the future from investments are considerable. It is not that I intend or wish to deceive anyone—God guard me from that!—but it seems to me that past expenditure to make a man employable should be considered, as also his disposition not to dissipate what he has, but to acquire more. And this is what I am counting on him to put his mind to when he is settled." Such a confidence after the experience of years was truly maternal.

A few days later Vincent informed Louise that he had spoken with Mme de Romilly and that the girl's dowry would be 15,000 livres, with hope of more after the deaths of her father and mother. He had given this information to Michel in the presence of the Duchesse d'Aiguillon, "who was of your opinion that they have not told the whole story. This good lady [the Duchesse] has been deputed by the girl's side to investigate the person and prospects [of Michel]. I have since seen Père Delahaie and confided this business to him. He will keep me informed for [Michel's] side."

At the time that Louise was thus engrossed in getting Michel settled once for all, she suffered bitter grief and humiliation over the defection, in what seems to have been scandalous circumstances, of three of her Sisters, known only as Anne-Marie, Renée and Mathurine. From Liancourt she besought Jeanne Loret, whom she had left in charge at the motherhouse, not to waste a minute in handling this matter, since "it is to be feared that the devil has great plans for the loss of these souls. Above all, Sister Anne-Marie must be prevented from leaving." Louise was for taking the strongest measures and asked Julienne to obtain Vincent's consent to incarcerate the girl, which would be no problem "if we had a strong room, but I see no other choice than to put her at Saint-Marie as if she were to make her retreat." The reasons for Louise's desperation were the fears that people would get the idea that anyone could enter and leave the Company with ease and that their subsequent behavior might hurt its reputation. She reminded Vincent that she had spoken to him "about this poor young Sister and you proposed to send her back [to her native village]. But she has no intention of going back: the advice Renée gave her was to allow herself to be put aboard the coach and then get out a short time after it left. These are bold spirits who can do much harm."

Vincent was not at all inclined to get excited over the situation. "You are too sensitive about your girls leaving . . ." he admonished Louise. "Our Lord does the Company a mercy to purge it of people like this . . . Also, you can be assured that none of those whom Our Lord has called to the Company will abandon her vocation. Why bother about the others . . . ? Let them go. You will not lack girls."

Despite this press of important matters, Louise had time for the smallest things. Julienne Loret was to buy wheat or farina if she could get it at a good price, "but if it is dear I think it would be better to wait." The weather was fine and she was anxious for the Sister gardeners to take advantage of it, especially for weeding the chicory. They should be careful, too, not to let the pigs run in a herd, especially in the garden, "so that we may see it green again," and they should measure out the feed for the cow and the other domestic animals, for too much could be harmful for them.

Despite all the talk about an emergency general assembly of the Ladies of Charity, nothing had been done about it, and the work of the foundlings was in great danger. Louise wrote Vincent three desperate letters in November, asking him bluntly whether they could "in conscience" continue to accept foundlings only to see them die. She implored action and described the impossibility of receiving these little babies.

> At present there are seven . . . who will not take the bottle and there is not a *double* to put them out to nurse, or any provision for sheets or linen, and no hope of borrowing any. The ladies make no attempt to help us and I am sure that they think we manage at their expense, which is most contrary to the truth . . . I know of only one way of being fair to those who are enduring agonies in this work, which is that, in the name of our Company, we should present a petition to Monsieur le premier président [Molé] to discharge us from receiving the children and to put them where he pleases . . . These ladies have no idea of what they are doing. Not one of them has sent anything.

Louise's indignation at length forced the convening of the assembly, and she sent Vincent a memorandum of what he should tell the ladies. She fired off another the day before the assembly was to meet, insisting that "we are at the point where we must have help without delay or quit entirely. Yesterday we had to supply money to the detriment of our house—nearly fifteen or twenty livres—for wheat for the children at Bicêtre, and we had to borrow more . . . Please! The ladies' assembly tomorrow must do something . . . ! I think that if someone were to speak to Madame le princesse [de Condé] about this extreme need, she would give something. It is pitiful that the ladies put themselves to such little trouble! They must think that we have means of subsistence or they would not be against throwing the whole work up and, therefore, I think they have made up their minds to do nothing at all."

Vincent was able as always to cajole the good women and the work managed to survive. Their hearts were of the best but, if the truth were told, their busy social lives and court interests prevented them from seeing in any depth its desperate straits as poor Louise and her overworked daughters had to.

At last a bride was found for Michel. She was Demoiselle Gabrielle Le Clerc, a daughter of the late seigneur de Chennevières and his late wife, Musset de la Rochemaillet.

There were to be difficulties, however, before the marriage could be arranged to everyone's satisfaction. Louise complained to Vincent in December of "the trouble widows have in discharging their duty after their husbands are gone." She still had not the money, promised by her relatives presumably, to conclude the affair. Moreover, the bride's marriage broker was pretending to cast his eyes on fairer fields, "which makes me somewhat afraid that they are thinking of breaking off with us. If that happens, I will not know what to say further."

Almost automatically she launched into a self-conscious but nonetheless fierce defense of Michel:

> All these difficulties are due to my son's lack of experience. He only needs a push and some independence in applying himself to work in good earnest. He has a lazy spirit like me. We have to be prodded into action. Whether it be things that have to be done, or things of our own choosing, we go at them in spurts . . . Monsieur de Marillac has seen the articles [of the marriage contract] and is well aware that they leave something to be desired but nevertheless advises me not to break off negotiations even though they do not grant what he told me to ask for, because he sees this matter as very greatly to our advantage. [She asked to consult with Vincent on Saturday], the day the uncle and the girl are scheduled to come and, I think, everything will have to be agreed upon. Your dear, good advice will help me greatly in coming to a decision.

Louise told the Comte de Maure that she understood and sympathized with the girl's fears, for she could not count on a life of wealth and ease, "there not being, all told, that little bit needed to raise a small family; and since in the ordinary run of things children come to those least able to support them, the thought of death and of leaving poverty-stricken orphans behind makes her hesitate to put herself in that danger."

The point on which everything turned was the position in the Court des Monnaies, which would give Michel a stable income but which Louise could not afford to purchase. The Comte de Maure gave some financial assistance—Louise did not hesitate to remind him that he had an obligation to do so because his in-laws had arranged her own marriage—and so did the Marillacs. The widow of René de Marillac in Carmel firmly advised Louise to approach Mlle d'Atri "to remind her of the services the late M. Le Gras rendered Mme her mother [Geneviève d'Attichy, duchesse d'Atri]." But it was Demoiselle Le Clerc's uncle René-Michel de la Rochemaillet who solved everything by resigning his own post in the Court des Monnaies in favor of Michel Le Gras.

On January 13, 1650, Louise asked Jeanne Lepeintre and "all our Sisters" at Nantes to offer Holy Communion "for the intention of my son, who, I think, will receive the Sacrament of Marriage one of these days. God has chosen for him what seems to be a very virtuous young girl, not from Paris." On the eve of the marriage Vincent inspected the contract and sent it back to Louise with the sole comment: "If you judge it necessary to name M. le prieur [Adrien Le Bon, former prieur de Saint-Lazare] and me in the contract, he should be named ahead of me." He prayed God to bless the couple and to "give you the dispositions He gave the Blessed Virgin when she went with Her Son to the marriage at Cana."

Michel-Antoine Le Gras and Gabrielle Le Clerc were married in the Church of Saint-Sauveur on January 18, 1650. After thirty-six years of anxiety, Louise could at last draw a deep breath of relief. In the next few months she still had some minor worry in scraping together the required tax for Michel's reception into his government job, but she managed it and he was formally installed in his post on July 14 of that year.

XV

Paris under Siege,
the Countryside in Flames

The last decade of Louise's life began with all the usual problems besetting her in force. The Sisters at Richelieu had sent some "fine lace" for the motherhouse chapel for which "our altar thanks you," she assured them, "but our debts weep!"

She had ever to combat the homesickness in Charlotte Royer and Françoise Carcireux. "You seem to be always worrying about your parents," she reproached them gently.

Sister Carcireux's father seems to have been something of a drifter. Louise told her now that he had wanted to go to Richelieu to see her but Louise had dissuaded him and he went instead to visit relatives at Beauvais, one of whom was president of the parlement there. The président had found work for his wandering cousin and had written to Louise promising to look after him to the best of his ability. As for Sister Royer's parents, who lived at Richelieu, Louise had heard nothing of them for some time but, she reminded the good Sister, no news was good news. "Nothing remains, then, dear Sisters, but to appreciate the graces God gives you and to work for your perfection . . ." she finished.

A Sister had returned from Bicêtre resolved on leaving the Company and Louise was troubled that she could find her no way of supporting herself except to send her to help the Sisters at Saint-Sulpice, who were understaffed—a solution that was not at all to Louise's liking. "I confess to being somewhat downcast by the quantity of difficulties caused by the attitude of a great part of our Sisters," she told Vincent. "I can assure you, Monsieur, that it gives me great cause for confusion before God and men, this inability of mine to support these good girls in doing good."

Sisters were dying with a frequency she would never get used to, the latest being Sister Florence—"only two years in the Company!" She took the opportunity of "the news of so many deaths" to urge Sister Jeanne Pangoy at Liancourt to renew her resolution "to do good to everyone since life is so short and we die only once and the judgment at the hour of death will perdure forever."

At Louise's behest Vincent himself wrote to Jeanne Lepeintre on February 23 to comfort her as best he could. This house at Nantes reflected in its own way the problems that afflicted the whole Company. The Sisters' quarters were too small: she had no recourse, he told Jeanne, but to go to the administrators. She wanted to be relieved of the burden of being Sister Servant: this consoled him, he assured her, "because anyone who is doing a good job asks from time to time to be relieved," and he directed her to trust in Providence "which will remove you from this office when it is expedient and which will give you the graces required to do it well so long as you exercise it." She asked again for the recall of Henriette Gesseaume. "Please have patience in this matter," he begged her, for there was no replacement at hand. She was very unhappy over the administrators' having hired boys to work in the kitchen. Vincent didn't like it, either, but, he shrugged, "if it is . . . a necessary evil, it must be borne for the love of God who permits it"—but that did not prevent her from keeping after the administrators until they removed them. Her greatest indignation was reserved for the effrontery of the administrators in having cut peepholes in the doors and windows to check on whether or not the Sisters were doing their work: he could only agree wearily that "that is annoying; but after you have tried to rid yourself of such a form of slavery, you must have patience," he urged. "Alas! my daughter, I don't know who is not watched!"

Louise continued to be vindicated in her judgment of Bicêtre as a poor place for the foundlings. To the unsuitability of the rooms and equipment was now added the difficulty of getting respectable nurses. War had taken its toll: some of these women had fallen victim to the blandishments of the soldiers and had been fired; others quit because of the large number of camp followers in the neighborhood, with "their bad language and extreme wantonness." Mme de Lamoignon and her daughter joined Louise in urging Vincent to put into effect the resolution he had taken to transfer the children back to Paris and to do it at once "in this Jubilee Year and not put it off until another time."

Worst of all, Louise reported to him, the Ladies of Charity were getting more and more highhanded and paying no attention to his rules and regulations for the work. For this reason, she urged, he and she both "must insist on utilizing one or two of your houses, the more so to save rent. Otherwise, if they are allowed to choose, the direction of the work will pass wholly and perpetually into the hands of others. Such a confrontation will completely expose their schemes. It has occurred to me that they think we could not pull out of serving the children because we are obliged to it by the thousand livres we hold in domain—and you know how wrong they are, since it was the intention of the donors that half of it belongs to us purely and simply for the subsistence of the Company, with no more obligation to the service of these little children than to other poor and the prisoners. It would be a good thing if they were to make an issue of that some day, and it might as well be now as some other time." It was obvious that the Marillac temper was aroused and that Louise was spoiling for a fight. At the heart of the matter was a resentment on the part of the ladies at her control of the work, and all of her correspondence treating of the foundlings shows that she was well aware of it.

Her advice prevailed and the children were removed from Bicêtre, apparently in April, some to the "Thirteen Houses" Vincent had built for his works in 1645, some to the Sisters' motherhouse, and some to private homes. By August Vincent had arranged with M. le procureur général Blaise Méliand to transfer the babies who were weaned, along with the older girls, to Les Enfermés, where two Sisters were put in charge of them. Vincent had been helped in his approach to the procureur général by a M. Biète and was so pleased with him that he told Louise: "M. Biète could look after all our affairs. He held his own with certain commissaires who were insisting that the foundlings be put in charge of the nurses."

Louise made an important visit to M. le procureur général Méliand in April to seek the formal registration by Parlement of the Act of Establishment of the Company. The reception he gave her delighted her. "He asked me whether we considered ourselves regulars or seculars," she reported to Vincent. "I made it plain to him that we considered ourselves only the latter. He said that that was without precedent. I alleged the daughters of Madame de Villeneuve [the Daughters of the Congregation of the Cross] and proved to him that they went everywhere. He showed no disapproval of our design, saying much good of the Company, but [said] that a matter of such importance required thought. I evidenced my pleasure in his acting in this way and *begged him, if it did not deserve to be or ought not to be continued, to destroy it utterly; but*

that, if it were good,. we begged him to establish it firmly . . . He replied: 'Let me think about it, not for months but for some weeks.' "
Neither the woman nor the noble in her could prevent her from expressing to Vincent her satisfacton that "he took the trouble to see us to the
carriage!"

Word came in late April that the administrators at Nantes had now
turned to thoughts of replacing the Sisters there with another religious
community. M. d'Annemont, one of the few who were friendly to the
Sisters, confirmed the news in a letter in which he offered to fight the
proposal, but Vincent informed him, he told Louise, that "it is my desire
and my prayer to God that the matter will succeed in favor of these good
religious if it is for the benefit of the poor and that we would agree very
willingly to the dismissal of the Daughters of Charity." He also asked
her to write M. d'Annemont in the same vein, so as "to honor and practice the counsel of Our Lord to the effect that, if they wish to take our
robe from us, we must give them our cloak."

Louise hastened to instruct Jeanne Lepeintre, on May 4, to instill in
the Sisters "great courage in rendering Him the fidelity He asks of them
in this situation so painful to nature." She understood what they were
suffering: "the uncertainness of events, the opposing factions, no one to
trust for comfort and advice . . ."

The administrators seem to have been extremely fickle in their plans.
In May they suggested that the Sisters stay on but that an on-the-spot
administrator direct the business of the hospital and that—for some obscure reason—a cook be hired. Louise was quite ready to accept a lay
administrator. In fact, she told M. Truchart that "there would be a great
advantage in having one . . . so long as his wife did not interfere in any
way with the service of the poor." As for the cook, she saw many disad-
vantages, especially insofar as she might threaten the privacy of the Sisters. An administrator was appointed, and Louise seized the opportunity
to remind the Sisters that there was now no reason whatever for them to
go traipsing about the town, "not even Sister Henriette, for the herbs
she needs can be brought in to her."

On top of the uncertainty at Nantes came news that the administrators at Angers had purchased another house to be turned into a hospital,
which they expected the Sisters to staff. On July 1 Louise asked M. de
Vaux to let her know "what it is all about. Too much responsibility for
them is to be feared. They will fail in the exactitude and propriety necessary in hospitals, and people will put the blame on them, not knowing

how small their number is. But what is most important is that the sick will be exposed to the danger of much suffering." This second hospital succeeded, but it was a long time before Sisters could be supplied for it.

Writing to the Sister Servant at Liancourt on September 20, Louise laid down beautiful and memorable guidelines for all superiors: "I beg you . . . to be aware of each Sister as an individual, to be their comfort in their little troubles by your cordiality and support. You must be very patient in offering them little remedies, the better to suffer with them in their trials and to point out to them the importance of going out of their way to do God's will which never wavers. You must be careful to change them without waiting for them to ask when they grow weary in an office. In short, it is most necessary to condescend in many things, to anticipate our Sisters' wishes without letting on to them. I am sure you understand that authority must be exercised not so much absolutely as charitably, and that we are Sisters Servants, which is to say that we bear the most intense pains of soul and body and give our dear Sisters who have trouble enough in putting up with us—sometimes because of our moods, at other times because of the repugnance nature and the evil spirit give them—as much consolation as we can."

The request made to Vincent to establish the Sisters in Vannes was followed up by a letter written to Louise on July 14, 1649, by the grand vicar, M. Eudo, asking for Sisters to staff a hospital there. Now, more than a year later, the request was granted by sending Anne Hardemont and Geneviève Doinel to found the new mission. They left Paris on October 22, 1650.

Two weeks later a letter to Sister Jeanne de la Croix at Serqueux spoke of another new foundation at Châlons. The four Sisters sent there met with a peculiar problem: they were deprived of the sacraments because their confessor was so deaf he could not hear their sins. Louise, no doubt suspecting some exaggeration on the part of the bewildered Sisters, suggested that they try to continue to go to confession to the deaf man, "but not . . . so often." In the meantime they should confess in the parish church or at the Capuchin monastery at Forges, she said. "If such can be done," she concluded with surprising liberality for the times, "seeing the example you owe the parish on feasts and on Sundays, it would be just as well to communicate every day."

Another little-known early mission of this period is conjectured from the address of a letter of November 8, 1650, to Sister Marie Gaudoin at Alois, or Les Alluets, in the canton of Poissy.

By December 10 things had quieted down again at Nantes and Louise directed Jeanne Lepeintre to "praise God . . . that His kindness ever works for the good of our Company so that it can fulfill God's holy will and that one of its special charges is to advance as well as it can the welfare of the hospital at Nantes." She wished, she wrote fervently, that Jeanne "could see my heart and know that distance increases rather than diminishes the close bond it pleased God's goodness to effect in our souls a long time ago . . ."

On January 7 of the New Year 1651 Louise sent news from home to the over-anxious Sisters at Richelieu: "Sister Charlotte, your father came to see us. He brought your baptismal certificate, which I enclose. He is well, also your mother, brothers, and sister-in-law and niece, thank God. They haven't had the time to write to you. He promises me he will write, and he greets you all. Here is a letter for you, Sister Françoise, from Monsieur Carcireux—but don't get upset: we have learned that he is not as much in need as he would make it appear."

They were affectionate and generous Sisters and Louise had occasion in this letter to thank them for an altar cloth they had made for the motherhouse chapel and in a letter of March 17 for a gift of thread and some apples.

They had asked to make perpetual vows, as some of the first Sisters had, and Louise's reply spelled out the custom of taking vows that has perdured in the Company to the present day. "As for your desire," she wrote, "it is most praiseworthy. For it is not enough to begin well; one must persevere, which I see to be your intention. We must, nonetheless, submit in this matter to the direction of our superiors, who for very cogent reasons have ordained it sufficient to make this offering for a year only, and to renew it each year. Don't you think, dear Sisters, that that would be most agreeable to Our Lord since, having your freedom anew at the end of each year, you can again make a new sacrifice of it?"

The next day Vincent was writing to encourage Sister Guillemine Chesneau and a companion, who had gone to start yet another new mission, a small hospital, at Saint-Etienne-à-Arnes. He assured them that everyone was in excellent health, but a note written to him by Louise on the same day gives him the lie. His own legs were ulcerating badly again. The tortured and constantly repeated treatment Louise prescribed for them in great detail must, however, have caused the holy patient at least equal discomfort and pain!

A council meeting was called on April 13 to appoint an assistant to replace Sister Hellot, who had died recently. Louise's choice fell on Sister Jeanne de la Croix because she was "a girl given to virtue and good example. She has great sweetness and charity toward the Sisters, and she works hard—all of which seems necessary in a Sister assistant in order to supply for my defects which prevent me from putting the first hand to the work as I should." Louise's frailty was indeed keeping her from an active participation in the administration of the motherhouse: it was now a rare occasion when she was able to preside at the spiritual exercises of the community.

Sister Jeanne was astonished at being invited to the next council meeting, held two days later in the parlor of Saint-Lazare, and asked in her humility to be excused—no one had bothered to inform her of her election! To her greater confusion, when the meeting began, she was called upon to give her opinion first. She demurred, representing that she was wholly inexperienced and that others more seasoned should speak first. "Sister, it is your turn to speak," Vincent replied kindly. "It is the custom to begin with the Sister seated at the right." Louise, who took the notes for the minutes, pointed out that "in this way he avoided saying that the last were asked to speak first, from which we should take example not to humiliate people we speak to. This [courtesy] is always evident in the conversations and conferences of our Most Honored Father and also customary in private conversations."

The most important matter discussed was the sending of a "Sister of judgment" to Chars. The Sisters there had at first lived in peace under the kindly direction of a curé who had died the previous year. His successor, an Oratorian, was a Jansenist who sought to bend the Sisters to his harsh views of Church doctrine by demanding searching communications of their interior life to be made to him, as well as frequent general confessions. Thus far they had resisted firmly, but their situation was now further imperiled by the death of their patroness, the Marquise d'O, and their utter dependence on the lord of the village, the Duc de Luynes, who was as zealous for Jansenism as the new curé.

Sister Julienne Loret was chosen to make "an exacting visitation" of this mission. She was to stay on as Sister Servant for two years.

Julienne left immediately. The following week Louise wrote her in an optimistic vein that "Monsieur le curé . . . has taken the trouble to come to see us this morning, and seemed to me to be reasonable. He is rather brusque, but he can only be reached by sweetness and submission in word, especially when you can do what he wants. When you cannot, he must be explained the reasons courteously and humbly, and I am sure he will be very easy to please." The Sisters who had already suffered him were not so sure, and they were to be proven right. Louise herself seemed not so sure actually, for, attempting to convince herself and the Sisters that "they would find it easy to go to confession to him or to one of his priests," she added: "Nevertheless, dear Sister, be prudent. It would be better not to go at all than to let them have their way."

On May 2 she sent word to Vincent that "Madame de Saint-Mandé has informed our Sisters that there would be an assembly today to discuss the little children. I beg you most humbly to be careful that the ladies do not take up the question of sending them all back to Bicêtre. It seems to me that several experiences should prevent us, at your good pleasure, from committing ourselves to that, and I fervently hope that the occasion will not arise of having to refuse it. The work is going so well that I cannot help telling you, Most Honored Father, that I am apprehensive of these ladies again taking control of everything for fear that they will interfere with the direction God has given it since they have had scarcely anything to do with it." Brother Ducournau in preserving this letter has written in the margin: "This shows that her [Louise's] direction alone made the work succeed."

At the assembly it was decided to buy a house in Paris for all the foundlings. Vincent asked Louise—in the interest of peace, no doubt— to enlist Mlle Viole's aid in looking for one. A house in the Faubourg Saint-Marceau was eminently suitable, he said, but the location seemed to him to be "at the end of the world. See what you can find in one of the nearer faubourgs." The house decided on was most conveniently located: it stood on the rue du Faubourg Saint-Denis, facing Saint-Lazare and around the corner from the Sisters' motherhouse.

Despite the proficiency she had attained in the spiritual life, Louise was still capable of being upset occasionally by what she read. During her annual Pentecost retreat that year she told Vincent that, "since the reading I have done in Granada's *Memorial* instead of [his] *Sinner's Guide*, my mind has been obsessed with the pains he represents, without being apprehensive of them, however, because of the too little fear I have. All the same, I seemed to be overwhelmed by I know not what all-encompassing terror. It diminished somewhat as I meditated on sin after reading the first chapter of the *Guide* and perceiving that I was worthy of contempt and only the words *God is He who is* gave me entire tranquillity— even though I was still aware of crimes against His goodness in myself.

Shall I continue this reading?" she asked prudently. She knew the folly of terror, while rejoicing in the humiliation of admitting that it had seized upon her, however much against her will.

She had reached a state of very high prayer, as retreat notes of this period show. "I persuaded myself vividly that God was present in my soul," she wrote with simplicity, "that he roused my soul to listen to Him, that He wished no other thoughts than those His truth wished overwhelmingly to inspire. In reflecting upon this soul which God had not drawn from matter, I discovered in it a sort of participation in the Divinity, both because of its nature which is spiritual and renders it like that of Jesus Christ, and because of its end which is to possess God." There is no mistaking the climate of illumination and union.

She wrote on June 9 to cheer up Sister Charlotte at Richelieu, who had been ill, and to congratulate her and Sister Françoise on pronouncing annual vows when M. Lambert had been there on visitation. She was so overburdened with the care of all her daughters that she could not remember whether these particular Sisters had "asked me for permission to write to your parents. You may do so. If you have spoken to me about anything else, remind me of it again because I no longer have your letter." She had bad news for Sister Françoise: "Your sister is in a most pitiable state of poverty . . . but by the grace of God she is bearing her suffering in peace. Pray for her and her three children. Your little brother has come to this city to try to be placed in Les Incurables [a hospital]. If we can help him, we will. Monsieur your father has gone back to Beauvais. Ask our good [God] earnestly for the graces he needs to make good use of all his troubles. His relatives do what they can for him. Sister Charlotte's family are all very well, thank God."

In June a minor storm broke with the resentment of certain persons of quality over the transfer from the parish of Saint-Jean-en-Grève of Sister Jeanne-Baptiste, who had been sent to open a new mission at Montmirail. (It is rather ironic that this village, where Vincent had begun the work of the Charities, had had to wait all these years for his daughters.) Mlle Amaury and Mme Fouquet, mother of the superintendent of finances—whom Louise noted as "having a bit of a temper"—were especially indignant over Sister Jeanne-Baptiste's change. "I tried to speak to them with the respect I owe them," Louise assured Vincent dryly, hinting that her own temper had been aroused. He advised her to inform M. Georget, the curé who had accompanied the ladies on their visit to Louise, that "you have learned that certain people from Saint-Jean are writing to this girl [Sister Jeanne-Baptiste], that you don't know whether it is the ladies or a young man who is seeking her in marriage . . . that if it is the ladies who are asking [her return], they do the other Sisters of the Company a great wrong by the bad example she is giving them [in receiving unauthorized mail] and that there is reason to fear that she might turn out like those other Sisters of Saint-Roch—one of whom, getting married, acquitted herself of her duty so badly that she made herself unbearable and obliged the ladies to chase her and to come to ask for other girls for the Charity." This is a curious reference: it would seem to hint that the ladies' doting on a particular Sister forced Vincent and Louise at least once to suffer her remaining at her post even in such bizarre circumstances.

On June 22 Louise wrote to encourage Sister Guillemine Chesneau, who had gone with three others to nurse the sick and wounded left in the wake of the fighting in Picardy. Because of the nature of the work, the Sisters were forced to live alone—which Guillemine minded very much. Louise reminded her of the Apostle John, "who wished so earnestly to follow Our Lord and to have the happiness of being with Him always but chose to renounce this comfort in order to carry out the work He gave him for the glory of God and the service of the neighbor." To add to Guillemine's wretchedness, someone had been trying to influence her to leave the Company. "It is true that the work God has given you to do is extremely hard and to all appearances without consolation," Louise wrote with compassion, "but you must find [your consolation] in the assurance that you are doing God's holy will and are assured that you continue to do so as long as your spirit is submissive." Her heart was the more moved in the secret knowledge she had that the council had decided not to send Guillemine a companion, in view of the temporary character of her assignment.

Louise had to comfort, also, the Sisters at Angers. Cécile Angiboust, the Sister Servant, and Sisters Claude and Marie were ill and the other Sisters were exhausted between worry and the extra burden of work. "I am sure, dear Sisters," Louise wrote, "that you have accepted this affliction from the hand of our common Father who knows what we need and afflicts and consoles us when He pleases. What do I say, dear Sisters? That if we cherish His holy will nothing can afflict us since we know that He loves us and wishes us well in all things." The Sisters had been disappointed when a visit from M. Duchesne to preach the Jubilee to them had been called off, and they were still being tormented by evil gossip.

"Oh! how good it is to suffer for justice, dear Sisters!" she rallied them. "But let us be very careful not to give cause willingly to those who accuse us; that is, let us give them no occasion for their evil, especially by our curiosity and interest in things we should leave alone."

The Jansenist curé at Chars continued to harass the Sisters, sometimes in the pettiest manner. "I agree vehemently with you in your complaint against this humiliation," Louise assured Julienne Loret on August 30, "and ask you to request Monsieur le curé's agreement to your having your own lock, assuring him that it is not from any lack of trust of Monsieur le vicaire but that propriety demands it."

M. Lambert was making a visitation of the distant houses and his report of the peace and piety of the Sisters at Angers rejoiced Louise's heart. His only complaints, she told Cécile Angiboust, were "of all the work you have to do and the [bodily] weakness of our Sisters. Please, most dear Sister, make greater use of your women and healthy servant girls, for I know that the gentlemen want you to."

On July 1 she wrote to encourage Jeanne Lepeintre in her work "of reclamation" at Nantes. "The trouble you have taken up to the present will not be lost," she promised her. "You know, the fine weather succeeds the rain."

For some time she had been mulling over in her mind the future of the Company and sat down on July 5 to inform Vincent of her conclusions. Divine Providence compelled her, she told him, "to speak with all simplicity about needs which could, as experience has shown us, sap the strength of the Company of the Daughters of Charity." She truly believed before God that she was the "principal cause" of the "general and particular faults" which could bring about its destruction, "both by my bad example and by my negligence and lack of zealous fidelity in acquitting myself of my duty." The Company's first need, therefore, was for more capable leadership, she insisted.

Its second need was "that the manner of life be reduced to writing, kept where our Sisters could read it, and guarded reverently . . ." It should also be read publicly at stated times, "and because there will ever be gross spirits in the Company . . . there should be an explanation of the intention with which each article is to be carried out."

Then she came to the heart of her convictions: "It must be realized that weakness and frivolity of spirit need to be supported by a firm establishment . . . and the cornerstone of this establishment, without which it would seem the aforesaid Company cannot last . . . is the necessity

of erecting the aforesaid Company under the name of Company or Confraternity entirely submissive to and dependent upon the venerable government of the Most Honored General of Messieurs the venerable
Priests of the Mission . . . so that, firmly joined to it, it will participate
in the good that it does . . . and will live by the spirit which animates
the aforesaid honorable Company [of the Mission]."

Vincent's reply to this latest example of Louise's undying vision of a
double family has been lost, but her continued firm insistence upon it
indicates that he did not, at least, forbid her to pursue it.

She was disturbed in mid-July because she had not heard from Jeanne
Lepeintre in a long time, and it made her fear that Jeanne was "ill or
offended. I would be very unhappy, dear Sister, to be the cause in any
way," she wrote Jeanne anxiously. "If I have failed to answer you or give
you some satisfaction you wished of me, I beg you to blame my memory,
which is failing rapidly, and not my affection . . ." Her "failing" memory was real enough at times, but it did not prevent her from reminding
Jeanne of something she had written her two weeks before!

On August 14 Louise wrote a note of apology to M. de Vaux for any
pain she might have caused him because of her disappointment in a girl
he had sent to the Company. "M. Lambert has strongly reproached me,
Monsieur, because of the liberty I took in letting you know my displeasure," she told the good abbé. "I assure you that this poor girl aroused
such compassion in me that if I could have been sure that she was innocent of the worst of which she was accused I would have taken any
measure to do what I could. In the end, Monsieur, because her father
took too long in coming for her to please her, she left us and entered
service in the town. Be assured, Monsieur, that in the displeasure God
permitted us, that of knowing that the trouble and the practice of charity you exercised for us in this matter were useless was more distressing
than any other consideration after the glory of God."

Despite the call-down from M. Lambert—who seems from this and
other instances to have been a prim and rigid character—it is obvious
that Louise, with all her polite regrets, considered that she had acted
wisely and justly—and the girl's subsequent actions proved it. In a letter
to Cécile Angiboust at Angers there is even a hint that Louise was not
overly confident of Lambert's judgment concerning candidates for the
Company. "As for the girls M. Lambert received, I have only to say that
if you believe them suitable, if, since his return, you have noticed nothing in them contrary to our vocation, you can send them," she instructed

Cécile. "But give us no idlers, no chatterers, or any who wishes to come to Paris for her own ends under the pretext of being a Daughter of Charity and with no will to serve God or perfect herself . . ."

A Sister at Saint-Jacques was dying and Louise asked Vincent to inform M. Lambert "of the blessing Our Holy Father has granted us and how to impart it so that our poor Sister can share in this great favor." She spoke, of course, of the plenary indulgence at the hour of death obtained by M. Portail in 1647. She also asked his permission to visit the dying Sister in the company of Mme de Marillac, "to see whether I can be of any use." She wished at the same time "to make the three holy stations in the rue Saint-Denis, all near one another, and if Your Charity can spare the time to speak to me on Saturday I would be very happy to communicate on Sunday for the Jubilee intention." Vincent replied on the back of her letter that he was ignorant of the procedure in conferring "that kind of indulgence Our Holy Father has granted you, but will find out." He was also uncertain whether the indulgence could be gained during a Jubilee year, "during which all other indulgences cease." As for her visit and stations, she could go if she had a carriage to take her.

On September 1 Louise wrote with a firmness bordering on annoyance to Julienne Loret at Chars that she "thought you had been told very clearly that Monsieur Vincent told me he does not want the bell rung for your exercises for many reasons which it would take too long to explain. All that you need to know is that it is ordered by obedience. His Charity tells me that you need not make any other excuse than that it is not the custom in any of our Sisters' houses [and you know the importance of not introducing novelties into communities]." She decided on second thought to give Julienne the reasons, which were practical ones: bells would disturb the sick in hospitals, and in houses where there were only two or three Sisters it was impossible because of duty to make many exercises together, and "who would the Sister call but no one?" The fact that three hundred years ago the Sisters made their exercises without being summoned to them is rather amusing in light of the newly discovered practice of doing away with bells in religious houses in the interest of personal freedom and responsibility! She thanked Julienne for some fruit she had sent but cautioned her, since she had "promised to send more, please line the basket with hay and put it even between the fruit, otherwise it will all be squashed. You did not say whether you had made the cake yourself. If so, you are a good baker. Our sick would thank you for it with all their hearts if they could write, and for the fruit, too."

On September 5, 1651, Vincent sent the first of his priests to Poland at the request of Queen Marie-Louise de Gonzague. M. Lambert headed this first group. Queen Marie-Louise was the daughter of the Duke of Nevers and Mantua; her mother was a princess of the House of Lorraine. Raised at the court of France, she was married in 1645 to Ladislav IV, King of Poland, and after his death in 1649 to his brother and successor Jan Casimir. It is not certain that she was a member of the Ladies of Charity before her marriage, but it is most probable because of her admiration for Vincent de Paul and his communities.

The letter of introduction which M. Lambert carried to the Queen makes the first mention that Daughters of Charity, too, were destined for Poland. Vincent assured her that "the Daughters of Charity Your Majesty has asked for hold themselves in readiness to depart." Actually they were not to leave until the following year.

Louise was surrounded with illness when she wrote Jeanne Lepeintre on September 22. Whatever the nature of the epidemic sweeping Paris, the motherhouse was so stricken with "sick and infirm . . . that it looks like we shall all die." Her son, also, had been gravely ill for eight days. Vincent had not escaped either, she told Jeanne, but was now "well enough, considering his age [seventy] and the press of business."

He lent Louise, as always, the great strength of his faith in helping her to bear these latest afflictions. "We must hope for Our Lord to spare [your son]," he wrote, "and I beg it of Him with all my heart and that He give you a portion of the generosity His divine goodness gave our worthy Mère de Chantal in similar circumstances." He prayed also that God would "sanctify and glorify . . . your sick daughters . . . The death of many martyrs was the seed of Christianity. I trust it will be the same with your daughters."

Michel Le Gras had always been a difficult patient, and Vincent expressed his happiness to Louise on September 19 that Michel had "decided to accept remedies . . . You would do well to call in M. Riollant and M. Vacherot if he has no aversion to him, for there is hardly any better. I approve of your sending a Sister to nurse him, indeed I think you should send two so that they can spell each other." He felt that she should by all means go to visit her son but he cautioned her, for fear of infection, "not to sleep there. It will suffice to spend two or three hours with him." He had already given orders that his own carriage stand ready to take her, "providing," he added humorously, "that a horse which was expected to die yesterday or the day before is in condition to go!"

As Michel's illness progressed, both the patient and his mother found fault with the doctor's treatment and Vincent was forced to reprimand her. "I make the same request I made you and Monsieur your son yesterday, that you submit to the doctor—but who can throw off opinions held from time immemorial!" he sighed. "Despite everything, people think that doctors kill more patients than they cure, God thus wishing to demonstrate that He is the supreme doctor of souls and bodies especially to those who refuse remedies. Nevertheless, when we are sick we must submit to the doctor and obey him. Perhaps, Mademoiselle, what you regard as bad for him is really good. Let us bow, please, to God's good pleasure."

Late in October Louise was at last able to tell Julienne Loret that "my son seems to be entirely cured but does not go out yet or eat meat in the evening."

Despite all her good qualities, Henriette Gesseaume, the pharmacist at Nantes, continued to be a problem. Perhaps because of what Louise called "a certain steadiness amid her failings," or in a tactful attempt to transfer her—which Jeanne Lepeintre had long requested—Vincent wrote her a surprisingly liberal letter on October 1, asking her, in the modern fashion, what she would like to do. "I have received your letter and much consolation at seeing you ready to go where Providence calls you . . ." he wrote approvingly. "Nevertheless, tell me, please, whether you would rather stay at Nantes than leave, or whether you are indifferent, or finally whether you still wish us [to make the decision] to change you. In the last case we have decided, Mademoiselle Le Gras and I, to send you to Hennebont for some time, according to the original plan, and I ask you to go there as soon as you receive this. But if you are content to continue serving the hospital where you are . . . let me know at once and stay there until our reply." Whether by her own preference or not, she stayed on at Nantes for the time being.

Louise was more worried lest Jeanne Lepeintre crack under the strain of trying to manage the turbulent mission—things were quiet for the moment, but ominously so—and her worry was increased when she unexpectedly received a letter from Jeanne written from Angers. Louise wrote at once for M. de Vaux's opinion of the girl, for, she confided, "I am afraid she has suffered some extraordinary oppression of mind . . ." Even after Jeanne had returned to Nantes with "fresh vigor," Louise was anxious for de Vaux's opinion as to whether she should "stay on at Nantes a while longer . . . or is in need of a change and of returning to

Paris for a time." Louise admitted to him that Jeanne had expressed the desire to return a long while before, "but for some time she has not spoken to me so openly and may be offended in some way, although I can't think why."

M. de Vaux had renewed his request for Sisters for the Hôpital des Enfermés at Château-Gontier, but Louise had to tell him respectfully once more that she could promise none for the present. A month later she wrote to congratulate him on finding others to fill the need. He had also forwarded to her a certain monastery's request for a Daughter of Charity, presumably as an infirmarian. "We can't do that," was Louise's short answer.

The promise of Louise's happy interview with M. le procureur général Méliand was never fulfilled, because the good man died shortly afterward. When his successor, Nicolas Fouquet, came to this piece of Méliand's unfinished business, the documents—the Act of Establishment and the approved Rules—were nowhere to be found. The situation was made more difficult by the death of Méliand's secretary also, so that no tie to the previous administration remained. The most exhaustive search of the procureur général's files, of Saint-Lazare and of the Sisters' motherhouse proved fruitless. "I have found no paper concerning the Establishment," Louise informed Vincent on November 25, "and I recollect that one day Your Charity was kind enough to give us a lecture on the petition which had been presented to Monseigneur de Paris with our rule appended. Thinking that it ought to be preserved in our house, I asked you for it. I think that what prevented us from keeping it here was that something still had to be done to it."

She took the occasion of this mysterious loss to insist once again upon her unfitness to be at the head of the Company and to express her conviction that God would continue to defer its formal establishment until she was removed. In her accustomed searching self-examination—to examine the conscience of the Company was to examine her own, for it was but the extension of herself—she found reasons to wonder whether God really intended its formal establishment: the untimely deaths of so many promising Sisters, the fear that ecclesiastical recognition might cause the Sisters to forget their "nothingness," the Sisters' faults, their failure to advance in perfection especially in regard to mortification of the senses and the passions. She harbored a final dread, born of her own spotlessness. Already, she told Vincent, she had watched with horror "three or four leave voluntarily to get married, thus opening the door of the Company to those thoughts close to impurity, a crime which would destroy the Company utterly if it took root, because it must flourish to honor Our Lord and the Blessed Virgin who are purity itself."

On the other hand, there were, she agreed, wonderful signs of God's approbation: the unquestioning merit of the work and the way He had blessed it, the evident signs of His directing hand, the willingness of the superiors to dismiss from the Company those who would harm it. The reason that gave her the profoundest confidence was simply stated: if the establishment had not been made "by the institutor God used to begin it . . . his successors would not dare to make it."

She finished this long communication by informing Vincent that she did have copies of "our original rule" and of the one submitted to the Archbishop, which she enclosed, and advised Vincent that the efficient Brother Ducornau "would know where to find either a copy or the original of the petition together with the Act of Establishment." Not even Ducornau's efficiency was able to turn them up, however, and Fouquet was forced to request Cardinal de Retz, who had succeeded to the See of Paris, to begin the process all over again. It meant a sufficiently long delay, but as things turned out, it proved to be God's way of granting Louise her most cherished dream for ensuring the Company's permanence.

Coste states, without citing his sources, that Louise has been accused of having had a hand in the disappearance of the Act of the Establishment and Rule, the accusation seeking verisimilitude from the fact of Louise's friendship with Fouquet's mother, whose good offices she allegedly sought, and from the fact that the new approbation by de Retz gave her what she wanted: the perpetual government of Vincent de Paul and his successors. As Coste says, however, even beyond the evidence of Louise's disclaimer of any knowledge of the documents' whereabouts in her letter of November 25, the charge, in the context of her character, is ridiculous.

December 21 was the anniversary of Antoine Le Gras's death and Louise "could not let the day go by without reminding Your Charity that it is twenty-six years since Providence put me in the state of corporal widowhood and favored me with the desire of being united to Him for time and eternity."

Although Vincent had congratulated Jeanne Lepeintre a few weeks earlier on what she had done to right things at Nantes and on "the calm you enjoy after the many storms and troubles which have shaken your little bark," Louise was still fearful for Jeanne's health and happiness. "What do you think about sending her to Saint-Malo?" she asked him. Circumstances apparently prevented it, for Jeanne stayed on at Nantes.

Changes in personnel had been made at Angers and Louise wrote Cécile Angiboust on December 30 bidding her to have patience with the new arrivals. "You know that changes are always difficult and that it is necessary sometimes to learn the customs and how best and efficiently to serve the poor. All I can tell you is that they are of good will and have done well in the places where they were stationed." And she counseled her to have ". . . great sweetness, condescendence and discretion, especially great reserve in expressing your feelings and in telling one Sister what you know about others. Sisters Servants must die to themselves in order to acquit themselves well of their charges." She cautioned her, as she had had occasion to do before, about her communications with the Bishop: "Do not abuse the honor he does you by overfamiliarity."

She conveyed in this letter the news of the death of Madame la présidente de Lamoignon, who had succeeded Mme Goussault as superioress of the Ladies of Charity and had guided them by means of "her three chief virtues of holy simplicity, perfect humility and great charity and liberality." The poor loved her so much that they would not let her be buried any place but among them in the Church of Saint-Leu.

Vincent had been premature with his congratulations to Jeanne Lepeintre on the peace at Nantes. The administrators were complaining again—this time that there were too many Sisters and that the expense of supporting them was too great (Louise retorted that there were no more than the administrators had asked for) and that despite this large number, the Sisters were still hiring women "to carry, change, and wash the linens . . . and even the dishes" (Louise asked Jeanne Lepeintre whether this accusation was true, "for if it is, it would put us in the wrong"). It was as she suspected, false.

She had sad news, she told Jeanne, for Sister Françoise, whose mother and grandmother had both died. "Her father is well, thank God, for he too had been very sick," she continued, offering some vestige of comfort: "Her two sisters in our Company are also quite well and bear their grief in a virtuous and Christian way. I beg her with all my heart to do the same, to give herself entirely to God for the accomplishment of His holy will and to see the cause of her sorrow in this admirable will and plan of Providence. Let her see no other good for her relatives than to die like good Christians as these good mothers did because of their deeds. It is unbelievable, the virtue and submission their father has shown in this situation." And she finished by asking Jeanne to assist Françoise "to bear her cross well."

Louise had been given a great joy in the year 1651 with the birth of a granddaughter, who was christened Renée-Louise in her honor but whom all the Sisters—who in their delight made her a "member" of the Company!—dubbed "the little Sister." The precise date of her birth is unknown, but it was before late summer, judging from a letter Louise wrote to Julienne Loret on January 7, 1652. Julienne had sent New Year's gifts for all the Sisters and Louise thanked her in their name. "As for your good cakes, the Company will think of you while eating them. The little Sister hasn't enough teeth for them yet," she added with a smile. "Here are the New Year's gifts Divine Providence has chosen for the two of you, and a little Saint-Julienne that I did not wish to put at hazard"—the Sisters drew lots for their gifts—"for fear she would not fall to you." She alluded to another of their holiday customs by informing Julienne that "Sister Ménard was queen."

The Sisters at Chars had described their beautiful crèche for Louise and she was happy that they had "housed the little Jesus so well. I am sure you have done the same for His new presence in your hearts, where I beg Him with all of mine to be pleased to take His good pleasure."

A few days later Louise fell "very ill of a *double-tierce* fever" which kept her in bed for three weeks. Even afterward it hung on, as she told Julienne Loret on March 11. Julienne, too, had been ill and Louise was anxious for her "to try to eat and to be sure to get the air, at least as much as your strength will permit."

The renewed civil war was spewing lawlessness and brigandage all over the country and the two Sisters at Chars were living in a constant state of anxiety and tension. Louise, so far away, could do no more than let them know that she was suffering with them "in their constant fear of the soldiers." She told another band of Sisters sent to nurse the wounded: "Be certain that while we sympathize with you, many are envious of the service you are rendering to God . . . Oh! dear Sisters, how many consolations you must have amid such weariness! Courage! Work hard for your perfection in the many occasions of meeting rebuffs with the exercise of sweetness and patience . . ." The sign of God's blessing, she told these Sisters in the field, was in the growing number of postulants, "so many that there were thirty at first table." God gives help when help is needed, especially to the innocent, and in all wars it was the innocent bystanders, especially the poor, who suffered—she went on to motivate them—and Daughters of Charity were needed to alleviate their famine and sickness and degradation.

The tragedy of the Fronde was that it need never have happened in the first place. Mazarin, keenly aware of his low birth, found pleasure in insulting the Princes of the Blood: at one point in 1650 he held Condé, Conti and de Longueville prisoners for months. The Princes in their turn—especially Condé—were so jealous of their prerogatives that they even alienated would-be allies. The malice of the Cardinal de Retz kept the pot boiling in Paris, where Parlement and the people never ceased demanding the presence of the Queen and the young King. To effect complete chaos, loyalty was nonexistent and the great men of the kingdom kept shifting allegiances so often that no one knew whom or what to support. It is little wonder that the rabble cried a pox on all—Princes, Parlement and Mazarin—and threw up their barricades!

The final misery of the capital was inevitable when, after the armies had made a shambles of the realm in two years of fighting up and down and across it, driving the terrified villagers and farmers inexorably toward Paris, Condé made the city the focal point of attack by fleeing there to join forces with Gaston d'Orléans, the King's seditious uncle. Vincent told M. Lambert on May 3 that "our public and private miseries . . . increase daily because the armies are close by—which spells complete ruin, and if God doesn't give us peace . . . we are on the eve of many hardships." Soup kitchens staffed by Vincent's priests and brothers and Louise's Sisters were already feeding large numbers of poor families, giving first call to those with the greatest number of children and infirm adults: 900 people in the parish of Saint-Hippolyte, 300 in the parish of Saint-Martin, and 600 in the parish of Saint-Laurent. Other parishes were as bad off, but there were only funds enough to provide for these three. In the parish of Saint-Médard alone there were 1,800 working-class families in dire need, not to mention the hordes of refugees lucky enough to reach the comparative safety of the capital. Those trapped in the suburbs outside the walls lived amid stark horror. To quote the official *Relations* of the time: "In these quarters you hear of nothing but murder, pillage, robbery, rape, sacrilege. The churches are no less plundered than those on the frontiers, the Blessed Sacrament no less hurled on the ground to appropriate the ciboria. Villages are deserted, most of the wheat trampled underfoot, the curé in flight and without a flock, the peasants hiding in the woods, where they suffer hunger and the justified fear of being killed by those who pursue them."

It goes without saying that the Sisters and their charges, the sick poor and the foundlings, suffered along with everyone else. On May 14, in the midst of the bloody battle being waged at Saint-Denis between the royal troops under Turenne and the *Frondeurs* under Condé, Vincent wrote to thank Mlle de Lamoignon for her "offers of lodging and safer accommodation for the poor children. The heat of battle, with men killed before their eyes right in front of their house, put such terror into the nurses that they fled, leaving everything—each one her little foster child and the other children alseep in bed—with the Daughters."

And Louise told Vincent: "This alarm has thoroughly frightened all of us. Many of our Sisters would like very much to go to confession today and I am afraid that we will not be able to have the priest from Saint-Laurent. If not, I ask you to do us the charity of sending us one after dinner.

"I don't think it's possible to go to buy wheat, there not being any in the neighboring villages, and furthermore there is great danger of the money being lost." She suggested his pursuing an idea he had had, that the magistrates of the city bring wheat to the Place de Grève and supply the purchasers with a safe-conduct of archers. "I don't think there is any other way of preventing these poor little children from dying from hunger," she finished.

Then she turned to the safety of the Sisters. "Most of the people of this faubourg have left. Shouldn't we follow their example? That, of course, would entail a lot of trouble. If there is any fear for our young Sisters, we could scatter them among the various parishes . . . As for me, I seem to be waiting for death and cannot keep my heart from leaping every time someone cries 'To arms!' Paris seems to have abandoned this faubourg, but I hope God will not abandon us and that His goodness will have mercy on us . . . I'm afraid our Bicêtre man hasn't gotten through. What shall we do about Sister Geneviève [Poisson], who is very much needed there to reassure our poor Sisters?"

Vincent sent an immediate reply. The plan for dispensing wheat in Paris was not feasible, he said, because the magistrates were "not masters of the people." He thought "there was no danger in our Brother Mathieu [Regnard] going on a tour of the villages" for wheat. Geneviève could return to Bicêtre safely because "things were not as volatile on that side of the city as on this one." Louise could, if she wished, disperse "the most timid" of the girls along the parishes but, he insisted, "I cannot persuade myself that the danger is as great as people say, or that the faubourg will be attacked . . . What Our Lord protects is well protected: the proper thing is to commit ourselves to His adorable Providence."

It may well have been a Sister working in one of the overcrowded hospitals who wrote Vincent the following heartrending note: "We are overburdened with work, and will drop if we do not have help. I am forced to trace these few lines at night while sitting up with our sick, there being no leisure during the day, and even as I write I am exhorting two who are dying. First I go to one to urge him, 'Raise your heart to God, my friend, ask His mercy.' That done, I return now to write one or two lines, then turn to the other: 'Jesus! Mary! My God, I hope in You!' And now I come back again to my letter. And so I go back and forth, writing to you with a distracted mind. This is why I beg you most humbly to send us another Sister." No one will ever know the name of this exhausted heroine. And she was only one of many, a memorable symbol of all. But Louise wrote to Barbe Angiboust at Brienne on June 11: "Since God chastises His people for their sins, is it reasonable that we should not suffer with the others? Who are we that we should be exempt from public calamities?"

On June 13 Vincent attended a general assembly of the Ladies of Charity, convoked to consider new ways of helping the refugees and presided over by the Archbishop of Reims. The ladies "have begun to assist them in body," he informed M. Dehorgny at Rome, "and I have offered to give them missions, according to the good maxim which advocates seizing opportunity where you find it." Although he admitted that the Congregation was not founded to preach missions in towns but only in the country, nevertheless, he argued, the countrypeople "have come to us, chased out and forced to leave the countryside by the rigors of war . . ."

People were now being fed at the rate of fourteen thousand or fifteen thousand a day, and priests and laity alike were protecting eight or nine hundred young girls by taking them into their presbyteries and homes, as well as in large houses, where they shut them away from the licentious soldiers and saved some of them from the temptation of taking to the streets. Amid all the wantonness and cruelty in the city there was a great and profound charity.

Peace rumors began to fly—and the populace grasped at them eagerly —in the wake of public processions ordered by the Archbishop. These processions for peace came to a glorious climax on June 11 with the "descent" into the city from her church on Mont-Ste-Geneviève of the *châsse* containing the relics of Ste Geneviève, faithful protectress of Paris in its moments of gravest peril. Vincent commented on the solemn ceremony at Notre-Dame that "there has never been seen a greater concourse of people in Paris, or more exterior devotion." Louise told Barbe Angiboust to ask the bearer of her letter to describe "the beautiful ceremony carried out today for the descent of the *châsse* of Sainte-Geneviève. Oh! how good it is to be faithful to God who renders so much honor to His good servants as a mark of His eternal affection! What he asks of you at the present moment, dear Sister, is great union and support among you . . . I pray you, Sister Barbe, old and worn out as you are," she wrote tenderly, "that if you see Sister Jeanne with too much work and cannot help her, do what you can, because we cannot send you another . . . because of the five thousand poor to whom we are dispensing soup—we are feeding two thousand, not counting the sick, in our own parish."

Vincent confirmed these figures in a letter written to M. Lambert on June 21. While his priests were housing and feeding refugee priests at Saint-Lazare, preaching missions in the churches and refuges of the city, and helping to distribute food wherever they could, he wrote, "the poor Daughters of Charity are playing a much greater role in the corporal assistance of the poor than we are. They prepare and dispense soup every day at Mademoiselle Le Gras's house to 1,300 bashful poor and in the Faubourg Saint-Denis to 800 refugees; and in the parish of Saint-Paul alone, for the five of these girls feed 5,000 poor, besides the sixty or eighty sick they are taking care of. Others are doing the same in other places."

On the twenty-third of the month he wrote to congratulate the Sisters at Valpuiseaux on their escape from harm. They had been in the thick of the fighting and had had to flee for their lives. "Blessed be God that you are back in your own house at last," he wrote almost in disbelief, "and that He has preserved you through so many dangers and perils! . . . It is as if, being dead, you had been brought back to life!" He brought them up to date on what had been happening at Paris, and begged them to keep well: "Mademoiselle Le Gras herewith sends you syrups and drugs to that end." He finished by assuring them that he would send them more Sisters but for the danger on the roads from the soldiers and from bandits as well as from the wolves, which had recently devoured three women in their neighborhood.

On July 5 Saint-Lazare was threatened by "an entire army"—Condé's —and M. Alméras in the seminary of Saint-Charles, located in the far corner of the sprawling property, was maltreated by eight soldiers, who ransacked all the rooms but were forced to disgorge all their loot by two of the Duc de Bourbon's men who happened along at the fortuitous moment. The fright of the Sisters across the road can be imagined.

Horrified beyond words at the destruction and misery he had witnessed for months, Vincent decided to risk himself once more as an emissary of peace. Off he went on another desperate errand to the court, which was now at Saint-Denis. The Queen received him as graciously as before but would not commit herself. The next day he wrote from Paris to Mazarin, representing as delicately as he could that the King's return to Paris and his own resignation would solve everything. Again it was all in vain. Indeed, Vincent's discouragement turned into disgust when he learned a few days later that the Duc de Bourbon, who had personally urged him to make the intervention, had himself bolted from the side of Condé and joined the Queen's forces.

Epidemics of virulent fever now began to sweep the courntryside in the wake of battle. They were especially rampant at Palaiseau, where Turenne had his headquarters for a time. "Those who fell sick first and did not die are now in need of convalescence, and those who were healthy are now sick," Vincent wrote despairingly to the Duchesse d'Aiguillon. "One of our priests has come expressly to bring me the news that the soldiers have cut all the wheat and there is none left to harvest. Nor are we any longer in the position to buy [any] . . . I beg you most humbly, Madame, to call a small assembly at your house today to get your heads together and see what is to be done. I will be there if I can." This was but one of the constant crises the Ladies of Charity met with a tireless generosity that bled them white.

On July 11 Louise informed Vincent of a request by Mme de Varize for two Sisters to take over a hospital at Châteaudun and for two more to serve the villagers of Saint-André. The good lady had already been promised two Sisters for her manor-village of Varize but the fighting had delayed their departure. She assured Louise that it was now possible to get them through the lines and they left to establish this new mission. Louise and Vincent were forced to refuse her requests for Châteaudun and Saint-André for the moment, however, alleging the need of supply-

ing Sisters to Etampes, which was more stricken by the war than many
other places, and to the Parisian parishes, where many of the sisters had
fallen ill from sheer exhaustion.

At Etampes the Sisters had heroically attacked the worst desolation
they had yet seen. They were operating four hospitals, two for the towns-
people and two for the peasants of the countryside, besides an orphanage
they had set up in one of the great town houses. Several of the Sisters
"died, victims of their devotion," at Etampes.

The house at Châteaudun was not to be established for two years, but
Louise was forced to reconsider her decision concerning Saint-André
when Mme la présidente de Herse came to join her entreaties to those of
Mme de Varize. She told Vincent that she would make an effort to
accommodate the wife of the président of Parlement, if he approved,
especially because the extra Sisters intended for Etampes had not been
able to get through and the Sisters destined for Poland could not leave.
Despite everything, however, Sisters seem never to have gone to Saint-
André.

Even the exercise of charity breeds quarrels and Vincent was able to
quash one that arose during that dreadful summer almost before it
began. The Queen of Poland had sent 12,000 livres for the relief of Paris
and had entrusted their distribution to Mlle de Lamoignon and Mère
Angélique Arnauld of Port-Royal. Because of Mlle de Lamoignon's
membership in the Ladies of Charity, a rumor started and quickly spread
that the ladies were to have entire responsibility for disbursing the alms.
When it reached Mère Angélique's ears, she immediately wrote to Mlle
de Lamoignon in protest, and that good lady turned to Vincent for help.
He easily cleared the air by explaining to her that the Queen had also
offered to allow the ladies to borrow up to 4,000 livres of the money if
they needed it for their works, promising to pay off the debt herself.

On August 16 Vincent decided to make his boldest effort for peace by
appealing to Pope Innocent X to intervene. The courage it took may be
measured by the almost absolute dependence of himself and his communities upon all the warring factions for the success of their ministries.

He drew for the Pope a picture of "the lamentable state of our country France" which stands as one of the most terrible indictments of the
Fronde: "The Royal Family torn by dissensions; the people split into
factions; the cities and provinces scourged by civil war; the villages, ham-
lets and towns pillaged, ruined, burned; the laborers incapable of reaping
what they sow, and sowing nothing for future years. Soldiers give them-

selves up to every excess with impunity. The people are exposed in turn not only to rapine and brigandage but even to murder and every kind of torture. Country people who escape the sword almost all die of hunger. Priests, spared no more than anyone else by the soldiers, are treated cruelly and inhumanly, tortured and put to death. Virgins are dishonored, religious, even, exposed to their lust and fury, temples profaned, ransacked or destroyed. Those left standing are for the most part bereft of their pastors, so that the people are almost entirely deprived of sacraments, Masses and all other spiritual aid. Finally—what is horrible to think of and still more horrible to put into words—the most august Sacrament of the Body of the Lord is treated with the utmost sacrilege even by Catholics, for in order to carry off the sacred vessels, they hurl the Holy Eucharist to the ground and trample upon it." Vincent's letter is preserved in the Vatican archives, but there is no record of an answer. Be that as it may, the Fronde began to fall apart soon afterward.

Despite all turmoil and upheaval, Louise went about the usual affairs of the Company with serenity. Writing to Jeanne Lepeintre at Nantes on August 24, she bade her inform the youngest Sister in the house, who had just arrived there, that she "should be at peace as far as her parents are concerned: her mother, sister and other relatives are all well, thank God . . ." She then instructed Jeanne to "encourage her in her work and especially in the observance of her rules. I am sure, dear Sister, that you do not fail to inculcate in the latest arrivals the respect they owe the older Sisters. That is so necessary that, if we do not look well to it, it can cause the greatest disorders in the community. Young souls must be formed to submission and interior mortification, otherwise there will be nothing but chaos, and the older Sisters will have good reason for any dissatisfaction they may have."

Vincent was disconsolate when he wrote to M. Blatiron at Turin on August 30. "They gave us reason to hope for peace," he sighed, "but right now they are not to be trusted. As soon as our sick get better, others take their place . . . It is estimated that for some time now ten thousand persons a month have died in Paris. Pray for us all, please . . . This year we will lose at least twenty-six or thirty barrels of wheat, even though we are hoarding the little that is left to us, and that is in constant and extreme danger because most of it is still in the barns in the country. May it please God to dispose of us and what we have for His glory!"

As in the greatest tragedies, there were bits of comic relief. On one occasion Brother Ducournau wrote to Vincent to decide two earth-shaking matters: "1⁰ The Daughters of Charity at Forges say that M. le curé wishes to give them the church chalice for safekeeping, and Mademoiselle Le Gras inquires whether they ought to accept or refuse it and, in case they accept it, whether an act should be drawn up testifying to the fact that M. le curé had entrusted them with it." "I don't think these formalities are necessary," was Vincent's laconic reply. "2⁰ They are sending little boys who have been naughty to the school to be dealt with by [the Sisters], as if their master could not chastise them. They ask what they should do." The rueful shake of the head is almost visible in Vincent's reply: "It is not even proper for the Daughters to allow boys in their school, let alone whip those that people send them!"

Vincent made his last effort for peace in September after the Coadjutor led an unsuccessful embassage to Louise XIV at Compiègne. The young King had not even deigned to receive them, but sent out word that he would return to Paris when those who were obstructing his return had decamped—a patent allusion to the Coadjutor himself. On the eleventh, Vincent wrote to Mazarin to assure him that Paris had come to its senses and "asked for the King and the Queen with a cry from the heart." And, forestalling the Cardinal's animosity for the wives of his enemies, he added that "even the Ladies of Charity, who are among the most distinguished citizens of Paris, tell me that, if Their Majesties draw near, they will go out, a regiment of women, to receive them in triumph." He did not stick at pointing out again Mazarin's own unpopularity, or at pricking holes in alternate plans the Cardinal might have, or even at suggesting that he should refrain from making himself part of the triumphal return. The Minister was furious and countered by dismissing Vincent peremptorily from the Council of Conscience—which could not have made the saint happier! Nevertheless, the Cardinal was no fool, and when peace came the following month, it came pretty much the way Vincent suggested it might.

The way was at last cleared for the Daughters of Charity to leave for their first mission outside France. Sisters Marguerite Moreau, Madeleine Drugeon and Françoise Douelle had long been destined for Poland. Ironically, their departure had been held up—why, is not clear—by the refusal of the Archbishop of Paris to allow the departure of the nuns of the Visitation who were to go with them. After waiting so long, the three Sisters were informed on September 5 that they were to be ready to leave the next day! Vincent sent them off in true missionary style. "How very few women and girls have received the call to minister to body and soul you have received today!" he exclaimed. "It is the call given to a Saint François Xavier in former times . . . Oh! my dear daughters, how great a vocation is yours! To raise up saints, both men and women, to Christ in this new realm where the faith is in grave danger although given protection by the shadow of a glorious throne which will [also] shield you."

Louise's first extant allusion to this historic event which marked the beginning of that mighty pilgrimage of her daughters to the remotest parts of the earth is in a letter written on October 26 to Barbe Angiboust at Brienne. "I don't think I told you that Divine Providence has finally called three of our Sisters to Poland to serve the poor," she wrote. "We have no news of their arrival as yet . . . You know there is always peril on the sea—which makes me recommend them to your prayers." Actually, they had been in Poland nearly a month as she wrote, and a letter from the Queen was on the way to Vincent expressing how "very satisfied" she was with what seemed to her "very good girls."

Louise had been happy to learn from Barbe that butter was "very cheap" at Brienne and asked her, if she could buy it "at no more than six sols a pound, to do us the favor of sending as much as you can, but no more than a hundred pounds." She saw distinct possibilities for the use of a type of honey Julienne Loret had sent her from Chars. "If this honey is naturally white or if there is a way to render it so . . ." she suggested, "it could be used for making syrups and even candy, since sugar is so extremely dear." And she sent a sheaf of recipes in which it could be used.

Although peace had been finally restored with the tumultous welcome given to the King when he entered Paris on October 21, the devastation and misery and poverty wreaked by the war would last a long time, so there were no prospects of rest for the Sisters. This depressing future after the terrible experiences of the long months just past, added to Louise's years—she was now sixty-one—took their toll and her strength failed more each day, so that it seemed that she lived only by the grace of God and her own indomitable spirit. Yet she continued to attend to whatever business she could.

She would never, as long as she lived, be able to accept with complete serenity the failings and especially the betrayal of her daughters. In these closing days of autumn she wrote in evident anguish to Vincent about "poor Sister Nicole from Montmirail" (one wonders sadly whether this was the same Nicole who had been Louise's cross in former years). Nicole, she said, had told "our Sisters that Mademoiselle Montdésir, Madame Tubeuf's daughter, had accepted her to serve the sick poor in the village of Issy, the place from which we withdrew our Sisters a long time ago now, and that she had no intention of abandoning either the habit or the coiffe and would dress always as one of our Sisters. All our Sisters are upset, and I am too, for I am fearful of this situation [insofar as my present lassitude permits me]." Couldn't the habit be taken from her, she implored? It could be done easily, she assured him, by the prudent intervention of Mademoiselle Viole.

Vincent, too, was tired and old and sick—he was seventy-one now—and the reply he scribbled across the bottom of Louise's note was definitely testy. "Do we have to get upset even over the whole Establishment, let alone over a habit, etc.?" he wrote angrily. "Is that necessary? In the name of God, Mademoiselle, let's cure ourselves of this failing! You feel the way you do because of exhaustion and weakness." Nevertheless, he grumbled, if Mlle Viole could turn the trick, let her try.

On December 14 Louise wrote to thank Barbe Angiboust for some small gifts she had sent from Brienne. "Your raisins are perfectly lovely!" she enthused. "You know well that I have no teeth to eat breads with!" She had good news of the Sisters at Paris: they had all recovered from their illness and "Monsieur Vincent, our Most Honored Father, goes along in apparent good health. We have every reason to ask God to preserve him for many years."

On Christmas Day she was able to assist at Vincent's Mass and assured Julienne Loret that she had not forgotten to ask him to include a special intention Julienne had requested. She was forced to ask Julienne's indulgence because she could not remember either the type or the quantity of blankets she had asked for, however—whether from age or the press of work, she was growing increasingly forgetful.

This preoccupation with humdrum things after the drama of the past months seemed to create a lull in Louise's busy life and even to presage quiet for the evening of it. But the lull was illusory and quiet would never be given her except in the depths of her heart, which was its true home.

XVI

The Misery of Champagne, Picardy—and Poland

The decision to recall Julienne Loret to Paris in January 1653 precipitated a new crisis at Chars. Julienne was one of the most valuable Sisters in the Company and she had been "wasted" on the small house of two Sisters at Chars only because Vincent and Louise had hoped that she might defeat the curé's efforts to ensnare the Sisters in Jansenism. She had indeed held him at bay but had not succeeded in stopping him from plaguing them altogether: they still suffered martyrdom in an effort to make their weekly confession, for example, and indeed were sometimes deprived of the sacraments for months at a time.

Now that the Company needed to make greater use of her talents, her persecutors decided to resist her change and enlisted the help of the Baronne de Chars, herself a close friend of the arch-Jansenist Arnauld, to prevent it. Vincent saw a chance to bargain. "Insist," he instructed Louise, "either that they promise you that the Daughters can adhere to their rule concerning confession—for to say that times for confession need not be specified means that the Church was deceived when she ordered the faithful to confess once a year—or else it will be necessary for you to hold firm in not giving them this good girl . . ." If that failed, he said, "see if you can break away rather than chance the spread of the spirit of the times in the little Company . . ." Neither the curé nor the Baronne de Chars, apparently, would make any concessions, because Julienne was recalled to Paris and sent shortly afterward as Sister Servant to Fontenay-aux-roses. The superiors could not act to withdraw the Sisters entirely because they did not want to offend Mme la présidente de Herse, who had founded the mission but was not at all sympathetic to the heresy of the other protoganists.

After the decision to recall Julienne had been made, Louise had been so eager to have her at Paris that she urged her "to get used to traveling by horseback or donkey, for to undertake a long trip on foot is impossible, besides having to wait for the roads to dry, which is a long way off."

In a letter of January 3 to M. Lambert, Vincent expressed his happiness that "the Daughters of Charity are at Warsaw and ready to set to work. May God bless and preserve them!" He told Lambert that he had been ready to begin a conference to the Sisters at the motherhouse when he had been summoned to an emergency assembly of the Ladies of Charity by the Duchesse d'Aiguillon and Mme de Herse to consider what they could do for Champagne, which had been "reduced to a pitiable state" by the armies of Condé, who had stubbornly retreated to that frontier province, and of Turenne, who had pursued him there. "I am afraid that we may not be able to make any great efforts," Vincent wrote in discouragement, "because we are already put to great expense in assisting this diocese, which is costing us six or seven thousand livres a week."

And he was forced to write the following week to M. Coglée, who was superior at Sedan in the heart of the distressed province: "I am greatly afflicted at the miseries of your frontier and at the number of poor people who are overwhelming you, but can do nothing more than to pray God to come to their aid—the which I do. It is impossible to add anything to the hundred livres allotted to you each month. Sedan is the only place in the frontier to which Paris continues its alms. It has been forced to forsake all others because of the extreme need in this diocese where the armies have stayed on a long time."

Indeed, the whole of Paris was giving the little it had to those who had less. Two storehouses had been set up in the city to receive the old clothes, linens, furniture, cooking utensils, foodstuffs and drugs brought by people of every class. These storehouses were the forerunners of the warehouses of the St. Vincent de Paul Society—and of the Salvation Army and other kindred organizations—found all over the world today.

The misery of Champagne, and of Picardy, was an old story dating back to 1635, when the Spaniards had begun their depredations and invasions of France's northern frontier. The armies of Condé and Turenne were only new perpetrators of old evils. The atrocities and cruelties and barbarous immoralities visited on the unhappy villagers and peasants were still those detailed by Vincent for Pope Innocent X.

One of Vincent's missionaries wrote a horrified eyewitness account of the utter desolation and degradation in 1651: "No tongue can utter, no pen express, no ear dare listen to, what we have seen in the early days of our visits . . . All the churches and most sacred mysteries profaned, vestments stolen, baptismal fonts broken, priests slain, maltreated or put to flight, all the houses demolished, the whole of the harvest carried off, the fields left without seeds or tillers, almost universal famine and death, corpses without burial and for the most part exposed as a prey to wolves. The poor who have survived this state of misery are reduced [after losing all their possessions] to gathering corn or barley in the fields which has just begun to sprout and is half rotten. The bread they bake resembles mud and is so unwholesome that the life they lead is a living death. Almost all of them are sick. They lie hidden in roofless cabins or holes into which they can scarcely squeeze, stretched for the most part on the bare ground or on rotten straw, without linen or clothes save a few wretched rags. Their faces are black and disfigured, and they resemble ghosts rather than men." Most horrendous of all, the poor people endured these unspeakable conditions for twenty-four years.

The Ladies of Charity played a major role in the relief of the stricken provinces. According to Coste: "During the early years the ladies received and dispatched ten, twelve, fifteen and even sixteen [this was the highest figure] livres a month, for flour was then very dear and the number of poor people greatest. At the end of 1652, poor parish priests received one hundred crowns a month. Abelly reckons the sum total expended by the Ladies of Charity between 1650 and 1660 at more than 600,000 livres in money, provisions, clothes, linen, bedding, shoes, medicines, tools, corn and church vestments. Hard and constant work was needed to amass such resources, and Saint Vincent, as usual, employed both natural and supernatural means. He celebrated Mass once a month in Notre-Dame that God might inspire the wealthy to give and to give generously, and the ladies who assisted at his Mass went to Holy Communion for the same intention. He also worked hard himself by begging from house to house; sometimes he returned home bent down under the weight of crowns collected; on some occasions he brought back as many as 1,800. It was heavy work but not fatiguing, for joy lightened the burden. He had also at times disappointments, which he cheerfully endured; he remarked on one occasion: 'Today after I had preached very well to a lady, I thought she would give me a large contribution. Do you know what I got? Four white crowns [twelve francs]. Now, what use is that?' "

The Daughters of Charity did their part by working in the hospitals and the hovels of the poor at Rethel, Saint-Etienne-à-Arnes, Sedan, Châlons, La Fère, Stenay, Montmédy and Calais.

It was for all practical purposes a gigantic Vincentian effort into which he deployed all his spiritual armies, and Louise was his trusted lieutenant.

Writing to Barbe Angiboust on February 8, Louise asked for prayers for the Sisters in Poland, who had been called upon, almost as soon as they arrived there, to nurse the victims of the plague, which was raging in Warsaw. Vincent had asked all the Sisters for prayers during a conference a few days before, and then went on to tell anecdotes about the "foreign missionaries." "After the [Queen] had given them some time to grow accustomed to the country and to learn a little of the language," he began, "she said to them: 'Now, Sisters, it is time to begin to work. There are three of you. I intend to keep one with me, and it is you, Sister Marguerite. The others will go to Krakow to serve the poor.' Sister Marguerite replied: 'Ah! Madame, what are you saying? There are only three of us to serve the poor, and you have in your kingdom plenty of other people more capable than we are to serve Your Majesty. Give us leave, Madame, to do here what God asks of us, just as we do elsewhere.' 'What! Sister, do you not wish to serve me?' 'Pardon me, Madame, but it is God who has called us to serve the poor.' " And Vincent exclaimed: "Isn't that beautiful, Sisters? O Savior of my soul! God has permitted this example in order to animate you! What, Sisters, to trample royalty under foot!"

Queen Marie-Louise was at times homesick for France and loved to chat with the Sisters about Paris and about Vincent and Louise. One day she began to talk about the foundlings and how, after they were raised, they might join the Company. Without thinking, Sister Marguerite exclaimed artlessly: "Forgive me, Madame, but our Company is not made up of such persons. Only virgins are admitted into it." And Vincent made use of the simple story to say: "It was God who made her talk like that, Sisters, in order to warn us that only pure and chaste persons should be members of the Company."

Both communities were shocked in early March to learn of the death on January 30 of M. Lambert. Louise was very conscious of how well and faithfully he had served the Company and asked the Sisters to offer up a Communion for the repose of his soul.

"Our poor Sisters of Poland have great need of prayers. There affliction is heavy . . ." she told Jeanne Lepeintre. "Although the Queen shows them much kindness, to the point that Her Majesty looks after them personally and uses them in works of charity, nonetheless, dear Sister, what must be their grief at having lost such a father!" Louise was pleased that some of the Sisters' pupils there had been so impressed by them "that already they dream of being Daughters of Charity!" And she added, more prophetically than she knew, that "if God gives His blessing, a great establishment will rise up there." The Polish province became, indeed, one of the largest in the Company and gave hundreds of actual and dry martyrs to the Church in the slave-labor camps of World War II.

A new and different work fell to the Company in March 1653—the care of old people. A rich bourgeois of Paris, who insisted on remaining anonymous, gave Vincent 100,000 livres for a work of charity of which Vincent was to make the choice. He decided on a home where poor old men and women of the working class who could no longer earn their living might end their days sheltered and at peace. He thereupon bought a house known as the Nom-de-Jésus, close by Saint-Lazare, and admitted to it in separate wings twenty men and twenty women. On the day appointed, Louise sent a note to inform him that "the little family has not failed to assemble, except one from each side who have not yet come. I think it necessary, Monsieur, that Your Charity take the trouble to welcome them tomorrow morning and have them make some devotion such as to adore the Holy Cross and give them a little talk on the Passion." Her suggestions were prompted by the fact that it was the Lenten season and the chapel was not ready: by April 3 permission to say Mass in the Nom-de-Jésus had not yet been sought from the Curé de Saint-Laurent.

One of the first to benefit from the charity of this house—which Louise often called, graphically, the *Pauvres Ouvriers* instead of by its proper name—was, fittingly enough, a relative of one of the Sisters. On May 23 Louise asked Cécile Angiboust at Angers "to tell Sister Elisabeth that her cousin Brocard has passed away in a very Christian manner. Monsieur Vincent saw him two or three times during his illness because we had put him in a hospice for workers which has opened in the neighborhood."

Louise's heart went out in a special way to the Sisters on the frontier because of the superhuman demands on them and her consciousness that many of them were alone. She tried as best she could to bring them back to Paris to rest, but this was not always possible. She told Anne

Hardemont at Châlons how astonished she was that the town magistrates had not yet made good their promise to give her the fare to return to the motherhouse. "Nevertheless," she cautioned, "Monsieur Vincent thinks you should wait for their consent." In her moments of discouragement Anne sometimes thought that her Sisters far away in the capital had forgotten her. "You must not doubt my great desire to see you," Louise insisted affectionately. "Indeed, it seems to me that your being hurt makes you closer to us." She agreed that Sister Jeanne at Etampes had "good reason to be vexed at being so long a time alone and of not receiving our news . . . It is constantly on my mind that you have deserved to come home for a long time and if it cannot be arranged very soon we will send you one of our dear Sisters . . . Remind yourself time and again of my very special affection and that our Sisters and I speak of you often with happiness at the service you render Our Lord and with sorrow when we think of you all by yourself."

Vincent sent for Jeanne to come home on September 20. "Mademoiselle Le Gras needs you," he wrote in welcome, "and your Company will be very eager to see you after the great and useful work you have done, for which I give thanks to God." She could not come at once because Mlle Rigault, who was going to take over her work, was still in Paris and Jeanne was forced to await her return to Etampes.

To those in the field who had the good fortune to live together Louise urged the necessity of living the common life in all its energizing spirituality. "Have you constant love for your little rules?" she asked the Sisters at Varize. "When you are interrupted in their practice to serve the neighbor, do you return to them determined to carry them out all the better? I am sure that you bear each other a mutual love, that your dear conversation—after you have done what you can for the poor—is to speak to each other of God, of the Company to which God has called you, and of the virtues you have admired in our Sisters." It was her chief work to console, to encourage, to instruct, to love. Vincent understood and strengthened her in turn. "You have cause to honor the varieties of grief and worry of Our Lord in the desert and the horrible temptations He suffered there," he told her during one of her little retreats snatched from the hurly-burly of life. "These give you reasons for consolation."

The trials that accompany the beginning of a great work were of an especially dangerous type for the pioneer Sisters in Poland. With the cessation of the plague, the Queen neglected to give them further work and, even more thoughtlessly, placed them in circumstances which were contrary to their rule, which threatened their common life and which outraged their sense of modesty. She sent a motley group of seventeen externs to live in their house. One had scurvy, the other adults had venereal disease. Among them were a mother and daughter of doubtful virtue and two boys of five, one of whom was already experimenting in vice with a little girl of the same age. "We dare not put into words the embarrassment we have suffered . . ." the Sisters wrote in anguish to Vincent, and added bitterly, "In France no one would expect us to minister to such people, but here we are happy to have them in our house!" They begged Vincent to tell them what to do. They told him with simplicity that a lady of the court had asserted that "the Queen would be good enough and kind enough to send us back without noticing that we were annoyed." And the brave girls avowed to him humbly: "Really we should not be upset or annoyed ourselves, because we have come under obedience." Despite their bravery, however, they were very unhappy. "Our greatest pain is not to have any work, which gives us cause to humble ourselves and to think often of the good advice you gave us when we left," they wrote with a heart-rending wistfulness, "especially concerning humility, charity and union among the three of us chiefly—in which we hope that God will do us the grace to keep us even unto death. We can tell you honestly that there is such a union among us that the three of us are as one."

Such a letter would hardly go unanswered, but the answer is lost. Much as Vincent's heart went out to them, the great distance made it almost impossible to help them and it would be a long time before he would be able to send them more Sisters, thus making the firmer establishment which proved to be their salvation. He was also hampered by the greatness of the personages involved and by the Polish Queen's connections with so many of his distinguished benefactors and aides in France. On August 15 he wrote to Nicolas Guillot, to whom he had confided the Sisters after the death of M. Lambert, to caution him "to abstain from speaking about [the matter] to others because it is a crime to discredit the conduct and intentions of the great and it is part of the piety of people like us to think and say only good things of those to whom we are under obligation." Vincent was a man of his age when it came to deference to the titled, but he was also a realist, and therefore his words can be read in sardonic context. He finished up his advice to Guillot by stating: "We are not of this world, there is nothing proper to us except to receive and carry out God's orders. It is enough for us to try to omit nothing that could advance His work, without blaming others for the delay."

On August 24 Louise wrote ecstatically to Vincent of the mystical favors God had bestowed on her during some days of recollection. "My heart is still full of the joy of understanding that I believe Our good God has given me concerning the words *God is my God!*" she wrote. "And the appreciation I have had of the glory all the blessed render Him on account of this truth will not permit that I hold off from speaking to you this evening, to ask your help in making use of this transport of joy and to have you assign me some practice for tomorrow, the feast of the saint whose name I have the honor to bear, the day of the renewal of my vows . . ."

Vincent wrote his reply in the margin while the messenger waited: "Blessed be God, Mademoiselle, for the caresses with which His divine Majesty has honored you. You should accept them with reverence and devotion and in anticipation of some cross He is preparing for you. His goodness is accustomed to warn souls He loves in this way when He is about to crucify them."

The cross Vincent foresaw—and which he promised to participate in —may well have been the wrangling that had already broken out in the house at Nantes. "I have great sorrow at what is going on among our Sisters," he had written to Jeanne Lepeintre on August 20. "The world and the evil spirit have excellent sport in bringing down you and them. God forgive . . . those who have brought about this division! When outsiders leave you at peace, you make war among yourselves! Oh, what a pity! I know very well that it is not your fault and that He does not blame you for the constant bickering . . . To remedy it I have asked M. Alméras to visit you . . . Tell no one . . ." On M. Alméras's recommendation, Sisters Anne and Louise were transferred and peace and union returned to the house

"At last Our good God has been able to make use of M. Alméras to remedy the troubles you have all endured for so long a time and especially you, dear Sister, whom Our Lord has chosen to carry this heavy yoke . . ." Louise wrote to Jeanne with satisfaction. "By order of Monsieur Vincent I have written to Sister Anne that she is to go to Richelieu at the first opportunity without any delay. I did not get around to writing to Sister Louise. It is enough for you to tell her on the day appointed

to accompany Sister Anne . . . It is not intended to keep the two together for long, but they will have to wait there [at Richelieu] for instructions as to what they are to do."

It had not helped things at Nantes that another Sister had defected
that same year, and everything had combined to bring a deep spiritual
depression upon Jeanne—who had been under a constant strain in this
unlucky house from the beginning—and she began to lose confidence in
herself. "I beg you with all my heart to make your own dear heart understand the confidence you must have in yourself especially as regards two
things," Louise wrote in gentle encouragement. "One concerns occur-
rences which you fear you don't understand enough; and the other the
resultant anxiety which gives you a repugnance for Communion and
your conviction that no one understands you." She cited for her comfort
the example of "the great Saint Teresa," who, when confessors of her
choice were unavailable, "had such simplicity and humility that she
asked advice very freely of those God had given her for her directors and
listened to them as if God spoke to her, contenting herself with what she
had to know, leaving the rest, without fretting about it, to God."

She took a further step to strengthen Jeanne's confidence by informing Vincent that it was M. Alméras's opinion that the Sister Servant
should be the one to distribute the appointments of house officers and
that "I believe this to be absolutely necessary for the maintenance of
peace and for putting the Sister Servant in the recognized position of
having the effective direction of others—which can be better understood,
perhaps, through an act of spiritual than of temporal obedience . . ."

In the end, however, it was decided to relieve Jeanne of the onerous
duty which she had discharged faithfully and as well as she could, of
which no more could be said of anyone.

Sisters Anne and Louise remained rather fractious even in their disgrace and decided to go to Richelieu by the long way around, via Angers.
They had no permission to do so but Louise instructed Cécile Angiboust
with a sigh to receive them. "Perhaps it is the desire to see you that
determines them to take this detour," she commented mildly.

One of the Sisters at Nanteuil displayed more of the politician than
might be expected in a country girl. She announced her departure from
the Company to go to Touquin-en-Brie to work for the poor there, presumably because the curé, a M. Gallais, made it more attractive for her
financially. M. le curé de Nanteuil was anxious to have her back and
enlisted Louise's aid to that end. Louise turned to Vincent. According to

the Abbé de Nanteuil, she told him, "Sister Judith is repentant and has offered to return if Monsieur le curé de Nanteuil will assure her of her livelihood." His laconic reply was worldly-wise: "The condition this girl lays down is its own negation. Her director is joking." M. de Nanteuil's pride, however, would not brook the triumph of M. de Touquin-en-Brie and, Louise told Vincent in distress some weeks later, he had threatened angrily to take the case to the Bishop of Nantes, who, as has been seen, was no friend of the Company. "I believe another will soon follow Sister Judith by the same path," she moaned. "It is my sins and bad leadership that bring on these disorders . . ." This kind of comic opera outraged Louise's sense of propriety—but Sister Judith was heard of no more, and the Company has survived.

The cabals of priests like these are typical of the trials that have been inflicted unnecessarily upon women's communities by self-important males. As if to prove the point, Louise had to ask M. de Vaux on November 12 "to take the trouble to investigate Monsieur Maillard. I am afraid that he is a little too prompt in judging that it is necessary for our Sisters to leave the Company in order to save their souls."

On the day she made this request, three Sisters—Marie-Marthe Trumeau, Anne de Vaux and Madeleine Micquel—left Paris for Nantes to replace Jeanne Lepeintre, Marie and Louise. Vincent made sure that they went neither unwarned nor unarmed. "You are going to a large hospital where there is more work to be done than elsewhere," he told them. "It is not like a parish in Paris where you have no other duty than to nurse a small number of sick people, or like country places where you have only to visit and instruct the poor." He was most blunt about the condition in which they would find the Company there: "Dissensions have arisen in this hospital by the instigation of evil spirits. Yes, Sisters, the devil has been strong enough to promote discord among our Sisters by his wiles, and you must remedy this by the union and concord existing among you." He gave them obedience as their chief support: ". . . a Daughter of Charity should be ready to do or not to do whatever the Sister Servant commands or forbids. I say the *Sister Servant*, because what another Sister says should not be listened to when her advice goes against that . . . Do what the Sister Servant says, and never what Marie or Jacquette or anybody else may say when the former has once given an order . . . Not indeed that the advice of our Sisters is to be despised. Oh, no! but those who give advice should remain in a state of indifference, whether their advice is taken or not."

He went on to warn them about the petulance of certain priests who boarded at the hospital, and did not neglect the Bishop himself: "He says you are religious, because he has been told you make vows. If he speaks to you about them, tell him you are not religious. Sister Jeanne, who is the Sister Servant, said to him: 'Monseigneur, the vows we take do not make us religious, because they are simple vows which may be taken anywhere, even in the world.' As a matter of fact, it cannot be maintained that the Daughters of Charity are religious, because they could not be Daughters of Charity if they were, since to be a religious, one should be cloistered. The Daughters of Charity will never be religious, and woe to whoever speaks of making them religious!"

It is astonishing that, in view of the enormous correspondence of Vincent and Louise and the many irons they had in the fire, they did not trip each other up more often. To avoid doing so, they had the prudent habit of letting each other see letters and documents concerning projects in which both were involved. At the end of 1653, for example, Louise showed Vincent a letter she had prepared as an answer to Abbé de Vaux's request for additional Sisters. "I wrote to M. l'abbé de Vaux of your oral promise to furnish girls for eight places before you could give him any," Vincent commented. "Consider, Mademoiselle, whether that doesn't contradict what you tell him, that I know nothing about this business." She tore up her letter and wrote another, making no mention of Vincent but detailing for the Abbé the reasons why she could not help him at the moment: the necessary changes at Nantes and Hennebont, the need of giving companions to four Sisters who had worked alone too long, and the supplying of six Sisters for the war-ravaged district of Sainte-Ménéhauld in Champagne by order of the Queen. "It will take six months to fulfill these pledges," she told him, but promised that "after that I will contact you before we engage ourselves any place else. Meanwhile, I hope God will grant us success in training the newcomers."

The war had created problems in recruiting vocations, she told him: "Since the war, we have had a lot of trouble in finding girls suitable for our works, and many, after a complete training program, have let themselves be carried away by their own desires and have withdrawn from the Company—all of which has hampered us for years . . . I tell you candidly, Monsieur, that right at the moment there are not three older Sisters at the motherhouse to assist in training others and that all the rest are either new or infirm."

In the opening months of 1654 it was found necessary to enlarge the outpatient facilities at Saint-Laurent. Louise wrote general instructions to the architect which had the effect of making him responsible for the spiritual edifice of the Company as well as its physical buildings, thereby neatly tying his hands against extravagance. "My absolute confidence that you will look favorably upon the favor I ask concerning our little plans makes me remind you again that it [the extension] be rustic and as unpretentious as possible," she wrote, but—well aware of artistic pride— she added in sympathetic flattery: "I know you will not be able to demean yourself to this without pain because you are used to building grand and lofty things. When you reflect on what I have told you, however, and on the Company's need in order to endure to appear poor and plain in everything, you will understand that it is Our Lord's work, Monsieur, and will be happy perhaps to contribute to its solidity by means of the talent God has given you . . ."

Her great tact was evident, too, in a reminder to a Sister Servant that it was not her prerogative to read letters the Sisters addressed to herself or Vincent but only those written to or received from others, which reminder made a pointed reference to a utopian dream for the Company: "It is also necessary in order to live in great union and charity, dear Sister, that when Sisters Servants write or receive letters they should so inform the Sister assistant, even to the point of reading to them whatever they wish—committed secrets excepted. For, dear Sister, there must be great equality, so that, when all is well established in the Company, it may be judged proper that the Sisters take turns being Servant for a year."

It can be imagined with what happiness Louis sat down on February 16 to summon home her old colleague and friend Barbe Angiboust. Besides the arduous work of nursing soldiers and civilians at Châlons and Brienne, Barbe had had to endure the pettiness and moods of her companion. "I cannot put into words the joy we all feel to have you back, dear Sister," Louise wrote in welcome. "I know that your poor body has need of this rest so it will be able to work elsewhere for God's glory." And she added with a mother's anxiety that all her children live at peace with one another: "I am sure you will do everything you should to satisfy your neighbor before you leave. I know your heart, and that it has never been stingy with humiliations in similar circumstances." The letter was not posted for a month because it was decided in the meantime to send immediate replacements for Barbe and for Sister Marie Poulet, stationed nearby. Before sealing it, Louise added a hasty postscript cautioning Barbe not to let on to the new Sisters of her difficulties with Sister Jeanne—which was the companion's name—for in any event Jeanne was being transferred to Montmirail.

Even the gods are sometimes half human, and Louise was forced that same March to reproach the irreproachable Julienne Loret because her letter "did not smell of the poor but of a scent which is not permitted Daughters of Charity." Sister Laurence at Bernay erred in another extreme. "When your heart is bursting to do more than you are accustomed to," Louise admonished her, "take the occasion to humble yourself saying: 'Let us do what is permitted us, thus being faithful to our Rules both interiorly and exteriorly,' and rest assured that Our Lord will be happy with you. Sometimes it seems that we should perform great penances, extraordinary devotions, and we fail to notice the great delight our enemy is taking in seeing us amuse ourselves with vain desires while we give short shrift to the ordinary virtues that occasion offers."

At the end of June, Marie-Louise of Poland wrote Vincent a letter which proved how right he had been the preceding November when he warned M. Guillot that if the Daughters of Charity should complain publicly of their mistreatment they would make an enemy of the Queen. "I admit that I am not entirely satisfied with one of the Sisters here," Her Majesty wrote. "Not that she is not a good girl, but she is too rude and quick of temper. People who stay with her have much to suffer because she has no tolerance, and everything proposed to her—except the care of children—shocks her . . . I hope that the new ones you intend to send me have a spirit of unswerving obedience." Moreover, Marie-Louise insisted that one of the new Sisters become Sister Servant the moment she arrived and that she in turn take her orders from the Queen's trusted lady in waiting, Mme de Villers.

As it turned out, nothing had to be done at the moment because the Sisters could not leave France. Vincent wrote to encourage the unhappy Sisters already there, who in their discouragement had fallen into bickering among themselves. "You are Daughters of Charity but you will be so no longer if you continue to live in misunderstanding, aversion or defiance, one toward the other . . ." he told them with that directness one must use with the emotional or hysterical. "You have enough to suffer from outsiders and from your ministry without making new crosses for yourselves at home; such crosses are the most bothersome and will make a small purgatory of your house, instead of the love that should make it a little heaven."

The new recruits for Poland stood by all that summer awaiting the opportunity of an escort. It was finally decided, on the advice of the Polish Queen herself, that they would not leave until the following spring.

In early August, Louise made a short retreat in preparation for her sixty-third birthday. The retreat was marred by the flight of a postulant from Arras who had asked permission of Sister Mathurine, the mistress, to go out to buy some linen and had never returned. Although Louise wondered, as usual, whether it was not partly her fault "for not having taken the trouble to visit her during her retreat, and for allowing her to eat with the other Sisters," nevertheless she accepted the loss with much more tranquillity than formerly. "Our good God knows what He wants and what is good for the Company," she wrote Vincent placidly.

At the same time she asked to make an entire review of her soul and spiritual life. "I will hold back nothing that could interfere with it," she assured him, "by the grace God has always given me to want you to have a complete understanding of all my thoughts, actions and intentions even as His goodness sees them . . ." She closed in great peace: "If God wishes that Wednesday, the anniversary of my birth, be also the day of my death. I indeed wish to prepare myself."

Her thoughts still dwelt on the peace of a happy death when she wrote the Sisters at Angers on August 15, feast of Our Lady's Assumption. "I ask Our Lord that you be ever according to His heart," she prayed, "and that you have today been very close to the Blessed Virgin in her death, by the most voluntary sacrifice possible of dying to yourselves so as to live more in God, giving all the rest of your days to His holy will."

Anne Hardemont, who had been back at the motherhouse for a rest, had returned to her frontier post at Sedan, Louise told the Angers community, taking with her Françoise Cabry, Jeanne-Marie and Anne Thibault "to nurse the wounded soldiers. It edifies them to see them [the soldiers] die like good Christians. Pray fervently to God for the King's army and ask a change of heart for the enemy."

Marie Joly had been summoned home by Louise and had refused to come. Vincent wrote to M. Martin, superior at Sedan, and enclosed a letter to her demanding her return "by the first coach." It was possible, he admitted to M. Martin, that she might still refuse, "because she has a temperament little inclined to docility and submission, and a mind of her own, and she might be too strongly attached to Sedan." In that case, he instructed Martin "to sound Monsieur le gouverneur out about commanding her to obey . . ." Then Vincent's indignation boiled over: "They tell me that she has boasted that she would not budge until I wrote to her. Up until now this little Company has enjoyed so great a spirit of submission that it has never known the like!" They were sending in Marie's place Sister Jeanne-Christine, "a very virtuous girl, sweet and intelligent, whom God has blessed wherever she has been."

Marie returned to Paris but Louise reported to Vincent on November 16 that she had disappeared after dinner without saying a word to anyone and might be on her way back to Sedan. She returned to the motherhouse the next day, however. On the eighteenth, Vincent wrote to warn M. Martin that "she is on retreat at present, but as she is very fickle it is to be feared that the temptation to go back to Sedan may seize hold of her again." If such should happen, Martin was to send her away at once. She was still at the motherhouse on the twenty-eighth, "resolved to dream of Sedan no more."

In November Louise turned her thoughts to Poland and the Sisters to be sent there in the spring. She was aware that the Queen intended to appoint a "directress" for the Sisters, undoubtedly the trusted Mme de Villers. She was not averse to the idea—the Ladies of Charity acted in this capacity in the confraternities—indeed, she felt that three or four should be appointed so that the work would not fail in the event of Mme de Villers's death, she told Vincent, and besides such an arrangement "would be closer to the establishments of Charity." Her determination to make a success of the Polish mission was evident from the caliber of the names she submitted to him for the post of Sister Servant there: Cécile Angiboust, Julienne Loret and Jeanne Lepeintre. She felt, she assured him, that the Sisters would fall in with M. Ozenne's instructions "not to meddle in anything beyond what they were charged with, but the difficulty will lie in the goodness and familiarity of the Queen. In speaking with our Sisters she might order them to do things which the Demoiselle [the directress]—be it to maintain her authority or for other good reasons—might not agree with or might perhaps absolutely forbid, thereby giving rise to contentions and jealousies." She well understood how easily differences could divide even the best-intentioned members of her sex.

On November 20 Vincent informed M. Ozenne that Louise and he had talked the matter over and had decided that it would be best for the directress to be chosen from among the Sisters themselves rather than from outside the Company, and that the Sister chosen should be guided in all things by himself as superior general. This wise decision precluded well in advance any fragmentation of the Company when, as Louise and he foresaw, it should extend itself throughout Poland.

Mme de Brou requested Sisters for Bernay, and Barbe Angiboust was sent to open a small refuge for poor girls there in November. On December 4 Louise cautioned her "never to consider establishing a hospital, or taking the sick into your house any more than taking pensioners, before you have written to Monsieur Vincent." The house provided for the Sisters was a very poor one. "You have suffered need and perhaps still do," Louise wrote in sympathy. "Doesn't this state of affairs console your heart indeed, dear Sister, joining you as it does to the state in which Our Lord and His holy Mother found themselves so often when on earth? Believe me, dear Sister, when I see establishments so grand that there are nothing but smiles at their opening, I immediately grow afraid." It is not hard to surmise that the beginning at Nantes was in her mind as she wrote!

At the same period a foundation was made under the patronage of the Duchesse de Liancourt at La Roche-Guyon. Anne Hardemont was the first Sister Servant, but her companion, Sister Claude, did not work out and had to be recalled. "Do the best you can," Louise counseled Anne, "but don't overburden yourself with work. I know that Madame has such a good heart that she would permit you to hire a woman to help you with the nursing and the laundry . . . Please, dear Sister, don't push yourself beyond your strength!" Two other Sisters, Claude Chantereau and Elisabeth, had been sent at the same time to nurse the wounded at Sainte-Marie-du-Mont near Caen on the lands of Louise's other great friend the Duchesse de Ventadour.

There was a flurry of excitement that same month over the possible abandonment of the mission at Chantilly because of the lack of financial support from its patrons, notably the Queen. The Sisters' rent had been owing for four years and the more than patient landlord had at length seized their meager furniture and was about to sell it. Louise was especially embarrassed, naturally, over the Queen's part in it. Whatever accord was finally worked out, the Sisters stayed on at Chantilly.

It was undoubtedly the habitual thoughtlessness of the Queen, not to say the stinginess she sometimes displayed, that caused Louise to write to the Sisters at Fontainebleau a few months later when the Queen was in residence there: "If Her Majesty wishes to speak with you, make no difficulty about it, even though the respect due her person makes you fearful of approaching her. Her virtue and kindness give the lowliest persons the confidence to tell her their needs. Don't, above all, fail to relate quite frankly those of the poor."

At the end of January 1655 Vincent assured M. Ozenne at Warsaw that Louise "was beginning to look around for Daughters of Charity suitable for Poland and to get them ready. However," he added dryly, "we cannot possibly find any with the qualities desired by the most serene Queen because it has pleased God to compose this little Company of persons of low condition [and] mediocre mind but—by His mercy—of good will which through His grace increases daily in them."

He wrote two days later to M. Coglée at Sedan to remind him that the strictest rule admitted of exception. "Monsieur Petigon, advocate of the King at Sedan, having done me the honor to write to me concerning a little child he has looked after up to the present to avoid its falling into the hands of the Huguenots, asked me at the same time to speak to the ladies about [assuming] the upbringing of this little boy—the which I have done. They are of the opinion that the Daughters of Charity should take him and raise him, even though they would not do so here. Therefore, Monsieur, please tell Sister Jeanne-Christine for me and for the Ladies of Charity of this town that she should take him in and raise him."

Louise was delighted to receive a letter from Barbe Angiboust's new companion, Sister Laurence Dubois, in "a hand other than that of Sister Barbe . . . Am I right in thinking that you are learning to write?" That being so, she instructed Sister Laurence kindly, "if you have some secret to confide to me, write it yourself and without any obligation of showing your letter [to Barbe]; nevertheless, because of the cordiality you owe her, inform her that you are writing. Don't be afraid that she will ask what you wish to tell us or that she will read it, for she knows well that she would offend God."

One of the Sisters at Saint-Germain had requested permission to make a journey—perhaps to visit relatives—on the pretext of illness and her need for a change. Louise had her doubts about the extent of the Sister's illness but conceded that "a change of air would do her a world of good . . ." She insisted firmly to Vincent, however, that it would be much better for her to make her sojourn at the motherhouse than elsewhere. "Permit me to say, Most Honored Father, that my heart is sensibly and often moved by the thought that the Company is on the brink of decline," she wrote, "and that I foresee many inconveniences if Your Charity permits this journey, similar permissions having been refused others for many reasons." Vincent readily accepted her view and the Sister found her change of air in Paris.

On the eve of the feast of the Annunciation—which was transferred, because of Holy Week, to April 4 that year—Louise reminded Vincent with a holy nostalgia that "tomorrow is our great feast on which we should recall *the grace God bestowed on this day upon five of the first Sisters whom His goodness wished to be wholly dedicated to Him for the work of the little Company, one of whom [Sister Turgis] is in heaven if Our Lord has shown her that mercy.*"

Three Sisters were petitioning to make their vows on the feast: two of them, Marguerite Chétif and Madeleine Raportebled, wishing—with the approval of Louise and M. Portail—to make them perpetually, and the other, Philippe Bailly, for one year. Although Vincent's reply is lost, there is no reason to suppose that he refused a request that came so highly recommended, especially in view of the fact that Marguerite and Madeleine were being considered for Poland.

Vincent was writing to Poland almost weekly now because of the negotiations for additional priests, brothers and Sisters, and because of the state of the country, in peril from the invading Russians and rebellion at home. Louise was certainly writing often to encourage her Daughters, also, but unfortunately her letters have been lost. On April 9 Vincent expressed his annoyance to M. Ozenne that "Sister Marguerite is so high and mighty and determined in her ways. In the name of God, Monsieur, help her to acquire a true spirit of humility and condescension in all things!" On May 7 he praised God "that the Daughters of Charity have opened their little schools," but was astonished "that they are not employed in ministering to the sick poor of the town." It was undoubtedly the vagaries of the Queen and Mme de Villers which prevented them.

Despite the gravity of the affairs in Poland there occurred—as is common amid the seriousness of life—a diverting incident. Queen Marie-Louise's friends in France had made her the gift of a little dog and Mme de Villers wrote to Louise asking her to care for it until the Sisters could bring it to Warsaw with them. Louise could not, of course, refuse, and Vincent took obvious delight in telling M. Ozenne that she was "rather disturbed" over the chore, because he added the information in his own hand as he read over the letter he had dictated to his secretary. As the months passed, however, the little pet apparently won her heart, for she actually took it to visit Vincent in the parlor of Saint-Lazare. "He likes one of the Sisters of Charity so much," Vincent told Ozenne, "that he won't look at any of the others—only at her; and if she goes out he cries and won't stop. This little creature throws me into great confusion at his single-hearted affection for the one who feeds him, knowing the little attachment I have to my sovereign Benefactor and my little detachment from all other things. You can assure the Queen that the girls are taking every care of [her dog]."

The Sisters were on the point of leaving for Poland in June when they were prevented again, this time by French officials because of the worsening military situation there.

The bad temper of the administrators of the hospital at Nantes, which had caused so much persecution and heartache to the Sisters, reached a climax in 1655 when Vincent and Louise finally decided to change Henriette Gesseaume. As has been seen, Henriette, although an excellent Sister, had nonetheless been at the center of every upset in the house, due to her inability to live with others. Perhaps for this reason—that she was their unconscious ally in the house—and because she was an experienced pharmacist, the administrators now made her recall a *cause célèbre*. They were categorically opposed to it. Further, they expressed the utmost indignation that no money had been sent from Paris to defray the cost of her journey there. And finally, they insisted, if she must go then she must be replaced with someone equally skilled and efficient.

The superiors looked so gravely upon this impertinence approaching blackmail that they began to think about recalling the Sisters altogether and called a special council meeting on April 8 to consider the matter. Besides Vincent and Louise, M. Alméras, M. Portail and Louise's three assistants were present.

Against the recall was the fact that the presence of the Sisters at Nantes seemed to be a true vocation since the Sisters had been invited by lawful authority and had responded in the spirit of dedicated service. In favor of it was the presumption that it was only a trial establishment —Louise, who had made it personally, held this opinion—which the constant problems had proved unsuccessful and contrary to God's will. When the vote was taken, Louise and M. Alméras were unconditionally in favor of recall, M. Portail and the Sisters assistants for giving the administrators one more chance by sending a seasoned pharmicist in Sister Henriette's place. Vincent voted with Louise and Alméras, but suggested recourse to prayer before making a definitive decision at their next meeting.

It was decided to make one more try. Nicole Haran was sent to replace Marie-Marthe Trumeau as Sister Servant; Henriette Gesseaume and Marie Thilouse were replaced by three Sisters whom Louise described as "of good disposition" and "very attached to their vocation." On May 22 she wrote: "I have great hopes for the establishment at Nantes, because persecution is a sign that a work is worthwhile." Her hopes were not in vain: this was the last major fracas at Nantes. The administrators came to realize, apparently, that they had pushed their luck to the limit and were unwillingly to tempt fate further.

With that major problem settled, Louise could turn her attention more fully to everyday affairs. "So there you are at court again, fulfilling the commands of our most excellent and devout Queen!" she wrote playfully to the Sisters at Fontainebleau, and she went on to caution them against letting daily contact with the great make them too familiar and forward. She was anxious, too, lest their hospital experience lead them to think they knew more than the doctors. "Does your familiarity with nursing care and your knowledge of remedies make you rash, or unwilling to accept advice and to follow their rules and obey their orders?" she asked. If so, they would be abusing God's grace.

She wrote to Barbe Angiboust "a tiny reproach for not informing me that you had received visits from your nephew." Vincent wanted to remind Barbe also "to get more information about girls who want to enter our Company." Some of Barbe's postulants had proven unsuitable and occasionally had to be sent home at community expense, to say nothing of those who worried the superiors by choosing to stay on in Paris, "where there is danger . . . for girls."

Sister Elisabeth at Angers had an oversensitive conscience and Louise wrote from experience to warn her that "we must not trust the first thoughts that come into our minds or pay attention to problems and difficulties which are often no more than passing temptations and proofs of our fidelity."

Sister Laurence at Bernay was worried about missing certain religious exercises even though it was due to work ordered by Sister Barbe. "You must come to realize that when she orders something the responsibility is more hers than yours," Louise wrote comfortingly. She understands well that it is to leave God for God when we leave our exercises for the service of the poor."

On June 23 she informed Barbe that "we will soon have Sisters at Les Petites Maisons to nurse the insane and the poor sick women there." She referred to a city hospital which occupied a block of houses from which it took its name. Some of the Ladies of Charity, notably Mlle de Lamoignon, took a personal interest in the work and it was undoubtedly their influence which brought control of the hospital into the hands of the Sisters. It would be autumn, however, before they were ready to assume this entirely new work.

Marguerite Chétif, Madeleine Raportebled and Jeanne Lemeret were named to go to Poland under the escort of M. Berthe and two lay brothers. In the letter of introduction carried by the Sisters, Louise told M. Ozenne: "You have asked for such accomplished [Sisters] that you will jump to the conclusion that these are absolutely perfect! In the name of God, Monsieur, don't make that mistake! Just take my word for it that they are very good subjects." Marguerite Chétif was to be Sister Servant and Louise lamented only her lack of poise: "If she had that, she would lack nothing in my opinion, except that she has no experience of court atmosphere or of the niceties of society, I am afraid. She goes along in a very plain manner, but there is no weakness of mind or of judgment in her, and she has all the prudence she needs and knows how to use it in such a way that no one has ever seen her do anything except with the greatest simplicity." Louise's opinion of Marguerite is especially interesting because she was unwittingly giving a very favorable nod to the woman who would succeed her as head of the Company.

Louise also wrote a long letter to the Sisters waiting in Poland. "My dear Sisters, you have already told me that you are but one heart in your three persons," she wrote with that tender charm and delicacy which were so much a part of her. "In the name of the Most Holy Trinity that you have honored and must continue to honor, I beg you to enlarge it to let our three Sisters enter into this cordial union in such a way that it will not be apparent who were the first or the last three." And she added in the same vein: "Will you permit me, dear Sisters, to ask something else of you that seems to me to be necessary? It is that you never speak Polish together without letting our Sisters know what you are saying . . . I believe, dear Sisters, that I could never rejoice enough in the union I expect among you in words, in actions . . . of such kind that there will never be any secrets among the six of you, and everything that goes on in your house . . . will always be secret as far as the outside world is concerned."

The band of missionaries waited nearly a month for news of a sailing via the North Sea and at length left Paris on August 19 to take ship at Rouen. They had scarcely gone when word reached Vincent of the invasion of Poland both by the Russians and by the Swedes, whom the Polish nobles joined against their King. The court fled Warsaw—and the Sisters with it—first to Krakow and then to Silesia. Vincent sent posthaste to his sons and daughters at Rouen to return to Paris to await more favorable news. It would be nearly two years before a second journey could be attempted.

At a conference to the Sisters on August 8, 1655, Vincent definitively established the Company according to the powers given him in the Act of Establishment by the Archbishop of Paris. The day before, Louise—well aware that officers general would be named at this historic assembly—sent Vincent a last desperate note begging him "not to speak of me in electing officers. The title of first assistant would say plainly enough that I am what I have been and would not prevent my being so no longer when God shows you the necessity for that." Her reasons were feeble enough, the chief being that she felt "I know not what repugnance to being recognized" and "named by the Company" its superioress.

She warned him, also, of "the repugnance most of our Sisters have for the very word confraternity," so that he might be prepared to explain to them how necessary the title was to ensure that "the Company never change its original form."

She was overjoyed at the one significant difference between the new Act of Establishment and the one of 1646, a difference that was due in overwhelming measure to her years of persistence and prayer. Gone was the article that put the direction of the Sisters in the hands of any priest the Archbishop of Paris might name. In its place Cardinal de Retz had written: "Inasmuch as God has blessed the work undertaken by our dear and well-beloved Vincent de Paul to bring this pious design to success, we have accordingly confided and committed and, by these presents, do confide and commit to him the government and direction of the aforesaid Society and Confraternity for his lifetime, and after him to his successors the generals of the aforesaid Congregation of the Mission." It was not, indeed, the complete exemption from the Ordinary of Paris that Louise would have liked and could conceivably be changed by a future archbishop; but, in the Providence of God, it was sufficient: because no prelate would attempt without the gravest reasons to withdraw from so revered an institute as the Congregation of the Mission was to become—especially in France—this definitive power given by a predecessor over the equally revered Company of the Daughters of Charity which had won the hearts of all the people. This disposition of 1655 served in fact for nearly 225 years until Pope Leo XIII gave it the virtue of his pontifical authority by a rescript of the Sacred Congregation of Religious dated June 25, 1882, which decreed that "nothing was to be changed in the government laid down for the Association of the Daughters of Charity which by pontifical indult pertains to the Superior General of the Congregation of the Mission, commonly called Lazarists, instituted by Saint Vincent de Paul."

Louise's humility suffered agonies of embarrassment the next day— Sunday, August 8, 1655—when the Company of the Daughters of Charity was formally constituted as an official institute of the Church according to its Act of Establishment. Not only did the Act itself acknowledge for posterity her part in the formation of the Company and describe in great detail her wise and prudent stewardship over it, but Vincent in his own official Act of Promulgation saw fit to repeat and confirm what the Act of Establishment had said. There was no question of allowing her to relinquish her post. The Act appointed her for life, and Vincent merely noted that "we have asked the aforesaid Demoiselle de Marillac to continue in the charge of Superioress and Directress of the aforesaid Confraternity for her lifetime as she has done with great benediction by the mercy of God from the establishment of this Confraternity until the present."

Nor was there any question of changing the title of Confraternity or Society because, as Vincent told the assembled Sisters, "His Grace the Archbishop has commanded it." Because of Louise's warning of the day before, however, he took the time to explain why: ". . . If the title of Congregation were given to you, there might be persons in the future who would wish to have the house cloistered and to have you become religious—as happened in the case of the daughters of Sainte-Marie [the Visitandines]. God has allowed poor girls to take the place of these ladies." How well he knew how to appeal to the human heart!

Although the Act of Establishment called for election of the other officers of the Company for a three-year term, Vincent used the authority it gave him to appoint the first officers. He named Julienne Loret first assistant; Mathurine Guérin, second assistant and treasurer; and Jeanne

Gressier, bursar. Subsequent events proved the wisdom of his choices. Little is known of Sister Gressier, who subsequently became first assistant; but Julienne Loret, whose capacities have already been noted, served as an assistant to Louise's successors Marguerite Chétif and Nicole Haran; and Mathurine Guérin—who was only twenty-four at the time of this first appointment—became superioress of the Company for six elected terms, from 1667 to 1694.

When all the exhortations, explanations and appointments were concluded the Sisters, led by Louise, advanced one by one to sign the historic document. Forty-one Sisters signed, and the humble origins of the Company were symbolically recorded in the nine or ten crosses made by those who could not write.

There were familiar names among them: Barbe Bailly, Geneviève Doinel, Madeleine Raportebled, Marie Vigneron, Marguerite Chétif, Marie Joly, Françoise Noret, Geneviève Poisson, Anne Hardemont, Philippe Bailly. Vincent signed last of all.

Then someone had the happy inspiration to add the names of all the Company who would surely wish to be identified, if only in spirit and by proxy, with this memorable moment. Accordingly the names of 102 Sisters out on the mission were written at the bottom. It is regrettable to note among those who were absent the names of Barbe Angiboust and her sister Cécile, Jeanne Lepeintre and Nicole Haran.

The strength of the Company on August 8, 1655, twenty-two years after its beginning, thus stood at 143 members, not counting the postulants and novices and the many who had died or had left the community in the intervening years.

Vincent concluded the conference by reminding the Sisters: " 'You have been chosen to be the foundation of your Company. You should then give yourselves wholly to God in thanksgiving for His having chosen you to be His spouses. You should give yourselves wholly to God to observe your rules. It now remains for us to find out whether you all desire to persevere in this observance.'

"All the Sisters answered, 'Yes.'

"Monsieur Vincent then said: 'Do you accept these regulations?'

" 'Yes, *Mon Père!* ' "

He then offered a beautiful prayer to Our Lady, Patroness of the Company: " 'O Blessed Virgin, you who speak for those who have no tongue and cannot speak for themselves, we beseech you, these dear Sisters and myself, to help this little Company. Advance and perfect a work which is the greatest on earth. I implore you on behalf of those who are present and absent. And, O my God, I make this petition to You through the merits of Your Son Jesus Christ that You may complete the work You have begun. Continue Your holy protection over this little Company. Continue to bestow all the blessings which You have been pleased to lavish on it up to now and grant, if it please You, the grace of perseverance to these good girls . . .' "

Louise might well have sung her *Nunc Dimittis* as she went to bed in quiet but all-encompassing joy that evening, but it would have to wait until she had done much more for God and His Church and the world and her daughters.

Her joy pervaded the whole Company and it was still in evidence when the new officers met a month later for Vincent's instructions. He was full of praise for Louise, uncommonly so, for he knew her tender humility. It was as if he must wound it so that posterity might have his personal judgment of this great woman.

He began routinely enough, listing the duties of the superioress, which, he said, culminated in her being "the soul which animates the members of the whole Company. She is a living rule who must be the model of what the others should do, teaching them as much by her good example as by her words. Well, that will be enough about Mademoiselle's office . . . there is no need to go any further since by God's grace she does and always has done what a good superioress should." But he could not prevent himself from going further and returned to Louise again and again. "Up until now," he said, "Mademoiselle has conducted affairs well by God's grace and so well that I don't know a religious house of women in Paris in the condition in which you find yourselves. All weep for what they ought to be, the daughters of Sainte-Marie and many others . . . Behold how Our Lord has blessed the good government you have had . . . ! You have certainly not had a superioress who let the house go by default: on the contrary, she has made you one . . . No, I tell you, I don't know of the like in Paris and it is due, after God, to the good management of Mademoiselle."

At this point Louise interrupted him in a desperate attempt to put a stop to his praise. "You know well, *Mon Père*, and our Sisters also," she cried out, "that if anything has been done it has been by the orders Your Charity has given me." It was a neat *touché* and Vincent was not inclined to engage in a duel of humility. He had said what he wanted to say.

In the course of the meeting Vincent gave a report of the Company's resources that was a true picture of its absolute poverty. "I repeat that there must be great care to conserve the little you have—which is not much," he urged. "The revenue from the coaches given by Madame la duchesse d'Aiguillon is very uncertain; so, too, what the King has given from the domain of Gonesse. That is why we must pray God to preserve the King. Your house is unlike others. They have other means. Look at the daughters of Sainte-Marie: they don't receive anyone who does not bring twelve or thirteen hundred livres with them. And all the other religious institutes receive large dowries. But you have nothing but your poor and the Providence of God—which is a great deal. And it is there you must put all your trust."

The conference of September 29, which continued the explanation of the Rule, was in a way an extended celebration of the great gift which had come to the Company in August. With his eye on the future, Vincent took a father's delight in testing the love and fidelity of his daughters. "You should be ready to go anywhere, because you are being asked for from all sides," he told them proudly. "You are being demanded insistently at Toulouse. Monseigneur de Cahors has written me to the same purpose and we shall have no peace or rest until some of you have gone to that district. In Madagascar our Gentlemen [the Priests of the Mission] beg us to send them Daughters of Charity to help them win souls . . . It is 1,500 leagues away and it takes six months to get there. Sisters, I am telling you this that you may see God's designs on you. So dispose yourselves, my Daughters, and give yourselves to Our Lord to go wherever it may please Him.

" 'Are you resolved to go everywhere without any exception?'

" 'Yes, *Mon Père*,' they replied.

" 'But are you really so disposed? If so, tell me.' "

The Sisters rose as one and repeated fervently that they were. Here was a wholehearted spirit of dedication and forgetfulness of self, the Charity of Christ that would and ever will in His goodness urge this little Company on to renew the face of the earth.

XVII

The Infirmities of Age, the Drive of Youth

In his conference of September 29, 1655, Vincent congratulated the Sisters on the works God had given them to do—the alleviation of the miseries of the poor, the instruction of the ignorant, the nursing of the sick and wounded, the raising of foundlings, the solace of prisoners—and dwelt on the recently accepted ministry of Les Petites Maisons.

"Is there any community that looks after poor lunatics?" he asked with obvious satisfaction. "You won't find one; and yet you have this happiness. The Gentlemen of the Great Council have decided that, for the better management of this great establishment of poor lunatics, they should appeal to the Daughters of Charity. As a matter of fact, they did not cease to press us until we had sent them some Sisters." Anne Hardemont was the first Sister Servant of this forerunner of the Company's modern psychiatric institutes. It was located on the site of the Bon Marché department store—known to all students of French grammar and composition!—which is directly opposite the present motherhouse of the Sisters in Paris.

Louise's health continued poor as ever, but daily she managed to gather her strength to address herself to the ever increasing affairs of the Company. She insisted that Barbe Angiboust, who had need of undergarments, send her the measurements "and we will make them, for there is usually such a diversity from one person to another due to the fashions that you would think they were from two different countries!" She sent Cécile Angiboust news of her family and of the unhappy lot of the Sisters in Poland. She apologized to Abbé de Vaux for having to write through her secretary because of weakness, and was in even greater confusion because they were not yet able to send him the extra Sisters they had promised. The Sister Elisabeth who had been so confused in her thoughts had actually left the Company for a short time but was back at the motherhouse, she told de Vaux, "with a great desire to persevere," and much of it was due "to the charity you showed her."

M. Portail had been taken ill while on a visitation of the Sisters' houses, and Louise wrote to him on September 26 half in jest that she did not know whether to pray for his "perfect health or languishing health. The first would prolong your return but, on the other hand, our Sisters at Sedan, Brienne, Montmirail and Nanteuil would benefit, while all at Paris would suffer in the same proportion . . ." She suggested to Vincent that they send a Sister to Chantilly whom she wished to get out of Paris "because of the importunities of her parents—not for fear of her losing her vocation, because she is in the Company a long time . . ." She also asked permission for Sister Françoise, "the gardener," to renew her annual vows for the seventh time "tomorrow, the feast of Saint-François."

On October 8 she told Vincent of her son's need for prayers for his increasing deafness. "I ask it only in conjunction with the grace for him to make a firm resolution not to allow God to be offended in the bosom of his little family. Good Brother Fiacre has promised to begin . . . a novena to the Blessed Virgin tomorrow." Michel's deafness eventually forced him to relinquish his hard-won post at the Court des Monnaies.

On the twenty-second, Louise confided to Vincent quite casually her opinion that "my *petit fièvre* is caused solely by my bad spleen, which is hardening and covers part of my stomach. If this is the key by which I will leave this world soon, I certainly need to be so afraid that I will get myself ready. To that end I look to your goodness, that I may not suffer shipwreck in the home port . . ." Her lifetime of illness was now causing serious breakdowns in the organs of her body which must have been accompanied by great pain. Yet, to the amazement of all, the strength of God continued to sustain her.

It was profoundly touching to see these two, Vincent and Louise, grown old together in the service of God and of the poor—he was seventy-four now and she ten years younger—ailing, yet forcing themselves to pursue the incredible burden of business which occupied them as much as from twelve to sixteen hours a day. It was an unspoken agreement between them that they were obliged to rally and support each other. Louise, well aware that she bore the chief responsibility for the Sisters, gave the tired old man no peace until he had given the Company

of the Daughters of Charity that full and authentic commentary on their
Rule which has sustained their profound and knowledgeable spirituality
to the present day.

He had given another conference on the Rule in October but exhaustion and the press of business had permitted no more. Now on the last
day of the month Louise wrote "in fear that Monsieur Béens would forget to propose a little conference to you for one of these feast days without endangering your health. I would not be so importunate," she
pleaded, "were it not for the great length and importance of the subject." She was extremely apprehensive lest he or she or both should die
before the task was completed. Vincent obliged with an exceptionally
long conference on November 2.

He collapsed again soon afterward and Louise requested special
prayers of the Sisters for his preservation. She expressed her own panic at
the thought of his death in her usual way by finding fault with the medical treatment he was getting. "Permit me to say," she wrote on November 14, "that it is absolutely necessary that your leg not be allowed to
dangle even for half a quarter of an hour, or that it feel the full heat of
fire. If it gets cold the fault can be corrected with warm linen wrapped
around your stockings." Her warnings that excessive bleedings and too
much physic were contributing to his general weakness were highly sensible. And, of course, she had her own pet remedies to offer. "Am I not
very rash to speak to you like this?" she finished affectionately. "But I
know what you are as you know that I am . . . your most humble and
grateful daughter." She added a postscript that was pure whistling-in-the-
dark: "I take half of a large cup of tea every day and find myself very
well. It gives me strength and appetite."

At the beginning of Lent of 1656 she was still insisting that tea had
given her back her appetite, even for Lenten fare, but admitted humbly:
"If it please you to dispense me again for a while, you would give me
great pleasure." Her pious subterfuge, however, was to use the dispensation to eat a larger quantity of eggs until such time as she would absolutely need meat.

She continued to dissemble her own infirmities, as when she assured
Vincent in March that "what appeared to be infirmity was only a pre-
caution against illness and too much care of my health. Indeed, it was
also a way of taking as much time off as I could." The good man must
have been vastly amused. She confessed more realistically to the Sisters
at Angers that their letters "had come in time to put the finishing touch

to my recovery from a grave illness I have suffered for the past month— for you must believe, dear Sisters, that nothing can gladden me like knowing of your good health and interior dispositions . . ." On March 26 she admitted to Vincent that she was still not feeling well but was afraid "of trying too hard to end my days comfortably."

On March 29 she asked Barbe Angiboust "to pray fervently in asking Our Lord to send laborers for His work since you would not believe how many places are asking for them, or the few we have to give." Nonetheless, she cautioned Barbe again, "we must be very careful to take only those truly called." She looked to the Ladies of Charity to supply in whatever way they could the dearth of Sisters. On April 8 she asked Vincent to lay before them at their assembly the next day—Palm Sunday—"how much spiritual good they could accomplish by visiting the poor galley slaves at the hours when our Sisters serve them their dinner —which is at a convenient enough hour for them to get back to their homes without their households being upset."

Barbe and her companion, Sister Laurence Dubois, were still living in the poorest and most unsatisfactory conditions at Bernay but Louise warned her on April 24 "to be careful not to be the one to insist on getting a house, because I understand that Madame de Brou no longer has anything to do with the matter and I am afraid of your having to pay for it."

The demands for Sisters, especially for places far distant from Paris like Agde and Cahors—whose Bishop, Vincent's pious but peppery friend Alain de Solminihac, was applying unbelievable pressure—added to the lack of Sisters and the consequent need for new seedbeds of vocations led the Company to a radical solution: the establishment of a "seminary or motherhouse like that of Paris from which girls could be sent to places far and near and could also be received there." The matter was thoroughly discussed at a council meeting held on April 25 in the parlor of Saint-Lazare and attended, besides Vincent and Louise, by M. Portail, the officers and two older Sisters. All agreed that such a new center for the Company was useful and indicated by Divine Providence. The Sisters insisted, however, that such "a motherhouse be always dependent on that of Paris," and Louise, backed by M. Portail, insisted further that "it be located in a place where there are Gentlemen of the Mission." It was decided to have special Masses, Communions and prayers offered for divine guidance before finally determining a matter of such importance. Four days later Vincent convened another council meeting to report that he had consulted Mme Fouquet, mother of Monseigneur d'Agde, about establishing the proposed motherhouse on a site opposite her son's seminary but that she had replied that a project already launched would occupy his time and his budget for some time. The matter of this second motherhouse was thereupon tabled, not to be revived while Vincent or Louise lived.

Louise relapsed into another grave illness in May and her life was despaired of. On May 17 Vincent told Sister Françoise Ménage at Nantes that "Mademoiselle Le Gras . . . has been close to death and is not yet entirely out of danger, but she is much better, thanks be to God." On June 9 he was able to inform M. Martin, who was now superior of the house at Turin, that "Mademoiselle Le Gras, who was on the point of leaving this life for another, has returned to her former state." It was not saying much, but at least she would not die yet. Louise herself told Françoise Ménage with a smile that "it is no longer [God's] good pleasure to wipe me from the face of the earth yet, although I have long deserved it . . ."

In this grave illness Louise's thoughts had been on her little granddaughter and, not surprisingly, on a way of giving her an attraction for the poor whom Louise herself loved so much. To this end she called in a lawyer and added a codicil to her will directing that, from the alms she had left to the discretion of the Congregation of the Mission, there be given "eighteen livres a year to my granddaughter for her lifetime to be used to serve a small dinner to the poor of her parish, at which dinner she will wait on them."

On June 14 Louise was at last able to inform M. de Vaux that she was sending the Sisters he had waited for so long and so patiently, but she expressed astonishment at "our Sisters being away, which makes it impossible for us for the moment to choose another fit to take Sister Cécile's place and gives me extreme displeasure. It will delay the departure of our Sisters [from here] until the beginning of next week . . ." For more than a year she had been waiting for the opportune moment to give Cécile a rest from her years of faithful service at Angers.

She was even more astonished "at the proposal of Messieurs les Pères of the Hôtel-Dieu to buy a fishmarket in which they plan to employ our Sisters! I can give no approval for such employment. I don't even know what it entails so that I can bring the proposal to the attention of Monsieur Vincent! Further, Monsieur, doesn't it strike you that great inconveniences are to be feared from such an increase of work?"

Barbe Angiboust had written on June 3 to tell Louise that "Providence had offered a hospital to the poor" of Bernay. "Our Lord be forever blessed . . . !" Louise replied with joy on the nineteenth, but cautioned Barbe "to be careful . . . in establishing the hospital, of anything contrary to the simplicity and humility of the Daughters of Charity which could interfere with the exact observance of the rule; and if they wish to burden you with things you would not ordinarily take care of— such as the management of temporalities, the purchase of general provisions—please consult Monsieur Vincent."

Vincent never liked the Sisters to be involved in the temporal management of their missions if it could be avoided. This was due beyond a doubt to the usual conditions under which they assumed works: generally they were "hired" to carry out the actual ministries connected with pious projects conceived and financed by public or private overseers, and Vincent was ever loath for them to assume more responsibility than they were asked to assume. He was also keenly aware that the rude origins of most of the Sisters made them unfit for even the least sophisticated aspects of administration. He instructed Sisters setting out for La Fère: "I don't know, Sisters, how the needs of the poor will be provided for in regard to their food and other requirements, but I beg you, as far as possible, not to accept such duties. If you cannot avoid handling money, present your accounts as soon as possible. Hence it is always necessary to write out a statement of what you have received and expended. It is absolutely essential for Daughters of Charity to be known as, and actually to be, persons who keep their accounts strictly."

Throughout that summer the ailing founders of the Company continued to urge each other on in pursuing their goal of a complete commentary on the Rule, and five lengthy and detailed conferences were held between June and September. Despite his seventy-five years, Vincent became the young, vivacious Gascon in the conference chair and the words tumbled out in rapid, lively and often earthy style, accompanied by indescribable mimicry, which unfortunately the printed page can only hint at. On July 23, for example, he completely devastated the female vanity which lurked even in the most dedicated religious heart:

> An unmortified Sister will not be satisfied with complaining when something is not to her liking or with mentioning it to a lay person, but will try to gratify her wishes. If she has shoes she does not like, she will procure others. If a dress is not made as she wants it, she must have another and of better material . . . Another will find that a collar does not come up to

her wishes; she will hand it back . . . Another will touch up her head-dress, draw out her hair to let people see she has some . . . ! Another may have a bodice of which the sleeves are a little frayed; not only will she complain about it, but she will have another made and perhaps of finer material than that worn in the community!

His entranced listeners laughed, clapped their hands with delight—and disapproved of such a silly Sister.

On July 25 Vincent thought it necessary, in this never ending attempt to form the Company to a devoted regularity, to reprimand Jeanne Le-peintre—now Sister Servant at Châteaudun—gently yet firmly for taking "a journey to Orléans for the benefit of the poor and to that other place where M. de Franqueville died to nurse him in his illness. I grant that these acts are good and laudable in themselves, but they ought not to be undertaken by anyone consecrated to God and bound by rule and spirit-ual direction without the consent of superiors. You know that, my daughter. And if you examine yourself carefully you will find either curi-osity or self-love behind these enterprises."

Louise wrote on July 31 to encourage Louise Christine and the Sisters at Montmirail, regretting that "there is no time left to speak with you heart to heart . . . but it is after ten o'clock at night." She was espe-cially touched at Sister Louise's "affection for my son's little family. His hearing has improved a great deal, by God's grace. His wife is well and [also] his little daughter, who had been dangerously ill, but God's good-ness gave her back to us. They are in the country. I ask you to pray to God for all their necessities, especially for their salvation." And with a "bonsoir, dear Sisters," her tired fingers put down the pen.

The Sisters at Bernay were so excited over their new hospital that Louise had to cool their ardor. She refused Sister Laurence Dubois's request for "the rule for hospitals" because "it would not be suitable for your place on account of the small number of sick you have." And a few days later she warned Barbe Angiboust more sharply "to be careful not to launch grandiose schemes because you don't know yet how many sick you will have, and to set up too much equipment and furniture would raise suspicions for which you could be blamed." She finished with the news that "Sister Marthe [Trumeau] from Nantes and Sister Elisabeth left Sunday to go to the army." They had been requested by the Queen for La Fère in the thick of the Champagne fighting.

Queens were not kept waiting in those royal days. The request, or rather command, had come on July 28 and the Sisters left on the thirtieth. Vincent had first appointed two other Sisters, who had balked at going, one most emphatically, the other more circumspectly—she alleged illness while piously proclaiming her "determination to go even though she should die." Vincent was not taken in and not only would he not force them to go, he would not allow them to go. At this point Marie-Marthe and Elisabeth arrived back at the motherhouse after their long journey from Nantes, promptly accepted the dangerous mission, and went to Saint-Lazare for instructions. Vincent was so moved at their eagerness to serve in contrast to the reluctance of the others that he gave them a long and tender conference all for themselves. "That God would have thought of you, dear Sister, in your native Champagne, and you in Poissy, as persons fit to be sent to a battlefield to serve Him!" he exclaimed. "That you, although poor country girls homely and ignorant, have been looked upon and chosen by Him for such great works! *Mais quoi!* a Queen has been thinking of you . . . !" He urged them as he had always urged others "to be very careful about the observance of your common rules insofar as the service of the sick permits, for you know that this is the chief business for which you should leave all else without, however, ceasing to do a part or what you can even if you cannot do the whole."

On August 8 Louise informed him that the Sisters had reached La Fère. The works were increasing at such a pace and the Sisters so insufficient in numbers and training that there was the temptation to overemphasize prudence. "But," she avowed, "—I don't know whether I deceive myself—*it seems to me that Our Lord would always prefer confidence to prudence for the preservation of the Company, and that this same confidence would effect prudent action in difficulties without anyone perceiving it was there.*"

In an effort to alleviate the shortage of vocations, Vincent called a council meeting in the parlor of Saint-Lazare on August 13. He asked the Sister Servant at the Enfants Trouvés to attend because he was anxious to explore the possibility of the older orphan girls being suitable for the Company. He was pained to discover that, despite their years of dedication to this work, the Sisters still tended to regard these poor children as "children of sin." There were girls old enough and pious enough for the Company, the Sister Servant admitted, but she thought that to give them the habit "would offend our Sisters and cause everyone to think that all Daughters of Charity were foundlings." Vincent reminded her very sharply of St. Peter's vision of the sheet filled with every kind of animal and of God's command to kill and eat because everything from the hand of God was clean. And he peremptorily cut off the discussion by announcing his intention of making a trial of these girls.

On August 25 he was forced to tell one of his priests at Rennes regretfully that "we cannot engage ourselves to give two Daughters of Charity in a month or two to the hospital at Saint-Malo because Mademoiselle has none ready and it takes a long time to train them well . . . I agree that if there were Daughters at Saint-Malo it would be a means of attracting others from there to the Company, but the impossibility of providing them for some time prevents it." There were, even then, three girls of that district who wished to join the Company and Vincent promised that "Mademoiselle Le Gras will be glad to receive them. She has a high opinion of Breton girls from her experience of former ones."

Louise sent Vincent a note to inform him that her cousin Michel de Marillac was "very ill of a cold and Madame his mother [the Carmelite] is most anxious for me to visit her for that reason. Madame her daughter-in-law not being in Paris increases her anxiety." Louise went with Vincent's blessing to comfort the good woman, who, cloister or no cloister, was at the moment a very worried mother.

On the eve of the Assumption Louise requested in another note, "to be delivered to Monsieur Vincent before he says Holy Mass," the usual permissions for certain Sisters to renew their vows the next day. The request had a special note of poignancy this time; one of the Sisters making the request had "grown hunchbacked in the service of the poor soldiers. She can no longer look forward to anything but a life of great pain, but she carries her affliction well, thank God."

Louise was disturbed by the visit of a certain M. Leheurt from Angers who had very little good to say about the Sisters there—she told Vincent —accusing them, and especially Cécile Angiboust, "of meddling by giving evidence against the Gentlemen [the administrators], of questioning penitents after their confessions, and of several other things of this nature." Louise was far from naïve and wrote at once to M. de Vaux that it was her opinion that "a persecution was being stirred up against the Sisters." She was right, and nothing more was heard of the matter.

Despite their unwillingness to take on new establishments at this time, Vincent and Louise decided to send two Sisters to Arras. They had been requested by the Bishop-designate Etienne Moreau and by the Ladies of Charity of Paris, whose fidelity in the service of the poor could not be denied. The Ladies had been moved to tears by the first-hand account of the misery suffered by the poor of Arras given by a young girl of the town who had walked all the way from Arras to Paris to make her plea.

Sister Marguerite Chétif was chosen to go as Sister Servant and Sister Radegonde Lenfantin as her companion. Vincent gave them their instructions at a conference on the day of the departure, August 30. He assured them that they "were going to people who serve God well and who are very charitable—yes, they are very good people indeed . . ." He was anxious that a confraternity of charity be established there but, remembering his experience in Beauvais years before, he cautioned that confraternities be established in each parish rather than one for the whole city: "Select the most suitable, with the Bishop's advice, then go on to another, and so on . . ."

The "good girl full of charity" who had come to ask for the Sisters was to return to Arras with them and Vincent suggested that "there may be others who would like to join you in visiting the sick. You may permit them to do so, but don't burden yourselves with too many at the same time. Two will be enough . . ." He bade them, however, to be careful to inform these lay helpers "from the start that you have your own little rules and that you must have privacy." He finished, in speaking of the willingness with which they should bear the contempt of others, by revealing a calumny against that most generous woman, the Duchesse d'Aiguillon: "Even if some were to say that you keep the money that belongs to the poor . . . humble yourselves, for if you were to wear a pearl necklace there would be people to say that you wore it at the expense of the poor, as they have said of the Duchesse."

Since this was to be an important establishment Louise, also, drew up for the Sisters a set of regulations that summarized clearly the practices of the Company in setting up new houses and in implementing the Rule. "In order that these regulations may be carried out exactly," she enjoined, "[the Sisters] shall read them at least once every eight days for the first three months and afterwards every month—and the Common Rules as well . . ."

Vincent had written ahead to M. Guillaume Delville, priest of the Mission at Arras, to inform him of the Sisters' departure on the next Amiens coach. "These girls are good servants of God," he reported with satisfaction. "I hope that He will bless their work." When the Sisters arrived at their destination it was learned that their young companion who had come to summon them, completely exhausted by her errand of mercy, had died on the way at Amiens. Vincent made her a priceless eulogy in wishing for the Sisters "the sweetness and zeal she had for the poor."

Toward the middle of September Louise had a weak spell while getting out of bed and fell heavily, apparently bruising or cracking a rib. She was in a great deal of pain and at length fever set in. Vincent informed Nicole Haran at Nantes on the twenty-seventh that she was still confined to bed and showed little improvement, but he ventured his usual optimism that "it would prove to be nothing . . ." He told Marguerite Chétif the same thing. On arriving at Arras, Marguerite had suffered an aridity of soul which, together with the inevitable trials that accompany a new work, gave her a sensible distaste for it. Vincent assured her that it was nothing more than the doubts and difficulties which the devil used to discourage any work that might "result in great service and honor to God." Passing on to business, he assured her that when M. Delville, who was at Douai giving a mission, returned he would instruct him to set aside two weeks for assisting Marguerite in negotiating the Act of Establishment of the house.

Marguerite wrote to Louise about the possibility of the Sisters' changing their headdress to conform to the costume of Arras. She must have been surprised to receive a long and decidedly negative reply, not from Louise, but from Vincent. "You speak of the embarrassment caused by appearing in church different from others, that everyone is looking at you—and I am afraid that it is pride that is causing you this embarrassment . . . You wish to bring about a division in your Company, which must be entirely uniform, because if the Arras women cover themselves in one way, in Poland and in France they cover themselves in another. If you are going to follow these fashions, just look at the variety you will have!"

Louise had not recovered sufficiently by the middle of October to take full charge of the affairs of the Company, but she aroused herself to protest against what Barbe Angiboust had told her was happening at Bernay. "*Mon Dieu*, dear Sister!" she exclaimed, "where are those responsible, or what has happened to the control exercized by the Ladies of Charity, if the sick are forced to go to the hospital? You will see how the bashful poor will be deprived of help . . . We are obliged insofar as we can to prevent this by humble and kind remonstrances." She could not forbear to ask Barbe, half teasing, about "this beautiful house you live in. Doesn't it sometimes make you afraid about your profession of lowliness and poverty?" Vincent, she assured her, "seems the same as usual but nevertheless his age and little infirmities oblige us ever . . . to pray for his preservation, which we have more need of than ever."

Françoise Carcireux at Richelieu had written to comfort Louise in her illness and now Louise thanked her "for the solicitude you have shown for the continuation of the life of this miserable body which so offends God on earth. His mercy seems to wish to prolong it a little longer but it cannot be for very long. That is why, dear Sisters, I ask you to show me your affection by making use of your good offices with Our Lord to procure my salvation which I can hope for if I do His holy will for the rest of my days. Ask this grace of Him for me. I promise to do the same for you, trusting that your fidelity to God in the observance of your Rules, which we hope to send you soon, will draw down upon you the fruit of our poor prayers . . ."

On November 8 Vincent was forced to deny a request for Sisters by Balthasar Grangier de Liverdi, Bishop of Tréguier. Citing the lack of Sisters, he stated bluntly: "Their work is so hard that many of them die from it." And, pointing out to him further that at least six other bishops were clamoring for Sisters for their dioceses, he promised him nevertheless that "we will do everything we can to send you some; I don't say eight at the same time, but two or three so as to begin with the hospital which is the most necessary."

Every Sister available was pressed into service during this long shortage. Louise sent an old Sister, "who knows how to bleed [patients] and conducts school very well," to fill a vacancy at Maule. "We had decided not to send her out from the motherhouse any longer both because of her age and because of other minor reasons which will make little difference at Maule," Louise told Vincent, "but I spoke to her this evening and have come to the conclusion that she could still go to this war without too much difficulty."

On All Saints' Day, Vincent was attacked by a violent recurrence of his fever and circulatory trouble. He managed to fight it off again, and late in the month Louise wrote joyfully to Barbe Angiboust inviting her "to praise God with us, dear Sister, for his improved health: there remains only an erysipelas which has settled in the leg. It brought on an extremely severe attack of fever lasting twenty-four hours and there have been a succession of small attacks since. We have every motive for asking God for his recovery . . ."

On November 25 Vincent wrote through a secretary to thank

"Mademoiselle Le Gras for her anxiety for my health and to pray Our Lord to restore her own. I have recovered from my little cold, thank God, and do everything I can for it," he continued virtuously. "I don't leave the room. I sleep in every morning. I eat everything they put before me and have taken some julep which Brother Alexandre gives me each evening." He added rather too pointedly that there was no further need for him to take the frequent cups of tea she had prescribed!

The Sisters at Arras seem to have been unusually fastidious: their latest problem had to do with what to eat and drink. On December 2 Vincent informed M. Delville that it was "unnecessary to change anything as regards the Daughters of Charity's eating habits. Mademoiselle Le Gras says that they have the safeguard of knowing how to mix sweet water which counteracts all other water and prevents them from getting sick. Therefore, those at Arras should stop drinking the bit of beer you have suggested so that they will be uniform with the others and so as to remove any pretext for some, dissatisfied with the ordinary beverage, to ask for wine."

As the year drew to a close, Louise learned of the death of Sister Claude Chantereau at Sainte-Marie-du-Mont on the lands of the Duchesse de Ventadour. This was the most isolated of all the missions and Louise worried constantly about the Sisters there. She took the occasion of Sister Claude's death to eulogize "these poor girls" who "show great proof of their fidelity to Our Lord. They are fifteen leagues from Caen in a region without messenger service so that they are sometimes three months without news from us and our letters are often lost, and despite that they live as if they were here."

Louise's tender heart was not reserved for her daughters. On February 9, 1657, she importuned Vincent for a young wife who had tried twice to see him in an effort to seek employment for her husband. "This good young woman is in such extremity that she is debating whether she can in conscience take advantage of a proposition made to her," she wrote with what imagined blushes, "and by someone you know who would raise your eyebrows—he promises to dissipate her worries . . ." The girl had not eaten for four days and Louise implored Vincent to interest the Ladies of Charity in her desperate situation before she lost her innocence. We can be sure that the poor girl was duly rescued from her dilemma.

On February 16 Louise artfully begged to be allowed "to continue the diet I began Lent with—eggs and bouillon." She insisted that this diet would "temper the heat of the blood by soothing somewhat the trouble I am having with my arteries again." She was too honest not to admit that she felt herself obliged to this mortified fare, "although I am afraid that it is prompted more by an attachment to my health than a desire to obey the precept . . ." We do not know whether he decided to humor her on this occasion.

He was delighted with the report from M. Delville at Arras that "the whole town is edified by and satisfied with the good Daughters of Charity, who take excellent care of the sick, observe the practices of their little Company faithfully and in this way draw down the blessing of God on their ministry . . ." He was disturbed to learn, however, that Marguerite Chétif had been ailing. "Perhaps she works too hard," he suggested anxiously, "and in that case she ought to moderate her labors and proportion them to her strength. I recommend that she do so."

Besides her illness, Marguerite was suffering still from desolation of spirit which now took the form of doubts about her vocation. Vincent's advice to her on February 18 is a classic reply to all beset with like temptations. "I tell you, Sister, it is simply a temptation of the evil spirit who, seeing the good you accomplish, tries to turn you away from it," he wrote firmly. "To judge whether God has called you to your present state, you should not concentrate on your present dispositions but on those you had when you entered. On several occasions at that time you felt the call within you. You prayed to God that you might know His will. You asked the advice of your directors. You made not only a retreat but a trial of living with Mademoiselle Le Gras. After all that, once you had voluntarily decided upon this way of life in God's sight and in response to His call, He showed you that this decision was most pleasing to Him by blessing ever since your person and your deeds so that you have been a source of edification at home and abroad." There can be little doubt that Marguerite's protracted spiritual trial had implications for the Company and its glorious future by way of preparing her to be its mother in a very few years.

On February 23 Vincent told M. Martin at Turin of the ambitious plan afoot in Paris to turn the vast complex of buildings known as the Salpêtrière—as well as Bicêtre, Le Refuge, La Pitié, Scipion and La Savonnerie—into "a great hospital for the feeding, instructing and housing of all poor beggars so that none will be seen any longer in the town or the churches." Vincent distrusted the plan from the beginning because the idea of forcing people to do anything was distasteful to him. He became even more opposed to it when, without consulting him or Louise, a royal edict placed the spiritual ministry of the proposed hospital in the hands of his Congregation and the nursing duties in those of the Daughters of Charity. After much prayer and thought he politely but firmly refused both assignments, alleging truthfully enough the lack of personnel—although at least two Sisters, Jeanne Lepeintre and Madeleine Ménage, seem to have worked at the hospital for a short time.

Vincent's instinct was right. Most of the professional beggars simply vanished from the city until the whole thing should blow over, and while the institutions continued to operate as almshouses their character of paupers' prisons was less and less insisted upon and ultimately lost. The project had been dear to the heart of the Ladies of Charity, who were among its prime movers and the chief allies of the state in trying to enlist Vincent's support. Despite its more or less inevitable outcome, they cannot be denied praise and even glory for their efforts and prodigious outlay of funds.

Early in March the Sisters at Chantilly sent the motherhouse a special treat in the form of some "wonderful fish." In accepting the gift with her usual courtesy, Louise made the delicate reproach that "if it could have been promptly returned, I would have asked that it serve as a little feast for your poor because you know very well that our Company does not indulge itself in this way. But since that was impossible your kindness has brought pleasure to several of our sick Sisters, among whom I divided it."

The Priests of the Mission had suffered a succession of deaths recently, notably that of M. Blatiron, the superior at Genoa, and on March 20 Louise sent Vincent a letter of sympathy. "Our Lord seems to be the only general proprietor of the Congregation of the Mission, disposing of its good subjects as He sees fit," she wrote. "And he has selected for an excellent mission him whom He has taken from us. What can we say? Nothing—except that I believe this new entry into heaven will draw great graces from God upon all the rest of the Company and this universal grief will produce its holy effects in many souls. Isn't it rash of me, Most Honored Father, to dare mingle my tears with your accustomed submission to the wishes of Divine Providence, my weakness with the strength God has given you to bear so well the sorrow God gives you so often?" And she finished by urging him gently not to fight the natural expression of grief: "For His love, give nature what it needs for its relief and what is necessary for your health."

He understood and was grateful. Writing to Nicole Haran at Nantes, he confided that Louise felt for him the more because she herself was dragged down by a heavy cold which she could not shake off. Nicole had done more to cheer him than anyone by telling him of her attraction for the mission in Madagascar. "I don't know whether [God] will take you at your word, but I know for certain that this kind of zeal is not displeasing to Him . . ." he assured her. No Sisters were to leave for Madagascar in the few short years left to Vincent and Louise.

During the last days of Holy Week Louise reminded Vincent that Anne-Marie-Louise d'Orléans, Duchesse de Montpensier—the flamboyant lady known to history as "La Grande Mademoiselle"—had again requested Sisters for a hospital at Saint-Fargeau. Louise thought the request should be honored both because of the high station of the petitioner as a Princess of the Blood and because "it is a long while since she made the first request, and they say that that district has great need of spiritual and corporal assistance." Vincent agreed and two Sisters were sent immediately.

This Holy Week letter also reveals how poor a table the first Sisters kept, for in it Louise asked Vincent whether she should grant the wish of her friend the Duchesse de Ventadour to be allowed to treat the Sisters to roast meat for their Easter dinner. The accustomed frugality of the Company is further revealed in a note which accompanied cloth for habits which Louise sent Barbe Angiboust. "If you have a worn habit," she asked Barbe, "please save it so that we can make linings out of it."

In April Louise was at last ready to fulfill the long-standing request of Alain de Solminihac, Bishop of Cahors, for Sisters, and she even withdrew an especially talented Sister from the foundling asylum to please him. Louise had been anxious because the good Bishop had said nothing about helping to defray the cost of the long journey—but her anxiety was dissipated in a most unexpected way when one of the Sisters chosen for the mission, frightened at the prospect of going so far away, bolted the Company and was never seen again. Her flight caused another year's delay because there was no one to replace her.

Jeanne Lepeintre, who had borne the brunt of the difficulties caused by the administrators at Nantes, was experiencing difficulties of another kind with the administrators at Châteaudun. The Sisters' quarters there were most unsuitable because of a lack of privacy: people wandered in and out like chickens in a peasant's kitchen. Again and again the administrators had reneged on their promise to remedy the situation and

Jeanne's patience was wearing thin. Nevertheless, Louise did not want an open quarrel and besought Vincent to caution Jeanne "not to seize the occasion for a refusal of obedience or to break the agreements with the gentlemen . . ."

On May 12 she informed Cécile Angiboust that one of the priests of the Mission would make a visitation of the house at Angers. "I wish it with all my heart," she wrote, "confessing to you and to all our dear Sisters my great sorrow at seeing the little advancement in perfection of your community." And she told Cécile tactfully where the blame lay: "When I become aware of some little disturbance among certain Sisters and have studied it carefully to discover the cause I must confess with simplicity that frequently I see it to be my fault—whether from a lack of cordiality or of setting the example I should. We must realize, dear Sister, that the name of *Servants* of our Sisters which Divine Providence gives us obliges us to be the first in practicing true and solid virtues of humility, support, work and exactitude in the rules and practices of the Company . . ."

In a note of June 12 Vincent sent Louise his regrets that he could not hear the confessions of two "good girls from Saint-Flour because of certain pressing business that has taken up the whole morning—and I have to go into the city after dinner." He suggested that, if they were unwilling to wait, M. Alméras would oblige them. Louise replied that they were quite willing to wait, because the older wished to make an interior communication—even if she had to do it in writing. "I see a great perfection in this soul and admirable qualities for the works to which God applies her," she continued. It was rare for her to commit herself to such a positive spiritual judgment, and the statement which followed it was unique: "She would have done and would do well now if she were to be put in my place." It is rather frustrating not to know the name of this Sister.

For some time Louise had been anxious for Barbe Angiboust to go to Saint-Marie-du-Mont to report on the state of that isolated mission and to encourage the Sisters there. She urged her on June 22 "to leave as soon as you can . . . if you think you have strength enough for the trip . . . Encourage our dear Sisters with all your heart, for I am afraid they have a great deal of work and little consolation." She showed how deeply worried she was by instructing Barbe "to come back this way"—although the distance would be much greater—"if the road is better than the one to Bernay." Barbe left for Sainte-Marie-du-Mont at once. On July 10 Louise was fussing over Sister Laurence Dubois left alone at Bernay: "I am worried . . . for fear you have much more work than you can do . . . Please let me know whether you have some good girl to stay with you at night . . . because that's the time when our enemies are most apt to attack in an effort to overcome us—which makes me confident that you will redouble your prayers and your diligence in the practice of virtue, and especially that you will keep your doors firmly bolted . . ."

Louise's thoughts dwelt on the protection and honor of her daughters in an even more profound way these days. Cardinal de Retz's Act of Establishment of the Company was being readied for the King's approval and subsequent registration by Parlement. Legalities move slowly and Louise took advantage of this to importune Vincent—as she did again now on July 22—"that it be stated in the letters accompanying the Seal or in the verification by Parlement that, considering the service the Company renders the public and considering the weakness of its sex and their labors in diverse places, the King or Parlement assume special protection over it—both the whole Company in general and each member in particular—defending them expressly against those who leave the said Company without the consent of the Superior and even against those who leave wearing the simple habit with permission"—country girls, after all, could hardly be forbidden to wear their native costume—"thus making it possible, if the necessity arose, to proceed juridically against such persons as being refractory to the ordinances of the King or of Parlement. If this suggestion is entirely ridiculous I know your goodness will excuse this fault along with my other usual ones . . ." Certainly Vincent would not consider ridiculous whatever might save the Company from the embarrassment brought upon it by girls who still pretended to belong to it, but whether or not an attempt was made to do as Louise suggested, no protective measures appeared in the letters patent of the King of November 1657 or in the parliamentary registration of December 16, 1658.

At a council meeting of July 21 to which the older Sisters of the house were invited it was finally decided to give up the mission at Chars. Despite the Jansenist persecution the Sisters had endured from the Oratorians who held the parish, Vincent and Louise had dragged their heels in withdrawing the Sisters, out of deference to Mme la présidente de Herse, who had brought them there. Louise now assured that great lady that they had taken "every possible means" to stay but could no longer suffer "the introduction of customs alien to the Church," and she proceeded to list the indignities the Sisters had endured: one had been refused Communion publicly at the altar rail; another had the host she presented at the offertory removed from the paten; they were permitted to communicate only once a week; months went by without the opportunity of confession; they were threatened with public penance at the door of the church; they were forced to carry out demands of the curé which were in direct contravention of their rules and the orders of their superiors. Although they had suffered in silence for the most part, they had balked at the curé's insistence that they whip one of their little pupils in front of her classmates—Louise and Vincent both frowned on corporal punishment except as a desperate measure—and on one occasion Sister Marie's nerves had snapped and she had roundly dressed down one of her priestly tormenters in the public street.

Having informed Mme de Herse of the decision taken, Louise wrote a respectful but firm notice of withdrawal to the curé, in which she again detailed all the offenses which were the reason for it.

The invasion of the Sisters' privacy continued at Châteaudun and Louise decided in August to send Barbe Angiboust there to replace Jeanne Lepeintre, who had failed to correct the situation. Actually poor Jeanne's powers were failing imperceptibly and within a year or two her mind would give way, nor was it surprising in light of the difficult tasks she had shouldered over the years. For the present, however, Louise appointed her Sister Servant of the Company's shortlived mission at the Salpêtrière.

Barbe was just the right person to deal with the problem at Châteaudun. Although naturally friendly and of an exceptionally gay and sunny disposition—or perhaps because of it—she had always taken a literal and uncompromising view of the rule which forbade men in the Sisters' quarters. Little more than a week after her arrival at Châteaudun, both Vincent and Louise were writing to congratulate her on getting the administrators to keep their promise of safeguarding the Sisters' privacy and on the steps she herself had taken to enforce it. Her approach was very direct: she simply took the intruder by the arm and escorted him to the door. His rank or office mattered nothing: a city magistrate had thus been thrown out of the house, as well as a priest, whom, when he had resisted, Barbe asked reproachfully: "Oh, Monsieur! Do you really wish to enter a place where there are only girls?" More vigorous resistance was offered by an altar boy who had run in to light his candle and when Barbe marched him out turned around and beat her. Even this urchin was back the next day to apologize.

Barbe's companion at Bernay, Sister Laurence Dubois, succeeded her as Sister Servant there and Sister Anne Levies was sent as her companion. Barbe's sister Cécile had still not been relieved of her duties at Angers and her health was again giving way under them. The most that Vincent and Louise could do for her at the moment was to order her to Richelieu for a rest. She had not gone by September 12, which caused Louise to write in astonishment to M. de Vaux, "since she has evidenced the desire [of going] so many times and even of coming to Paris! You know how important it is to carry out the orders of superiors, Monsieur." Cécile now begged Louise to let her come home and on October 13 Louise informed Barbe that she had granted the request, expressing the hope that Cécile might visit her on the way, "because she will be here a long time." Sister Claude was appointed acting superioress at Angers in her absence.

Vincent depended on Louise for the fine points of housekeeping at Saint-Lazare. On September 2 he asked her "to buy blankets at the price of nine francs," and added dryly: "I don't doubt that those which the draper offers at eight and a half livres are of the quality of wool that the said demoiselle [Louise] writes"—he was dictating to a secretary—"and that they are worth still less. The draper has to make a profit over and above the workman's price. Our good Brother who went earlier had trouble believing that. He knows nothing about business. We need sixty blankets. I send six hundred livres approximately." Louise knew something about business. She noted on the bottom of his letter: "There were only 45 eleven-livres coins, which makes only 495 livres." By October 5 she had managed to purchase fifty-two blankets out of this.

A charming note of this period asks Vincent to allow her "to pretend to be one of the bashful poor and to beg you for the love of God to do me the charity of giving me the alms of a little visit, of which I have great need . . ." And in a postscript she presses politely: "If Your Charity could come today?"

There was good news from Poland. The King's forces were prevailing and it looked like the country would soon be reunited and at peace once again. Vincent told M. Ozenne on September 7 of his consolation in

knowing that his priests and the Daughters of Charity were giving spiritual and temporal comfort to the soldiers who were laying seige to Krakow.

Communication with the Sisters at Varize had become as uncertain as
with the Sisters at Sainte-Marie-du-Mont. Louise had asked Barbe Angiboust on September 2 whether she had had any news of them and now,
on the fifteenth, assured her that "you would give me great pleasure if
you made a little trip to Varize and gave good advice in your usual sweet
and kind way to Sister Claude, as regards both her health and her out-
look. I would be relieved to know how Monsieur le prieur and she get
along." On the same day she wrote to admonish the Sisters at Chantilly
—who, she felt, were bothering their spiritual directors unnecessarily—
"not to abuse" their goodness "by giving them too much trouble, for you
know that we do not call upon our superiors here except when there is
need of the sacraments or some other necessity."

On the twenty-second she wrote affectionately to Marguerite Chétif at
Arras, who had made her some kind of gift—perhaps of a Mass for her
intention: "I have learned of the kindness you have done me who do not
merit it, except that friendship does not expect repayment or a like recognition. I thank you therefore very humbly, dear Sister, for the testimony you have given me of yours which is most dear [to me]." Mlle de
Lamoignon had donated money for bread for the poor of Arras, she told
Marguerite, and expressed concern for the needs of the Sisters, "which
leads me to say, dear Sister, that you must suffer no inconvenience, asking me for what you need and borrowing until you receive it."

On September 28 she was again urging upon Vincent, who was ailing
as usual, her cure-all tea—"at least during your retreat . . . If you will
not make this little trial for your health, I will complain to Our good
God . . ."

She was pleased to learn from the Sisters at Angers that M. Ratier was
very faithful in giving them conferences, and regretted that she could
not send them a set of the conferences given by Vincent because "to
write them out in full would take a Sister who did nothing else." She
urged them to preserve M. Ratier's conferences and instructed them in
the procedure followed at the motherhouse: "A Sister . . . writes down
as much as she can while [the conference] is being given and then,
making a fair copy, fills it in by enlisting the memory of others."

She had cause to reprimand the Sister Servant at Saint-Denis and minced no words. "Well! Look at you, fallen in such a clumsy way again!" she began. "You represent Sister Anne's fault in a different manner than it happened. This Sister became angry at seeing a number of cats around the two of you at prayer time and you say that they displeased 'another Sister.' *Mon Dieu*, Sister, how good it is to tell the truth! Have I not asked you to get rid of these animals and you have not troubled yourself? And," she finished in fine sarcasm, "a Sister fails to obey you promptly!" The reprimand given, however, she reverted to her usual compassion: "Please, Sister, don't grow discouraged at sight of your faults. We would never know ourselves unless we managed to correct ourselves without that. Console yourself then in the hope that the retreat will do you good."

She was just as ruthless in pointing out to Françoise Carcireux "the desire of self-satisfaction hiding within you under the fine appearance of seeking great perfection. We deceive ourselves very much if we think we are capable people and still more if we seek to acquire perfection by our own efforts and by a continual search or scrupling to identify every movement and disposition of our soul. It is good to apply ourselves exactly to this scrutiny once a year in defiance of ourselves and with a recognition of our own insufficiency; but to make a continual hell for our soul by picking at ourselves and giving an account of every thought is a useless work, not to say a dangerous one." And she added with humble remembrance: "I am telling you what was once told me."

Vincent sent instructions for the Sisters' preparation for Christmas. "To spend Advent well," he advised, "use R. P. Souffrand's book [*L'Année Chrétienne*]. Have the treatise on this season read to our Sisters at table and let them say the prayers and perform the practices in it which are pleasing to them. Permit them to add some little act of penance to those they are doing now—that is, any who ask the permission of you." She must have been dismayed when she read the next sentence: "As for yourself, for your penance bear your infirmities for the love of God and don't even think of performing any others!"

On December 18 Louise was in an unusually gay mood writing to Barbe Angiboust. She reeled off a breathless string of questions, wanting to know "if you have received two letters we sent about two weeks ago by messenger, and if you have had news of our Sisters at Varize recently, and if everybody is settling down to accept your reform, and if your cordiality and sweetness is drawing persons of quality to the hospital to do good there." Cécile was "very well, thank God!" she assured Barbe, "although she has a great deal to do." Cécile had been sent to Les Petites Maisons as acting Sister Servant in Anne Hardemont's place.

Early in 1658 Vincent was thrown head first from his carriage, an affront to his seventy-seven years that incapacitated him for weeks. On hearing the news, Louise immediately wrote M. Portail about "the defects I have noted in that carriage . . . The doors are hung too low on the frame and the whole chassis of the carriage is raised too high by the sling, which, while it heightens efficiency, nevertheless gives you such a shaking that at times when I have been in it I have been afraid the jolting would hurl me out the door . . ." Because of Vincent's prominence, the news of his accident spread far and wide and he even had a letter of sympathy from his disciple Jacques-Bénigne Bossuet in far-off Metz.

In the first weeks after the accident Louise was careful to burden Vincent as little as possible with day-to-day business and so, when Brother Ducournau passed on to her a letter addressed to Vincent by the Sisters at Saint-Fargeau, who were anxious to garner recruits for the Company, she penned the reply herself. "It is necessary to represent to girls of Saint-Fargeau who ask to be received into the Company," she instructed the good Brother to write in Vincent's name, "that it is not a religious community, or a hospital where she stays put, but goes continually in search of the sick poor in divers places at set times and precise hours. That [its members] are clothed very meanly with never anything to put on their heads unless it be a linen cornette in great necessity. That there must never be any other intention in coming to the Company than simply that of serving God and the neighbor. That it is necessary to live in continual mortification of body and spirit. That they have the intention of observing all the rules exactly and especially unquestioning obedience. That they understand that even when they travel around Paris they will not be allowed to visit the homes of their acquaintances without permission. That they must have the price of their journey and their first habit." It was a clear challenge to anyone who wished to be a Daughter of Charity uncompromisingly stated by a Company that sorely needed every member.

Brother Ducournau also asked Louise about a request Vincent had received from her friend the Duchesse de Ventadour for two more Sisters for La Fère. Louise rejected the reasons advanced by the Duchesse but recommended that, since the two Sisters there were not well, a helper be sent them in the person of Sister Julienne Allet.

Vincent dictated an addition to Louise's reply to the Sisters at Saint-Fargeau. He was afraid, he told the Sisters, that "the two little pensioners take up too much of your time. You know that it is not customary for your Company to receive them and you should not have taken on the responsibility of these children without our permission. If you say Her Royal Highness [the Duchesse de Montpensier] commanded you to receive them, perhaps it was because you did not give her to understand that it was against your rule, because if she had known that, she would have waited until she had written to Mademoiselle Le Gras and received her reply."

The work at Nantes was getting ahead of the Sisters, and Vincent wrote on January 18 to promise Nicole Haran another Sister even if the administrators should not request one. "If no one there can make them understand that you are too few for so many sick," he stated emphatically, "we will send a missionary to Nantes soon, with God's help, and he will impress upon them the excessiveness of your duties and the danger you are in of dying [from them]." The heavy work load was taking its spiritual toll, too, and Nicole worried over the fact that they were missing daily Mass with alarming frequency. "You have no reason to be scrupulous about losing Mass to assist the poor," Vincent assured her, "because God prefers mercy to sacrifice. I have but two things to ask from God for you and your Sisters: the first is that He give you a great solicitude for the salvation and solace of the sick, and the second that He give you the grace to love and support one another . . ."

Louise sent Vincent a private note on February 1 demanding to "know the truth about your health" and begging him not to get up prematurely. He was coming along surprisingly well, considering his years and the seriousness of his fall. On that same day he wrote to commend M. Delville at Arras for preventing the town officials from "giving our Daughters of Charity the care of the sick soldiers lodged in the Hôtel-Dieu . . . since religious are not only capable of such an assignment but entirely willing to undertake it. And according to Mademoiselle Le Gras's wish and the tradition of the Company, you ought not to allow these two Daughters to go to nurse the sick in the said Hôtel-Dieu under the direction of religious, both because the aforesaid religious ought to perform that task themselves . . . and because the Daughters of Charity are destined only for the abandoned sick who have no one to help them . . ."

On February 4 Louise sent Vincent "this little book you asked me for. Permit me to request, Most Honored Father, that the authorship be kept secret—not that I fear that anything in it is contrary to faith: but might it not be interpretated as a fault to have spent time in this manner, or again, to appear as being engaged in colloquoy with a woman?" Because of Louise's diffidence it is legitimate to ask whether this work was hers—perhaps in the form of her questions and Vincent's answers concerning spiritual matters. Was it the compilation of her spiritual notes which have been published since under the title of *Pensées?* The reference to a colloquoy would challenge this latter supposition. Whatever the nature of this mysterious book, it seems certain that its circulation was strictly private and limited.

Sister Brigitte had been appointed Sister Servant at Angers and Louise requested her on February 13 to "appoint certain times for our Sisters to talk with you individually—at least once each month, when you should grant them only a quarter of an hour." She did not want the worthwhile practice of spiritual communication to turn into a marathon of confidences and direction!

On the sixteenth, Louise came to the assistance of Laurence Dubois at Bernay, who had been caught in the crossfire of a squabble between the Ladies of Charity of the parishes and those of the Hôtel-Dieu there. Laurence must do her best to smooth over the differences without getting herself embroiled, Louise counseled, and above all "you must not weigh their social stations in paying them respect. It should be enough for you that they have been taken into the Company [of the Ladies of Charity] to honor them as Mothers of your Masters the Poor, even when they do not pull their load. If you knew, dear Sister, what abasement, what sweetness and submission Our Lord expects from Daughters of Charity, you would be upset at not practicing them." She had a special word of advice for Sister Anne, who was inclined to be lazy: "If you are ill I repeat what I have said many times, that work is a necessity and that idleness causes sin in the soul and sickness in the body."

Some of Vincent's priests would pass through Nantes on their way to take ship for Madagascar and Vincent seized the opportunity to have them conduct a visitation of the Sisters' house and hospital. Louise sent a letter with them imploring the Sisters to open their souls to "these good gentlemen." In the same letter she encouraged Sister Françoise

Ménage and Sister Andrée to write to her, "but for the love of God," she begged, "learn how to spell so that I can read your letters easily and give the answers you request!"

In April Vincent's legs grew much worse and Louise, fearing for his life, sent around to the houses for prayers.

Marguerite Chétif, still in her distress of soul, now got it into her head that Louise was dissatisfied with her. Patiently, Louise wrote to assure her of her amazement "at these thoughts that have taken possession of you against all the reasons I have to be confident of your affection and that you should have of mine, for I tell you that you have never seemed to belong to God or to love your vocation more than at present."

The Duchesse de Ventadour has decided to endow a new hospital on her lands at Ussel and Vincent and Louise promised her two Sisters for it. Anne Hardemont was appointed Sister Servant, and Louise suggested as her companion "the little Sister who had been destined for Cahors. We are sure of her determination to serve God, she is exact as to her rules [and] she knows how to write . . ." This was Avoie Vigneron. The Duchesse personally escorted the two Sisters to Ussel about the middle of May. Louise reminded M. Portail on the eleventh that "they should take with them a copy of the principal articles concerning establishments, particularly as to wholehearted dependence [on their superiors] in spirituals, [and] the preservation of style and color in habits, that they will not be associated with anyone else in their ministry to the poor either at home or abroad; and since it is not an established hospital, an article stating that their maintenance will be kept separate from that of the poor will be necessary—if Monsieur Vincent judges it proper."

The Duchesse had first entertained an ambitious plan to establish a second motherhouse and novitiate at Ussel, but Vincent and Louise had dissuaded her because there were no priests of the Mission in the neighborhood to supply the direction.

On the feast of Pentecost, June 9, Louise made another of her vain pleas to be relieved of office. She began casually by reminding Vincent that this was the day for "carrying out the election of officers." She granted that the Act of Establishment specifically stated that she was to remain in office for life, but rather lamely proposed that "*if Your Charity judges proper*" they could start "to make the office elective . . ." She thought the other officers should be retained because it took "three or four months for them to get used" to their duties. Vincent's reply was to hold no elections of any kind that year.

The violence of the Fronde was still a reality on the northern border of the realm, where the armies of Turenne and Condé were still locked in conflict. The Sisters summoned to La Fère on a temporary basis in 1656 had been nursing the wounded for two years, with no end in sight. Indeed, the recent Battle of the Dunes and an epidemic which swept through the armies in its wake had greatly increased the carnage and devastation and the Queen now called for more Daughters of Charity. Vincent referred to it in a Pentecost conference: "The Queen has called for you to go to Calais to nurse the poor wounded soldiers. What a motive for humbling yourselves is the thought that God wishes to make use of you for such great things! Ah! My Savior! Men go to war to slay their fellowmen, and you, you go to war to repair the harm they are doing." Although he expressed confidence that "many of you . . . are quite ready to go . . ." it would seem that the four or five chosen had already left, because he commented later in the same conference: "Those Sisters who went to the Queen—that was martyrdom because, although so far they have not died, nevertheless they exposed themselves to the danger of death, and did so for the love of God, like all the other dear Sisters who have spent their lives serving the poor. That is martyrdom."

The Queen had asked for six Sisters but only four could be spared because, at her request also, four others had to be found for Metz. The Sisters who went to Calais were Françoise Manceau, Marguerite Ménage, Marie Poulet and Claude Muset.

How drastically Louise's health had failed was pathetically evident in a letter she wrote to Françoise Carcireux on June 25 begging her pardon for not having answered her letters. "Please accept the little recommendation I made you to help me not to commit this fault any more," she asked Françoise humbly. "That is, dear Sister, to make it easier for me to read your letters by lining up each thing you want at the head of the letter. Not that it isn't a great comfort to me when you do me the honor of telling me your news in detail—but I am at such an extreme of weakness that I have great trouble reading. I am very upset that I can't remember everything you asked me in your other letters."

She was constantly "very ill" now, as she herself admitted. The prospect of death, which heightened every day, increased the anguish she always felt over faults in the Company and drove her constantly to the only weapon she had left, her pen. On July 5 she reproached the Sisters at Chantilly for their "wholesale forgetfulness of your obligations. The desire God has given me for your perfection makes me suffer more than I can tell you. For the love of God, think a little of the shortness of life and the misery of souls who appear before God covered with sins and infidelities. I commend this lesson to myself as well as to you because I have not overcome myself or detached myself from satisfactions that are contrary to God or renounced the evil use of my senses and passions . . . No one will rise with Jesus Christ who does not first die to these things."

Yet she constantly warned against the futility of discouragement or of anger with oneself in the battle for perfection: such a course, she insisted, "often ends in imaginary virtue, makes you bad-tempered and, by trying too hard, leads to disgust for solid virtue."

The fact that she was so desperately ill did not affect her habitual solicitude for her daughters' peace of mind regarding their loved ones. She assured Sister Andrée at Nantes that God was showering graces on "your good mother and all her family. It seems to me that that tells me something about you, too, because it is customary for God to watch over the near and dear of those who are faithful to Him." She reminded Sister Ménage that she had kept her informed regularly of how her sisters and all her family were doing since "your good father died" and that they continued "as well as ever."

For Sister Anne, who was suffering from earache, she prescribed "a drop of oil of rue in the ear before she retires and some cotton to keep it in. There is nothing better."

Anne Hardemont and Avoie Vigneron were very unhappy at Ussel. The establishment of a new house is always difficult and they had allowed themselves to grow discouraged, which led to complete dissatisfaction with themselves and everyone else. Vincent wrote on August 10 to deny emphatically something Anne had gotten into her head: "You have let yourself imagine that Mademoiselle Le Gras sent you there to punish you. O *Dieu!* Sister, that is far from the truth! I know the esteem and affection she has for you and that she wished to procure your good in sending you with a lady of great piety [the Duchesse de Ventadour] for the service of God and the solace of his poor members." Indeed, he told her, "if you had been here you would have been sent to Calais, where . . . all have fallen ill and two have died . . ." The plague had been no respecter of the Sisters and had carried off Françoise Manceau and Marguerite Ménage.

In the emergency caused by their deaths, Vincent and Louise set to work immediately to find four more Sisters for Calais. Henriette Gesse-aume, who was now at the Hôtel-Dieu, met Vincent in one of the wards and begged him to send her. Touched at the self-sacrifice of this Sister who had contributed her share of dissension to the house at Nantes, he nonetheless hesitated because she was over fifty. The next day, however, he told her she could go and she and her companions set out the day afterward, Sunday, August 4. Seeing them off, Vincent wept openly as he asked them: "What did [Our Lord] come into this world for, if not to save people? And what are our dear Sisters doing if not trying their best to save the lives of all these poor people of which others wished to deprive them? Isn't that what our Sisters have done and are doing now, and some of them have even lost their lives while doing it? Oh, how happy they are for having lost their lives for such a noble object!"

He went on to speak frankly of what lay ahead of them: "What are you about to do, Sisters? You are going to take the place of the dead. You are going to martyrdom, if God is pleased so to dispose of you." Reminding them that people had once thought that the Church would fail because of its many martyrs, he expressed the conviction that "the blood of our Sisters will bring many more to the Company and merit God's grace to sanctify those who remain." Two of the Sisters were very young—it was perhaps their first mission—but, he told them, St. Igna-tius had sent novices into the army as chaplains and when someone asked him where a holy priest had made his novitiate he answered: "In the army." Vincent smiled on the youngsters and bade them: "Don't be afraid. You will make a good novitiate. You will do far more, because you will live and die as martyrs . . ." He finished, choked with emotion: "Embrace our dear Sisters who are still at Calais . . . Greet them on Mademoiselle's behalf and mine and tell them we are grateful even unto tears for the service they have rendered God and the poor."

Having twice tried to smooth Anne Hardemont's ruffled feathers, Vincent made the same attempt with Avoie Vigneron on August 24. She was constantly in tears and fired off one complaining letter after the other, both to Vincent and to M. Portail. She also began feverishly mak-ing novenas but abandoned that project when, she decided, the more she prayed, the less she obtained. She obstinately refused to write to Louise, blaming her—as Anne had done—for all her troubles and angrily reject-ing her gentle urging to forget self in the pursuit of virtue. In light of all this, Vincent's restraint and kindness in dealing with her was admirable and was eventually to have its effect.

Queen Anne of Austria had commissioned Vincent's priests to preach a mission at Metz in Lorraine, where—according to his judgment—"to tell the truth the people are not bad but the poor souls have a certain grossness of mind in regard to divine things which they have contracted from associating with the Huguenots and Jews who dwell in that city." It was hardly an ecumenical age!

Pleased with the success of the mission, the Queen asked Vincent: "What shall we do for Metz?"—she meant in the way of establishing piety on a permanent basis and alleviating the poverty of the people, who had been greatly reduced in circumstances by the wars. She answered her own question by requesting a permanent house of the Daughters of Charity there. Madeleine Raportebled, Marie Papillon, Marguerite Rechaut and a Sister Barbe were chosen to establish it.

Vincent bade them goodbye on August 26, telling them: "You are going . . . to make known to all, to Catholics, to heretics and Jews, the goodness of God, because when they see that our good God takes such an interest in His creatures as to establish a Company of persons who devote themselves to the service of the poor—which is not to be found in their religions—they will be compelled to confess that God is a kind Father." He warned that "the hardness of mind" of the citizens "has caused pity to be almost banished from the city" and that "the vice of avarice . . . has a strong hold there. I say this to our shame: even priests lend out money at interest, not directly, like the rest of the people, but through others, so that in this way they may hide their avariciousness." But the sight of the Sisters' example, he assured them, would have a good effect in combating this vice, "for when the people see women working, as Daughters of Charity should work, for their neighbor, without hoping or seeking for any other recompense than God, they will see how blind they are to attach so much importance to the goods of this world."

He left them with the injunction to be always humble. "If people ask you where you are going, don't say that the Queen has sent you. No, that would be contrary to humility." Louise was even more fearful of the fuss being made over them. The Premier Président de Metz had arranged to meet them outside the town and to lodge them in his own house the first night. Couldn't they decline this hospitality from so great a gentleman, Louise asked? Vincent thought not, because the Président would be offended. But, she persisted, would they have to eat at his table "even if they arrived late and should go to bed?" In that case Vincent thought they might excuse themselves, "giving as the reason that it is not customary for poor girls to be present at the table of the great."

The demand for Sisters continued. Vincent told M. de Beaumont at Richelieu that they were "asking for them on all sides. Four prelates and several towns have made us requests which we cannot honor." And Louise wrote Geneviève Doinel at Chantilly that "I think I am more upset than you that we cannot send you a Sister as soon as we both would like. We owe more than ten to different places—yours included." She was indeed especially anxious to supply a Sister for Chantilly because no one there could read and she was very unhappy with outsiders reading her letters to the Sisters.

Although she had been relatively free of worry about her son since his marriage, she now came to realize that she had inherited the problems of her in-laws. "I don't know whether my son has spoken to you about Champlan [where her daughter-in-law's family lived]," she wrote Vincent on September 19, "but Monsieur his brother-in-law told me he was going to speak with you about it and wants me to go there on fairly important family business having to do with a cooling of friendship between my daughter and her de la Prontière and Lestang cousins—which could cause trouble if it continues . . ." Vincent thought "it would do good to make this little trip to bind the hearts of the family together again and more tightly." So the poor, sick old lady had to traipse off to Champlan to make peace. In a subsequent note Louise informed Vincent that she had better stop to see "Madame de Marillac the Carmelite," whose convent was quite near Champlan, because the family had been offended when she had failed to stop on a former journey.

There was another act of charity to be done. A religious in Paris had fled her convent and needed advice and, Louise told Vincent, if one of his priests was not available, she was prepared to go to the distraught woman herself. In either case the poor thing was not left desolate. In fact, Louise was able to inform her friends a couple of weeks later that she had made a retreat and had returned to her convent.

Louise was anxious for news from Calais. When she had heard nothing by October 7, she wrote to Henriette Gesseaume. She was especially concerned about the Sisters who had survived the plague. "If Sister Claude's stomach flux continues," she instructed Henriette, "make her a large drink of chicory roots with a little barberry thorn . . . It is a prompt remedy but," she admitted, "it is hard to drink unless accompanied by a remembrance of Our Lord's drink on the Cross."

The Duchesse de Ventadour returned to Paris in October and Louise was happy to learn that, despite the uncertain start, things were going well at Ussel. She wrote to commiserate with them in the trouble they were having getting used to the native food, which centered around a kind of greasy soup, but she felt constrained to caution Sister Avoie that "when you sing together to divert yourselves, be careful that no one can hear you outside . . ."

Word had reached Paris that "it has pleased God to dispose of M. Ozenne, superior of our poor family in Poland," Vincent informed M. Cabel at Sedan. "A violent fever snatched him from earth to heaven on the eve of the Assumption . . . He was very candid, amiable and exemplary, and God is now his reward." It was a heavy blow for the priests and Sisters on the Polish mission, who had already suffered so much.

The time had finally come to send the Sisters so long requested, nay demanded, by Vincent's friend Alain de Solminihac, Bishop of Cahors. Adrienne Plouvier and Louise Boucher were selected for this farthermost mission within the boundaries of France. Sending them off on November 4, Vincent recalled rather ruefully: "I think it is four years since Monseigneur de Cahors first urged me so strongly to send him Sisters that he grew quite vexed with me because Mademoiselle Le Gras had no way of satisfying his wishes." Monseigneur was indeed a testy character and Vincent warned the Sisters "that you may well stand in need of mortification if Monseigneur de Cahors doesn't think you are doing your duty well . . . so that you may humbly receive his reproof's and corrections because the great austerity with which he treats himself may render him a little severe." That this was an understatement is evident from the added Gascon witticism: "Monseigneur is a man who would make it a matter of conscience to pay a compliment!"

With all this, Monseigneur was "looked on as a saint in his own country." The regard of his countrymen was well deserved, for Pope Pius XI declared him "Venerable" in 1927. He was perhaps typical of his province. As Vincent further warned the Sisters, they would have need of great humility "to combat the demon of this country, which is pride. The demon who rules over this countryside is a demon of pride, wrath, passion and self-sufficiency . . . You will see persons there who are almost always in a rage, who fly into a passion on the slightest occasion, and you must combat this vice by your meekness. Moreover, the people are self-sufficient and love to talk at great length."

The mission was another landmark for the Company because it was the Sisters' first orphanage for older children. Vincent hailed it as "one of the greatest works you have yet undertaken. You have Sisters in parishes and in the hospitals in Paris, in the home for convicts, in the foundling hospital, but so far you have had no work like this."

On November 11 Louise invited Geneviève Doinel to Paris for a change of air. She had indeed been ill but there was a further reason: the house at Chantilly was still in financial straits and Louise wanted to discuss the matter. She thought the situation "very strange" because, as she put it delicately, "I knew that they have the means of paying us." The patroness of the mission was, of course, the Queen herself. It was Louise's intention to straighten the matter out once for all by going with Geneviève to Mme Fouquet, mother of the superintendent of finances.

She was sending Sister Etiennette on a visitation of the house at Angers and asked Vincent to instruct her thoroughly in "making herself easy to approach by the Sisters who wish to speak with her, in keeping secret everything communicated to her, in preventing insofar as she can the softnesses of mind and body which seek only satisfactions, in holding the line in regard to exactitude of rule without harming the service of the poor, in being pleasant . . . and"—she concluded—"all the rest which you know better than I who do nothing worthwhile." He gave Etiennette her instructions at the Sisters' conference the next day.

On the eve of the feast of the Immaculate Conception, Louise was moved interiorly—how intensely was evident in the frequent underscoring of her words—to witness to Vincent "in the name of the whole *Company of our Sisters* that we deem ourselves very happy to *have you place us tomorrow on the holy altar* under the protection of the Blessed Virgin, and *to beg Your Charity* to obtain for us the grace *ever to be able to recognize her as our only Mother* since her Son has *never permitted up to the present* anyone else to usurp this title in an official act."

Vincent responded by giving the Sisters a feast-day conference on the Rosary. Pointing out that it was made up of Paters and Aves, prayers composed by Our divine Lord and the Holy Spirit through the instrumentality of Our Lady and St. Elizabeth, and that it was highly indulgenced, he concluded: "It is your breviary. Hence you should take great care to say your Rosary. Now as all priests should recite their office in accordance with the intention of the Church, so you, too, should take great care to recite your Rosary in accordance with the intention of the Company that God may sanctify it and bless its work and all its labors for the service of the neighbor. Priests do not undertake to say any prayers which might prove prejudicial to their obligation to read the office, and so you, too, should not undertake to say any prayers which might deprive you of the time needed for saying your Rosary . . . Resolve, then, never to fail to say it."

Peace had returned to Poland and Vincent wrote on December 13 to assure M. Desdames, who had assumed the direction of the Sisters upon the death of M. Ozenne, that he would send two more Sisters as soon as winter was over. Sister Françoise and Sister Madeleine had had a falling out and Desdames was minded to send Françoise home, but Vincent would not allow it because "of the bad noise her return would make, the personal danger [of the trip], the effect on the others, the expense of the journey, the difficulty of replacing her and so many other difficulties. Do what I have asked you to—separate them. Employ Sister Françoise in a hospital or in some other work which prevents frequent communication with Sister Madeleine."

Vincent's legs were deteriorating badly and kept him confined to his room nearly all the time now. Louise was extremely worried and showed it in her usual way by sending him, a few days before Christmas, more detailed prescriptions for obtaining relief. He thanked her and assured her he would be very faithful in following them. She responded with another remedy especially prepared for him by the Sisters but wrote in distress on Christmas Day that "although our remedy was ready by ten o'clock, I forgot it entirely until noon." She was even more deeply distressed at being deprived of his spiritual direction and bewailed "my indifference to my interior state and everything which pertains to the service of God and my salvation . . ."

She was, for that matter, as sick or sicker than he, and her misery was increased by the shocking news that Barbe Angiboust was gravely ill and close to death. Vincent was also deeply grieved but, he told Louise, he saw no point in sending a Sister to Châteaudun as they had done in similar cases because, whether Barbe lived or died, the crisis of her illness would have been passed by the time the Sister got there.

Barbe died on December 27 in the Hôtel-Dieu at Châteaudun. She was fifty-four. All of Châteaudun went into mourning and, her companion Sister Anne Bocheron reported, "the people came in crowds the whole day long to sprinkle holy water on her remains, and she looked so lovely that some persons asked me if she had been painted. All the gentlemen and the members of the Board were present at her funeral, together with a great crowd of people, and they even touched her corpse with their rosary beads."

Barbe had indeed been a great woman and a great Daughter of Charity. When a conference was devoted to her virtues on the following April 27, those who had lived with her attested eloquently and in detail to her exact observance of the Rule, her lack of human respect, her humility, her poverty, her love of her Sisters and her gay cheerfulness with them, and her complete dedication to the poor. She was an incomparable loss to the Company and to Louise herself, who requested a special high Mass for her, since she was "one of the oldest in the Company and very faithful to her vocation." This loss was one of the chief reasons for Louise's writing to Vincent in a letter she began on the last day of the year 1658 and had not the strength to finish until the next day: "I begin the year very feebly and sorrowfully in mind and body."

XVIII

"Things Still to Be Done"

The memory of Barbe Angiboust lay like a weight on Louise's heart as she began her own last full year of life. "It has pleased God to afflict us," she wrote with simple sadness to Nicole Haran at Nantes and bade her hold Barbe up as a model to the Sisters "to animate them for the conquest of a blessed eternity." She dwelt on Barbe's last hours for Marie Donion at Brienne: "Her devotion throughout the whole of her illness, the conformity of her will to God's will, her patience as she saw herself dying at the feet of Jesus Crucified . . ." There was a pride in her words as she told Laurence Dubois at Bernay that God had "honored [Barbe] with the highest witness of the true Christian and servant of God" in her agony.

Her personal sense of loss was laid bare in her reminder to Nicole Haran that "we needn't always feel joy and consolation in order to please God, for the Son of God accomplished the work of saving everyone through sorrows and griefs."

Unfortunately, it was not always her dead daughters who brought her "sorrows and griefs": those left behind provided their share. Far from being soothed by Vincent's gentle correction, Anne Hardemont and Avoie Vigneron had grown increasingly insolent toward her. She suffered the insolence in silence, although it broke her heart. Vincent, however, rebuked them sharply, all gentleness dissipated by his indignation at the insults offered this holy mother he so deeply revered and loved. He told Avoie acidly.

> You are a little too handy with your advice, and you have on occasion lost the respect you owe Mademoiselle. I know very well that your heart has not failed in its respect but, in your attempt to justify yourself over some little reproach she made you, your words have been too bold. *Mon Dieu*, Sister! If you have no reverence and submission for your superiors, for whom will you have them? She has not complained, but I must speak

to you in this way so that you will treat her as your good mother who esteems and cherishes you.

He was much more severe with Anne as "one of the oldest in the Company whom Providence has led to Limousin to perform works of mercy, and who no sooner arrives in the place when she wants to return out of sheer imagination and cries without ceasing because they leave her there . . . !"

What was worse, not content with complaining to her superiors, he went on, she had to go weeping to outsiders and now "without doubt the whole province knows it!" Mademoiselle, he told her plainly, "is your mother who has a right to give you the instructions she deems proper and who has received graces from God to do so. And now you are pouting so that, in your own words, you don't wish to write to her. Be careful, Sister! That is the behavior of a mutinous and proud spirit . . . !"

The letter had its effect, because Anne wrote humbly the following month to ask whether she should go to nurse a lady of quality who was ill. Vincent told her no, while praising her "return to doing nothing without our permission." He promised her that God would now give her "peace and contentment" at last.

There were attacks from other quarters, too, but as these were leveled at the Company, Louise would not be silent but bridled to its defense. "Certain delicate souls in the Company have a repugnance for this word *Confraternity* and would prefer *Society* or *Community*," she wrote scornfully to Vincent. "I take the liberty to insist that this word is essential to us and can aid stability greatly, so that nothing will be changed, and it signifies our secularity; also, that Providence has added *Society* and *Company* to teach us that we ought to live regularly by observing the rules we received at the establishment of our Confraternity in the way they have been explained to us."

All these trials were part of a final purification to which God was subjecting her soul. On February 1 she cried out to Vincent: "If God did not render me insensible by my very sorrow at seeing myself forsaken, I would suffer great pain. What affects me is not to have understanding enough to make use of it according to God's plan, or the means of utilizing the privation I have perhaps merited!" She referred specifically to the separation that both their illnesses enforced but also to a deeper abandonment of which the separation was but a symbol. Vincent was restored to her toward the end of that month when his legs improved enough for him to go out of doors again.

No matter her personal trials, she never ceased giving herself completely to her daughters. On February 23 she asked Sister Jeanne de la Croix to watch with special care over Sister Sulpice, "whom I know to be a good child, but because she is of a very gay and naïve temperament you must keep an eye on her in that dangerous place [Châteaudun] . . . I know very well that all her intentions are good, even so far as her recreations are concerned, but the world doesn't take them that way. I especially ask that if you assign her to cooking she not be left alone in the bakehouse or in places that can be entered from outside."

She regretted that the Sisters at Roche-Guyon could not make their retreat, "but this is the true harvest time for the little pupils when they can be instructed and prepared well to spend the holy season of Lent devoutly—the which will dispose them to make their Easter duty well, especially those who will be making their first Communion. I also ask you—if your duties permit—to teach the big girls on feasts and Sundays and to encourage them to visit you, for they sometimes have as much need of instruction as the little ones—but it must be given tactfully and sweetly without making them ashamed of their ignorance . . ."

On March 11 she admonished Marie Donion at Brienne not to deprive herself "of what is necessary for nourishment. You frightened Sister Geneviève seeing you so thin, but she doesn't realize that it's natural with you. Nevertheless, be careful not to live in want. Borrow money freely when you need it. I well know that you will not abuse it."

She expressed her own astonishment that Nicole Georgette should be surprised "at all the slanders they make up against us, for we are Christians, and further, Daughters of Charity . . ." She was "saddened" to learn that Nicole had quarreled with "Monsieur le curé, who is a man of holy life, and so learned, and to whom we are deeply obligated because of his charity and the good will he has always shown our Sisters."

She was disappointed when illness prevented her from attending Vincent's Mass on her favorite feast of the Annunciation, but said simply, "I did not deserve it." She asked, at least, "to recommend my children to you." Vincent replied in kind. He was "ashamed" that his own illness had "put him in the way of not thanking Mademoiselle Le Gras for all the nice things she does for me." (His weakness forced him to write his most intimate thoughts through a secretary.) "I do so now with full appreciation and beg God to be her reward." He knew she would be pleased that he was "better, thanks to God's grace and your help"—he fell naturally into the more personal pronoun. He preferred to think, he continued, that his improvement was due not so much to the doctor's treatment as to Louise's "prayers and the novena her kindness has made for me. Charity never seems so estimable as when she performs it. God be praised for manifesting Himself so beautifully in the said demoiselle, whom I thank with all my heart once again!"

Word came in August that Queen Marie-Louise de Gonzague had provided the Sisters with a large house in Warsaw for the instruction of poor girls. Vincent wrote on the twenty-sixth to thank her, telling her that "Mademoiselle Le Gras and I have been very touched, as have most of the daughters of this Company who assembled two days ago for a conference I gave . . ." This house became the motherhouse of the Polish province and served as such for more than two hundred years. The conference completed the authentic commentary on the Rule, that precious and unique heritage for which the Daughters of Charity must thank their good mother, who, knowing its incomparable value, literally harried the poor, sick old man until it was done.

François Fouquet, Archbishop of Narbonne—and brother of the superintendent of finances and son of Vincent's and Louise's great friend the Baronne de Maupeau—had been requesting Sisters at least since 1656 when he was Bishop of Agde. It had been decided at last—at the council meeting of April 25, 1659—to grant his request. The Sisters were chosen and prepared for their departure in early September. On September 7 Louise sent an agitated note to Vincent recommending that they add Sister Marie-Marthe Trumeau to the band. "One of our Sisters has reminded me that none of the Sisters named—with the exception of Sister Carcireux—is a worker," she explained. "It is a fact that the temperament of the others is extremely sluggish and I am afraid that they will fail to do the work, and that will raise a storm! Further, because of the way things are going at Cahors, I think it may be necessary to send Sister Carcireux there to keep Monseigneur happy." She apologized for her oversight, which, she said, was caused by "my thinking only of the great need." It is not surprising that, at sixty-eight and in her constant state of exhaustion, her powers should show signs of failing.

Marie-Marthe Trumeau was finally decided upon for Cahors, and Françoise Carcireux, Anne Denoual and Marie Chesse for Narbonne. This establishment differed from others in that, as Vincent admitted to the Sisters in his farewell instruction, "I cannot tell you what you are going to do because I do not know, nor, I think, does this good Archbishop, although I am certain that you are going for the glory of God and the service of your neighbor. He may, perhaps, establish a hospital and I also think He will have a Confraternity of Charity established in the city . . ." In her parting words Louise reminded them, if a hospital was decided on, "not to forget to provide for the bashful poor who would receive no comfort because they would never go near the hospital, however they tried to force them, and therefore the establishment of the Charity is absolutely necessary."

As usual, Vincent forearmed them with his knowledge of the citizens of Narbonne: "The people there are clever and hard to please. You must expect to be laughed at. They are good, but all their inclinations tend to what is evil. The vice of impurity is, above all others, prevalent there. And therefore, my dear Daughters, you must use great precautions by your modesty, reserved language and refusal to listen to any impropriety." And he proceeded to give them a sound lesson in the psychology of evil-minded men: "Oh, how dangerous it is to listen to men! Remember I have often told you that their conversation at first is good and devout, but that is to ensnare you. Be very much on your guard. Never remain alone with them. Never let them see that you listen to them with pleasure . . . and never give them reason to think that you esteem or like them, because where there is esteem there is a first step toward, or a snare for, affection."

On the last day of the previous December Louise, conscious of her fast-failing strength, has spoken urgently to Vincent "of things still to be done to secure the spiritual stability of the Company" and offered to send him "a memorandum I have drawn up—for which I ought to blush for shame." She had misplaced the memorandum in the intervening months and now she drew up another, begging him "not to let anyone see it for fear they will make fun of it."

Louise's thoughts were still on Barbe Angiboust in November. Time had dulled her sorrow, so that when two Sisters who had been with Barbe when she died visited the motherhouse, Louise never tired of hearing them retail Barbe's virtues, and repeated what they said in the letters she wrote to distant missions. It was probably her doing that Vincent had the Sisters stay on until the next conference, scheduled for November 11, so that all the Parisian Sisters might have the edification of hearing of Barbe's holy life and death from eyewitnesses. Thus the faithful Barbe was accorded an honor granted only to one other—Louise herself—two conferences on her holy life.

M. Portail was aging fast now and was as regularly ill as Vincent and Louise. He had retired to a little hermitage at the end of the garden at Saint-Lazare for rest and quiet and to make his soul. Louise wrote to him there on November 29 about the Rule, which, despite her age and infirmities, she was constantly polishing as practice pointed up its strengths and weaknesses. She was especially apprehensive lest a worldly softness encroach upon the Company's dedication to poverty and mortification. She now felt, she told Portail, that

> the thirteenth article needs more check than rein; for if the minute a Sister falls ill a chicken or some veal must go into the pot—and they be waited on in their beds like ladies . . . ! Perhaps you will be as amazed as I was to learn that one of our Sisters made, or had made, a dressing gown and that her sister who had been ill wore it yesterday when she got up! This was at Saint-Médéric. Such a thing is very nice indeed—but it is fine for demoiselles and *bourgeoises* of Paris—which we are not! And, Monsieur, it will have many imitators.

She finished with the practical request that when he transcribed the rules again he use "heavier paper to give the [book] weight and substance, and if it were covered with parchment it would stand up better." As the feast of the Immaculate Conception approached, her thoughts turned as they ever did to Mary as the guardian of chastity in the Company and she requested Vincent "to ask pardon of Our Lord—out of love of His choice of His most blessed Mother—for all the interior and exterior failings against purity, and [to beg] that true purity His mercy wishes it to have." And this purest of souls added: "As I am the most at fault, don't I need the strongest intercession?"

Louise continued to see little of Vincent, as she told Mathurine Guérin at La Fère, "because his infirmities and never-ending business, added to the inclement weather, keep him to his room." It was a grievous separation for her. She could not forbear mentioning it with affectionate sadness, when she wrote on Christmas Eve, to remind him that the next day was

> the day when Mass is said for the entire Company's needs and intentions, *which Your Charity knows. Permit me* to say, my Most Honored Father, that my incapability of doing anything good *prevents me from having anything* worthwhile to offer Our Lord *beyond my poor renewal* [of

vows]—except the privation of the only consolation *His goodness has given me* for thirty-five years and which I accept for love of Him *in the manner His Providence* ordains, hoping from His goodness *and from your kindness the same assistance* by interior voice. I ask it *through love of the union of the Son of God to human nature*—without, however, losing hope of the honor of seeing you when it can be done without detriment to the little health God gives you.

Friendship enables heart to speak to heart, but the holy friendship of these great souls had so welded their hearts in a mystical union that she could actually ask him, though absent, to direct her by interior voice! The calm request opens up wondrous possibilities and speculations as to what passed between these two holy, house-bound old people united heart to heart and the two hearts in God—as Vincent had once expressed their relationship and as the relationship of François de Sales and Mme de Chantal had been shown him in vision.

Louise's weakness was so great that during the Christmas season she was able to visit the community's Christmas crib only on her way back to her room from Mass. Geneviève Doinel and Marie-Marthe at Chantilly had asked her "to look for them" at the crèche, where they would be in spirit. She assured them when she wrote on December 28 that she "believed most lovingly" that they were there, "united with our Sisters." And she described for them where the crèche had been set up that year —"in the little grotto at the feet of Jesus Crucified in a large niche which seems to us to represent Bethlehem better than in former years."

On December 30 she sent a letter of encouragement and counsel to Françoise Carcireux, whose duties as Sister Servant were made especially difficult by the great distance between Narbonne and Paris. Yet Louise gave her the wise and homely advice she would give the Sister Servant in the next parish. One word of advice was particularly memorable. "It seems to me that I should not be speaking of this to you," she wrote apologetically, "but my own inability to do anything has made me see very clearly the difference between a Sister Servant who says, 'Let us do,' and one who is content to say, 'Do,' and doesn't put her own hand to the work. The first one puts herself on an equal plane with her Sisters and the second isolates herself from her peers and from work and billets them like soldiers under her authority." The force of Louise's lesson—a model for the doctrine of authority taught by Vatican Council II—is evident in its implementation by Sister Servants of the Daughters of Charity to this day.

The year of Louise's completion of her work and summons to glory began as usual. There was to be no retirement for her, no laying down of the burden by her tired hands and racked body. She would do everything she was supposed to do as well as she could until God said "Enough."

Her first letter of that year of 1660—written on January 3 to Sister Jeanne de la Croix at Châteaudun—was really only a note apologizing for the long time since her last letter, due to the press of business and the enervating effect of illness, and assuring Jeanne that "neither my heart nor my will has failed or will ever fail with God's help to remember and love you, since we are so intimately united in the love of our dear Jesus."

On January 4 she asked Vincent "to allow me to greet Your Charity very humbly in this New Year and to request in this way your holy blessing to help me be faithful to God so long as it pleases His goodness to leave me on earth." She enclosed a New Year's present which was most fitting in view of the suffering and death the year would bring them both—a picture of "Jesus crowned with thorns. My one thought is that nothing will do more to sweeten your all-encompassing suffering than this model . . ." She was anxious to have a detailed account of his condition and was ready with a new remedy which was "very good for babies and old people"—she was not one to ignore the fact that they were both reduced to that fragile state that marks the beginning and the end of human life. She finished by reassuring him that "Our Lord has put me in the state of bearing everything peacefully enough."

The extent of her deterioration was evident in a letter she wrote to Mathurine Guérin at La Fère: she repeated herself and left out parts of sentences, which had to be supplied by the context. It was probably a question of failing eyesight, added to the general weakness which had become habitual, for she begged Mathurine to "excuse my mistakes; you know that I can't reread my letters." It was not senility, because she continued to address herself to current business: the drawing up of a suggested paragraph for a will in which Mme de Glou was making provision for the works of the Company; instructions to Marguerite Chétif concerning the use of a new book, La Paroissienne Charitable, by the Curé de Saint-Laurent; the sending of a copy of the Rule and a list of the Sisters' pious practices to Abbé de Vaux.

She continued her efforts to impart a vigor to the Company that would ensure its permanence after she and Vincent were gone. She was uneasy, she confessed to him, about certain signs that could lead to its decay: "First of all, I have noticed that the ladies of several parishes are beginning to be suspicious of [the Sisters], although I am fairly certain that no one has given them cause—unless it be some who, out of their eagerness to solace the poor, accept the alms for distribution from the ladies without feeling obliged to consult the officers, which offends them." She recognized, of course, that these were human foibles that would not ordinarily bring permanent harm to the work.

What worried her much more deeply was the possibility of a change in the nature of the Company. She insisted upon

> the necessity of rules forever obliging to the poor, simple, and humble life, lest the adoption of a more expensive way of life and of practices tending toward public acceptance and partial cloister should set off a novel search for the means to subsist in such fashion—since it would be a very interior community but not concerned with action—and such houses would be acquired as would inhibit going out and poor attire. It is a fact that certain ones are murmuring among themselves that this cap, this title of Sister, rather than commanding respect invite contempt. I know not only Daughters of Charity but others obliged to carry out God's design through the spiritual and corporal service of the sick poor who are greatly disposed to this [other] manner of life so dangerous to the continuation of God's work—the which, my Most Honored Father, your goodness has most firmly sustained against all opposition.

In a letter written on February 7 to M. de la Fosse at Troyes, Vincent confirmed Louise's concept of the nature of the Company and stated quite clearly his priests' responsibility toward it. After stating his own Congregation's dedication to "the corporal and spiritual ministry to poor people," he continued:

> That being established and the Daughters of Charity entering into the disposition of Providence as a means God gives us of doing by their hands what we could not do by our own—through the corporal assistance of the sick poor and the supplying by their mouths of some word of instruction and encouragement toward salvation—we have, then, the obligation of helping them toward their own progress in virtue in order that they may acquit themselves well in their charitable works.
>
> There is this difference between them and religious, that religious have for their end their own perfection while these Daughters are used just like us for the salvation and comfort of the neighbor. And if I say *with us* I say nothing contrary to the Gospel but most comfortable to the practice of the primitive Church since Our Lord looked after certain women

who followed Him and we find in the *Canon of the Apostles* that women were charged with the sustenance of the faithful and were connected with the Apostolic ministries.

He thus unequivocally stated the vision of Louise and himself of the Company as an *aggiornamento,* a return to the fountainhead of early Christianity.

On February 4 Louise's last agony began. The wasting away of the past year had left her whole body vulnerable to any attack. On that fateful morning her left arm swelled suddenly, with what seems to have been a gangrenous infection: the shrunken tissues and collapsed veins could no longer support life. Her temperature shot up alarmingly and the Curé de Saint-Laurent, Nicolas de Lestocq, was hastily summoned. There was much running about in the house, with other messengers despatched to Michel and his family and to the Sisters in the neighboring parishes.

When M. le curé arrived, everyone crowded into the sickroom to assist at the Last Rites. Louise herself felt the solemnity of the moment more deeply than any. Michel had been the first charge God had given her, and after she had been prepared for judgment and heaven, she called him first to her bedside along with his wife and little girl, who was now nine years old. "I pray the Father, Son and Holy Spirit, by the power God has given fathers and mothers to bless their children, to bless you, detach you from all earthly things and unite you to Himself," she murmured lovingly and dismissed them with the injunction "to live like good Christians." Her beloved religious daughters had their blessing next and the injunction to love their vocation and their masters the poor.

When she lasted through this first day and the next, it became obvious that she was going to die slowly and the house went back to its accustomed order as it began the long deathwatch. Louise's agony was the first of the triple passions that were to deprive the Company in a matter of months of its director, its mother and its father.

Two days later, on February 6, M. Portail had a dangerous weak spell in his little hermitage in the garden of Saint-Lazare. His release came much more rapidly than Louise's. Vincent detailed his last illness and death for M. Desdames in Poland in a letter of March 5: "He died on Saturday the 14th of the month, the ninth [day] of his illness, which began with a spell of weakness that changed to continual fever and other complications. He preserved a clear mind and speech. He had always been afraid of death but, seeing its approach, he met it with peace and resignation and told me several times when I visited him that no trace of his fear remained. He died as he lived, in the good use of suffering, the practice of virtue, the desire of honoring God and of finishing his days like Our Lord in the accomplishment of His will."

He confessed to M. Desdames that this loss of his first co-worker was a sore blow to his heart, which was aggravated by Louise's illness, of which he "didn't dare hope" for a favorable outcome.

His hopes had brightened by March 3, however, when he told Mathurine Guérin that Louise was "better. Her chief trouble has been a massive inflammation of the left arm on which it has been necessary to make three incisions, the last one yesterday. She suffers greatly, as you can imagine, and while she has no more fever she is not for all that out of danger because of her age and weakness. They are doing everything they can to save her—but that is up to God who, having preserved her for twenty years against all human odds, will preserve her still if it is for His glory."

Louise's improvement can be ascribed to the Sisters' simple, pious faith. The abatement of the swelling and consequent drop in temperature had followed the application of two relics: a stole St. Charles Borromeo had worn, and a tiny portion of the heart of St. François de Sales.

But the gangrene was all through her and on the ninth she suffered another relapse, which was the prelude to death. On the twelfth she sent a Sister to ask M. le curé to bring her Holy Communion, which, strangely enough, she had not received since her first attack on February 4. The only valid explanation seems to be that her physical condition would not permit it. When the Sister returned with the welcome news that the curé would come in the morning, she cried out in joy and spent the rest of the day preparing herself. The next day the Sisters knelt around her bed to assist at her second Viaticum, and when she had received her Lord, M. de Lestocq urged her to bless her daughters once more. Looking on them fondly, she said:

> My dear Sisters, I never cease asking God's blessing on you and praying Him to give you the grace of perseverance in your vocation that you may serve Him in any way He wishes. Take great pains to serve the poor,

and especially to live together in great union and cordiality, loving one another in imitation of the union and life of Our Lord. And beg the Blessed Virgin fervently to be your only Mother.

It was her official farewell, but it said nothing new. When she added that if she lived to be a hundred she would say the same things, she only confirmed what she had told them over and over for twenty-six years.

She had accepted the torments of the last month with a peace that was no surprise to anyone who knew her, saying in her matter-of-fact way that "it was quite reasonable for evil to dwell where sin abounds," that "God was exercising His justice" upon her and that "where He exercises justice, He exercises mercy."

Her one deep regret was that Vincent, dying himself, had not been able to come to her and now, seeing death so near, she indulged herself to the extent of sending to ask a farewell word in his own hand. In reply he sent one of his priests with the verbal message that she was going before him and that he hoped to see her in heaven.

This action has evoked much nonsense about its being an act of heroic and total renunciation of human affection—even Gobillon permits himself this pious reflection—and some have unfairly condemned Vincent for his seeming harshness and lack of feeling. The facts of the case are open to much more simple and normal interpretations, all of them plausible taken singly or together. In the first place, Vincent was mortally tired and there should be nothing surprising about a seventy-nine-year-old man in his weakened condition being literally unable to lift his hand, let alone write a message, on a given day. Second, there can be no doubt of his personal grief over the imminent separation from the person he loved most dearly in the world, and it is quite conceivable, indeed quite in keeping with his warm, vivid temperament, that he might be afraid to trust his emotions once he took pen in hand. Third, and perhaps closest to the truth, who can say what volumes were unspoken in that simple message passed between persons who understood each other's slightest glance? Louise accepted the message with complete tranquillity: no one has recorded that the least shadow of regret crossed her face.

Word spread quickly that the end was near. All day Saturday and Sunday Louise's family and friends, the first ladies of Paris as well as the least, flocked to her sickroom. The Duchesse de Ventadour moved into the house determined to stay with her friend to the end. All this hubbub depleted completely the flicker of strength left in Louise, as well as distracting her from the great act of dying. On Monday the fifteenth, at six o'clock in the morning, she asked her daughters and the Duchesse to draw her bed curtains and leave her in peace, promising to call them when her hour had come. Only the priest of the Mission Vincent had sent in his place remained in the room.

At the priest's direction Louise prayed in the language of Job: "Have mercy on me, for the hand of the Lord has touched me"—and of David: "Look upon me and have pity on me because I am alone and miserable." At one point the pain became unbearable and she cried out: "Take me!" Gently, the priest held the cross before her eyes and asked if Jesus had asked to be taken. "Oh no, He stayed," she replied meekly. "So will I, until my Lord comes in search of me." And once, seized with momentary fright, she moaned: "O my God! I must appear before my judge!" When the priest consoled her with the words of the Psalm: "I have raised my soul to You, O my God! I trust You"—she finished the verse in peace: "I will not be ashamed, for I do not stand confounded in my hope."

At eleven o'clock she gave the signal for the curtains to be drawn back and the Sisters summoned. The final agony lasted half an hour, during which she lay quiet, her eyes fixed on heaven, while the murmur of the prayers for the dying rose around her. At the priest's request she gave her daughters a final blessing. As the moment of death approached, he imparted to her the apostolic blessing she had received from Pope Innocent X in 1647. She signed to them once more to close her bed curtains, and fifteen minutes later, alone with God, she just stopped breathing.

Her body lay in state there in her bedroom the remainder of that day and all day Tuesday to accommodate the throngs that converged on the house from every corner of Paris. She was buried on Wednesday, March 17, in the Chapel of the Visitation in the Sisters' parish church of Saint-Laurent, on the spot which had been her favorite place of devotion. Vincent had promised her that she would be buried in the cemetery next to the church of Saint-Lazare, but he now gave into the wishes of the curé, who insisted that she be buried in her parish church. Actually, it was more fitting, because all her daughters who had died since the new motherhouse had been opened were buried in the cemetery alongside the church. Her wish that her funeral cost no more than theirs, however, was scrupulously respected, as was her other request that a cross with the words *Spes Unica* mark her grave. A similar cross was placed on the outside wall of the chapel, facing her daughters' graves as a sign of their union.

Vincent ordered a solemn requiem to be celebrated for her several days later in the church of Saint-Lazare. Besides the priests of the Mission and the Daughters of Charity, it was attended by the ordinands on retreat in preparation for priesthood. It was an especially happy tribute, because she had been accustomed to offer her prayers and Communions for the ordinands during the days of their priesthood retreats and had enjoined the same practice on her daughters in her will.

Not long after Louise's burial a strange phenomenon began to be noticed at her tomb. At first it was talked about in awed whispers and then proclaimed throughout Paris: a mist was frequently seen to rise from the tomb, accompanied by the delicate but unmistakable odor of violets and irises. Gobillon himself, who was to succeed de Lestocq as curé of the parish, attests to it as an eyewitness. He adds further that he made an exhaustive personal investigation before coming to the conclusion that it could not be explained by natural causes. The most touching and beautiful aspect of it was that the fragrance clung to the Sisters' clothes and was carried into the confraternity halls and the hospital wards where the patients inhaled it with joy.

SOURCES

The sources are keyed by page and line numbers, the latter in parentheses.

CHAPTER I

Page
3. (28) Baunard, pp. 3–4.
4. (1) Louis Brochard, *Saint-Gervais*, p. 397. (12) Sister Geoffre, *Parisien. Beatificationis et Canonizationis Servae Dei Ludovicae de Marillac etc.*, Positio Super Introductionis Causae. (17) Jean Guy, *Sainte Louise de Marillac*, p. 17. (18) AN, "Minutier Central," Etude LXVIII, registre 98. (23) Jean Guy, *op. cit.*, p. 19. (33) Jean Calvet, *Louise de Marillac*, p. 15. It is interesting to note that, while Calvet's demonstration of Louise's illegitimacy in 1958 caused something of a sensation, Canon Brochard's reference to her birth in his *Saint-Gervais* (p. 397) in 1938—". . . Louise, fille naturelle de . . . Louis"— passed unnoticed.
5. (14) Calvet, pp. 15–16. (17) *Ibid.*, p. 16. (23) AN, *ibid.* (30) Calvet, p. 17. (32) *Parisien. Beatificationis etc.*, *ibid.*, "Declaratio R. D. Antonii Fiat, Sup. Gen. Congreg. Missionis circa actum baptismatis Servae Dei." (36) *Ibid.*
6. (7) Carl J. Friedrich, *The Age of the Baroque*, p. 46.
7. (3) It would appear that the family order of births was as follows: Charles (n.d.), Marie (n.d., possibly Aug. 28, 1560), Louis (1561 or 1562), Michel (Oct. 9, 1563). Eduoard Everart, in his *Michel de Marillac, sa vie, ses oeuvres*, sets Oct. 9, 1563, as the date of Michel's birth (p. 1), but changes his opinion in the Appendix (p. 197). However, Brochard's testimony, in his *Saint-Gervais* (p. 397), that Michel was baptized on Oct. 12, 1563, would make Everart's first choice the right one. (5) Everart, *op. cit.*, p. 4. (17) "Marlhac est la 'vraye et ancienne orthographe' du nom patrimonial"—*ibid.*, p. 1, footnote 1. (18) Nicolas Lefèvre de Lezeau, *Histoire de la vie de Michel de Marillac*, Chap. 1.
8. (20) Everart, *op. cit.*, pp. 1–4, and *Notes Généalogiques sur la famille de Marillac*. Everart bases his genealogy of the Marillacs on the research of Nicolas Lefèvre de Lezeau and Bellaigue de Bughas. (28) Baunard, p. 41. (29) Brief of Pope John XXIII, March 15, 1960.
9. (2) AN, *ibid.* An *arpent* (acre) equalled from ¾ to ⁵⁄₄ of the modern acre. (9) *Ibid.* (15) Some biographers make this aunt also Louise's godmother, but without evidence. (32) Michael de la Bedoyere, *François de Sales*, p. 218. (36) Bremond, Vol. II, p. 300.
10. (33) For a detailed treatment of Poissy, cf. Poinsenet, *op. cit.*, pp. 15–26.
11. (10) Bremond, Vol. II, pp. 292–326; Poinsenet, *France Religieuse du XVIIᵉ Siècle*, pp. 22ff. (20) Poinsenet, *De l'Anxiété à la Sainteté, Louise de Marillac*, p. 14. (29) Guy, pp. 16–17.
12. (3) Poinsenet, *op. cit.*, p. 20. (21) Calvet, *op. cit.*, p. 19. (37) *Ibid.*, p. 10 *et al.*
13. (7) AFC, V, "Vocation à la souffrance" (SLDM, p. 895). This quote has

been widely used by biographers but without an exact citation of Louise's words. It is especially to be noted that in every instance they have omitted the words: "Sa bonté a voulu que j'en fusse marquée dès ma naissance même . . ." —which seem to be a unique allusion to the circumstances of her birth.

CHAPTER II

14. (2) *Registres paroissaux de Saint-Paul*, 1595. (3) AN, X2Bm 1179. (4) Everart, *Notes Généalogiques sur la famille de Marillac*, p. 4; Bremond, Vol. I, pp. 119–20. (7) Cf. Bremond, *op. cit.*; Poinsenet, *France Religieuse du XVIIᵉ Siècle*; and de la Bedoyere, *François de Sales, et al.*

15. (23) *Ibid.* (36) *Ibid.*, "Minutier Central," Etude LXVIII, registre 98.

16. (8) The *auditeur* who made the award was Jean Alméras, father of René Alméras who was to succeed Vincent de Paul as superior general of the Priests of the Mission and the Daughters of Charity. (9) AN, *ibid.* (21) *Ibid.* (29) *Ibid.*

17. (3) Calvet, *op. cit.*, p. 22. (5) Cf. p. 11. (10) Gobillon, pp. 6–7. (25) Poinsenet, *op. cit.*, p. 24: "La maîtresse étant pauvre, elle lui proposa de prendre de l'ouvrage des marchands, et travaillait pour elle, encourageant ses compagnes à en faire autant. Elle se chargeait même des bas ouvrages de la maison, comme serrer le bois et sacquitter de tâches ménagères confiées d'ordinaire aux domestiques."

18. (17) Cf. p. 17. (23) Calvet, *op. cit.*, pp. 23–4. (26) *Ibid.*, p. 23.

19. (2) Bremond, Vol. I, pp. xvi–xvii, and Vol. II, pp. 1ff. (13) *Memoire sur la fondation, le gouvernement et l'observance des carmelites dechaussées, publié par les soins des carmelites du premier monastère de Paris*, II, 24. (16) Cf. Everart, *op. cit.* (37) Poinsenet, *op. cit.*, pp. 31–3.

20. (11) *Ibid.*, p. 33. (12) Guy, p. 47. (14) Everart, *Michel de Marillac, sa vie, ses oeuvres*, p. 28, pp. 197–8. (16) Guy, p. 48. (19) Baunard, p. 11, *et al.* (22) Gobillon, p. 8; Calvet, *op. cit., et al.*

21. (8) Cf. *ibid.*, pp. 17–19. (24) AN, *ibid.* (25) *Ibid.* (29) *Ibid.* (31) Calvet, *op. cit.*, p. 28.

22. (6) Gobillon, p. 9. (26) Cf. the fury of Madame, sister-in-law to Louis XIV, and the shock of the court when the King forced her son the Duc de Chartres to marry his illegitimate daughter Mlle de Blois. Lucy Norton, *Saint-Simon at Versailles*, pp. 3–10. (35) Brochard, pp. 143, 213, 395, 397, 409, 424–5.

23. (5) The designations did not then, as they do now, have anything to do with marital or single status. *Madame* was reserved for wives of the nobility, *Mademoiselle* for the wives of the *bourgeoisie* and lower. (35) AN, *ibid.* It is interesting to note that all of Louis de Marillac's brothers and sisters were present. Michel and Louise Hennequin were his full brother and sister; Louis and Valence were his half brother and half sister. (40) Brochard, p. 135.

CHAPTER III

26. (12) Not to be confused with the sixteenth-century French Queen who was a distant cousin. (25) Cf. Van Dyke's portrait of Henrietta of England with her pet dwarf (National Gallery, Washington, D.C.).

27. (28) Cf. Everart, *op. cit., et al.*

28. (5) R. P. Chalumeau, C.M., *Guide de Saint Vincent de Paul à travers Paris*, pp. 26, 56. (11) Baunard, pp. 13–14; Calvet, *op. cit.*, p. 32. (14) Chalumeau, p. 26; AFC, II, 96 (SLDM, p. 117). (18) Guy, p. 54. (30) AFC, V, "Son Règlement de vie dans le monde" (SLDM, p. 888).

29. (3) Gobillon, pp. 10–11. (11) AFC, VI, "Témoignage de la femme Delacour." (20) Gobillon, p. 11. (34) Baunard, p. 15. (38) Gobillon, p. 20. For the history of this famous Congregation, cf. Poinsenet, *France Religieuse du XVIIᵉ Siècle*, pp. 256ff. (30) *Registres de la paroisse Saint-Merry*, "Acte de baptême du 19 Octobre 1613."

30. (27) AFC, "Testament de Mlle Le Gras. (32) Cf. pp. 32–4. (37) AFC, II, Le Gras to Rebours, n.d.; Gobillon, p. 21.

31. (1) Gobillon, *ibid.* (10) AFC, VI, "Témoignage de la femme Delacour." (21) *Ibid.*, V, "Son Règlement de vie dans le monde."

32. (14) Bremond, Vol. I, pp. 118ff. (20) Cf. Poinsenet, *De l'Anxieté à la Sainteté, Louise de Marillac*, p. 43. (36) Baunard, pp. 16–17; AFC, II, 96, 274 (SLDM, pp. 117, 362–3).

33. (19) Cf. Bremond, *passim*; Baunard, p. 117, *et al.*; Leonard, *op. cit.*, pp. 181–183, 550–2; Everart, *Notes Généalogiques sur la famille Marillac*. (38) AFC, *ibid.*, 96 (SLDM, p. 117).

34. (3) *Ibid.*, 274 (*Ibid.*, pp. 362–3). (12) Carl J. Burkhardt, *Richelieu, His Rise to Power*, p. 97. (14) *Ibid.*, pp. 100–1. (37) Baunard, p. 16. (23) *Ibid.*

35. (13) Calvet, *op. cit.*, p. 34. (23) Baunard, p. 17. (26) AFC, *ibid.* (*Ibid.*). (32) Cf. Calvet, *op. cit.*, p. 35. (36) Cf. pp. 43–4.

36. (3) Gobillon, p. 17. (12) de la Bodeyere, pp. 215ff.; Baunard, p. 20. (39) de la Bodeyere, pp. 218–21; AFC, *ibid.* (*Ibid.*).

37. (23) Cf. esp. Theodore Maynard, *Apostle of Charity*, pp. 142–6.

38. (2) Gobillon, p. 182. (3) *Parisien, Beatificationis etc.*, Positio supra Introductione Causae. (14) *Conferences*, Vol. IV, p. 315. (23) For St. Vincent de Paul's extremely low opinion of himself, cf. Saint Vincent de Paul, *Entretiens Spirituel aux Missionaires*, ed. by André Dodin, C.M., pp. 1003–11. (25) Cf. AFC, II–V, *passim* (SLDM, *passim*). (39) *Ibid.*, V, "Son Règlement de vie dans le monde" (*Ibid.*, p. 888).

39. (1) *Ibid.*, VI, Camus to Le Gras, n.d. (7) *Ibid.* (15) Bremond, Everart, *passim*. (24) AFC, VI, Marillac to Le Gras, Sept. 12, 1619. (30) *Ibid.*, Marillac to Le Gras, March 6, 1620. (33) Calvet, p. 36. (36) AFC, *ibid.*

40. (7) Gobillon, p. 20. (11) *Ibid.*, pp. 20–3. (22) ASJPH, VIII, 60. (30) Gobillon, p. 20. (36) AFC, I–II, *passim*, II, 96 (SLDM, p. 117), *Testament de Mlle Le Gras*.

41. (11) Gobillon, pp. 14–21; Baunard, p. 24.

42. (2) AFC, VI, Camus to Le Gras, n.d. (10) *Ibid.*, Camus to Le Gras, n.d. (13) AFC, V, "Grande tentation suivie d'une grace singulière" (SLDM, pp.

875–6). (15) Calvet, *op. cit.*, pp. 40–1. (20) St. Augustine, *Contra Mendacium,* Cap. X, Tom. IV, *post initium.* (23) Gen XXII. (24) Matt I, 19–21. (28) AFC, VI, 1002b. (30) Cf. p. 87. (36) AFC, V, "Grande tentation suivie d'une grace singulière" (SLDM, pp. 875–6).
43. (15) *Ibid.* (19) *Ibid.*
44. (8) *Ibid.*

CHAPTER IV

45. (3) II Cor 12:7. (8) Cf. p. 43. (18) The definitive life of St. Vincent de Paul, crowned by the French Academy, is *The Life and Works of Saint Vincent de Paul,* 3 vols., by Pierre Coste, C.M., tr. by Joseph Leonard, C.M., Westminster, 1952 (the original, *Monsieur Vincent, le grand saint du grand siècle,* was published at Paris, 1932). A most readable life, also authoritative, is *Saint Vincent de Paul* by Jean Calvet, tr. by Lancelot C. Sheppard, New York, 1951.
46. (11) ACM, de Paul to Comet, July 24, 1607. (16) *Ibid.* (19) *Ibid.* (30) *Ibid.*
47. (2) *Ibid.* (19) Calvet, *Saint Vincent de Paul,* p. 34.
50. (14) *Conferences,* Vol. I, pp. 216–17. (35) Louis Chaigne, *Vincent de Paul,* pp. 38–9. (39) Cf. p. 88.
51. (1) Cf. p. 38. Aside from Vincent's growing fame, the Hôtel de Gondi on the rue de Pavée was in Louise's parish of Saint-Sauveur and not far from her own house. (21) AFC, VI, 1002. (25) Cf. Poinsenet, *op. cit.,* p. 60. (32) Gobillon, p. 28.
52. (31) The reference is, of course, to the healing pool of Bethsaida (Jn 5:1–13). (37) AFC, *ibid.,* 1000.
53. (2) Baunard, p. 34; Poinsenet, *op. cit.,* p. 62. (6) Baunard, Poinsenet, *ibid.* (19) Baunard, Poinsenet, *ibid.*
54. (8) Gobillon, pp. 21–3. (19) *Ibid.,* p. 24. (23) *Ibid.,* pp. 26–7. (31) Baunard, p. 36.
55. (1) Cf. I Cor 7:33. (6) AFC, *ibid.,* 1004. (17) *Ibid.,* 1007. (26) Cf. Eph 5:23–32. (28) Gobillon, p. 38.
56. (8) AFC, V, "Esprit de foi et abandon à Dieu" (SLDM, p. 898). (14) *Ibid.,* "Testament de Mlle Le Gras." (20) *Ibid.* (23) *Ibid.*

CHAPTER V

57. (10) Cf. p. 68. (12) AN, *ibid.;* cf. also pp. 26–7. (14) Everart, *Notes Généalogiques sur la famille Marillac,* p. 5. (16) Cf. pp. 45–6. (19) AFC, *ibid.* (22) *Ibid.*
58. (3) *Ibid.* (18) *Ibid.* (21) Chalumeau, p. 25. (25) *Ibid.,* p. 39. (28) Baunard, p. 41. (30) Chalumeau, p. 38; cf. Gobillon, p. 29.
59. (4) Saint Vincent de Paul, *Entretiens Spirituels aux Missionaires,* pp. 420–421. (10) Baunard, p. 30. (16) Cf. pp. 43, 52. (19) Baunard, *ibid.*
60. (5) ACM, 12 (LSVDP, pp. 53–4). (10) LSVDP, p. 522, Footnote 1. (21)

ACM, 104 (LSVDP, pp. 67–8). (34) Calvet, *Louise de Marillac*, p. 51; Baunard, p. 55. (37) Cf. p. 33.
61. (6) ACM, 22 (LSVDP, p. 54). (19) *Ibid.*, 29 (*Ibid.*, pp. 55–6). (23) *Ibid.* (*Ibid.*).
62. (7) *Ibid.* (*Ibid.*). (13) AFC, II, 1 (SLDM, pp. 5–6). (21) *Ibid.* (*Ibid.*). (25) Baunard, p. 42. (30) AFC, *ibid.* (SLDM, *ibid.*). (33) ACM, 355 (LSVDP, pp. 80–1).
63. (24) AFC, *ibid.*, 2 (SLDM, pp. 6–7). (30) ACM, 378 (SVDP, pp. 555–556).
64. (3) *Ibid.*, 22 (LSVDP, p. 54). (12) *Ibid.*, 24 (SVDP, p. 40). (20) AFC, V, "Renoncement a soi-même" (SLDM, p. 909). (34) *Ibid.*, "Son Règlement de vie dans le monde" (*Ibid.*, p. 889).
65. (2) *Ibid.*, "Premiere Retraite," 1 (*Ibid.*, p. 883). (10) *Ibid.*, 2 (*Ibid.*, p. 884). (12) *Ibid.*, 3 (*Ibid.*). (20) *Regulae seu Constitutiones Communes Congregationis Missionis, passim.* (32) AFC, *ibid.*, 4 (*Ibid.*, p. 885).
66. (1) *Ibid.* (*Ibid.*). (11) *Ibid.*, 6 (*Ibid.*, p. 886). (16) *Ibid.*, 7 (*Ibid.*).
67. (13) AFC, *ibid.* "Acte de Protestation" (*Ibid.*, pp. 876–7). The *Act*, while conventionally paragraphed in the original, has been presented here in legal format because its language and intent certainly permit such a presentation, and to emphasize the logical gradation of its points. (29) 2 Cor 5:14. (35) Cf. p. 43.
68. (3) AFC, *ibid.*, "Son Règlement de vie dans le monde" (*Ibid.*, pp. 887–90). (21) Cf. p. 28.
69. (1) Cf. p. 31. (2) Cf. p. 43. (6) For divergent views, cf. Baunard, p. 53, Calvet, *op. cit.*, pp. 52–3. (20) ACM, 266 (LSVDP, p. 76). Father Coste seems to have dated this letter much too late. While noting that "the general tone of the letter is surprising at such a late date," he nevertheless fixes the date of the letter between 1636 and 1642, "the two extremes of Louise de Marillac's stay at La Chapelle." The context of the letter, however, seems to indicate that Louise is still in the world and reflects a state of soul more characteristic of earlier years. Vincent says only that he will hear her confession at La Chapelle; indeed, it is indicated that she is still living on the rue Saint-Victor: "Will you be able to get a carriage? If not, I shall try to send to Saint-Victor." That the carriage was intended for Louise's use and not for his own is further indicated by the fact that he habitually rode horseback at this period of his life. It would seem that Vincent was out of Paris and La Chapelle was selected as their halfway meeting place. His reference to "little Le Gras" would seem to date the letter certainly before 1628, when Michel would have been fifteen. (23) *Ibid.*, 49 (*Ibid.*, p. 58). (33) AFC, *ibid.*, "Sur les privileges singuliers de la Conception Immaculée de la Sainte Vierge" (*Ibid.*, pp. 877–9).
71. (8) *Ibid.*, "Louange a la très Sainte Vierge, Mère de grâce et de misericorde" (*Ibid.*, pp. 880–1). (10) Words applied to Blessed Elizabeth Ann Seton in foretelling her religious community; cf. ASJPH, VIII, 153. (16) Cf. Joseph I. Dirvin, C.M., *St. Catherine Labouré of the Miraculous Medal; A Woman Clothed with the Sun*, ed. by John Delany, "The Lady of the Medal"; *La Scapulaire Verte*, Paris, 1944. (18) AFC, *ibid.*, "Deuxième Retraite" (*Ibid.*, pp. 901–8). (22) *The Introduction to a Devout Life.* (28) ACM, 107 (Joseph

Leonard, C.M., *St. Vincent de Paul and Mental Prayer*, pp. 64–5). Since this letter seems to be a companion to Letter 266 (cf. *Ibid.*, p. 85, Footnote 2, we must disagree with the date assigned it by Father Coste. The reference to the change of residence is not conclusive since, as noted by Father Chalumeau, Louise moved twice during this period (cf. p. 58). (35) Cf. Leonard, *ibid.*, pp. 64–5, Footnote 6.

72. (25) ACM, 266 (LSVDP, p. 76). (34) AFC, *ibid.*, "3ᵉ Journée" (SLDM, p. 903). (37) *Ibid.* (*Ibid.*).

73. (3) *Ibid.* "4ᵉ Journée" (*Ibid.*). (4) *Ibid.*, "7ᵉ et 8ᵉ Journées" (*Ibid.*, p. 906). (11) ACM, 50 (SVDP, Tome I, pp. 86–7). (20) AFC, *ibid.* (*Ibid.*). (23) Cf. p. 62. (27) For a discussion of what prompted this letter, cf. Leonard, *op. cit.*, p. 63, Footnote Letter 27.

74. (3) Matt 7:15–21. (6) ACM, 27 (Leonard, *op. cit.*, pp. 63–4).

CHAPTER VI

75. (13) Gobillon, p. 29.

76. (8) AFC, *ibid.*, "Esprit de foi et abandon à Dieu" (SLDM, p. 898). (15) *Ibid.*, "Sur le détachement considéré en Saint-Fiacre" (*Ibid.*, p. 912). (29) ACM, 96 (LSVDP, p. 67).

77. (2) Cf. p. 61. (7) ACM, 18 (SVDP, Tome I, p. 33). (10) *Ibid.*, 22 (LSVDP, p. 54). (13) *Ibid.*, 34 (SVDP, *ibid.*, pp. 69–70). (18) *Ibid.* (*Ibid.*). (23) AFC, *ibid.*, "effets de la venue de Saint-Esprit" (SLDM, p. 892).

78. (2) *Ibid.*, "Résignation à Dieu dans ses peines intérieures" (*Ibid.*, p. 894); Phil 4:7. (18) *Ibid.* (*Ibid.*). (28) *Ibid.*, "Volenté de Dieu" (*Ibid.*, p. 895).

79. (1) ACM, 38 (SVDP, *ibid.*, pp. 72–3). (9) *Ibid.*, 31 (*Ibid.*, p. 68, and Footnote 1). (10) The passage runs: "Esto nobis, Domine, in precinctu suffragium, in via solatium, in aestu umbraculum, in pluvia et frigore tegumentum, in lassitudine vehiculum, in adversitate praesidium, in lubrico baculum, in naufragio portus, ut, te duce, quo tendimus prospere perveniamus et demum incolumes ad propria redeamus." (28) ACM, 39 (LSVDP, pp. 57–8). (30) Cf. pp. 49–50; cf. p. 48. (38) Cyprian W. Emmanuel, O.F.M., *The Charities of St. Vincent de Paul*, pp. 104ff.

82. (20) *Ibid.*, p. 168. (33) Cf. pp. 75–6.

83. (8) Quoted in Baunard, p. 74. (10) Cf. his oils of French peasant life in the Louvre and the National Gallery of Art, Washington, D.C. (18) Cf. Baunard, pp. 74–5. (23) Cf. Gobillon, pp. 33–5. (33) ACM, 40 (SVDP, *ibid.*, p. 75).

84. (8) Cf. Jacques Ruppert, *Le Costume*, II, Chap. V. (27) Gobillon, p. 35. (25) *Conferences*, Vol. I, p. 71.

85. (30) AFC, *Catéchisme*.

86. (4) ACM, 40 (SVDP, pp. 75–6). (21) *Ibid.* (*Ibid.*). (33) *Ibid.*, 41 (*Ibid.*, p. 77). (36) *Ibid.* (*Ibid.*). (38) Calvet, *op. cit.*, p. 59.

87. (9) AFC, II, 4 (SLDM, p. 4). (20) Gobillon, p. 36. (22) ACM, 42 (SVDP, pp. 77–8). (24) *Ibid.* (*Ibid.*). (27) *Ibid.*, 43 (*Ibid.*, p. 79). (34) Cf. pp. 61–2.

88. (6) ACM, *ibid.* (SVDP, *ibid.*). (13) *Ibid.*, 53 (*Ibid.*, p. 90). (17) *Ibid.*, 45

(*Ibid.*, p. 80). (19) *Ibid.*, 44 (*Ibid.*, p. 80, Footnote 1). (35) *Ibid.*, 46 (LSVDP, p. 58).

89. (6) *Ibid.*, 47 (SVDP, *ibid.*, pp. 82–3). (8) *Ibid.* (*Ibid.*). (12) *Ibid.* (*Ibid.*). (16) *Ibid.*, 57 (*Ibid.*, pp. 94–5). (32) Burkhardt, p. 160; Everart, *Michel de Marillac, Sa Vie, Ses Oeuvres*, pp. 50ff.
92. (13) Burkhardt, Chap. XVIII and XX. (17) Cf. pp. 98, 101–3; 195. (24) *Saint-Simon at Versailles*, sel. and ed. by Lucy Norton, p. 97. (37) ACM, 58 (SVDP, *ibid.*, pp. 95–9, Footnote 1).
93. (6) *Ibid.* (*Ibid.*). (14) *Ibid.*, 59 (*Ibid.*, pp. 99–100). (21) *Ibid.* (*Ibid.*). (23) SVDP, p. 99, Footnote 2. (28) ACM, 60 (SVDP, p. 101). (32) *Ibid.* (*Ibid.*).
94. (9) *Ibid.*, 61 (*Ibid.*, pp. 101–3). (12) *Ibid.*, 63, 64, 65 (*Ibid.*, pp. 103–7). (17) *Ibid.*, 67 (*Ibid.*, pp. 108–9). (31) *Ibid.* (*Ibid.*). (36) *Ibid.*, 64 (*Ibid.*, pp. 104–6).
95. (2) *Ibid.*, 62 (*Ibid.*, p. 103). (7) *Ibid.*, 66 (*Ibid.*, pp. 107–8).

CHAPTER VII

96. (17) *Ibid.*, 71 (LSVDP, p. 63).
97. (4) *Ibid.*, 69 (SVDP, pp. 110–12). (12) *Ibid.* (*Ibid.*). (17) *Ibid.*, 75 and 77 (*Ibid.*, pp. 118–19 and 120–1). (21) *Ibid.*, 75 (*Ibid.*, pp. 118–19). (35) *Ibid.*, 81 (*Ibid.*, pp. 122–5). (39) *Ibid.* (*Ibid.*). (45) *Ibid.* (*Ibid.*).
98. (38) *Ibid.*, 84 (*Ibid.*, pp. 128–9).
99. (7) *Ibid.* (*Ibid.*). (19) *Ibid.*, 83 (*Ibid.*, pp. 126–7). (21) *Ibid.*, 88 (*Ibid.*, pp. 134–5). (23) Cf. *Ibid.*, 81, 82, 84, 85 (*Ibid.*, pp. 122–5, 125–6, 128–9, 129–31) *et al.* (25) *Ibid.*, 86 (*Ibid.*, pp. 131–3). (28) *Ibid.* (*Ibid.*). (30) *Ibid.*, 88 (*Ibid.*, pp. 134–5). (34) *Ibid.*, 85 (*Ibid.*, pp. 129–31). (37) *Ibid.*, 88 (*Ibid.*, pp. 134–5).
100. (17) *Ibid.*, 92 (*Ibid.*, pp. 141–3). (21) Cf. extant portraits of Michel de Marillac, e.g., in *L'Auvergne Historique*, Jouvet, Riom. (38) Calvet, *op. cit.*, pp. 28–9.
101. (9) ACM, *Ibid.* (SVDP, *ibid.*). (28) Belloc, *op. cit.*, cf. pp. 304–13. (39) Baunard, p. 117.
102. (4) ACM, 101 (SVDP, *ibid.*, pp. 150–1). (10) *Ibid.*, 103 (*Ibid.*, p. 152). (11) Cf. SVDP., *ibid.*, p. 150, Footnote 3. (22) ACM, 105 (SVDP, *ibid.*, pp. 153–4). (24) *Conferences*, Vol. IV, p. 320. (28) Cf. Baunard, p. 114 and Everart, *op. cit.*, p. 175. (29) Everart, *op. cit.*, Chapter XVIII, pp. 178ff.
103. (3) ACM, 106 (SVDP, *ibid.*, pp. 154–5). (7) *Ibid.*, 108 (*Ibid.*, pp. 156–8). (13) Vincent wrote "Poulaillon" mistakenly, as he did regularly. (14) ACM, 109 (SVDP, *ibid.*, pp. 158–60). (23) *Ibid.* (*Ibid.*). (25) *Ibid.*, 85 (*Ibid.*, pp. 129–31). (29) *Ibid.*, 110 (*Ibid.*, pp. 160–1). (35) *Ibid.* (*Ibid.*).
104. (2) *Ibid.*, 111 (*Ibid.*, pp. 161–2). (19) *Ibid.*, 113 (*Ibid.*, p. 165). (22) *Ibid.*, 116 (*Ibid.*, pp. 167–8). (32) SVDP, *ibid.*, p. 166, Footnote 2.
105. (4) ACM, 115 (SVDP, *ibid.*, p. 166). (8) SVDP, *ibid.*, p. 166, Footnote 2. (22) ACM, 131 (SVDP, *ibid.*, pp. 185–6). (25) The Hôpital de la Santé or Hôpital Sainte-Anne for the plague-stricken. (29) ACM, 132

398 ஒ Sources

(SVDP, *ibid.*, pp. 187–9). (35) Cf. *Conferences*, Vol. I, p. 71. (38) ACM, *ibid.* (SVDP, *ibid.*, also Footnote 9).

107. (11) Jerome Lallemont, who was later superior of the *Mission du Canada* and died at Quebec in 1673.
108. (21) ACM, 135 (SVDP, *ibid.*, pp. 191–6).
109. (2) *Ibid.*, 136 (*Ibid.*, pp. 196–8). (11) *Ibid.*, 137 (*Ibid.*, pp. 198–9). (23) *Ibid.*, 138 (*Ibid.*, pp. 200–1).

CHAPTER VIII

110. (8) *Ibid.*, 139 (*Ibid.*, p. 201). (18) Louis Abelly, *Vie du Venerable Serviteur de Dieu Vincent de Paul*, Vol. II, pp. 246ff.
111. (2) ACM, 141 (SVDP, *ibid.*, pp. 202–3). (14) *Ibid.*, 140 (*Ibid.*, pp. 201–202). (32) *Ibid.*, 147 (*Ibid.*, pp. 212–13). (35) SVDP, *ibid.*, p. 213, Footnote 3.
112. (9) AFC, V, "Oblation de la Compagnie des Filles de la Charité à la Vierge" (SLDM, pp. 837–8). (21) ACM, 151 (SVDP, *ibid.*, pp. 217–18). (31) *Ibid.*, 152 (*Ibid.*, pp. 218–19).
113. (37) Gobillon, pp. 51–2.
114. (7) AFC, *ibid.*, "Sur la vocation des Filles de la Charité: estime de cette vocation" (SLDM, p. 839). (19) Gobillon, p. 11. (24) Cf. pp. 67ff. (26) Cf. p. 73. (33) Cf. pp. 87–8.
115. (1) Cf. p. 96. (6) Cf. p. 109. (23) AFC, *ibid.* (SLDM, p. 840).
116. (23) *Conferences*, Vol. II, p. 213. (35) AFC, *ibid.* (SLDM, *ibid.*). (39) *Conferences, ibid.*, p. 203.
117. (3) AFC, *ibid.* (SLDM, *ibid.*). (6) *Conferences, ibid.*, p. 206. (24) *Ibid.*, Vol. I, pp. 13–14.
118. (3) *Ibid.*, Vol. III, p. 126. (13) *Ibid.*, Vol. IV, p. 261. (21) AFC, *ibid.* (SLDM, p. 839). (30) The difference between a private and a public vow has nothing to do with the total dedication promised by the vow, but is a canonical establishment of ecclesiastical identity and its effects. A public vow is received in the name of the Church by an authorized official and establishes one as a religious with consequent rights and obligations. A private vow, not officially accepted or recognized by any Church deputy, has no ecclesiastical effect whatever.
119. (10) *Common Rules of the Daughters of Charity*, Paris, 1658, 1954, no. 2. (32) AFC, *ibid.*, "Difficultés de cette vocation" (SLDM, p. 843).
120. (11) *Conferences*, Vol. III, pp. 161–2. (15) *Ibid.*, p. 175. (21) Chalumeau, p. 38. (25) *Conferences*, Vol. I, p. 74.
121. (30) *Ibid.*, pp. 74–85.
122. (4) *Ibid.*, pp. 84–5. (21) Chalumeau, p. 29.
123. (7) Emmanuel, pp. 172ff. (17) SVDP, *ibid.*, p. 229, Footnote 2.
124. (3) ACM, 159 (SVDP, pp. 229–31). (32) *Ibid.*, 161 (*Ibid.*, pp. 232–3).
125. (5) Gobillon, p. 52. (26) ACM, 162 (SVDP, pp. 233–4). (31) Such a remedy sounds strange to modern ears, but it must be weighed in the context of the seventeenth-century, when the medicinal effects of Holy Communion

were not so emphasized as now. That Vincent held no extreme positions concerning the privation of Communion may be judged from his uncompromising attack on the Jansenistic opinions of Arnauld.

126. (2) ACM, 163 (SVDP, pp. 234–5). (8) *Ibid.* (*Ibid.*). (10) Emmanuel, p. 177. (15) ACM, *ibid.* (SVDP, *ibid.*). (29) SVDP, *ibid.*, p. 41, Footnote 1. (33) ACM, 164 (SVDP, pp. 235–6).

127. (7) *Ibid.*, 167 (*Ibid.*, p. 238). (14) *Ibid.*, 168 (*Ibid.*, p. 239). (17) Cf. p. 92. (28) ACM, 169 (SVDP, *ibid.*, pp. 239–40). (32) *Ibid.*, 170 (*Ibid.*, p. 241). (38) *Ibid.* (*Ibid.*).

128. (3) *Ibid.*, 169 (*Ibid.*, pp. 239–40). (13) AFC, I, 4 (SLDM, pp. 8–11). (15) ACM, 171 (SVDP, *ibid.*, pp. 241–2). (18) *Ibid.* (*Ibid.*). (35) *Ibid.*, 173 (*Ibid.*, pp. 244–5).

129. (2) SVDP, p. 243, Footnote 6. (27) ACM, 174 (SVDP, *ibid.*, pp. 245–7). (30) *Ibid.*, 177 (*Ibid.*, pp. 249–54).

130. (2) AFC, *Recueil de diverses pièces appartenants à la conduite et direction des Dames de la Charité de Paris* (*c.* 1700). (21) ACM, *ibid.* (SVDP, *ibid.*).

131. (6) Emmanuel, pp. 148–9, 174–5. (29) Coste, Vol. I, pp. 241–2.

132. (14) ACM, 182 (SVDP, *ibid.*, pp. 277–8).

135. (5) Barbe Angiboust, most famous of the early Sisters, had joined the Company on July 1 at the age of twenty-nine. (33) *Conferences, ibid.*, pp. 1–11.

CHAPTER IX

136. (24) ACM, 176 (SVDP, *ibid.*, pp. 248–9).

137. (9) *Ibid.*, 185 (*Ibid.*, p. 281). (24) *Ibid.*, 200 (*Ibid.*, pp. 300–1). (34) *Ibid.*, 210 (*Ibid.*, pp. 312–13). (39) AFC, I, 5 (SLDM, p. 11).

138. (12) ACM, 199 (SVDP, pp. 299–300). (16) *Ibid.*, 210 (*Ibid.*, pp. 312–13). (21) *Ibid.*, 213 (*Ibid.*, pp. 314–15). (27) *Ibid.* (*Ibid.*). (32) Cf. p. 93. (38) ACM, 203 (SVDP, pp. 304–5).

139. (10) *Ibid.*, 214 (*Ibid.*, p. 315). (22) *Ibid.*, 215 (*Ibid.*, p. 316). (31) *Ibid.*, 217 (*Ibid.*, pp. 317–18). (36) *Ibid.*, 218 (*Ibid.*, pp. 318–19).

140. (3) *Ibid.*, 219 (*Ibid.*, p. 320). (11) *Ibid.*, 221 (*Ibid.*, pp. 321–3). (20) Gobillon, p. 74. (34) Baunard, pp. 184–5. The autograph quoted is in AFC, V, "Volenté de Dieu" (SLDM, p. 896). (37) Coste, *ibid.*, pp. 389–90.

141. (4) Cf. p. 137. (12) ACM, 219 (SVDP, *ibid.*, pp. 320–21). (34) *Ibid.*, 221 (*Ibid.*, pp. 321–3). (39) *Ibid.*, 222 (*Ibid.*, pp. 323–4).

142. (4) *Ibid.*, 223 (*Ibid.*, pp. 324–6). (21) *Ibid.* (*Ibid.*). (29) *Ibid.* (*Ibid.*). (36) *Ibid.* (*Ibid.*).

143. (5) SVDP, p. 327, Footnote 1.

144. (27) ACM, 224 (SVDP, *ibid.*, pp. 327–32). (36) *Ibid.*, 227 (*Ibid.*, pp. 334–5).

145. (17) Cf. C. V. Wedgwood, *The Thirty Years War*, pp. 393–4, and SVDP, *ibid.*, p. 339, Footnote 2. (20) ACM, 231 (SVDP, p. 339).

146. (3) *Ibid.*, 232 (*Ibid.*, pp. 339–41). (12) *Ibid.*, 235 (*Ibid.*, pp. 343–4). (21) *Ibid.*, 236 (*Ibid.*, p. 344). (25) *Ibid.*, 239 (*Ibid.*, pp. 346–7). (28) Gobillon,

p. 75. (35) ACM, 234 (SVDP, *ibid.*, pp. 342–3). (38) Gobillon, p. 76.
147. (2) ACM, 231 (SVDP, *ibid.*, p. 339). (10) Cf. Wedgwood, *loc. cit.*, and SVDP, p. 339, Footnote 2. (28) ACM, 229 (SVDP, *ibid.*, pp. 336–7).
148. (23) AFC, II, 96 (SLDM, pp. 117–18). (28) *Ibid.* (*Ibid.*) and SVDP, pp. 344–6. (35) ACM, 242 (SVDP, *ibid.*, pp. 350–1).
149. (6) *Ibid.*, 248 (*Ibid.*, pp. 358–9). (11) *Ibid.*, 253 (*Ibid.*, pp. 364–6). (12) *Ibid.*, 255 (*Ibid.*, pp. 367–8). (16) *Ibid.*, 241 (*Ibid.*, pp. 348–9). (17) Cf. AFC, *ibid.* (SLDM, *ibid.*) and ACM, 238 and 247 (SVDP, *ibid.*, pp. 346 and 357–8). (24) *Ibid.*, 242 (*Ibid.*, pp. 350–1). (27) *Ibid.*, 247 (*Ibid.*, pp. 357–8). (28) *Ibid.*, 248 (*Ibid.*, pp. 358–9). (30) *Ibid.*, 251 (*Ibid.*, pp. 362–363). (38) *Ibid.* (*Ibid.*).
150. (4) *Ibid.*, 253 (*Ibid.*, pp. 364–5). (13) *Ibid.*, 254 (*Ibid.*, p. 366). (20) *Ibid.*, 255 (*Ibid.*, pp. 367–8). (22) Cf. p. 187. (23) ACM, *ibid.* (SVDP, *ibid.*).
151. (15) AFC, *ibid.*, 6 (SLDM, pp. 11–12). (25) ACM, 258 (SVDP, *ibid.*, pp. 371–2). (38) *Ibid.* (*Ibid.*).
152. (4) *Ibid.*, 262 (*Ibid.*, pp. 380–1). (8) *Ibid.* (*Ibid.*). (10) SVDP, *ibid.*, p. 380, Footnote 5. (17) ACM, 263 (SVDP, *ibid.*, p. 381). (40) Gobillon, pp. 78–9.
153. (27) ACM, 264 (SVDP, *ibid.*, pp. 381–2). (32) *Ibid.*, 265 (*Ibid.*, pp. 382–383). (35) SVDP, *ibid.*, p. 383, Footnote 3. (19) *Ibid.*
154. (6) ACM, 267 (SVDP, *ibid.*, pp. 385–6). (16) *Ibid.*, 273 (*Ibid.*, pp. 391–393). (20) *Ibid.*, 274 (*Ibid.*, pp. 392–3). (27) *Ibid.*, 278 (*Ibid.*, pp. 396–8). (38) *Ibid.*, 279 (*Ibid.*, pp. 399–400).
155. (9) *Ibid.*, 283 (*Ibid.*, pp. 407–8). (15) *Ibid.*, 275 (*Ibid.*, pp. 393–4). (18) Cf. *Ibid.*, 278 and 280 (*Ibid.*, pp. 396 and 400–1). (22) *Ibid.*, 280 (*Ibid.*, pp. 400–1). (31) *Ibid.*, 283 (*Ibid.*, pp. 407–8).
156. (10) *Ibid.* (*Ibid.*). (25) *Ibid.*, 286 (*Ibid.*, pp. 411–12). (36) *Ibid.*, 285 (*Ibid.*, pp. 410–11).
157. (9) *Ibid.*, 288 (*Ibid.*, pp. 417–18).

CHAPTER X

158. (22) SVDP, XIII, p. 798. (24) *Ibid.* (29) *Ibid.*, p. 775.
159. (6) *Ibid.*, p. 798; cf. also p. 775. (9) *Ibid.*, p. 775. (12) *Ibid.*, p. 798. (13) *Ibid.*; cf. also Gobillon, pp. 85–6. (15) Gobillon, p. 86. (22) SVDP, *ibid.* (27) ACM, 239 (SVDP, Vol. I, pp. 419–20). (33) *Ibid.*, 290 (*Ibid.*, pp. 421–3). (38) *Ibid.*, 289 (*Ibid.*, pp. 419–20); also SVDP, p. 419, Footnote 4.
160. (5) ACM, 289 (SVDP, pp. 419–20). (19) SVDP, p. 420, Footnote 5. (29) ACM, 290 (SVDP, pp. 421–3). (32) AFC, *ibid.*, 7 (SLDM, p. 13). (37) ACM, *ibid.* (SVDP, *ibid.*).
161. (17) SVDP, p. 421, Footnote 3, and ACM, 307 (SVDP, pp. 449–51). (24) *Ibid.*, 290 (*Ibid.*, pp. 421–3). (36) AFC, *ibid.* (SLDM, *ibid.*).
162. (33) ACM, 295 (SVDP, pp. 433–5).
163. (4) *Ibid.*, 296 (*Ibid.*, pp. 435–6). (8) *Ibid.*, 297 (*Ibid.*, pp. 436–7). (11) AFC, *ibid.*, 31 (SLDM, pp. 38–40). (12) *Ibid.* (*Ibid.*). (19) ACM, *ibid.*

(SVDP, *ibid.*). (22) Coste, Vol. II, p. 259. (29) AFC, *ibid.*, 89 (SLDM, p. 111). This letter is wrongly assigned in the 1960 edition of Louise de Marillac's letters to the year 1643. It is obvious from the references to Mme Goussault in letters 301-4 (ACM; SVDP, *ibid.*, pp. 441-5) that it belongs to 1638. (37) ACM, 301 (SVDP, *ibid.*, pp. 441-2).

164. (1) *Ibid.*, 302, 303 (*Ibid.*, pp. 442, 443). (5) *Ibid.*, 302 (*Ibid.*, p. 442). (6) *Ibid.*, 305 (*Ibid.*, pp. 445-6). (19) *Ibid.*, 304 (*Ibid.*, pp. 444-5). (21) *Ibid.*, 305 (*Ibid.*, pp. 445-6). (24) *Ibid.*, 309 (*Ibid.*, pp. 454-5). (31) *Ibid.*, 310 (*Ibid.*, pp. 455-6). (37) *Ibid.*, 327 (*Ibid.*, p. 481).

165. (2) *Ibid.*, 349 (*Ibid.*, pp. 506-7).

166. (30) *Conferences, ibid.*, pp. 116-27. (36) Cf. p. 262.

167. (1) Gobillon, p. 75. (5) ACM, 296 (SVDP, pp. 435-6). (9) Cf. pp. 117-118. (12) ACM, 297 (SVDP, pp. 436-7). (16) *Ibid.*, 290 (*Ibid.*, pp. 421-3). (20) *Ibid.*, 303 (*Ibid.*, p. 443). (37) *Ibid.*, 312, 313 (*Ibid.*, pp. 458-9, 459-60).

168. (3) *Ibid.*, 313 (*Ibid.*, pp. 459-60). (6) *Ibid.* (*Ibid.*). (10) *Ibid.*, 310 (*Ibid.*, pp. 455-6). (18) Gobillon, pp. 79-80. (25) *Ibid.*, pp. 80-2; cf. also *supra*, pp. 87ff. (37) ACM, 313 (SVDP, pp. 459-60).

169. (1) *Ibid.* (*Ibid.*). (2) *Ibid.*, 314 (*Ibid.*, pp. 460-1). (4) *Ibid.*, 301 (*Ibid.*, pp. 441-2). (6) *Ibid.*, 314 (*Ibid.*, pp. 460-1). (19) *Ibid.*, 315 (*Ibid.*, pp. 461-2). (27) *Ibid.*, 319 (*Ibid.*, pp. 467-8). (32) *Ibid.*, 320 (*Ibid.*, pp. 468-469). (35) *Ibid.*, 325 (*Ibid.*, pp. 478-9). (38) *Ibid.* (*Ibid.*).

170. (3) *Ibid.*, 327 (*Ibid.*, p. 481). (6) Cf. p. 300. (15) ACM, 335 (SVDP, pp. 493-4). (30) *Ibid.*, 337 (*Ibid.*, pp. 494-5).

171. (4) AFC, *ibid.*, 8 (SLDM, pp. 14-15). (12) ACM, 338 (SVDP, *ibid.*, pp. 495-6). (17) *Ibid.*, 344 (*Ibid.*, pp. 501-2). (22) *Ibid.*, 345 (*Ibid.*, 502-3). (36) *Ibid.*, 351 (*Ibid.*, pp. 508-9).

172. (7) *Ibid.*, 352 (*Ibid.*, pp. 509-11). (9) *Ibid.*, 353 (*Ibid.*, pp. 511-12). (18) Baunard, p. 302.

173. (9) ACM, 354 (SVDP, pp. 513-14). (24) *Ibid.*, 355 (*Ibid.*, pp. 515-17). (27) *Ibid.* (*Ibid.*).

174. (7) *Ibid.* (*Ibid.*). (16) *Ibid.*, 357 (*Ibid.*, pp. 517-18). (24) *Ibid.* (*Ibid.*). (27) *Ibid.* (*Ibid.*). (33) Cf. p. 151. (39) ACM, 359 (SVDP, pp. 519-20).

175. (5) *Ibid.*, 373 (*Ibid.*, pp. 544-5). (11) *Ibid.* (*Ibid.*). (13) *Ibid.* (*Ibid.*). (33) *Ibid.*, 379 (*Ibid.*, pp. 557-8).

176. (2) AFC, III, 152 (SLDM, pp. 203-4). (10) ACM, 378 (SVDP, *ibid.*, pp. 555-6). (11) Cf. p. 63. (14) ACM, *ibid.* (SVDP, *ibid.*). (16) Wedgwood, p. 400. (23) SVDP, p. 551, Footnote 13. (28) ACM, 371 (SVDP, pp. 542-3). (37) AFC, II, 10 (SLDM, p. 17).

177. (3) ACM, 375 (SVDP, *ibid.*, pp. 546-7). (6) Cf. pp. 291-3. (24) AFC, *ibid.*, 9 (SLDM, p. 16). (35) ACM, 386 (SVDP, *ibid.*, pp. 569-70).

178. (15) *Ibid.*, 387 (*Ibid.*, pp. 570-1). (19) *Ibid.*, 388 (*Ibid.*, pp. 572-3). (27) *Ibid.*, 382 (*Ibid.*, pp. 560-1). (30) *Ibid.* (*Ibid.*). (38) *Ibid.*, 391 (*Ibid.*, pp. 576-7).

179. (4) *Conferences, ibid.*, p. 187. (5) *Ibid.*, Vol. III, p. 127. (6) *Ibid.*, Vol. II, p. 218. (10) *Ibid.*, Vol. I, p. 63. (17) AFC, III, 11 (SLDM, pp. 17-20).

CHAPTER XI

180. (5) Coste, Vol. I, p. 405, Footnote 7. (11) *Ibid.*, p. 405, and SVDP, *ibid.*, p. 612, Footnote 3. (22) *Ibid.*, Footnote 1.
181. (6) ACM, 393 (SVDP, *ibid.*, pp. 580–1). (19) *Ibid.* (*Ibid.*). (25) *Ibid.*, 399 (*Ibid.*, p. 584).
182. (17) AFC, *ibid.* (SLDM, *ibid.*). (21) ACM, 409 (SVDP, *ibid.*, pp. 601–2). (24) *Ibid.* (*Ibid.*). (28) *Ibid.*, 410 (*Ibid.*, pp. 602–4).
183. (8) *Ibid.* (*Ibid.*).
185. (16) SVDP, XIII, pp. 539–47. (28) ACM, 411 (SVDP, I, pp. 605–6). (34) *Ibid.* (*Ibid.*).
186. (4) AFC, IV, 12 (SLDM, p. 23). (16) ACM, *ibid.* (SVDP, *ibid.*). (27) *Ibid.*, 414 (*Ibid.*, pp. 609–10). (33) *Ibid.* (*Ibid.*). (38) *Ibid.* (*Ibid.*).
187. (14) *Ibid.*, 415 (*Ibid.*, pp. 611–12). (20) *Ibid.*, 416 (*Ibid.*, p. 613). (28) *Ibid.*, 419 (*Ibid.*, II, pp. 6–7). (30) *Ibid.*, 420 (*Ibid.*, pp. 7–8). (34) *Ibid.*, 419 (*Ibid.*, pp. 6–7).
188. (1) *Ibid.*, 420 (*Ibid.*, pp. 7–8). (5) *Ibid.*, 421 (*Ibid.*, pp. 9–10). (8) SVDP, p. 9, Footnote 3. (20) ACM, 417 (SVDP, *ibid.*, pp. 1–2). (22) SVDP, *ibid.*, p. 7, Footnote 3. (23) ACM, 419 (SVDP, *ibid.*, pp. 6–7). (32) *Ibid.*, 426 (*Ibid.*, pp. 19–20). (39) *Ibid.*, 425 (*Ibid.*, pp. 18–19).
189. (3) *Ibid.* (*Ibid.*). (4) *Ibid.*, 426 (*Ibid.*, pp. 19–20). (6) *Ibid.*, 432 (*Ibid.*, p. 26). (10) *Ibid.*, 426 (*Ibid.*, pp. 19–20, and p. 20, Footnote 3). (15) SVDP, *ibid.*, p. 9, Footnote 1. (18) AFC, *ibid.*, 14 (SLDM, pp. 24–5). (19) *Ibid.*, 15 (*Ibid.*, p. 25). (21) ACM, 425 (SVDP, *ibid.*, pp. 18–19). (28) *Ibid.*, 421 (*Ibid.*, pp. 9–10). (30) *Ibid.*, 422 (*Ibid.*, pp. 11–12). (38) *Ibid.*, 419 (*Ibid.*, pp. 6–7).
190. (6) Cf. pp. 158–9. (29) SVDP, XIII, pp. 774–8. (31) ACM, 419 (SVDP, II, pp. 6–7).
191. (2) SVDP, *ibid.*, p. 32, Footnote 19. (8) ACM, 437 (SVDP, *ibid.*, p. 36). (18) *Ibid.*, 444 (*Ibid.*, pp. 42–4, and p. 42, Footnotes 2–4). (29) AFC, *ibid.*, 16 (SLDM, pp. 25–6). (39) *Ibid.*, 17 (*Ibid.*, pp. 26–7).
192. (7) *Ibid.*, 18 (*Ibid.*, pp. 27–8). (12) *Ibid.* (*Ibid.*). (15) SLDM, p. 999, 18, Footnote 2. (20) AFC, *ibid.* (SLDM, *ibid.*). (31) *Ibid.*, 19 (*Ibid.*, pp. 29–30). (38) SVDP, XIII, pp. 779–85.
193. (19) *Ibid.* (29) AFC, II, 60 (SLDM, pp. 76–7). (31) *Ibid.*, IV, 21 (*Ibid.*, p. 31). (33) *Ibid.*, 20 and 21 (*Ibid.*, pp. 30–1). (36) *Ibid.*, 21 (*Ibid.*, p. 31).
194. (1) *Ibid.*, 22 (*Ibid.*, pp. 31–2). (10) *Ibid.*, III, 23 (*Ibid.*, p. 32). (13) *Ibid.*, II, 24 (*Ibid.*, p. 33). (31) *Ibid.*, 25 (*Ibid.*, pp. 33–4).
195. (2) *Ibid.*, IV, 29 (*Ibid.*, pp. 36–7). (16) ACM, 471 (SVDP, *ibid.*, pp. 93–4). (23) *Ibid.*, 472 (*Ibid.*, pp. 94–5). (25) *Ibid.*, 478 (*Ibid.*, pp. 108–109). (26) *Ibid.*, 480 (*Ibid.*, pp. 109–11). (31) Cf. *ibid.*, 411, 421, 479, 480, 481 (*Ibid.*, I, pp. 605–6; II, pp. 9–10, 109, 109–10, 111). (32) Cf. *ibid.*, 441 (*Ibid.*, pp. 39–40). (33) Cf. *ibid.*, 450 (*Ibid.*, p. 53). (37) *Ibid.*, 469 (*Ibid.*, p. 91). (39) *Ibid.* (*Ibid.*); *Ibid.*, 481 (*Ibid.*, p. 111).
196. (5) *Ibid.*, 482 (*Ibid.*, p. 112). (11) *Conferences*, *ibid.*, p. 13. (20) *Ibid.*, p. 12. (33) *Ibid.*, pp. 16–17. (36) Cf. pp. 249ff. (39) ACM, 483 (SVDP, *ibid.*, p. 113).

197. (3) *Ibid.*, 484 (*Ibid.*, pp. 114–15). (14) AFC, V, "Avis pour les Soeurs chargées des offices interiers de la communauté" (SLDM, pp. 984–5). (23) *Ibid.* (*Ibid.*, pp. 985–6).
198. (6) *Ibid.* (*Ibid.*, pp. 986–7). (25) *Ibid.* (*Ibid.*, pp. 988–9). (31) *Ibid.*, "Pour les Filles de la Charité attachées à l'Hôtel-Dieu de Paris, et pour celles des Hôpitaux" (*Ibid.*, pp. 989–90). (38) *Conferences, ibid.*, p. 16.
199. (4) ACM, 432 (SVDP, *ibid.*, p. 26). (5) Cf. p. 189. (7) Cf. pp. 104–5. (10) Coste, Vol. II, p. 317. (14) Cf. p. 105. (26) Cf. Coste, *ibid.*, pp. 315ff.
200. (25) AFC, *ibid.*, "Règles pour les Filles de la Charité qui ont soin des Galériens, pouvant servir à toutes sortes de prisons" (SLDM, pp. 991–2).
201. (16) *Conferences*, Vol. IV, pp. 249–50. (30) AFC, II, 33 (SLDM, pp. 41–42). (32) ACM, 487 (SVDP, *ibid.*, pp. 121–2). (34) AFC, *ibid.* (SLDM, *ibid.*). (39) ACM, 482 (SVDP, *ibid*, p. 112).
202. (9) AFC, *ibid.* (SLDM, *ibid.*). (12) ACM, *ibid.* (SVDP, *ibid.*). (20) *Ibid.*, 491 (*Ibid.*, pp. 129–31). (22) *Ibid.* (*Ibid.*). (29) *Ibid.*, 494 (*Ibid.*, pp. 133–134).
203. (2) AFC, *ibid.*, 7 *bis* (SLDM, pp. 13–14).

CHAPTER XII

204. (11) ACM, 494 (SVDP, pp. 133–4). (17) *Ibid.*, 503 (*Ibid.*, pp. 146–7). (21) *Ibid.*, 494 (*Ibid.*, pp. 133–4).
205. (2) AFC, IV, 44 (SLDM, p. 55). (11) *Ibid.*, 45 (*Ibid.*, pp. 56–7). (20) *Ibid.*, 34 (*Ibid.*, pp. 42–3). (25) ACM, *ibid.* (SVDP, *ibid.*). (30) *Ibid.*, 491 (*Ibid.*, pp. 129–30). (36) *Ibid.*, 506 (*Ibid.*, pp. 149–50).
206. (14) *Ibid.*, 509 (*Ibid.*, pp. 156–7). (34) AFC, II, 36 *bis* (SLDM, pp. 47–8). (39) *Ibid* (*Ibid.*).
207. (2) ACM, 513 (SVDP, *ibid.*, pp. 160–1). (6) *Ibid.*, 509, 510, 511 (*Ibid.*, pp. 156–7, 157–8, 158–9). (22) *Ibid.*, 510 (*Ibid.*, pp. 157–8). (28) *Ibid.*, 519 (*Ibid.*, pp. 165–6). (33) *Ibid.*, 516 (*Ibid.*, pp. 162–3). (35) *Ibid.*, 518 (*Ibid.*, pp. 164–5). (36) *Ibid.*, 519 (*Ibid.*, pp. 165–7).
208. (1) *Ibid.*, 533 (*Ibid.*, p. 179); AFC, *ibid.*, 38 (SLDM, pp. 50–1). (10) ACM, 519 (SVDP, *ibid.*, pp. 165–7, also p. 166, Footnote 3). (14) *Ibid.*, 528 (*Ibid.*, pp. 174–5); cf. also pp. 200–1. (18) ACM, *ibid.* (SVDP, *ibid.*). (21) *Ibid.*, 529 (*Ibid.*, p. 175). (22) *Ibid.* (*Ibid.*). (39) *Ibid.*, 530 (*Ibid.*, p. 176).
209. (6) *Ibid.*, 534 (*Ibid.*, pp. 179–80). (13) SVDP, *ibid.*, p. 180, Footnote 3. (19) AFC, IV, 37 (SLDM, pp. 49–50). (25) *Ibid.*, 47 (*Ibid.*, pp. 58–9). (30) *Ibid.*, II, 38 (*Ibid.*, p. 50).
210. (5) *Ibid.*, 39 (*Ibid.*, pp. 50–1). (20) *Ibid.*, 41 (*Ibid.*, p. 52).
211. (2) *Ibid.*, IV, 47 (*Ibid.*, pp. 58–9). (7) *Ibid.* (*Ibid.*). (16) *Ibid.*, II, 67 (*Ibid.*, pp. 86–7); SVDP, *ibid.*, p. 179. (22) *Ibid.*, AFC, *ibid.* (SLDM, *ibid.*). (35) ACM, 535 (SVDP, *ibid.*, pp. 181–2).
212. (5) SVDP, *ibid.*, p. 184, Footnote 4. (8) ACM, 536 (SVDP, *ibid.*, pp. 182–183). (9) SVDP, *ibid.*, p. 184, Footnote 4. (23) Dirvin, *St. Catherine Labouré of the Miraculous Medal*, pp. 60–1. (39) *Conferences*, Vol. I, pp. 42–7.

213. (4) ACM, 546 (SVDP, *ibid.*, pp. 191–2). (32) AFC, *ibid.*, 48 (SLDM, pp. 59–60, also p. 1001, 48, Footnotes 1–4). (37) *Ibid.* (*Ibid.*).

214. (6) ACM, 558 (SVDP, *ibid.*, p. 206). (15) *Ibid.*, 564 (*Ibid.*, p. 214). (21) Elizabeth Stopp, *Madame de Chantal*, pp. 244–5.

215. (6) SVDP, XIII, pp. 125–8. (10) ACM, 569 (SVDP, II, pp. 218–23). (17) *Ibid.*, 568 (*Ibid.*, pp. 217–18). (34) *Conferences, ibid.*, pp. 48–52.

216. (9) AFC, IV, 55 (SLDM, pp. 69–70). (12) *Ibid.*, 59 (*Ibid.*, pp. 75–6). (14) *Ibid.*, 66 (*Ibid.*, pp. 85–6). (21) *Ibid.*, 55 (*Ibid.*, pp. 69–70). (32) *Ibid.*, 57 (*Ibid.*, pp. 72–3). (34) *Ibid.*, III, 64 (*Ibid.*, pp. 80–2). (39) *Ibid.* (*Ibid.*).

217. (4) *Ibid.*, II, 68 (*Ibid.*, pp. 87–8). (12) Cf. p. 211. (18) Cf. *supra.* (28) AFC, *ibid.*, 128 (SLDM, pp. 161–3); SVDP, pp. 259–62. (31) Cf. ACM, 546, 550 (SVDP, *ibid.*, pp. 191–2, 197–8, also p. 198, Footnote 1); AFC, *ibid.*, 35 (SLDM, pp. 43–4). (34) Cf. SVDP, *ibid.*, p. 258, Footnote 1.

218. (1) AFC, III, 102 (SLDM, pp. 123–4, also p. 1009, 102, Footnote 2). (4) *Conferences, ibid.* (17) ACM, 592 (SVDP, pp. 258–9). (25) AFC, V, "Conduite admirable de la divine Providence sur la Compagnie" (SLDM, pp. 913–915). (31) *Ibid.* (*Ibid.*). (34) Cf. pp. 29, 75–6, 96–7, 109, 111–15, *et al.*

219. (21) Cf. p. 179; *Conferences*, ibid., p. 63. (29) AFC, IV, 62 (SLDM, p. 78). (36) *Ibid.*, 63 (*Ibid.*, pp. 78–80).

220. (2) *Ibid.*, 65 (*Ibid.*, pp. 84–5). (8) *Ibid.* (*Ibid.*). (11) Cf. p. 216. (13) Cf. p. 195; also ACM, 533, 546 (SVDP, *ibid.*, pp. 179, 191–2). (30) AFC, III, 64 (SLDM, pp. 80–2).

221. (2) *Ibid.*, II, 64 *bis* (*Ibid.*, pp. 82–3). (4) ACM, 601 (SVDP, *ibid.*, pp. 268–269). (5) Cf. pp. 208, 216–17. (7) Cf. p. 217. (8) AFC, *ibid.* (SLDM, *ibid.*); ACM, *ibid.* (SVDP, *ibid.*). (25) Coste, *ibid.*, pp. 152–3.

222. (3) ACM, 611 (SVDP, *ibid.*, pp. 289–90). (11) *Ibid.*, 614 (*Ibid.*, p. 294). (16) *Ibid.*, 615 (*Ibid.*, p. 295). (21) *Ibid.*, 616 (*Ibid.*, pp. 295–6). (25) *Ibid.*, 617 (*Ibid.*, pp. 296–7). (37) AFC, III, 70 *bis* (SLDM, pp. 90–1).

223. (2) ACM, 620 (SVDP, *ibid.*, pp. 300–1). (8) AFC, II, 73 (SLDM, pp. 93–94). (12) *Ibid.*, 76 (*Ibid.*, pp. 97–8). (24) *Ibid.*, 77 (*Ibid.*, pp. 99–100). (34) *Ibid.* (*Ibid.*).

224. (3) *Ibid.*, IV, 78 (*Ibid.*, pp. 100–1). (12) *Ibid.*, 80 (*Ibid.*, pp. 102–3). (15) SLDM, p. 1006, 80, Footnote 1. (24) AFC, III, 82 (SLDM, 104–5). (29) ACM, 656 (SCDP, *ibid.*, pp. 383–4).

225. (6) AFC, *ibid.*, 97 (SLDM, pp. 118–19). (11) SVDP, *ibid.*, p. 383, Footnote 2. (29) AFC, II, 85 (SLDM, p. 107). (39) Cf. ACM, 617 (SVDP, *ibid.*, pp. 296–7), *et al.*

226. (7) SVDP, p. 401, Footnote 3. (11) AFC, *ibid.*, 86 (SLDM, pp. 107–8); SVDP, pp. 401–2. (21) AFC, III, 88 (SLDM, pp. 110–11). (29) *Ibid.*, II, 90 (*Ibid.*, pp. 111–12). (32) Cf. *Ibid.*, 85, 87 (*Ibid.*, pp. 107, 109); ACM, 657 (SVDP, *ibid.*, p. 385), *et al.* (33) AFC, *ibid.*, 90 (SLDM, pp. 111–12).

227. (3) *Ibid.*, III, 93 (*Ibid.*, p. 113). (9) *Ibid.*, II, 31 (*Ibid.*, pp. 38–40); ACM, 695 (SVDP, *ibid.*, pp. 438–40). (14) AFC, IV, 95 (SLDM, pp. 116–17). (19) *Ibid.*, 98 (*Ibid.*, pp. 119–20). (35) *Ibid.*, 99 (*Ibid.*, pp. 120–1). (38) *Ibid.*, II, 101 (*Ibid.*, pp. 122–3).

228. (4) *Ibid.* (*Ibid.*). (14) *Ibid.* (*Ibid.*). (16) *Ibid.*, III, 102 (*Ibid.*, pp. 123–4). (23) *Ibid.*, IV, 103 (*Ibid.*, pp. 124–6). (26) *Ibid.*, 104 (*Ibid.*, pp. 126–7).
229. (5) Cf. Coste, Vol. III, Chap. XLVII–XLVIII. (11) AFC, II, 286 *bis* (SLDM, p. 380); SVDP, *ibid.*, p. 465. (14) *Ibid.*, Footnote 1.
230. (2) AFC, III, 104 *bis* (SLDM, pp. 128–30). (15) *Ibid.*, 105 (*Ibid.*, pp. 130–132). (19) *Ibid.*, IV, 107 (*Ibid.*, p. 134). (23) *Ibid.*, 108 (*Ibid.*, pp. 136–7). (24) SVDP, *ibid.*, p. 478, Footnote 3. (35) AFC, II, 109 (SLDM, p. 137). (37) *Ibid.* (*Ibid.*).
231. (7) *Ibid.*, 110 (*Ibid.*, pp. 138–9). (9) Cf. p. 111. (20) AFC, *ibid.*, 111 (SLDM, pp. 139–40). (25) *Ibid.*, 113 (*Ibid.*, p. 141).
232. (2) *Conferences, ibid.*, pp. 152–3.

CHAPTER XIII

234. (5) *Ibid.*, pp. 160–79. (9) *Ibid.*, *passim.* (11) Cf. Calvet, *op. cit.*, pp. 159ff. (23) AFC, *ibid.*, 118 (SLDM, pp. 147–8); SVDP, *ibid.*, pp. 524–5. (25) AFC, III, 119, and II, 120 (SLDM, pp. 149–51). (35) *Ibid.*, 120 (*Ibid.*, pp. 150–1); SVDP, *ibid.*, pp. 528–9. (37) AFC, *ibid.* (SLDM, *ibid.*); SVDP, *ibid.*
235. (20) AFC, III, 121 (SLDM, pp. 151–3). (25) *Ibid.*, II, 123 (*Ibid.*, p. 154); SVDP, *ibid.*, pp. 541–2.
236. (27) AFC, *ibid.*, 124 (SLDM, pp. 154–6); SVDP, *ibid.*, pp. 542–3. (29) Cf. pp. 225–6. (32) AFC, *ibid.*, 125 (SLDM, pp. 156–7); SVDP, *ibid.*, pp. 545–6.
237. (21) AFC, *ibid.* (SLDM, *ibid.*); SVDP, *ibid.* (34) ACM, 771 (SVDP, *ibid.*, pp. 546–7). (39) SVDP, *ibid.*, p. 547, Footnote 1.
238. (5) *Ibid.*, pp. 547–8. (26) ACM, 773 (SVDP, *ibid.*, pp. 548–53).
239. (14) *Ibid.* (*Ibid.*). (17) Cf. SVDP, *ibid.*, p. 553, Footnote 4, and Coste, Vol. I, p. 350. (21) SVDP, XIII, p. 551. (23) Cf. pp. 218–19. (38) AFC, *ibid.*, 130 *quater* (SLDM, p. 171).
240. (4) *Ibid.*, IV, 129 (*Ibid.*, p. 164). (7) *Ibid.*, II, 129 *bis* (*Ibid.*, p. 165); Coste, *ibid.*, p. 419. (9) *Ibid.* (11) AFC, *ibid.*, IV, 130 (SLDM, p. 170). (18) *Ibid.*, III, 130 *bis* (*Ibid.*, p. 169). (20) *Ibid.*, 130 *ter* (*Ibid.*, p. 170). (27) *Ibid.*, II, 131 (*Ibid.*, p. 172). (38) *Ibid.* (*Ibid.*).
241. (1) *Conferences, ibid.*, pp. 214–66. (4) *Ibid.*, p. 214. (40) *Ibid.*, pp. 214–15.
242. (3) *Ibid.*, p. 224. (15) *Ibid.*, p. 225. (27) AFC, *ibid.*, 132 *bis* (SLDM, pp. 174–5).
243. (2) *Ibid.* (*Ibid.*). (7) *Ibid.*, 137 (*Ibid.*, pp. 182–3); SVDP, *ibid.*, pp. 574–5. (15) SVDP, *ibid.*, pp. 575–6. (32) *Ibid.*
244. (1) AFC, *ibid.*, 132 *ter* (SLDM, pp. 175–7); *Ibid.*, 132 *quater* (*Ibid.*, pp. 177–8); SVDP, *ibid.*, pp. 588–91. (3) AFC, *ibid.* (SLDM, *ibid.*). (11) *Ibid.*, III, 134 (*Ibid.*, pp. 179–80). (15) ACM, 803 (SVDP, *ibid.*, pp. 588–591). (16) AFC, *ibid.*, 133 (SLDM, pp. 178–9). (29) *Ibid.* (*Ibid.*). (35) SVDP, *ibid.*, p. 599, Footnote 5. (38) AFC, II, 140 (SLDM, pp. 186–7).
245. (2) *Ibid.*, III, 141 (*Ibid.*, pp. 187–8). (10) SVDP, *ibid.* (22) AFC, *ibid.*, II,

140 (SLDM, pp. 186–7). (23) Cf. p. 247. (25) SVDP, XIII, pp. 589–603.
247. (7) *Ibid.* (36) AFC, *ibid.*, III, 144 (SLDM, pp. 190–2).
248. (5) *Conferences, ibid.*, pp. 230–1. (22) AFC, II, 159 (SLDM, pp. 211–20). (30) ACM, 830 (SVDP, III, p. 5). (37) AFC, *ibid.* (SLDM, *ibid.*).
249. (5) Cf. pp. 196ff. (6) AFC, *ibid.*, 145 (SLDM, pp. 192–3). (15) ACM, 832 (SVDP, *ibid.*, pp. 7–11). (23) AFC, *ibid.*, 159 (SLDM, pp. 211–20). (31) *Ibid.*, IV, 178 *bis* (*Ibid.*, pp. 246–7). (34) *Ibid.*, 182 *bis* (*Ibid.*, pp. 253–5). (35) ACM, 833 (SVDP, *ibid.*, pp. 11–14).
250. (6) AFC, II, 159 (SLDM, pp. 211–20). (11) *Ibid.* (*Ibid.*). (18) *Ibid.*, 138 (*Ibid.*, pp. 183–4). (30) *Ibid.*, 159 (*Ibid.*, pp. 211–20). (38) *Ibid.*, 147 (*Ibid.*, pp. 195–6).
251. (5) *Ibid.*, 159 (*Ibid.*, pp. 211–20). (16) *Ibid.* (*Ibid.*). (19) *Ibid.* (*Ibid.*). (27) *Ibid.* (*Ibid.*). (35) *Ibid.*, 148 (*Ibid.*, pp. 197–9).
252. (13) *Ibid.*, III, 149 (*Ibid.*, pp. 199–200). (22) *Ibid.*, 150 (*Ibid.*, pp. 200–1).
253. (6) ACM, *ibid.* (SVDP, *ibid.*). (37) AFC, II, 151 (SLDM, pp. 201–2).
254. (20) *Ibid.*, III, 152 (*Ibid.*, pp. 203–4). (26) ACM, 836 (SVDP, *ibid.*, pp. 16–17). (27) SVDP, *ibid.*, p. 17, Footnotes 5 and 6. (32) AFC, *ibid.*, 154 (SLDM, pp. 205–6). (35) SLDM, p. 1014, 155, Footnote 1. (37) AFC, II, 155 (SLDM, pp. 206–8).
255. (7) *Ibid.* (*Ibid.*). (19) *Ibid.* (*Ibid.*). (23) ACM, 841 (SVDP, *ibid.*, p. 23). (39) AFC, *ibid.*, 159 (SLDM, pp. 211–20).
256. (8) *Ibid.*, III, 160 (*Ibid.*, pp. 220–1). (18) *Ibid.*, 161 (*Ibid.*, pp. 221–3). (24) *Ibid.*, 162 (*Ibid.*, pp. 222–3). (30) *Ibid.*, 163 (*Ibid.*, pp. 223–4).
257. (2) *Ibid.*, 166 (*Ibid.*, pp. 226–7). (6) Cf. p. 239. (8) SVDP, XIII, pp. 557–565.

CHAPTER XIV

258. (4) AFC, *ibid.*, 166, 168 (SLDM, pp. 226–7, 231–2). (8) SLDM, p. 1015, 169, Footnote 1. (18) AFC, *ibid.*, 169 (SLDM, pp. 232–3).
259. (2) *Ibid.*, 171 (*Ibid.*, pp. 234–5). (6) *Ibid.*, 172 (*Ibid.*, pp. 235–6). (22) *Ibid.*, II, 173 (*Ibid.*, pp. 237–8). (28) SVDP, III, p. 171, Footnote 7.
260. (23) Cf. AFC, *ibid.*, 181 (SLDM, pp. 250–1). (31) ACM, 939 (SVDP, *ibid.*, pp. 174–80). (37) AFC, *ibid.*, III, 174 (SLDM, pp. 240–2).
261. (8) *Ibid.*, II, 179 (*Ibid.*, pp. 247–9). (15) Cf. ACM, 954, 955, 956 (SVDP, *ibid.*, p. 199). (20) AFC, V, "Aux Soeurs allant à Montreuil-sur-Mer" (SLDM, pp. 977–81); SVDP, *ibid.*, p. 206, Footnote 1. (23) *Ibid.*, XIII, pp. 629–45.
262. (1) *Ibid.* (8) AFC, *ibid.* (SLDM, *ibid.*). (13) *Ibid.*, II, 213 (*Ibid.*, p. 294); ACM, 966 (SVDP, *ibid.*, pp. 208–9). (26) AFC, *ibid.*, 181 (SLDM, pp. 250–251). (30) *Ibid.*, 213 (*Ibid.*, p. 294); SVDP, *ibid.*, pp. 208–9. (32) AFC, III, 204 (SLDM, pp. 284–5).
263. (6) *Ibid.*, III, 181 *bis* (*Ibid.*, pp. 251–2). (11) *Ibid.*, 182 (*Ibid.*, pp. 252–3). (25) ACM, 969 (SVDP, *ibid.*, pp. 210–11). (39) AFC, II, 188 (SLDM, p. 262); SVDP, *ibid.*, p. 211.
264. (7) AFC, III, 181 *bis* (SLDM, pp. 251–2); SVDP, XIII, pp. 629–30. (16)

AFC, *ibid.*, (SLDM, p. 256). (19) *Ibid.*, 185, 186 (*Ibid.*, pp. 256–9). (36) *Ibid.*, 185 (*Ibid.*, pp. 256–8).

265. (6) *Ibid.*, 187 (*Ibid.*, pp. 260–1). (27) *Ibid.*, 189 (*Ibid.*, pp. 262–4).

266. (18) ACM, 973 (SVDP, III, pp. 213–15). (21) AFC, *ibid.*, 186 *bis* (SLDM, p. 259). (23) *Ibid.*, 189 (*Ibid.*, pp. 262–4). (26) *Ibid.*, 186 (*Ibid.*, pp. 258–259). (35) *Ibid.*, II, 192 (*Ibid.*, pp. 267–8); SVDP, *ibid.*, pp. 228–30. (38) AFC, III, 193 (SLDM, pp. 268–9).

267. (13) *Ibid.*, II, 199 (SLDM, pp. 276–7).

268. (32) SVDP, XIII, pp. 646–59.

269. (3) AFC, III, 200 (SLDM, p. 277). (11) *Ibid.*, 200 *bis* (*Ibid.*, p. 278). (20) *Ibid.*, 201 (*Ibid.*, p. 279).

270. (3) *Ibid.*, II, 202 (*Ibid.*, pp. 281–2). (12) *Ibid.*, 203 (*Ibid.*, pp. 282–3). (19) *Ibid.*, 206 (*Ibid.*, pp. 285–6). (30) *Ibid.*, III, 208 (*Ibid.*, pp. 288–9). (39) SVDP, *ibid.*, pp. 659–70.

271. (6) AFC, *ibid.*, 210 (SLDM, pp. 290–1). (11) *Ibid.*, 210 *bis* (*Ibid.*, p. 292). (21) *Ibid.*, II, 211 (*Ibid.*, p. 293). (38) SVDP, III, p. 360, Footnote 2.

272. (3) ACM, 1063 (SVDP, *ibid.*, pp. 360–1). (4) For a discussion of the relationship between Anne and the Cardinal, cf. SVDP, *ibid.*, p. 360, Footnote 2, and Calvet, *Saint Vincent de Paul*, pp. 142–5, *et al.* (19) For a good treatment of the Fronde, cf. Calvet, *op. cit.*, pp. 182–95. (25) AFC, III, 214 (SLDM, pp. 295–6). (34) *Ibid.*, 215 (*Ibid.*, pp. 296–7). (36) *Ibid.* (*Ibid.*). (38) *Ibid.*, 216 (*Ibid.*, p. 297).

273. (5) *Ibid.*, 219 (*Ibid.*, pp. 300–1). (10) *Ibid.*, 218 (*Ibid.*, pp. 301–2). (12) *Ibid.*, 220 (*Ibid.*, pp. 302–3). (15) *Ibid.* (*Ibid.*). (18) *Ibid.* (*Ibid.*). (21) *Ibid.* (*Ibid.*). (22) *Ibid.*, 216 (*Ibid.*, p. 297). (37) *Ibid.*, 221 (*Ibid.*, pp. 303–4).

274. (13) SVDP, *ibid.*, p. 361, Footnote 4. (15) ACM, 1063 (SVDP, *ibid.*, pp. 360–1). (25) AFC, II, 222 (SLDM, p. 304). (32) *Ibid.* (*Ibid.*); SVDP, *ibid.*, pp. 387–8. (34) AFC, III, 223 (SLDM, p. 305). (37) *Ibid.*, 224 (*Ibid.*, pp. 305–6). (39) *Ibid.*, 226 (*Ibid.*, pp. 307–8).

275. (5) *Ibid.*, 230 (*Ibid.*, pp. 311–12). (10) *Ibid.*, 233 (*Ibid.*, p. 315). (26) *Ibid.*, II, 232 (*Ibid.*, pp. 313–14).

276. (13) *Ibid.*, III, 234 (*Ibid.*, pp. 316–17). (21) *Ibid.*, 235 (*Ibid.*, p. 319). (39) ACM, 1087 (SVDP, *ibid.*, pp. 402–4).

277. (5) *Ibid.* (*Ibid.*). (9) SVDP, *ibid.*, p. 402, Footnote 1. (13) ACM, 1089 (SVDP, *ibid.*, pp. 406–8). (16) *Ibid.*, 1086 (*Ibid.*, p. 401). (18) SVDP, *ibid.*, p. 403, Footnote 2. (23) ACM, 1088 (SVDP, *ibid.*, pp. 405–6). (38) *Ibid.*, 1090 (*Ibid.*, pp. 408–10).

278. (5) SVDP, *ibid.*, pp. 414–15. (12) ACM, 1094 (SVDP, *ibid.*, pp. 419–20). (15) *Ibid.*, 1096 (*Ibid.*, pp. 421–3). (17) *Ibid.* (*Ibid.*). (20) SVDP, *ibid.*, p. 415, Footnote 18. (24) *Ibid.*, p. 422, Footnote 2; cf. pp. 504–5. (32) ACM, 1097 (SVDP, *ibid.*, pp. 423–6). (35) *Ibid.*, 1099 (*Ibid.*, pp. 427–8). (39) AFC, II, 242 (SLDM, p. 325); SVDP, *ibid.*, pp. 426–7.

279. (5) AFC, IV, 240 (SLDM, p. 323). (8) ACM, 1097 (SVDP, *ibid.*, pp. 423–426, and *ibid.*, p. 424, Footnote 3). (28) Cf. pp. 250ff. (33) Cf. p. 256. (39) AFC, II, 242 (SLDM, p. 325).

280. (3) ACM, 1101 (SVDP, *ibid.*, pp. 430–3). (5) AFC, III, 246 (SLDM, p. 328). (10) ACM, 1103 (SVDP, *ibid.*, pp. 435–7). (16) *Ibid.* (*Ibid.*). (22) SVDP, *ibid.*, p. 437, Footnote 4. (26) ACM, 1103 (SVDP, *ibid.*, pp. 435–7). (33) *Ibid.*, 1105 (*Ibid.*, pp. 448–9). (35) SVDP, *ibid.*, p. 449, Footnote 3.
281. (2) AFC, II, 247 (SLDM, pp. 329–30). (9) *Ibid.*, III, 249 (*Ibid.*, pp. 331–332). (13) *Ibid.*, 250 (*Ibid.*, pp. 332–3). (17) *Ibid.*, 253 (*Ibid.*, pp. 336–7). (20) SVDP, *ibid.*, p. 452, Footnote 2; cf. also AFC, *ibid.*, 250 (SLDM, pp. 332–3). (29) *Ibid.*, 252 (*Ibid.*, pp. 334–5). (32) *Ibid.*, 253 (*Ibid.*, pp. 336–7).
282. (13) *Ibid.*, 254 (*Ibid.*, p. 338). (31) *Ibid.*, II, 255 (*Ibid.*, p. 339); SVDP, *ibid.*, pp. 477–8.
283. (2) ACM, 1132 (SVDP, *ibid.*, pp. 479–80). (22) AFC, III, 256 *bis* (SLDM, pp. 340–1). (28) ACM, 1132 (SVDP, *ibid.*, pp. 479–80). (33) AFC, *ibid.*, 259 (SLDM, p. 343). (37) *Ibid.*, 261 (*Ibid.*, pp. 344–6).
284. (15) *Ibid.*, II, 266 (*Ibid.*, pp. 349–50); SVDP, *ibid.*, pp. 508–9. (17) AFC, *ibid.*, 267 (SLDM, pp. 350–1); SVDP, *ibid.*, pp. 510–11. (28) AFC, *ibid.*, 263 (SLDM, pp. 346–7). (36) SVDP, *ibid.*, p. 517, Footnote 6.
285. (19) AFC, *ibid.*, 272 *bis* (SLDM, pp. 360–1); SVDP, *ibid.*, pp. 516–17. (26) AFC, *ibid.*, 274 (SLDM, pp. 362–3). (31) *Ibid.* (*Ibid.*). (35) *Ibid.*, 267 (*Ibid.*, pp. 350–1). (37) SVDP, *ibid.*, p. 516, Footnote 2.
286. (3) AFC, III, 275 (SLDM, pp. 365–6). (9) ACM, 1177 (SVDP, *ibid.*, pp. 544–5). (11) SVDP, *ibid.*, p. 544, Footnote 3. (14) AFC, II, 279 (SLDM, p. 371); SVDP, *ibid.*, pp. 595–6. (15) *Ibid.*, p. 595, Footnote 4.

CHAPTER XV

287. (4) AFC, III, 277 (SLDM, pp. 368–9). (17) *Ibid.* (*Ibid.*). (21) *Ibid.*, II, 277 *bis* (SLDM, p. 369). (25) *Ibid.* (*Ibid.*). (27) *Ibid.*, III, 280 (*Ibid.*, p. 372).
288. (4) *Ibid.* (*Ibid.*). (26) ACM, 1192 (SVDP, *ibid.*, pp. 613–17).
289. (6) The reference is to a grant made to the Company by Louis XIII in July 1642: cf. Coste, Vol. II, pp. 271–2. (12) AFC, II, 283 (SLDM, pp. 373–5). (20) SVDP, IV, p. 170, Footnote 3. (27) ACM, 1218 (SVDP, *ibid.*, pp. 21–2).
290. (5) AFC, *ibid.* (SLDM, *ibid.*). (10) ACM, *ibid.* (SVDP, *ibid.*). (16) *Ibid.* (*Ibid.*). (21) AFC, III, 284 (SLDM, pp. 376–7). (30) *Ibid.*, 286 (*Ibid.*, pp. 379–80). (33) *Ibid.*, 289 (*Ibid.*, pp. 383–4).
291. (2) *Ibid.*, IV, 288 (*Ibid.*, p. 382). (19) *Ibid.*, III, 290 (*Ibid.*, pp. 385–6). (20) Cf. p. 280. (25) AFC, *ibid.*, 291 (SLDM, p. 386, and *ibid.*, p. 1028, 291, Footnote 1). (27) *Ibid.*, 292 (*Ibid.*, p. 387). (36) *Ibid.* (*Ibid.*). (39) *Ibid.*, 294 (*Ibid.*, p. 389, and *ibid.*, p. 1029, Footnote 1).
292. (8) *Ibid.*, 296 (*Ibid.*, pp. 390–1). (10) Cf. p. 287. (16) AFC, *ibid.*, 297 (SLDM, pp. 393–4). (20) *Ibid.*, also 300 (*Ibid.*, also pp. 395–6). (30) *Ibid.* (*Ibid.*). (34) ACM, 1330 (SVDP, *ibid.*, pp. 161–2). (38) AFC, II, 301 (SLDM, p. 397); SVDP, *ibid.*, pp. 162–3.
293. (6) SVDP, XIII, pp. 671–3. (22) *Ibid.* (32) *Ibid.*, pp. 673–80.

294. (7) AFC, III, 302 (SLDM, p. 398). (18) Ibid., II, 303 (Ibid., pp. 398–9). (20) SLDM, p. 1029, 303, Footnote 1. (26) ACM, 1338 (SVDP, ibid., p. 170). (28) SVDP, ibid., p. 170, Footnote 3.

295. (1) AFC, II, 305 (SLDM, p. 403); SVDP, ibid., pp. 201–2. (12) AFC, "Troisième Retraite" (SLDM, p. 922). (27) Ibid., III, 306 bis (Ibid., pp. 404–5). (36) Ibid., II, 307 (Ibid. pp. 405–6); SVDP, ibid., p. 212.

296. (9) ACM, 1370 (SVDP, ibid., pp. 213–14). (26) AFC, III, 309 (SLDM, pp. 407–8). (29) SVDP, XIII, ibid.

297. (4) AFC, ibid., 310 (SLDM, pp. 408–9). (10) Ibid., 311 (Ibid., p. 410). (16) Ibid., 313 (Ibid., p. 412). (20) Ibid., 314 (Ibid., pp. 413–14).

298. (6) Ibid., II, 315 (Ibid., pp. 414–15). (17) Ibid., III, 316 (Ibid., p. 416). (30) Ibid., IV, 322 (Ibid., pp. 421–2).

299. (3) Ibid., III, 323 (Ibid., p. 423). (8) Cf. p. 261. (18) AFC, II, 323 bis (SLDM, pp. 424–5). (39) Ibid., III, 324 (Ibid., pp. 425–6).

300. (3) ACM, 1401 (SVDP, ibid., pp. 246–9, and ibid., p. 246, Footnote 1). (7) Coste, Vol. I, pp. 331–5. (9) Ibid., p. 332, Footnote 91. (13) ACM, ibid. (SVDP, ibid.). (20) AFC, ibid., 328 (SLDM, pp. 429–30). (28) ACM, 1405 (SVDP, ibid., pp. 253–4). (39) Ibid., 1406 (Ibid., p. 255).

301. (11) Ibid., 1407 (Ibid., p. 256). (14) AFC, ibid., 331 (SLDM, pp. 432–3). (17) Ibid., IV, 330 (Ibid., pp. 431–2). (29) ACM, 1411 (SVDP, ibid., pp. 259–60). (36) AFC, ibid., 329 (SLDM, pp. 430–1).

302. (4) Ibid., 330 (Ibid., pp. 431–2). (7) Ibid., 329 (Ibid., pp. 430–1). (8) Ibid., 330 (Ibid., pp. 431–2). (11) Ibid., 329 (Ibid., pp. 430–1). (20) Cf. Coste, ibid., p. 360. (26) AFC, II, 333 (SLDM, pp. 434–6); SVDP, ibid., pp. 274–5.

303. (15) AFC, ibid. (SLDM, ibid.); SVDP, ibid. (18) Coste, ibid. (31) Ibid., pp. 360–1. (36) AFC, ibid., 335 (SLDM, pp. 437–8).

304. (1) ACM, 1428 (SVDP, ibid., pp. 279–80). (2) AFC, ibid. (SLDM, ibid.). (15) Ibid., III, 330 (SLDM, pp. 431–2). (20) Ibid., 337 (Ibid., pp. 439–440). (21) Ibid., 339 (Ibid., pp. 445–6). (30) Ibid., 338 (Ibid., pp. 441–3).

305. (3) Ibid. (Ibid.). (21) Ibid., 339 (Ibid., pp. 445–6). (23) Ibid., 340 (Ibid., p. 447). (32) Ibid., 342 (Ibid., p. 449). (38) Ibid., 344 (Ibid., pp. 450–1).

306. (3) Ibid. (Ibid.). (20) For a detailed account of the climax of the Fronde, cf. Coste, Vol. II, Chap. XLII. (24) ACM, 1494 (SVDP, ibid., pp. 376–9).

307. (2) SVDP, ibid., p. 378, Footnote 2. (6) Ibid., p. 382, Footnote 1. (11) ACM, 1498 (SVDP, ibid., pp. 381–3). (33) AFC, II, 348 (SLDM, pp. 455–6).

308. (6) ACM, 1501 (SVDP, ibid., p. 386). (17) SVDP, ibid., p. 389. (22) AFC, III, 353 (SLDM, pp. 462–3). (32) ACM, 1509 (SVDP, ibid., pp. 397–9). (39) Ibid., 1510 (Ibid., pp. 400–3, and ibid., p. 402, Footnote 9).

309. (8) ACM, ibid. (SVDP, ibid., and ibid., p. 401, Footnote 6). (19) AFC, ibid., (SLDM, ibid.). (29) ACM, 1511 (SVDP, ibid., pp. 403–7).

310. (2) Ibid., 1512 (Ibid., pp. 408–10). (8) Ibid., 1515, 1516 (Ibid., pp. 417–419, 419–21). (12) SVDP, ibid., p. 423, Footnote 1. (15) ACM, 1518 (SVDP, ibid., p. 423). (19) SVDP, ibid., p. 423, Footnote 6. (29) ACM, 1519 (SVDP, ibid., pp. 424–5).

311. (3) AFC, II, 408 (SLDM, pp. 522–3). (8) SVDP, *ibid.*, p. 435, Footnote 5. (15) AFC, *ibid.*, 350 (SLDM, pp. 457–8); SVDP, *ibid.*, p. 428. (29) ACM, 1533 (SVDP, *ibid.*, pp. 445–6, and *ibid.*, p. 446, Footnote 1).
312. (13) SVDP, *ibid.*, pp. 455–9. (28) AFC, III, 351 (SLDM, pp. 458–60). (37) ACM, 1542 (SVDP, *ibid.*, pp. 462–3).
313. (11) *Ibid.*, 1546 (*Ibid.*, pp. 468–9). (16) SVDP, *ibid.*, p. 473, Footnote 1. (26) ACM, 1551 (SVDP, *ibid.*, pp. 473–8). (27) SVDP, *ibid.*, p. 478, Footnote 14. (38) Cf. Coste, Vol. I, p. 441.
314. (5) AFC, 1056. (12) *Ibid.*, 354 *bis* (SLDM, p. 464). (15) SVDP, *ibid.*, p. 487. (19) AFC, *ibid.* (SLDM, *ibid.*). (24) *Ibid.*, 354 (*Ibid.*, pp. 463–4).
315. (15) *Ibid.*, II, 356 (*Ibid.*, pp. 465–6). (22) *Ibid.*, III, 356 *bis* (*Ibid.*, pp. 466–7). (25) *Ibid.*, III, 358 (*Ibid.*, pp. 469–70).

CHAPTER XVI

316. (2) *Ibid.* (*Ibid.*). (9) SVDP, XIII, pp. 733–7. (20) ACM, 1538 (SVDP, *ibid.*, pp. 536–7). (23) AFC, *ibid.*, 359, 396 (SLDM, pp. 470–1, 512).
317. (3) *Ibid.*, 359 (*Ibid.*, pp. 470–1). (6) ACM, 1584 (SVDP, *ibid.*, pp. 537–541). (15) *Ibid.* (*Ibid.*). (24) *Ibid.*, 1585 (*Ibid.*, pp. 542–3). (28) *Ibid.*, 1584 (*Ibid.*, pp. 537–41, and *ibid.*, p. 539, Footnote 7. (36) Cf. pp. 311–312.
318. (14) Coste, Vol. II, p. 413. (15) For a complete account of the condition and relief of Picardy and Champagne, cf. *ibid.*, Chap. XLI. (37) *Ibid.*, p. 408.
319. (2) *Ibid.*, pp. 426, 436–9. (9) AFC, *ibid.*, 360 (SLDM, pp. 471–2). (33) *Conferences*, Vol. II, pp. 194–202.
320. (8) AFC, *ibid.*, 363 (SLDM, pp. 476–8). (24) SVDP, *ibid.*, pp. 552–3, and *ibid.*, p. 552, Footnote 2. (27) AFC, II, 364 (SLDM, p. 478). (30) *Ibid.* (*Ibid.*). (35) *Ibid.*, III, 365 *bis* (*Ibid.*, pp. 480–1).
321. (8) *Ibid.*, 362 (*Ibid.*, pp. 475–6). (15) *Ibid.*, 362 (*Ibid.*, pp. 475–6). (19) ACM, 1656 (SVDP, V, p. 15). (21) *Ibid.*, 1658 (*Ibid.*, pp. 18–19). (30) AFC, *ibid.*, 368 (SLDM, pp. 484–5). (35) ACM, 1617 (SVDP, IV, p. 590).
322. (22) *Ibid.*, 1626 (*Ibid.*, pp. 602–3).
323. (3) *Ibid.*, 1648 (*Ibid.*, V, p. 405). (13) AFC, II, 369 (SLDM, pp. 485–486). (19) *Ibid.* (*Ibid.*). (29) ACM, 1650 (SVDP, *ibid.*, pp. 6–7).
324. (3) AFC, III, 372 (SLDM, pp. 488–9). (5) ACM, 1647 (SVDP, *ibid.*, pp. 3–4). (18) AFC, *ibid.*, 370 (SLDM, pp. 486–7). (25) *Ibid.*, 373 (*Ibid.*, pp. 489–90). (28) ACM, 1685 (SVDP, *ibid.*, pp. 51–2). (33) AFC, *ibid.*, 374 (SLDM, pp. 490–1).
325. (4) *Ibid.*, II, 379 (SLDM, pp. 496–7). (10) *Ibid.*, 380 (*Ibid.*, pp. 497–8). (18) *Ibid.*, IV, 382 (*Ibid.*, pp. 499–500).
326. (11) *Conferences, ibid.*, pp. 263–6. (22) ACM, 1692 (SVDP, *ibid.*, pp. 58–9). (31) AFC, *ibid.*, 399 (SLDM, pp. 514–15). (39) *Ibid.*, IV, 401 (*Ibid.*, pp. 517–18).
327. (15) *Ibid.*, II, 392 (*Ibid.*, p. 509). (26) *Ibid.*, III, 395 (*Ibid.*, pp. 511–12).
328. (4) *Ibid.*, 398 (*Ibid.*, pp. 513–14). (8) *Ibid.*, 404 (*Ibid.*, pp. 519–20). (16)

Ibid., 406 (*Ibid.*, p. 521). (20) Cf. ACM, 1769 (SVDP, *ibid.*, pp. 44–6). (29) *Ibid.*, 1757 (*Ibid.*, pp. 162–3).

329. (2) *Ibid.*, 1761 (*Ibid.*, pp. 167–8). (4) *Ibid.*, 1768, 1770, 1771 (*Ibid.*, pp. 177–8, 178–81, 182–3). (6) *Ibid.*, 1773, 1774 (*Ibid.*, pp. 184–5, 185–6). (22) AFC, II, 411 (SLDM, p. 525). (29) *Ibid.*, III, 412 (*Ibid.*, p. 526). (35) *Ibid.* (*Ibid.*).

330. (10) ACM, 1788 (SVDP, *ibid.*, pp. 206–8). (19) AFC, II, 418 (SLDM, pp. 531–2); SVDP, *ibid.*, pp. 223–4; ACM, 1809 (SVDP, *ibid.*, pp. 234–5). (37) AFC, *ibid.*, 416 (SLDM, pp. 529–30).

331. (5) ACM, 1803 (SVDP, *ibid.*, pp. 227–9). (18) AFC, III, 419 (SLDM, pp. 532–3). (28) *Ibid.*, 422 (*Ibid.*, p. 538). (31) *Ibid.*, and 421 (*Ibid.*, and pp. 537–8). (36) *Ibid.*, II, 81 (*Ibid.*, pp. 103–4); SVDP, *ibid.*, p. 240, and *ibid.*, Footnote 3.

332. (7) AFC, III, 432 (SLDM, pp. 546–7). (14) ACM, 1831 (SVDP, *ibid.*, p. 266). (25) *Ibid.*, 1833 (SVDP, *ibid.*, pp. 268–9). (34) AFC, *ibid.*, 425 (SLDM, pp. 540–1).

333. (6) *Ibid.*, II, 428 (*Ibid.*, pp. 543–4); SVDP, *ibid.*, pp. 419–20. (7) AFC, *ibid.* (SLDM, *ibid.*); SVDP, *ibid.* (14) Cf. p. 125. (18) AFC, *ibid.*, 430 (SLDM, pp. 545–6); SVDP, *ibid.*, pp. 353–4. (30) ACM, 1861 (SVDP, *ibid.*, pp. 357–61). (32) *Ibid.*, 1870 (*Ibid.*, pp. 372–7).

334. (11) *Ibid.*, 1861 (*Ibid.*, pp. 357–61). (14) *Ibid.*, 1882 (*Ibid.*, pp. 390–1).

335. (4) SVDP, XIII, pp. 687–93. (10) AFC, III, 433 (SLDM, pp. 547–8). (23) *Ibid.*, 435 (*Ibid.*, pp. 549–50). (30) *Ibid.*, 436 (*Ibid.*, pp. 550–1). (35) *Ibid.*, 438 (*Ibid.*, p. 552).

336. (2) *Ibid.*, 439 (*Ibid.*, p. 553). (4) *Ibid.*, 440 (*Ibid.*, pp. 554–5). (13) ACM, 1901 (SVDP, *ibid.*, pp. 406–7). (24) AFC, II, 446 (SLDM, pp. 558–559).

337. (2) *Ibid.*, III, 447 (*Ibid.*, pp. 559–62). (10) ACM, 1907 (SVDP, *ibid.*, pp. 411–13). (25) AFC, II, 445 (SLDM, p. 558); SVDP, *ibid.*, pp. 405–6. (36) *Ibid.*, XIII, pp. 569–72.

338. (12) Cf. Coste, Vol. I, p. 362, Footnote 68. (26) SVDP, *ibid.*, pp. 572–7. (35) *Conferences*, Vol. III, p. 89.

339. (1) SVDP, *ibid.* (7) Coste, *ibid.*, pp. 364–5. (12) *Ibid.*, p. 363. (22) SVDP, *ibid.*

340. (7) *Conferences*, *ibid.*, p. 91; Coste, *ibid.*, p. 364. (39) SVDP, *ibid.*, pp. 693–701.

341. (12) *Ibid.* (30) *Conferences*, *ibid.*, pp. 92–105.

CHAPTER XVII

342. (11) *Conferences*, *ibid.*, p. 99. (22) AFC, III, 450 (SLDM, pp. 563–4). (24) *Ibid.*, 451 (*Ibid.*, p. 565).

343. (1) Cf. p. 335. (3) AFC, IV, 452 (SLDM, p. 566). (9) *Ibid.*, II, 453 (*Ibid.*, pp. 567–8). (12) *Ibid.*, 496 (*Ibid.*, p. 612). (15) *Ibid.*, 455 (*Ibid.*, p. 570). (20) *Ibid.*, 456 (*Ibid.*, pp. 570–1). (22) SLDM, p. 1040, 456, Footnote 1. (28) AFC, *ibid.*, 457 (SLDM, pp. 571–2).

344. (10) *Ibid.*, 459 (*Ibid.*, p. 573); SVDP, V, p. 460. (12) *Conferences, ibid.*, pp. 120–34. (14) AFC, III, 461 (SLDM, pp. 575–6). (27) *Ibid.*, II, 462 (*Ibid.*, p. 576). (33) *Ibid.*, 467 (*Ibid.*, p. 583); SVDP, *ibid.*, pp. 554–5). (37) *Ibid.*, 467 bis (*Ibid.*, p. 584).

345. (3) *Ibid.*, III, 468 (*Ibid.*, p. 584). (5) *Ibid.*, II, 470 (*Ibid.*, p. 585). (10) *Ibid.*, III, 471 (*Ibid.*, pp. 586–7). (16) *Ibid.*, II, 472 (*Ibid.*, pp. 587–8); SVDP, *ibid.*, p. 589. (22) *Ibid.*, III, 473 (*Ibid.*, pp. 588–9). (29) SVDP, XIII, pp. 711–15. (39) *Ibid.*

346. (4) *Ibid.*, pp. 717–19. (6) Cf. ACM, 2063 (SVDP, V, pp. 610–11). (8) *Ibid.*, 2068 (*Ibid.*, pp. 616–18). (11) *Ibid.*, 2076 (*Ibid.*, pp. 624–6). (17) AFC, *ibid.*, 478 (SLDM, p. 593). (25) *Ibid.*, "Testament de Mlle Le Gras" (*Ibid.*, p. 943). (31) *Ibid.*, IV, 479 (*Ibid.*, pp. 593–5). (39) *Ibid.* (*Ibid.*).

347. (9) *Ibid.*, III, 480 (*Ibid.*, pp. 595–6). (25) *Conferences, ibid.*, p. 178.

348. (5) *Ibid.*, pp. 163–4. (18) ACM, 2109 (SVDP, VI, pp. 39–45). (27) AFC, *ibid.*, 489 (SLDM, pp. 604–5). (31) *Ibid.*, 488 (*Ibid.*, pp. 603–4). (37) *Ibid.*, 489 (*Ibid.*, pp. 605–6).

349. (8) Cf. *Conferences, ibid.*, p. 173. (20) *Ibid.*, pp. 173–9. (28) AFC, II, 490 (SLDM, pp. 606–7).

350. (3) SVDP, XIII, p. 730. (13) ACM, 2128 (SVDP, VI, pp. 65–6). (17) AFC, *ibid.* (SLDM, *ibid.*). (26) *Ibid.*, 492 (*Ibid.*, p. 608). (34) *Ibid.*, IV, 494 (*Ibid.*, pp. 609–10).

351. (3) SVDP, *ibid.*, p. 90, Footnote 1. (5) AFC, "Aux Soeurs qu'on envoyait à Arras" (SLDM, pp. 981–4). (26) *Conferences, ibid.*, pp. 197–201. (33) AFC, *ibid.* (SLDM, *ibid.*). (37) ACM, 2130 (SVDP, *ibid.*, pp. 67–72).

352. (3) *Ibid.*, 2143 (*Ibid.*, p. 90). (9) *Ibid.*, 2148 (*Ibid.*, pp. 95–6). (12) *Ibid.*, 2152 (*Ibid.*, pp. 100–2). (29) *Ibid.*, 2160 (*Ibid.*, pp. 113–15).

353. (3) AFC, III, 497 (SLDM, pp. 613–14). (14) *Ibid.*, 511 (*Ibid.*, pp. 630–631). (22) ACM, 2165 (SVDP, *ibid.*, pp. 121–2). (30) AFC, II, 547 bis (SLDM, pp. 672–3). (38) *Ibid.*, III, 511 (*Ibid.*, pp. 630–1).

354. (7) ACM, 2173 (SVDP, *ibid.*, pp. 136–7). (17) *Ibid.*, 2178 (*Ibid.*, pp. 142–143). (26) AFC, *ibid.*, 505 (SLDM, pp. 623–5). (36) *Ibid.*, II, 512 (*Ibid.*, p. 631).

355. (5) *Ibid.*, 514 (*Ibid.*, 634). (14) ACM, 2213 (SVDP, *ibid.*, p. 189). (29) *Ibid.*, 2214 (*Ibid.*, pp. 190–2). (38) *Ibid.*, 2218 (*Ibid.*, pp. 237–9).

356. (16) Coste, Vol. II, Chap. XXXVI. (24) AFC, III, 515 (SLDM, pp. 634–635). (39) *Ibid.*, II, 516 (*Ibid.*, pp. 635–6).

357. (7) ACM, 2227 (SVDP, *ibid.*, pp. 251–2). (16) AFC, *ibid.*, 403 (SLDM, p. 519); SVDP, *ibid.*, pp. 262–3. (21) AFC, *ibid.* (SLDM, *ibid.*); SVDP, *ibid.* (24) AFC, III, 517 (SLDM, pp. 636–7). (33) *Ibid.*, II, 518 (*Ibid.*, pp. 637–8); Coste, Vol. I, p. 457.

358. (4) AFC, *ibid.*, 522 bis (SLDM, pp. 640–1). (17) *Ibid.*, III, 523 (*Ibid.*, p. 642). (22) ACM, 2282 (SVDP, *ibid.*, p. 318). (29) AFC, II, 528 (SLDM, pp. 647–8); SVDP, *ibid.*, p. 319.

359. (1) AFC, III, 530 (SLDM, pp. 651–2). (8) *Ibid.*, 531 (*Ibid.*, pp. 652–3). (26) *Ibid.*, II, 532 (*Ibid.*, pp. 655–6); SVDP, *ibid.*, pp. 270–1. (32) *Ibid.*, p. 271, Footnote 2. (39) *Ibid.*, XIII, pp. 733–7.

360. (15) AFC, *ibid.*, 527 *bis* (SLDM, pp. 646–7); cf. also *ibid.*, 535 (*Ibid.*, pp. 657–8). (18) *Ibid.*, 529 *bis* (*Ibid.*, pp. 650–1); cf. also *ibid.*, 527, III, 529 (*Ibid.*, pp. 645–6, 648–50). (24) Coste, *ibid.*, p. 338. (26) AFC, *ibid.*, 537 (SLDM, p. 659). (31) *Conferences*, IV, pp. 244–56. (34) ACM, 2343 (SVDP, VI, p. 404); AFC, *ibid.*, 539 (SLDM, pp. 660–1).

361. (4) Coste, *ibid.*, p. 451. (7) AFC, *ibid.*, 540 (SLDM, p. 661). (10) *Ibid.*, IV, 541 (*Ibid.*, p. 662); ACM, 2361 (SVDP, *ibid.*, p. 436). (13) AFC, *ibid.*, 543 (SLDM, pp. 663–4). (14) *Ibid.*, II, 545 *quater* (*Ibid.*, pp. 669–670). (17) *Ibid.*, III, 549 (*Ibid.*, pp. 675–6). (18) *Ibid.*, 554 (*Ibid.*, pp. 680–1). (30) ACM, 2362 (SVDP, *ibid.*, pp. 436–7) and *ibid.*, p. 437, Footnote 2. (35) AFC, II, 558 (SLDM, pp. 684–5); SVDP, *ibid.*, p. 455.

362. (3) ACM, 2368 (SVDP, *ibid.*, pp. 444–6); cf. also *ibid.*, 2372 (*Ibid.*, pp. 452–5). (6) AFC, III, 542 (SLDM, pp. 662–3). (11) *Ibid.*, 544 (*Ibid.*, pp. 665–6). (15) *Ibid.*, 545 (*Ibid.*, pp. 666–7). (25) *Ibid.*, 545 *bis* (*Ibid.*, pp. 667–8). (29) *Ibid.*, II, 545 *quater* (*Ibid.*, pp. 669–70). (37) *Ibid.*, III, 554 (*Ibid.*, pp. 680–1).

363. (12) *Ibid.*, 556 (*Ibid.*, p. 682). (23) *Ibid.*, 557 *bis* (*Ibid.*, pp. 683–4). (32) ACM, 2474 (SVDP, *ibid.*, pp. 631–2).

364. (2) AFC, *ibid.*, 557 (SLDM, p. 683). (3) *Ibid.*, 550 (*Ibid.*, pp. 676–7). (4) SVDP, XIII, p. 737. (11) AFC, II, 560 (SLDM, pp. 688–9). (14) SVDP, VII, pp. 84–5. (33) AFC, *ibid.*, 561 (SLDM, pp. 689–90).

365. (2) *Ibid.* (*Ibid.*). (12) ACM, 2511 (SVDP, *ibid.*, pp. 49–51). (26) *Ibid.*, 2512 (*Ibid.*, pp. 51–2). (29) AFC, *ibid.*, 562 (SLDM, p. 690).

366. (2) ACM, 2522 (SVDP, *ibid.*, p. 65). (7) AFC, *ibid.*, 563 (SLDM, p. 691). (18) *Ibid.*, III, 564 (*Ibid.*, pp. 691–2). (34) *Ibid.*, 565 (*Ibid.*, pp. 692–3).

367. (3) *Ibid.*, 566 (*Ibid.*, p. 694). (5) *Ibid.*, 570, 571 (*Ibid.*, pp. 697–8, 698–700). (11) *Ibid.*, 571 (*Ibid.*, pp. 698–700). (13) SVDP, *ibid.*, p. 142, Footnote 2. (17) AFC, II, 573 (SLDM, p. 701); SVDP, *ibid.*, p. 142; *Ibid.*, Footnote 3. (26) AFC, *ibid.*, 574 (SLDM, p. 702). (30) Coste, *ibid.*, pp. 454–5; AFC, III, 578 (SLDM, p. 706). (38) *Ibid.*, II, 577 (*Ibid.*, p. 704).

368. (20) *Conferences*, *ibid.*, pp. 124–39. (24) ACM, 2610 (SVDP, *ibid.*, pp. 184–5, and *ibid.*, p. 185, Footnote 2). (34) AFC, *ibid.*, 577 *bis* (SLDM, p. 705).

369. (8) *Ibid.*, 580 (*Ibid.*, pp. 708–9). (12) *Ibid.*, 581 (*Ibid.*, pp. 709–10). (24) *Ibid.* (*Ibid.*). (36) ACM, 2641 (SVDP, *ibid.*, pp. 232–4). (38) Coste, Vol. II, p. 438.

370. (7) *Ibid.* (29) *Conferences*, *ibid.*, pp. 164–71. (39) ACM, 2646 (SVDP, *ibid.*, pp. 240–3).

372. (2) *Conferences*, *ibid.*, pp. 172–8. (5) ACM, 2625 (SVDP, *ibid.*, pp. 209–210). (8) AFC, *ibid.*, 590 (SLDM, pp. 717–18). (11) *Ibid.*, 588 (*Ibid.*, pp. 715–16). (22) *Ibid.*, II, 591 (*Ibid.*, pp. 718–19). (26) *Ibid.*, 593 (*Ibid.*, p. 721). (30) *Ibid.*, 591 (*Ibid.*, pp. 718–19). (32) *Ibid.*, III, 597 (*Ibid.*, pp. 724–5). (39) *Ibid.*, 596 (*Ibid.*, pp. 723–4).

373. (7) *Ibid.*, 598 (*Ibid.*, pp. 725–6). (12) ACM, 2675 (SVDP, *ibid.*, pp. 281–283). (28) *Conferences*, *ibid.*, pp. 191–5. (31) *Sacra Rituum Congregatio:*

Index ac Status Causarum Beatificationis Servorum Dei et Canonizationis Beatorum, MCMLXII, p. 6.

374. (4) *Conferences, ibid.* (7) Cf. p. 331. (9) AFC, *ibid.,* 599 (SLDM, pp. 727–8). (20) *Ibid.,* II, 600 (*Ibid.,* p. 728); SVDP, *ibid.,* p. 367. (21) ACM, 2724 (SVDP, *ibid.,* p. 368). (30) AFC, *ibid.,* 602 (SLDM, pp. 729–30).

375. (5) *Conferences, ibid.,* pp. 228–31. (16) ACM, 2748 (SVDP, *ibid.,* pp. 400–2). (20) AFC, *ibid.,* 603 (SLDM, pp. 730–1). (21) ACM, 2755 (SVDP, *ibid.,* pp. 409–10). (27) AFC, *ibid.,* 604 (SLDM, p. 731). (33) ACM, 2761 (SVDP, *ibid.,* p. 419). (34) *Conferences, ibid.,* p. 244.

376. (2) *Ibid.,* p. 280. (8) *Ibid.,* pp. 244–56. (14) AFC, *ibid.,* 605 (SLDM, pp. 731–2).

CHAPTER XVIII

377. (5) AFC, III, 695 *bis* (SLDM, pp. 735–6). (8) *Ibid.,* 607 (*Ibid.,* pp. 736–738). (11) *Ibid.,* 608 (*Ibid.,* pp. 738–9). (15) *Ibid.,* 605 *bis* (*Ibid.,* pp. 735–6).

378. (2) ACM, 2767 (SVDP, *ibid.,* pp. 429–30). (14) *Ibid.,* 2768 (*Ibid.,* pp. 430–3). (19) *Ibid.,* 2786 (*Ibid.,* pp. 453–4). (29) AFC, II, 609 (SLDM, pp. 739–40). (35) *Ibid.,* 609 *bis* (*Ibid.,* pp. 740–1).

379. (2) *Ibid.,* III, 610 (*Ibid.,* pp. 741–2). (11) *Ibid.* (*Ibid.*). (20) *Ibid.,* 611 (*Ibid.,* pp. 742–3). (25) *Ibid.,* 613 (*Ibid.,* pp. 743–4). (31) *Ibid.,* 614 (*Ibid.,* pp. 744–5). (35) *Ibid.,* II, 615 (*Ibid.,* pp. 745–6).

380. (8) ACM, 2791 (SVDP, *ibid.,* pp. 460–2). (14) *Ibid.,* 2950 (*Ibid.,* VIII, pp. 92–3). (24) SVDP, XIII, p. 751. (35) AFC, *ibid.,* 628 (SLDM, pp. 757–8). (38) *Conferences, ibid.,* p. 268.

381. (6) *Ibid.,* pp. 268–70. (10) AFC, III, 628 *bis* (SLDM, pp. 758–9). (24) *Conferences, ibid.* (29) AFC, II, 605 (SLDM, pp. 731–2). (31) *Ibid.,* 629 (*Ibid.,* pp. 759–60). (39) *Ibid.,* III, 634 (*Ibid.,* pp. 765–7); *Conferences, ibid.,* pp. 273–81.

382. (18) AFC, II, 638 (SLDM, pp. 769–70). (28) *Ibid.,* 639 (*Ibid.,* p. 771).

383. (7) *Ibid.,* 644 (*Ibid.,* pp. 776–7). (14) Cf. p. 61. (15) Cf. pp. 214–15. (24) AFC, III, 647 (SLDM, pp. 779–80). (36) *Ibid.,* 647 *bis* (*Ibid.,* pp. 780–2).

384. (11) *Ibid.,* 648 (*Ibid.,* pp. 785–6). (24) *Ibid.,* II, 649 (*Ibid.,* pp. 786–7). (30) *Ibid.,* III, 651 (*Ibid.,* pp. 789–91). (34) *Ibid.,* II, 649, 654 (*Ibid.,* pp. 786–7, 793). (36) *Ibid.,* III, 651 (*Ibid.,* pp. 789–91).

385. (6) *Ibid.,* 652 (*Ibid.,* pp. 791–3). (17) Cloistered nuns were called Madame. (22) AFC, II, 655 (SLDM, pp. 793–5).

386. (3) ACM, 3077 (SVDP, *ibid.,* pp. 237–40). (27) Coste, Vol. I, p. 464.

387. (8) ACM, 3091 (SVDP, *ibid.,* pp. 257–9). (11) *Ibid.,* 3078 (*Ibid.,* pp. 240–1). (20) *Ibid.,* 3089 (*Ibid.,* pp. 254–6).

389. (23) Cf. p. 261.

390. (20) Gobillon, pp. 174–87.

BIBLIOGRAPHY

Archives de la Congregation de la Mission, Paris, France

Lettres et Papiers Autographes de Saint Vincent de Paul.

Archives des Filles de la Charité, Paris, France

Vol. I—Lettres Autographes de Saint Vincent de Paul à Mademoiselle Le Gras (Louise de Marillac); Lettres aux Filles de la Charité. Vol. II—Lettres Autographes de Louise de Marillac à Saint Vincent de Paul, Etc. Vol. III—Recueil des Lettres de Louise de Marillac aux Filles de la Charité. Vol. IV—Lettres de Mlle Le Gras à M. L'Abbé de Vaux. Vol. V—Ecrits Autographes de Louise de Marillac; Notes sur Divers Sujets. Vol. VI—Autographes-Lettres et Pièces Diverses Concernant Louise de Marillac, Mlle Le Gras. Vol. VII—Autographes-Pièces Diverses. Recueil de diverses pièces Appertenants à la Conduite et direction des Dames de la Charité de Paris: (Circa 1700).

Archives Nationales, Paris, France

Minutier Central, Etude LXVIII, registre 98, "Le Contrat du mariage d' Antoine Le Gras et Louise de Marillac."
X2B, 1179, "Procès (Louis vs. Antoinette de Marillac).

Archives of the Procurator General at the Holy See, Congregation of the Mission, Rome, Italy

Sacra Rituum Congregatio. *Parisien. Beatificationis et Canonizationis Servae Dei Ludovicae de Marillac Viduae Le Gras Confundatricis Puellarum Charitatis*, Roma, 1895–1908: Positio Super Introductione Causae; Positio Super Non Cultu; Positio Super Fama in Genere; Positio Super Validitate Processum; Positio Super Virtutibus; Nova Positio Super Virtutibus; Novissima Positio Super Virtutibus.

Abelly, Louis. *La Vie du vénérable serviteur de Dieu, Vincent de Paul*, 3 Vol., Paris, 1664.

Agnel, Arnaud d'. *Saint Vincent de Paul, A Guide for Priests*, tr. by Rev. Joseph Leonard, C.M., London, 1932.

Barine, Aruede. *La Grande Mademoiselle*, New York and London, 1902.

Battifol, M. *Richelieu et le roi Louis XIII*, Paris, 1934.

Baunard, Msgr. Louis. *La Vénérable Louise de Marillac*, Paris, 1898.

Bedoyère, M. de la. *François de Sales*, London, 1960.

Belloc, Hilaire. *Charles I*, Philadelphia and London, 1933.

———. *Louis XIV*, New York and London, 1938.

———. *Richelieu*, New York, 1939.

Brantôme, M. l'Abbé de. *The Book of the Ladies*, tr. by K. Prescott Wormeley, London, 1899.

Bremond, Henri. *Histoire Litteraire du Sentiment Religieux*, 12 Vol., Paris, 1916–1938.

Brochard, Chanoine Louis. *Saint-Gervais, Histoire de la Paroisse d'après de Nombreux Documents Inédits*, Paris, 1938.

Broglie, Prince Emmanuel de. *The Life of Blessed Louise de Marillac, Co-Foundress of the Sisters of Charity of Saint Vincent de Paul*, tr. by Rev. Joseph Leonard, C.M., London, 1933.

——. *La Bienheureuse Marie de l'Incarnation*, Paris, 1913.

Burckhardt, Carl J. *Richelieu, His Rise to Power*, tr. by Edwin and Willa Muir, New York, 1940.

Calvet, Jean. *Louise de Marillac, A Portrait*, tr. by G. F. Pullen, New York, 1959.

——. *Saint Vincent de Paul*, tr. by Lancelot C. Sheppard, London, 1952.

Canitrot, Etienne. *Le Plus Familier des Saints, Vincent de Paul*, Paris, 1947.

Chaigne, Louis. *Saint Vincent de Paul*, tr. by Rosemary Sheed, New York, 1962.

Chalumeau, R. P., C.M. *Guide de Saint Vincent de Paul à Travers Paris*, Paris, 1960.

Corbie, Arnauld de. *Monsieur Vincent*, récit historique, illus. de 16 photos, hors-texte tirées du film de Maurice Cloche, Paris, 1948.

Coste, Pierre, C.M. *The Life and Works of Saint Vincent de Paul*, 3 Vol., tr. by Joseph Leonard, C.M., Westminster, 1952.

Daniel-Rops, Henri. *Monsieur Vincent*, Biographie illustré par Jean Servel, Maquette et photos de René Perrin, Lyon, 1959.

——. *Monsieur Vincent, The Story of St. Vincent de Paul*, tr. by Julie Kernan, New York, 1961.

——. *The Catholic Reformation*, 2 Vol., tr. by John Warrington, New York, 1964.

Delarue, Jacques. *The Holiness of Vincent de Paul*, London, 1960.

de Paul, St. Vincent. *Entretiens Spirituels Aux Missionaires*, textes réunis et présentés par André Dodin, C.M., Paris, 1960.

——. *Letters of St. Vincent de Paul*, tr. and ed. by Joseph Leonard, C.M., London, 1937.

——. *Saint Vincent de Paul, Correspondance, Entretiens, Documents*, Tomes VIII, edition publiée et annotée par Pierre Coste, Prêtre de la Mission, Paris, 1920.

——. *St. Vincent de Paul and Mental Prayer, A Selection of Letters and Addresses*, tr. by Joseph Leonard, Priest of the Congregation of the Mission, London, 1925.

——. *The Conferences of St. Vincent de Paul to the Sisters of Charity*, tr. by Joseph Leonard, C.M., Westminster, 1952.

de Sales, François. *Introduction to the Devout Life*, tr. and ed. by John K. Ryan, Garden City, 1955.

Dirvin, Joseph I., C.M. *Mrs. Seton, Foundress of the American Sisters of Charity*, New York, 1962.

——. *St. Catherine Labouré of the Miraculous Medal*, New York, 1958.

Dodin, André. *Saint Vincent de Paul*, Paris, 1949.

——. *Saint Vincent de Paul et la Charité*, Paris, 1960.

Emmanuel, Cyprian W., O.F.M. *The Charities of St. Vincent de Paul, An Evaluation of His Ideas, Principles and Methods*, Chicago, 1923.

Evelyn, John. *Diary and Correspondence*, 4 Vol., London, 1854.

Everart, Edouard. *Michel de Marillac, Sa Vie, Ses Oeuvres,* Riom, 1894.
———. *Notes Généalogiques sur la Famille de Marillac,* n.d.
Farrow, John. *Pageant of the Popes,* New York, 1942.
Feillet, Alphonse. *La misère au temps de la Fronde et Saint Vincent de Paul,* Paris, 1862.
Flinton, Sister Margaret. *Sainte Louise de Marillac, L'Aspect Social de Son Oeuvre,* Tournai, 1957.
Friedrich, Carl. *The Age of the Baroque, 1610–1660,* New York, 1962.
Giordani, Igino. *St. Vincent de Paul, Servant of the Poor,* tr. by Thomas J. Tobin, Milwaukee, 1961.
Giraud, Victor. *St. Vincent de Paul,* tr. by Joseph Leonard, C.M., Dublin, 1955.
Gobillon, Nicolas. *La Vie de Mademoiselle Le Gras, fondatrice et première superieure de la Compagnie des Filles de la Charité,* Paris, 1675.
Guerard, Albert. *France in the Classical Age, The Life and Death of an Ideal,* New York and Evanston, 1965.
Guichard, J. *Saint Vincent de Paul, esclave à Tunis; étude historique et critique,* Paris, 1937.
Guy, Jean. *Sainte Louise de Marillac, Femme au Grand Coeur, Ame de Feu, 1591–1660,* Paris, 1960.
Huxley, Aldous. *Grey Eminence, A Study in Religion and Politics,* New York, 1966.
———. *The Devils of Loudon,* New York, 1965.
Kittler, Glenn D., *The Papal Princes, A History of the Sacred College of Cardinals,* New York, 1961.
Lavedan, Henri Léon Emile. *The Heroic Life of Saint Vincent de Paul,* tr. by Helen Younger Chase, London, New York, 1929.
Lefèvre de Lezeau, Nicolas. *Histoire de la vie de Michel de Marillac,* Bibl. Ste-Geneviève, Mss. L, f. 12, 2 Vol., Paris, n.d.
Leonard, Joseph, C.M. *St. Vincent de Paul and Mental Prayer,* London, 1925.
Loth, Arthur. *Saint Vincent de Paul et sa mission sociale,* Introduction by Louis Veuillot, Appendices par Ad Baudon, P. B. et L.B., E. Cartier (et) Auguste Roussel, Paris, 1880.
Lough, John. *An Introduction to Seventeenth Century France,* London, 1954.
Lovat, Alice Mary (Weld-Blundell) Fraser, Baroness. *Life of the Venerable Louise de Marillac (Mademoiselle Le Gras), Foundress of the Company of Sisters of Charity of St. Vincent de Paul,* preface by Father Bernard Vaughan, S.J., London, 1916.
Magne, Emile. *La vie quotidienne au temps de Louis XIII,* Paris, 1946.
Marillac, St. Louise de. *Correspondance, Meditations, Pensées, Avis,* Paris, 1961.
Matt, Leonard von. *St. Vincent de Paul,* tr. by Emma Craufurd, Chicago, 1960.
Maynard, Theodore. *Apostle of Charity, The Life of St. Vincent de Paul,* New York, 1939.
McLaughlin, Arthur. *St. Vincent de Paul, servant of the poor,* Milwaukee, 1965.
Ménebréa, André. *Saint Vincent de Paul, le Maître des Hommes d'Etat,* Paris, 1944.
———. *St. Vincent de Paul, le savant; la révolution inaperçue,* Paris, 1948.
Mourret, Fernand, S.S. *A History of the Catholic Church,* tr. by Newton Thompson, St. Louis and London.
Neale, J. E. *The Age of Catherine de Medici,* New York, 1962.

Norton, Lucy. *Saint-Simon at Versailles*, sel. and tr. from *Memoirs de M. le Duc de Saint-Simon*, New York, 1958.

Ogg, David. *Europe in the Seventeenth Century*, New York, 1960.

Poinsenet, M. D. *De L'Anxiété à la Sainteté, Louise de Marillac*, Paris, 1957.

———. *France Religieuse du XVIIe Siècle*, Paris, 1958.

Prunel, Chanoine L. *La Renaissance Catholique en France au XVIIe Siècle*, Paris, 1928.

Purcell, Mary. *The World of Monsieur Vincent*, New York, 1963.

Ranum, Orest A. *Richelieu and the Councillors of Louis XIII, A Study of the Secretaries of State and Superintendents of Finance in the Ministry of Richelieu 1635–1642*, Oxford, 1963.

Redier, Antoine. *La vraie vie de saint Vincent de Paul*, Paris, 1927.

Redondo, Jose. *Misionologia de San Vicente de Paul ano tricentario 1660–1960*, Mexico, 1960.

Retz, Cardinal de. *Oeuvres*, 11 Vol., Paris, 1870–1920.

Richemont, Comtesse de. *Histoire de Mademoiselle Le Gras, Louise de Marillac*, Paris, 1882.

Ruppert, Jacques. *Le Costume*, "La Renaissance-Le Style Louis XIII," Paris, 1931.

Shannon, G. J., C.M. *Saints in Social Service, A Woman Named Louise: A Priest Called Vincent*, n.d.

Sheedy, J. P., C.M. *Untrodden Paths: The Social Apostolate of St. Louise de Marillac*, London, 1958.

Stopp, Elizabeth. *Madame de Chantal, Portrait of a Saint*, Westminster, 1963.

Suenens, Leon Joseph Cardinal. *The Nun in the World, Religious and the Apostolate*, tr. by Geoffrey Stevens, Westminster, 1963.

Tanquerey, Adolphe. *The Spiritual Life, A Treatise on Ascetical and Mystical Theology*, Baltimore, 1930.

Trouncer, Margaret. *Mère Angélique*, New York, 1957.

Ward, Barbara. *Faith and Freedom*, New York, 1958.

Wedgwood, C. V. *Richelieu and the French Monarchy*, London, 1949.

———. *The Thirty Years War*, New York, 1961.

Woodgate, M. V. *Saint Vincent de Paul*, Westminster, 1958.

Common Rules of the Daughters of Charity, Paris, 1658, 1954.

Course of Meditations for all the Days of the Year for the Use of the Congregation of the Mission by a Priest of the Same Congregation, Paris, 1889, manuscript copy, Perryville, 1941.

Fêtes et Saisons, Numéro 61, Juin-Juillet 1961, "Paris, Carrefour des Saints," Paris, 1961.

La Grammaire des Styles, "Le Style Louis XIII," ed. Henry Martin, Paris, 1929.

La Medaille Miraculeuse, Novembre-Decembre 1959, Numéro Special, Paris, 1959.

Les Missions des Lazaristes et des Filles de la Charité, Numéro Special, Paris, 1953.

Life of Mademoiselle Le Gras (Louise de Marillac), Foundress of the Sisters of Charity, tr. by a Sister of Charity, New York, Cincinnati and St. Louis, 1884.

INDEX

Place names are in italics.

of second motherhouse, 346; and finances at Chantilly, 374

FOUQUET, M. LE PROCUREUR-GÉNÉRAL NICOLAS, unable to find Company documents, 302ff.; requests renewal of process of approbation, 303

FOURÉ, SISTER JEANNE, appointed infirmarian at foundling hospice, 247

FRANCIS OF ASSISI, ST., relationship between Vincent and Louise compared to relationship of St. Clare to, 61

FRANÇOIS, SISTER MARGUERITE, among first band of Sisters at Angers, 189; falls ill of the plague, 192; death, 192

FRANÇOIS I, KING OF FRANCE, betrayed by Connétable de Bourbon, 7

FRANÇOISE, SISTER, Louise gives spiritual advice to, 222

FRANÇOISE, SISTER, "the gardener," Louise approves renewal of vows by, 343

FROGET, GEORGES, rector of seminary of Saint-Nicolas, offers to accept Michel Le Gras, 175; and Michel Le Gras's intention to take tonsure, 181

FRONDE, start, 271ff.; fresh outbreak of, 275

GACHIER, M., and debt owed the Le Gras', 57–58

GALLAIS, M., Curé de Toquain-en-Brie, and defection of Sister, 324–325

GALLEY SLAVES, Vincent almoner of, obtains hospital for, enlists Louise's aid for, 104ff.; priests of Saint-Nicolas minister to, 105; Louise learns of new apostolate with, 189; beginning of Company's ministry to, 371ff.; Barbe Angiboust transferred to work of, 208; Sister assists Barbe Angiboust in work of, 217; Ladies asked to visit, 345

GAUDOIN, SISTER MARIE, at Alois, 291

GENEVIÈVE, ST., blesses arms against Attila the Hun, 7; possessed the virtues of village girls, 121; relics carried in peace procession, 309

GENEVIÈVE OF THE HÔTEL-DIEU, SISTER, suggested as replacement for defecting Sister, 149; hypochondria of, 150; asked to aid refugee from Lorraine,

176; proposed for visitation of Parisian houses, 247

GEOFFRE, SISTER MARIE, archivist of Daughters of Charity, testifies concerning Louise's birthplace, 4

GEORGETTE, SISTER NICOLE, counseled by Louise, 379

GERMAINE, schoolmistress at Villepreux, 93; on tour with Louise, 99; considered for school at Villeneuve, 104; loss bewailed, 138

GERSON, recommended for Louise's retreat reading, 71; suitability of, 71; prescribed for Sisters' retreat, 220

GESSAUME, SISTER HENRIETTE, reported as lackadaisical, 143; permitted journey, 154; problem with, 186; desires to nurse soldiers, 211; destined for Sedan, 217; sent to Saint-Sulpice, 221; considered for Saint-Gervais, 412; considered for Issy and Fontenay, 223; proposed for visitation of Saint-Sulpice, 247; sent to Nantes, 256; quarrels with chaplain, 266; cause of trouble, 279; reprieved at Nantes, 280; recall asked for, 288; need not go out to shop, 290; transfer proposed to, 301; transfer triggers last major quarrel at Nantes, 334ff.; volunteers for Calais, 370; Louise asks news from, 372

GOBILLON, NICOLAS, Curé de Saint-Laurent, first biographer of Louise, on her birthplace, 3; on Louise's stay in *pension*, 16ff.; on Louise's charity in world, 29; on meeting between Louise and François de Sales, 35; on Louise's freedom from mortal sin, 37–38; on Louise's care of husband, 40; credits Camus for securing Vincent as Louise's director, 51; on Louise's conduct at husband's death, 54; and Louise's "novitiate," 75; on origins of Company, 213; on advantages of move to La Chapelle, 140; on work of retreats, 152; on Louise's work with foundlings, 159; on Louise's prayer-life, 168; on Louise's deprivation of last note from Vincent, 388; on remarkable phenomenon at Louise's tomb, 390

periments with headdress, 208–209;
relieves Sister Servant from office because of illness, 209; reluctant to
readmit Madame Pelletier to Company, 209; blames self for faults of
Sisters, 209–210; inaugurates free
schools for Parisian poor, 210; promises to procure uncle's books for Abbé
de Vaux, 210–211; interested in "Devils of Loudun," 211; cheered by work
of Sisters at Sedan, 211; desires spiritual advice on birthday, 211; receives
unfavorable report on house at Richelieu, 211; comments on Vincent's reply to Sister, 212; learns of praise
accorded new house at Fontenay, 212;
and unique form of correspondence
with Vincent, 213; and imprudence of
priest, 213; and question of episcopal
approval for Sisters, 213; last visit with
Madame de Chantal, 213; and custom
of opening mail, 213–214; on visitation of houses, 214; Vincent apolo-
gizes to, 214; gives Abbé de Vaux
advice on Sisters' devotions, 215–216;
defends Sister at Angers, 216; fears
lawsuit over Sister's transfer, 216; con-
sults Vincent, 217; saved from fall of
ceiling, 217–218ff.; her essential role
in foundation of Company, 218–219;
asks Abbé de Vaux's charity toward
widow, 219; prescribes for Sisters' retreat at Angers, 220; writes news of
Company, 220; Sisters' complaints of,
220–221; felicitates Vincent on feast
day, 221; and transfer of Sisters, 222;
visits Duchesse de Liancourt and
neighboring charities, 222; gives spiritual advice to Sisters at Angers, 222;
and need for vocations, 222–223; worried over stability of Sisters, 223–224;
first uses community motto, 224; prescribes for Sister Martin, 224; writes
to dying Sister, 224; and proposal to
recommend son to de Retz, 225; and
proposal of Bicêtre for foundlings, 226;
comforts Sister in illness, 226; urges
Vincent to spare himself, 227; in-
structs Abbé de Vaux concerning visi-

tation, 227; suggests house for
foundlings, 227; and interior trial,
228; consoles Sister Claude, 228; worries over Vincent's increased burdens,
228–229; and first use of community
seal, 229; rebukes Sisters at Angers,
229; wishes to recall Madame Turgis,
230; and missing son, 230; and proposed approbation of Company, 231;
visits Chartres, 231; in anguish over
son, 231; and equality of Sisters, 231–
232; and custom of discoursing on
virtues of deceased Sisters, 233; reaches
high sanctity, 234; written correspondence with Vincent slackens,
234; afflicted over Sister's faults, 235;
on Sisters' dowries, 235; depressed over
personal and community problems,
236ff.; states reasons against Bicêtre,
236; and formal petition for approbation of Company, 237; opposes other
control over Sisters than Congregation
of the Mission, 239; favors title
Daughters of Charity for Sisters, 239;
continued anguish over son, 239; rebukes Sisters at Liancourt, 240; lists
subjects for conferences, 240; alerts
M. Portail to problems at Angers,
242–243; given assistant, 242; donates
painting to Vincent, 243; asks Vincent
to permit Marian chaplet devotion to
Sisters, 243; and ill-starred foundation
at Mans, 243–244; gives financial accounting of motherhouse, 244; and
first council meeting of Sisters, 245ff.;
conducts first Sisters to Nantes, 247ff.;
leaves instructions for motherhouse,
247; asks M. Portail for complete
rule, 248–249; defends Sister at Angers, 249; and financial duel with
Angers administrators, 249; visits Ladies at Ingrandes, 250; refuses candidate for Company, 250; advises Sister
Lepeintre, 252; accepts Sisters' confessor designated by Vincent, 252; learns
of son's grave illness, 252; experiences
new calm, 253; amused at Ladies'
reaction to her journey, 253; writes to
Sister Hellot about son's illness, 253–

Cefte ville eft vn autre monde
Dedans vn monde floriffant,
En peuples et en biens puiffant
Qui de toutes chofes abonde.